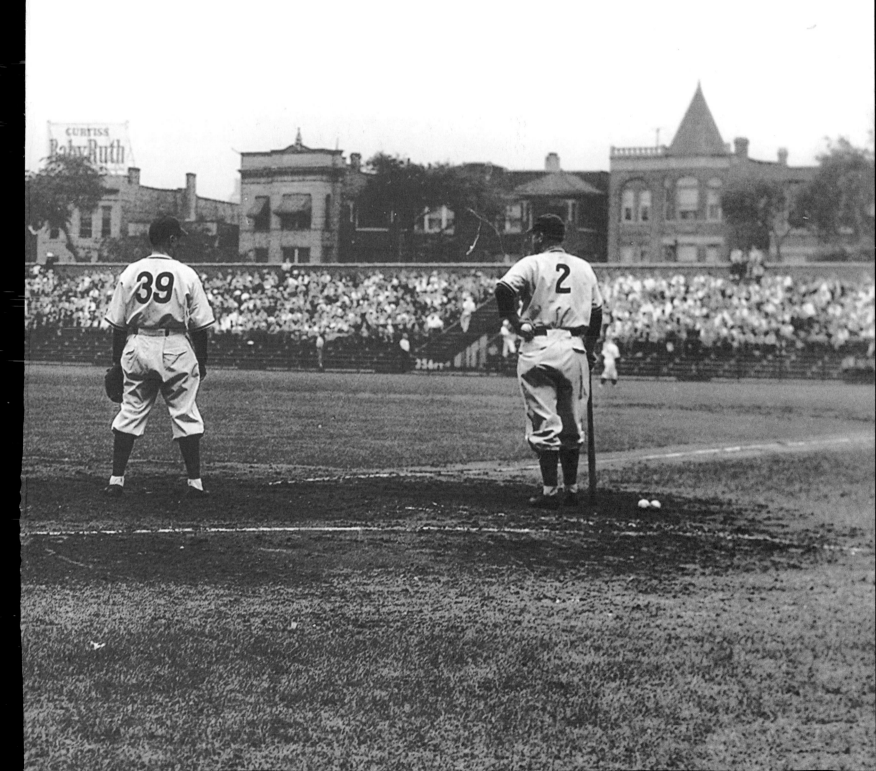

THE
CUBS

ALSO BY THE AUTHORS

The Dodgers: 120 Years of Dodgers Baseball
Yankees Century: 100 Years of New York Yankees Baseball
Red Sox Century: The Definitive History of Baseball's Most Storied Franchise
Ted Williams: A Portrait in Words and Pictures
DiMaggio: An Illustrated Life
Jackie Robinson: Between the Baselines

EDITED BY GLENN STOUT

The Best American Sports Writing,™ *1991–present* (series editor for annual volumes)
The Best American Sports Writing of the Century (with David Halberstam)
Chasing Tiger: The Tiger Woods Reader
Impossible Dreams: A Red Sox Collection
Top of the Heap: A Yankees Collection

BY RICHARD A. JOHNSON

A Century of Boston Sports
The Boston Braves: 1871–1953
The American Game: Baseball and Ethnicity (co-editor with Lawrence Baldassaro)
Fall Classics: The Best Writing about the World Series' First 100 Years (co-editor with Bill Littlefield)

BY GLENN STOUT, CHARLES VITCHERS, AND ROBERT GRAY

Nine Months at Ground Zero:
The Story of the Brotherhood of Workers Who Took On a Job Like No Other

THE
CUBS

THE COMPLETE STORY OF
CHICAGO CUBS BASEBALL

TEXT BY **GLENN STOUT**

PHOTOGRAPHS SELECTED AND EDITED BY

RICHARD A. JOHNSON

HOUGHTON MIFFLIN COMPANY

BOSTON NEW YORK

2007

For information about permission to reproduce selections from this book, write to Permissions, Houghton Mifflin Company, 215 Park Avenue South, New York, New York 10003.

www.houghtonmifflinbooks.com

Library of Congress Cataloging-in-Publication Data
Stout, Glenn, date.
  The Cubs : the complete story of Chicago Cubs baseball / text by Glenn Stout ; photographs selected and edited by Richard A. Johnson.
      p. cm.
Includes index.
ISBN-13: 978-0-618-59500-6
ISBN-10: 0-618-59500-7
1. Chicago Cubs (Baseball team)—History. I. Johnson, Dick, date. II. Title.
GV875.C6S86 2007
796.357'640977311—dc22   2007009421

Printed in the United States of America

Book design by Julia Sedykh
Typefaces: Swift, Knockout, and Cyclone

DOW 10 9 8 7 6 5 4 3 2 1

Illustration Credits
ASSOCIATED PRESS: 210, 241, 321, 327, 349, 359, 374, 377, 379, 385, 386, 387, 388, 390, 391, 393, 394–95, 396, 398, 403, 404, 406, 407, 408, 409, 410, 421, 422, 425, 426, 428. BOSTON PUBLIC LIBRARY: 50–51. *BOSTON HERALD*: 209, 232, 238. BRACE PHOTO: iii, vi, 102, 152–57, 218, 231, 236, 257, 274, 281, 285, 303, 305, 328, 380, 430. COLLECTION OF RICHARD A. JOHNSON: xii–xiii, xx, 12, 15, 20, 34, 84, 112, 120, 122, 136, 137, 181, 189, 190, 199, 206, 207, 228–29, 233–34, 237, 244–45, 272–73, 277, 290–91, 297, 310–11, 341. CORBIS: 322, 335. CORBIS-BETTMANN: 264. CORBIS-REUTERS: 360, 401, 384. NATIONAL BASEBALL HALL OF FAME: iv–v, 2, 6, 17, 25, 26, 28, 31, 35, 36, 37, 38-39, 40, 43, 44, 52, 59, 60, 67, 72, 75, 76, 77, 78, 86–87, 93, 96, 99, 101, 107, 109, 111, 114, 117, 119, 125, 126, 129, 134–35, 138, 140, 143, 144–45, 147, 149, 150, 151, 159, 161, 162, 163, 164, 166, 168, 170, 172, 175, 176, 182, 184, 186, 187, 191, 193, 194, 196, 200, 201, 216–17, 222, 225, 227, 240, 242, 248, 252–53, 254, 255, 256, 258, 260–61, 267, 268, 278, 284, 286, 288, 301, 302, 306–7, 313, 314, 323, 324, 337, 344, 350, 351, 352. STEPHEN GREEN/CUBS: 318, 330, 336, 338–39, 347, 348, 354–55, 357, 368, 370–71, 405. TRANSCENDENTAL GRAPHICS: xvi, 9, 10, 13, 19, 30, 33, 46, 49, 62, 68, 88 90, 105, 246. PENNY MARSHALL: 417–18. RICK TELANDER: 293–94.

Endpapers
FRONT: National Baseball Hall of Fame
BACK: Brace Photo

To Cubs fans everywhere, who all deserve better.

And for Siobhan and Saorla.

GLENN STOUT

To the memory of Paul Emil Dietrich (1926–2001),
Mentor, Friend, and Eternal Optimist
who skipped school in Hammond, Indiana, on September 28, 1938,
to attend the "Homer in the Gloamin'" game with his dad.
He loved his Cubs to the end.

And to my home team, as true blue as the Cubbies:
Mary, Minna, Lizzy, Amy, Tania, Cordelia, Clare,
Arrika, Madeline, Bobby, Bob, Nick,
KC, Cooper, and Toby Phillip Jenkins.

RICHARD A. JOHNSON

CONTENTS

ACKNOWLEDGMENTS

The authors would like to extend thanks to editor Susan Canavan, Will Vincent, Beth Burleigh Fuller, Cindy Buck, Julia Sedykh, and everyone else at Houghton Mifflin for their help and understanding over the course of this project, and to agent John Taylor Williams and Hope Denekamp of Fish and Richardson for their support. Special thanks also go out to Patricia Kelly, Tim Wiles, Jim Gates, and Ted Spencer of the National Baseball Hall of Fame, Aaron Schmidt of the Boston Public Library, Mary Brace of the George Brace Collection, Cubs photographer Stephen Green, Tom Shaer, Mark Rucker of Transcendental Graphics, Mike Andersen, George Castle, Al Thiebeault of the *Boston Herald*, Michele Lee Amundsen, and Carolyn McGoldrick of AP Images. The many writers who have covered and written about the Cubs throughout their history all deserve our unending gratitude for their efforts. We are also grateful to the staff of the Chicago Public Library, to Denise Bousquet for her research assistance and attentiveness, to David Wheat and Jack Pickens for their hospitality, and to Shaun Kelly, Jack Lamabe, Scott Turow, William Nack, Rick Telander, John Schulian, Penny Marshall, and Howard Bryant.

Only the Cubs remain.

Until recently, a common history has linked the Chicago Cubs, Boston Red Sox, and Chicago White Sox. All three teams had gone almost a century since winning a world championship, and in the interim all had experienced a string of almost comical bad luck and futility. Boston fans traced their frustration back to 1918 and included the seasons of 1946, 1948, 1975, 1978, 1986, and 2003 in their litany of pain. White Sox followers counted the days since 1906 and the dark era of the Black Sox scandal that followed soon after and had not even experienced a pennant since 1959.

Cubs fans cite 1908, an era they know only through old newspapers, an era so far back in the distant past that there were no airplanes then, no radio. The blues had yet to take root in Chicago. Wrigley Field had not been built. The Model T was still on the drawing board, and the Loop was still a shining marvel, impervious to rust. The Chicago Bears football club did not exist because neither did the National Football League. Notorious gangster Al Capone was just a runny-nosed kid in Brooklyn. Carl Sandburg was an unknown poet and political organizer. Put it this way— in 1908 the New York Yankees had yet to win a single pennant, never mind the World Series. They have since won twenty-six world titles.

The Cubs have won none.

It was not always this way. In 1908 the Cubs were kings. They had supplanted New York's Giants as baseball's most dominant and successful franchise, won three straight National League pennants and two consecutive world championships, and averaged 107 wins in each of the three previous seasons. The "Cubs" moniker seemed too

tame for such a potent ball club. Scribes sometimes called them the "Bruins," and even that name failed to encompass the terror other clubs felt when facing the powerful National League champions. All baseball cowered before them.

So in the name of God, what the hell happened? The Red Sox shed their past by winning the World Series in 2004, and the White Sox—the *White Sox*, for crying out loud!—did the same in 2005. And when the Red Sox and White Sox won the World Series, their nonagenarian fans who remembered the last time it happened became instant celebrities.

No one alive today remembers the 1908 Cubs with any clarity. No one.

Now only the Cubs remain. Only the Cubs and their fans do not know what it is like to experience a world championship. The club of Tinker and Evers and Chance, Charlie Weeghman, William Wrigley, Hack Wilson, Gabby Hartnett, Ernie Banks, Fergie Jenkins, Leo the Lip, Bruce Sutter, Greg Maddux, Harry Caray, Ryne Sandberg, and Mark Grace. They stand alone, singular in their discontent, confounding the "friendly confines" and the laws of probability, if not the laws of nature itself, checking off their failure season after season, now in its *ninety-ninth* straight year, a near-century of perennial agony and frustration. For over this time the Cubs have also been the club of Rabbit Maranville, P.K. Wrigley, the "College of Coaches," Kenny Hubbs, Ernie Broglio, Don Young, the Tribune Company, Kerry Wood's tender elbow, Sammy Sosa's corked bat, and Steve Bartman.

They have been loved, but they have not won. That is the short version of the story.

The longer version follows.

This book tells the story of the Cubs and tries to explain how and why they have come to be so loved, how and why they have not won, and how and why the latter does not seem to affect the former. The challenge of this book is to explain how, in the face of such record failure, the Cubs still inspire more joy than angst, more pleasant memories than pain. They are baseball's last unsolved mystery, the final conundrum, a historical enigma, baseball's oldest story, with an ending that has yet to be written.

That makes them as irresistible to a historian as they are to their fans. For in the end their story, against all odds and logic, is not quite a tragedy.

At least not yet. But it's getting close.

Well over a decade ago, my colleague and close friend Richard Johnson and I conceived of this series of illustrated team histories, which began with *Red Sox Century* (2000) and continued with *Yankees Century* (2002) and *The Dodgers* (2004). The Cubs posed a special challenge, for their history begins in the game's dark ages, and perhaps that explains why no previous narrative history has ever attempted to tell their entire story. Nearly two-thirds of their history is, in a sense, almost pre-historical, virtually without living witnesses.

Fortunately, there is still a wealth of material available from which to reconstruct their story. As with our previous books, newspaper accounts preserved on microfilm and now online have served as the primary resource material for this book. I spent a glorious week in the microfilm department at the Chicago Public Library making thousands of copies from various Chicago newspapers; through the miracle of modern technology, I also spent countless hours online plumbing the depths of the *Chicago Tribune*, the *Sun-Times*, and the *Daily Herald*—all of which are substantially available in electronic form—as well as the archives of other newspapers from around the country, slowly extracting the story of the Cubs from millions of words of agate type. Similarly, I read as many books about the Cubs as possible to create a road map and framework for the story, as well as to identify both areas for additional exploration and areas that had been ignored by others.

The Chicago Cubs organization was not consulted about the project, nor was this project done with its approval. In our experience, independence has proven more valuable than the kind of controlled access that comes when one partners with a subject. Interviews did not play an overly significant role in this book—as previously stated, most Cubs history is without witnesses, and to change approach as we came up on the modern era would have been jarring. Interviews were used primarily as background and include conversations I have had with Cubs players and their opponents periodically over the last twenty years while pursuing a variety of other projects. I have often found that conversations with fans and others are just as enlightening as those with players, and all these perspectives have combined to inform this project.

Richard Johnson's inimitable explorations in Cubs imagery mirrored my own excursions into print, and he shares my belief, earned over the two years we have spent on this project, that the Cubs are at least as worthy as their peers of a book of this scope. We only hope that we are worthy enough to write it. I trust the readers will let us know. We have been honored that Scott Turow, Penny Marshall, William Nack, the estate of Mike Royko, Rick Telander, and John Schulian agreed to add their insight to this project with their essays.

The best part of any project of this type is, of course, what you learn along the way, and I have to say that in that regard this book has not been disappointing. Ever since I was a young boy, along with my dreams of one day playing in the major leagues, I would occasionally fantasize that I knew someone who had done that, or that I would find a distant uncle or cousin who had.

While writing this book, that actually happened. My brother, while researching a family genealogy, informed me that we were related to a former big leaguer. In fact, he was a former Cub, the Depression-era pitcher Clyde Shoun, nicknamed "Hardrock." It seems that several generations ago the Shouns and the Stouts both sprouted from the same small northeastern Tennessee town, Mountain City, and that some generations back a Stout and a Shoun married, making Clyde Shoun and myself something like fourth cousins twice removed. That's close enough for me, and I hereby claim my Cubs birthright.

Although I have been living in the Northeast for the past twenty-five years, I am a native of the Midwest and was born and raised in a small town outside Columbus,

Ohio. Several months after I graduated from college, I was back in Columbus pouring concrete for a living, precisely what I had been doing before attending college. I determined that it was time to leave and decided that I would move to a city with an old ballpark, a place where I could go see major league baseball just about anytime I wanted, something I had never been able to do.

At the time, the choices were few, and I quickly narrowed my potential destination to either Chicago or Boston. I had, in fact, made the decision to go to Chicago before changing my mind at nearly the last minute, when I decided that I'd had enough of the Midwest and would try my luck nearer the ocean. I went to Boston, spent many hundreds of hours in Fenway Park, and have since returned to the Midwest only for funerals and holidays.

In the course of researching this book, I spent a few weeks in and around Chicago—it was really the first time I had been back to the Midwest for any length of time since I left. It was a bit different than I remember—Chicago, after all, is quite a bit more cosmopolitan than a small town outside Columbus, Ohio—but I was also struck by the friendly and open nature of the people. Living in the Northeast, I had grown accustomed to being greeted with suspicion, sometimes even after living years in a place, and I had long ago developed the persistent defensive wariness that characterizes so many who live out this way.

But from the instant I stepped off the plane in Chicago, I realized that veneer was not needed anymore. It seemed that I never took more than a few steps without ending up in a conversation that might have started with a simple pleasantry but, once the Cubs were mentioned, morphed into one of those talks where you look at the clock and wonder where the time went and whether you have enough change for one more beer.

This was nowhere more true than in and around Wrigley Field, a place I had never been before I began this book. Wrigley was all that it was advertised to be and quite a bit more—instantly comfortable, like an old chair. I felt surrounded by friends, something I have never, ever felt in Fenway Park, which over time has become increasingly standoffish and full of "us against them" antagonism.

Although I don't regret that instead of taking a left to Chicago I took a right to Boston, I must admit that when I was visiting Chicago I could not help but wonder how different my life might have been had I taken that other direction. Then, wandering through a near-empty Wrigley Field one day, as the sun set behind the third-base grandstand and cast long shadows out across the outfield and bathed the bleachers in the golden glow of late summer, I knew exactly what would have happened had I decided, twenty-five years before, to move to Chicago.

I would have been right where I was, in Wrigley Field.

—GLENN STOUT
Alburgh, Vermont
December 2006

THE
CUBS

Baseball . . . is the very symbol, the outward visible expression,
of the drive and push and rush and struggle of the living, tearing,
booming nineteenth, the mightiest of all the centuries!

—MARK TWAIN, greeting the Chicago club
at the end of their world tour, 1889

1867–1897

THE CAPTAIN'S CLUB

It was humiliating.

Never before had a game of baseball in Chicago been the cause of such enthusiasm. Or heartbreak. On July 27, 1867, several years before the team that would become the Chicago Cubs was born, the Nationals baseball club of Washington met Chicago's finest, the Excelsiors, at Dexter Park. That morning, reported the *Chicago Tribune*, "the match, and nothing but the match, occupied everyone's mind. . . . One heard of it at the breakfast table . . . it crept into the saloon, was heard at the courts and out-of-the-way-offices." By 2:30 P.M., nearly ten thousand rabid fans, "men and boys, tops and labor-stained workmen, women and handsome girls . . . were there, drawn by the one purpose of manly contest between muscle."

Within only a few minutes, that same crowd was red-faced with embarrassment. Their beloved Excelsiors, the best ballplayers in Chicago, already trailed by the miserable score of 37–0. By 4:00 P.M., the game was over and the

The National League's first championship team in 1876 featured the impressive talent of Hall of Fame pitcher Albert Goodwill Spalding (47–13), second baseman Ross Barnes (.429 batting average), and slugging catcher Deacon White, who led the fledgling league with sixty RBIs.

sullen crowd had slunk away. The final score was irrefutable. Nationals 49, Excelsiors 4.

But these same fans, despite their disappointment, were not angry. One sober observer in the *Tribune* noted the obvious. "The Nationals," he wrote, "are professional athletes, while the Excelsiors are but amateurs." Indeed, most if not all of the players on the Nationals held nominal "no-show" jobs that allowed them to play ball full-time at a good wage. That was no surprise, for over the previous year or so such "professionalism" had crept into what had previously been a game played by amateurs. While some members of the National Association of Base Ball Players, the fledgling organization that ruled the game, fled the group in horror over the next few years to form their own amateur circuit, Chicago found this new form of the game surprisingly attractive and responded with a "if you can't beat them, join them" attitude.

Chicago was absolutely mad for baseball. Since its founding in 1830, the city had grown to become a civic force of nature, a wide open, sprawling municipality of more than one-quarter of a million people, hub of the largest railroad network in the world. Four decades of unbridled growth had taught Chicagoans to expect rapid success in all arenas and nothing less. Baseball would be no exception to this rule. The throbbing metropolis swept up the game in the wake of the Civil War like it swept up everything else.

Although a variety of primitive "ball" games similar to cricket had long been played in all corners of the country, in the 1850s a more organized, orderly, and genteel version of the game had emerged in the Northeast and New England. But that style simply didn't fly in Chicago. The city was not a place of exclusivity, of mannered gentlemen amiably pursuing pastoral pastimes, but of brawling adolescents driving and pushing and struggling. It was a city where the bounties of the prairie intersected with industry, where immigrants and plowboys clawed and scratched for survival. Chicagoans didn't wait; men made themselves and created their own story. And when baseball met Chicago, Chicago changed the game just like it changed everything else.

Perhaps no other city in America needed baseball quite as badly as Chicago. For most workers, there was little that was appealing about life in Chicago beyond dim faith in the potential, someday, for a better life. Living conditions were appalling. New arrivals often found themselves packed into wood shacks on swampy, fetid back streets they shared with livestock. Nearly one-tenth of the population—twenty-five thousand people—made their living working seven days a week slaughtering animals.

To these Chicagoans, baseball was a balm, a chance to escape the squalor for a few hours, to gaze upon a pastoral scene of green and allow time to unfold at a more leisurely pace. Going to the ball game was the only opportunity most Chicagoans had to revisit their rural roots.

In 1868 the Cincinnati Red Stockings, ably manned by the Wright brothers, Harry and George, shed any remaining pretensions of "amateur" status. As one observer noted, they "threw down the gauntlet of defiance to the National Association of Base Ball Players" and announced that henceforth they would be a wholly "professional" organization. They quickly secured the services of the best players in the game and became a juggernaut, going undefeated for the next year and a half.

The men of Chicago looked upon the Red Stockings with both envy and unabashed jealousy. Cincinnati, dubbed "Porkopolis" owing to its primary industry, had long been the dominant city of the Midwest, but Chicago had begun to trump it in importance and thought it should do the same in regard to baseball. Recalling the recent defeat of the Excelsiors, Chicago's most notable baseball cranks decided that what was good enough for Cincinnati could be just as good, if not better, for Chicago.

They were determined to make Chicago the preeminent city of the Midwest, if not the entire nation, in everything, including baseball. Over the ensuing decades, that goal would consume a city.

The team that would eventually evolve into the Chicago Cubs was born on October 1, 1869, in a posh meeting room in the Briggs House, one of Chicago's finest hotels. No other team in existence today can trace its history back so far. The Cubs are truly baseball's oldest story.

On that evening, some fifty-odd men—mostly merchants, assorted financiers, and members of the Chicago Board of Trade—met with one goal in mind. Under the name of the "Chicago Base Ball Club," they intended to "get together a professional baseball nine; a nine which should play ball and nothing else, a nine which should beat the world." Under the leadership of chairman S. W. Tanner, they set a goal of raising $10,000 from investors to secure and maintain a club. Within just a few weeks, no fewer than thirty players from around the country had contacted the group and expressed interest in playing for Chicago.

The first known player to sign with the club was James Wood, a second baseman and former member of Brooklyn's Eckford club. He was named captain and given the responsibility of recruiting other established players to man the Chicago nine. Chicago, with resources that eventually approached $20,000, was more than successful as it plucked many of the best players from the most powerful eastern clubs—which included virtually any team based east of Chicago. By March, the *Tribune*, which had originally been skeptical of the venture, offered, "There is not a man of the ten who is not as good as the best of the other clubs . . . there is not a man the other clubs deem weak."

They proved it in their first contest in St. Louis on April 29 versus the Unions, romping to a 47–1 victory and in the process earning their first nickname. As described by the *Tribune*, they took the field adorned in blue caps bearing a white star, white flannels trimmed in blue with the letter "C" on the chest, and "stockings of pure white British thread [and] shoes of white goatskin." The name "White

Stockings" was suggested by the "showy purity of the hose" and immediately adopted by both the press and the fans.

After a month training in the hinterlands against lesser competition, the White Stockings debuted in Chicago at Dexter Park on Forty-second Street and Halsted on June 3, playing a "practice game" against the Forest City Club of Cleveland. Club officials laid out the field, which lay alongside the grandstand of the racing course and was affectionately referred to as "the Stables." Plans called for seating for twelve thousand fans, expandable to up to thirty thousand in a pinch; the diamond was touted by the *Tribune* as "nearly as perfect as could be desired."

The massive crowd was not disappointed. Despite playing without captain Wood, who was incapacitated with what the *Tribune* called a "sprained limb," the White Stockings scored seven eighth-inning runs to swamp Forest City, 15–9.

Throughout most of the summer, similar successes were matched by defeats, but most looked toward September 7 to provide a true gauge of their club's power. On that date, in Cincinnati, the White Stockings were scheduled to meet the Red Stockings. It mattered not that the Red Stockings were not quite the powerhouse they had been in 1869 and that star shortstop George Wright was sidelined

A CUB
BY ANY OTHER NAME

One of the first problems the Cubs cause any historian is determining their proper name. Although one can track the history of the franchise back at least as far as 1871, the name "Cubs" is, in historical terms, a relatively recent phenomenon. The team existed for more than thirty years before the name "Cubs" was adopted.

Much of the confusion stems from the fact that the Cubs were the original White

Stockings (never, at the time, the "White Sox"!) and that after the Cubs abandoned the name it was later adopted by the American League club. Genealogically, however, today's White Sox are completely unrelated to the White Stockings of the nineteenth century.

The problem is further complicated by the fact that since the White Stockings were, for many years, the only major league team in Chicago, baseball writers and newspaper headline writers were not concerned about confusing the reader and used all manner of nicknames, some of which were actually used by the public— such as the "Colts" and the "Orphans"— and others of which were almost certainly

used only in print, such as the "Microbes," the "Remnants," and the "Zephyrs."

As often as not, in everyday conversation nineteenth-century baseball fans usually referred to the team simply as either "Chicago" or "the Chicagos." When the American League put a team in Chicago, however, it became impossible to tell which team "Chicago" referred to. Although some fans undoubtedly called the NL team the "Nationals" and the American League team the "Americans," the "Cubs" and the "White Stockings" soon became the preferred terms, and the "Cubs" was formally adopted in 1907 when Frank Chance insisted that writers refer to his team by that name.

Adrian "Cap" Anson was the most accomplished player of his generation and played his entire twenty-two years for the club that would soon be known as the Cubs. He was the first major leaguer to reach 3,000 hits, retiring in 1897 with 3,041, a total that is still the Cubs' all-time career hit record.

templated to give this pig a suitable bringing up and when he has reached the enormous dimensions to which all things Chicagoan attain, his unctuous purpose will be forwarded to Cincinnati as a salve for her wounded pride." Indeed, in less than one season a champion ball club had been created from whole cloth and now, in the estimation of its fans, stood atop the baseball world.

Humiliated by the defeat to Chicago and other losses, the Red Stockings disbanded in the offseason as Harry Wright jumped to the Boston club and brought many of his teammates with him. The most powerful of the remaining clubs, whose number included the White Stockings, pulled out of the four-hundred-club NABBP and in March 1871 formed a new organization, the National Association of *Professional* Base Ball Players (NAPBBP), a nine-team league of sorts. Each club would play all others in a five-game series, with the championship awarded to the team that won the most series rather than the most total victories.

The White Stockings threw themselves into the championship effort, building a new ball grounds at the corner of Randolph Street and Michigan Avenue, what was then lakefront property. For much of the year, everything went according to plan. At a time when pitchers still tossed the ball underhanded from a box forty-five feet away from the batter, George Zettlein was one of the best hurlers in the league, and the White Stockings entered the final month of the season, October, battling the Athletics of Philadelphia and the Boston Red Stockings for the NAPBBP championship.

But sometime in the early morning hours of October 8, in a barn on DeKoven Street owned by Patrick and Catherine O'Leary, a small fire of unknown origin quickly turned into a large one. Over the next thirty-six hours, three and a half square miles burned in the center of Chicago, killing three hundred people and leaving one hundred thousand homeless.

The White Stockings were among the fire's victims. Virtually all tangible evidence of the ball club went up in smoke, including their ballpark, club office, and records.

Yet the White Stockings did not fully disband. While Chicago rebuilt, the players joined other clubs and the White Stockings, as an organization, simply went dormant, for Chicagoans faced challenges much more press-

by an injury. They were still baseball's dominant team, the standard against which all others were measured.

The headline in the *Tribune* on September 8, 1870, told the story—"White Above Red"—and a special dispatch offered that "the mission of the White Stockings has been accomplished. The organization was affected with a direct view of beating the Red Stockings, and they have done it," topping Cincinnati, 10–6. Three thousand fans met the White Stockings at Union Depot when they returned to Chicago a day later, and the players celebrated by parading their trophy through the streets—a month-old swine they dressed in red stockings and a placard that read: PORKOPOLIS, SEPTEMBER 7, 1870. The *Tribune* noted that "it is coning than the fortunes of their baseball team. By 1874 enough of the city had been rebuilt that it was possible to think of baseball once again.

While the White Stockings slumbered, the National Association had changed, and not for the better. In short, it was foundering. In Chicago's absence, the Boston Red Stockings had dominated the league, winning the championship in both 1872 and 1873 and entering the 1874 season as a clear favorite. That hurt attendance, and with the championship all but decided, other teams and players sought out alternative reasons to play. Gambling was rampant among both fans and players, and it affected the integrity of the game itself. No one could be sure if a given contest was played on the square. At the same time, many players began reaping the benefits of celebrity. As a fair number of these first professionals, flush with cash, drank their way into oblivion, the game was wracked by scandals.

Although the players themselves were nominally in charge of the Chicago club, after the fire they virtually abandoned it, as did many of the original investors. When the club re-formed, new blood and new money kept the team afloat as the team occupied a new ballpark of sorts, the Twenty-third Street Grounds, and resumed play in the NAPBBP, now known popularly as the National Association.

Foremost among these new investors was William A. Hulbert. Born in 1833 in Burlington Flats, New York—not far from Cooperstown, baseball's mythical ancestral home—Hulbert had moved to Chicago with his parents in 1834. He attended Beloit College, married well, joined the Board of Trade, and by his midforties was a wealthy man. He represented the new, postfire Chicago, a city in the midst of a frenzy of rebuilding that recognized few limits.

Hulbert saw opportunity everywhere he looked in his adopted home, once saying, "I'd rather be a lamppost in Chicago than a millionaire elsewhere," because there was so much opportunity in Chicago that a man hardly needed to move to succeed. A fan of baseball, Hulbert invested in the dormant White Stockings and by 1874 was one of the team's officers.

But he didn't like the way the National Association was operated. Hulbert, a businessman, believed that players simply weren't qualified to run their own baseball associa-

tion and were squandering its profit potential. Since players signed one-year contracts, salaries were kept high, but they demonstrated little loyalty, and most of the talent fled east. Under these circumstances, many teams were unable to become competitive, and that hurt the competitive balance of the entire league. Quite simply, the National Association didn't know how to run or grow a business.

The White Stockings finished the 1874 season with a record of 28–31, in fifth place, and eighteen and a half games behind champion Boston; in 1875, although the league had expanded to thirteen teams, the White Stockings were barely competitive while Boston was almost unbeatable, going 71–8 over the season. The NAPBBP began to fall apart—seven clubs disbanded and failed to finish the season.

As the season sputtered along, Hulbert, who had been named president of the White Stockings, sensed an opportunity. Impatient with the performance of the re-formed White Stockings and angry over what he believed was NA bias in favor of the eastern teams, Hulbert decided to bring a championship club to Chicago by any means necessary.

There was only one way to do that quickly, and that was by signing players from other clubs. He started at the top, and with pitching, for even back then good pitching was the key to victory.

Earlier that season, when Boston had visited Chicago, Hulbert met with Boston pitcher and Rockford, Illinois, native Albert G. Spalding. After starring with the Forest City Club, Spalding had joined the Red Stockings in 1871 and become one of the best players in the league, and certainly its best pitcher at a time when the ball was still tossed underhanded from a distance of forty-five feet. Spalding wasn't particularly fast—some hurlers at the time had mastered a discreet and technically illegal "wrist snap" that enabled them to put a surprising amount of speed on the ball—but he had good control and was a master of changing speeds. Hulbert appealed to Spalding's midwestern roots and was pleased to learn not only that Spalding was not averse to leaving Boston for Chicago, but that he shared Hulbert's belief that the NA didn't know what it was doing. Excluding himself, of course, Spalding believed the players had no idea how to run their association. He favored a more centralized system in which team owners ran the show and players were merely employees. Hulbert was thinking along precisely the same lines.

In midseason, Hulbert secretly signed Spalding to a contract for the 1876 season, naming him team captain as well, which at the time made Spalding, in effect, both field manager and general manager. He also received a healthy raise plus 25 percent of gate receipts. He was now vested in the club.

Spalding knew a good deal when he saw one. Knowing that a winning team would draw big crowds and maximize his contract, Spalding convinced teammates Deacon White, Cal McVey, and Ross Barnes to join him in Chicago, and he also recruited another midwesterner, Adrian Anson, a member of the Philadelphia-based Athletics and a young player of considerable promise and flair. Together, Anson and Spalding would tower over the game for the remainder of the century like no other men.

Word of the signings soon leaked out, and the ensuing uproar made the remainder of the 1875 season even more problematic. Disgruntled Boston fans caustically referred to Spalding and the others as "secessionists," a potent insult less than a decade after the Civil War. Some members of the NAPBBP wanted the contracts voided and the White Stockings and any other club that had signed players in midseason expelled from the association.

Hulbert and Spalding did everything but twist the ends of their mustaches. This was exactly what they wanted. Chicago was a significant market, and Spalding was the marquee player of the era. Without either, the association had no credibility, as some other association members were well aware. Using the *Chicago Tribune* as a mouthpiece, the two started a drumbeat of criticism against the NAPBBP, citing problems for which Hulbert and Spalding just so happened to have solutions. Their argument resonated with some other clubs, and in the offseason Hulbert and Spalding proposed a solution: forming an entirely new organization, a league of the most powerful existing teams that would be controlled by the club owners rather than an association of players.

On February 2, 1876, Hulbert met in New York with other disgruntled club representatives from Boston, Cincinnati, Hartford, Louisville, New York, Philadelphia, and St. Louis. They thought of themselves as revolutionaries and looked to the nation's forefathers as their model.

Spalding wrote a constitution that echoed the Declaration of Independence:

> We the undersigned Professional Baseball Clubs of the United States, by our representatives in convention assembled, in the City of New York this 2d day of February, a.d. 1876, lamenting the abuses which have insidiously crept into the exposition of our National Game, and regretting unpleasant differences that have arisen among ourselves growing out of an imperfect and systemized code, with a view of relieving ourselves from the incubus of such abuses . . . hereby announce that we have this day organized ourselves into a "National League of Professional Baseball Clubs."

Those who have since tried to find some supernatural foundation for the misfortune that would later haunt the team that became the Cubs would do well to begin their search here. Hulbert's coup wrested control of baseball away from the players and forever placed it in the hands of the capitalist owners. For better or worse, simmering tensions and distrust between players and management have dogged baseball ever since and continue to do so today. One can, rightly, trace that back to Hulbert.

All of a sudden, the NAPBBP didn't have clubs in the nation's biggest cities, and it would survive in name only. The new league quickly distanced itself from its forebear, sloughing off lesser clubs in favor of those representing larger cities. Each club in the eight-team circuit contributed $100 toward the creation of a central league office, based in New York, that would handle scheduling and manage league affairs, and Morgan Bulkeley was elected league president. The new circuit tried to clean up baseball's tawdry image, banning Sunday baseball and the sale of alcohol at the ballpark, paying umpires a standard fee of five dollars per game, and raising admission from twenty-five cents to fifty cents to keep the riffraff out of the park.

That spring the White Stockings worked out indoors at the Athenaeum until the weather warmed, while the club opened its offices at 1039 Wabash Avenue, just around the corner from the ballpark on the corner of Wabash and Twenty-third. In the first game of the season, Spalding, who also served as the team's manager, twirled a shutout, beating Louisville 4–0, then threw another shutout on May 10, when the club played its first home game in the ramshackle Twenty-third Street Grounds. The White Stockings, paced by the batting of Ross Barnes and Adrian Anson and the pitching of Spalding, who won forty-seven games, easily outdistanced the competition, winning the pennant by six games with a record of 52–14.

For Hulbert, Spalding, and Chicago, it was a win-win-win situation. Chicago drew more fans than any other club. Spalding was heralded as a managerial genius. He cashed in on his notoriety in the rapidly growing city and opened a sporting goods business with his brother.

Unfortunately, Chicago's success did not spread to the rest of the league. A postseason series against second-place St. Louis failed to excite fans, and much as had happened in the NAPBBP, the first few seasons of the NL were marred by financial problems and defections. When the New York Mutuals and Philadelphia Athletics failed to complete their final western road trips, they were booted from the league.

Even the White Stockings were not completely immune from trouble. Before the start of the 1877 season, Spalding, all of twenty-six years old, decided to retire from the mound and transfer to first base. He claimed that he was beginning to slip, a perception shared by no one else in the game. In reality, he was smitten with the business end of baseball. His sporting goods business was taking a great deal of his time, and pitching required too much mental and physical energy. Playing first base allowed Spalding to give his business the attention it needed.

Thus, Spalding inaugurated another grand tradition of Chicago Cubs baseball, one since followed by both later owners, such as Philip K. Wrigley, and the Tribune Company. For much of their history, the Cubs have taken a backseat to the larger business interests of management. Spalding used the White Stockings to position himself to make money regardless of how well the White Stockings played. Wins and losses were less important than profit potential, a circumstance that, over time, Cubs fans would find as recognizable as Wrigley Field's outfield ivy.

The club signed St. Louis pitcher George Bradley to replace Spalding, but there had been a reason Spalding was known as "the King of the Pitchers." The White Stockings finished the season with a record of only 28–33 and

placed fifth in the now-six-team league as Boston recaptured the title.

Spalding's supposed baseball acumen took a beating over the course of the season, and he jumped from the sinking ship, retiring as a player at the end of the season. But his business acumen remained acute. He wore a fielder's glove all season—one of only a few players to do so at the time—and thus helped to popularize a piece of equipment that he just happened to manufacture and sell at his store. He convinced the other clubs that the league

Cap Anson was known as much by his imperious leadership methods as by his playing chops. A giant of his times, standing at six-foot-two and weighing over two hundred pounds, the powerful first baseman was a popular figure for cartoonists of the day.

Albert G. Spalding was one of a handful of nineteenth-century players whose performance and vision transformed the game of baseball from a sleepy town-green ritual into a genuine, blood-and-guts, big-city spectacle. In roughly a decade, Spalding went from being merely a great pitcher to one who dominated his sport like no other. In his spare time, he founded the greatest sporting goods empire of the nineteenth and early twentieth centuries while also helping to establish organized baseball as America's national pastime.

needed to use a single, standard ball and secured a contract to supply the NL with just such an "official" baseball, one that Spalding could then also sell to others. He also acquired rights to publish the *National League Guide*. In short, in less than two years he had not only remade the game but gained a virtual monopoly over the manufacture and sale of baseball equipment. He retired as an active player at age twenty-seven to run his business and serve as a club official, probably the first professional ballplayer in America to parlay his skill on the diamond into an even more lucrative career in the game off the field.

The White Sox didn't miss him on the field, for in 1878, as shortstop Bob Ferguson took over as team captain, the club actually improved by a few games to finish at .500. The club also moved into a new ballpark, Lakefront Park, on the same site as the park that had burned in the Great Fire. It was hardly an improvement over the Twenty-third Street park, for the site had been used as a dump after the fire, and all manner of debris now worked its way out of the ground over the course of the season. The new park did, however, sport one of the shortest fences in baseball, less than two hundred feet down the lines; the home run, previously a baseball rarity, became somewhat less so.

Just before the end of the season, however, Ferguson was informed that he would not return as team captain. He was prone to throwing temper tantrums, and over the course of the season the players had tuned him out. In Spalding's last season, he had mentored Adrian Anson, and the White Stockings probably should have given him the job instead of Ferguson. Now they did. The face of the White Stockings was about to take center stage.

Anson, by now nicknamed "Cap" owing to his status as team leader, was the first "Mr. Cub." Perhaps more than any Cub ever, Anson and the ball club became synonymous. Under Anson, the White Stockings would evolve into a powerhouse at a time when baseball was transforming itself from a game that would appear archaic today into its modern form. Anson was one of the few players to survive, and even thrive, during this transition. More than any other player, the young Anson, with his broad shoulders, wide, open face, and handlebar mustache, was the face of baseball in the nineteenth century.

By 1879 he already had a well-deserved reputation as not only a talented player but an innovative one. He is credited with being the first third-base coach, standing in foul ground, ribbing the opposition, and giving instructions to base runners. Some baseball historians also give him credit for inventing the hit-and-run play. He was a pioneer in using signs, platooning players, using a pitching rotation, and holding a formal spring training. A strapping six-foot-two, Anson weighed more than two hundred pounds, making him a giant in this era. A speedy runner in his youth, Anson, who primarily played first base after taking over for Ferguson, was best known as a hitter. In a twenty-seven-year career, he would hit over .300 twenty-four times and be nearly as dominant a player in his era as Ty Cobb and Babe Ruth were in theirs, a feat made even more impressive by the fact that Anson was simultaneously considered the game's best field general.

But it was Anson's personal charisma that really set him apart. He was strong-willed, disciplined, confident, and combative; at times he exhibited arrogance that even bordered on the obnoxious as he argued with umpires, baited other players, and berated his own teammates. Fans in other cities taunted him with cries of "Cry-Baby," but Anson was unaffected by the jeers. Had any other man in the game acted the way Anson did, he'd have been smacked down. But Anson, like Cobb and Ruth, could get away with behaving the way he did because he could back it up with his play. He fit Chicago, for like the city he represented, Anson admitted to having no equal. He was bigger than the game, a fact that would prove to be his greatest fault. Anson, by the force of his personality, would soon draw the color line in baseball.

As Anson was taking command in the winter before the start of the 1879 campaign, the league went through its annual reshuffling before settling on an eight-team lineup. Indianapolis withdrew, and Milwaukee went broke and was booted from the league, replaced by clubs from Cleveland, Syracuse, and Buffalo. The White Stockings once again took advantage, acquiring several key players from the disbanded nines.

Under Anson's lead, the White Stockings got off to a terrific start in 1879. At the end of June, their record stood at 23–4, and they held first place by five and a half games. The pennant seemed all but certain.

Contemporary Cubs fans can probably infer what followed next. First, pitcher Terry Larkin, who had thrown

nearly 1,500 innings over the previous three seasons, was bothered by a sore arm; he would even stop in the middle of a game to apply ice. Then, in early August, with their record at 35–12 and still leading by five and a half games, the White Stockings took a day off and traveled to Dubuque, Iowa, to play an exhibition for $150. Catcher Frank "Silver" Flint lost a nail on his thumb to a foul ball, and as the *Tribune* reported a few weeks later, "Anson's liver was affected. The thumb recovered but the liver is still out of condition. . . . These are not ordinary times and just now that liver and its workings are the source of great anxiety. . . . Everybody knows what the trouble is and people go around the streets with fearful forebodings." Chicago lost not only the game but whatever magic had blessed the first half of the season.

The undefined "trouble" remained just that. Anson's "liver trouble" knocked him out of the lineup and back to his farm in Marshalltown to recuperate. The White Stockings thoroughly collapsed: the league's best team from April to July was terrible for the remainder of the season, going 11–21 and finishing an astonishing ten and a half games back of first-place Providence with a record of 46–33. Thus, another Cub tradition, the late-season swoon, was put firmly in place.

Fortunately, Anson recovered just as quickly as he had been stricken. In late October, the White Stockings, Cincinnati, and Rochester embarked on a barnstorming tour of California organized by Spalding, sometimes playing each other, sometimes playing local clubs. Anson got a good look at Cincinnati's Mike Kelly, who had hit .348 in 1879 while playing the outfield, third base, second base, and catcher.

Everything Kelly did on the field impressed Anson. Like Anson himself, Kelly was big, nearly six feet tall, but he was much faster and a better all-around athlete. Already a strong hitter, Kelly's speed, instinct, and versatility set him apart. As one contemporary said of him, "His strongest advantage was that he was always ready. He could take advantage of a misplay which others wouldn't see until afterward." He played aggressively at a time when few players did, taking the extra base, stealing, and putting pressure on the opponent, while his ability to play all over the diamond made him invaluable. Anson had taken note of how his club broke down at the end of the 1879 season.

THE NEW BASE-BALL GROUNDS AT CHICAGO, ILLINOIS.—Drawn by W. P. Snyder from a Sketch by L. Braunhold.—[See Page 299.]

The White Stockings' home at Lakefront Park, as depicted in *Harper's Weekly*. Note the lake view in the grandstand shown in the bottom left corner.

When he was ill, there had been no adequate replacement, and in one September game the White Stockings had been so debilitated by injuries that they had to borrow a player from the opposing team. Kelly's adaptability could provide some insurance.

Kelly shouldn't have been available. At the end of the season, the club owners entered into a secret agreement that allowed each to "reserve" five players from one season to the next; by agreeing not to attempt to sign players on reserve from other clubs, the owners effectively kept salaries down. But Cincinnati manager Cal McVey, a former member of the White Stockings, didn't think the fun-loving Irishman took the game seriously. He was right. As talented as Kelly was on the field, his off-field behavior did not bode well for a long career. Ruggedly handsome, Kelly was keenly aware that he was attractive to the ladies, and he loved the nightlife, fast living, and alcohol even more than baseball. For all his ability, he *played* baseball,

he didn't work at it, an outlook he carried over into his private life. If Anson was the face of the game on the field, the rakish Kelly was the ultimate player off the field. They called him "King" Kelly, and he took his title seriously.

Perhaps Anson saw a bit of his younger self in Kelly, for as a young man, Anson too had earned a considerable off-the-field reputation before settling down. Anson swept in and signed him to a contract. But if he expected Kelly to settle down in Chicago, he would be disappointed.

Anson made one other move in the offseason. Pitcher Terry Larkin was finished. To replace him, Anson signed not one but two pitchers—speedballer Larry Corcoran and curveball artist Fred Goldsmith.

Never before had a team had *two* frontline pitchers. One was generally considered sufficient, with a backup who was only used rarely. As a result, in a season that now lasted more than eighty games, top starting pitchers sometimes threw five hundred to six hundred innings out of a possible seven hundred or so. Even though the rules still required a pitcher to throw underhanded, most were exhausted by the end of the season and lasted only a few years before breaking down completely.

Using two pitchers in some kind of rotation was groundbreaking. Not only did the strategy protect the health of both pitchers, but Corcoran and Goldsmith used contrasting pitching styles. According to the rules at the time, pitchers were not allowed to bend the arm at the elbow, but most utilized a technically illegal but widely accepted wrist snap to impart speed and put spin on the ball. Corcoran was considered a speed pitcher. Goldsmith, on the other hand, lacked Corcoran's speed but was a pioneer of the curveball. In fact, until his death, Goldsmith took issue with those who credited Candy Cummings with the invention of the pitch. Teams that faced Goldsmith and Corcoran back to back had to adapt to their differing styles, and on occasion Anson even used one man in relief of the other in the same game, making that adaptation even more difficult.

From top to bottom, the 1880 White Stockings were revolutionary. In a sense, they were the first modern team, a perception supported by the fact that in four of the next five seasons Chicago would win the championship.

Anson's innovations didn't stop with the pitching rotation. He recruited a team of giants. In an era when few players stood more than five-foot-seven or -eight, fully half of his squad stood six feet tall or more, intimidating the opposition before the first pitch was thrown. His ball club was also better trained. Before the start of the season, Anson put his team through what could be considered the first organized spring training. He worked the club hard and put into place the style of play he wanted them to use during the season. For instance, for a number of years Anson himself had occasionally been making use of the "hit-and-run" play when he was at bat. Now he instructed others in the strategy, and in 1880 Kelly and White Stocking outfielders George Gore and Abner Dalrymple made use of the play as well. Anson also pioneered the use of hand signals to communicate with players on the field. Pitcher Larry Corcoran picked up on the approach, and after he developed a curveball of his own, he began to signal to his catcher which pitch was coming next by moving around the chaw of tobacco in his cheek.

Still, it was Kelly who really put the White Stockings over the top, for he was one of the most creative players in baseball history, one whose skills were made even more pronounced by an equal measure of baseball savvy and raw talent. He found a way to exploit every possible advantage during a game, such as cutting corners when he ran the bases if he noticed the umpire looking the other direction. In one particularly notable act of tactical brilliance, Kelly was sitting on the bench when the opposition lofted a foul ball in his direction. The King sprang to his feet, called out, "Now catching, Kelly," and caught the ball. The out stood, for there was no rule against making a substitution in the midst of a play. And rather than slide directly into the base, Kelly developed the flamboyant "hook"

Chicago utility man Michael "King" Kelly was one of nineteenth-century America's two reigning sporting gadfly/superstars (along with John "I can lick any man in the house" Sullivan) and was constantly celebrated on tabloid front pages for activities both on and off the field. His sale to the Boston Beaneaters in 1887 not only established a financial threshold for baseball greatness but inspired one of baseball's greatest nicknames, "$10,000 Kelly."

KING KELLY, THE FAMOUS CATCHER AND ALL-AROUND BALL-PLAYER.

slide, which deceived the fielder into reaching out to make the tag as Kelly hooked the base with his free leg, a signature move that later inspired the popular song "Slide, Kelly, Slide." Together, Anson's leadership and Kelly's dynamism created a devastating combination.

From their opening day 4–3 win over Cincinnati, the White Stockings were the class of the league, a step ahead. Corcoran and Goldsmith stayed strong all year, Kelly played all over the diamond, and the White Stockings were one of the most dominant teams in the history of the game, leading the league in virtually every important statistical category. A twenty-one-game winning streak from June 2 through July 8 gave them a gaudy 35–3 record and effectively settled the pennant and championship, for as yet there was no such thing as a World Series. The club cruised to a final mark of 67–17, finishing fifteen games ahead of second-place Providence. The *Tribune* offered that over the course of the year the White Stockings had displayed "the finest illustration of the beauties and the possibilities of the noble game of baseball that the American people have witnessed since the sport was devised," and that Anson was "almost infallible in judgment . . . no field captain ever so fully possessed the confidence and regard of his men as does Capt. Anson." That was no hyperbole.

There was no reason to make any changes, and the White Stockings made none in 1881, beginning the campaign virtually unchanged despite the fact that the pitching distance was increased to fifty feet to make hitting a bit easier. They dominated once more and romped to another pennant, this time by nine games, with a record of 56–28.

There seemed to be no end in sight to Chicago's dynasty. Every key player on the team was still under age thirty. But on April 10, 1882, team president William Hulbert passed away. Hulbert was rightly hailed as the founder of the National League and, as the *Tribune* noted, "the brains and backbone of that organization." Albert Spalding took over as team president.

The White Stockings, in an anomaly, got off to a slow start in 1882 and were below .500 into mid-June before turning the season around. They won seventeen of their last eighteen games to sweep to another pennant, edging out Providence by three games.

The victory was not without controversy. In the last month of the season, the Worcester franchise nearly went under. Afraid that would result in an unbalanced schedule and cast doubt on the championship, Albert Spalding set up a nine-game postseason series between Chicago and Providence to decide the title. But when Worcester unexpectedly did finish the season and Chicago finished three games ahead, Spalding tried to back out. Providence, however, demanded that the postseason series be played.

Other clubs also wanted a crack at the White Stockings. Another professional league, the American Association, had been formed, and champion Cincinnati also challenged the White Stockings. Spalding agreed, looking at the two-game set as a tune-up for the Providence series, while Cincinnati viewed the game as a referendum for the new league. It was, in the broadest sense only, the first "world series," a meeting between two league champions.

Unfortunately, because Anson didn't take the games very seriously, they were stripped of any lasting significance. In the first contest in Cincinnati, Mike Kelly wasn't even in town, and Anson let pitcher Larry Corcoran play shortstop. Cincinnati swept to a 4–0 win. Chagrined by the loss, the White Stockings put some effort into game two. Corcoran pitched and threw a shutout to win 2–0. They declared victory and then took off for their series with Providence.

The White Stockings, with nothing to gain, would have preferred to retire for the year. Anson made that clear in game one. This time he let outfielder Hugh Nicol play short and put Corcoran in left field. The *Tribune* observed that the White Stockings played in a "don't care sort of manner," and Providence won easily, 10–4.

In fact, the White Stockings lost all three games played in Providence; then the series left for first Philadelphia and then New York before returning to Chicago, by which time the *Tribune* was referring to it as the "Hippodrome Folly," an arranged exercise signifying nothing but greed on the part of the two participating teams. Most fans sensed that Chicago had lost the first three games simply to ensure a full complement of games, and as the series continued and Chicago won four of the next five games, interest in the series waned. The finale was played in, of all places, Fort Wayne, Indiana. The White Stockings won, 19–7, in a game the press described as "a great disappointment. . . . It was poorly played and the players seemed to take no inter-

In 1882 the Chicago White Stockings became the first National League franchise to win three straight pennants. Included in this nattily attired ensemble are future Hall of Famers King Kelly and Cap Anson. Anson led the team with a .362 batting average, while Kelly led the league with thirty-seven doubles and played shortstop—his second position in three seasons. Pitching aces Fred Goldsmith and Larry Corcoran led the three-man staff with twenty-eight and twenty-seven victories, respectively.

est in it." Still, with three straight pennants, the White Stockings were the greatest team in the history of the game to that point, and manager Cap Anson was widely acknowledged as the man responsible for that. Sadly, however, Anson himself would soon provide reason to ignore those accomplishments.

Up to this point, the participation of African Americans in the national pastime had, on rare occasions, been tolerated. Although none were on the roster of a National League club, a handful of African Americans played organized baseball in lesser leagues, most notably pitcher Bud Fowler in the New England League and Moses Fleetwood Walker, a catcher from Oberlin College and the University of Michigan who played for Louisville in the Northwestern League.

That situation began to change in 1883. And Cap Anson was a significant reason why.

The White Stockings began the 1883 season in search of their fourth straight pennant. Fred Pfeffer took over at second base. The Chicago press soon began referring to the foursome of Pfeffer, Anson, Tommy Burns, and Ned Williamson as the "Stonewall" infield—an impenetrable barrier that was considered the best in the game for much of the next decade. Anson added fleet outfielder Billy Sunday as a fourth outfielder. Sunday, like Anson, was a Marshalltown, Iowa, native, but after only a few years as a hard-living member of the White Stockings, Sunday had a change of heart, became born-again, and left baseball to become famous as an evangelist.

Otherwise, the White Stockings were little changed. In the offseason, Lakefront Park had received a complete makeover and was now the finest ballpark in the land, with seats for ten thousand spectators, including plush luxury boxes. It also featured the smallest playing field. Nowhere was it more than 300 feet to the fence, and down the lines it was considerably less—180 feet in left and 196 feet in right. In fact, the fences were so close that balls hit over the fence were counted as doubles, not home runs. Clubs from New York and Philadelphia replaced Worcester and Troy as NL members, and the eight-team league added nearly twenty games to the schedule.

After a quick start, the White Stockings slumped in June and nearly fell out of the pennant race. In August, as they struggled to save the season, one game, an exhibition with Toledo on August 10, would eventually overshadow every other game in Cap Anson's career.

Before accepting the engagement, Anson and Spalding reportedly informed Toledo that the Chicago players would not share the field with the club's African American catcher, Moses Walker. Indeed, in 1881 the White Stockings' second baseman, Fred Pfeffer, playing for Louisville, had walked off the field rather than face a semipro club that featured Walker behind the plate.

When the White Stockings arrived in Toledo, the question appeared moot, for Walker had a sore hand and was not even in the lineup. He would watch the proceedings from the bench.

But that wasn't good enough for Anson. As the *Toledo Blade* later reported, the White Stockings, reacting "with the swagger for which they are noted," announced that they wouldn't share the field "with no damn nigger." Anson protested the longest and the loudest and tried to bully Walker out of the ballpark.

Yet Toledo manager Charles Morton refused to be intimidated. In fact, he inserted Walker into the lineup, in right field.

Anson roared, but Morton told him in no uncertain terms that the White Stockings would either play or not be paid. Anson relented, but not before he was overheard telling Morton, "We won't never play no more with the nigger in." The White Stockings then defeated Toledo 7–6 in extra innings as Walker went hitless.

But the damage was done. Anson had articulated baseball's latent racism, brought it to the surface, and given it a face—his own. This wasn't Fred Pfeffer walking off the field. It was Cap Anson, the game's biggest star and greatest manager, taking a very public stand. Although the incident got little ink outside of Toledo, word of Anson's stand traveled fast, and he would soon find occasion to reaffirm his viewpoint.

The specific genesis of Anson's racism has never fully been explained. He avoided the subject in his autobiographical writings and apparently never broached the topic off the diamond except to make the claim that he had been the first white child born in Marshall County, Iowa, which previous to its settlement by Anson's father had been Indian territory. While it is true that Anson's brand of racism was commonplace at the time, even in the North, and shared by the vast majority of professional baseball players, Anson cannot be considered blameless. For it was he, and no one else, who made race an issue on this occasion and several others. In fact, he went out of his way to do so publicly. He was fully aware that he was one of baseball's most prominent figures, a stature he cultivated and relished. He had to know that if he took a stand on the issue, others would look to his example, just as they looked to his example in regard to his strategic innovations. In fact, he may well have hoped for just that result.

At the same time, one cannot blame Anson alone. Albert Spalding was club president and perhaps the only bigger name in the game, and he was probably the only man in the game who could have disagreed with Anson. He did not. Yet Spalding has received a pass in regard to race. Ironically, the sporting goods company Spalding founded would eventually owe much of its success to the marketing of its product to African Americans.

Although Anson's racism would taint both his own personal reputation and that of the White Stockings of the era, at the time it had no negative impact on either. The White Stockings, despite a late-season surge in 1883, missed out on another pennant, finishing second to Boston.

They would follow suit in 1884, opening the season with twenty road games and winning only six to effectively end the season. Goldsmith and Corcoran, despite

Anson's use of a pitching rotation, both began to wear down, and matters weren't helped by a rule change at Lakefront Park. In 1884 balls hit over the fence were home runs, not doubles. Anson himself hit five over a two-game period, and the club hit 142, paced by Ned Williamson's 27—a record at the time. Unfortunately, Chicago's opponents found the fence just as easy to reach, and the White Stockings enjoyed little advantage.

Before the year was over, however, Anson found a pitcher to lead the White Stockings into a new era—Harvard graduate John Clarkson. Clarkson was so impressive that by the time the White Stockings opened the 1885 season, Fred Goldsmith was gone and Corcoran was relegated to secondary duty as Clarkson became the White Stockings' number-one hurler.

That wasn't the only change. Beginning in 1885, pitchers were allowed to throw overhand, although the batter could still call for either "high" or "low" pitches. The City of Chicago, which owned the land, sold Lakefront Park, and the White Stockings hurriedly built a replacement, West Side Park, at the corner of Congress and Throop Streets. Although the stands were much bigger than Lakefront Park, the field was still undersized, particularly down the lines, where it was barely two hundred feet to the fences, still the shortest distance in the league.

Paced by Clarkson, whom Anson used in about two-thirds of Chicago's 112 games, in 1885 the White Stockings resumed their march to the pennant. But they had a rival that was fully their equal, the New York Giants, a team that had been created by a virtual merger between the American Association Metropolitans and the National League Gothams. Pitchers Tim Keefe and Mickey Welch were the near-equal of Clarkson, and first baseman Roger Connor led the league in batting. Between them, the two clubs led the league in absolutely every significant statistical category. They were so dominant, in fact, that only one other club, Philadelphia, finished above .500—but still some thirty games out of first place.

The pennant came down to a final four-game series between the two clubs beginning on September 30. Chicago led going in, with a record of 84–21 to New York's 81–23, and needed to win only two of the games to clinch the pennant. The Giants, meanwhile, needed to take three of four and then hope that Chicago ended the season in

a tailspin. Incredibly, this was the first time the league championship had come down to such a series.

Ten thousand fans turned out at West Side Park, which included representatives of most teams in both the NL and the American Association and reporters from the *New York World*, *Herald*, and *Times*, along with a host of Chicago scribes. Fans packed the stands and even squeezed onto

Second baseman Fred Pfeffer, along with first baseman Cap Anson, shortstop Tommy Burns, and third baseman Ned Williamson, was part of the infield unit referred to by Chicago sportswriters as the "Stonewall" infield. Pfeffer, nicknamed "Dandelion Fritz," helped lead Chicago to pennants in 1885 and 1886.

SAVIOR OF THE GAME

William Hulbert's role in the early history of baseball is obvious and undeniable, and virtually every historical account of the game in the nineteenth century makes note of his significance. To say that Hulbert was the preeminent nonplaying baseball figure of the nineteenth century would not be an overstatement. During his lifetime, he was often referred to as "the Savior of the Game" for his role in the creation of both the reserve clause and the National League. Hulbert, as much as any other man, turned baseball into a business. Everyone who makes money from the game today should, in part, thank Hulbert.

Why then was William Hulbert not elected to the National Baseball Hall of Fame until 1995? It all goes back to 1876.

Although Hulbert was responsible for the creation of the National League, at the time the new league was primarily seen as the brainchild of Hulbert and other western baseball interests based in St. Louis, Cincinnati, and, most significantly, Chicago. To succeed, the National League needed to court teams from baseball's eastern strongholds in the Northeast. So, rather than become league president himself, Hulbert agreed that the first league president should be a representative of these eastern clubs. Morgan Bulkeley, whose father founded the Aetna Insurance Corporation, was the principal financier of the Hartford, Connecticut, team. With some reluctance,

he agreed to serve as the National League's first president, but only after extracting a promise from other club owners that he would have to serve no more than one year in the role. They agreed, and Bulkeley assumed the presidency.

A year later, as promised, he stepped down, and now Hulbert, who had by then earned the trust of his colleagues, took over as president. Unfortunately, his tenure proved to be tragically short. On April 10, 1882, at the age of forty-nine, Hulbert died of a heart attack. In the meantime, Bulkeley's connection to baseball ended when he stepped down as NL president. Although he went on to an accomplished career, later serving as mayor of Hartford and governor of Connecticut and as a U.S. senator, he had nothing whatsoever to do with baseball for the remainder of his life.

Fast-forward to 1936. The National Baseball Hall of Fame was scheduled to open in 1939 as part of baseball's celebration of its spurious one-hundredth anniversary in 1939. But in order to have a Hall of Fame, the game needed men to honor. In 1936 members of the Base Ball Writers Association of America (BBWAA) were given the authority to elect players from the twentieth century to the Hall, and in 1936 they elected the first five players—Ty Cobb, Babe Ruth, Honus Wagner, Christy Mathewson, and Walter Johnson. A "Veterans' Committee" was created to consider figures from the nineteenth century, but in 1936 the group failed to agree on any honorees.

A year later, in 1937, the Veterans' Committee was replaced by a "Centennial Commission" to select nonplayers for admission when the museum opened in 1939. American League founder and longtime president Ban Johnson was an obvious choice and

received widespread support. Politically, however, the commission thought it advisable to balance Johnson's election with that of his National League counterpart. Although Hulbert, like Johnson, deserved credit as league founder, the commission chose to balance the selection of one league's first president with the selection of the other. Morgan Bulkeley, who was still a familiar name to many members of the commission because of his political career and great personal wealth, was selected to enter the Hall of Fame at the same time as Ban Johnson.

Hulbert's crime, apart from engineering the election of Bulkeley, was to die too soon. After his death in 1882, he was rather rapidly forgotten. Baseball was virtually ignored as a serious topic for historians until the 1950s, and in the interim his contributions to the game were all but forgotten.

Historian Harold Seymour and his wife Dorothy virtually created the field of baseball history in 1960 with the publication of the book *Baseball: The Early Years*, an expanded version of Seymour's history thesis from Cornell University. Hulbert's key role in baseball's early history was brought to light, and over the next thirty-five years other historians, many of them members of the Society for American Baseball Research, filled out the Hulbert biography. Finally, in 1995, the Veterans' Committee saw the light and at long last selected Hulbert for inclusion in the Hall of Fame.

the playing field, causing special ground rules to be put into effect, while those without tickets tested the strength of nearby rooftops. Newspaper offices in both New York and Chicago were mobbed by fans awaiting the posting of dispatches and special bulletins.

It was over quickly. New York won the coin toss and chose to take the field behind pitcher Mickey Welch, against whom, the *Tribune* noted, "the Chicago boys have heretofore gone down before like saplings in a storm." On this day, though, Chicago wielded stronger lumber. With Kelly and Gore on second and third and two out, Pfeffer sent one into the overflow crowd for three bases, scoring two. Williamson and Burns followed with hits, and the White Stockings had four first-inning runs. New York never recovered, and Chicago, behind pitcher Jim McCormick, who had taken over for Corcoran in midseason, went on to win, 7–4.

The Giants desperately needed a win the following day, but now they had to face Clarkson, already the winner of fifty-one games. Anson, who could afford to gamble, had wisely withheld his ace from the first contest. New York, which now needed to sweep the remaining three games, countered with Tim Keefe.

The second game was closer, but for New York the result was the same. Chicago won, 2–1, the margin of victory a home run by Pfeffer. For all intents and purposes, the season was over.

But not for Chicago. Now that the White Stockings were virtually guaranteed a pennant, the club agreed to meet American Association champions St. Louis in a series scheduled to last either seven or nine games. Each club owner put up $500, with the winning players to split the $1,000. Players from both clubs shared receipts from the first two games of the series, and Spalding and St. Louis owner Chris Von der Ahe split the gate receipts of the remaining contests.

That arrangement proved critical, for the series should have, and could have, been the first real World Series. But the players rightly concluded that Spalding and Von der Ahe were making most of the money, and as a result the players treated the series with disdain and indifference. So did Spalding, for that matter. He didn't even attend the start, traveling to New York instead for the annual league meeting.

Copyright 1887
Goodwin & Co.

Clarkson, P.

In 1885 Hall of Fame pitcher John Clarkson enjoyed one of the greatest seasons in major league history as he forged an astonishing 53–16 won-lost record and helped lead Chicago to its fifth pennant in the first decade of the National League. In four seasons in Chicago, the right-hander set a franchise record for career winning percentage (.705) as he won 136 games and lost only 57.

Game one was played in Chicago on October 14, before a crowd of only two thousand; even fans sensed that the players weren't taking the game seriously. The most entertaining part of the whole day was the foot-racing and ball-tossing contest held before the game. Ned Williamson won the ball toss with a throw of 133 yards, 1 foot, and 4 inches, and Fred Pfeffer circled the bases in just a shade under 16 seconds. Then the two clubs played to a 5–5 tie as the White Stockings conveniently scored four runs in the final inning.

The second game, in St. Louis, was little better. In the sixth inning, with St. Louis leading 4–2, a bad call by the umpire led to hundreds of fans storming the field, which forced the White Stockings to wield their bats in order to hold their position. St. Louis finally walked off the field in protest, and the White Stockings claimed victory by forfeit.

The series rapidly deteriorated as the players appeared to be tired of the whole mess and just wanted to go home. Anson lost control of his club—outfielder George Gore had shown up for game two drunk—and indifference ruled. After another game in St. Louis, the series went on the road, where fans showed little interest in the contests. The series ended—finally—on October 24. Chicago pitcher John Clarkson "overslept"—likely a euphemism for a hangover—and missed his ride to the game, and Chicago lost, 13–4. Although both teams had agreed that the final contest would be definitive, afterwards Anson decided that, in fact, the series, which ended 3–3, was a draw and should be considered as such, and besides, the players from both teams had already agreed to split the $1,000 purse. Whatever.

In 1886 Detroit pushed Chicago, but the White Stockings still managed to win their fifth pennant in seven seasons, this time by two and a half games with a record of 90–34. St. Louis won the AA pennant again, and the two clubs again decided to try a postseason series. This time

The West Side Grounds was initially used solely as a venue for Sunday baseball; all other games were played at the South Side Grounds, owing to its proximity to the World's Fair. Starting in 1894, the West Side Grounds was used for all games.

Baseball Game in West Side Ball Grounds, Chicago

Von der Ahe and Spalding did their part to drum up interest by issuing a series of challenges and counterchallenges before finally settling on a winner-take-all purse of at least $15,000, presumably enough to keep fan interest high and ballplayers sober.

Fat chance. After the White Stockings won game one, 6–0, they lay down in game two, 12–0, as pitcher Jim McCormick was reportedly dead drunk and pitched that way. Anson wanted to give him another chance in game three, but once again he was too drunk to take the mound. Clarkson pitched most of the game, but in the late innings St. Louis hitters became so compliant that Anson let Ned Williamson mop up.

The series lurched to its drunken conclusion amid charges of "hippodroming," fixes, and other complaints, never more obvious than in the final game. Chicago led that contest 3–0 entering the seventh inning as Clarkson was twirling a no-hitter, only to lose 4–3 in ten innings as the White Stockings suddenly and inexplicably made mistake after mistake before Curt Welch scored the winning run on a wild pitch. Spalding was so angry with his team that he refused to give them train fare back to Chicago.

In fact, the loss so disgusted Spalding that it caused him to reconsider his role in the game. Over the next few seasons, he would slowly extract himself from an active role in the management of baseball.

Up to this point, he had put up with a certain level of competitive insolence from his players. As long as the White Stockings were winning—and making money— Spalding and Anson had both overlooked the occasional hangovers, bouts of drunkenness, and other scandals of high living that infected the club. But no longer. The Series against St. Louis had been the last straw.

King Kelly drew the bulk of their ire, for not only was Kelly a drunk, a gambler, and a womanizer, but even worse, his behavior seemed to have little effect on his play, which made discipline impossible to enforce. In fact, although Kelly had spent most of the 1886 season drinking more often and harder than ever, he had responded with his greatest season ever, hitting .388, scoring 155 runs in 118 games, and knocking out 175 hits. A performance like that led others on the team to follow his example and excuse their own behavior and ignore Anson's admonitions to hew to the straight and narrow. John Clarkson, the young

pitching star, was the latest recruit to show signs of falling. Spalding was determined to purge his club of alcohol.

Outfielder George Gore was the first to go. Despite the fact that Anson considered him one of the best players in the game and would later name him to his all-time team, Gore's drinking made him morally expendable, and on November 24 he was sold to the Giants. That same day veteran outfielder Abner Dalrymple, who had slumped in 1886, was shipped to the new Pittsburgh franchise.

If Spalding hoped those deals would inspire sobriety in Kelly, he was disappointed. If anything, the star outfielder became even more belligerent. Kelly and Spalding spent much of the fall sparring in the press, and when the White Stockings gathered in Hot Springs, Arkansas, for spring training in early February, Kelly and pitcher Jim McCormick were absent. Just as well, for Spalding demanded that every player in camp take a pledge of total abstinence. Kelly had no intention of complying, a point he made clear a few days later when he met with Spalding and asked for the $375 bonus Spalding had promised if Kelly behaved in 1886. Spalding not only refused to pay the bonus but reminded Kelly that he had been fined $225 over the course of the season for drinking and he wouldn't be getting that back either.

A few days later, Kelly and McCormick let the club owner know how they felt. McCormick told the press that he could get more money "to walk the streets," while Kelly hurled insults Anson's way over his declining skills and said, "If Mr. Spalding refuses to let me go, I will retire on my laurels. But if he should decide to release me, I would be pleased to become a member of the New York Giants."

It didn't take a genius to see that Spalding's sword would soon be swinging in Kelly's direction. Despite his reputation, Kelly had plenty of suitors. New York's interest was obvious, but Spalding feared that if he sent them Kelly, the Giants would head off the White Stockings in the pennant race.

Kelly's Irish heritage made him particularly attractive to Boston. They contacted Spalding, who started negotiating with their club president. Boston had finished more than thirty games behind Chicago in 1886, and it was unlikely that Kelly would come back to haunt the White Stockings. Spalding received $10,000 for Kelly, and Boston had to kick in another $5,000 to get the player to agree on a contract. The King would prove to be the most popular player Beantown had ever seen and would respond with several stellar seasons, but eventually drink would take its toll. In less than a decade, Kelly would be dead. As Anson later said of the popular star, Kelly had but "one enemy, that one being himself."

McCormick was next. Despite the fact that he had gone 20–4 in 1885, including sixteen straight wins, Spalding did not forget McCormick's sodden performance against St. Louis. McCormick was shipped to Pittsburgh in exchange for another pitcher, young George Van Haltren.

The White Stocking dynasty was finished. Spalding and Anson never made up for their losses, and sportswriters started calling the ball club "the Colts" in reference to the relative youth of Anson's new players.

The White Stockings remained competitive for much of the 1887 season before finishing in third place behind Detroit and Philadelphia. For many Chicago fans, the most memorable moment of the season came when King Kelly made his return with Boston on June 24. All of Chicago went ga-ga—five thousand fans surrounded Kelly's hotel just to watch him leave for the game, and someone hired a band that serenaded him with the song "See the Conquering Hero." Ten thousand more turned out at the ballpark and watched Kelly knock out three hits, but he also made two errors and was thrown out stealing in the 15–13 Chicago win. Afterwards, Kelly claimed to come up lame. When it appeared as if he might sit out the second contest, Spalding and Anson, knowing that another huge crowd was in the offing, paid Kelly a visit at his hotel. Kelly told them that if he didn't have to run the bases, he could play. Anson and Spalding, despite the fact that they were in the midst of a pennant race, and knowing that Boston, sans Kelly, would be much easier to defeat, agreed to allow Kelly to use a pinch runner whenever he got on base. Kelly responded with three hits in front of another crowd of ten thousand as the White Stockings squeezed out an 8–7 win.

Still, despite their preseason pledge of sobriety, the remaining White Stockings went their own way too often and ignored Spalding and Anson. In the same game in which Kelly used the pinch runner, Chicago shortstop Ned Williamson tried to beg out, claiming he too was lame. When Spalding told him he was needed and would still

play, Williamson reluctantly agreed, then pulled his ticket to the races from his pocket and tore it up in Spalding's face.

History, however, remembers the White Stockings of 1887 for another reason. On July 19, Chicago visited Newark of the International League for an exhibition game. Newark newspapers announced that the club's best pitcher, George Stovey, would face the White Stockings.

That was all Anson needed to know. Stovey was black. Just a few days earlier, the International League, a minor league founded in 1886, responded to pressure from white ballplayers and announced that despite the fact that five African American ballplayers were already in the league, the league would approve no more contracts for African Americans, although those already playing could remain active. At the same time, Stovey's prodigious talent was undeniable. He was rumored to be on his way to the New York Giants.

Anson put a stop to that. Once again, he refused to take the field with a black player, reportedly saying, "Take him out or I get off." Newark, unlike Toledo, capitulated, pulling Stovey from the contest and offering the excuse that he had "complained of sickness."

Anson's stand emboldened others in organized baseball to take a similar position. Later that year, St. Louis backed out of a scheduled exhibition against the all-black Cuban Giants when the St. Louis players objected, and the New York Giants never made a move to sign Stovey. Although a few African Americans would play another season or two in the minor leagues, the color line was being drawn, and Anson, who regularly referred to African Americans as "darkies," "coons," and "niggers," stood vigilant along the border.

The White Stocking players seemed to sense that the Chicago club was on the wane. Before the beginning of the 1888 season, John Clarkson let Spalding and Anson know that he wanted to play for Boston, and he threatened legal action against organized baseball's "reserve clause," the contractual agreement that, in effect, bound a player to a team for life. Then as now, the reserve clause was key to baseball's financial success. Although it would eventually be given legal status under baseball's antitrust exemption, in 1888 that was not yet the case, for as the *Tribune* noted, "The best legal authorities agree that the reserve rule is an unlawful compact." Spalding didn't want to risk a legal fight, so he accommodated Clarkson, selling him to Boston on April 3 for $10,000.

That sank the White Stockings. Clarkson won thirty-three games for Boston and led the league in innings pitched. His replacement in Chicago, George Van Haltren, won only thirteen and began a transition to the outfield as the White Stockings, still with the best offense in the league, burned through ten pitchers during the season, an extraordinary number for the era. After leading the league through June, they faltered and finished nine games behind New York.

The game was beginning to pass by Anson and Spalding. Both had been involved in the game virtually from the start and had seen baseball evolve from a mannered contest in which gloveless gentlemen pitched underhanded from a distance of forty-five feet to a big business in which men threw overhand as hard as they could from fifty-five feet away. In 1887 the right of the batter to call a low or high pitch was withdrawn, and in 1888 the league settled on the four-ball walk and three-strike strikeout. Anson was still one of the most productive hitters in the league, but as a manager he failed to keep pace with changing styles of play and found it more difficult to motivate the next generation of players. In the field, he was beginning to slow, and his glove work at first base, while never exemplary, now occasionally drew critical comment. Opponents had started to refer to him as "Old Man," a moniker Anson tried to enjoy. On at least one occasion, he played while wearing a false white beard and wig.

Spalding was increasingly interested in the longer view. Before the start of the 1888 season, he had announced that he intended to take the White Stockings and an all-star squad he would dub the "All Americas" on a worldwide tour. Spalding referred to them as "baseball missionaries," and they were, for he was a smart enough businessman to know that if he could manage to spread the game of baseball to Europe and beyond, the demand for his sporting goods products would grow.

The tour began in Chicago on October 20, then moved on to California. The ballplayers left San Francisco by boat on November 18 and traveled to Hawaii, New Zealand, and Australia before crossing the Indian Ocean for Ceylon. They continued on to Egypt, where the players were

BATTING CHAMPIONS

1876	Ross Barnes	.429
1880	George Gore	.360
1881	Cap Anson	.399
1884	King Kelly	.354
1886	King Kelly	.388
1912	Heinie Zimmerman	.372
1945	Phil Cavarretta	.355
1972	Billy Williams	.333
1975	Bill Madlock	.354
1976	Bill Madlock	.339
1980	Bill Buckner	.324
2005	Derrek Lee	.335

famously photographed on the Sphinx, then crossed the Mediterranean to play in Italy, France, and England before returning in April to New York, where they were greeted with a welcome-back banquet at Delmonico's. The tour lost money and did little to popularize the game, but it did make the Spalding name somewhat more familiar overseas. However, the tour also left the White Stockings both exhausted and undermanned—Ned Williamson ruined his knee while playing a game in Paris, tearing it up while sliding on a rock-strewn field. His loss proved critical, for

Anson considered him "the best all-around ballplayer the country ever saw." Anson's Colts—as nearly everyone now called them—were never really in the pennant race in 1889 and barely finished above .500.

At the end of the season, the National League faced its most significant challenge to date as John Montgomery Ward, president of the fledgling Brotherhood of Base Ball Players, organized a third major league to compete with the National League and the American Association, the Players' League. The innovative circuit sought to free players from the confines of the reserve clause and break the monopoly of club owners. In short, the Players' League rejected the league created by Spalding and Hulbert in favor of one in which players and management shared the responsibility and the risk of operating a club.

When half the players in the NL jumped to the new league, no team was more affected than the White Stockings. They lost nearly every player on the roster apart from Tommy Burns and Anson, who owned stock in the club. Meanwhile, the new league placed a team in Chicago, the Pirates, providing the White Stockings with real competition.

The end result weakened both the American Association and the National League, and it made the White Stockings contenders again. Unfortunately, no one cared as fans turned their back on the club. Even though the White Stockings won forty of their last fifty games to finish only six games behind first-place Brooklyn, league attendance dropped nearly in half, and barely 100,000 fans turned out to see the White Stockings for the season. After earning a profit of more than $200,000 from 1883 through 1889, Chicago lost $65,000 in 1890.

Between the Players' League, the National League, and the American Association, there simply were not enough fans to provide financial support for twenty-five major league teams. National League club owners helped prop each other up and in general were better financed than either the Players' League or the AA. Although the Players' League, which had the best players, was an artistic success, at the end of the season it folded.

Most players who had left the White Stockings wanted to return, but Spalding wouldn't hear of it—in his eyes, they were disloyal, and he wanted nothing to do with them. In fact, Spalding wanted less to do with running the

club, period. The world tour had been exhausting, and over the previous few years he had taken heat in the press for selling Kelly and Clarkson and losing everyone else to the Players' League. On March 25, 1891, Spalding resigned as team president and named James Hart, a crony from his real estate investments and former manager of clubs in Louisville and Milwaukee, as the new team president.

Anson was dismayed. He'd always believed that he would take over for Spalding, but Spalding, after making the transition from player to owner himself, was a true believer in baseball oligarchy, particularly after the Players' League debacle. Anson, despite his many years in the game, was just a player, and Spalding considered him unsuitable to take on a significant role in club management. Embittered but with few options, Anson stayed on.

There was, however, one additional benefit to the demise of the Players' League. The Pirates' ballpark, South Side Park, on the corner of Thirty-fifth and Wentworth (virtually across the street from where Comiskey Park would later be built), was available. Not only was the new park better than West Side Park, but the annual rent of $1,500 was only 20 percent of the cost to play on the West Side and the park was more convenient to public transportation and closer to the site of the 1893 World's Fair, which promised to increase traffic. The ballpark itself was an improvement over West Side Park, although in 1891 the club used both diamonds, playing on the West Side on Mondays, Wednesdays, and Fridays and on the South Side the remainder of the week. (They were banned from playing on Sunday in either location.)

Paced by pitcher "Wild Bill" Hutchison, who won 44 games, and Anson, who led the league with 120 RBIs, the surprising White Stockings surged into first place and stayed there. In mid-September, with only fifteen games remaining, they led second-place Boston by six and a half games, and the pennant seemed certain.

But this was Chicago, and as Cubs fans would have ample opportunity to learn over the ages, a pennant is never less likely to fly in Chicago than when it looks like a sure thing. The White Stockings inexplicably lost nine of their next fifteen games, while Boston won eighteen in a row, including a key five-game series against New York in the last week of the season. Chicagoans thought it smelled when the Giants inexplicably failed to use their three top stars, Buck Ewing, Roger Connor, and Amos Rusie, in the contests, and they were right.

When National League owners had conspired with one another to prop each other up financially during their war with the Players' League, club ownership became murky as owners who had money took team stock from those who did not in exchange for financing. As a result, most owners ended up owning pieces of several clubs, what critics called "syndicate baseball." Chicagoans believed that New York threw the final set of games because Boston owner Arthur Soden owned a portion of the Giants. Ironically, that arrangement had first been championed by Albert Spalding, who himself owned even more stock in the Giants than Soden. Anson later wrote that there was a "conspiracy" against his club, and president Hart sent a letter to league officials in which he complained, "Were I under indictment for murder, with the circumstantial evidence against me as strong as it appears to be against the New York club, I should expect to be hanged." Needless to say, Hart lived and Boston retained the pennant when the NL dismissed Hart's charge.

In the offseason, the American Association collapsed, leaving the National League as the only major league. The circuit added four teams, bringing the number of league members up to twelve. Teams scrambled to sign the remaining AA alumni who were suddenly without contracts.

The White Stockings, however, missed out and were further damaged when Fred Pfeffer and Tommy Burns were released, leaving Anson as the only remaining member of the "Stonewall" infield. At age forty, he was the second-oldest player in the game and known far and wide as "the Grand Old Man of Baseball."

But Anson's tenure as the most respected man in the game was over. All of a sudden, the Cubs were also-rans as over the next six seasons Boston and Baltimore traded the pennant back and forth. In 1893 baseball virtually completed its evolution into its modern form when the pitching distance was pushed back to sixty feet, six inches, the same distance in use today. While Anson, as a hitter, was able to keep pace with the changes, he was less successful doing so as a manager. He found modern players less disciplined than in his younger days and was repeatedly angered when they went over his head in regard to disciplinary matters. As a strategist, he still managed as if the White Stockings were a team of sluggers playing in old Lakefront Park. As his own playing skills eroded, he tended to undervalue what he himself could not do very well anymore, like run the bases or cover ground at first base. Baltimore manager Ned Hanlon, who made aggressive use of the steal, bunt, and hit-and-run play, became the consensus pick as baseball's best manager.

Although Anson still managed to pick up some valu-

In 1889 Albert G. Spalding brought his world baseball tour, which included many Chicago players, to Egypt, where players posed near the Sphinx for this iconic nineteenth-century portrait.

OLD JUDGE CIGARETTES Goodwin & Co., New York.

Standing all of five-foot-nine and weighing only 175 pounds, right-handed pitcher "Wild" Bill Hutchison (often spelled Hutchinson) was one of the dominant pitchers of his era while leading the league in victories for three consecutive seasons with won-lost totals of 42–25 (1890), 43–19 (1891), and 37–34 (1892).

able individual ballplayers, uncovering such stars as short-stop Bill Dahlen, outfielder Bill Lange, and pitcher Clark Griffith, over time Chicago slipped back as too many of Anson's prospects proved ill adapted to succeed in the modern game. The dynasty of the 1880s had been relegated to the history books. From 1892 to 1897, the White Stockings were never in the pennant race.

At first, Chicago hardly noticed. Since the Great Fire, the city had been rebuilt and never looked back, exploding in an orgy of stockyards, factories, and hustle and bustle and a fair measure of good old-fashioned out-and-out hus-

tle. Chicago was a dangerous place, vice-ridden and violent, but by the 1890s the city was both looking ahead and looking to change its reputation, pouring its resources into the so-called White City, the Hyde Park site of the Columbian Exposition of 1893, the World's Fair. While the fair was in swing, the White Stockings were but a footnote. Although the vast number of tourists in Chicago pushed baseball attendance in 1893 up to nearly 250,000 fans, that was less than the number of people who attended the World's Fair on the Fourth of July alone.

Before the 1893 season, Albert Spalding decided to build a new ballpark, the West Side Grounds, on land he owned on Polk and Lincoln Streets on the West Side. Although he was no longer team president, he still wielded significant influence. He then rented the $30,000 ballpark back to his own club for $6,000 a year, although in 1893 it was used only on Sundays before the club moved there virtually full-time in 1894. For the first time, the White Stockings had a large, symmetrically shaped home. It was 340 feet to the outfield fence down the line, and 560 in center field. The era of the cheap home run was over, at least for a while.

But the new park was not without its problems. Spalding separated the twenty-five-cent bleacher seats from the fifty-cent pavilion seats with barbed wire and also strung a barbed-wire fence eight feet high between the bleachers and the field to keep fans from interfering with play. That was all fine and well, but the effect was to create a cage that virtually penned the crowd in.

On August 5, 1894, a huge crowd was on hand watching Chicago play Cincinnati. In the seventh inning, with Chicago leading 8–2, Anson struck out. As he did, fans noticed a commotion in the bleachers along the left-field line—a small fire had broken out in the loose paper and other debris beneath the wooden stands.

In less than a minute, flames were licking up between the planks. As the *Tribune* noted the next day, it was then that "the stampede began. There was a rush, a scramble for the exits: the flood of men choked them in an instant." Some five thousand fans were trapped between the fire and the barbed wire.

A few managed to scramble calmly over the fence and onto the field, but in seconds the crush of people pinned hundreds against the fence as the crowd went into full-blown panic and men climbed over each other to try to escape. The scene was ghastly: the *Tribune* reported that "the wires were strung with hair and strips of skin and flesh." Some Chicago players grabbed bats and went to work on the fence, trying to pry holes in the wire mesh. Fortunately, just as the fire began to reach the mob, according to the *Tribune*, "the terrific pressure from the crowd forced the wires from their staples." The fence collapsed, and hundreds tumbled onto the field and away from the flames. Although the *Tribune* reported that "it seemed as if the entire field was covered with bleeding men," no one was killed, although at least five hundred were reported to have been "more or less seriously hurt," and area hospitals were swamped. One-half of the stands were destroyed before the fire was put out. Had the fence not given way, many hundreds would have died. The fault was almost certainly Spalding's, but no one publicly dared lay the blame at the feet of the powerful club owner.

They didn't blame Anson for the fire either, but that was about all. The club finished the 1894 season thirty-four games behind; after bouncing back to win more than they lost in 1895 and 1896, the club slumped to ninth place with a record of 59–73 in 1897.

After the 1895 season, Anson had cashed in on his notoriety by starring in a play called *The Runaway Colt*. Now, as the club lurched toward the end of the 1897 season, many were calling for the Grand Old Man of Baseball to run that way again.

Anson did not want to go. He refused to admit that he was slowing down as a player and that he had lost the respect of his team, who often made him the butt of their jokes and rolled their eyes when he tried to give them advice. Opposing players openly mocked Anson for his wooden play in the field, and in a season in which the league batting average was .292 and Baltimore's "Wee Willie" Keeler hit .424, Anson hit only .285, with no power. Still, he put himself into the lineup day after day, usually batting cleanup.

The end was awkward, as everyone in Chicago, save Anson, saw it coming. His contract with the club expired on January 31, 1898. Although the newspapers openly reported that Hart planned to hire former Chicago third baseman Tommy Burns as manager in 1898, and Hart and Burns were known to be close, Anson kept saying that he intended to play and manage another year. Spalding interceded and took him on a month-long trip to England, hoping Anson would get the message and resign, but "the Old Man" never took the hint.

The end came at midnight on January 31. As the *Tribune* reported the next day:

Adrian Constantine Anson is no longer the head of the Colts. With the expiration of his contract last night Anson's connection with the club ceased. He has not said a word, but has waited for the club to act while they waited for him to move. The veteran died an easy death. . . . How many runs he has batted across the plate, how many times he has stepped upon the rubber and how many cheers his unfailing bat has brought down only the recording angel can guess.

"TRIO OF BEAR CUBS"

The modern history of the Chicago Cubs began at 12:01 A.M., February 1, 1898. Cap Anson and Albert Spalding had cared for the ball club from its infancy through an idyllic childhood resulting in six National League pennants by 1886, followed by an awkward and increasingly lonely adolescence. Now it was time to grow up, not only for the Chicago ball club but for the National League. In only a few short years, the team would forge an entirely new identity.

Although Chicago traditionally had some of the best attendance figures in the NL, elsewhere attendance was stagnant in the twelve-team league, which now included teams in Chicago, New York, Boston, Philadelphia, Brooklyn, Cincinnati, St. Louis, Washington, Louisville, Pittsburgh, Baltimore, and Cleveland. Fan interest in a few cities—most notably Washington and Cleveland, where neither team had been in a pennant race for years—had dwindled to almost nothing. Since the demise of the Players' League

On September 15, 1902, the first double play recorded by the famed trio of Tinker, Evers, and Chance was made against the Reds at the West Side Grounds. According to legend, shortstop Joe Tinker (left) and second baseman Johnny Evers barely spoke to each other off the field but played well enough to inspire poetry and help the Cubs win four pennants and back-to-back World Series in 1907 and 1908.

and the American Association, the NL, with no challengers, had become arrogant. Baltimore and Boston dominated the league, a situation that didn't really bother most owners. Ownership of individual clubs had become so convoluted, with virtually every magnate owning a stake in several teams, that it hardly mattered to them which team won. So-called syndicate baseball more or less ensured that everyone would make money.

No club owner would admit it, but by 1898 the National League was moribund. The game had entered the "dead ball era," an epoch that featured little offense and spawned "scientific" or "inside" baseball—runs scored by way of the bunt, steal, and sacrifice. Although the press warned that the game was losing fans, the National League was blind to its own growing set of problems. Every club had the same admission charge of fifty cents and treated fans as if seeing a ball game was a privilege. On the field, too many players fought and scrapped and acted like bullies. Off the field, alcohol and gambling fueled increasingly volatile behavior.

It was no different in Chicago. Under new manager Tommy Burns, the situation didn't change. Shortly after he was hired, when asked what alterations he intended to make to the team, Burns told the Chicago press, "We stand pat"—a fitting description of the entire league. Burns made a halfhearted effort to make a few deals but had no

incentive to make wholesale changes. Former manager Cap Anson's departure left a hole at first base; Burns merely moved third baseman Bill Everett, a fine hitter but an atrocious fielder, across the diamond and shuffled the deck at a few other positions, but he did nothing dramatic. The big addition to the club would eventually prove to be catcher and outfielder Frank Chance, whom center fielder Bill Lange had discovered in California, but for the time being Chance was only a part-time player. Big, rangy, and fast, Chance would take a few seasons to make his mark. He did, however, make a notable debut. In his first game on April 29, 1898, he caught Clark Griffith. Entering the ninth inning, Griffith was twirling a shutout and Chicago led Louisville, 16–0. But Griffith considered shutouts unlucky. When two Louisville hitters lofted pop-ups near home plate, Griffith ordered Chance to let the balls drop. Louisville scored two meaningless runs, saving Griffith from the hazard of bad luck. This was the kind of nonsense National League fans were getting tired of seeing.

In Anson's absence, the press gave the club a new name—"the Orphans." The use of the name "Cubs" was still several years away. Although the team featured the

---

The West Side Park, surrounded by a curious array of outlaw bleachers erected on neighboring rooftops, was the site of the Cubs' greatest triumphs.

1898

best pitching staff in the league and finished the 1898 season twenty games over .500—a marked improvement—the club didn't sport much of an offense and still failed to contend for the pennant.

Even if they had been in the running, it didn't much matter, for in 1899 syndicate baseball made a complete mockery of the National League. A conspiracy of owners dismantled the powerful Baltimore Orioles—who had finished second to Boston in 1898—and sent their best players to Brooklyn to create a powerhouse there. Not wanting to be left behind, St. Louis, Cleveland, Cincinnati, and New York entered into similar alliances, creating instant contenders out of St. Louis and Cincinnati while relegating New York and Cleveland to the second division. The Cleveland Spiders, in fact, became perhaps the worst team in the history of baseball. They would win only 20 games in 1899 while losing 134 to finish an astonishing 84 games out of first place.

Chicago didn't have much of a chance either. On January 25, just a few weeks before the creation of the Brooklyn powerhouse, team president James Hart made that virtually certain. At Burns's suggestion, Hart dealt shortstop and team captain Bill Dahlen to Baltimore for Gene DeMontreville. The deal completely backfired. Dahlen went on to star in Brooklyn for much of the next decade, while DeMontreville fizzled in Chicago. Burns then made a serious faux pas. When it came time to name a new team captain in the place of Anson, who had held that title for years, Burns said, "I think I will appoint myself." The players were dumbfounded. Traditionally, captains were active players, as Anson had been. Burns hadn't played in a decade. The players rebelled, elected outfielder Jimmy Ryan team captain, and began to question Burns's authority and judgment.

The Orphans played the 1899 season as if they truly had been abandoned, barely making it to .500 and finishing twenty-six long games behind Brooklyn. At the end of the season, Bill Lange, dubbed "Little Eva" by his teammates for his dancer's grace, decided to retire.

Perhaps no player in the history of baseball has ever made such a poor decision at such an inopportune time. Lange was at his peak. At age twenty-eight, he had a career batting average of .330 and perhaps another decade of baseball ahead of him. Had he stayed in the game, in all

Outfielder Bill Lange is shown in the Chalmers automobile awarded him by Chicago's baseball writers. In 1900 he gave up a promising career at age twenty-eight to marry Gail Geiselman, whose wealthy father disdained ballplayers. Not only did Lange spend his entire seven-year career with the Cubs, but his lifetime batting average of .330 is third in franchise history.

likelihood he would have had a plaque in the Hall of Fame.

He gave it all up for love. The San Francisco native had fallen for Gail Geiselman, the daughter of a wealthy San Francisco businessman who looked at all ballplayers with disdain. He would allow Lange to marry his daughter on one condition—that Lange retire and join his father-in-law in business. Lange agreed, but appeared to regret the decision at a banquet held in his honor at the end of the season as he broke down in tears. Although Lange went on to become a wealthy man, he was not so lucky in love. A few years later, he and Gail divorced.

In only two years, Burns had lost the services of two star ballplayers and replaced neither one, something the Orphans could ill afford. There had been rumors since midseason that Hart was looking to make a change, and he didn't wait very long. In late November, Burns "resigned," and Hart hired Tom Loftus to manage the club in 1900.

Loftus was an odd choice. As a player, he'd been something of a career minor leaguer, playing a total of only thirty-three games in the major leagues. But since 1880 he'd found more or less steady employment as a manager

HOME RUN CHAMPIONS

Year	Player	HR
1884	Ned Williamson	27
1885	Abner Dalrymple	11
1888	Jimmy Ryan	16
1890	Walt Wilmot	13
1910	Frank Schulte	10
1911	Frank Schulte	21
1912	Heinie Zimmerman	14
1916	Cy Williams	12
1926	Hack Wilson	21
1927	Hack Wilson	30
1928	Hack Wilson	31
1930	Hack Wilson	56
1943	Bill Nicholson	29
1944	Bill Nicholson	33
1952	Hank Sauer	37
1958	Ernie Banks	47
1960	Ernie Banks	41
1979	Dave Kingman	48
1987	Andre Dawson	49
1990	Ryne Sandberg	40
2000	Sammy Sosa	50
2002	Sammy Sosa	49

in places ranging from Dubuque, Iowa, and Milwaukee to Columbus, Ohio. Most recently, he'd served as a manager in Ban Johnson's upstart Western League, which was starting to make some noise. In fact, Loftus had first become acquainted with Hart when, at Johnson's behest, he'd started exploring the possibility of placing a Western League franchise in Chicago, one that he was likely to own at least in part. Hart may well have decided to hire him as a way to thwart such a move.

That would soon prove a vain desire. On March 8, 1900, the National League elected to drop four teams, reducing the number of ball clubs in the league to eight. While the move was intended to strengthen the remaining clubs, in the end it had the opposite effect. Ban Johnson was ambitious. He had no intention of running a minor league for the rest of his life. Eventually he wanted to turn the Western League into a second major league. By dropping four teams, the NL had just opened up some new territory for Johnson to exploit.

A week later, Johnson made his move, transferring his Grand Rapids club to Cleveland and announcing that he had also put a team in Chicago, where he installed Charles Comiskey, who had operated several Western League franchises, as team owner. He also renamed his new circuit, dropping the regional name "Western League" for the more formidable "American League."

At this point, Johnson still hoped to work things out with the NL. He promised to abide by the "National Agreement," honor existing contracts, and not compete for players. Hart, in turn, was surprisingly compliant and decided not to challenge the new club. In fact, he even met with Comiskey to work out mutually beneficial details. The new club agreed to locate on the South Side, leaving the North and West to the Orphans, and Hart got Comiskey to agree not to use the name "Chicago." Comiskey agreed—and immediately chose the abandoned moniker "White Stockings" for his team, the same franchise that is today known as the White Sox.

In reality, even if Hart had wanted to stop Johnson and Comiskey, there was little he could have done. Spalding still retained a portion of the club, and the Western League used sporting goods too. Besides, the American League White Stockings provided the Orphans with a natural rival. Hart realized that once the club was established, they could play each other in exhibitions certain to draw big crowds.

But Hart did not account for the impact of the White Stockings on attendance over the course of an entire season. Then again, no one in the National League correctly gauged the threat of Johnson's new league. For the National League, complacency had become a way of life.

The Orphans stumbled through another season, sometimes playing well, but just as often playing poorly. Their performance on the final day of the season was unintentionally symbolic. Before a crowd of only seven hundred, they played host to Cincinnati in what the papers correctly referred to as Chicago's "last game of the century." The game was nominally important—if Chicago swept, they could conceivably finish in fourth place, while Cincinnati was trying to keep out of the cellar. But as the *Tribune* noted, "The occasion was more like a wake than anything else. . . . The Chicago team played in dead march time while the Red danced jigs all around them."

The Orphans dropped both games, 13–4 and 9–1. That was bad enough, but the manner in which they were defeated made it appear as if that had been the goal. Across two games the club made seventeen errors and played with such an obvious lack of enthusiasm that by the middle of the first game the few fans in attendance were openly questioning the motivation of the players. During one quiet stretch, one crank got the crowd laughing when he yelled out, "Are any of you stiffs engaged for next year?" a question that spawned dozens of imitators over the remainder of the afternoon. By the time Chicago pitcher Jack Taylor was hit by a line drive in the ninth inning of game two, the *Tribune* reported, "The crowd had

Jimmy Ryan anchored the Chicago outfield for fifteen seasons before retiring with the franchise lead in triples (142) and a .310 batting average. In 1899 his teammates on the Orphans elected him captain, in part as a protest against manager Tom Burns.

tired even of sarcasm." Fatigue had also struck the Orphans, for not a man remained on the bench to replace Taylor, forcing the umpires to call the game. "Another century is coming," reported the *Tribune*, "and perhaps in that Chicago might win another pennant." The reporter was referring to the Orphans, for across town the White Stockings had already hoisted the American League flag.

Ban Johnson took the game's temperature and decided it was time to move. Just after the end of the season, he

moved teams into Baltimore and Washington and announced that the American League was minor no more. He was ready to join the big leagues.

The National League owners laughed so hard they nearly choked. In January, Johnson asked the NL to accept him as an equal partner and stated his intention to accept the same playing rules and respect the reserve clause. The National League was still so convinced of its own superiority that it saw no reason to speak with him. Johnson was sent off like a beggar.

One colleague of Johnson's later described him as someone who "always remembers a friend but never forgets an enemy." Now the NL was Johnson's enemy, and he was determined to take it by force. The brushoff meant war. He had the financial backing to outbid the National League for talent, and he intended to do so. The players were more than eager to switch leagues—ever since the demise of the Players' League they'd been treated like slaves. Johnson targeted the best.

The turn of the century saw the Cubs become a dynasty, and many of their stars national celebrities. In this Gillette advertisement, Frank Chance and Johnny Kling are featured prominently.

For the remainder of the winter and into the spring, baseball remained in the news. Almost every day another player or two jumped from the National to the American League, usually at twice the salary. Johnson's insurgency grew as he placed teams in Philadelphia and Boston to go head to head against NL clubs in those cities as well.

The NL owners were slow to react—at first, many didn't even try to stop their stars from leaving, clinging to the false hope that Johnson was bluffing and the players would remain loyal to the NL. By the time they realized that both assumptions were entirely wrong, it was too late.

And nowhere was it more too late than in Chicago. Hart and Spalding balked at paying a penny more for "their" ballplayers. Meanwhile, Johnson, knowing that his new White Stockings had to compete head to head against the National League club, gave Comiskey carte blanche in going after Orphan players.

One by one, the Orphans ran away to the South Side and points farther east and north. Pitchers Clark Griffith and Nixey Callahan and outfielder Sam Mertes joined the White Stockings. Third baseman Bill Bradley and outfielder Jack McCarthy went to Cleveland. Pitcher Ned Garvin joined Milwaukee, and catcher Roger Bresnahan jumped to the Baltimore Orioles. About the only talented players to remain with the club were pitcher Jack Taylor and Frank Chance.

Since the Orphans had fled en masse, the Chicago press needed a new, more appropriate name for the club. They selected the obvious, dubbing the team "the Remnants." Some reporters tried to look on the bright side. One looked at those players who remained and proclaimed, "The anarchic element on the team is gone"—but so was all the talent. Before the season was a month old, the *Tribune* was already referring to the Remnants as "tiresome."

Desperate times spawned desperate measures. On May 3, the Remnants tried to plug a hole and purchased pitcher Rube Waddell from Pittsburgh. An immense talent, the left-hander would eventually win consecutive league strikeout titles and help lead two teams to pennants. Unfortunately, Chicago would not be one of these teams.

Normally, a pitcher of Waddell's skill is rarely available at any price. When one is, there is usually a reason. In regard to Waddell, there were several. As Philadelphia manager Connie Mack once said of him, Waddell "had a two-million-dollar body and two-cent head."

At the very least, he was one of the more eccentric men to ever play in the major leagues. At worst, he may have been mentally ill or disabled. Waddell not only marched to his own drummer, but danced and sang and did somersaults. Since turning pro in 1897, he'd already driven several managers to distraction, jumping his club at a moment's notice to go fishing, drinking to excess, and acting like he was living in an altogether different world that only occasionally intersected with that of his teammates. The sound of a fire bell could send him racing down the street—or out of the ballpark—searching for the fire. On his way to the ballpark, he would become distracted and spontaneously join a sandlot football game.

Waddell had pitched well with Pittsburgh in 1900, but in 1901 the Pirates were flush with pitching and didn't need Waddell, or his distractions, and made it known that he was available. Loftus had seen Waddell pitch in the minor leagues and was convinced that his potential could offset his problems. Besides, the Remnants needed pitching, and they were willing to put up with just about anything.

Waddell got off to a quick start. Before he ever stepped onto the field in Chicago, he took in a game from the stands, watching his old and new teams square off. Nothing wrong with that. But he did so while brandishing a revolver, which alarmed some of his former teammates, for Waddell had promised to "get even" over some unknown transgression when he was traded. They played and won the game while nervously looking over their shoulders, keeping an eye on Waddell.

In four seasons as Cubs manager, former Boston Nationals manager Frank Selee never won a title before tuberculosis forced him to retire. He did, however, lay the groundwork for the dynasty led by player-manager Frank Chance.

His performance whetted the appetite of the home crowd, and two days later, on May 5, fourteen thousand turned out to watch Waddell pitch in a Chicago uniform for the first time. He lost, 4–2, but Chicago fans cheered his every move and left the game thoroughly entertained, for Waddell played the game with a heavy accent on the word "played."

For a brief period of time, it appeared as if the Remnants might become respectable, but apart from Waddell's

Joe Tinker may have been only a .259 lifetime hitter, but he did have the distinction of being remembered in a poem that brought him to Cooperstown, as well as of playing shortstop for the greatest dynasty in Cub history.

occasional brilliance, little went right, and with each defeat, fan interest waned. By September, even Waddell was bored. It was fall, and in his mind autumn meant fishing.

He jumped the club and after a few days appeared in the uniform of a semipro team from Gray's Lake (now Grayslake), just northwest of Chicago. They had enticed him away from the Remnants by promising that he could go fishing six days a week as long as he pitched for them on the seventh day, an easy pledge to make for a team from a town named after a lake. In Waddell's world, Chicago's proximity to Lake Michigan just didn't compare. Still, the pitcher apparently gave the ball club the opportunity to match the Gray's Lake offer. When Loftus and company chose not to, Waddell, whom the *Tribune* referred to as "aboriginal man," decided it was "greater to be a big toad in a small puddle and fish than have to report for morning practice." Despite the fact that Waddell was signed for the 1902 season, the Remnants soon suspended him. His career in Chicago was over. Two years later, Waddell, apparently fished out, reemerged as a star pitcher for Connie Mack's Philadelphia Athletics and was eventually inducted into Baseball's Hall of Fame.

In fact, many National League careers ended after the 1901 season, for few teams—apart from Pittsburgh, which galloped to the pennant by nearly thirty games—met expectations. Attendance had dropped almost everywhere, and someone had to take the blame. In Chicago, the pennant-winning White Stockings outdrew the Remnants by an almost two-to-one margin; the Remnants drew only 200,000 fans, less than half of what they had drawn in 1898.

Of course, the National League owners didn't blame themselves for the slide—that was what managers were for. At the end of the season, Boston fired Frank Selee, even though in twelve seasons his club had won five championships.

That got Hart's attention. He knew Selee and admired him. In fact, Selee had succeeded Hart as Boston manager twelve years earlier. The more Hart thought about Selee, the less he thought of Loftus, for not only had the club finished the season 53–86—only a game out of last place—but without Waddell they were in even worse shape, and there were disturbing rumors that Loftus wanted to play a role in the American League. He viewed the situation in Chicago as hopeless, a poisonous attitude that spread to his players. As soon as the season ended, outfielders Danny Green and Topsy Hartsell and pitcher "Long Tom" Hughes all decided to jump to the American League. Loftus followed them, quitting on October 25 before eventually popping up as a part owner of the Washington Senators. Hart gave Selee a three-year contract to assume command.

For the first time since Anson had manned the club in his youth, Chicago had a manager who knew what he was doing. Selee was an excellent judge of talent, enjoyed contacts throughout the game, and had a record of performance that was beyond reproach. Chicago's horrible record in 1901 gave him carte blanche to make changes in 1902.

He started with what he knew best—his own players from Boston. Before the start of the season, he brought over second baseman Bobby Lowe and outfielder Jimmy Slagle. During spring training, he began experimenting with Frank Chance—who'd drifted from catcher to the outfield—at first base, and Jack Taylor emerged as his number-one starting pitcher. Everywhere else Selee held a virtual tryout camp. Players came and went on a daily basis, phenoms appearing out of nowhere and disappearing just as quickly.

Foremost among his problems was shortstop. Incumbent Barry McCormick had taken his seventy-two errors and jumped to St. Louis in the AL. At first Selee planned to play Lowe at short, but he changed his mind. Early in spring training, Snapper Kennedy seemed to have the inside track, but when Kennedy came up with a sore arm, Selee asked his strong-armed rookie third baseman, Joe Tinker, to give the position a shot.

Tinker had been acquired in the offseason from Portland in the Pacific Northwest League, and Selee had been impressed with his demeanor. Even though he too had a sore arm, Tinker did as he was told.

The transition wasn't easy for the young infielder. He struggled in the field during his first few seasons and made even more errors than the departed McCormick. Selee could live with that, for Tinker, a hard worker, showed steady improvement. At the plate, he was a tough out, and he was particularly adept at the hit-and-run play. Tinker gave Chicago a real shortstop for the first time since the trade of Bill Dahlen.

Notre Dame product Ed Reulbach enjoyed a tremendous rookie season in 1905, winning eighteen games with an ERA of 1.42. Included in his victories were two epic complete-game marathons: eighteen innings on June 24 over the Cardinals and on August 24 over the Phillies.

Selee made so many changes that spring that it soon became obvious that the name "Remnants" no longer applied. Neither did the nickname "Orphans," for Anson was now five years removed and only a few players remained from his tenure. The newspapers sometimes called the club "the Nationals," or "the Nats," to distinguish them from the White Stockings—who were now also known as the "White Sox"—but the name didn't catch.

On March 27, an anonymous reporter from the *Chicago Daily News* anointed the club with a new name when he wrote: "Frank Selee will devote his strongest efforts on the teamwork of the new Cubs this year." The term "cub" was common slang for a young ballplayer, and it very well may be the typesetter who should get credit, for had the word not appeared with the capitalized "C," it might not have stood out. "Cubs" did catch on, however, and the newspaper began using the term more and more often.

Not every newspaper followed suit as over the next few years other names received tryouts in the press. The *Tribune* favored another youthful name, preferring to call the ball club either the "Colts" or, later, the "Zephyrs," in reference to the speed of the players and the blustery Chicago weather. Another publication dubbed the ball club the "Microbes," owing to the small size of so many Chicago players. None of these names resonated with the public the way "Cubs" did. Although the name would not become official for another five seasons, it can safely be said that by the end of the 1902 season, if one walked into a Chicago saloon and complained about "the Cubs," most patrons would have known the conversation was about baseball, not bears. For that reason, they will be referred to in this narrative as the Cubs from this point on.

And somewhat surprisingly, that conversation probably would have been tinged with optimism. For despite using more than thirty players over the course of the season, including twenty rookies, in 1902 the Cubs improved to 68–69. While still thirty-seven games behind pennant-winning Pittsburgh, for the first time in a generation there was reason for optimism. Jack Taylor won twenty-three games and was one of the best pitchers in the league, Slagle and outfielder Davy Jones provided surprising offensive punch, while Tinker settled in at shortstop, Chance saw his playing time at first base start to increase, and Johnny Kling, a holdover, held down the catcher's spot.

When the Cubs were short an infielder owing to injury late in the year, one more important piece arrived. At the end of August, the Cubs purchased diminutive shortstop Johnny Evers from Troy, New York.

For the first time, the combination of Joe Tinker, Johnny Evers, and Frank Chance was in place, albeit not quite in the same place that writer and poet Franklin P. Adams would later preserve them for all time in his well-

Mordecai Peter Centennial Brown was better known by his nickname of "Three-Finger." When he was seven, the right-hander lost his forefinger and part of his middle finger in a grain grinder on his family's farm in Nyesville, Indiana. Despite his handicap, Brown could pitch, and he would develop amazing control of a variety of pitches that spun from his hand in a flurry of drops and curves.

"Trio of Bear Cubs"

known poem "Baseball's Sad Lexicon." They appeared in a game together for the first time on September 1, 1902. Chance played first base, Evers played shortstop, and Tinker accommodated the youngster by moving to third base. They didn't turn a double play, so as yet the world was unaware of the satisfying iambic pentameter of the phrase "Tinker to Evers to Chance."

In time Evers would move to second base and complete the "trio of bear Cubs, fleeter than birds," later memorialized by Adams. Evers was the perfect fit, an excellent bunter and base stealer who got the ball club moving. He was also a steady fielder; dubbed "the Crab" for the way he scurried after ground balls, Evers had a personality that fit his nickname, for the pugnacious infielder made few

"TINKER TO EVERS TO CHANCE"

These are the saddest of possible words:
"Tinker to Evers to Chance."
Trio of bear cubs, and fleeter than birds,
Tinker and Evers and Chance.
Ruthlessly pricking our gonfalon bubble,[1]
Making a Giant hit into a double—
Words that are heavy with nothing but
    trouble:
"Tinker to Evers to Chance."

The above poem, entitled "Baseball's Sad Lexicon" by Franklin Pierce Adams, is baseball's second-best-known piece of verse, surpassed in popularity only by Ernest L. Thayer's classic "Casey at the Bat." But like Thayer's poem, the popularity of Adams's verse was hardly instantaneous.

Adams published the poem in his column "Always in Good Humor" in the *New York Mail* on July 10, 1910. A native of Chicago, Adams later told people that he wrote the poem while traveling to the Polo Grounds to see the Cubs play the Giants, probably a month earlier in June, and originally titled it "That Double Play, Again." At

the time the poem was first published, the Giants were in Chicago playing the Cubs, a series that may have inspired Adams to publish his timely stanza.

The phrase itself, "Tinker to Evers to Chance," is more than descriptive. It is precisely the way the double plays turned by the trio were notated in box scores of the era—verbal shorthand akin to "6–4–3." The phrase was occasionally used in Chicago at the time as a metaphor denoting cool efficiency.

The poem, however, was little known. At the time it was first published, it did not appear in Chicago and inspired no comment. Not until the death of Frank Chance in 1924 did the poem begin to become widely known. Then the *Tribune* erroneously credited the poem to its own columnist Hugh Keough, but Mrs. Franklin P. Adams contacted the newspaper and informed editors that her husband had written the poem, although she believed he had done so in 1908, not 1910.

The poem was occasionally reprinted after that, but it finally received wide distribution in March 1947 when *New York Times* columnist Arthur Daley reprinted it in a col-

[1] The obscure word "gonfalon" means pennant.

Frank Chance was one of the best athletes to ever play major league baseball, and his skill as an amateur boxer gained him universal respect on the rough diamonds of the dead ball era. Chance's speed led to the all-time Cub stolen base record of 400, and his steady bat (.297 lifetime average) and superb fielding made him a superstar. In eight seasons as player-manager of the Cubs, he led them to four pennants and two world championships.

umn about Evers. When Joe Tinker died a year later—the last of the three men to pass away—the poem was widely reprinted and became a part of popular culture. It is widely credited with helping both Johnny Evers and Joe Tinker earn admission into the Hall of Fame.

friends. The antipathy between Evers and Tinker was legendary. They shouldn't have shared a line in a novel, much less one in a poem. Evers later admitted, "Tinker and myself hated each other, but we loved the Cubs."

While things were looking up for the Cubs, the future was not so rosy for the National League as a whole. American League president Ban Johnson had the senior circuit by the short hairs, and the pain was being felt everywhere. In the offseason, the National League sued for peace, and in January, after a protracted period of negotiations, the two leagues agreed to coexist, abiding by the same set of rules and respecting each other's contracts. Albert Spalding, who in recent years had had less and less to do with the Cubs, sold out to Hart, severing his ties with the club. For the Cubs, these changes came at a fortuitous time. They were on the rise in 1903, while the White Sox were beginning to slip.

As part of the agreement between the two leagues, a few Pittsburgh players were redistributed, which brought the Pirates back to the pack and gave the other NL clubs a chance. Pittsburgh still won the pennant, but this time by only six and a half games over second-place New York.

The Cubs were a surprising third. Chance, who hit .327, became a bona-fide star at first base, while Evers and Tinker settled in at second and short. But the real difference was pitching.

Rookie "Tornado Jake" Weimer came out of nowhere to win twenty games, even besting New York Giant legend Christy Mathewson 1–0. Bob Wicker, after failing to stick with the St. Louis Cardinals, found Chicago more to his liking and also won twenty games.

Almost 400,000 Cub fans made their way to the West Side Grounds to see the show. The Cubs' combination of speed, pitching, defense, and just enough hitting fit the dead ball era perfectly.

Peace between the two leagues helped everyone make money, and the desire to keep up the bottom line didn't end with the regular season. Champion Pittsburgh agreed to play American League champion Boston in the first "world's series," a best-of-nine affair.

Although the Cubs had finished the season in third place and the White Sox ended the American League season in seventh place, both clubs decided it would be good business if they too met at the end of the season. As did the

two clubs in Philadelphia and St. Louis. The Giants and Dodgers both refused to play the American League's New York representative, the Americans, but Cleveland and Cincinnati met in a cross-state rivalry. None, however, were as ambitious—or as greedy—as the two Chicago clubs. They decided to play a virtual second season, meeting an incredible fifteen times.

These were not meaningless contests. Fans and baseball writers alike saw the series of games—rightly or wrongly—as a referendum on the relative strength of the two leagues. Interest in the contests was intense, and local bookies were swamped. Although the Cubs had finished the 1903 season with the better record, many observers believed the American League was the stronger circuit, and the White Sox were favored.

The players, however, were not quite as concerned with bragging rights. After a 154-game season, they were not particularly anxious to continue, and even though their contracts extended into October, they weren't thrilled with the idea of playing more without getting paid more.

It showed in their play. As the *Tribune* noted after game one, "Chicago's Colts [Cubs] met their local rivals . . . for the first time in baseball history on the west side grounds and there was absolutely nothing to it." Pitcher Jack Taylor scattered three hits, and his team backed him up with eleven runs as the Cubs won in a shutout. When the Cubs followed up with two more wins, they appeared to be the superior club, although, to be fair, several key White Sox players were injured and did not play.

Then things got funny. Taylor was drilled in his second appearance in game four and appeared unconcerned. As the White Sox pulled back into the series, observers noted that the two clubs seemed determined to keep things close, a perception that increased the next two times Taylor pitched and was shelled: suddenly one of the game's best pitchers couldn't get an out. The old charge of "hippodroming" returned. Crowds remained large, but White Sox president Charles Comiskey felt the need to offer his players $2,500 if they won to ensure that they stayed motivated.

On October 15, the White Sox won, 2–0, to even the series at seven games apiece, potentially setting up a one-game finale to decide everything. This game should have been the biggest in the history of Chicago baseball to that time.

Well, if a tie is like kissing your sister, the Cubs and the White Sox were locked in an unholy embrace. The Cubs stopped being paid on October 15, and they stopped playing. Game fifteen was never played. The series ended in a 7–7 tie, filling the pockets of both Hart and Charles Comiskey, but deciding nothing. It was clear to everyone that, while the series had been entertaining, in essence it had been a big fraud. When the *Tribune* tried to argue that the cancellation of game fifteen by the Cubs somehow proved that the club wasn't interested in money, the argument fell flat, for the paper also argued that "the White Stockings could not have won much more glory by playing and winning the decisive game." Huh?

The rumor mill that ran back and forth between the South Side and the West Side knew the truth, and so did James Hart. Jack Taylor had been on the take, something he admitted a year later when he said, "Why should I have won? I got $100 from Hart for winning, and I got $500 for losing." Both Hart and Selee were incensed, and they made it clear that Taylor was available in trade, as the *Tribune* noted, "for a man equally good and perhaps equally dissatisfied with his surroundings."

They succeeded on December 12, acquiring a pitcher who would prove to be not only "equally good," but better and not at all dissatisfied to be in Chicago. The last-place St. Louis Cardinals badly needed pitching, and Taylor, who had not failed to finish a game he started since June 1901, was certain to eat up a lot of innings. The Cubs were so eager to get rid of him that they packaged the hurler with giant rookie catcher Larry McLean and in return received catcher Jack O'Neill and pitcher Mordecai Peter Centennial Brown, who had won thirteen games for the Cards.

Brown, who already had one of the most memorable names in the game, was even more notable for his descriptive nickname "Three-Finger." At the age of seven, Brown inadvertently stuck his right hand into his uncle's corn shredder (a machine that cut corn into silage), which cut off his index finger at the first joint and damaged his pinkie finger. A few weeks later, Brown fell and broke the other two fingers on his hand. When the hand healed, it resembled a claw—the pinkie finger was paralyzed, his index finger was half gone, and the other fingers were bent and twisted.

Fortunately for Brown, the injury proved to be beneficial for throwing a baseball. His odd grip gave him an advantage, allowing him to impart spin on the ball with little effort. Throwing sidearm, Brown had a curveball that acted something like a forkball, tumbling toward the plate and then dropping or darting dramatically, and his fastball had a natural sink. Good thing, because Brown didn't throw particularly hard. The pitcher was wise enough to recognize the source of his talent too—he eventually acquired the corn shredder from his uncle and put it on display. He made Cub fans forget all about Taylor, and his acquisition would prove to be as significant as that of any other player on the squad.

The Cubs started the 1904 season in California, holding spring training in Los Angeles, which led the *Tribune* to marvel that "it rains so seldom here they don't even have clouds of smoke . . . [and] management does not even have rain checks printed." While the weather was spectacular, the real reason for training in California was to allow the team to barnstorm back to Chicago, bringing big league baseball to the hinterlands and hauling back the proceeds. After leaving Los Angeles, the team traveled to San Francisco, Sacramento, Ogden (Utah), Denver, Colorado Springs, and Omaha, among other places along the way.

A quick start in 1904 had fans thinking of a pennant. The ball club moved into a tie for first place after beating Christy Mathewson and the Giants on May 20, but a series of injuries soon knocked the club back.

The worst of these was to Frank Chance. A right-handed hitter, Chance liked to crowd the plate, and whenever he was hit by a pitch, he became more determined not to be intimidated or to back off. As a result, he became a target.

On May 30, the Cubs played the Reds in a doubleheader in Cincinnati. In game one, Chance and Reds pitcher Jack Harper got caught in a game of chicken. Every time Chance stepped into the box, Harper brushed him back. By the time Chance stepped to the plate in the ninth inning, he'd already been hit twice.

Harper came inside again. This time the pitch froze Chance, and it hit him flush on the side of the head. He was knocked out cold. The invention of the batting helmet was still decades away. He fell to the ground and for several minutes did not move. Then, incredibly, he not only stirred but stood, took his base, and stayed in the game.

He played the second contest as well and was hit twice more by Reds pitcher Win Kellum. Even with his eye blackened, Chance nevertheless played errorless ball and managed a hit. But he looked ghastly. The *Tribune* noted that "if the blow had been an inch farther back, it would have killed him."

Eventually it may actually have played a role in his death. The pitch from Harper was perhaps the worst of the hundred-plus pitches known to have hit Chance in his career. If that wasn't dangerous enough, Chance fancied himself a boxer. He spent much of the offseason in the ring, earning quite a reputation as an amateur. The accumulation of blows, both pugilistic and pitched, eventually caused him to lose much of his hearing and caused headaches that later led him to undergo risky brain surgery. He died young, at age forty-seven.

The next day, blurred vision and a headache forced him out of the lineup. Catchers Johnny Kling and Jack O'Neill were also injured. By the time everyone was healthy, the Cubs had fallen behind the Giants. They would go on to finish the season in second place with an impressive record of 93–60, but still thirteen games behind New York.

In the meantime, Selee kept tweaking his ball club. They had enough pitching, but in order to compete with the Giants, who had outscored the Cubs by almost a run a game, the team needed some offense.

Lucky for them, they had a terrific advantage. Selee was friendly with University of Illinois athletic director George Huff, who was well connected in the sports world, particularly in the upper Midwest. He served as the Cubs' chief scout and was a genius at ferreting out talent as the Cubs took geographic advantage of being on major league baseball's northern and western edge, a location that gave them something of an advantage in acquiring western talent.

But Huff's connections also stretched to the east. In August, he signed outfielder Frank Schulte, who was hitting .335 for Syracuse of the New York State League. Although Schulte didn't crack the starting lineup until

In his first eight complete seasons with the Cubs, "Three-Finger" Brown averaged twenty-four wins per season with an ERA under two runs per game.

1905, he soon became a fixture in right field and earned the nickname "Wildfire," not for his style of play but for his favorite horse.

Each move made Selee's club a little stronger. In the offseason, the club spent $15,000 spiffing up West Side Park, giving it a paint job and adding one thousand seats to the bleachers and several hundred more in the grandstand by adding a few rows in front of the stands and moving the press box to the roof. The players got a new brick clubhouse featuring the latest rage in comfort—showers—and fear of fire caused the club to replace the wooden walkways around and beneath the stands with concrete walks.

Not only is third baseman Harry Steinfeldt the answer to one of the most-asked baseball trivia questions of all time (name the other member of the infield with Tinker, Evers, and Chance), but he also won five pennants in his five seasons with Chicago.

Despite the addition of Schulte, offense was still an issue for the Cubs in 1905. Once again they got off to a quick start, only to fall back when they stopped scoring runs. Still, baseball in Chicago was booming. The Cubs and White Sox were among the top draws in the game, and more than one million fans turned out to see the two teams play in Chicago in 1905, more than watched big league baseball in New York, which was home to three clubs. Hart, who'd bought out Spalding several years before and also ran the lucrative Chicago Gravel Company, decided it was time to retire. He wanted to cash out.

The ball club was a prize. The Chicago market was huge, growing, and already profitable. The first to learn that the club was on the market was a former newspaperman turned press agent for Giants owner John Brush, Charles Murphy, whom the press called "Chubbie Charlie." When Brush mentioned to Murphy that Hart was thinking about selling, Murphy quickly met with Hart, secured an option to buy, and even agreed to pay the club owner a fee for negotiating the sale.

All Murphy needed was cash. He had only $15,000 in the bank and needed an investor who was both wealthy and secure enough to allow Murphy to run the club. Incredibly, Murphy knew just such a guy.

From his newspaper days in Cincinnati, Murphy was friendly with Charles P. Taft, the half-brother of U.S. President William Howard Taft. Taft agreed to front Murphy another $90,000 or so to make the deal happen. As part of the arrangement, Hart received a $5,000 brokering fee, and Frank Chance, a Murphy favorite, was given stock in the club. The deal was announced on July 15 but would not be fully consummated until November. Until then, Hart still ran the club, but Murphy's views were usually taken into account.

A crisis soon tested that arrangement. Manager Frank Selee had never been in robust health. In fact, he had tuberculosis, a malady that certainly wasn't helped by the humid Chicago summers combined with the cloud of pollutants and other toxins that often hung over the city. A bout of appendicitis put him in the hospital in July and left him weak, and indeed, he never completely recovered. Selee stepped down, a move the press at once described as temporary but inferred was permanent. It was also reported that as soon as Selee could travel he was expected to spend the rest of the year in either Colorado or New Mexico for health reasons.

Frank Chance, whom the players had elected team captain, took over. Most realized that he was no interim solution. Murphy in particular was in awe of his first baseman. At the end of the season, as soon as the deal became official, Murphy named him manager. He then asked Chance what the club needed.

When Murphy took over, he told Chance, "I want to win the biggest prize in baseball," to which Chance responded, "You don't want to do it any worse than I do." The Cubs were chasing the Giants, Murphy's old employer, and there was nothing Murphy wanted more than the opportunity to beat his old team, at any price. For the moment, money was no object. Murphy wanted to win and wanted Chance to tell him what—and who—it would take to do that.

Chance could tell that Selee's ball club had peaked. The once-young Cubs were getting a little gray in a few places, namely in the outfield, at third base, and behind the plate. And as players like third baseman Doc Casey and outfielder Jack McCarthy aged, their sinking batting averages dragged the team down. The addition of Schulte in 1905 had helped, but Chance knew that if the Cubs were to continue to improve in 1906, they needed more offense and more youth.

Chance knew exactly whom he wanted. Brooklyn outfielder Jimmy Sheckard was easily the Dodgers' best player. Only twenty-six years old, Sheckard had just one problem—inconsistency. He tended to follow a fine year with a bad one. He'd been only average in 1905, so the Dodgers didn't know what to expect next. They were in disarray anyway, because Charlie Ebbets was battling Ned Hanlon for control of the franchise.

Behind the plate, Chance had his eye on Pat Moran of Boston. Kling was fine defensively but had hit only .218 in 1905, and backup Jack O'Neill hit only .198. Moran was much better than O'Neill, and younger than both men. Kling couldn't catch every day anyway Moran, at the very least, could give the club some insurance.

In December, Murphy went to New York for the annual league meeting and met with Ebbets. Half the teams in the league were after Sheckard, which should have led Ebbets to wonder if it was wise to make a trade, but the Dodgers needed players, plural, and Sheckard, for all his talent, was just one guy. The Cubs dealt from a position of strength and sent Jack McCarthy, Doc Casey, pitcher Button Briggs,

and outfielder Billy Maloney to Brooklyn for Sheckard. Another deal delivered Pat Moran from Boston.

Chance was still without a third baseman, apart from rookie Hans Lobert. That was okay, however, because Chance already had his eye on a replacement.

Cincinnati third baseman Harry Steinfeldt had been one of the best third basemen in the league in 1904, before hurting his leg; when he slumped in 1905, he ended up in manager Joe Kelley's doghouse. It was common knowledge that the Reds were looking to move him.

The Cubs offered Cincinnati young Hans Lobert, a fine prospect, but the Reds wanted more. Jake Weimer had won eighteen games for the Cubs in 1905, but at age thirty-one he was the oldest man on the staff, which made him expendable. The Cubs packaged Weimer with Lobert, and the Reds gladly parted with Harry Steinfeldt.

For all intents and purposes, the Cubs were complete. The addition of Steinfeldt to the "trio of bear cubs," Tinker, Evers, and Chance, gave Chicago the best infield in baseball. All four players were either at or near their peak. The outfield of Sheckard, Schulte, and Slagle was almost as accomplished, if not quite as amenable to literary hyperbole. Every man on the team could run, and they were all schooled in the finer points of inside baseball, bunting, stealing, and using the hit-and-run. Three-Finger Brown, young Ed Reulbach, and Carl Lundgren headlined a pitching staff that, while lacking the star power of New York's tandem of Mathewson and Joe McGinnity, was just as effective, and rookie Jack Pfiester, whom Murphy purchased from Omaha, was one of the game's great prospects.

Murphy looked at his club and was effusive. "Unless we are crippled by accidents," he said, "I certainly think we will make a bid for the flag."

For perhaps the last time in club history, that sentiment was not just wishful thinking.

PEERLESS

They didn't stop. Not for a day, not for an hour, not for a second. From 1906 through 1908, the Chicago Cubs may have been the best baseball team ever. They won games incessantly, by every available method, as if possessed. And after every win, they looked for ways to be even better. Win begat win begat win.

No other team has ever won more games in a three-year period. Such success seemed to fit their city, for just as Chicago seemed on the brink of becoming a world-class city, so too did the Cubs seem poised to assume a place atop the world of baseball.

The history of the Cubs, however, has never been simple. There is, it seems, always a qualifier or two. The 1906 Cubs, perhaps the best club of that time period, won everything but a world championship. While that would come later, in both 1907 and 1908, when one looks back at the era it is nevertheless difficult to do so without seeing this greatest team in Cubs history as underachievers. As great as they were, the 1906 Cubs should have been even greater, and for all their success,

The 1906 World Series was the battle of Chicago and the first subway series in major league history. In this rare action photograph, Cub left-hander Jack Pfiester is shown pitching to White Sox player-manager Fielder Jones in the third game of the Series.

including world championships in 1907 and 1908, the Cubs of this era have been remembered, not for the joy their success delivered, but for the perennial frustration that was born during those seasons.

It has been all downhill ever since that time.

Before the start of the 1906 season, although the Cubs appeared to have improved, they still seemed to lag behind the world champion New York Giants by a substantial margin. After winning the pennant in 1904, the 1905 Giants were dominant in every way, finishing nine games ahead of second-place Pittsburgh and thirteen games above the Cubs. In the World Series, they embarrassed the Philadelphia Athletics, taking the series four games to one and outscoring the A's 15–3. Had it not been for a few errors, Philadelphia not only wouldn't have won a game but wouldn't even have *scored*—New York's team ERA for the Series was 0.00. Paced by manager John McGraw, star pitcher Christy Mathewson, and a potent offense built around outfielder Mike Donlin, the Giants didn't feel the need to change in 1906. Although a few players were beginning to show their age, none seemed likely to collapse. New York was so confident that they opened the season wearing uniforms that stated the obvious—the phrase "World's Champions" was emblazoned across their chests.

The Cubs found such overconfidence galling, which may have provided just the spark the team needed. The Cubs already knew they were good, but just as the city of Chicago needed New York to set an example for its own grandiose expectations, the Cubs needed the Giants to push them into greatness. From the very start of the 1906 season, both the ball club and the press sensed that all that stood between the Cubs and a championship was the team from New York, and if the Cubs could beat the Giants, a championship would logically follow. Before opening day, the *Chicago Daily News* found it necessary to note that "everybody will pull for the Cubs . . . against McGraw's arrogant Giants, who have captured the flag twice in succession and are touting themselves with brass horns to repeat."

The Cubs opened the season on April 12 in Cincinnati with a smart 7–2 victory, then stumbled. Two weeks later, the club's record was a well-deserved 6–6, and the Giants led the league.

The Cubs soon hit their stride, however, winning ten in a row to keep pace with the Giants and, for one day, on May 7, edging into the lead. But they lost the next day and fell back.

Few teams ever win championships solely on their own merits. They win when they have enough talent to take advantage of the misfortune of competitors. The Cubs had enough talent: Tinker, Evers, Chance, Steinfeldt, Schulte, and Sheckard were all in their prime, offensively and defensively, something Cub pitchers appreciated. The Cubs scooped up everything and committed the fewest errors in the league, helping Cub pitchers give up the fewest hits in baseball. The team didn't beat itself through errors, whether mental or physical. It had to be beaten.

All the Cubs lacked was a bit of misfortune to befall the Giants. Fortunately for them, that happened on May 15 in a game between the Giants and the Reds that would turn out to be the most important game of the regular season for the Cubs.

New York pitcher Hooks Wiltse was magnificent that day, striking out twelve in the 4–1 New York victory, including four in the fifth inning after Jim Delahanty reached first base when catcher Roger Bresnahan dropped a third strike. Wiltse, who had been a spot starter in both 1904 and 1905, seemed poised to blossom into one of the best pitchers in baseball. The Giants needed him, for Christy Mathewson, who had won thirty-one games in 1905, missed the first few weeks of the season with diphtheria and was still weak when he returned. Nevertheless, the Giants had played their way into first place, and now, with Mathewson returning to form and Wiltse joining McGinnity atop the Giants pitching rotation, New York seemed on the verge of taking off.

But in the seventh inning, outfielder Mike Donlin, who already had two hits and was hitting almost .350, lofted a fly ball into right field. The Cincinnati outfielder missed making the catch and overran the ball. Donlin rounded first and headed for second, sliding into the bag with a hustling double. But he paid a price for his aggressiveness. His leg was broken, and his teammates had to carry him off the field.

No one, except perhaps Mathewson, was more important to the Giants. Not only was Donlin New York's best position player and best hitter, but he set the tone for the club—he was the player who could best translate manager John McGraw's fiery passion into action on the field. In

1905 Donlin had done it all, hitting .356, stealing 33 bases, smacking out 54 extra-base hits, and leading the league with 124 runs. At age twenty-eight, he was in his prime.

Donlin's loss initially seemed to inspire the Giants. After the Cubs had edged back into first place, on May 20 New York came into Chicago and took three of four games to tie for the top spot.

But the effort exhausted them. By May 28 the Cubs had moved into first. A few days later, they made a move to secure their position: in a pitcher swap, they sent Bob Wicker to the Reds for Orvie Overall. The move worked out brilliantly. Wicker would go on to lose fourteen games for the Reds while Overall won twelve for the Cubs.

On June 5, the Cubs traveled to New York with first place at stake once again. They led the Giants by a game and a half with a record of 31–15 to New York's 29–15. The Cubs took the first game, 6–0, and the second, 11–3, before facing Mathewson in game three. The Giants desperately needed a win.

It wasn't even close. Jimmy Slagle led off and worked Mathewson for a walk. Then Sheckard singled. Schulte beat out an infield hit, and Chance reached on a fielder's choice. Steinfeldt singled, and when Tinker doubled to chase Mathewson, McGraw brought in McGinnity. He was no more effective. The carnage continued, and by the time the Cubs were out, the score was 11–0. They went on to win 19–0. Although the Giants won the following day, Donlin proved to be irreplaceable, and the Cubs would not be bothered by New York again in 1906. From that point on, Chicago was competing only with history.

For the style of play in vogue during the dead ball era, the Cubs had everything. Almost every player in the lineup possessed more or less the same skills and knew how to bunt, move runners along, steal, and take the extra base. At the same time, they also had the most power in the league, which they led in extra-base hits. Steinfeldt in particular led the way with the best season of his career.

But the Cubs really shone on the pitcher's mound. The team ERA was 1.75—half a run better than any other team in the league—paced by Brown's stingy mark of 1.04. The pitching staff gave up the fewest hits, had the most strikeouts, and collected thirty shutouts.

Moreover, the Cubs led the league in brains. They outfought every other team in the game. Evers and catcher

CHICAGO BASE BALL CLUB OF 1908.
WORLD'S CHAMPIONS.

1—Slagle	7—Overall	13—Steinfeldt
2—Reulbach	8—Hofman	14—Howard
3—Evers	9—Fraser	15—Pfeister
4—Schulte	10—Tinker	16—Brown
5—Moran	11—Lundgren	17—Chance
6—Kling	12—Sheckard	18—Durbin

Little did Cub fans know that when their 1908 team captured their second consecutive World Series title over the Detroit Tigers, it would be their last world championship of the century. Led by player-manager Frank Chance, who batted .421 in the Series, and pitchers Mordecai Brown and Orval Overall (two wins apiece), the Cubs dominated Detroit, winning by four games to one.

Johnny Kling were master sign stealers, and Chance knew how to walk the line as player-manager. At times he was one of the boys, organizing team poker games, which he believed helped keep the "mental faculties" sharp, and he often picked up the tab at the bar. Yet he knew when to crack down; when the team was on the road and most likely to stray, he enforced a hard and fast 11:30 P.M. curfew, and if a player wasn't at breakfast by 9:00 A.M., he didn't eat. Chance knew precisely what his players could do and could not do. Every move he made seemed to work. The press started calling him "P.L."—shorthand for "Peerless Leader." The name fit.

The result was a team that was as close to unbeatable as any team in baseball history. The Cubs lost three games in a row precisely *once* all season long, and two in a row only four times. They were dominant at home (56–21) and even more dominant on the road (60–15). They went 27–13 in close, one-run games and were even better in blowouts, beating the opposition thirty-three times by five runs or more while losing by that margin or greater only six times. They even stayed healthy. No one on the club suffered from a serious injury all year.

As June gave way to July and August, the Cubs, already dominant, kept improving. As if they needed more pitching, on July 1 another trade brought back Jack Taylor. Like Overall, he too went 12–3 over the balance of the season. They entered August with an already gaudy record of 66–28, and then lost only *eight games* during the rest of the regular season, winning forty-seven. The Cubs clinched the pennant on September 19, breaking the record set by the Giants the year before. They finished the year with a record of 116–36 and a winning percentage of .763, still the best of all time.

Fans were so giddy on the West Side that they hardly noticed that on the South Side the White Sox were doing pretty well too, playing tortoise to the Cubs' hare. In late July, the Sox were barely a .500 team, mired in sixth place, and as late as August 2 they were still treading water, in fourth place by nine games, trailing Cleveland, New York, and first-place Philadelphia. Then they caught fire, winning nineteen in a row, including twelve games against Philadelphia and New York, which vaulted them into first place and earned the team a new nickname.

The 1906 Cubs achieved the greatest regular-season record ever with 116 victories and 36 losses. The loss in the World Series to the White Sox "hitless wonder" team ranks as one of the biggest upsets in sports history.

M. BROWN.   J. PFEISTER
GESSLER. J. TAYLOR.   H. STEI
C. LUNDGREN.

CHICAGO NATIONAL LEAG

OFMAN   C. G. WILLIAMS   O. OVERALL.   E. REULBACH.   J. KLING.
LDT.   J. McCORMICK.   F. CHANCE.   J. SHECKARD.   P. MORAN.   F. SCHULTE
WALSH.   J. EVERS.   J. SLAGLE.   J. TINKER.

E BALL CLUB 1906   THE "CUBS"--PENNANT WINNERS

Evers to Chance.   1906

In barely six seasons with the Cubs, Orval Overall became one of the best pitchers in franchise history. Not only did he win three World Series games against no losses in the consecutive-year triumphs over the Tigers in 1907 and '08, but he also enjoyed a cumulative won-lost record of 50–22 for the three consecutive pennant-winning seasons from 1906 to 1908. In the 1908 World Series, Overall batted .333 while winning two games, including the clincher.

On August 21, the *Tribune*'s Hugh Fullerton, Chicago's leading sportswriter, wrote, "To those who have not seen the White Sox in their wonderful winning streak, it is a wonder how they score so many runs on so few hits." From that day on, the 1906 White Sox would be known as the "hitless wonders." It was an apt description, for despite a team batting average of only .230, the White Sox were opportunistic, and like the Cubs, they were well served by their pitching staff.

It was a great time to be a baseball fan in Chicago. When the White Sox clinched the pennant on October 3, Fullerton wrote, "Chicago is the baseball center of the earth. Since last night a combination pennant pole marking the site of Chicago has served as the earth's axis and around it something less than 2,000,000 maddened baseball fans are dancing a carmagnole of victory." But despite the Cubs' apparent superiority, Fullerton cautioned that the teams were closer than it appeared. "The National League team won because it was the best team," he wrote. "The American League team won because it is the gamest, best handled and most scientific team." Fullerton was one of only a few men brave enough to risk public ridicule by giving the White Sox a chance to win. By contrast, the Cubs, from all appearances, looked unstoppable, and gamblers installed them as a two-to-one favorite to win the World Series.

But there were the smallest of cracks in that formidable facade. The Cubs ended the season with an exhausting road trip, spending nearly a month on the road, riding the trains and staying in hotels. Then, in the last week of the season, with only three games between September 30 and October 7, the Cubs hardly played at all; the schedule was so slack that on October 5 they played an exhibition game in Youngstown. The club was so tired of twiddling its thumbs that Chance even allowed several Chicago players to leave the team to visit their families and conduct other personal business.

The schedule and pace of play hurt both pitchers and hitters. Three-Finger Brown, who had been magnificent all year long, took his last turn on the mound on September 24 and then was allowed to rest for more than two weeks before the start of the World Series on October 9. Lundgren and Reulbach also had more than a week's rest. After scoring runs in bunches, Cub hitters struggled as well over the last ten days of the regular season. The club hadn't played an important game since early June and returned to Chicago on the evening of October 7 with only one full day to gear up for the Series and all its attendant pressures. By the time the Series began, the sharp edge the Cubs had hewn all season long had been dulled.

The White Sox, meanwhile, spent most of September and early October playing at home, and the tight pennant race kept them driving hard. Every game they played over the last two months had mattered. They entered the Series confident, in battle-tested condition, happy to be considered underdogs, and determined to prove everyone wrong. Not even a late-season injury to shortstop George Davis, who had a bad back, or second baseman Frank Isbell's sprained ankle knocked them off stride. The whole season had been a struggle, and they had always found a way to persevere.

They were also not quite the "hitless wonders" most people imagined them to be. While their offensive performance over the course of the season paled in comparison to that of the Cubs, over the final two months the White Sox had averaged nearly four runs a game—a full half-run per game better than their performance through July and nearly the equal of the Cubs. And from August onward, White Sox pitchers tossed an incredible eighteen shutouts and held the opposition to only one run ten times.

Few noticed at the time, but by the time the Series began the two Chicago clubs were much closer in ability than it initially appeared. The Cubs were a little flat and a little overconfident. They were already planning a few post-Series exhibition contests to cash in on their expected victory and selling tickets for a victory banquet featuring Cap Anson, Billy Sunday, and the governor of Illinois. The South Siders, meanwhile, had been improving all year long and, unlike the Cubs, were not looking beyond their next game, much less the Series.

All Chicago was agog at the spectacle scheduled to begin on October 9 at West Side Park. City hall employees were given the day off. The Board of Trade closed at 1:15 for game one, and members boarded special "tallyho" cars capable of carrying fifty men at a time to the ballpark. Every car line was packed, and thousands of fans milled around the outside of the park looking for tickets. The *Tribune*'s Charles Dryden commented that "the Big town on the lake is baseball dizzy, which is several degrees worse than batty." Cartoons in Chicago newspapers showed fans pouring toward the ballpark, each one offering up the imaginary ailment that would "prevent them from being at the office," such as "melancholia," "nettle rash, "insomnia," and, in a nod to local journalists, "writer's cramp." Any fan left on the fence could buy a button sporting a bear cub wearing white stockings.

Five hundred police officers were assigned to crowd control—fifty of them stood outside on "anti-scalper duty," and one hundred were stationed inside the park to keep the aisles clear. Local hotels reported that at least two thousand out-of-towners were in Chicago to take in the contests, including the most famous group of baseball fans in the world, Boston's vaunted "Royal Rooters," led by barkeep Mike "Nuf Ced" McGreevey.

The lucky ones already had tickets. The unfortunate paid scalpers an unheard-of four dollars, over twice the regular cost, for every game had been sold out ever since the White Sox clinched the pennant. The Series would alternate between West Side Park and the White Sox home field, South Side Park, which the press also called Comiskey Park, sending fans west and south and then west again.

For game one, most fans wished that the game was being played much farther south, as in Florida. Dryden observed that "the air in the ball park was ideal for putting up ice . . . the fanatics came in rigged out like Peary parties. Men in bearskin coats and carrying extra wraps squatted in boxes and on the open field seats. There was no hint of summer." Chance tabbed Three-Finger Brown to pitch for the Cubs. His counterpart, White Sox player-manager Fielder Jones, had previously announced that spitball artist Ed Walsh, who had tossed ten shutouts during the regular season, would start for the Sox, but when he looked up at the sky and saw snowflakes, he decided it was too cold for Walsh and gave the ball to twenty-game winner Nick Altrock. Jones hoped the left-hander could quiet the Cubs' predominantly left-handed lineup. The weather did not deter the fans, however. More than twelve thousand turned out—so many that some had to be put onto the field and special ground rules put into place turning any ball that reached the crowd in fair territory into a double.

The result was a typical dead ball era contest, a game that turned on the smallest event. Brown was particularly sharp at the start and struck out three of the first six men he faced, but the Cubs were no more successful against Altrock. In the fifth inning, the White Sox broke through in typical fashion.

White Sox third baseman George Rohe shouldn't even have been playing. He was only in the lineup because Davis's injury had forced regular third baseman Les Tannehill over to shortstop. Rohe opened the inning with a hard line drive over Steinfeldt's head down the third-base line. The ball shot out to Sheckard, who kicked the ball under a bench down the left-field line. By the time he was able to extract it, Rohe was on third base with a triple. He scored two batters later when Patsy Dougherty squibbed a pitch about thirty feet in front of home plate. Brown fielded the ball and threw home, but Kling dropped the rushed toss and the White Sox led, 1–0.

In the sixth, they scored a second run. After Altrock walked and was sacrificed to second, Fielder Jones singled. Altrock was gunned down at home by Solly Hofman's throw, but Jones advanced to second and scored on Frank Isbell's single. For the White Sox, two runs were the equivalent of a deluge.

The Cubs couldn't compare. They scratched out one run in the sixth but were overanxious against Altrock. He held them at bay for the rest of the game and won, 2–1. Excited White Sox fans stormed the field after the game and carried Altrock away, the hero of the moment, as the Cubs slunk off.

Although no Cub would admit to being worried, local bettors weren't so sure, and a surge of money on the White Sox brought the odds down to even money. But Reulbach was magnificent for the Cubs in game two at Comiskey Park, holding the White Sox to only one hit while the Cubs raked Doc White and Frank Owen for ten hits; Jones, owing to the weather, had held back Walsh again. The Cubs won in a rout, 7–1, and their fans breathed a sigh of relief. Returning to their home ballpark for game three, all was right with the world. But it was even better for the White Sox.

As the *Daily News* reported, when the teams arrived at the ballpark, "there was joy in the hearts of the players . . . when they felt the warmth of the sun." But there was more joy in the White Sox dugout than in that of the Cubs, for the change in the weather allowed the White Sox to use Walsh. Just a few years before, Jack Chesbro of the New York Americans had become the first to master the spitball, and in 1904 it helped him win a record forty-one games. Walsh was one of a number of pitchers who subsequently adopted the pitch, and the most successful. Batters were still trying to figure out how to hit it. The ball "squirted" out from the fingers and tended to drop and dip dramatically just as it reached the plate.

Initially, however, it seemed as if the Cubs would get to Walsh, for in the first inning Hofman singled and Schulte doubled. Unfortunately for the Cubs, before Schulte's hit Hofman was thrown out stealing, and after that the Cubs never really threatened. That was it. For the rest of the game, it was the Cubs who were hitless and wondering. Meanwhile, over the first five innings Cub pitcher Jack Pfiester was even better than Walsh, giving up only one hit.

In the sixth inning, Tannehill led off with a single, bringing up the pitcher. Walsh tried to sacrifice, Pfiester didn't give him a pitch, and Walsh walked. Center fielder Eddie Hahn came to bat, and Jones once again flashed the sign for a sacrifice bunt. Pfiester threw and Hahn squared around, but Pfiester's pitch tailed in. As the *Tribune* noted,

Hahn "sacrificed his nose to the great cause . . . Eddie was hit squarely on the side of his nose, breaking the bone as if it were made of clay." Hahn had to leave the game and was taken to the hospital.

Pfiester was in serious trouble, but he got Fielder Jones to foul out and struck out Frank Isbell. With two down, the Cub infield retreated to normal depth as game one hero George Rohe stepped in.

According to the *Tribune*, "The noise was deafening . . . [and] more than 13,000 pairs of eyes were glued upon those two men, Rohe and Pfiester, pitted against each other in a death struggle." Pfiester's first pitch cut over the heart of the plate and Rohe jumped on it, smacking another line drive over Steinfeldt's head. The ball then skipped into the crowd, and the umpire ruled it a three-base hit, clearing the bases. The White Sox led, 3–0, and a few innings later took the game by that same score.

Now the Cubs were nervous and the White Sox were increasingly confident. Sox owner Charles Comiskey was ebullient. "We have tamed the sluggers and the giant killers," he told the *Chicago Daily News*. "Instead of their being full of confidence we have them on the defensive with manager Chance wearing a worried look." Chance's counterpart, Fielder Jones, was all smiles. George Davis was feeling better, and now Jones had to decide what to do about hot-hitting George Rohe. It was the first time all year he'd had too many hitters.

He left Rohe in the lineup in game four, benching Tan-

nehill, but Three-Finger Brown rendered that move moot by giving up only three hits. Altrock was nearly as good as the Cubs continued to struggle at bat, but they managed to tie the Series in the seventh inning when Chance drove the ball over Hahn's head in center field for a triple, then Evers singled him home for the only run the Cubs needed in the 1–0 victory.

Interest in game five was intense. Crowds pushed their way into the ballpark by the thousands before Charles Murphy ordered the gates closed, leaving thousands locked outside waving dollar bills in the wan hope that would somehow get them inside. In the ballpark, fans spilled all over the field, kept at bay by a pair of real bear cubs contributed by the Board of Trade that were paraded on leashes around the field. Outside the park any nearby resident with a rooftop granting a view of any kind was getting two dollars a perch.

For a few moments after the game started, Cubs fans considered that money well spent. The Cubs, who thus far had lost every game on the West Side and won every one at Comiskey Park, were determined to change their luck. Chance ordered his team to wear their gray road uniforms for the game. Although the White Sox opened the game

---

The West Side Grounds was the site of four World Series in which the Cubs finished with a cumulative home record of 4–6 with one tie. Despite winning two of these Series, the Cubs have never clinched a world championship in their home ballpark.

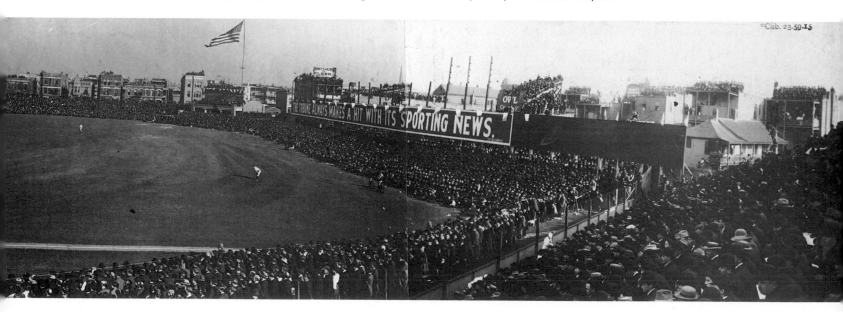

with a single run in the first off Reulbach, the Cubs exploded in the bottom half of the inning for three runs off Walsh. The Cubs, at last, appeared to be putting the White Sox in the mirror.

That was an illusion. In the third inning, Isbell and Davis cracked back-to-back doubles, driving Reulbach from the game in favor of Jack Pfiester on their way to tying the score with two runs. Then, in the fourth, when Pfiester started the inning by walking Walsh and then gave up three straight hits, Chance turned to Orvie Overall. He fared little better. The hitless wonders were suddenly hitting everything, and every pitcher the Peerless Leader led to the mound was getting killed. If not for six errors by the White Stockings, the 8–6 final score would not have been nearly so close.

The Cubs were on the brink not only of disaster but of embarrassment. To lose to the White Sox was bad enough, but to be *beaten* by them was something else entirely. The Cubs could not afford another loss.

Chance was desperate. Half his pitching staff was shot, and the other half did not have Chance's confidence. Pfiester, Reulbach, and Overall had all pitched the day before, and Brown had had only one day's rest. Chance simply did not trust Jack Taylor or Carl Lundgren in such a big game. So for the first time all year he made the wrong call. He gave the ball to Brown for the third time while Jones countered with Doc White.

It was over early. After the Cubs scratched out a run in the top of the first, the White Sox came storming back in the bottom of the inning to score three runs. The big play was a ground-rule double by George Davis over the head of Frank Schulte. Schulte, knowing that he couldn't reach the ball, had tried to pull a fast one. He pulled up short, lurched at the ball as it went over his head, then came racing in to argue with umpire Silk O'Loughlin.

Schulte claimed that a policeman holding back the crowd had pushed him, preventing him from making a play. But O'Loughlin wouldn't be dissuaded, and a Cub fan in the area later told the *Daily News* that "not a soul touched him [Schulte]. In fact the crowd spread and let him come on back. . . . Without any exaggeration the ball cleared Schulte's hands by two feet." Schulte, however, didn't back down from his story and was still complaining about it days later, telling the *Daily News*, "I'm sorry now I

didn't get that policeman's number before I ran to the infield," as if that would have made any difference.

It didn't matter anyway. The White Sox scored another four runs in the second to put the game away. The Cubs lost game six, 8–3, to lose the Series, four games to two. The White Sox, not the Cubs, went barnstorming that winter. Sox fan Bessie Brown memorialized the Series in song for the *Daily News*. Choosing "The Star-Spangled Banner" as her model, her song ended: "The championship pennants, oh long may they wave / O'er the grounds of the Sox and the Cubs' gloomy grave." Another Sox aficionado hung crepe over the door of the Cubs office and a sign that read: TOLD YOU SO. Even Giants manager John McGraw, who wasn't happy that Chance had at least temporarily taken over the crown as the game's best manager, did a dance on that gloomy grave. He told reporters that if Donlin and Mathewson had been healthy, the Giants were still the better team, and that "the Cubs used bad judgment. . . . After Lundgren and Taylor had helped the Cubs win the pennant I believe manager Chance should have used one or both of them in the world's series." In retrospect, McGraw was right.

The Cubs seemed unable to swallow the defeat, and for the next few weeks excuse after excuse continued to pop up in the papers—Schulte kept complaining about the cop, Steinfeldt had been ill the whole series, etc., etc.

Fortunately, however, the Cubs did not overreact to the loss. After all, they had won 116 games. One bad week wasn't enough to tear the team apart. The only significant activity took place at West Side Park. The crowds at the Series had nearly burst the place apart, so in the offseason the club renovated, doubling the capacity of the grandstand and adding five times the number of box seats.

Apart from that, the Cubs stood pat the following year, in 1907. The only blip came in the spring when Joe Tinker was sidelined with appendicitis. Solly Hofman filled in until he was healthy, and later did the same for Schulte when he was knocked out of the lineup with a torn groin muscle.

It made no difference. The Cubs were a machine and opened the season winning twenty-four of their first twenty-nine. Unfortunately, so did John McGraw's Giants, even with the loss of Mike Donlin, who had decided not to play in 1907.

There was bad blood between the two teams, and nearly

every contest was marred by a disagreement of one kind or another. On May 21, the Cubs and Giants were tied for first place when the Cubs invaded the Polo Grounds for a three-game series. Brown beat Mathewson in the first game as the Cubs inched into first place, but the Giants took the top spot back the next day with a 7–1 win.

The big news came in the fourth inning after the Giants' Cy Seymour beat out an infield hit and then decided to steal second. According to the *Daily News*, "Instead of sliding he jumped in feet first . . . his spikes struck Tinker in the face, ripping off a bunch of skin, cutting him on the face and elbow. . . . Tinker responded to Seymour's alleged intentional spiking with a smash in the face with his fists." Perhaps inspired by such rough play, the Cubs beat the Giants the next day, despite the fact that McGraw used all six of his pitchers in an attempt to stop them.

By June the Cubs had shed the Giants and pulled ahead, and by mid-July they had opened up a lead of more than ten games. From there the team cruised to a second consecutive pennant, winning "only" 107 games but finishing seventeen games ahead of Pittsburgh as the Giants slumped to fourth. Another World Series was in the offing for the Cubs.

In the American League, the White Sox failed to repeat and were headed off by the Detroit Tigers, led by their sensational twenty-year-old outfielder Ty Cobb. In his first full season, Cobb had led the league in hits, RBIs, batting average, and stolen bases. The perfect ballplayer for the dead ball era, Cobb keyed the best offensive attack in baseball in 1907. He pushed the "scientific" style of play as far as possible, endowing it with his own legendary aggressiveness. Cobb didn't steal a base like most other ballplayers, sliding demurely away from the tag. He stole bases like a thief lurking in the dark and then appearing out of nowhere, sticking his spikes in the fielder's ribs and daring him to make the tag. He was always looking to take the extra base, always trying to intimidate the opposition. That aggressiveness had gone a long way to making the Tigers American League champions, but the Cubs, thanks to McGraw's Giants, were accustomed to that style of play. Their strategy, when pushed, was to push back—hard.

Before the start of the Series, baseball's ruling National Commission informed the players that their share of the gate would come from the proceeds of the first four games, leading Germany Schaefer and Ty Cobb of the Tigers to ask innocently, "What about a tie?" The commission, thinking such a result most unlikely, told the players that in the remote chance that one of the first four games ended in a tie, the players would also share the proceeds of that contest, a not-insignificant windfall. The extra game would mean more money for all. The players filed that small nugget of information away.

If anything, Cub fans were even more excited about the World Series of 1907 than they had been in 1906. This was their chance to make up for the previous year's loss. Pressure for tickets was so intense that the *Tribune* sold tickets for game reenactments at the First Regiment Armory on Sixteenth and Michigan Avenue. The plan was to tell the story of the game "by means of a unique system of lights which will show the plays on a large board, fourteen feet square."

This time in the days before the start of the Series, the Cubs stayed quiet and allowed the opposition to do all the chirping, something ebullient Detroit manager Hughie Jennings was quite capable of. He announced, "I believe the Tigers are the best baseball team the world has ever seen," a pronouncement that did not sit well with Chance and the Cubs. The Cubs were well aware that over the past two seasons they had won 223 games. The Chicagoans were further put off by all the attention the press lavished on young Cobb—the *Daily News* pronounced him a "phenomenal baserunner" and asked, "Will Cobb outgeneral such men as Overall, Brown . . . Chance and Evers?" The Cubs were determined to answer that question with a resounding no.

On the morning of October 6, all streetcars headed toward the West Side of Chicago were crowded to overflowing, and by 12:20 P.M., more than two hours before the game, the ballpark was reportedly already nearly full.

For the next two hours the crowd still came, filling up every seat, blocking every sidewalk, flooding surrounding streets, and taking possession of every nearby tree, pole, and rooftop. They weren't all Cub fans, for it was only a short trip from Detroit to Chicago by train, and thousands of Tiger fans had made the trip. Indeed, when the Tigers clawed their way into the park and onto the field, they were greeted by thousands of cheers. So, too, did the crowd greet the Cubs, who had eschewed all manner of superstition and wore brand-new uniforms made just for the Series.

Each manager went with his big winner in game one: Jennings picked twenty-five-game winner "Wild Bill" Donovan to start for Detroit, while Chance picked Orvie Overall, winner of twenty-three games.

Both pitchers were up to the task. Although each club mounted several potential rallies, by the eighth inning the Cubs held a narrow 1–0 lead. Then Chicago suffered a rare defensive lapse. With one out, Davy Jones legged out an infield hit, stole second, and went to third when Joe Tinker bobbled Germany Schaefer's ground ball. Both scored on Sam Crawford's double, and Crawford went to third when Johnny Kling fumbled the throw-in. The Cubs nearly doubled Crawford up after Cobb grounded to Overall, but Steinfeldt dropped the throw during the rundown, and Crawford came on to score on a sacrifice fly. Detroit had scored three runs on only one solid hit.

By the bottom of the ninth, the Tigers still led, 3–1. Then things got a bit strange. Now the Tigers seemed determined to give a few runs back. After Chance singled, Donovan hit Steinfeldt. Kling popped out, and then Evers was safe when the third baseman made an error. After Schulte grounded out, scoring Chance, pinch hitter Del Howard struck out. That should have been the ball game, a 3–2 Detroit win.

The one weak link in the Detroit lineup was catcher Boss Schmidt, who had a bad arm. The Cubs had figured out that he couldn't throw and were already on their way to a record sixteen stolen bases during the Series. Now they learned that he couldn't catch either. He didn't even touch the third strike. The ball rolled to the backstop, and Howard made it to first as Steinfeldt scored.

The score was tied, the same convenient scenario envisioned by Cobb and Schaefer a few days before, as an official crowd of almost twenty-five thousand fans suddenly looked like a windfall. The game entered extra innings.

Detroit went out easily enough in the next three innings, but the Cubs nearly ruined everything by mounting a threat each time they came to bat before bending over backwards to end it. In the tenth, Steinfeldt, on deck, interfered with catcher Schmidt as Jimmy Slagle tried to score, ending the inning and prolonging the tie. In the eleventh, Chicago loaded the bases with one out before Heinie Zimmerman struck out and Reulbach, on in relief of Overall, conveniently hit into a force-out. And in the twelfth, as twilight came on, with one out and Jimmy Sheckard at first, Chance belted a line drive to third base. Schaefer, at third, made what the *Tribune* called a "spectacular jumping catch," and Chance was out.

Someone forgot to tell Sheckard, or else he chose not to believe his eyes. He was running on the pitch, and Schaefer easily doubled him off first base for a double play. Then umpire Hank O'Day called the game because of darkness. The tie was in, and players from both teams reaped the benefit of the big crowd.

To many observers, the outcome was suspicious, but not particularly troubling. Iffy play in postseason series was a standing tradition, and the result drew little comment at the time. Few begrudged the players for trying to take advantage of a rule that would help them earn some extra money, and once the tie game had been played, the players probably played the remainder of the Series straight.

Besides, in the end, playing for the tie backfired. It backed up every subsequent game in the Series, and fans who had bought tickets and made plans to attend were caught unawares. Attendance slumped, and in the long run the players probably earned less with the tie than without it.

Chicago took command in game two. Jack Pfiester scattered nine hits, and the Cubs walked off with a 3–1 win. But that wasn't enough for Chance and the Cubs.

After the Cubs stole four more bases, some observers speculated that Detroit, if not for Schmidt, was actually the better team. After the embarrassment of losing the Series in 1906, Chance didn't just want to win—he wanted to win definitively and without question. As the *Daily News* noted, "Manager Chance is bent on demonstrating to the baseball world that the Cubs can bat themselves to victory without relying on their fleetness on the bases."

So before game three, as Chance explained later, "I told my men to cut out the baserunning for this one game, for I wanted to show the baseball world we could beat that club in straightaway batting." As requested, the Cubs played station-to-station baseball and never tried to steal as Reulbach pitched the Cubs to a 5–1 win. West Side Park was only half full, however, for the game, the third in the Series, hadn't originally been scheduled for Chicago. There was no advance sale, the day was cold and blustery, and Detroit fans who had bought round-trip excursion tickets to Chicago missed the game completely. The *Tribune* even reported that some Chicago fans "did not know yesterday's game was to be played here," and by the time they did it was too late to attend.

As they left for Detroit, the Cubs, up two games to none, were confident. The *Daily News* reported that "the Cubs themselves, almost to a man, feel they have the World Series clinched," and Chance told reporters, "I don't think there's anything to it now." Bill Donovan was the only Detroit pitcher who gave the Cubs any trouble, and Ty Cobb, thus far, had been more kitten than Tiger. As the *News* observed, "Unless Schmidt can brace up and stop the base running of the Cubs, Detroit will lose."

Once the Cubs got to Detroit, it was all Chicago. Overall beat Donovan 6–1 in game four in a contest made notable by the Cubs' defensive play. In the third inning, Donovan lined a long drive that Frank Schulte caught on one bounce. He came up throwing. Chance, playing with a dislocated finger on his throwing hand after being hit in the first inning, made a leaping catch, came down on the bag, and Donovan was out.

On the morning before game five, after a sleepless night, Chance visited a doctor, who reset the dislocation and wrapped the finger in bandages. Chance sat out the game, but it hardly mattered. Most Detroit fans considered the situation hopeless, followed suit, and sat out the game as well. Only a little more than seven thousand spectators turned out for the game, the second-lowest total ever to watch a World Series game.

Three-Finger Brown, who had been bothered by a sore arm late in the season, made the most of his only appearance in the Series. He scattered seven hits and, on the rare occasion he was in trouble, was able to bear down and notch a strikeout, getting Ty Cobb twice. Meanwhile, the Cubs scored single runs in both the first and second innings, stealing three bases in the process.

Boss Schmidt had the honor of making the final out, popping up to Joe Tinker, who made a nice play in short left field. Brown's 2–0 shutout gave the Cubs their first world championship under that name.

Left fielder Jimmy Sheckard was nearly blinded in the spring of 1908 when, during a clubhouse fight with rookie Heinie Zimmerman, he was hit in the face by a bottle of ammonia that shattered, covering his eyes with the toxic liquid. Fortunately, he recovered and played another six seasons in the majors.

The on-field celebration was subdued. Not only was the outcome expected, but thousands of Tiger fans had left the ballpark early, making the end of the game feel like some midseason exhibition in the hinterlands.

The Cubs waited until they returned to Chicago to celebrate, and then they were the beneficiary of some largesse by Tiger owner William Yawkey. The small crowds after game one had cut so deeply into the players' share of receipts that the losing Tigers would earn barely $1,000 each for the Series. Yawkey, who had made his money in lumber and mining, felt bad for his club and threw another $15,000 into the kitty, almost doubling their take to $1,945.96.

This was a potential source of embarrassment for Cubs owner Charles Murphy, because now the Tigers, for losing, stood to earn more money than the Cubs did for winning.

Heinie Zimmerman's Cubs career was nearly over before it started following his infamous clubhouse brawls with teammates Jimmy Sheckard and Frank Chance. However, in ten seasons in Chicago Zimmerman was both a valuable utility man and a third baseman. In 1912, while playing third base, he enjoyed a career season, leading the league in batting average (.372), home runs (fourteen), and, depending on which statistical records you accept, RBIs. His triple crown is disputed by some who claim that he had only 99 RBIs as opposed to 103.

Murphy responded by kicking in just over $7,000 of his own cash to ensure that the Cubs would make more than the Tigers, each man earning $2,142.85.

After two straight pennants and a world championship, the Cubs had every reason to expect that the 1908 season would bring more of the same. No other team in the National League seemed capable of heading them off. Even second-place Pittsburgh needed to make up seventeen games on the Cubs, a team in its prime and one that showed no sign of slipping. But just as the Cubs had taken advantage of a key injury to the Giants in 1906, in 1908 both the Pirates and New York were able to take advantage of some aching Cubs. The Giants were helped further by the return of McGraw's prodigal son, Mike Donlin. He picked up where he had left off almost two years earlier and was again one of the best players in the league.

At first, however, it looked as if the Cubs would run away with another pennant. Through May 30, they had a stellar record of 22–12 and were well in front as the Phillies, Pirates, and Giants all struggled to stay above .500.

But there were a few cracks in the facade. Evers was hurt, Jimmy Sheckard had sore ribs, and Solly Hofman was hobbled by a bad knee. Rookie Heinie Zimmerman was filling in for Evers and playing well, but in the third inning of the first game of a double-header against St. Louis, Cardinal right fielder Shad Barry rocketed a line drive back at Orvie Overall. According to the *Tribune*, Overall "managed to block it with his mitt, then picked up the ball threw his man out at first, after which he collapsed and was unable to continue." While twisting his body to block the drive, Overall had pulled a muscle in his rib cage and would miss several weeks.

The Pirates next came to Chicago, and after the Cubs took game one, they lost the second contest and lost another player when Sheckard, already hurt, sprained an ankle. That was bad enough. The real damage came the following day. As the *Boston Globe* reported, Sheckard arrived at the clubhouse "with the intention of treating his ankle. As he pulled the cork out of the ammonia bottle it exploded near his face, some of the ammonia going into his eyes. He immediately lost the use of his eyes and they became badly swollen." Initially the Cubs feared Sheckard would lose his sight. At the same time, Heinie Zimmerman was hospitalized with some unknown malady.

Except that's not what happened, and if one read the Chicago newspapers, one never learned even that much. The real story wasn't revealed for several months, not until the pennant race was much warmer. It was New York catcher Roger Bresnahan who apparently tipped off a couple of New York writers, and the true story subsequently made its way into print.

Sometime before the game in Pittsburgh, as the Cubs gathered in the clubhouse, Zimmerman, the rookie, and Sheckard began to argue over something insignificant since lost to the ages. At some point, Sheckard picked up an object and tossed it in Zimmerman's direction.

The rookie responded in kind. He reached out for the nearest object and threw it at Sheckard.

Zimmerman had grabbed a bottle of ammonia, which hit Sheckard in the forehead and shattered, sending the liquid into his eyes and sending the outfielder, screaming, to the ground.

Frank Chance looked at Sheckard, looked at Zimmerman, and exploded in a rage, attacking the youngster with his fists. Zimmerman fought back and quickly gained the upper hand, blackening both of Chance's eyes before a mass of Cubs took Chance's side and beat the now-outmanned Zimmerman so badly that he followed Sheckard to the hospital.

The end result left the Cubs crippled. They lost the next two games to the Pirates, then dropped three of four to the Giants a short time later. Had they not been so decimated by injuries, there is little doubt that the Cubs would have cruised to another title. As it was, suddenly there was a pennant race in the National League.

It wasn't just any pennant race either. It was one of the closest pennant races in the history of the game, the subject of innumerable articles and several books on its own. For the Cubs and their fans, however, the pennant race, in the end, paled in importance to the result.

Throughout the rest of June and into July and August,

the Cubs, Pirates, and Giants stayed in a knot atop the National League as none of the three teams managed to pull away. The Cubs were in ambulance mode, for besides the injuries already cited, outfielder Frank Schulte was in and out of the lineup with some illness. In addition, pitcher Carl Lundgren, who had won thirty-five games over the past two seasons, suddenly couldn't get anyone out. The Giants had their troubles too, as "Iron Joe" McGinnity was showing fatigue and could pitch effectively only once a week. But the Cubs had one advantage that neither the Giants nor the Pirates could match: Johnny Evers's brain. It would prove to be the difference in the season.

On September 4, the Cubs played the Pirates in Pittsburgh. Three-Finger Brown of the Cubs and Pittsburgh pitcher Vic Willis were magnificent, each holding the opposing team at bay and sending the scoreless game into extra innings.

In the bottom of the tenth, Pittsburgh player-manager Fred Clarke led off with a single and was then sacrificed to second. Honus Wagner followed with a smash to the hole between first and second, but Evers made a brilliant stop. Wagner still made first base, but Clarke was forced to stop at third base.

Pittsburgh first baseman Warren "Doc" Gill stepped up to the plate. A career minor leaguer, Gill was in the midst of a modest tryout as the Pittsburgh first baseman, the one weak spot in the Pirate lineup. Gill would appear in only twenty-seven games in 1908 and never played in the major leagues again. Nonetheless, his career is evidence that one need not play a long time in the major leagues to have a significant impact on the history of the game.

Brown threw Gill a curveball, which hung and smacked the ballplayer in the ribs, loading the bases. Owen Wilson, up next, then lined a ball into short center field. Playing second base, Evers waved at the ball, but it was out of his reach.

Clarke ran across home plate. Wagner ran toward third, saw the ball land free, and then touched the base as he looped back toward the Pirate dugout. Wilson ran to first base, crossed the bag, then turned toward the Pirate dugout. Warren Gill took off for second base, saw the ball get past Evers, then slowed, turned, and jogged after Wilson. He did not reach or touch second base.

No one noticed but Johnny Evers. In an instant, he saw

Umpire Hank O'Day made the courageous and controversial out signal after determining that the Giants' Fred Merkle hadn't touched second base after stroking the apparent game-winning hit against the Cubs in a critical late-season game. This call turned the 1908 National League pennant race on its ear and helped deliver the Cubs' third straight pennant.

that since Gill had never touched second base, he could still be forced out at that base. Evers called for center fielder Jimmy Slagle to throw him the ball, and Slagle did so. Then Evers ran to second, stood on the bag and started calling for umpire Hank O'Day. He wanted Gill called out.

But O'Day too had turned away as soon as the run scored and was over by the dugout getting a drink of water. As Evers stood on the bag with the ball, Joe Tinker got to O'Day and told him what had happened. The umpire

looked up, shrugged, said, "Clarke has crossed the plate," and left the field. Pittsburgh won, 1–0.

Or did they? Evers was technically correct, although since time immemorial it had been common practice to allow the run to score on such a play. The situation wasn't even unfamiliar, for it was a baseball rules puzzler that was often presented as such in newspapers—including the *Chicago Tribune* only a few months before.

After hearing from Chance, Charles Murphy protested the game and gathered affidavits from various witnesses and submitted them all to league president William Pulliam. But even Murphy sensed the protest was futile, telling *Tribune* beat writer I. E. Sanborn, "I do not expect the protest will be allowed."

He was right. A few days later, Pulliam dismissed the complaint, saying, "I think the baseball public prefers to see games settled on the field and not in this office." But Evers filed the play away—he knew he was right. So too did umpire Hank O'Day. A Chicago native, O'Day had once pitched for a team sponsored by Al Spalding before moving on to Washington and New York. He had Cap Anson to thank for his umpiring career, for he had filled in one day when the regular ump failed to show and earned Anson's praise. Widely considered one of the best umpires of the era, O'Day, although he had refused to change his call, knew that Evers was correct. Knowing he had been out of position, he was embarrassed by the play.

The stage was now set for one of the most infamous plays in baseball history. After taking the first two games of a four-game series with Pittsburgh on September 18, the Giants appeared to have the pennant locked up. With just over two weeks remaining in the season, they now led the Pirates by six games and the Cubs by five. With two more games coming up against Pittsburgh, followed by a four-game set with the Cubs, the Giants, playing at home and with a favorable schedule, were perfectly positioned to put away both teams.

That didn't happen. The Pirates clawed their way back into the race by beating the Giants two in a row. Then the Cubs came into New York for a double-header on September 22 and beat the Giants 4–3 and 3–1 as Three-Finger Brown shut down the Giants in relief of Overall in game one and went the distance in game two, leading the *New York World* to comment that "the only thing for McGraw to do to beat Chicago is to come up with a pitcher with only two fingers." The victories gave the Cubs a chance. The *Chicago Daily News* crowed that Chance had "outgeneraled" McGraw, and W. A. Phelon of the *Chicago Journal* summed things up nicely when he wrote, "There is no joy in Manhattan," even as he looked ahead at the schedule and cautioned Cub fans, "It is well not to become too hilarious." The sweep set up one of the most famous games in baseball history.

New York's Polo Grounds was perhaps the most intimidating ballpark in America, and it was full to overflowing on September 23 when Jack Pfiester squared off against Christy Mathewson. New York fans, while confident of victory, were still a bit worried when the starting lineup was announced before the game. First baseman Fred Tenney, who had gone hitless the day before, had a sore back. McGraw replaced him in the lineup with nineteen-year-old Fred Merkle. It was the only game Tenney would miss all year long.

Both pitchers were up to the task: entering the fifth inning, the game was scoreless. Then Joe Tinker drove a sinking line drive to right field. Mike Donlin raced in toward the ball to try for a shoestring catch, but the ball fell short. As the *New York Herald* reported, with subdued irony, "Two or three ardent fans in a perfectly polite manner suggested to Mike that if he had stretched his anatomy on the greensward he might have stopped the ball." He did not, and Tinker raced around the bases to put the Cubs ahead, 1–0.

Fortunately for Donlin, one inning later he pulled the goat horns off his head. Buck Herzog beat out an infield hit and took second when Steinfeldt's throw went astray. Bresnahan bunted him to third; then Donlin singled up the middle to tie the game.

It stayed tied at 1–1 until the bottom of the ninth. Pfiester, pitching with a pulled ligament in his arm, probably shouldn't have even been on the mound. With one out, Art Devlin singled, and then Moose McCormick dribbled the ball to Evers. Evers threw to Tinker, but it was too late to continue on to Chance. Fred Merkle stepped in and singled, sending McCormick to third.

Al Bridwell came to bat with the game and, it would turn out, the season on the line. He rapped a single past Evers into right-center field.

McCormick ran home and crossed the plate. Bridwell ran to first and, as soon as he touched the bag, took off for the clubhouse in right-center field as the crowd was already pouring onto the field in celebration. Fred Merkle started for second, saw the fans racing onto the field from every direction, and made his break for the clubhouse too.

Evers was watching. And this time, fortunately, so was O'Day. Evers screamed for Solly Hofman to throw him the ball, and the center fielder launched it his direction, but it went wide. Iron Joe McGinnity, who had been coaching third for the Giants and watching Evers, hauled it in. Tinker and Evers both raced over to McGinnity and tried to wrestle the ball away, but McGinnity sensed what was happening, pulled away, and chucked the ball into the crowd.

Evers later claimed that he was able to retrieve the ball from a "tall stringy middle-aged gent with a brown bowler hat on" when teammate Floyd Kroh knocked the man out with an overhand right. At any rate, somehow Evers did end up with a ball in his hand. He fought his way through the crowd, still celebrating what they believed to be a win, to second base. O'Day was waiting. Evers touched second base, O'Day said, "The run doesn't count," and all hell broke loose.

At least that's the way Evers remembered it. Newspaper reports at the time are somewhat less clear and perhaps biased, for according to some it was Frank Chance who wrestled McGinnity for the ball and Chance who grabbed Hank O'Day, hauled him out to second base, told him the run didn't count, and, since the crowd had taken over the field, wanted O'Day to rule the game a forfeit in Chicago's favor. At any rate, by the time O'Day tried to leave the field, the crowd had learned of the decision and reacted like the rioters at the Haymarket. O'Day barely escaped assault, and once he was safely off the field, he reiterated that the run did not count and that the game, a tie, was over.

The Giants were livid afterward. McGraw whined, "How can umpires decide it's no game. . . . [They] can't make rules. . . . It's a simple case of squeal. We won fair and square." Merkle, for his part, claimed he had touched second, and Bob Emslie, the second umpire that day, wisely said he hadn't seen anything.

The Cubs, to their credit, did not get "too hilarious." They knew that the decision would be decided by the

CUBS PITCHING RECORDS

Victories	29	Mordecai Brown (1908)
Losses	23	Tom Hughes (1901)
ERA	1.04	Mordecai Brown (1906)
Games	84	Ted Abernathy (1965), Dick Tidrow (1980)
Starts	42	Ferguson Jenkins (1969)
Complete games	34	Jack Taylor (1902)
Shutouts	8, 9	Mordecai Brown (1906, 1908), Orval Overall (1909), Pete Alexander (1919), Bill Lee (1938)
Saves	53	Randy Myers (1993)
Innings pitched	363.1	Pete Alexander (1920)
Relief innings pitched	136.1	Ted Abernathy (1965)
Hits allowed	347	Nixey Callahan (1900)
Runs allowed	195	Nixey Callahan (1900)
Earned runs	155	Guy Bush (1930)
Home runs allowed	38	Warren Hacker (1955)
Bases on balls	185	Sam Jones (1955)
Strikeouts	274	Ferguson Jenkins (1970)
Winning percentage (10 or more decisions)	.941	Rick Sutcliffe, 16–1 (1984)
Consecutive games won	14	Ed Reulbach (1909), Rick Sutcliffe (1984)
Consecutive games lost	13	Robert McCall (1948)
Consecutive scoreless innings pitched	44	Ed Reulbach (September 17–October 3, 1908)
Consecutive saves	19	Tom Gordon (2001)
Hit batters	22	Nixey Callahan (1900)
Wild pitches	26	Larry Cheney (1914)

league and that there was no way of telling how it would rule. Even the Chicago papers, which were usually quite boosterish, didn't go overboard. Some, in fact, sided with New York. In the *Tribune*, Charles Dryden blamed "minor league brains" for stealing a game he felt the Giants had fairly won.

To the surprise of some, the next morning NL president Pulliam declared that the game was a tie, but his ruling had little meaning, for Giant owner John Brush immediately filed an appeal. Meanwhile, the Cubs had to go back into the den to play the final game of the series.

Perhaps no team in the history of the game had faced a more hostile crowd than the Cubs did the next day. Thousands of fans showed up early for the show, and Chance gave them one. He and Charles Murphy had concluded that if the previous game was a tie, as Pulliam had ruled, the Cubs and Giants should be playing a double-header to make it up. Twenty thousand Giants fans were already on hand when Chance dutifully sent the Cubs out onto the field at 1:30, two hours before the game was scheduled to begin. The early arrivals in the stands hooted them off the field.

The real game started at 3:30 P.M. Incredibly, umpire Hank O'Day even showed up to arbitrate the contest. Although a few fans applauded him for his courage when he took the field, the *New York Herald* reported that "the names hurled at 'Hank' O'Day when he took the field must have kept some 'rooters' up all night thinking up the epithets," and Chance, too, was a target of jeers. The Giants won the raucous contest, 5–4, and with that, as the *Daily News* reported, it was "back to the peace and quiet of Brooklyn" for the Cubs.

Two separate seasons now played to conclusion as the events of September 23 were hashed out. On the field, the Giants, Cubs, and Pirates fought for the pennant. In the league offices, the Cubs and Giants battled it out alone. Depositions and affidavits flew back and forth at a dizzying pace as each statement that Merkle had failed to touch second base was matched by one that claimed he had, just as each statement that Evers had retrieved the ball was matched by one that he most assuredly had not. Each observer had seen the end in a different way, colored by his own prejudice, and it was up to the league to sort it out. The Giants wanted the outcome of the game to be decided in their favor. The Cubs, not content with a mere tie, wanted a forfeit declared in their favor.

That strategy may have been a mistake, it may have been an act of genius, it may have been a simple sign of greed, or it may have been a bit of all three. By shooting for the works and arguing for a forfeit, the Cubs clearly overreached. But at the same time the ploy gave the league an out—a tie game was an effective compromise, one neither club was asking for. And as the league considered what to do about the knotted contest, they began to realize that, if the game had to be replayed, everyone involved would have an opportunity to make a bit of extra profit.

Meanwhile, the Cubs, Giants, and Pirates all waltzed toward the end of the season in a death grip that got tighter every day. The Giants, who still led the league and simply needed to continue winning to render the September 23 game moot, immediately dropped two games to Cincinnati and then stumbled against Philadelphia, losing three of eight games, all to pitcher Harry Coveleski, whom the *Chicago Daily News* heralded as the "idol of Chicago fans." The players liked him too, for the *News* also reported that not only did the Cub players send him a congratulatory telegram, but "the members of the team will take up a collection for him and send him a financial reward." At the same time, while the Giants were stumbling, the Pirates had won eleven of twelve and the Cubs had won eight of nine.

That set up a playoff of sorts. On October 4, the Cubs and Pittsburgh were scheduled to play a makeup game. A Pittsburgh win would deliver the pennant directly to the Pirates. But if the Cubs won, and the Giants won the last three games of their season against the Braves, then the Cubs and Giants would be tied, pending the decision on the game of September 23. For the moment, then, Giants fans were in the awkward position of rooting for the Cubs to beat Pittsburgh. The Giant organization, realizing this, opened up the Polo Grounds, and nearly four thousand fans showed up to watch a reenactment on an electric scoreboard set up near home plate.

Deep in the bowels of the National League offices in Cincinnati, nothing much was happening beyond the gathering of evidence and a lot of hoping and intense praying that Pittsburgh would beat the Cubs and render the whole dispute moot. According to league rules, the matter of the tie game would be considered by the league's board of directors, which consisted of Murphy, Pittsburgh owner Barney Dreyfuss, Charlie Ebbets of Brooklyn, Gerry Hermann of Cincinnati, George Dovey of Boston, and president Pulliam—hardly an unbiased crew. They wisely held off holding a hearing until after October 4.

But as Harvey Woodruff of the *Tribune* put it, "With baseball ruin, absolutely blank nothingness as the price of defeat, with a league pennant and a chance for world honors" at stake, before one of the biggest crowds in club history, the Cubs defeated Pittsburgh 5–2. The disposition of the tie game versus the Giants now loomed over everything. Although the Giants still had three games with Boston remaining, in the event the Giants won all three and ended the season in a tie with the Cubs, the board had to reach a decision one way or the other.

The board finally met on October 5 to consider the matter. Pulliam started the meeting by booting both Murphy and Dreyfuss, since the decision affected their clubs, which left Hermann, Dovey, and Ebbets to hash things out with him. They started by sorting through a stack of affidavits, then took testimony from both umpires, then tried and failed to reach a decision, for according to league bylaws, the decision had to be unanimous. Reportedly, after a few hours of deliberations, two members of the board wanted to award the game to New York, while the other two supported Pulliam's decision to call the game a tie and make the two clubs play it over. Meanwhile, the Giants beat Boston.

The board met again on October 6. Clearly, there was only one way out, only one solution that would not appear as if the board was favoring one club over the other. As George Dovey put it, "The fair way . . . is to have them play it over"—and, as it turned out, blame Merkle for the whole mess rather than admit that, in reality, when Pulliam had failed to uphold the Cubs' protest a month earlier, he had given his tacit approval to the long-standing tradition of dashing off the field as soon as the run scored. In its public statements, the board concluded that "there can be no question that the game should have been won by New York had it not been for the reckless, careless inexcusable blunder of one player, Merkle. . . . The New York club lost a well-earned victory as a result of a stupid play by one of its members." In the event that the game had a bearing on the pennant race, the board ruled that the Cubs and Giants would meet in New York on October 8 and replay the contest.

The decision angered both teams equally. Both the Cubs and the Giants felt wronged. In New York, they griped that the Giants were being "legislated" out of a championship. In Chicago, Murphy and Chance were particularly upset by the possibility that the pennant would be decided by a single game, played in New York no less. Chance noted that "the [league] constitution provides that in such cases a three-game series shall be played. . . . The board of directors wants to hand the pennant to New York. . . . They order this one game in the belief that Mathewson can beat us." Charlie Murphy in particular salivated at the potential windfall of a multigame playoff, for even if the Cubs were to lose, he would win, and the Cubs feared facing Mathewson in a single game. But the Giants apparently held more sway with the board of directors and reportedly lobbied for the single contest, leading some members of the press to refer to the NL as "Brush League," in reference to the perceived power of the New York owner. Besides, if the Pirates somehow ended up tied with both clubs, a three-way, three-game playoff would take at least another week to finish, pushing back the World Series.

Fortunately for everyone except the Pirates, the Giants swept Boston in their last regular-season series to finish in a tie with the Cubs, 98–55, half a game ahead of Pittsburgh, guaranteeing that the winner of the replay would win the pennant. At the same time, the White Sox, behind Ed Walsh's forty wins, narrowly missed out on an American league pennant. On October 2, in a virtual dead heat with Cleveland, Walsh twirled a four-hitter and struck out fifteen, only to lose 1–0 when Cleveland's Addie Joss threw a perfect game. The White Sox hung on and were not eliminated until October 6, losing the flag by one and a half games to Detroit.

All attention now focused on the Cubs-Giants playoff game that would decide it all—the pennant, the possible world champion, and the reputation of poor Fred Merkle for the rest of time. Although neither his teammates nor his manager held him at fault, the press was already referring to the infamous play as "Merkle's Boner," a name that survives to this day.

For Chicago fans, the game was even bigger than that,

although no one could have guessed that one hundred years later the game would figure in what remains the Cubs' last world championship. It is only by the narrowest of margins that Cub fans aren't hearkening back to 1907—Merkle's Boner and the playoff game that resulted from that contested play have thoroughly overshadowed the details of the 1908 World Series in baseball history. And that is entirely appropriate, for the great rivalry of the day was that between the Giants and the Cubs. They were the best two teams in baseball, the most powerful, and the most storied, and it was almost destiny that they met in such a game with so much at stake.

The odds and almost everything else were against the Cubs. Until the Giants beat the Braves on October 7, it was uncertain whether there would even be a playoff game the next day. The Cubs were still in Chicago because, if the Giants lost to the Braves, the Cubs had to be in Detroit the next day to begin the Series. As soon as word of the Giants' victory over Boston reached Chicago, the Cubs raced to the LaSalle Street station and boarded the Twentieth Century Limited for New York. In normal circumstances, that was a trip of twenty-eight hours, so the Cubs were forced to order a "relay" of special, more powerful locomotives to ferry the club east as fast as possible, cutting some ten hours off the overnight journey and ensuring their arrival at 9:30 A.M.

Cubs fans were half-crazed with excitement. After witnessing the scene at the train station, where thousands of fans virtually carried the Cubs onto the train as they arrived, City of Chicago coroner Peter Hoffman predicted that if the Cubs didn't beat the Giants, the overwrought behavior of Cubs fans would lead to "tragedy, despair and insanity." Although he was reportedly smiling as he made that prediction, he also cautioned that it was not unthinkable that some fans might commit suicide if the Cubs lost.

The players were just as frantic. One player announced that when the players woke at dawn the next morning, "we are going to try to find a hunchbacked colored man at sunrise if such a man can be found along the railroad track. We will take him along, for such a person is the surest kind of baseball luck."

They didn't find such a person, but were greeted at nearly every stop by fans. In Elkhart, Indiana, the crowd blocked the tracks. They wanted a firsthand look at Three-

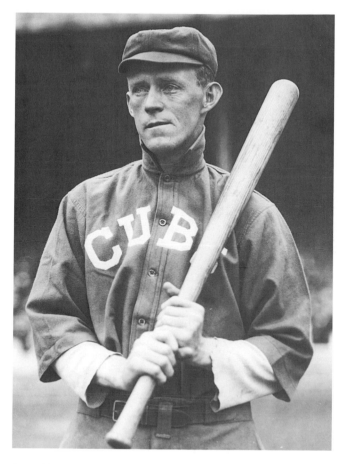

Second baseman Johnny Evers was nothing less than James Cagney in spikes. Upon his arrival in Chicago, Evers weighed slightly over one hundred pounds and was soon nicknamed "the Crab" by teammates for his short fuse and overall cranky attitude. In a dozen seasons with the Cubs, Evers forged his Hall of Fame credentials while helping to lead his team to four pennants and two world championships.

Finger Brown's famous appendage, which they knew only through the descriptions in the newspaper. Brown obliged, and the train continued on its journey.

When the Cubs arrived in New York, they were greeted by a city in baseball frenzy. By 11:00 A.M., more than five thousand fans were waiting for the gates to open. Although the league had earlier announced that no fans would be allowed on the field, the crush was so intense that by 1:00 all seats were filled and the overflow had spilled over into the outfield. The Cubs arrived a few moments later and were greeted with an ear-splitting cacophony of jeers, boos, and hisses. The greeting made the reception the Cubs had received a few weeks earlier

Orval Overall arrived in Chicago from the Reds in 1906 with a spotty career won-lost record of 20–27. However, the right-hander soon helped lead the Cubs to pennants in four of his first five seasons in Chicago. Arm trouble ended his career before the age of thirty. He made a brief comeback in 1913, when he pitched just eleven games.

seem tame. Chance was the particular target of the crowd's wrath. Moments after stepping onto the field, he was hit in the neck by a beer bottle, which drew blood.

Outside it was bedlam, and some later estimated that as many as one-quarter of a million fans milled around the park. Fans climbed up on the Eighth Avenue El, blackened the roof of every nearby building with even the smallest obstructed view of the park, and covered the bluffs that overlooked the park like ants at a picnic. When a train would momentarily pause outside the park, in seconds fans would commandeer the roofs of the cars, only to be spirited off when the train suddenly started and headed downtown. All around the park the police and fire department skirmished with fans.

There were rumors in both Chicago and New York that the game was fixed, and there were certainly attempts to do so. In fact, someone had tried to bribe the Phillies just a few days after the disputed tie, and Philadelphia catcher Red Doonin had been kidnapped in a failed attempt to prevent him from playing in a series. Before the playoff game, Giants team physician Joseph Creamer allegedly offered umpire Bill Klem $2,500 to ensure a New York victory. Although Creamer denied the charge, he was later banned from the game for life. Three-Finger Brown received numerous death threats, and Joe Tinker was cautioned not to make any side bets on his own ball club. In saloons near the Polo Grounds, vast handfuls of money changed hands as rumors swirled that key Cub players were on the take.

Inside the park, gamesmanship was the order of the day. When the Cubs took the field for their customary twenty minutes of fielding practice, after only five minutes McGraw sent his club onto the field. When Chance refused to take his team off the field, Joe McGinnity threatened him with a bat. According to Giant outfielder Fred Snodgrass, the Giants hoped to bait Chance into a fight and get him tossed from the game before it even started. But Chance held off, even as New York police ordered his team from the field.

Everything seemed to be conspiring against a Cubs victory. Not only were they exhausted from the trip, but in the final days of the season McGraw had gambled and kept Mathewson off the mound. Now he was fresh. Three-Finger Brown begged Chance for the ball, but he'd pitched nearly every day for two weeks and had a sore arm. After seeing Philadelphia's Harry Coveleski, a left-hander, beat the Giants three times in a week, Chance decided to go with his left-hander with the sore ligament, Jack Pfiester, who had pitched in the tie game and already beaten the Giants three times in 1908, forever earning him the nickname "Jack the Giant Killer."

When Mathewson strode across the field just before the start of the game, wearing a full-length duster to protect him from the cold, the crowd erupted. The scene resembled not so much a baseball game as a contest at the Roman Coliseum—with the crowd at fever pitch, Mathewson the emperor, and the Cubs, hoped New York fans, about to be torn asunder by their beloved Giants.

The Cubs went quietly in the first as the crowd kept up a constant, surging roar that rattled from the ballpark to the bluffs and back again, draping the game in a constant tumult. When the Giants stepped in against Pfiester, the roar somehow grew even louder.

With the first pitch he threw, Pfiester struck New York first baseman Fred Tenney. He next got ahead of Buck Herzog, two strikes to no balls, and then lost the plate, walking him. Roger Bresnahan struck out, but Kling dropped the third strike.

The Giants then made a sandlot mistake. A runner can take first base on a dropped third strike only if it is unoccupied. But Bresnahan broke for first. Seeing him do so, Herzog broke for second. Kling threw to first, and Herzog was out, doubled off first base.

Up stepped Mike Donlin. He drilled the ball past Chance down the right-field line. The Cubs thought it landed foul, but the umpires disagreed and Donlin pulled into second as Tenney scored to give the Giants a 1–0 lead. As one press report noted, "The monster crowd was bellowing great hoarse volumes of delight" toward the Cubs.

Chance didn't hesitate. This moment could be the ball game. There was no tomorrow if the Cubs didn't win today, and with Mathewson on the mound, he knew that a run or two could prove insurmountable. He waved for Three-Finger Brown and a dejected Jack Pfiester walked off. It was the kind of move for which Chance had earned the name "Peerless Leader," for as the *Tribune* put it, "It was no kindergartner's problem Brownie was called upon to face. . . . Unconscious of everything, careless in his bearing, the man who had faded and touched off many a death

dealing blast in Indiana's coal mines walked to his position." Brown struck out Art Devlin to end the threat.

The game remained scoreless until the third. Before pitching to Joe Tinker, Mathewson repositioned his outfielders, moving them back, but Cy Seymour, in center field, didn't move far enough. Joe Tinker smacked the ball over his head and raced around the bases. Seymour should have let the ball roll into the crowd. According to the ground rules in effect that day, Tinker would have been awarded second base. But Seymour reached the ball before it made the crowd, and Tinker kept running, beating the relay to third base.

Mathewson now pitched as if rattled. Kling singled Tinker home, and then Brown sacrificed Kling to second. Sheckard flied out, and then Mathewson chose to walk Evers and pitch to Schulte. He singled, Chance followed with a double, and by the time Steinfeldt struck out, the Cubs led 4–0. Giants fans were stunned into silence. Back in Chicago, the crowd at Orchestra Hall watching the electronic reenactment was roaring. Getting one or two runs off Mathewson was miracle enough. Four runs was a deluge of biblical proportions.

Brown gave the Giants only one opportunity to catch up. In the seventh inning, two hits and a walk loaded the bases, bringing up Mathewson. McGraw pinch-hit for the pitcher, who over the course of the season had completed thirty-four of his forty-four starts. But Larry Doyle popped up, and Brown escaped the jam, giving up only one run.

The final two innings sped by. Less than two hours after taking the field, the Cubs were finally champions of the National League. Some Chicago fans poured out of the stands and surrounded the Cubs, while disgruntled Giants backers tossed cushions and fruit. Others turned violent. One bold crank raced up and struck Chance with his fist from behind, breaking cartilage in his throat. Solly Hofman was hit in the face by a pop bottle, and Steinfeldt and Pfiester were also attacked.

The Cubs had precious little time to celebrate. As soon as the game ended, they left for Detroit. The World Series would begin in less than forty-eight hours. And for the second time in two days, the Cubs would take the field as the underdog, for most observers assumed that after beating back the Giants, the Cubs would, at least for a game or two, stumble before the Tigers. Detroit was little changed from the year before, apart from the emergence of pitcher Ed Summers and the improved throwing of catcher Boss Schmidt. The Tigers were still a team built around offense, and Ty Cobb had proven that his performance in 1907 was no fluke by leading the AL in 1908 in hits, doubles, triples, and RBIs.

Yet Detroit was still no match for the Cubs. The contest against New York had driven the Cubs to a fever pitch. They were running hot, burning adrenaline, and carrying the momentum of three seasons, 322 wins, three pennants, and one world championship. They were just about as close to an unstoppable force as baseball has ever seen.

The Tigers didn't have a chance.

Game one in Detroit was played under wretched conditions, in a cold driving rain. Absolutely no one outside of Detroit would have blamed the Cubs had they mailed the game in and then tried to regroup for game two. But over the past few weeks, the Cubs had developed an "us against the world" mentality. They played every inning of every game. Ed Reulbach took the mound opposite lefty Ed Killian of the Tigers as Hugh Jennings tried to offset the lefty-laden Cub lineup, which included the entire outfield as well as Johnny Evers.

The Tigers struck first, scoring a first-inning run on a single by Cobb, but in the third the Cubs appeared to break the game open, driving Killian from the mound on a couple of hits and Tiger defense that the *Tribune* described as "full of blowholes." After the Cubs hit in the top of the seventh, they led 5–1.

Then the Tigers finally got going. All game long the Cubs defense had bailed out Reulbach. But in the seventh, Detroit drove Reulbach from the game and drew to within one. First Overall and then Brown came on in relief, but in the bottom of the eighth the Tigers scratched back for two runs when Chance, playing despite the throat injury, dropped a throw and Evers tossed a relay wild. The Tigers were three outs away from a 6–5 win, and relief pitcher Ed Summers, one of the first knuckleball artists, had the Cubs befuddled.

That was enough for the Cubs. No team was better when all looked bleak. With one out, Schulte legged out a hit on a ground ball to short. Up came Chance, eager to make up for his earlier miscue. He ripped what the *Daily News* termed a "vicious single" to center.

Steinfeldt singled to load the bases, bringing up Hofman, who worked Summers to a full count, then ripped a hit to left. Schulte and Chance scored, and the Cubs were in front, 7–6.

Now the Tigers were reeling, and the Cubs knew it. Tinker and Steinfeldt worked a perfect delayed and perhaps accidental squeeze play, one that, as I. E. Sanborn wrote, "completed the utter rout of the Tigers," for both Summers and catcher Schmidt went after the ball, leaving the plate unguarded. A double steal and another single by Kling and suddenly Chicago was ahead 10–6 and the Cubs had shed the Tigers as if they were so many kittens trying to climb up their leg.

Back in Chicago for game two, Overall and Wild Bill Donovan matched each other for seven innings before Joe Tinker drove the ball over Cobb's head and into the crowd for a home run, keying a six-run outburst as the Cubs won going away, 6–1.

In game three, Chance made the most important decision of the series. Reulbach was sick with a cold, Overall had already pitched twice, Brown was still recuperating from his end-of-the-season grind, and Pfiester was still bothered by the pulled ligament and, according to some reports, a stab wound suffered on the Polo Grounds field after the playoff game. Rest could help Overall and Brown, but not Pfiester. He was, quite literally, sacrificed as Chance decided to withhold both Brown and Overall from game three, no matter what. Pfiester failed to win the game but gamely stayed on the mound until the final inning of the 8–3 loss. He should have gotten a medal, for although Chicago had lost the battle, Pfiester's effort put the Cubs in fine shape for winning the war. It may have cost the pitcher his career as well, for after three seasons as a dominant pitcher, Pfiester was never the same and would play only three more seasons.

In game four, the Cubs were back to normal—and normal meant Three-Finger Brown. It was as if the Cubs, with the end of the long season in sight, collectively decided, "Enough," and chose to end things as swiftly and smoothly as possible. Finally pitching with a little rest, Brown was magnificent. He gave up four hits, and the Cubs won game four, 3–0.

Needing only one more victory, Chance turned to Overall, and the Cubs won game five in Detroit in almost clinical fashion before just over six thousand fans, the smallest crowd in Series history as Detroit fans had little desire to see the Tigers mauled once more. In the top of the first, the Cubs scored the only run they needed when Evers, Schulte, and Chance singled. When Detroit came to bat, Overall walked the first Detroit hitter. A strikeout and a single put runners on first and second, but that was only a tease. The pitcher struck out the next three hitters, including Cobb and Claude Rossman, who reached base on a passed ball before Overall fanned Germany Schaefer, giving him four strikeouts for the inning and thoroughly demoralizing the Tigers. Over the remainder of the game, he scattered two hits and three walks. The Tigers threatened only once, in the fifth, after the Cubs had scored another run, but Overall snuffed the rally with another strikeout, this time making Tiger outfielder Sam Crawford his victim.

The game ended quietly on a high foul pop-up to Johnny Kling off the bat of Boss Schmidt. The entire con-test had taken only an hour and a half. A few jubilant Cubs fans in the outer reaches of the stands did their best to whoop it up as the workmanlike Cubs escaped to the club-house, pausing only briefly to accept the subdued congrat-ulations of the Tigers. For the second year in a row, they were champions, the first team in modern baseball history to have won the World Series in back-to-back seasons. To a man, they knew full well that they probably should have won the Series in 1906 as well. Looking ahead, there seemed to be no reason that at least another champi-onship or two was in the near future.

In the *Tribune*, I. E. Sanborn tapped out the obvious. "What those gray clad modest young warriors have accom-plished," he wrote, "will be remembered longer than any of them lives."

Few words ever written about the Cubs have proven to be so accurate, but not in a way Sanborn or anyone else could possibly have imagined.

DYNASTY'S END

At the conclusion of the 1908 season, the Cubs were, by every criterion, a dynasty. Although the Giants and Pirates had pushed them to the brink, their performance under pressure in the final weeks of the season, coupled with their dominance over the Tigers in the World Series, seemed to announce that, as of yet, there were no real challengers to the Cub empire. They reigned supreme, the best club in all baseball, and the best club of all time.

How soon it would all begin to unravel. Like many waning dynasties, the Cubs organization was incapable of looking at itself with any kind of perspective. The problem wasn't arrogance, but neither was the organization honest about any self-appraisal. In recent years, the Cubs had thrived because they were a team in the truest sense: each player did his part, and no one was a star dramatically superior to everyone else. While that was the team's greatest strength, as time went on it was also its greatest weakness. The heart of the ball club had already been together for five seasons, and they were get-

Pitcher James L. "Hippo" Vaughn gained immortality on May 2, 1917, when he and Reds pitcher Fred Toney matched each other in one of the greatest games in major league history. Fewer than two thousand fans braved the cold at Weeghman Park (Wrigley Field), but they were rewarded with a double no-hitter through nine innings. In the tenth, the Reds managed two hits to win by a 1–0 score. Vaughn finished the season with a career-best 23–13 won-lost record.

ting older. That "trio of bear Cubs" and their companions had matured and were about to enter their golden years, with all the attendant infirmities. They did not know it yet, but their best was in the past, and in only a few short years the club would be in a battle for its survival.

The entire team began to erode, so slowly at first that it was virtually invisible. When the decay finally became obvious, replacing one or two players was an insufficient response—it was already too late. The entire organization needed an overhaul. The Cubs would collapse together before rising again with a new owner, in a new ballpark, with an entirely new group of players and a new personality.

But never again in their history would the word "dynasty" be used to describe the Cubs. Their best had come and gone.

The offseason before the 1909 campaign delivered the dynasty's first casualty. Since first joining the club, catcher Johnny Kling had been automatic. A heady catcher best known for his rifle arm and a quick snap throw from his knees that he allegedly learned from Negro League star Bruce Petaway, Kling was a given, a steady performer Cubs fans never worried about. He hit well enough to maintain his position, he shut down the opposition's running game, and he managed the pitching staff without creating a ripple of dissent. He was essential and everywhere, like oxygen, but also just as easy to overlook.

That was the problem. Kling was tired of being overlooked, at least financially. He was one of several Cubs who had discovered that their notoriety as ballplayers was more lucrative off the field than on. An accomplished billiards player, in 1908 and 1909 Kling had won the world's pro billiards championship—a popular table even bore his name. Before the 1909 season, he invested tens of thousands of dollars in a four-story billiard hall in his hometown of Kansas City, Missouri, and he told both Johnny Evers and Harry Steinfeldt that he was thinking about leaving baseball. His contract, however, ran through 1909. Instead of retiring, he asked Charles Murphy for a leave of absence, claiming his net worth of $100,000 made a baseball career unnecessary and telling the press, "They [the Cubs] can get along without me."

Murphy, incredibly, agreed. After all, it saved him some money. In all likelihood, what Kling really wanted was a raise from his salary of $3,000, which was much less than many other Cubs were paid. While it was true that he was a billiard champion and his hall was profitable, his request for a leave seems to indicate that, all things being equal, Kling would have preferred to play ball. In fact, in April 1907 he'd tried the same strategy, saying he was retiring to play billiards, only to return to baseball once it became clear the ploy wouldn't result in a better contract.

Of all the members of the Cubs organization, fame, success, and financial rewards had gone to Charles Murphy's head more than any other man. Although he'd borrowed heavily to get into the game, and Frank Chance had supplied the mental acumen that had created the greatest team in the game, Murphy was beginning to think that he was the genius. Allowing Kling to walk away was an enormous mistake. Lew Archer and Pat Moran split the position in 1910, but neither was the equivalent to Kling.

The Cubs stumbled out of the gate as both Boston and Philadelphia briefly held on to first place in April before Pittsburgh took over on May 5. Then the Cubs awoke and, with the best pitching in the league, made a furious run, but the Pirates were on a roll. No matter how well the Cubs played, the Pirates played just a little better and for most of the summer held a comfortable lead of between five and ten games. They took the season series from the Cubs thirteen games to nine and finished six games ahead of Chicago, winning the pennant with 110 victories. The Cubs, despite 104 wins, finished second.

Had Murphy or Chance been paying much attention, they'd have noticed that even though the Cubs won 104 games, they had begun to slide—their offense was only average in 1909. But it was easy to blame that on the absence of Kling. Besides, Murphy had other matters on his mind.

As his wealth grew, so did his ego. And as his ego grew, so did his desire for more wealth. Armed with a string of pennants and championship banners, Murphy now fancied himself as much of a magnate as legends like the Giants' John Brush and Pittsburgh's Barney Dreyfuss. Murphy and Charles Taft helped bankroll sportswriter Horace Fogel's successful effort to buy the Phillies. Taft owned the Philadelphia ballpark, and Taft and Murphy controlled fully two-thirds of the stock. It was legal, but against league rules—Murphy was clearly conflicted. From that point onward, profit, not wins and losses, was Murphy's primary goal. As the Cubs aged, Murphy kept salaries low and chose not to acquire youthful replacements.

Kling returned in 1910, accepting a $700 fine imposed by the league as a penalty for not fulfilling his contract in 1909, but he was never the same player again and would play only two more seasons with the Cubs. Still, he helped in 1910. Pittsburgh's pitching collapsed, and although the Cubs didn't capture first place until May 25, once they did they didn't look back: after opening up a big lead in mid-July, they cruised to yet another pennant, besting New York by thirteen games as they won 104 games. The big difference was rookie pitcher Leonard Cole, whose mound performance earned him the nickname "King."

In a late-season appearance in 1909, Cole twirled a shutout for the Cubs, and in 1910 he picked up where he'd left off, winning twenty games while losing only four. But he didn't inspire confidence in Frank Chance. Despite a sparkling ERA of 1.80, Cole struggled with his control, and in the clubhouse he was exposed as something of a dimwit: the young pitcher was the butt of jokes that he not only never saw coming but never even recognized as they went over his head. Chance even banned him from team poker games because his style of play became so erratic that it was obvious he not only didn't understand the rules but was incapable of doing so. Humorist and short story writer Ring Lardner, who covered the Cubs for the *Chicago Tribune*, later used Cole as partial inspiration for the character of Jack Keefe in his "Alibi Ike" series.

Connie Mack's Athletics captured the American League pennant, but the Cubs seemed little concerned. All year long the club had fought through injuries, but now almost everyone was healthy—save for Johnny Evers, who had broken his leg on October 1, but Heinie Zimmerman was a capable replacement. Before the Series, Murphy was so confident of victory that he said, "Class always tells. . . . The [Cubs'] superiority is greater than it really seems." The A's, after all, were entering the Series undermanned. Outfielder Rube Oldring, like Evers, had a broken leg, and star pitcher Eddie Plank had a sore arm. Chance was even more secure than Murphy. He told the press that he planned to have Orvie Overall start game one, saving Brown for game two, after which the Cubs expected to have an insurmountable two-game lead. According to Lard-

New Cubs owner Charlie Weeghman (right) greets manager Fred Mitchell (left) and star purchase Grover Cleveland Alexander. Alexander's playing time was limited during the Cubs' pennant-winning season of 1918, owing to military service. In nine seasons with Chicago, Alexander won 128 games, including a league-leading 27 in 1920.

ner in the *Tribune*, Cole wouldn't even pitch, and Chance "isn't figuring on the Philadelphia pitchers at all."

Both men were mistaken, and it didn't take long for them to realize just how wrong they were. In game one, Philadelphia pitcher Chief Bender shut down the Cubs on only three hits, while the A's knocked Overall out of the box in the third inning, winning 4–1. The next day Jack Coombs walked the tightrope all game long, stranding fourteen Cubs. Three-Finger Brown was in a car accident on his way to the game and pitched as if he expected to be hit again. The A's accommodated him on their way to a 9–3 win. The Cubs were on their heels, and no one in Chicago was very happy about that. When, on the off day, a pedestrian spotted Chance in his car and hurled a few epithets his way, the skipper jumped from his automobile and put his boxing skills to use.

But it was the Cubs who were knocked to the floor when the Series resumed. Mack surprised everyone by bringing back Coombs on one day's rest, and he won again, 12–5, as Chance got himself thrown out of the ball game for disputing a home run. Chicago saved face with a 4–3 victory in extra innings in game four as Cole finally got the call and pitched well, but the A's exploded for five runs in the eighth inning of game five to defeat the Cubs in the Series, four games to one.

Cub fans were shocked, as was the organization, which tried to act as if the defeat had never happened. Murphy was particularly garrulous. With Fogel acting as his toady, Murphy was beginning to throw his weight around in league affairs, complaining about umpires and generally irritating everyone. The Cubs were rapidly displacing the Giants as the team most disliked by everyone else.

The loss to the A's revealed a crack in the Cub facade, and players soon began spilling out. Overall was the first to go. He had pitched only three innings in the Series, had struggled with arm trouble, and was dissatisfied with his contract. He retired soon after the Series, saying, "I'm just tired of the job and I don't want any more of it." Then, in the spring, Harry Steinfeldt figured that five years of steady service was worth a two- or three-year contract. Murphy disagreed. On March 14, moments after he signed a one-year deal with Steinfeldt, Murphy shipped the third baseman off to Cincinnati. Pitcher Jack Pfiester was ineffective, and all of a sudden the Cub roster was a little thin. It wasn't long before it got a great deal thinner.

Anything that could go wrong in the life of Johnny Evers did, or was about to. Late in the 1910 season, he'd been in a car accident in which his best friend was killed. Then came the broken leg. As he recovered, he turned his attention to his then-flourishing business. Already the pro-

This advertisement appeared in the *Chicago Daily News* on September 3, 1916, promoting a Labor Day pitching duel between Christy Mathewson of the Reds and the Cubs' Mordecai Brown. In what would be the final career start for both legendary pitchers, the Reds lifted Mathewson to his 373rd career victory with a 10–8 win.

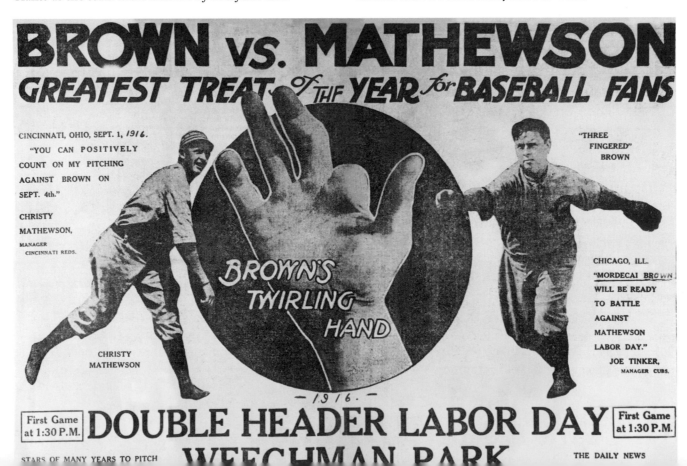

prietor of a shoe store in his hometown of Troy, New York, Evers tried to expand and invested heavily in a bigger store in Chicago with club treasurer C.G. Williams. At first, it seemed like a great success. At the grand opening just before the start of the World Series, the store attracted such a large crowd that police had to be called in. Lardner covered the opening, but when he asked Evers if his broken leg was keeping him from attending the Series, Evers answered oddly, saying, "It's my brains I'm afraid of."

He wasn't kidding. Evers was mentally ill, likely suffering from depression. In the offseason, things only got worse. After the initial crush, few patrons visited the new shoe store, and he discovered that his partner back in Troy had gambled away their profits. Evers was forced to close the Chicago shop just before spring training, a situation not helped by the illness of Williams, who had to withdraw with a nasty skin rash caused by a staph infection.

Evers was a mess. Unfortunately, his situation was not uncommon. The early history of baseball is littered with players who suffered from mental illness of all kinds, ranging from manic depression to full-blown psychosis. In 1898 Martin Bergen, a catcher for the Boston Nationals, axed his wife and children to death while in the throes of a paranoid delusion, and in the waning days of the 1903 season Pittsburgh pitcher Ed Doheny was sent to an asylum after trying to attack someone with a stove poker. He never got out and died in the asylum a few years later.

Sadly, few players received help for their problems. At the time there was little relief beyond the kind that came in a bottle, either served in taverns or dispensed by drugstores, which sold concoctions that often included drugs like morphine and cocaine. Such solutions did nothing but make the problems worse. Players were taught to remain stoic, for any sign of weakness, particularly mental or emotional weakness, could cut short a career. Club owners already had little patience for ballplayers who balked at "playing hurt" with physical injuries, and ballplayers suffering from mental or emotional problems received even less sympathy from them. Evers was expected to buck up and go on.

He couldn't. In early May, just before a game with Cincinnati, Evers collapsed in the clubhouse. The Reds won, 18–2, and the headline in the *Tribune* was strangely prescient: "The Most Useful Trick of the Mind Is Remem-

One of the more underrated and multi-talented players of the Cubs dynasty was catcher Johnny Kling. Not only did he backstop three consecutive pennant winners, but he also left the Cubs for a season to pursue a career in billiards. He returned in 1910 and played one final season with Chicago before being traded to the Boston Braves.

bering What to Forget." Evers couldn't forget anything and found it impossible to concentrate. He left the club. Fortunately, in Evers's case time proved to be the best medicine. He would return to limited duty before the end of the season and go on to continue his career, playing another six seasons.

Chance was the next to go. Getting hit in the head by baseballs and then taking punches in the boxing ring had taken a toll. He was out of sorts all year, complaining of headaches and double vision. Some of the Cubs even noticed that when he spoke he was developing a slurring lisp.

Over his dozen seasons with the Cubs, Johnny Evers's statistical accomplishments seem modest, with only two seasons in which he batted .300 or higher. The Hall of Famer is listed on only one Cub all-time career offensive category and holds seventh place on the all-time stolen base list. However, Evers's greatness lay beyond the realm of statistics, as he was nothing less than the spiritual and competitive driving wheel of four pennant winners and two world championships.

Before a game in Cincinnati on July 1, Chance felt dizzy and had a splitting headache. While taking infield practice, he stumbled and fell to the ground. His teammates had to help him to his feet, and a doctor was summoned from the stands. At first, Chance blamed the heat, but the headaches and dizziness failed to abate. Eventually, doc-

tors determined that the problem was a blood clot in his brain.

For all practical purposes, Chance's career was over. He'd play only eleven more games scattered across the next few seasons. Although he would continue as Cub manager and Vic Saier would fill in capably at first base, losing Chance the player would prove to be a nearly fatal blow for the ball club. Chance's demise as a player further empowered Charles Murphy. The owner began to take a more active role in on-field affairs.

For the time being, the Cubs seemed unaffected by the loss. Incredibly, they hung on in the pennant race with the Giants into late August before finally falling back, finishing the year in second place with ninety-two wins.

Yet their time of dominance was over. In the offseason, third baseman Jim Doyle, who had proven to be an adequate replacement for Steinfeldt, died following an emergency operation for acute appendicitis. A dark cloud began to gather around the Cub franchise, one that some would argue has yet to lift.

In 1912 the Cubs were mere pretenders, the oldest team in the league. Three-Finger Brown wore out, and King Cole, who had a bad arm, contributed nothing before being traded. Evers bounced back to hit .341, the best mark of his career, and Heinie Zimmerman batted an astounding .372, but everyone else was ordinary. The Cubs would finish in third place, eleven and a half games behind the Giants.

Charles Murphy thought he knew why. Instead of viewing the third-place finish as the rather remarkable performance it was, Murphy found it disappointing. The problem, thought Murphy, was Chance. Murphy believed that Chance had lost control of the team and led it into alcoholism.

On September 23, Murphy announced that the club was adopting a "total abstinence" rule—no Cub would be allowed to drink or smoke cigarettes in the upcoming season. In fact, each man would have to sign a pledge to that effect. In a letter to the *Tribune* the next day, Murphy tried to explain how he came to that decision. He claimed that while attending a National League meeting in 1909, Pittsburgh president Barney Dreyfuss, who had ordered his players to sign a sobriety pledge, told Murphy it was the best thing he had ever done. Then Dreyfuss added, "Drinking too much booze cost your club the flag." Murphy's letter went on to relate several veiled stories about various unnamed Cubs who had failed to perform owing to drunkenness before he added, "There is not nearly so much drinking among the White Sox." And that was just the beginning. According to Murphy, the Cubs also ate and smoked too much.

The press, a traditionally booze- and tobacco-fueled industry itself, sided with Murphy and cited Frank Schulte as a player who "failed to keep in his best condition at all times." Influential columnist Hugh Fullerton wrote, "We always found the Cubs around the hotel"—presumably at the bar.

Chance responded with what the *Tribune* termed "hot fire," defending his club to the hilt, but his contract expired at the end of the season, and now that he could no longer play, he was expendable. His request for a three-year deal as manager went unanswered. Murphy let him dangle for several weeks. The Cubs then fell to the White Sox in the city series, and the two men exchanged insults in the press. It soon became clear that there had been bad blood between them for years—Chance chided Murphy for being a tightwad and for his failure to use his profits to build the Cubs a new, first-class, concrete-and-steel ballpark like those that were being built virtually everywhere else, and Murphy called Chance a "utility infielder." Murphy then set up a number of conditions for the next Cub manager, all of which by definition excluded Chance. On October 24, Murphy finally announced that Johnny Evers would be the next Chicago manager, and he gave Evers a four-year contract worth $10,000 annually.

The dynasty was done. Without Chance to serve as a buffer, Murphy's oppressive reign drove the Cubs' few remaining players away. They were either traded or let go if they dared ask for more money or balked at signing the foolish sobriety pledge. Ed Reulbach was traded to Brooklyn. Joe Tinker was sent to Cincinnati. Three-Finger Brown, as if being punished, was released to minor league Louisville, and Jimmy Sheckard was sold to the Cardinals. Chance ended up as manager of the Yankees, but not before National League president John Tener and the other owners had to intercede to clear the way.

Cub fans had never really trusted Murphy since the 1908 World Series, when many suspected that he had fun-

neled tickets to scalpers in exchange for kickbacks. But a winning team had made it easy to overlook the owner. That wasn't the case anymore, and in short order Murphy had managed to alienate both Cub fans and the remaining Cub players.

The next group to abandon Murphy was his fellow owners. They had put up with him as long as attendance held, for the Cubs were traditionally the second-best draw in the league, just behind the Giants. But in 1912 attendance had started to erode. That was costing them money. Over the next few months, Murphy would find friends hard to come by.

It rained on opening day, and the game was canceled. That was just as well, for a smallpox scare temporarily made it seem likely that the Cubs would have to be vaccinated and placed under quarantine. That might have been for the best, because Evers didn't have much to work with in 1913. Larry Cheney emerged as one of the league's better pitchers, and for the second year in a row the Cubs outperformed their talent, again finishing in third place, thirteen and a half games behind the Giants. For that, Evers thought he deserved a raise. After all, the baseball situation was rapidly changing.

A new league, the Federal League, had cropped up in 1913 as an outlaw minor league based in the Midwest. But in 1914, following the model of Ban Johnson's American League, league president James Gilmore, after being rebuffed by organized baseball when he suggested a merger, decided to make the Feds a major league: he added two clubs, moved east, and went head to head against the AL and NL in St. Louis, Pittsburgh, Brooklyn, and Chicago. The Feds also began raiding the established teams of talent, sending salaries through the roof. Evers, as a bona-fide star, figured he deserved a few extra thousand to stay in the NL.

Murphy disagreed. In fact, Murphy had disagreed with just about everything Evers did in 1913, and now, with the Federal League threat on his doorstep, Murphy wanted out of Evers's salary. He decided that Evers's contract could be effectively split in two: retaining Evers as a player at a smaller salary, he would name a new, cheaper manager.

He selected Hank O'Day, the Chicago native, former player, and umpire. Murphy had apparently made the decision some days earlier, because when the announcement was made to the press, one of Murphy's toadies distributed a "telegram" that was in reality a press release the *Tribune* called "one of Murphy's well-known interviews with himself." It made the spurious claim that O'Day's appointment had already been "well received in baseball circles."

Evers exploded and released a statement that read, "I will never play for Murphy again under any conditions," and added, "I have been approached by the Federals and have held conferences with several of them." Evers inferred that he preferred to stay in the National League but believed that, by hiring O'Day, Murphy had broken his contract. Now Evers wanted to be declared a free agent.

His threat got the attention of the other owners. They didn't want Evers to jump to the Feds or challenge his contract in court in an effort to be declared a free agent. The reserve clause, which bound a ballplayer to a team for life, was the foundation of major league baseball and had to be protected at all costs. They began to examine the chain of events that led to Evers's dismissal and O'Day's hiring and eventually concluded that Murphy was wrong when he interpreted Evers's request for a raise as a resignation. In fact, Murphy had fired him, then messed things up even more by hiring O'Day without giving Evers the ten days' notice his contract required. It was a fine mess.

Evers wasn't about to be granted free agency, but the owners bent over backwards to accommodate him. Over the next few weeks, the magnates disposed of the situation by arranging a trade of Evers to the Boston Braves at the same salary he had been receiving in Chicago, plus a bonus to keep him happy. Then they went after Murphy. Expulsions of owners were not unprecedented. After the 1912 season, NL owners had expelled Horace Fogel after he publicly charged that other owners had entered into a conspiracy to deliver the 1912 pennant to the Giants.

They knew precisely how to get Murphy to take leave of baseball—with cash. Charles Taft, Murphy's sponsor, agreed to buy out Murphy's 53 percent interest in the team for a bit more than $500,000 and then take bids from other buyers. Murphy's knees went weak when he heard the offer, which he immediately accepted, saying in a statement that "Mr. Taft offered me more money for my 53 percent of Cubs stock than I ever thought there was in the world. I accepted without quibbling. I am through with baseball and its controversies and squabbles. I'm the hap-

piest man in the world tonight." Murphy's star-crossed tenure was over.

While he did very little right while at the helm of the Cubs and a great deal wrong, the bottom line is irrefutable: not only has no other owner of the Cubs—before or since—been more successful, *but no major league team*, under any owner, has ever won more games than the Cubs during the time Murphy owned the team. Nevertheless, one can argue that Murphy had little to do with that, for dynasty had been delivered to him ready-made, the logical result of Frank Selee's foresight and Frank Chance's leadership.

Over the next few months, Murphy's happiness only increased. The threat posed by the Federal League was real, and Murphy had gotten out of baseball just in time. Millionaire Charles Weeghman, who owned a successful chain of lunchrooms in Chicago, had acquired the Chicago Federal League franchise. He moved aggressively, signing the old Cub favorite Joe Tinker as manager and second baseman and making plans to build his own ballpark.

Weeghman got a leg up on both of Chicago's established major league clubs with the extravagant groundbreaking ceremony he organized on March 4, 1914. Weeghman pulled out all the stops by hiring a band, inviting dozens of politicians, and making the ceremony open to the public. Some five thousand baseball fans chose to attend the ceremony on Chicago's North Side at the corner of North Clark and Addison. Chicago mayor Carter Henry Harrison was a surprise no-show, but Chicago's building commissioner, Henry Ericsson, pinch-hit for the mayor, and at Weeghman's invitation, at 10:20 A.M., the first spade of dirt was turned over at the new park. A club official cracked a bottle of champagne over the spade, the band played "The Gang's All Here," and the assembled dignitaries scrambled for a favorable place in front of the camera. Moments later, men from the Blome Construction Company started in on the heavy work. Few of those in attendance could have imagined that, as of this date, no subsequent champagne has flowed on that site in celebration of a world championship.

The new ballpark, which took less than two months to complete, was a masterstroke, yet at first there wasn't anything particularly special about it apart from the fact that it was not the West Side Grounds. Like the new White Sox home, Comiskey Park, built in 1910, Weeghman Park was made of concrete and steel, a technological innovation that allowed for a bigger structure. It was spacious and airy and featured brick facades, a covered grandstand, wide aisles, concourses, and baseball's first concession stand beneath the stands. The distant outfield fences measured 345 feet in left, 440 feet in center field, and 356 feet in right.

Above all else, it was safe. In recent years, a spate of fires in the older wooden parks had made some fans hesitant about entering such firetraps, and longtime Cubs fans recalled the earlier fire at the West Side Grounds. The old parks were becoming impossible to insure, and Weeghman correctly sensed that once curious Chicagoans experienced the comforts of a new ballpark, they'd be more likely to change their allegiance from the Cubs to his Federal League "Whales." The White Sox, owing primarily to their new park, had recently been outdrawing the Cubs despite putting an inferior product on the field.

But it was not the ivy-covered "friendly confines" that most fans recognize today as beloved Wrigley field, for Wrigley, more than other ballparks of the period, has undergone extensive changes over the years. There were no bleachers when the ballpark opened, and no one thought that one day home runs would drop over the fences with regularity, or that the ever-present wind would be a boon to offense one day and a detriment the next, or that one day the ballpark would become the city's major tourist attraction, on par with the art museum or any other cultural institution. It has evolved just as the city of Chicago and the game of baseball have evolved. The sentimental place it holds in the hearts of many Cub fans today was not yet in evidence, nor would it be, for at least a generation.

The presence of the Whales suddenly made the Cubs seem even older and stodgier. Charles Murphy had retained ownership of the West Side Grounds and did minimal upkeep to the park, and Charles Taft was just a caretaker. He didn't put any real effort into building a ball club, and as long as the Whales were around, no one else was interested in buying the Cubs. The 1914 Cubs were average in almost every way: a solid, stolid ball club almost completely void of personality. Only Zimmerman and Schulte remained from the glory years, and although

CUB HOME BALLPARKS

1870	**DEXTER PARK** independent professional club—some games played at Ogden Park
1871	**UNION BASE-BALL GROUNDS** member of the National Association
1872–73	No home: club dormant due to Great Chicago Fire
1874–77	**TWENTY-THIRD STREET GROUNDS** as member of the National Association and National League
1878–84	**LAKEFRONT PARK**
1885–91	**WEST SIDE PARK I**
1891–93	**SOUTH SIDE PARK II** use overlapped use of both West Side Parks
1893–1915	**WEST SIDE PARK II**
1916—PRESENT	**WRIGLEY FIELD** 1060 West Addison Street

pitcher James "Hippo" Vaughn won twenty games for the first time, he wasn't exactly a drawing card.

The Cubs finished in fourth place with a record of 78–76. But the number that really mattered went through the turnstiles. After drawing more than 500,000 fans each season from 1908 through 1912, in 1913 attendance had slumped to only 419,000. But in 1914, with the nearby Whales playing in a brand-new ballpark and battling Indianapolis for the pennant until the final day of the season, Cub attendance fell to just over 200,000 fans. The White Sox were hurting too, but despite finishing in sixth place, they still drew nearly a half-million fans.

The Cubs weren't the only club to suffer. Virtually every team in both the American and National Leagues suffered losses at the gate, and the Feds, particularly in those cities, like Chicago, that were already home to at least one major league team, weren't exactly rolling in dollar bills either as competition for both fans and players proved costly.

Charles Weeghman was better positioned than most of his fellow owners in the new league. Although league president Gilmore eventually hoped to secure recognition of the Feds as a third major league, Weeghman wasn't convinced of the league's long-term future. Just after the end of the 1914 season, he spent some weeks negotiating with Taft, trying to arrange a purchase of the Cubs. If successful, he planned to shut down the Whales and move the Cubs into his ballpark. After several weeks, however, the deal fell through.

"It looks like war, doesn't it?" said Weeghman afterwards. "We are going right ahead with our plans for next season. . . . I certainly shall not entertain for a minute any plan to finance a minor league team in Chicago." He was throwing down the gauntlet. If the NL didn't want him, he intended to bury the Cubs.

All the Cubs did in response was shuffle the deck. O'Day was let go, and catcher Roger Bresnahan, who had joined the club at the tail end of a successful career in 1913, was named manager. In 1915 the club was as stagnant as attendance at West Side Grounds. After a quick start that carried them into first place as late as early July, for the second year in a row the Cubs struggled to play .500 baseball and drew only 200,000 fans.

Meanwhile, the Whales won the Federal League pennant, and when both the White Sox and Cubs refused a challenge to play a city series, Weeghman declared that his team was the champion of Chicago baseball. Over the next few months, the Whales would secure that claim.

As the 1915 season neared its conclusion, the NL, the AL, and the Federal League all wanted peace—no one was making any money. Weeghman, as one of the league's savvier and better-funded owners, entered into the negotiations.

At the cost of about $500,000, organized baseball paid off the Federal League. Two Fed owners, Phil Ball of St. Louis and Weeghman, were allowed to buy existing franchises and merge them with their Federal League clubs. Ball purchased the St. Louis Browns, while Weeghman bought the Cubs for $500,000. Almost overlooked at the time was the fact that he soon took on several partners. As Weeghman said later, "I told my friends and associates to name the four biggest businessmen in Chicago, and then I said I would go out and see them personally regarding taking stock in the purchase of the Cubs." The three men were J. Ogden Armour of the meatpacking company that bore the Armour name, Julius Rosenwald of Sears and Roebuck, and William Wrigley, president of the chewing gum company. Before the start of the 1916 season, another five men were added to the roster of directors, and the worth of the Cubs was estimated at more than $1 million.

All of a sudden, Weeghman controlled nearly fifty ballplayers and the ball club was rolling in capital. The Cubs had a chance again. He immediately named Whale manager Joe Tinker the new manager of the Cubs and abandoned the West Side Grounds for Weeghman Park, which for the next few seasons would be known as Cubs Park. Although some members of the press wondered if Cub fans would travel en masse to the ballpark on the North Side, most Cub fans were thrilled. With the influx of talent from the Whales supplementing the roster of the Cubs, a pennant seemed within reach.

Yet few realized that the Federal League was a major league in name only and that few Federal League stars would duplicate their performance in either the National or American League. After all, a pitcher like Three-Finger Brown, whose major league career seemed over, had reemerged in the Federal League and been a big winner—Brown had won seventeen games for the Whales in 1915 and sported one of the lowest ERAs in the league.

Even though the Whales had arguably been the best team in the league, few of their players even made the Cubs in the spring of 1916. Outfielders Max Flack and Les Mann joined Cub Cy Williams in the outfield, but Dutch Zwilling, who had been the Whales' best hitter, couldn't solve National League pitching, and none of the Whale hurlers, including veteran George McConnell, who had led the Feds with twenty-five wins, made much of an impact on the Cubs.

Cub fans didn't care. In the sunshine in Cubs Park, out from under the stifling ownership of Murphy and Taft, fans turned out in abundance. Attendance more than doubled in 1916, up to nearly a half-million fans. In fact, that was Weeghman's only problem: the size of the crowds. At the time, fans were given leather-covered cushions to sit on. Early in the season, exuberant fans discovered that when the leather-covered rectangles were thrown spinning through the air, they sailed far and true, not unlike today's Frisbee. When the game lagged, groups of fans delighted in starting fights with one another, using the cushions as weaponry. As sportswriter James Cruisenberry observed, "It isn't that the cushions are damaged, but that several patrons have been injured. . . . One woman at Sunday's game between the Cubs and the Pirates was struck across the face . . . knocked senseless and dangerously cut. . . . It cost the Chicago club a neat sum of money to settle with her." Weeghman halted the practice when he convinced Chicago police to arrest the cushion tossers.

Foul balls created another problem. The close confines of Cubs Park led to an inordinate number of foul balls reaching the stands. Throughout the major leagues, it was common for ushers to chase down the errant balls, pry them from the hands of fans, and return them to the field of play.

Not so in Chicago. Weeghman quickly tired of seeing his ushers and fans in mortal combat over a ball that cost only a dollar or two. Beginning in 1916, he ordered his ushers to allow patrons to keep the baseballs. The ushers were even happier than the fans, and boys who lived on the North Side were kept supplied with baseballs as dozens of fans went home happy each day.

Good thing, because what was taking place on the field delivered no such joy. Although the Giants, Braves, and Phillies all fought it out with pennant-winning Brooklyn for the title, the Cubs never got going. At least Weeghman tried, however. Over the course of the summer, the Cubs made not less than five deals that delivered nine players, among them New York's star second baseman Larry Doyle.

Several deals were strictly for cash, and the only players of note the Cubs gave up were Wildfire Schulte, who was no longer very wild, and Heinie Zimmerman.

Unfortunately, the deals made no difference in 1916. The Cubs finished far back in fifth place, twenty-five and a half games behind the Dodgers and almost twenty games behind the fourth-place Giants. When the Cub stockholders met after the season, they weren't happy, and increasingly the directors felt the need to throw their weight around. Weeghman had begun selling off small bits of his stock and was quickly becoming just another member of the board, president in name only.

The board got what it wanted. Manager Joe Tinker took the fall. The board then sent Weeghman east with express instructions not only to return with a manager, but with a manager who was either John McGraw of the Giants, George Stallings of the Braves, or Fred Mitchell, a former pitcher of no great distinction who was best known for serving as pitching coach for Stallings when the "miracle" Braves surged to the pennant in 1914.

McGraw and Stallings wanted nothing to do with the Cubs, but Mitchell was looking to move up and accepted the Cubs' offer. He then cautioned fans to be patient, for although he thought the roster "has the makings of a good team and has some good pitching material . . . if we get up around the leaders in a year and a half I will feel that we will have done as well as could be expected." Hardly a vote of confidence in his own ball club.

In the spring, Mitchell installed his system. He was a micro-manager who advocated what he called "percentage baseball," abolishing such traditional approaches as the hit-and-run play. His players were expected to follow orders that were delivered on nearly every pitch. Mitchell did all the thinking.

It worked—for a while. The Cubs opened the 1917 season with a rush, winning twenty-two of their first thirty-one to surge into first place. They then lost five in a row to fall out of the race.

In retrospect, the best game of the season—and one of the most remarkable in baseball history—took place on May 2 at Weeghman Park, when Hippo Vaughn and Fred Toney of the Reds squared off before just over three thousand fans. Yet the game had zero impact on the season and, in fact, was nearly overlooked at the time. Still, what happened that day had never happened before, and has never happened since.

Over the past several seasons, Hippo Vaughn had been one of the few bright spots on the Cub roster. The burly pitcher, who gained his nickname from his ungainly, hippopotamus-like, rolling walk, had labored in the major leagues for parts of five seasons, learning his trade, before finally finding success with the Cubs in 1914. He wasn't

---

Although Jim Thorpe made his name as an Olympic gold medalist and pro football pioneer, he also gained some fame on the baseball diamond. In the famed double no-hitter thrown by the Cubs' Hippo Vaughn and Reds teammate Fred Toney, Thorpe hit the grounder that resulted in the Reds' lone run when Cub catcher Artie Wilson failed to make the out on Vaughn's toss to home as Larry Kopf touched home.

overpowering but relied on command, mixing his fastball with a curve and a changeup. He was a pitcher, not a thrower, and anchored the Cubs' pitching staff.

Opposing him that day was Reds pitcher Fred Toney. Like Vaughn, he too relied more on guile and control than on pure stuff. Toney threw what sportswriters of the day termed a "crossfire"—throwing sidearm across his body.

Each pitcher was in command from the start. Vaughn was more dominant, striking out ten for the day as opposed to only three by Toney, but neither man was ever in trouble. Moreover, although each walked two men and Vaughn gave up a base runner on an error, through nine innings neither pitcher gave up a hit. In fact, neither team even had to make a difficult play. The game unrolled so matter-of-factly that Vaughn later said that he didn't realize until the eighth inning that both he and Toney were throwing no-hitters.

Vaughn struck out Toney to end the ninth and earn his no-hitter, having faced the minimum twenty-seven batters, for the Cubs had turned two double plays. A few moments later, Toney collected his no-hitter as well, sending the game into extra innings. For the first and only time in major league history, two pitchers had thrown a no-hitter in the same game. Then the spell was broken.

With one out in the tenth, Cincinnati shortstop Larry Kopf hit a line drive to right field. Fred Merkle, who had come to the Cubs in a trade, raced to his right but came up just short as the ball dropped for the first hit of the game. After a fly-out, Red first baseman Hal Chase lofted a ball to center field. Cy Williams misjudged the fly and dropped it for an error, sending Kopf to third.

Jim Thorpe, the Native American Olympian, came up next. He topped the ball toward third. Vaughn fielded it, didn't think he had enough time to catch Thorpe, and flipped the ball home. Although Vaughn later claimed that Cub catcher Artie Wilson "froze" on the play and failed to catch Vaughn's toss home, costing the pitcher the game, according to sportswriter James Cruisenberry, "the ball hit Wilson on the shoulder at about the same time Kopf crashed into him." Chase tried to score too, but Wilson recovered and tagged him out.

Vaughn trailed 1–0. Toney calmly took the mound, struck out two of the last three Cub hitters, and walked off with a 1–0, ten-inning no-hitter. Were the same event to take place today, it would be the subject of banner head-lines and wall-to-wall coverage. At the time, however, despite its rarity, the Chicago papers treated the game rather matter-of-factly. The game earned only a one-column headline in the *Tribune* that touted Toney's no-hitter but failed to mention Vaughn's accomplishment.

In fact, as the season droned on, all major league baseball began to be viewed as something less than a life-or-death situation. The assassination of Serbian Archduke Ferdinand in 1914 had sparked the Great War, which had slowly spread to encompass Europe, and by the spring of 1917 the United States had been pulled into the conflict. Although no American troops would reach Europe until October, the Selective Service Act had been passed, and with each passing day, the war had a greater impact on American life. Already, thousands of Americans, including scores of baseball players, were getting married, joining the reserves, or finding friendly doctors to diagnose them with flat feet in order to avoid the draft.

Attendance was already suffering. Although teams were drawing better than they had during the war with the Federal League, the American economy had slumped and fans were watching their wallets. The Cubs finished in sixth place, twenty-four games behind pennant-winning New York, and watched as the rejuvenated White Sox, behind star outfielder Joe Jackson, beat the Giants in the World Series. Although the 1917 season had unfolded as if oblivious to the war, as soon as it was over the war began to have an enormous impact on baseball, one that, improbably, would soon launch the Cubs back into the World Series.

A number of owners had lost money in 1917. Some, like Connie Mack of Philadelphia, looked toward the future with uncertainty. The war loomed over everything. The U.S. government was espousing a "work or fight" mentality, meaning that anyone not working to support the war was expected to do his part in the service, a philosophy that would soon gain legislative backing. In that context, baseball was superfluous, and some were calling for the suspension of play. Mack decided to cut his losses and over the next few months sold off the heart of his ball club, intending to rebuild after the war, when the economic climate would be more certain. Most other owners were a bit less reactionary, but still acted conservatively.

They didn't throw in the towel, but they did keep expenses to a minimum and trades were rare.

The exceptions were the Boston Red Sox under their ebullient owner Harry Frazee—and the Cubs. Frazee went on a spending spree and picked up many of Mack's discards. The Cubs, feeling some pressure after the White Sox success, were nearly as aggressive. In the offseason, they added Braves pitcher Lefty Tyler—Mitchell's protégé—and Philadelphia outfielder Dode Paskert, and in a trade that also included a record $55,000 payment they picked up the Phillies' star battery of catcher Bill Killefer and the great pitcher Grover Cleveland Alexander. Weeghman also made a play for star Rogers Hornsby, but the Cardinals turned him down.

On paper, this made the Cubs instant contenders—Alexander had won thirty games in 1917, and Tyler was solid, while Killefer and Paskert were upgrades over Artie Wilson and Cy Williams. But that was the problem in 1918. The roster on paper did not always match the roster on the field.

Most Americans assumed that the United States would quickly tip the balance when it entered the war and that American troops would only be needed for a few weeks or months at most. In fact, many American papers ran headlines that tallied the American presence in the war by days. But as the spring of 1918 approached, the body count went up, and it began to be clear that the war would require more from America than many had thought, many ballplayers went into a panic. They worried that unless they joined the reserves or took a job in the war industries, they'd be drafted. By New Year's Day, seventy-seven major leaguers were in the service.

The public took note, and many of those players who stayed behind were regarded as cowards and labeled "slackers." When former Giant outfielder Harry McCormick returned from his tour of duty, he reported that "the feeling among the boys over there seems generally to be that the ballplayers haven't acted on the level . . . there has been too much evasion, too much hanging back, too much sidestepping . . . the boys are generally incensed." Indeed, such feelings were so intense that the soldiers' newspaper, *Stars and Stripes*, eventually stopped printing scores and standings.

Baseball did what it could to offset the perception. In

spring training, players did drills using bats instead of bay-onets and raised money for various war charities, but these were mostly empty gestures. Ball clubs filled their depleted rosters with aging, career minor leaguers and others who were somehow unfit for service. As the season approached, baseball seemed to take the attitude that if it stayed quiet and didn't rock the boat, perhaps the public wouldn't notice.

The Cubs were lucky. By opening day, their roster was intact—not a single frontline player had joined the mili-tary. In contrast, the Boston Red Sox had lost fifteen play-ers, and most other clubs were missing at least two or three stalwarts.

Both the Cubs and Brooklyn jumped out to a quick start as everyone else struggled. But Grover Cleveland Alexander had been drafted. He reported for duty on April 30 after pitching in only three games.

Fortunately, the Cubs could absorb the loss. On May 18, provost marshal Enoch Crowder issued the "work or fight" order that compelled able-bodied workers to serve in either the military or an industry the government had decided was "essential" to the war effort. While entertain-ment industries like the motion pictures and theater had successfully lobbied to be declared "essential," baseball had made no such argument, and Crowder's ruling cast baseball into the "unessential" category.

Now baseball's ruling National Commission, the three-headed hydra that ran baseball and consisted of both league presidents and an owner, leapt into action. They sent a representative to Washington to try to get Crowder to reverse his ruling, but the commission didn't have the contacts necessary to make such a lobby successful. If any-thing, the effort only angered Crowder and the public, because baseball appeared to be asking for "special" treat-ment.

Meanwhile, on June 6, as baseball began to make plans to suspend the season, the Cubs took over first place and started to open up some ground. At about the same time, Red Sox owner Harry Frazee, whose Red Sox were also fighting for first place, began to pull some strings. Frazee,

Patriotic ceremonies were common at major league parks during the First World War. Here, the Cubs stand with troops at Weeghman Park on opening day in 1917.

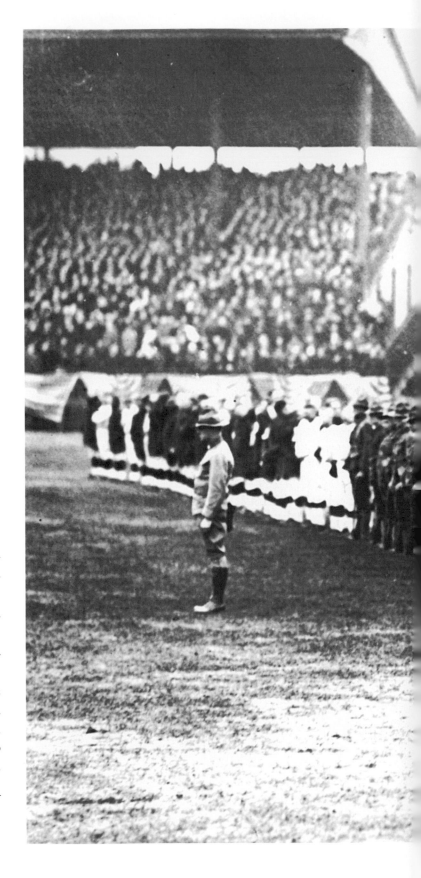

The Cubs rented Comiskey Park for the 1918 World Series, thinking the larger seating capacity would result in bigger profits. Instead, they gave up their home-field advantage to a Red Sox club used to playing in the expansive, self-proclaimed "Baseball Palace of the World."

who had made a fortune as one of the most successful Broadway producers of the era, knew everybody. He went to Washington and met with Secretary of War Newton Baker and convinced him that baseball, like the theater, was good for the nation's morale. Newton was sympathetic, and in July the government informed baseball that it would not enforce the "work or fight" order for ballplayers until October, as long as the season ended by September 1. Baseball was free to continue the season and, in a later ruling, play the World Series at the conclusion of the abbreviated season.

There was joy in Boston and Chicago, but little interest elsewhere. Many baseball fans had a cynical view of the Cubs and Red Sox as two ball clubs that had crassly tried to buy pennants with cash while their countrymen gave their lives on the battlefield. Even Chicago and Boston fans were conflicted. Although the Cubs drew more than five thousand fans per game, that was nearly two thousand fewer than they had drawn in 1916, and attendance was down in Boston also. In Chicago, fans had a special incentive to stay away: on at least one occasion federal agents manned the gates and demanded to see the draft cards of every draft-age man in attendance.

Despite it all, the Cubs were playing grand baseball. In a league weakened by the draft, Cub pitching was dominant. Vaughn was the best pitcher in the league, Tyler thrived under Mitchell's tutelage, former Fed star Claude Hendrix had the best season of his career, and "Shufflin' Phil" Douglas, who probably had the best stuff in baseball, took up the slack after the loss of Alexander. Douglas was a notorious, absolutely out-of-control drunk who was prone to disappearing, but when he was sober—or close to sober—he was one of the best pitchers in the game.

The Cubs were no less successful at the bat. The whole lineup feasted upon subpar pitching. Fred Merkle, rookie shortstop Charlie Hollocher, Max Flack, and outfielder Les Mann all had the best seasons of their otherwise mediocre careers. Over the final weeks of the season, as it became ever more likely that the Cubs and Red Sox would meet in the World Series, most observers correctly gave the Cubs a slight edge. Even Red Sox partisan Paul Shannon, who covered the Red Sox for the *Boston Post*, gave the edge to the Cubs. He not only thought that the Cubs were better than Boston but offered that "the 1918 Red Sox are the weakest team to represent the Hub in the American League in the past ten years."

Shannon was right. The Cubs *should* have taken advantage and won the 1918 World Series. But as modern observers know, in regard to the Cubs "should win" and "won" are not part of the same language. Although virtually everything tilted the Cubs' way, Weeghman and Mitchell couldn't leave well enough alone.

Foremost among Chicago's advantages was the schedule. Owing to wartime travel restrictions, the National Commission decided to start the Series in Chicago with three games before both clubs traveled to Boston for its conclusion, giving the Cubs an initial home-field advantage.

But Weeghman squandered that edge. When he looked at the World Series, he saw dollar signs and little else. No one knew it yet, but he was maneuvering to get rid of the Cubs—and looking for a final big score before doing so. Although fan interest had been tepid all season long, he somehow thought that Weeghman Park, with its capacity of eighteen thousand fans, would be overwhelmed. Weeghman asked the White Sox for permission to rent Comiskey Park, with nearly twice the capacity, believing he would reap a windfall in extra ticket sales. The White Sox agreed.

The home-field advantage was gone—the Red Sox were more accustomed to Comiskey Park than the Cubs. Also lost was any offensive advantage the Cubs enjoyed. Playing in Weeghman Park, the Cubs had the best offense in baseball. But Comiskey Park was enormous. Doubles and triples that rattled off the fences on the North Side were catchable farther south.

Fred Mitchell played a role in the decision as well. All season long Mitchell, who still lived just outside Boston, where he had an apple orchard, had heard about the batting exploits of Boston's star pitcher turned sometime-outfielder, Babe Ruth. Facing subpar pitching, Ruth was baseball's greatest slugger in 1918 with eleven home runs, fifty extra-base hits, and a .555 slugging percentage. Mitchell, intimidated by Ruth's power, believed that he would have a harder time reaching the fences in Comiskey Park.

In fact, Mitchell was so worried about Ruth that he decided to abandon most of his pitching staff. Aware that Ruth had some difficulty hitting left-handers, as did Harry Hooper, Boston's second-most-dangerous hitter, Mitchell decided to use left-handed pitching almost exclusively against Boston, which meant favoring Hippo Vaughn and Lefty Tyler over Claude Hendrix and Phil Douglas. Both decisions would prove disastrous.

A strange symmetry would soon begin to reveal itself. Beginning in 1918 and persisting until the present day, the Cubs and the Red Sox have inexplicably been bound together as time after time their individual histories have proceeded in more or less a parallel fashion.

The Cubs warmed up for the Series playing an August 26 exhibition game against a team representing the Great Lakes Naval Training Station. Douglas pitched, and the Cubs won, 5–0. Having already clinched the pennant, the Cubs had plenty of time to prepare for Boston and set their pitching rotation. So did Boston, for although the Indians pressed them until the final week, the Series was not scheduled to begin until September 4, almost a week after the end of the regular season.

Unfortunately, it rained on the morning of the fourth, pushing the game back a day. Owing to the weather and the delay, a surprisingly sparse crowd of just over nineteen thousand fans turned out on the blustery day for the ball game, the first sign that the 1918 World Series would be neither an artistic nor an economic success. Ruth immediately announced that he didn't care where he played by knocking the first pitch he saw during batting practice over the right-field wall of Comiskey Park.

Fred Mitchell and Boston manager Ed Barrow then both tried the same ruse. Neither had announced his choice to start the game, and each sent two men out to warm up: Vaughn and Tyler started tossing for the Cubs, while Ruth and Joe Bush warmed up for the Red Sox.

The big surprise was Ruth, who drew the starting nod when the batteries were announced before the game. He'd won only thirteen games in 1918, and the smart money believed that the Cubs were much better against left-handed pitching. But Ruth had been Boston's best pitcher down the stretch, and Ed Barrow had been reading the newspapers. He already knew the Cubs were going left-handed during the Series, and he had already figured out a

CUBS CHICAGO NATIONAL LEAGUE BALL CLUB

SEASON 1918

Champions National League 1906 1907 1908 1910

ESTABLISHED 1876 CHAMPIONS OF THE WORLD 1907—1908

5¢ OFFICIAL SCORE CARD

The "All-Year-'Round Soft Drink"

Non-Intoxicating   Non-Alcoholic

Bevo

THE BEVERAGE

for Sale in this Park

CHICAGO BRANCH—ANHEUSER-BUSCH
2367 Logan Boulevard   Phone Armitage 20

Cubs manager Fred Mitchell graced the cover of the 1918 World Series program. The Series, played under the threat of a player walkout and in the shadow of the coming influenza epidemic, may have been baseball's worst ever.

man botched the play, Mann took off for third, beating his throw, and Paskert took second. But that was about the only bad play that Whiteman, a native of Peoria, Illinois, would make.

Ruth worked Fred Merkle carefully, and he walked to load the bases, bringing up Charlie Pick. Pick lifted the ball to left field, but Whiteman made amends, catching the dying line drive on the run to bail Ruth out. Ruth then settled down.

Meanwhile, Vaughn struggled, falling behind nearly every hitter. In the fourth inning, Boston finally broke through. Shean walked, and after a botched sacrifice attempt, George Whiteman and Stuffy McInnis both singled, scoring Shean and giving Boston a 1–0 lead.

In a contest the *Tribune* termed "monotonous," that was it. The Cubs mounted a middling threat in the sixth, only to have Whiteman—again—end the rally with a running catch to secure Boston's 1–0 victory. Apart from that, the only matter of interest was Cub coach Otto Knabe. All game long he berated Ruth in the crudest terms possible, and after the game Ruth went looking for him.

Game two was far more engaging as Knabe, who had escaped Ruth the day before, again provided the entertainment, this time aiming his barbs at Red Sox coach Heinie Wagner. After Boston went down in the second inning, instead of returning to the Boston bench, Wagner came looking for Knabe.

Before anyone realized what was happening, Wagner was in the Cub dugout throwing haymakers. Then the Cubs folded in over the two men before Boston's reinforcements could cut across the diamond and come to Wagner's rescue. After some delay, Wagner emerged muddied but not bloodied from the confrontation. *Baseball Magazine* later reported that "fans who could see it [the fight] declared that when they heard two Germans were fighting, they merely encouraged them to beat each other up."

But the battle did ratchet up the intensity of the Series, and the rest of game two was played as if baseball were a contact sport. In the Chicago third, the Cubs broke through against Joe Bush.

With one out, Merkle walked, and then Pick, trying to bunt, beat the throw to first. Third baseman Charlie Deal popped up a bunt attempt, but Bill Killefer doubled to score one run and then Tyler helped himself, driving a single to

response—Ruth would pitch, because if he didn't appear on the mound, he wouldn't appear in the Series at all. Instead of using Ruth in the outfield, Barrow had decided to go with minor league journeyman—and right-handed hitter—George Whiteman in the outfield, along with Harry Hooper and Amos Strunk. He even had Ruth bat ninth, the usual pitcher's spot.

Neither Vaughn nor Ruth was sharp at the start. In the bottom of the first, with two out, Les Mann hit a bounding ball to second, which took a bad hop over Red Sox second baseman Dave Shean's head for a single. Then Dode Paskert ripped a single to left field. When George White-center that scored Pick and Killefer. Boston threatened in the ninth when Strunk and Whiteman hit back-to-back triples, but Tyler held on for the 3–1 win as Ruth stayed on the Boston bench and the Cubs knotted the Series.

A victory in game three was critical for Chicago. If they lost, Boston, with the rest of the Series scheduled for Fenway Park, would have home-field advantage.

But Fred Mitchell was determined to stick to his all-lefty strategy. He brought back Vaughn on one day's rest, while Boston countered with submariner Carl Mays.

Vaughn didn't pitch badly, but Mays was better. Boston pushed across two runs in the fourth after Vaughn hit Whiteman, and the Sox scratched out four singles, not one of which was hit hard. Chicago's best chance came in the bottom of the inning when Paskert nearly hit a home run, only to have—guess who?—George Whiteman grab the ball out of the front row. The Cubs scored one run in the fifth on a couple of hits, but Mays stopped them after that. The Red Sox won, 2–1.

The only happy Cub was catcher Bill Killefer. Before the game, Cub stockholder William Wrigley called Killefer over and said, "I guess I owe you some money." Killefer didn't know what he was talking about until Wrigley reminded him that during spring training Wrigley had bet Killefer $1,000 against a ten-cent cigar that the Cubs wouldn't win the pennant. "All I want to know," asked Wrigley, "is whether you want a separate check or whether I should have it added to your final paycheck." Killefer, due to join the Army at the end of the Series, gladly accepted the money, but told Wrigley he'd forgotten all about it.

A few hours later, at eight o'clock, both teams boarded the same train for the twenty-seven-hour trip to Boston. Normally, the two clubs would have had little to do with one another, particularly after the bad blood in game two, but the long journey caused tempers to cool.

Players from both clubs finally had a chance to look over some documents distributed by the National Commission. As they pored over the papers, the players came to understand that they were playing the World Series for a whole lot less than they thought they were.

Before 1918, the players had shared 60 percent of Series receipts, resulting in a payout of several thousand dollars each, often $5,000 or more for each player on the winning team while the loser received approximately 70 percent of that amount. But in 1918 the commission, acting on behalf of the owners, changed the distribution. Now the players would share only 55.75 percent of the receipts, and only from the first four games. Only 60 percent of that amount would go to the players of the two pennant winners; the rest would go to players on the teams that finished second, third, and fourth.

The rest? That went to the owners, who further stood to benefit by using the fact that half the players in the league now received an end-of-the-year "bonus" that would help keep salaries down. In addition, the commission also ordered each player to donate 10 percent of his Series share to the war charities.

Although the players were not protected by a union and hadn't been consulted, they were neither naive nor stupid. They didn't mind sharing the proceeds with charity, but they could do the math and blanched at taking what was, in effect, a pay cut of between 40 and 70 percent, depending on the number of games played, in order to subsidize the owners and deflate salaries.

Boston's Harry Hooper and Dave Shean spent much of the trip to Boston conferring with Les Mann and Bill Killefer, pondering how to react. Killefer had to wonder if Wrigley's recent largesse had been designed to influence the team leader's reaction. Regardless, the players were united. After consulting with members of each team, the players reached a consensus. Either the commission backed down or the players would strike. There would be no game four.

Arriving in Boston at midnight, the players immediately went to bed, but as the Associated Press reported, "When they came down to breakfast it was apparent that all the members of both teams were brimful of determination. . . . In spite of the intense rivalry the players of the two teams were united in declaring that they would back up to the limit the joint committee which they appointed on the train coming from Chicago." According to AP, in addition to the other cuts, the commission had originally set a minimum payout of $2,000 per player for the winning team and $1,400 for the losers, but now was even backing off that because ticket sales to the Series were slow. Now the guarantees were only $1,200 and $800.

After breakfast, the four player representatives sought

out the National Commission (which served the same role as today's commissioner): AL president Ban Johnson, NL president John Heydler, and August "Gerry" Hermann, the owner of the Cincinnati Reds. The players told the commission that they had no intention of playing and requested a formal meeting to air their grievances.

The commission was taken aback, but proved fast on their feet. The three men expressed complete ignorance of the entire matter and told the players they were powerless to change the agreement without consulting with all sixteen owners. That was a lie, and the players knew it, but when the commission agreed to a formal meeting the next day, the players reluctantly decided to play game four.

The Cubs in particular had reason to play. The night before, as the train chugged its way into Boston, Babe Ruth had decided to have a little fun. He'd raced through the cars plucking straw hats off the heads of passengers, then punching out the crown, a stunt Ruth found highly amusing.

Apparently, not every passenger felt the same way. Although reports varied, Ruth either miscalculated and punched through a hat and straight into the steel wall of the train, or else someone—maybe teammate Walt Kinney, maybe another passenger—resisted, causing Ruth to take a real swing, which missed and lost a battle with the wall of the car.

Whatever happened, the result was the same. The middle finger of Ruth's pitching hand was swollen to twice its normal size. Ruth had been penciled in to pitch game four. If he was hampered by the finger, or couldn't pitch at all, the advantage tilted toward the Cubs.

The Cubs stuck with Lefty Tyler. But when the game started, Ruth was on the mound for Boston. He'd had the finger drained, and it was stained with iodine, but he had convinced Barrow he could pitch.

He could, but just barely, as he lacked both his usual command and speed. Unfortunately for the Cubs, Boston's defense kept bailing him out as the Cubs proved too anxious. In the first inning, Flack was picked off first to end a rally, and in the third he was picked off second to kill another scoring chance. Shortstop Everett Scott stopped another rally in the fourth when he robbed Paskert of a hit, and in both the fifth and the seventh innings double plays killed the Cubs.

Tyler, meanwhile, appeared in complete command before falling apart in the fourth. After walks to Shean and Whiteman put two men on, Ruth came up with two outs.

It was Lefty Tyler versus the left-handed Ruth, and all odds seemed to favor the Cubs. Thus far, Ruth had done nothing with the bat in the Series, and now he was swinging virtually one-handed, for his swollen finger made it almost impossible for him to grip the bat with his left hand.

Still, Tyler pitched Ruth carefully—perhaps too carefully. He fell behind 3–0, and then Ruth watched two strikes pass by, as if he realized he had one good swing and was determined to wait for the perfect pitch.

He got it on the next pitch. As *Boston Post* reporter Paul Shannon wrote, "A report like a rifle shot rang through the park. Twenty-five thousands rose as one man, and while the bleachers shrieked in ecstasy, the Cubs right fielder [Flack] taken unawares dashed madly for the center field stands." Shean and Whiteman scored easily, and Ruth slid into third for a triple. Boston led, 2–0.

Tyler then settled down, not giving up another hit through the seventh inning. In the top of the eighth, the Cubs finally got to Ruth. Killefer walked, and then Mitchell pinch-hit for Tyler, inserting fellow pitcher Claude Hendrix. The move made perfect sense, for Hendrix was one of the Cubs' best hitters and, in fact, led the team in slugging in 1918. Hendrix singled.

Both men then advanced on a wild pitch as Ruth, who had walked six and struck out none, was obviously laboring. With Hendrix in scoring position, Mitchell put in pinch runner Bill McCabe.

With the infield in, Flack grounded out to first as both runners held, then Charlie Hollocher hit one in the hole between first and second. Boston second baseman Dave Shean, who was only able to play in the Series because he was on leave from the Navy, got to the ball, but his only play was at first base as Killefer scored. Mann followed with a hit to left to tie the score, but Paskert grounded out to end the inning. Still, the Cubs had finally broken through against Ruth, whose scoreless-inning streak in Series play, which was almost completely overlooked at the time, was halted at twenty-nine and two-thirds innings.

Phil Douglas, not Hendrix, took over for Tyler in the eighth. He was probably sober, but he played as if he were

Cub first baseman Fred Merkle is tagged out by Red Sox third baseman Fred Thomas in action at the 1918 World Series at Fenway Park. Merkle (.278) was one of but four starting players on either side to hit above .250 in a Series that saw the winning team bat just .186 to the loser's .210.

under the influence, holding the lead for all of five minutes.

Wally Schang led off with a single, and when Killefer failed to catch a Douglas pitch cleanly, he advanced to second. Harry Hooper then laid down a bunt, which Douglas fielded and promptly threw away, and Schang came around with the go-ahead run.

The Cubs had one last chance in the ninth but blew it just as they had so many other chances in the ball game. After Merkle singled and pinch hitter Rollie Zeider walked, driving Ruth from the game in favor of Joe Bush, Chuck Wortman, who had all of seventeen at-bats all year and no sacrifices, bunted too hard to Stuffy McInnis at first base. McInnis threw across the diamond to nail Merkle. Turner Barber then hit for Killefer and grounded into a double play. Ball game, and the Cubs trailed in the Series three games to one.

As soon as the game ended, however, the players again took up their grievance with the National Commission. Hooper, Heinie Wagner, Les Mann, and Bill Killefer went together to the Copley Plaza Hotel.

The commission had had twenty-four hours to get their story straight, and they were in fine form. The meeting

lasted all of five minutes as the commission again told the players they had no authority in the matter. They also passed out a press release that read, "We are powerless to change the situation. The legislation has been enacted by the American and National Leagues, and the other teams figuring in the split could bring suit against the National Commission and beat the suit if we were to make any change." With that, they patted the players on the head and sent them off to bed, confident they had the situation under control.

They didn't. The players were committed, and with each brushoff they grew more determined. Later that evening, they decided to try to meet once more with the commission, and unless the issue was resolved, they wouldn't play game five.

By this time, word of the snafu was becoming public knowledge. The press was four-square on the side of management—the *Chicago Daily Journal* referred to the players as the "bolsheveki of baseball."

The next morning the team of revolutionaries went to the Copley Plaza once again. An exasperated Ban Johnson sent them away once more, saying they could all meet again after game five.

The players knew better. If Boston won game five, the point was moot—the Series would be over, and there would be no meeting. The representatives went to the ballpark and explained the situation to the players of both teams. They were all in agreement. As far as they were concerned, there would be no game five.

Meanwhile, the commission was already celebrating their victory in the bar of the Copley Plaza, toasting each other on their combined brilliance. But as game time approached and some twenty thousand fans began to pour into Fenway Park, the field remained empty. Word traveled fast, and at about 2:00 P.M. the commission gulped down one last drink and hustled over to Fenway Park. Extra police had already been called in to handle the crowd, which was growing more restless by the minute as rumors spread that the players were on strike.

At 2:45, the commission met with Hooper, Shean, Mann, and Killefer on neutral ground, in the umpires' room, as a handful of sportswriters squeezed in behind them. The players were ready for a sober discussion of the issues. The commission was incapable of having a sober discussion about anything.

Hermann suddenly assumed powers he hadn't admitted to having and threatened the players, telling them that if they didn't play, he'd cancel the Series and not pay them a damn thing. He wasn't worried about being sued. Hooper tried to explain that as far as the players were concerned, the amount of money really wasn't an issue—they were willing to give it *all* to charity. It was a matter of principle. They wanted the traditional split restored for the benefit of those players who would play in the World Series in the future.

The commission recoiled at the foul notion that principle meant more than money, and observers from the press noted that the commission wasn't really in any condition to understand much of anything anyway. Ban Johnson, in fact, was bawling, pleading between tears for the players to take the field, telling Harry Hooper, "I did it, Harry. I did it, I went to Washington and had the stamp of approval put on this Series. I did it, Harry, I did it."

Actually, he hadn't, but when Hooper opened his mouth to argue, Johnson just kept blubbering. Then the AL president played the patriotic card, imploring the players to take the field for "the soldiers in the stands"—some of whom were, in fact, now on the field, having been pressed into service to try to prevent the crowd from rioting.

Reporter Nick Flately of the *Boston American* captured the tone perfectly in his story about the meeting. According to his description, Hermann piped up, saying, "'Let's arbitrary this matter, Mister Johnson,' then he launched forth into a brilliant exposition of the history of baseball's governing board. Expert reporters took notes for a while, then quit, befuddled."

So did the players. There was no sense arguing with three men who were seeing double and slurring every single word. On his way out the door, Hooper made the commission promise that the players wouldn't be punished for the delay. Boston Mayor John Fitzgerald—President Kennedy's grandfather—took the field and announced to the crowd that the players "have agreed to play for the sake of the public and the wounded players in the stands."

The crowd booed lustily, and when the players took the field, they fielded insults from every direction. Some fans just left, disgusted.

Then came the game. The players were on the field, but since they weren't sharing in the receipts of the contest, they played as if anxious for the Series to end. Boston fans took out their anger over the strike on the Red Sox, cheering Hippo Vaughn the whole game, and the Red Sox responded by making outs early and often. The Cubs scored a run in the second and two in the eighth, and just over one hour and forty minutes after it started, game five was history. The Cubs won, 3–0, and trailed the Red Sox three games to two. The Chicago press thought it was a great game, while Boston sportswriters were less impressed and all but wrote that the Red Sox had played to lose.

The end result was that no one cared anymore who won the Series. The strike, which the public didn't understand, soured many people on the Series, since most of the press reports sided with the owners and compared the players, unfavorably, to the sacrifice of the soldiers. The *Daily Journal* called the strike "the blackest of black eyes baseball has ever received" and charged that the players "tried to bluff the commission into paying them more money than the Series has taken in to date." That was a lie, but few fans knew better.

One more game remained. Fenway Park was only half full on the afternoon of September 11 when Tyler, on one day's rest, squared off opposite Carl Mays.

There was little glory for the Cubs. In the second inning, with two on, George Whiteman roped a line drive to Max Flack in right field. Flack dropped the ball, and two runs scored. Flack then opened the fourth with a single and came around to score, but the Cubs got no closer as Whiteman, who continued to play remarkable baseball, squelched their last best chance when he nabbed Barber's drive to left, turning a somersault as he dove for the ball, then left the game to a rousing ovation with a wrenched neck as Ruth trotted out as a meaningless defensive replacement. One inning later, Les Mann grounded out to second, and the Boston Red Sox were champions of the world.

Whiteman, not Ruth, was heralded as the hero of the Series. The right-handed hitter had feasted on Tyler and Vaughn while catching everything hit his direction. Cub observers blamed the loss on too many errors, both mental and physical, by the Cubs players. Weeghman and Mitchell's missteps were overlooked.

Chicago fans yawned. By the end of the Series, only a few dozen fans were showing up at the newspapers to watch the game replayed on the big board. The *Daily Journal* reported glumly that "interest was plainly at zero . . . baseball is not an essential during a time of war."

The Cubs quickly returned to Chicago, since each man had only a few days to either report to the service or find "essential" work. After all the push and pull over money, the Cubs earned, depending on which newspaper one believed, either $574.62 or $671.09 each, while each member of the champion Red Sox took in $1,001.52, and each still had to donate a portion to the war charities. Both figures were the lowest in Series history, as was the total of nineteen runs scored in the Series—ten by the Cubs and only nine for Boston.

As soon as the Series ended, the National Commission forgot all about their promise not to take retribution on the players. They denied the winning Red Sox their Series medallions, the equivalent of today's rings. The players, and then their descendants, petitioned for the medallions for years, only to be turned down by every baseball commissioner through Fay Vincent before baseball, belatedly, changed its mind in 1993.

Perhaps the worst World Series in history was over. At the time, no one could envision that decades later Boston fans would look back on it with nostalgia as their team went eighty-six years before winning another championship and that Cubs fans, who are still waiting, would look at 1918 almost a century later as one of the first in a string of lost opportunities.

In fact, within days after the Series ended, it was almost as if it had not been played at all. As the first pitch was being thrown, the Spanish influenza was arriving in Boston, carried there by the soldiers returning from Europe. Within a few days, scores of people began dying in Boston as the pandemic took hold. Among its victims would be Series umpire Silk O'Loughlin and several Boston sportswriters who had covered the Series.

The disease spread rapidly to Chicago, probably by the soldiers returning to the Great Lakes Naval Training Station, and perhaps by the fans, sportswriters, and players returning to Chicago from Boston. In October alone, more than ten thousand Chicagoans would die of the disease, and by the time the pandemic finally ended in the spring of 1919, a total of more than twenty thousand Chicagoans would be dead.

There was some good news, however. On November 11, the Great War came to an end. Baseball would soon return to normal. Unfortunately for the Cubs, "normal" no longer meant what it once did. The 1918 pennant would prove to have been an anomaly. The Cub dynasty was long gone, and in the future a world championship would remain a distant dream.

WRIGLEY IN AND WRIGGLING AWAY

Wrigley.

No other name has ever been so closely linked to the Chicago Cubs, and in the entire history of baseball, few other families have been so closely linked to a team, for so long and so intimately—and with so much ambivalence—as the Wrigleys have been linked to the Cubs.

The relationship between the Wrigley family and the Cubs began in 1915 when William Wrigley first purchased stock in the ball club, and it continued, officially, until 1981, when the Wrigley family sold the ball club to the Tribune Company. But in a larger sense, the ball club still operates under the Wrigley umbrella—the ballpark still bears the Wrigley name, and the Wrigley era, for better or worse, still influences how the team is operated and how the Cubs are perceived by their fans. In general, history has been kind to William Wrigley, but that has perhaps more to do with how he contrasts with his son, Philip K. Wrigley, than with any achievements of his own. The senior Wrigley looks so good only because the son was far worse.

William Wrigley Jr. was a master marketer who parlayed a job selling his family's soap into heading up the company that sold one of America's most recognized brands, Wrigley chewing gum. Starting in 1915, he bought stock in the Cubs and soon bankrolled majority owner Charles Weeghman's burgeoning restaurant business. Within a few years, Weeghman ceded his Cub stock to Wrigley in lieu of loan payments, and the Cubs had a new owner.

WRIGLEY

NOTHING GREAT IS EVER ACHIEVED
WITHOUT ENTHUSIASM

—framed sign on the desk
of William Wrigley Jr.

William Wrigley Jr. was similar to many of the men who bought baseball teams in the first few decades of the twentieth century. Few were self-made men. Most, like Wrigley and Detroit Tiger owner William Yawkey, represented a second generation of wealth. In this later generation, the virtues of hard work and sacrifice began to be supplanted by a desire to enjoy family wealth and all the privileges it entailed. After all, fun was a virtue too.

The motivation for anyone considering buying a major sports franchise is rarely financial. The main incentive is that the buyer, usually a wealthy but otherwise unknown mover and shaker, instantly becomes famous and recognizable, gains a degree of free advertising for his or her business, and is able to take some public pleasure in the trappings of success. That is precisely why George Steinbrenner bought the Yankees, why John Henry bought the Boston Red Sox, and why William Wrigley bought the Cubs. Before he did so, he was rich, but relatively unknown outside business and financial circles. Afterwards, he was as recognizable as any player.

Wrigley was born in 1862 in Philadelphia, where his father, William Wrigley Sr., owned and operated a small factory that produced scouring soap. Although Wrigley liked to spread the fiction that he was a self-made man, in fact his father, while not wealthy in the extreme, was nevertheless rich, and young Wrigley was well provided for.

He did, however, have a pronounced independent streak. At age eleven, he reportedly ran away from home for a summer, settling in New York, selling newspapers, and sleeping on the streets. Shortly after he returned home, at age thirteen, he convinced his father to allow him to go on the road as a "drummer," or traveling salesman, peddling the family soap.

The gregarious young Wrigley was a natural-born salesman, and he quickly grew his father's business, becoming a full partner at age twenty-one. By the age of thirty, Wrigley had noticed that the nation's population was shifting westward. In 1891 he transferred the company to Chicago to take advantage of lower transportation and shipping costs.

The city was perfect for Wrigley. Twenty years after the Great Fire, Chicago was still booming and bursting with anticipation over the coming World's Columbian Exposition, scheduled to open in 1893. In those heady times, a successful outsider could quickly become an insider, a track that never would have been available to Wrigley in Philadelphia, where old money and genealogy mattered.

Not so in Chicago. There a man could remake himself. Wrigley's many years on the road as a salesman had endowed him with a bit of the faux conviviality of the huckster, a shtick that played well in Chicago, a city accustomed to touting its own. In less than a decade, Wrigley was as much a Chicagoan as anyone else.

Wrigley was also a pioneer in what we now know as marketing. He built the family business by offering vendors a premium with each order in excess of $100, some trinket they could then give away to cus-tomers and use to increase sales. But Wrigley's selection of premiums occasionally proved faulty. In one instance, he ordered 100,000 green handbags to distribute, but vendors quickly discovered that after one or two ladies in a community received the bag, no one else wanted one, and so the vendors returned them to Wrigley by the thousands, almost wiping him out. On another occasion, Wrigley tried giving away small silver-plated cologne bottles, but they were poorly made and quickly tarnished. Once again, Wrigley took a bath and teetered on bankruptcy.

By then, Wrigley's clients not only expected a premium, but demanded it. The soap by itself was not enough to ensure sales, and after these two disastrous premiums, it was sitting on the shelves gathering dust. This time Wrigley chose to give away a common but useful product, baking soda, which proved so successful that he soon added baking soda to his product line. That meant he needed another premium. This time he selected a paraffin-based chewing gum manufactured by a company named Zeno.

The baking powder and soap flew off the shelves, and Wrigley's clients kept asking for more gum. According to the *Chicago Daily News*, Wrigley "reasoned that while 100 pounds of the soap his father manufactured was worth only $5, 100 pounds of chewing gum was worth $100. It could be shipped anywhere, made to pay its freight and still could be retailed at a price within everybody's reach." Wrigley entered into a partnership with Zeno and began to produce his own product, shifting from a paraffin gum base to a chicle base and introducing several new flavors and brands—first Lotta, Vassar, and Sweet Sixteen Orange, then Juicy Fruit and Spearmint.

The Wrigley Company was now a success, but the chewing gum industry was crowded: seven or eight manufacturers were battling one another in the market-place, each trying to gain an edge from a product that sold for a penny or two. As Wrigley put it, "Anybody can make gum. Selling it is the problem."

But selling was never a problem for Wrigley. He worshiped at the altar of advertising, adopting the motto "Tell 'em quick and tell 'em often" and comparing advertising to the operation of a furnace, saying, "You've got to keep on shoveling coal. Once you stop stoking, the fire goes out." He took his own advice to heart. Unlike other companies in his industry, Wrigley invested heavily in advertising. A neon sign in Times Square touting his gum reportedly cost him $100,000 a year in electricity. He distributed millions of free samples—including samples to soldiers in World War I. Alongside a commuter rail line between Trenton and Atlantic City, New Jersey, Wrigley linked some 117 billboards that together stretched nearly a mile. In 1915 he distributed 14 million copies of a booklet for children that rewrote Mother Goose nursery rhymes to tout Wrigley gum. He was soon selling $30 million worth of gum each year on every continent but Antarctica, with factories in Chicago, New York, Toronto, London, Frankfort, and Sydney. As one observer noted, "He taught the world the chewing gum habit"—for which thousands of dentists have since expressed their ever-lasting thanks.

Yet that wasn't enough. Wrigley's wealth gave him great power, and he used it. He branched out, bankrolling John Hertz, later of Hertz Rent-A-Car, in his first business, the Yellow Cab Company, and even the name of the company bore Wrigley's influence—the color yellow was selected after a marketing survey identified it as the easiest color for

pedestrians to spot. He also backed a theater chain that eventually morphed into Paramount. He bought real estate, owned a hog farm, raised his own mint and spearmint for flavorings, and by 1915 was easily one of the richest men in Chicago.

But few people outside the business world and the Board of Trade knew who William Wrigley was. His name first appeared in the *Chicago Tribune* in 1895 when his chewing gum storehouse blew up because a gas pipe cracked during a cold spell, ruining his stock. Over the next twenty years, his name appeared in the newspaper just over one hundred times, usually in the brief "society" notes.

That's where the Cubs came in. In 1915, as Wrigley traveled by train from Cincinnati to Chicago, an associate began ribbing him about the Cubs, asking how it was that, if Chicago was such a potent commercial center, the Cubs were controlled by a Charles Taft, a Cincinnatian. Later that year, when Weeghman bought the team and began looking for investors, Wrigley remem-

bered that conversation on the train and anted up.

After he bought into the Cubs, William Wrigley's profile increased exponentially—over the next fifteen years his name appeared in the *Chicago Tribune* nearly one thousand times. Wrigley himself came to epitomize the boosterish, can-do, entrepreneurial image of Chicago as a place brimming over with energy, optimism, and commerce. As club owner, he sought to remake the Cubs in that same image—essentially as an extension of his own personality by applying the same mixture of enthusiasm, advertising, cash, and bombast that had made Wrigley chewing gum as common as oxygen.

All Wrigley had ever known was success. He was convinced he could turn the Cubs into a championship team and sell them to the public just as he sold chewing gum.

How could he possibly fail?

Among the many improvements that William Wrigley made to the Cubs was creating an almost festive atmosphere at Wrigley Field. Among the amenities fans enjoyed was the Cubs Band led by Jack Bramhall, pictured here in uniform.

In the offseason between 1919 and 1920, Cubs outfielder Lee Magee was without a contract. After coming over from Brooklyn midway through the 1919 season in exchange for Pete Kilduff, Magee hit .292 for the offensively anemic Cubs. A big league regular for nearly a decade, he expected to be offered a contract.

The Cubs, however, chose not to do so. And neither did any other team in baseball.

Suddenly and without public explanation, Magee was persona non grata in baseball. The reason? In 1917, while with Cincinnati, Magee had been close to first baseman Hal Chase. A wonderful player considered the greatest-fielding first baseman of his era, Chase was also a notorious gambler. There had long been rumors not only that he bet against his own team, but that he threw games or arranged for them to be thrown for personal gain. That was quite a bit more serious than a gentlemen's arrangement between teams in the World Series to ensure the Series lasted seven games. In 1918 the Reds finally suspended Chase for "indifferent play," a euphemism for fixing games.

Magee got tarred by the fallout, as did former Cub Heinie Zimmerman. After the 1919 season, no team in baseball approached Chase, Zimmerman, or Magee to offer a contract.

Chase and Zimmerman accepted their blackballing and effectively chose to retire, but Magee fought back. On March 6, he announced that he was going to sue baseball because he had been "unlawfully blacklisted." Two weeks later, Magee threatened to go public, saying, "I'm going to burn my bridges behind me and jump off the ruins. If I'm barred, I'll take quite a few noted people with me. I'll show up some people for tricks turned ever since 1906. And there will be merry music in the baseball world."

Baseball didn't like being threatened. NL president John Heydler challenged Magee to provide evidence to back up what Magee termed "the biggest bomb in baseball history." Magee took him up on the offer and on April 14 in Cincinnati filed suit against the Cubs, seeking $9,500 in damages against the club's share of receipts for opening day in Cincinnati.

August Hermann, the president of the Reds, called the suit "a joke," but the Cubs weren't laughing. Magee had suddenly put Chicago, the Cubs, and gambling in the cross hairs. The Cubs didn't do much to help matters by providing a distraction: instead, they lost ten in a row immediately after winning nine straight in late May and then played thoroughly uninspired baseball for the balance of the 1920 season, finishing tied for fifth place. As they played out the season, with all the talk swirling around Chicago, baseball had to take action.

The Cubs—probably at the behest of the National Commission—drew more attention to themselves in mid-May when they contacted the Chicago police department and asked for their help rooting out gamblers at Cubs Park. Several detectives went undercover, dressing like workingmen, and were told to "hang around and get a line on the gambling situation."

The object of their investigation was telling. They didn't try to tempt players or infiltrate any of the gambling syndicates that controlled the big action in Chicago—those outfits were already paying protection and acting with impunity. Instead, the investigation focused on the little guys at the ballpark.

The detectives didn't have to look very hard, for if they didn't know about the gamblers in the bleachers already, they were deaf, blind, and dumb. Every day, as soon as the park opened, a collection of fifty or so street urchins grabbed bleacher seats and staked out their territory. As game time approached, a similar number of adults appeared and gave each boy a dollar to give up their spot so they could all sit together. As the *Tribune* later described it, "first bets were placed on the game, then came bets on other things . . . balls, strikes, fouls, hits, errors, balks."

A week later, on May 23, the detectives had enough evidence to mount a big raid. As the Cubs and Phillies finished the first inning of play, the undercover detectives rounded up the forty-seven evildoers and hauled them off.

It was a joke. Even newspaper stories describing the raid played the story as a piece of high comedy, albeit under banner headlines. According to one report, while escorting their prisoners to jail, the detectives kept cracking gambling-related jokes, telling one prisoner, "fifty cents says you're going to the cooler. . . . Who wants fifty cents?" One poor sap pled innocent, admitting to detectives he was playing hooky from work and had attended the game with a dollar his wife gave him that morning. With only thirteen cents remaining in his pocket, he was let go.

Baseball, however, acted as if this "raid" was a potent shot across the bow that was certain to send gamblers scurrying out of every big league park like so many rats before a hungry cat. Ban Johnson told reporters that the league had hired a detective agency to root out gambling at every ballpark in the league, and in fact, three fans had been arrested at the Polo Grounds that same day. Gee whiz, three whole live gamblers.

Of course, in this instance the cat was so well fed that it had no real desire to work for its meal, and the raids had no effect whatsoever. The crackdown was simply a meaningless show of force. Within a day or two, it was business

STRIKEOUT CHAMPIONS

1880	Larry Corcoran	268
1885	John Clarkson	308
1887	John Clarkson	237
1892	Bill Hutchison	316
1909	Orval Overall	205
1918	Hippo Vaughn	148
1919	Hippo Vaughn	141
1920	Pete Alexander	173
1929	Pat Malone	166
1938	Clay Bryant	135
1946	Johnny Schmitz	135
1955	Sam Jones	198
1956	Sam Jones	176
1969	Ferguson Jenkins	273
2003	Kerry Wood	266

as usual in Chicago and everywhere else. Magee went to trial in early June and lost not only his lawsuit but also whatever shred of reputation he had left. James Costello, a Boston gambler, testified that before Magee was traded to the Cubs in 1918, he had approached the gambler and told him that he and Chase had arranged a fix in the first game of a double-header between the Reds and Braves the next day. As a show of good faith, Magee had even given the gambler a $500 personal check. The check gave the Cubs all the evidence they needed in the lawsuit, and Magee lost. He never played another major league game.

One would have thought that with all the scrutiny brought to bear on gambling on baseball in Chicago that season, any Cub players involved in gambling would have shut down and kept such activities down for the duration of the year. That wasn't the case. Gaming was so ingrained within the national pastime that those predisposed to affect the outcome of games saw absolutely no reason to stop.

On August 31, the sixth-place Cubs were scheduled to play the last-place Phillies, a matchup between the Cubs' Claude Hendrix and Phillies ace Lee Meadows. The game between the two also-rans had absolutely no impact on the pennant race—it was the kind of game few attend and even fewer care about.

But just a few hours before the game, William Veeck received several anonymous phone calls and telegrams, all from Detroit, all bearing the same message, some using the same exact words, and all warning that the game had been fixed and there was heavy betting on Philadelphia. In fact, earlier that day the odds had swung from 6–5 in favor of Chicago to 2–1 in favor of Philadelphia. One of the telegrams even named pitcher Claude Hendrix as the compromised player, while another suggested that the Cubs pitch Alexander to thwart the plot. Similar messages were

On August 31, 1920, pitcher Claude Hendrix was scheduled to start for the Cubs in a seemingly meaningless game against the Phillies. Prior to the game, Cubs executive Bill Veeck received several anonymous phone calls and telegrams, all from Detroit, warning that the game had been fixed, with heavy betting favoring the Phillies. Responding to one message that suggested the Cubs start Grover Alexander (whom Veeck called "a man above all suspicion") instead of Hendrix, Veeck and manager Fred Mitchell benched Hendrix, and the Cubs still lost, 3–0.

1925

sent to Wrigley and manager Fred Mitchell. Clearly, someone in Detroit was upset and wanted revenge.

Veeck immediately called Mitchell into his office. The two decided to do exactly what their anonymous correspondents suggested: they benched Hendrix in favor of Alexander, whom Veeck later called "a man above all suspicion." Veeck and Mitchell then called Alexander into the office, informed him of the rumors, and offered him $500 extra if he won the game, an odd offer to a man above suspicion who would presumably need no extra incentive. At the same time, Mitchell benched Fred Merkle in favor of Turner Barber.

Alexander didn't come through, at least not in the way Veeck and Mitchell had hoped. Chicago lost, 3–0, as Meadows twirled a shutout and Chicago second baseman Buck Herzog made a critical error. The gamblers in Detroit were pleased.

Veeck tried to keep the story quiet; baseball was still more interested in keeping scandal private than cleaning the game up. But two days later, the *Chicago Herald Examiner* received an anonymous letter, also postmarked in Detroit. Someone clearly wanted the scandal exposed. The author of the letter revealed the whole rotten mess and wrote that "every fellow mixed up with baseball gambling hung around the tickers chuckling over the result of that game." In the irony department, that same day the Cubs played an exhibition in Marion, Ohio, for Republican presidential candidate Warren Harding at the behest of Wrigley and Cubs stockholders Albert Lasker and Henry Sinclair. Harding would go on to be elected president, then be brought down in the so-called Teapot Dome scandal, in which it would be revealed that Sinclair had purchased leases of federal land from Harding's Secretary of the Interior.

The letter inspired the newspaper to conduct a quick investigation. On September 4, the *Herald Examiner* published a front-page story that charged that gamblers had earned more than $50,000 on the contest. The other Chicago papers—which, like newspapers in every other big league city in America, had always reported the odds in big games and often made note of who was betting how much—quickly got on board. They expressed their complete and utter shock and dismay that there was a hint of gambling in baseball.

James Cruisenberry, in the *Tribune*, gave a detailed account of how baseball and gambling were tied together in Chicago, leaving little doubt about the veracity of the story. Cruisenberry's source offered that "thousands are bet every day within twenty-five yards of city hall." If one extended that to the rest of the city, then on any given day hundreds of thousands of dollars, if not millions, were changing hands in everything from office pools to larger wagers.

Veeck now had to take action, very quickly and very publicly. He had already hired private detectives to look into the disputed game of August 31, and now he released copies of the telegrams. But it was too late to stop the momentum of the rapidly expanding scandal. Cruisenberry recruited Fred Loomis, a successful and trusted Chicago businessman, and wrote a letter under his name that was published in the *Tribune* and called for a legal investigation.

They got one. On September 7, a Cook County grand jury convened to investigate not only the game of August 31 but the whole question of baseball and gambling, including the 1919 World Series.

The snowball was rolling downhill. New York Giants pitcher Rube Benton was called to testify and stated that late in the 1919 season Heinie Zimmerman and Hal Chase had offered him $800 to throw a game against the Cubs and that Chicago second baseman Buck Herzog was also in on the plot. That drew Herzog into the proceedings, and he sang as loud as he could to save his own skin.

He blew the lid off everything, revealing that the World Series of 1919 between the Reds and the White Sox had been fixed. The investigation took a dramatic turn, veering away from the Cubs and toward the White Sox. The Black Sox scandal, baseball's biggest black eye this side of steroids, and one that would result in the banning of eight men from baseball, was under way.

That development was most convenient for the Cubs. Baseball in Chicago was rotten to the core, and the smell was almost as bad on the North Side as it was at Comiskey Park. When even Charles Weeghman was called to testify, he revealed that he too had known of the Series fix from a gambler friend, but, whoops, no, he hadn't bothered to tell anyone. Few paid any attention to that, however, for as the investigation veered south, the Cubs' involvement in the game of August 31 and other gambling events was nearly forgotten.

In retrospect, one cannot help but wonder just how deeply the Cubs were involved in gambling at the time, for so many of those involved—Magee, Zimmerman, Herzog, Hendrix, and Weeghman—were closely connected to the Cubs. Later evidence intimated that Alexander too may have been in on the thrown game and that perhaps the call and telegrams, all part of an elaborate plot of misdirection, were sent to ensure that Mitchell pitched Alexander rather than Hendrix. After all, despite the change, according to the letter sent to the *Herald Examiner*, the gamblers in Detroit had still "chuckled" over the results.

At any rate, as the spotlight rapidly moved to Comiskey's White Sox, the Cubs organization wriggled off the hook and escaped the scandal relatively unscathed, with no lasting blot on the reputation of the franchise. In the offseason, they sacrificed Claude Hendrix, just as they had earlier done with Magee. Like Magee, Hendrix found himself blacklisted and never played another game in the major leagues.

Herzog also paid a price. Although he was benched for the remainder of the regular season, in late September he played for the Cubs in an exhibition in Joliet. All game long some fans jeered him as a cheat. When he got into his car to drive back to Chicago, one enraged fan climbed onto the running board and screamed at him, calling him "a crooked ballplayer" to his face. Herzog climbed out of his car and the two scuffled, soon joined by several other fans. Someone pulled a penknife, and Herzog emerged with minor knife cuts to his palm and calf. Although not badly wounded, like Magee and Hendrix, Herzog never played another game of major league baseball.

Every day the grand jury stayed in session the news got worse for the White Sox. In the end, eight players would be banned from the game, and in response, baseball would scrap the National Commission in favor of the single commissioner system. Judge Kenesaw Mountain Landis was named the first commissioner of baseball in November.

Although various other threads of the grand jury investigation pointed in a dozen directions, those other leads weren't actively pursued. The 1919 World Series bore the brunt of scrutiny. As a result, the White Sox franchise was decimated. The franchise would pay a dear price both on the field and at the turnstiles.

All this was good news for the Cubs, or should have been. For most of the next eight decades, there would be little question that the Cubs were Chicago's dominant franchise. In less than a decade, as the impact of the Black Sox scandal set in, the White Sox would almost cease to matter. In fact, the rise of the Yankees as the dominant power in the American League can be attributed in part to the fall of the White Sox, which effectively left them noncompetitive.

Yet in a strange way the Cubs never seemed to take full advantage of the White Sox demise. In time they simply

Charles Leo "Gabby" Hartnett arrived in Chicago in 1922 and dazzled fans with his rocket throwing arm. He took over starting catching duties in 1924 after Bob O'Farrell fractured his skull.

assumed their position at the top of the Chicago baseball universe, but did little to expand upon it. They could have, and probably should have, crushed the White Sox forever. Instead, they took the easy way out.

The demise of the White Sox made it comfortable for Wrigley and the Cubs at the gate, in the press, and on barstools throughout Chicago. The club didn't have to work very hard to achieve success. Winning was nice but, as would become clear over time, not really necessary—the Cubs soon started outdrawing the White Sox by a comfortable margin and would continue to do so until the 1950s. For the remainder of the century, the White Sox had to win to draw a crowd in Chicago, a trait still in evidence to the present day. The Cubs, however, were held to a different standard. They didn't have to win—simply not being the White Sox was enough to ensure the loyalty of their fans and, by and large, the favor of the press. It was that simple, and over time a comfortable largesse would slowly creep over the club like so much ivy.

In November 1920, Fred Mitchell was fired—too much had gone on under his nose for him to remain as Chicago's manager. He returned to Boston, where he became manager of the Braves. Wrigley and Veeck brought back Johnny Evers. Since managing the Cubs in 1913, he had supposedly matured, and in recent years Evers had been New York Giants manager John McGraw's right-hand man.

Evers's second tour of duty as Cubs manager would prove no more successful than the first. The loss of Herzog and Hendrix hurt, and both Lefty Tyler and Hippo Vaughn gave evidence that their careers were near the end; the two pitchers won a combined six games in 1921. Even Alexander slumped. Evers didn't make it past midseason, when he was replaced by former catcher Bill Killefer. The Cubs limped home in seventh place, 64–89, thirty long games out of first place.

That should have been the stimulus for a complete makeover. Instead, the Cubs did nothing. To be fair, Wrigley was not yet in complete control of the ball club. Although he owned more stock than anyone else, he did not yet control a full 50 percent and wasn't entirely free to do what he wanted. Albert Lasker, the advertising man, still owned a substantial piece of the Cubs, and Lasker had his ideas too. As a result, little was accomplished, but then again, there was little incentive to do anything.

The big news in the offseason came from Wrigley. In 1919 he purchased Catalina Island off the California coast just south of Los Angeles. Over the next few years Wrigley would spend $16 million transforming the property, in the words of one contemporary report, "into a fairyland," building roads, hotels, a casino, and other amenities that would make the island a playground for the well-to-do.

Lasker finally sold Wrigley enough shares to give him complete control of the franchise, and one of Wrigley's first moves was to make Catalina the spring training home of the Cubs, even if it meant blasting away part of a mountain and spending $60,000 to build a field that was used only a few weeks a year.

The result was comfortable enough, but the lack of convenient competition resulted in a training camp with the emphasis on "camp." Killefer sent the players on long hikes in the hills, leading one rookie, tired of walking along the slopes, to ask the manager whether or not the base paths in the National League were banked.

The rookie was Charles "Gabby" Hartnett, a catcher whose nickname stemmed from the fact that he rarely talked. Hartnett was born in Woonsocket, Rhode Island, and had grown up playing in the mill leagues of the Blackstone Valley in Rhode Island and neighboring Massachusetts. He was first signed by Worcester of the Eastern League; after only one season, he was bought by the Cubs. Although it would take Hartnett several seasons to establish himself as a big league regular, he would eventually become one of the team's all-time greats.

Hartnett was one of a host of Cubs rookies that spring when Wrigley, finally able to act on his own, was casting a wide net for prospects. Hartnett opened the season splitting the catcher's job with Bob O'Farrell, and a number of rookie pitchers joined Alexander on the Cub pitching staff, including Vic Aldridge, Virgil Cheeves, George Stueland, Percy Jones, and Tony Kaufman, none of whom were over the age of twenty-two. For the first time in a long time, there was some reason for Cub fans to look to the future with optimism.

First, however, they had to revisit the past. On April 14, Cap Anson died.

His death provided a measure of just how much the Cubs—and Chicago—had changed. For more than two decades, Anson and the Cubs, whether they were known as the White Stockings, the Colts, or the Orphans, had been synonymous. Anson, along with Spalding, had carried baseball in Chicago from its infancy on into adulthood.

Yet now, only twenty-five years since he retired as a player, Anson was an anachronism. Chicago had shed its nineteenth-century trappings and now resided solidly in the twentieth century. Many young Chicagoans didn't even know who Anson was. The few who did knew him only as some kind of character, someone who used to be a somebody.

The years had not been particularly kind to Anson. After leaving the Cubs, he was lost. The Giants hired him as manager, but he lasted only twenty-two games. Baseball had changed, but Anson hadn't. It was that simple.

He had some money, but the Anson name didn't mean much off the diamond. He sponsored and occasionally played for a semipro team, Anson's Colts, to stay close to the game and keep his name before the public. But every business he touched failed, including an ice rink, a soda plant, and a pool parlor. Then he tried his hand at politics; after winning an election to city clerk he was quickly dumped, for he failed to understand (or perhaps understood too well) how politics worked in Chicago.

Organized baseball recognized his role in the game and magnanimously offered him a pension, but Anson was too proud and turned it down. He ended up back in the theater, in vaudeville, slowly dropping lower on the bill. But he never stopped being Cap Anson, which still meant something to a few people. For his last act, Ring Lardner Jr.

Wrigley Field in the 1920s bore little resemblance to the ivy-covered shrine at the corner of Clark and Addison. This picture shows the pregame ceremony prior to opening day 1923.

and George M. Cohan helped him put together an act that included Anson's daughters. It was probably Lardner who wrote the self-deprecating lines of a song the daughters sang that was acutely accurate:

Cap Anson the greatest man that baseball ever knew
The pitchers feared him and the bleachers cheered him
And he led the league in 1492.

Now that he was dead, Chicago paused for a moment. Anson's funeral was one of the biggest in the history of the city. Dozens of baseball luminaries turned out, including Commissioner Landis, and anybody who had ever been anybody in Chicago turned out to mourn the past, but when it was done, that was it. Anson was gone and quickly forgotten. Two monuments, of a sort, carried on: the Cubs, and the lily-white nature of the major leagues.

Under Killefer, the 1922 Cubs were, to a degree, a success. First baseman Ray Grimes, in only his second season with the Cubs, hit .354 and led the team in almost everything. The Cubs finished above .500 with a record of 80–74, "only" thirteen games behind the first-place Giants. But those numbers were deceptive.

The Cubs fell behind the Giants early and never really challenged for anything, apart from a few brief days in July when, after a spate of games against Fred Mitchell's hapless Boston Braves—against whom the Cubs went 18–4 for the year—they edged into third place. When they played anyone else, however, the results weren't quite as impressive. The first-place Giants were a cut above the Cubs.

Wrigley seemed to recognize the wisdom of having a backup plan in the event that the Cubs weren't able to crack the top spot. He was already in the midst of an orgy of spending: in addition to the Cubs and Catalina Island, he had also added the Pacific Coast League Los Angeles Angels to his portfolio and embarked on the construction of the gleaming white Wrigley Building, one of Chicago's first skyscrapers and, briefly, Chicago's tallest building at twenty-nine stories. Now the Cubs were the object of his largesse.

To this point, Wrigley Field was still known as Cubs Park. While comfortable and spacious, it was not distinctive in the least. It was a simple field surrounded by a plain, single-tier grandstand that stopped short of the outfield. But in the offseason after the 1922 season, it began its transformation into the classic ballpark still appreciated today.

On November 8, the Cubs announced a massive expansion plan. Wrigley hired Zachary Davis, the original architect, to expand the park's seating capacity.

Given carte blanche, Davis made full use of his powers. Wrigley first acquired a block of land at Clark and Addison that allowed Davis, in effect, to back the ballpark up. He broke up the original grandstand into three sections, then moved the section of stands behind home plate back some seventy feet, also moving back home plate. The left-field stands were actually elevated—placed on rollers and moved out sixty feet toward Waveland Avenue. Wooden bleachers down the lines were torn down and replaced with steel structures. In effect, when the three sections were tied together, the result was a brand-new grandstand with additional box seats placed on the field. The playing field itself was excavated and lowered three feet to improve sight lines. Although it was still 447 feet to the center-field fence, in left field the bleachers reduced the distance to a cozy 325 feet. At the cost of $350,000, Wrigley had, in effect, a brand-new ballpark, with a capacity of 31,000, an increase of 14,000.

Unfortunately, it made little difference on the field. For all their good intentions, Wrigley and Bill Veeck were not baseball men. In the business world, Wrigley was far ahead of the curve—he was among the first, for instance, to use saturation advertising—and as an employer he was surprisingly progressive, instituting the five-day workweek and setting up pension, revenue sharing, and insurance plans for his employees.

As the administrator of a baseball team, however, he showed no such vision. Oh, he was good to his employees, but he overpaid players to such a degree that they had little incentive to perform. One quote from Wrigley was particularly telling, as it inadvertently pointed out his personal dilemma as a club owner. "Baseball," said Wrigley, "is too much of a sport to be a business and too much of a business to be a sport." Exactly. Wrigley himself apparently couldn't decide exactly what approach to take in regard to the Cubs—whether to treat them dispassionately as a business or as a paternalistic pastime. As a result, his approach vacillated back and forth, particularly during his first five or six years at the helm. It showed on the field—where the team was slow to adapt to the lively ball era and the sudden new importance of the home run as an offensive weapon—and in the front office, where his decision to hire the inexperienced Veeck cost the team a chance to win for several seasons as Veeck learned the administrative side of the game. But it certainly didn't help when the club suddenly lost its two best players in the middle of the 1923 season.

Ray Grimes was an emerging star and had finished second to Rogers Hornsby in the 1922 batting race while setting a major league record with an RBI in seventeen straight games. But he had also hurt his back, and he was so troubled by the injury in 1923 that he finally underwent an operation for a slipped disc. It didn't work. Grimes, whose twin brother Roy also played in the major leagues, as would his son Oscar, was never the same.

More troubling was the case of Cub shortstop and captain Charlie Hollocher. After joining the Cubs in 1918, Hollocher was one of the best shortstops in baseball. In 1922 he hit .340 and seemed poised to become one of the all-time greats.

But Hollocher's health was a constant issue. Early in his career, mysterious bouts of "nervousness" and resulting "stomach ailments" constantly knocked him from the lineup, but in 1921 and 1922 he seemed to have overcome his troubles and played nearly every game.

In the spring of 1923, however, Hollocher jumped the team, first complaining of the flu and then returning home because of his stomach trouble. When the season was a month old, Hollocher rejoined the team, but despite sporting a batting average well above .300, he was in and out of the lineup again with the same ailments.

In August it became too much. Hollocher jumped the team again, leaving manager Bill Killefer a note that read, "Feeling pretty rotten, so made my mind to go home and take a rest and forget baseball for the rest of the year. No hard feelings, just didn't feel like playing any more. Good Luck." He was done for the year, and after a brief return in 1924, done with baseball. For the rest of his life, he was periodically stricken with the same stomach trouble that drove him from the Cubs, which was never diagnosed. In all likelihood, Hollocher was either afflicted with mental illness or a real physical malady that doctors of the day

Cub captain and shortstop Charlie Hollocher was one of baseball's tragic figures. Early in his career, bouts of "nervousness" and recurring bouts of "stomach ailments" curtailed his playing time. After playing two full seasons in 1921 and 1922, he seemed poised for greatness after batting .340 in 1922. In 1923 illness caused him to jump the team. But he played another half-season before retiring at age twenty-eight the following season.

were powerless to cure. Sadly, abdominal pain drove him to suicide in 1940.

The Cubs continued to tread water in 1923, finishing three games better but in fourth place. In 1924 they somehow clung to first place into mid-June, but then collapsed completely to finish in fifth place once again.

Wrigley and Veeck were getting impatient. Wrigley had plenty of money and was more than willing to spend it to acquire ballplayers, but he found few sellers of major league talent, and Veeck kept missing the mark on minor leaguers. Wrigley and Veeck now decided that it was time to try to create a winner through trades.

During the offseason, Veeck attended a dinner in Pittsburgh honoring Pirate owner Barney Dreyfuss. Dreyfuss expressed interest in Cub pitcher Vic Aldridge, a steady if not spectacular performer whose success depended on his curveball. Veeck, mindful of the Cubs' need to replace Hollocher and Grimes, countered by asking for both Pittsburgh's starting shortstop and first baseman, Rabbit Maranville and Charlie Grimm. He was shocked when Dreyfuss, telling him that Grimm and Maranville were too "lighthearted" for his taste, agreed. In return, Dreyfuss also asked for a minor league first baseman and the poor-fielding Cub second baseman George "Boots" Grantham, but Dreyfuss also threw pitcher Wilbur Cooper—a twenty-game winner—into the deal.

Veeck's knees went weak. On paper, the Cubs had just fleeced the Pirates, gaining the right half of the infield plus a number-one starter from a team that had just finished three games out of first place in exchange for a backup first baseman, a .500 pitcher, and a good-hit, no-field second baseman. Grimm was a .300 hitter, and Maranville, while not much of a hitter, was widely considered to be perhaps the greatest-fielding shortstop of his time. Any way you added that up, from Veeck's perspective the Cubs had come out ahead. Wrigley and Veeck were so excited

that they stopped dealing and started counting off the days on the calendar until opening day.

Of course, it didn't work out that way. When Dreyfuss called Maranville and Grimm "lighthearted," what he meant was that Maranville was a drunk and Grimm, though a teetotaler, played wingman for Maranville in a never-ending roving party that sucked a number of other Pirates into their maelstrom. He'd been trying to trade Maranville for a year, but no one wanted him until Veeck took the bait. The Pittsburgh Pirates had finished third not because of Maranville and Grimm, but in spite of them. Dreyfuss was convinced that with those two out of the way the Pirates were a first-place team.

And that's where the Pirates, with Grantham hitting .326 while playing first base and Aldridge leading the team with nineteen wins, finished in 1925. The Cubs? Well, the

Like any number of major league owners, William Wrigley Jr. loved the limelight and delighted in sitting behind the Cub dugout, where he would cheer favorites such as Rogers Hornsby. Wrigley renamed Weeghman Park as Wrigley Field and as a result sold a lot more chewing gum. He died in January 1932, just before the Cubs won their third pennant under his ownership.

Cubs finished last. But at least they had some fun on the way down.

Maranville and Grimm set the tone during spring training on Catalina Island. In one celebrated incident, Grimm lay on the ground and held a golf tee in his mouth for photographers as Maranville, who didn't often golf, posed above him, driver in hand. To everyone's surprise, Maranville then struck the ball cleanly, nearly giving Grimm a heart attack.

Only a few weeks into camp, Maranville broke his leg while sliding, which gave him even more time to create havoc. By the time the Cubs hit the mainland, the party hats were being passed around as the new arrivals realized that the Cub roster already included some kindred spirits, such as Grover Cleveland Alexander, who medicated his epilepsy and the shell shock he developed during World War I with alcohol.

Alexander was, without question, one of the greatest pitchers in the history of the game, winner of 373 games, 128 of those with the Cubs. Hall of Fame pitcher Burleigh Grimes once said of Alexander that, "if anybody was ever a better pitcher than that guy, I don't know who it was." When Chicago first acquired him from Philadelphia in 1918, he had won thirty or more games three seasons in a row. The Cubs expected that to continue.

It didn't. Alexander was one of the few ballplayers in World War I to serve in real combat. An artillery sergeant, he had spent several harrowing months in the trenches of the front lines, never knowing if the next shell he heard overhead would be his last.

A heavy drinker before the war, Alexander appeared to have aged twenty years when he returned to the United States. The constant bombardment left him almost deaf in one ear. He was jumpy and nervous, he suffered from epilepsy, and his drinking had increased.

His fastball was gone, but he still knew how to pitch. On the mound, he was all business, determined and methodical, never wasting a pitch, with a fine curveball and a sinker. While Alexander was never quite as dominant for Chicago as he had been in Philadelphia, winning more than twenty games only twice, he helped keep the Cubs above water, often turning a second division team into one somewhat more respectable.

In 1925, despite fifteen wins, Alexander couldn't do anything to help. Wilbur Cooper, who had won 202 games for the Pirates, won only 14 in a Cub uniform. Maranville thoroughly enjoyed his convalescence, and Killefer quickly lost control of the team. He was fired on July 6. Then Wrigley and Veeck showed their lack of baseball acumen. When Veeck met with the team to announce the new manager, he stunned everyone, including the man he selected, when he announced that Maranville would take over. They'd just given the inmate the keys to the asylum.

It didn't take Rabbit long to display his management style. He celebrated his appointment by getting drunk on the train with his players and dousing most of them with water. He then got into an argument on his way to the ballpark and almost spent his first game as Cub manager in jail.

He didn't last two months as the Cubs sank under his watch. On September 3, Maranville was fired and coach George Gibson was named interim manager. He didn't want the job but agreed to stay on through the end of the season. Maranville went from manager to backup shortstop.

Apart from Gabby Hartnett, who hit twenty-four home runs and emerged as a full-fledged star, most of the Cubs played as if they didn't care, and the team finished in last place for the first time.

Something had to change.

the consumption of alcohol. Prohibition, which had been in effect since 1919, was nowhere less effective than in and around Chicago, where gangsters had quickly taken over the bootleg liquor market and speakeasies had sprung up on every corner. The Cubs, it seemed, knew the password for every single one.

Everywhere but at the gate, William Wrigley's reign had been a disaster. But he had done one thing right. In 1925 he allowed home games to be broadcast on the radio. He wasn't being particularly visionary, for he didn't foresee the eventual impact that broadcasting would have on the game. Wrigley's only goals were to spread the Wrigley brand and, as he put it, "tie up the entire city." That he did, allowing five separate stations to broadcast the games, making it almost impossible to avoid the broadcasts.

To his surprise, the broadcasts did far more than he intended. In Chicago, housewives stuck at home used the broadcasts as background noise, discovered they could tell their husbands about the game when they came home at night, and became true fans. "Ladies' Day" at Wrigley Field became a mob scene. Outside Chicago, listeners in the hinterlands found live descriptions of big league baseball exotic, and the Cubs' market expanded dramatically. Cars full of families began pulling up at Wrigley Field, and attendance at a Cubs game began to be viewed as an essential part of any visit to Chicago.

The Cubs were quickly becoming the dominant team in the Chicago market, which was second only to New York in size. It was hard to see, but if only the Cubs could win they would be positioned to adopt the same place in the National League that the Yankees held in the American. Of course, the Cubs didn't have a hitter like Babe Ruth or a manager like Miller Huggins, but they were on their way.

Wrigley and Veeck had to do something after 1925. Since they were unwilling and unable to fire each other, they had little choice but to find another manager. After all, if they had learned anything in 1925, it was that in times of stress you could always fire the manager.

Thus far, none of their choices for the top spot had been very inspired, none had been very successful, and after the disaster of 1925, no one was politicking for the job. At the time, most big league managers were either old-time baseball men schooled in the dead ball era, like Huggins, John McGraw, Brooklyn's Wil Robinson, or the Athletics' Connie Mack, or big stars, either still active or recently retired. In 1926 Ty Cobb, Eddie Collins, George Sisler, Tris Speaker, and Rogers Hornsby were all managing in the major leagues.

Between Evers, Killefer, Bresnahan, and Maranville, the Cubs had just about run out of former stars, and no established veteran manager was available. Veeck and Wrigley were forced to look elsewhere.

For Veeck, that meant looking where he was most comfortable. Early in his sports writing career, he had worked for the *Louisville Courier Journal* in Louisville, Kentucky, and was still friends with local sportswriters. For several years,

JOE McCARTHY'S TEN COMMANDMENTS OF BASEBALL

1 Nobody ever became a ballplayer by walking after a ball.

2 You will never become a .300 hitter unless you take the bat off your shoulder.

3 An outfielder who throws in back of a runner is locking the barn after the horse is stolen.

4 Keep your head up and you may not have to keep it down.

5 When you start to slide, slide. He who changes his mind may have to change a good leg for a bad one.

6 Do not alibi on bad hops. Anybody can field the good ones.

7 Always run them out. You can never tell.

8 Do not quit.

9 Do not fight too much with the umpires. You cannot expect them to be as perfect as you are.

10 A pitcher who hasn't control hasn't anything.

his old cronies back in Louisville had been touting Joe McCarthy, now in his seventh year at the helm of the Louisville Colonels of the American Association. In July 1925, McCarthy's name had even surfaced in a report in the *Tribune* speculating that he would soon replace Maranville as manager of the Cubs. Wrigley disputed the report at the time, but admitted that "such a move had been discussed" the previous year.

As soon as the 1925 season ended, those discussions resumed. While the Cubs and White Sox played each other in the city series—won by the Cubs in six games—Veeck again contacted McCarthy.

Only thirty-five years old, McCarthy had begun his baseball career as a second baseman at Niagara University before he turned professional in 1907. Over the next few seasons, he played for various minor league clubs, including those in Toledo, Indianapolis, Wilkes-Barre, and Buffalo. It was while McCarthy was playing in Buffalo that he first drew attention to himself for his baseball savvy. Manager Billy Clymer noted, "He plays any position with equal facility and uses his head as well as his hands." The Federal League appeared to provide McCarthy with a route to the major leagues, and in 1915 he reportedly signed with the Buffalo club, but the league collapsed. McCarthy landed with Louisville, first as a player, then as player-manager. It soon became obvious that his future was at the helm, not at second base.

Still, even after he led the club to a pennant in 1921, the major leagues remained a remote dream. Virtually every major league manager had played in the major leagues himself, and players looked down on those who had not. Indeed, had anyone but William Veeck been involved in the decision, McCarthy probably would have remained in the minor leagues for the rest of his baseball career.

But after the Maranville debacle, Veeck liked the idea of hiring McCarthy, who had a reputation for being serious and, compared to the Rabbit, sober. McCarthy insisted on discipline and drilled his players relentlessly in the fundamentals, expecting them to know the right way to play the game. Yet McCarthy also had his quirks. He didn't think much of Polish players or southerners, who he thought were hotheads and drunks, or pipe smokers, who he believed were too complacent. He tended to distrust pitch-

When Cub president Bill Veeck offered the Cub manager's job to Joe McCarthy prior to the 1926 season, McCarthy had already paid his dues with a dozen years of managing successfully in the minors. Within three years, McCarthy had retooled the Cubs as National League champions by acquiring minor league outfielders Hack Wilson and Riggs Stephenson and in another deal spending $200,000 and trading five players for Rogers Hornsby.

ers and rarely settled on a set rotation, preferring to go with the hot hand. Yet at the same time, he loved having a set lineup, which eventually earned him a reputation as a "push-button" manager who simply wrote out the lineup card and let his team play.

His Colonels had captured the AA pennant in 1925 and defeated Baltimore in the Junior World Series. Several Louisville players, such as Yankee center fielder Earle Combs, had thrived under McCarthy and gone on to become stars. Besides, the Cubs had absolutely nothing to lose.

McCarthy was introduced to the Chicago press corps on October 13, 1925. Wrigley underscored the significance of the appointment by saying, "We'll win the pennant in 1926 if Bill Veeck and I have to get into the lineup ourselves." Veeck then added that although he didn't intend to spend a million dollars on the four best hitters in the league, money would be no object, and he would acquire some players for his new manager "if we have to spend $1,000,000 for forty new men."

McCarthy was circumspect at this first press conference, saying, "It would be difficult for me to say just what will be done to fill up the gaps in the lineup," but he'd been paying close attention to the Cubs. He knew who he didn't want on the roster and, just as important, knew a few players he did. After seven years with Louisville, he was as familiar with minor league talent as anyone in baseball.

McCarthy had still one more advantage going for him. At age thirty-five, he'd seen baseball evolve from the dead ball era into a game increasingly driven by power. Unlike some of the more experienced major league managers, who stubbornly insisted on playing "scientific" dead ball baseball to the bitter end, McCarthy had no trouble integrating the change into his approach. In fact, his last club in Louisville had been the most power-laden club of his tenure there, and the most successful. He could see the future, and it lay in the ball sailing over the fence. Under McCarthy, the home run, for the first time, would become an important part of the Cubs' repertoire.

Wrigley and Veeck gave the new manager free rein to make any changes he wanted, and McCarthy got right to work. No one's spot on the roster was safe.

Maranville was the first to go. Not only had he slipped as a player, but the undisciplined shortstop was not McCarthy's kind of guy, and it would have been awkward for the former manager to stick around. The Dodgers picked him up on waivers, and a few weeks later the Cubs picked up a capable if unspectacular replacement from St. Louis in veteran Jimmy Cooney.

McCarthy wasn't satisfied with simply shuffling the deck with retreads. He trusted his own eyes. He'd seen some talent in the minor leagues, and he wanted it in Chicago. Hack Wilson had been trying to crack the New York Giants' lineup for several seasons. Only five-foot-six, Wilson, who had gone to work in a factory while still a child and virtually raised himself, was one of the strongest men in the major leagues, with a barrel chest sitting atop a pair of spindly and surprisingly swift legs. After the Giants' Billy Southworth was injured in 1924, Wilson had taken over in center field, hit .295, and cracked forty-one extra-base hits in just over half a season.

But Giants manager John McGraw didn't appreciate Wilson's talent, and when Southworth recovered, he got his old job back. Halfway through the 1925 season, Wilson was optioned back to Toledo.

Wilson hit .343 for the Ohio club, and McGraw fully intended to bring him back up to New York in 1926. Fortunately for the Cubs, New York club secretary Jim Tierney failed to file the appropriate paperwork to transfer Wilson to the New York roster, leaving him exposed in the annual minor league draft. The Cubs grabbed him, and all of a sudden the Chicago outfield was surprisingly potent.

When the Cubs convened for spring training on Catalina Island, McCarthy quickly took command. After Maranville's reeling reign, McCarthy's steadiness and calm was appreciated by many of the Cubs. McCarthy didn't play favorites, no one was a star, and everyone was treated like an adult until he proved otherwise. If you performed and played well, McCarthy was easy to play for—if you produced, you were in the lineup.

Although the Cubs were better in 1926, they weren't quite a contender, something McCarthy soon realized as he continued to tinker with the Cub roster. On the mound, Wilbur Cooper looked finished, and in the clubhouse the veteran was dismissive of McCarthy. The manager let him go in early June.

That should have sent a message to Grover Cleveland Alexander. He wasn't pitching very well either and, like Cooper, rolled his eyes at the manager. Alexander was accustomed to doing things his way and wasn't about to change.

In mid-June it all came to a head. When Alex wasn't pitching, which was often owing to a chronically sore arm, he was drinking. On June 15, the Cubs were in Alexander's hometown of Philadelphia, and the pitcher spent a long evening draining bottles before showing up at the ballpark completely stewed.

McCarthy was out of patience. "This isn't the first time by any means," he said of the pitcher's alcoholic stupor. "This is the sixth time this has happened in the last nine or ten days. . . . Any pitcher may drink and get away with it when he is winning . . . [but] he has been drawing a big salary and hasn't been any use to us." McCarthy meant what he said. Drinking was fine with him as long as you did your job every day. Hack Wilson had already spent a night in jail after being picked up in a speakeasy raid, and

McCarthy had done nothing—Wilson was hitting. But Alex wasn't pitching well. McCarthy suspended him indefinitely, something Alexander didn't discover for almost twenty-four hours—he was already off on another bender.

When he finally showed up, the Cubs sent him back to Chicago to dry out. A week later, however, McCarthy decided that, dry or not, the Cubs were better off without him. Even if Alexander came back to pitch well, the young manager felt that he needed to make a statement. The trading deadline had passed, so the club put him on waivers.

In retrospect, that was a cardinal error. St. Louis claimed Alexander for $4,000. Allowing a rival to acquire a player of Alexander's ability was a serious gaffe, one that tipped the balance of power in the National League. In the long run, it may also have cost the Cubs a chance at a dynasty. If Alexander had remained a Cub, he might have been the difference, not only in the 1926 pennant race, but in several subsequent races and, perhaps, several World Series. Later in his career, McCarthy would grudgingly admit that special players—like Ted Williams, whom McCarthy managed in Boston—needed special treatment.

In St. Louis, Alexander was reunited with former Cubs manager and catcher Bill Killefer, who now served as a Cardinal coach. Alexander sobered up enough to win nine games and help lead the Cards on a second-half surge that captured the National League pennant. Much to the chagrin of the Cubs, Alexander would pitch winning baseball for the Cardinals for several seasons, and St. Louis soon became a particular nemesis of the Cubs.

At about the same time, the Cubs added another player who would prove to be a difference-maker. Riggs Stephenson had played part-time for five seasons with the Cleveland Indians, mostly at second base. He could hit, finishing the 1924 season with an average of .371, but in 1925 he had clashed with manager Tris Speaker, who thought Stephenson's arm wasn't worthy of the major leagues. Stephenson ended up playing outfield back in the American Association, where McCarthy noticed his bat. In the middle of the 1926 season, with Stephenson hitting a robust .385 for Indianapolis, the Cubs acquired him for cash and two prospects.

Stephenson went directly into the outfield, and the Cubs were suddenly a much better team: Stephenson hit

Jackson "Riggs" Stephenson is one of the greatest batters not enshrined in the Baseball Hall of Fame. His .336 career batting average ties him for second on the Cubs' all-time list with Bill Madlock. In two World Series for Chicago in 1929 and 1932, he batted .316 and .444, respectively.

Right-hander Charlie Root was one of the greatest pitchers in Cub history, with a franchise-leading 201 victories achieved over sixteen seasons. Root is shown here at a day given in his honor in 1941 when he was presented with a station wagon purchased with the many thousands of dimes donated by fans. He also received a pet pig from his teammates.

for fan comfort in the spring and fall, when the wind tended to blow in off the lake.

In the offseason, McCarthy continued to exercise his knack for sifting gold from the coal of minor leaguers. Outfielder Earl Webb, who'd played with Wilson in Toledo, was picked up in the draft, and the Cubs also added Toledo shortstop Woody English, buying him for $50,000.

The real difference-makers in 1927, however, were Hack Wilson and Charlie Root. Wilson emerged as a bonafide star, tying Cy Williams for the league lead in home runs with thirty. Root, meanwhile, may not have been the best pitcher in the league, but he was the most valuable. McCarthy rode him like a draft horse.

Root set the tone for the season on opening day, when he beat Alexander and the Cardinals 10–1 and Earl Webb cracked two home runs, the first two hits of his major league career. Over the first half of the season, the Cubs, Giants, Pirates, and Cardinals all battled for first place, but the Cubs edged ahead at the beginning of August and then went on a run. When Root shut out the Dodgers on August 16 for his twenty-second win, the Cubs led by six games and fans began to look forward to a matchup between the Cubs and the potent 1927 Yankees in the World Series. Those who thought the Cubs might be New York's equal were not without credibility.

If McCarthy had a flaw, however, it was the way he wielded the whip down the home stretch. The rest of the Cubs' rotation—Sheriff Blake, Hal Carlson, and Guy Bush—were all talented, but McCarthy had fallen in love with Root's tenacity and durability. Whenever he had a chance, he gave Root an extra start, and in the late innings, with the game on the line, McCarthy hardly had to say a word—Root was already getting warm.

For two-thirds of the season the strategy worked brilliantly, but from the middle of August onward Root began to wilt, and the Cub lead shrank accordingly. Twenty-two years later, while managing the Boston Red Sox, McCarthy would make a similar error that may have cost his club a pennant—overusing pitcher Mel Parnell down the stretch in 1949. That mistake would mark the beginning of the end of McCarthy's career. In 1927, however, a similar error went all but unnoticed.

To be fair, McCarthy's use of Root was not out of the mainstream. Most big league managers at the time treated

.338, while Hack Wilson knocked twenty-one home runs and pitchers Charlie Root and Guy Bush each proved they could win in the major leagues. Although the team wasn't a serious contender and finished in fourth place, fans turned out in droves, both to see the ball club and to bask in the increasingly comfortable accommodations of Wrigley Field. From 1926 through 1928, Wrigley spent nearly $1 million on further improvements, most notably the addition of a second deck, which not only expanded the capacity of the park but also cut down on the wind that blew through the stands, a particularly important factor

their top starter in similar fashion, and the relief ace had yet to emerge. The nature of the game was changing, but not even McCarthy fully comprehended yet just how much. Although McCarthy was embracing the power game on the offensive side of the diamond, he failed to note that the lively ball made the game much harder on pitchers. The days of using an ace like Root in almost one-third of a team's games was just about over.

His dependence on Root cost the club the pennant. After Root's twenty-second win, the Cubs lost twenty-four of the next thirty-five, falling out of first place on September 1 when they lost to the Pirates, 4–3. Root, in a performance one newspaper oddly described as "wabbly," managed to win his twenty-fifth game on September 8, but over the final three weeks he won only once more. The Cubs tried to fill the gap by acquiring veteran Art Nehf from the Reds, but it was too late.

A few days later, it was all but official. After the Cubs fell to Brooklyn 6–5 on September 13, Irving Vaughn wrote in the *Tribune*, "Old Man Pennant Hope packed his luggage yesterday, waved good-by to the Cubs and said he probably wouldn't be back."

The Cubs finished fourth again, eight and a half games behind the pennant-winning Pirates, who went on to lose the World Series to the Yankees in four games. Meanwhile, Grover Cleveland Alexander won twenty-one games for second-place St. Louis, leaving one to wonder where the Cubs might have finished in 1926 and 1927 had McCarthy and Alexander managed to get along.

No one in Chicago was asking those kinds of questions. They rarely did, and it would be years before they started. Compared to their counterparts in cities like New York and Boston, Chicago's sporting press was surprisingly compliant. After all, Wrigley made their life comfortable, and Veeck was one of their own, a former ink-stained wretch made good. The writers primarily competed with each other in a contest over who could heap the most praise on the Cubs. Like Cub fans, more than one million of whom streamed through the gates in 1927, the men who covered baseball in the Chicago papers seemed so mesmerized by the creature comforts of Wrigley Field that they rarely raised a critical eye—and even more rarely put that point of view on the page in black and white.

In a way, self-deception was a way of life in Chicago. A generation before, everyone had blanched upon learning about the miserable conditions in the meat industry and the stockyards from exposés such as Upton Sinclair's *The Jungle*. But they liked eating fresh meat and making money, so they put up with it. In the 1920s, everyone recoiled in horror at the carnage that the gangsters were causing on the streets, but they liked drinking booze, so they put up with the gangsters. Chicago baseball fans liked Wrigley Field, so each time the Cubs lost they looked the other way and looked toward next year.

In the offseason, McCarthy picked up one more player that fans could look forward to: former Pittsburgh center fielder Hazen "Kiki" Cuyler. At the start of the 1927 season, Cuyler had manned center field for the Pirates between the two Waner brothers, Lloyd and Paul. Since becoming a regular in the Pirate outfield in 1924, Cuyler had been the best outfielder in the league, a player whom the influential *Reach Guide* accurately described as "one of the greatest ballplayers of the day. Cuyler can do everything—hit, throw, cover the ground and run the bases." In his first three seasons, he hit a robust .354, .357, and .321.

Shortly after the start of the 1927 season, however, Cuyler ran afoul of new Pirate manager Donie Bush, whom he derided as a "busher." Then the manager moved Cuyler to second in the batting order. He slumped, and the two clashed again. Finally, Cuyler failed to slide into second base on a double play. In response, Bush benched him. Cuyler sat for the rest of the season, including during the 1927 World Series, in which he did not appear.

When the season ended, the Pirates put him on the trading block. The Cubs jumped at the deal, giving up infielder Sparky Adams and outfielder Pete Scott.

All of a sudden, with Cuyler joining Wilson and Stephenson, the Cubs had one of the best outfields in all of baseball. Hartnett was already one of the game's premier catchers, the infield was solid, and when the club purchased rookie pitcher Pat Malone, the best pitching prospect in the minor leagues, the Cubs suddenly had one of the deepest pitching staffs in the game, with Root, Sheriff Blake, Guy Bush, Malone, and Art Nehf. When "hot stove" discussion turned to the 1928 National League pennant race, those discussions started with the Cubs. In two seasons McCarthy had turned the Cubs completely around.

The only real worry was Root. As Irving Vaughn noted in the *Tribune*, in 1927 the pitcher "probably threw more baseballs than any man in the major leagues." In fact, Root, who usually carried about 180 pounds on his five-foot-ten frame, finished the 1927 season weighing barely 160 pounds. He'd carried the team in 1927 and in the off-season wanted more money. The Cubs agreed with little argument, and Root showed up for spring training looking as if he'd taken his raise in calories, weighing 190 pounds and pitching poorly.

The Cubs lost on opening day but soon gained momentum and swept into first place on the strength of a thirteen-game win streak. With a record of 22–12, all signs

---

On November 28, 1927, the Cubs made one of the best trades in their history when they dealt infielder Sparky Adams and outfielder Pete Scott to the Pirates for future Hall of Fame outfielder Hazen "Kiki" Cuyler. In eight seasons with the Cubs, Cuyler batted a strong .325 and contributed to three National League championships.

pointed toward continued success, because the Cubs weren't even at full strength. Malone hadn't won a game, Charlie Root was struggling with his waistline, and Gabby Hartnett was injured and had yet to appear. The Cubs had been winning because the offensive power of the outfield lived up to its billing, and because Art Nehf, as one reporter put it, "has been sipping at the fountain of youth." Once Root and Malone got going, a pennant seemed all but certain.

It was not to be. The Cubs' tenure in first place lasted only a few days. Then a flu bug swept through the clubhouse, knocking out Stephenson and fourth outfielder Cliff Heathcote. St. Louis swept past the Cubs, and Chicago, despite hanging close, was never able to catch up. Malone finally got going, but Nehf slumped, and Root never got untracked. The 1927 season had taken a toll, and he simply didn't have the stamina—or the stuff—to pull off a repeat performance. Although he'd remain a valuable pitcher for a number of years, he never again pitched as well or as often as he had in 1927.

The Cubs were getting better, but clearly they were still a little short. Wrigley was getting older too, and although few knew it, his health was starting to fail. He was impatient for a pennant and rolling in dough, so he decided to use some cash to hurry things along.

The great Rogers Hornsby, arguably the best hitter in baseball and certainly the greatest right-handed bat, had just concluded his first season with the Boston Braves. Hornsby had first starred for St. Louis, hitting .402 over a five-year period from 1921 through 1926. But as soon as the Cards won the World Series, Hornsby was shipped off to the New York Giants, where he lasted only a year before going to Boston.

Why? Hornsby was a certified pain in the neck, a player who, despite all his talent, was sometimes not worth the trouble. He had the temperament of an artist and was thoroughly tactless. Only Hornsby knew what was good for Hornsby, and he couldn't understand why other players couldn't do what he could do at the plate, and he let them know it. He didn't drink or smoke or go to the movies and thought anyone who did was cheating themselves. As he once said of himself, "If you live like I do, you can be a great player too." Hornsby not only believed his own hype, but lived it.

Even though Hornsby had hit .387 in Boston, the Braves won only fifty games, were going bankrupt, and had already tired of Hornsby's attitude. At the end of the season, for the third time in three seasons, Hornsby was available.

Wrigley had lusted after Hornsby for years and had once offered the Cardinals a reported $300,000 for his services. Boston owner Judge Emil Fuchs knew that, and he approached Veeck and proposed a deal, asking for $200,000 and five players.

Veeck thought it was too much, and told Wrigley as much, but Wrigley overruled him. Although the actual dollar amount exchanged is still unknown—some sources at the time claimed that "only" $120,000 changed hands—Wrigley opened his wallet.

Before the deal, both men consulted with McCarthy, who apparently gave his okay, but it had to give him pause. A jaded veteran who could undermine his manager's authority, Hornsby had precisely the kind of temperament that McCarthy had spent several seasons getting rid of. Then again, Hornsby was a .400 hitter, so perhaps a little undermining was worth it.

The Cubs and Braves agreed to a deal in mid-October, then waited a few weeks until the Boston City Council gave its annual approval for Sunday baseball. Finally, on November 7, 1928, Rogers Hornsby became a member of the Chicago Cubs. In addition to the cash, the Cubs gave up five players, only one of whom, pitcher Percy Jones, was a proven major leaguer. A millisecond after the deal was made official, the Cubs became odds-on favorites to win the World Series, not only in 1929 but for several years thereafter.

In the offseason, Wrigley prepped Wrigley Field as if he were preparing it for the World Series, installing a new flagpole in center field and new foul poles, placing pennants that read WRIGLEY FIELD on the roof, resodding the entire field, and repainting every seat in the stands. Spring training went off almost without a hitch, and McCarthy announced, "I have never had so many pitchers in shape." The only questions seemed to be the batting order and whether or not Gabby Hartnett's sore arm would recover in time to start the season. As it was, he would end up missing almost the entire year, and his absence would be almost enough to cost the team the pennant.

For the first half of the season, the Cubs, Giants, and Pirates all fought it out for the lead, with no team able to forge ahead. Hornsby was everything the Cubs had expected—hitting near .400 and slugging better than any hitter in the league, he simultaneously made almost every other batter in the Cub lineup better. Cuyler, Wilson, and Stephenson all responded with what were arguably the best seasons of their career to date.

The only problem was behind the plate. In a season in which everyone in baseball seemed to be able to hit—ten of the sixteen clubs would hit .290 or better—no one the Cubs put behind the plate could do the job. Mike Gonzalez was barely hitting his weight, and rookie Earl Grace was no better.

On July 6, the Cubs fell to the Braves 3–1 and trailed the Pirates by half a game. After the game, McCarthy learned that the Braves were putting veteran catcher Zach Taylor on waivers. The Cubs picked him up, and for the rest of the season he played, as one scribe put it, "as steady as a time piece," hitting .274.

In a razor-thin pennant race, Taylor proved to be the difference. After he joined the club, the Cubs outscored every team in the league by at least fifty runs. On July 25, the Cubs took over first place for good in spectacular fashion.

The Cubs raced out to a 4–0 lead over the Giants, but in the sixth inning New York erupted for seven runs, knocking Guy Bush from the game. The game appeared over.

Then the Cubs came storming back. After Heathcote and Hornsby started the seventh with hits, Hack Wilson, in the words of the *Tribune*'s Irving Vaughn, "gave until his back muscles hurt and the ball went hurtling like a meteor," landing on the center-field side of the right-field bleachers to tie the game as the Cubs went on to win 8–5.

After that point, there was no turning back. Within three weeks, the Cubs' lead approached ten games as neither the Pirates nor the Giants could keep pace. Fans poured into Wrigley Field in record numbers, drunk on the display of offense the Cubs put on every day: battering the bleachers with baseballs, Hornsby hit .380 with thirty-nine home runs, Wilson matched him and hit .345, and both Cuyler and Stephenson hit better than .360. On Ladies' Day in August, a mob of more than thirty thousand women and twenty thousand men overwhelmed the turnstiles and stormed the park, occupying every available space in what was probably the largest crowd in Wrigley Field history. Some estimated that more than sixty thousand fans pushed their way inside. For the season, the Cubs drew nearly one and a half million fans, an all-time record. They clinched the pennant on September 18, won the pennant by ten and a half games, and took aim on the world championship.

In the American League, the Philadelphia Athletics had done a fair imitation of the Cubs, scoring runs in bunches behind sluggers Al Simmons and Jimmie Foxx, albeit with somewhat better pitching. Paced by George Earnshaw and Lefty Grove, they beat the mighty Yankees, who finished second, by eighteen games. As a result, the A's were installed as 7–5 favorites in the World Series.

Had the touts known who Connie Mack planned to start in game one, however, they'd have given the game and the Series to the Cubs. On a day when every single person in Philadelphia and Chicago—including the more than forty thousand fans who crowded into Wrigley Field—expected Mack to send either Earnshaw or Grove to the mound, Mack threw the biggest pitching surprise in World Series history. He passed over not only Earnshaw and Grove but his number-three, -four, and -five starters as well. Instead, he sent a pitcher out to the mound who had appeared in only eleven games all year long and hadn't started a game since July—thirty-six-year-old veteran Howard Ehmke. As Edward Burns later wrote in the *Tribune*, "According to all the conventions of baseball and decency Joe McCarthy has the right to sue Connie Mack for even thinking about running in this old dark horse, Howard Ehmke. The whole thing was unethical."

It was also absolutely brilliant. At one time, Ehmke had been a star of sorts, winning twenty games for a last-place Red Sox team and once throwing a no-hitter. But for most of his career he had been a distinctly .500 pitcher best known for his command and change of speed because he didn't have a fastball. As he grew older, Ehmke pitched as if bored and ready to go to bed, throwing slow, slower, and slowest from overhand, three-quarter, sidearm, and even submarine deliveries. The *Tribune* called him "one of the boys who has been waiting around for a ride back to the minors." It was widely assumed that he would retire at the end of the season.

But as the World Series approached, Mack looked at the Cubs and saw an aggressive, primarily right-handed hitting team that feasted on fastballs. Then he looked at the right-handed Ehmke and saw the perfect counterattack. He told his pitcher he planned to start him in the first game of the World Series and over the final weeks of the season even sent Ehmke off to scout the Cubs in person.

By game one of the Series, which opened in Chicago on October 8, the veteran had plotted his strategy. The Cubs, expecting Earnshaw or Grove, were all geared up for fastballs and salivating at the opportunity.

They didn't get any, at least not as fast as they expected. They licked their chops at the start, but after Ehmke set the side down in the first, he started the second by fanning both Cuyler and Stephenson. The Cubs threatened in the third when third baseman Norm McMillan singled and English doubled, but Ehmke struck out Wilson to end the threat.

That was it. With each passing inning, the Cubs hitters became more and more frustrated.

Through the eighth inning, the Cubs never really threatened again. The wind was blowing in, and on the rare occasion they hit the ball solid, it fell into the waiting arms of the A's.

Root, meanwhile, was just as good for the Cubs. The game was scoreless until Jimmie Foxx drilled a home run off Root in the seventh. He left for a pinch hitter in the eighth, but in the ninth Woody English botched two double plays, which led to two more runs. The Cubs trailed 3–0 with only three outs to go.

Wilson started the inning with a vicious line drive back to Ehmke. He threw Wilson out, but the line drive, which struck him near the groin, also broke his spell. Cuyler reached on an error and then scored when Stephenson singled. The Cubs were on the board, and when Charlie Grimm followed with a hit, Mack's gamble seemed just that.

Due up next was catcher Mike Gonzalez, who'd come in for Taylor. McCarthy called for pinch hitter Footsie Blair, then sent Chuck Tolson out to hit in the pitcher's spot.

That move exposed McCarthy's Achilles' heel. During the regular season, he ran out the same lineup day after day and rarely needed to use pinch hitters. But it was different in the Series. Time and time again in his managerial

career, in big games, particularly those in the postseason, McCarthy was forced to turn to players he'd rarely used in the regular season, and they usually weren't ready.

Blair grounded into a force-out. Ehmke exhaled. Tolson stepped in and swung through the first pitch as Ehmke calmed down. Tolson then worked the count to three balls and two strikes. As Ehmke started his wind-up, Stephenson and Blair took off. If Tolson hit a long single, the game would be tied.

He hit only air, whiffing on another slow pitch, Ehmke's thirteenth strikeout of the day. The Cubs lost, 3–1, and in a matter of minutes got sick of answering questions about why they hadn't hit Ehmke. They didn't have an answer.

The next day Mack sent Earnshaw and then Grove after the Cubs, while McCarthy countered with Pat Malone. But after seeing Ehmke, Earnshaw and Grove suddenly seemed faster than usual. Another thirteen Cubs fanned as the A's rolled to a 9–3 win.

The Series was virtually over. On the train ride to

By 1929 second baseman Rogers Hornsby had already captured seven National League batting championships in his first thirteen major league seasons. Arriving in Chicago just prior to the 1929 season, Hornsby proceeded to destroy the franchise single-season offensive numbers by topping the list for batting average (.380), runs scored (156), hits (229), and on-base percentage (.459).

Philadelphia for game three, the sportswriters began casting around for reasons to explain the Cubs' demise and found a few players willing to talk. Before the Series, McCarthy had former Cub Joe Tinker scout the A's, and Tinker had told McCarthy to pitch both Al Simmons and Mickey Cochrane inside. In game two, the two men combined to go 3-for-6, with four runs scored and four RBIs. Rogers Hornsby made it known that he thought that was entirely the wrong strategy, that the two players should have been pitched outside, and Cubs officials openly wondered why McCarthy had asked Tinker to scout the A's rather than an active player like Hornsby. After all, Ehmke's scouting report had made the Cubs look foolish.

And the Last Shall Be First

In six seasons with the Cubs, slugger Hack Wilson led the National League in home runs four times and averaged 32 home runs and 122 RBIs per season while batting .322. In 1931 he was traded to the Cardinals, who immediately dealt him to the Dodgers. In Brooklyn he enjoyed one last good season in 1932 (.297, 23 home runs, 123 RBIs). Within two years, he was out of baseball and working as a laborer in Baltimore.

As bad as it was being down two games to none, it would get worse for the Cubs. Back in Philadelphia for game three, Bush beat Earnshaw 3–1 to give the Cubs hope, and for the first six and a half innings of game four, the Cubs romped, pummeling Jack Quinn and Rube Walberg for eight runs. Root, meanwhile, gave up three inconsequential hits.

He took the mound in the seventh needing only nine more outs to keep the A's from scoring nine runs to tie the Series. Syndicated baseball writer Ed Burns put it best: "It remained for our beloved Cubs to furnish the greatest debacle, the most terrific flop, in the history of the World Series."

Root was pitching smartly, making sure he threw strikes. When Al Simmons led off the inning with a long home run, it drew only yawns from the Cubs and a smattering of applause from the A's crowd. Many were already on their way to the exits.

Foxx then followed with a single, and Bing Miller lofted a lazy fly ball to center. But in the late afternoon at Shibe Park in the fall, the sun hung over the grandstand, blazing straight into center field. Hitters loved it. Center fielders did not.

Two innings before, in the fifth, Wilson had dropped Jimmie Dykes's fly ball after losing it in the sun. He was wearing sunglasses, but they hadn't done much good.

Now he lost another fly, putting Miller on first and sending Foxx to second. Dykes followed with a single, as did Joe Boley, and all of a sudden the score was 8–3 and those Cubs fans who had made their way to Philadelphia started getting nervous.

They exhaled when George Burns, pinch-hitting for the pitcher, popped up, but when Max Bishop singled, McCarthy came out and sent Art Nehf on in relief of Root. He wasn't getting hit hard, but the Cubs needed to stop the A's momentum.

Nehf got Mule Haas to hit another ball to center, this time a line drive. For the third time, Wilson lost the ball in the sun, this time blindly reaching out for the ball with his bare hand. He missed it. The liner rolled to the wall, and all the A's rolled home, including Haas.

Now you could see it coming. Nehf walked Cochrane, violating McCarthy's Tenth Commandment, and McCarthy turned to Sheriff Blake, but the deluge was under way. Two more hits followed, then Pat Malone came on and hit a batter before Dykes doubled, putting the A's ahead 10–8. Malone struck out the next two hitters to end the inning, but it was far too little, way too late.

In the last two innings, the stunned Cubs went down like statues before Lefty Grove. Contemporary fans might argue, but the biggest choke in the history of the Cubs—and the World Series—was over and in the books for all time.

After the game, McCarthy covered for Wilson, saying, "He just couldn't see it. It wasn't his lack of ability or hindsight." Wilson said simply, "Couldn't see the balls, couldn't see the balls."

Game five was the final insult. Few teams ever recover from such grotesque losses. The headline in the *Tribune* put it succinctly: "Malone Great for Eight Innings, Then Folds Up." The Cubs nursed a 2–0 lead into the ninth, when Mule Haas cracked a two-run home run, and then Al Simmons doubled home Bing Miller to snatch another defeat from the jaws of victory. The A's were champions, and the Cubs—not for the last time—were infamous in failure.

No one knew what to say or how to say it. Some tried to blame Stephenson for not catching Dykes's double that gave the A's their final two runs in their ten-run comeback, and others looked to third baseman Norm McMillan, who barely missed fielding two singles that same inning. Wilson wore his miscues like a dark cloud, but William Wrigley put it all on Joe McCarthy. Franklin P. Adams even updated "Baseball's Sad Lexicon" to account for the collapse, penning a self-parody:

> These are the boys I elected to praise,
>   English and Hornsby and Grimm
> These are the boys that were sunk by the A's
>   English and Hornsby and Grimm.
> Daily accomplishing plays that are double.
> Pounding the pellet out into the stubble,
> Still to A's they are not any trouble—
>   English and Hornsby and Grimm.

In reality, there was plenty of blame to go around, and as Adams pointed out, much of it should have been shouldered by the Cubs hitters. Apart from Wilson, who hit .471, and Grimm, no one else had done much. Without question, however, Connie Mack had outmanaged Joe McCarthy. Pitching Ehmke in game one was the masterstroke that set up everything that followed.

The offseason was marked by public paralysis and private acrimony, a situation not helped when the stock market collapsed. The Wrigley Company would weather the Depression better than most, but Wrigley still lost a fortune, which hardly brightened his mood. The A's had exposed the Cubs as a complacent team that waited for something to happen, but the club did nothing to remedy the situation in the offseason other than pick up Braves third baseman Les Bell on waivers and look forward to Hartnett's recovery from the sore arm that had kept him

out of the lineup in 1929. If he bounced back, it would mean another potent bat in the Cub lineup.

But Wrigley couldn't let the 1929 Series go. Still blaming McCarthy for the loss, he was suddenly convinced that McCarthy's lack of major league playing experience was the cause. To remedy the situation, Wrigley and Veeck started taking on a more active role. They shoved former catcher Ray Schalk on McCarthy to serve as a coach. McCarthy froze him out. According to the *Daily News*, Schalk was "never taken into the councils on the matters of running the team."

McCarthy sensed what was happening. Before the start of the season, he told Chicago sportswriter Warren Brown that sometime during the 1930 season he expected to be fired.

The stakes were high in 1930, all or nothing, with perfection and a world championship on one side and total disaster on the other. There was no middle ground or wiggle room.

The disasters started early. Spring training might as well have been held in Wrigley's hospital on Catalina Island. Over the winter, Rogers Hornsby had a growth removed from his right heel and expected to be fully recovered by spring training. He wasn't. Hornsby was sent home when the heel started acting up, and he would get off to a slow start. Les Bell came down with a sore arm. Just after the start of the season, Guy Bush fell on his elbow while fielding a ground ball and was out of the lineup for several weeks, and Stephenson hurt his shoulder trying to make a diving catch. The Cubs sputtered.

Then came the worst disaster that can befall any ball club. On May 27, pitcher Hal Carlson, a member of the Cubs since 1927, went to bed in his room at Chicago's Carlos Hotel, where he kept an apartment. He had warmed up earlier that day but had not seen any action.

Since joining the Cubs, Carlson, who had won as many as seventeen games for the Pirates, had been something of a disappointment. After winning twelve games in 1927, Carlson's health had failed. He missed most of the 1928 season recovering from a bad case of the flu, and in 1929 another illness cost him half the season.

In the middle of the night, he summoned the Cubs' clubhouse boy, who resided in the same hotel, and complained of great pain. Within an hour, he was vomiting blood. An ambulance was called, and Carlson was rushed to the hospital, but it was too late. He died of a stomach hemorrhage later that morning, leaving a wife and four-year-old daughter.

The May 29 game between the Cubs and Cardinals was postponed, so that the players could attend Carlson's funeral in Rockford, and rescheduled as the first game of a double-header the next day. In the third inning of that game, another disaster hit. Rogers Hornsby broke his ankle.

Fortunately for the Cubs, if there was any season in which the team could afford to lose a player like Hornsby, it was 1930. Everybody would be hitting the lively ball as six teams in the NL, including the Cubs, hit better than .300 for the season. Still, the loss hurt.

In the midst of that litany of disaster, there were some positives. In combination, they were just enough to keep the Cubs in contention.

Pitcher Pat Malone blossomed into one of the best pitchers in the league, though McCarthy would overuse him in much the same way he had overused Root several years before. But it was at the plate that the 1930 Cubs really made their mark. Gabby Hartnett put together one of the best offensive seasons by a catcher in history, hitting .339 with 37 home runs and 122 RBIs. Teammate Kiki Cuyler arguably had the best season of his career, hitting .355, stealing 37 bases, knocking 50 doubles, scoring 155 runs, and knocking in 134.

So what? No one noticed, and today few remember what either Hartnett or Cuyler did in 1930. For in comparison with Hack Wilson, their performances were almost pedestrian.

One season after he helped cost his team the World Series, Hack Wilson put together one of the greatest seasons any hitter has ever had, picking up the slack from the loss of Hornsby and almost making up the difference all by himself. How good was he in 1930? If one could divide Wilson's production in 1930 between two players, each would still have a season to be proud of—a total of 56 home runs and a major league record 191 RBIs can do that. Hornsby's absence brought Wilson to the plate time and time again with runners on base as he hit fourth behind leadoff hitter Blair (who scored 97 runs), English, and Cuyler (who both scored more than 150). McCarthy later claimed, "We didn't lose a game all year when Wilson came to bat in the late innings." That wasn't much of an exaggeration. Forty of Wilson's home runs and 140 of his RBIs came in Cub victories.

Wilson's performance also led everyone to begin to realize that Wrigley Field was a pretty good place to hit. The lively ball made the ballpark small, particularly in the so-called power alleys in left-center and right-center. In midsummer, the wind often picked up in the late afternoon, blowing like an express train toward the outfield. Wilson was the first to master the park: he hit thirty-three of his fifty-six home runs at home.

In short, for one season Hack Wilson in Chicago was the right-handed equivalent of Babe Ruth in New York, and for much of the year there was some speculation that, indeed, Wilson would crack Ruth's home run record of sixty in a single season. Not only did Wilson keep up with Ruth's 1927 home run pace, but entering September he actually led the Babe's pace with forty-six home runs. In 1927, however, Ruth picked up that pace by hitting an incredible seventeen home runs in September alone. Wilson hit only ten, but he still set a major league record for a right-handed hitter, one that would stand until both Sammy Sosa and Mark McGwire shattered it in 1998.

Unfortunately, Wilson shared other traits with Babe Ruth, most notably his penchant for alcohol and late nights, but he didn't have the Babe's stamina. Five years of burning the candle at both ends was about all Wilson's body could take, and the 1930 season was the final flame-up. Wilson's bat disguised the fact that his other skills were already starting to erode. He didn't run very well anymore, had diminished range in center field, and, as demonstrated in the 1929 World Series, had trouble tracking the ball. In 1930 he led all NL outfielders in errors. Wilson himself once admitted, "I never played drunk. Hung over? Yes, but never drunk." Well, 1930 may have been the last season Wilson's hangovers didn't control his destiny.

In spite of Wilson's performance at the plate, the Cubs just couldn't quite get it done in 1930—something was always going wrong, sometimes in ways that boggled the mind. On July 13 in Boston, for instance, the Cubs lost game one of a double-header, 2–1, and were losing game two, 3–0, before erupting for four runs in the top of the ninth to take the lead.

Then the Braves started stalling. As Ed Burns reported: "[Lieutenant] McCluskey of the Commonwealth stepped in under the Sunday law which makes it wicked for ball fans to enjoy themselves after 6 P.M." Known as "blue laws," such ordinances were vestigial remnants of the Puritan legacy of Boston, where baseball had once been banned altogether. Incredibly, as the clock struck six, police officer McCluskey enforced the law. The score reverted to that of the last full inning, and the Cubs lost a game they should have won.

Still, the Cubs hung in the pennant race, chasing Brooklyn for much of the year before surging into first place in mid-August. Wrigley and everyone else sensed a pennant. When Charlie Grimm was hobbled, the Cubs moved quickly, picking up veteran George Kelly from the American Association; Kelly would go on to hit .331 for the season.

Unfortunately, about the same time the Cubs caught fire, so did the St. Louis Cardinals. After playing .500 baseball for much of the year, the Cards made a trade for pitcher Burleigh Grimes. Suddenly they couldn't lose.

In late August, the two clubs met in a memorable three-game series. As Grantland Rice wrote in his syndicated column, if the Cubs prevailed, "they should have enough to work on for the remainder of the season bumping along hostile roads." In other words, the pennant should be theirs.

The heart of the Cubs' batting order in 1929 was as formidable as any in National League history, with (left to right) Rogers Hornsby (.380), Hack Wilson (.345), Kiki Cuyler (.360), and Riggs Stephenson (.362) providing significant punch for a team that not only won the pennant but also led the league in runs with 982 and batted .303 as a team.

HACK WILSON IN 1930

RBI by RBI   **BOLD** = Cub wins

DATE	RBI #	SCORE	AB	H	HR	RBI	HR #
Apr 15	**1**	**Cubs 9 @ Cardinals 8**	**4**	**1**	**0**	**1**	**0**
Apr 21	**4**	**Cubs 9 @ Reds 1**	**5**	**1**	**1**	**3**	**1**
Apr 22	7	Cubs 3 vs. Cardinals 8	4	1	1	3	2
Apr 25	**9**	**Cubs 6 vs. Reds 5**	**5**	**3**	**1**	**2**	**3**
Apr 28	**10**	**Cubs 7 vs. Pirates 4**	**2**	**1**	**0**	**1**	**0**
Apr 30	**11**	**Cubs 5 vs. Pirates 2**	**4**	**1**	**1**	**1**	**4**
May 4	**13**	**Cubs 8 vs. Phillies 7**	**3**	**3**	**0**	**2**	**0**
May 6	**15**	**Cubs 3 vs. Dodgers 1**	**3**	**1**	**1**	**2**	**5**
May 7	**19**	**Cubs 9 vs. Dodgers 5**	**4**	**2**	**0**	**4**	**0**
May 8	**20**	**Cubs 7 vs. Dodgers 4**	**4**	**2**	**1**	**1**	**6**
May 9	**22**	**Cubs 6 vs. Giants 5**	**4**	**3**	**0**	**2**	**0**
May 10	25	Cubs 4 vs. Giants 9	3	2	1	3	7
May 12	26	Cubs 12 vs. Giants 14	2	1	1	1	8
May 13	**29**	**Cubs 9 vs. Braves 8**	**2**	**1**	**1**	**3**	**9**
May 15	31	Cubs 8 vs. Braves 10	5	2	0	2	0
May 18 (GAME 1)	**34**	**Cubs 9 @ Cardinals 6**	**3**	**2**	**2**	**3**	**10, 11**
May 20	35	Cubs 3 @ Cardinals 16	4	1	1	1	12
May 22	**36**	**Cubs 12 @ Pirates 5**	**4**	**2**	**0**	**1**	**0**
May 24	**37**	**Cubs 5 @ Pirates 3**	**4**	**1**	**0**	**1**	**0**
May 26	39	Cubs 2 vs. Reds 8	4	1	1	2	13

DATE	RBI #	SCORE	AB	H	HR	RBI	HR #
May 28	**41**	**Cubs 6 vs. Reds 5**	**3**	**1**	**0**	**2**	**0**
May 30 (GAME 2)	**42**	**Cubs 9 vs. Cardinals 8**	**3**	**1**	**1**	**1**	**14**
May 31	**44**	**Cubs 6 vs. Cardinals 5**	**5**	**1**	**0**	**2**	**0**
June 1	**49**	**Cubs 16 vs. Pirates 4**	**5**	**4**	**2**	**5**	**15, 16**
June 3	**50**	**Cubs 15 @ Braves 2**	**4**	**1**	**0**	**1**	**0**
June 4	**51**	**Cubs 18 @ Braves 10**	**5**	**2**	**0**	**1**	**0**
June 5	**52**	**Cubs 10 @ Braves 7**	**6**	**2**	**1**	**1**	**17**
June 6	**53**	**Cubs 13 @ Dodgers 0**	**5**	**2**	**0**	**1**	**0**
June 7	55	Cubs 9 @ Dodgers 12	4	1	1	2	18
June 10	56	Cubs 2 @ Phillies 6	2	1	0	1	0
June 12	58	Cubs 3 @ Phillies 5	2	1	0	2	0
June 14	**60**	**Cubs 8 @ Giants 5**	**3**	**1**	**0**	**2**	**0**
June 16	**61**	**Cubs 8 @ Giants 5**	**4**	**1**	**0**	**1**	**0**
June 19	**64**	**Cubs 10 vs. Braves 4**	**4**	**1**	**1**	**3**	**19**
June 21	**66**	**Cubs 5 vs. Braves 4**	**5**	**3**	**1**	**2**	**20**
June 22	67	Cubs 2 vs. Braves 3	4	1	1	1	21
June 23	**72**	**Cubs 21 vs. Phillies 8**	**6**	**5**	**1**	**5**	**22**
June 24	**73**	**Cubs 6 vs. Phillies 1**	**5**	**2**	**0**	**1**	**0**
July 1	74	Cubs 5 vs. Giants 7	3	2	1	1	23
July 2	76	Cubs 8 vs. Giants 9	5	2	0	2	0
July 4 (GAME 2)	77	Cubs 1 @ Pirates 5	3	0	0	1	0
July 5	**80**	**Cubs 12 @ Pirates 3**	**4**	**3**	**0**	**3**	**0**
July 6 (GAME 1)	81	Cubs 4 @ Reds 5	3	2	1	1	24
July 6 (GAME 2)	82	Cubs 7 @ Reds 8	4	2	0	1	0

DATE	RBI #	SCORE	AB	H	HR	RBI	HR #
July 16 (GAME 1)	**84**	**Cubs 6 @ Dodgers 4**	**3**	**1**	**0**	**2**	**0**
July 18	**85**	**Cubs 6 @ Dodgers 2**	**5**	**3**	**1**	**1**	**25**
July 19	**87**	**Cubs 5 @ Dodgers 4**	**3**	**1**	**1**	**2**	**26**
July 20	88	Cubs 5 @ Giants 13	4	1	1	1	27
July 21	**91**	**Cubs 6 @ Giants 0**	**5**	**2**	**2**	**3**	**28, 29**
July 24	**92**	**Cubs 19 @ Phillies 15**	**5**	**2**	**0**	**1**	**0**
July 25	**93**	**Cubs 9 @ Phillies 5**	**3**	**1**	**0**	**1**	**0**
July 26	**98**	**Cubs 16 @ Phillies 2**	**5**	**3**	**3**	**5**	**30, 31, 32**
July 27	99	Cubs 5 @ Reds 6	2	1	0	1	0
July 28 (GAME 1)	**101**	**Cubs 3 vs. Reds 2**	**4**	**1**	**0**	**2**	**0**
July 28 (GAME 2)	**102**	**Cubs 5 vs. Reds 3**	**4**	**1**	**0**	**1**	**0**
July 29	104	Cubs 3 vs. Reds 4	3	1	1	2	33
Aug 1	**106**	**Cubs 10 vs. Pirates 7**	**3**	**1**	**0**	**2**	**0**
Aug 2	107	Cubs 8 vs. Pirates 14	5	2	1	1	34
Aug 3	109	Cubs 8 vs. Pirates 12	4	2	1	2	35
Aug 5	**111**	**Cubs 5 @ Cardinals 4**	**3**	**1**	**1**	**2**	**36**
Aug 7	**114**	**Cubs 6 @ Cardinals 5**	**3**	**2**	**0**	**3**	**0**
Aug 10 (GAME 1)	**118**	**Cubs 6 vs. Braves 0**	**4**	**2**	**2**	**4**	**37, 38**
Aug 10 (GAME 2)	**121**	**Cubs 17 vs. Braves 1**	**4**	**2**	**1**	**3**	**39**
Aug 13	123	Cubs 5 vs. Dodgers 15	4	2	1	2	40
Aug 14	**125**	**Cubs 5 vs. Dodgers 1**	**3**	**2**	**0**	**2**	**0**
Aug 15	**126**	**Cubs 4 vs. Dodgers 3**	**4**	**1**	**0**	**1**	**0**
Aug 16 (GAME 1)	**129**	**Cubs 10 vs. Phillies 9**	**5**	**2**	**1**	**3**	**41**
Aug 17	**131**	**Cubs 5 vs. Phillies 4**	**3**	**1**	**0**	**2**	**0**

DATE	RBI #	SCORE	AB	H	HR	RBI	HR #
Aug 18	**135**	**Cubs 17 vs. Phillies 3**	**5**	**4**	**1**	**4**	**4**
Aug 19 (GAME 1)	136	Cubs 8 vs. Phillies 9	4	3	1	1	43
Aug 20	138	Cubs 8 vs. Phillies 10	2	0	0	2	0
Aug 21	140	Cubs 6 vs. Giants 13	5	1	0	2	0
Aug 22	**141**	**Cubs 12 vs. Giants 4**	**3**	**1**	**0**	**1**	**0**
Aug 23	**144**	**Cubs 4 vs. Giants 2**	**3**	**1**	**0**	**3**	**0**
Aug 26	**148**	**Cubs 7 vs. Pirates 5**	**3**	**2**	**1**	**4**	**44**
Aug 27	151	Cubs 8 vs. Pirates 10	5	2	0	3	0
Aug 30	**157**	**Cubs 16 vs. Cardinals 4**	**3**	**3**	**2**	**6**	**45, 46**
Sept 3	158	Cubs 6 @ Pirates 9	5	3	0	1	0
Sept 4	**159**	**Cubs 10 @ Pirates 7**	**5**	**2**	**0**	**1**	**0**
Sept 5	160	Cubs 7 @ Pirates 8	5	0	0	1	0
Sept 6	**164**	**Cubs 19 @ Pirates 14**	**6**	**3**	**1**	**4**	**47**
Sept 11	165	Cubs 1 @ Dodgers 2	4	1	1	1	48
Sept 12	**171**	**Cubs 17 @ Phillies 4**	**5**	**5**	**1**	**6**	**49**
Sept 15 (GAME 1)	172	Cubs 11 @ Phillies 12	5	2	0	1	0
Sept 15 (GAME 2)	**173**	**Cubs 6 @ Phillies 4**	**3**	**1**	**1**	**1**	**50**
Sept 17	**177**	**Cubs 5 @ Giants 2**	**4**	**3**	**2**	**4**	**51, 52**
Sept 19	**178**	**Cubs 5 @ Braves 4**	**4**	**1**	**0**	**1**	**0**
Sept 20	179	Cubs 2 @ Braves 3	3	1	0	1	0
Sept 22	**182**	**Cubs 6 @ Braves 2**	**4**	**2**	**1**	**3**	**53**
Sept 26	**185**	**Cubs 7 vs. Reds 5**	**4**	**2**	**1**	**3**	**54**
Sept 27	**189**	**Cubs 13 vs. Reds 8**	**4**	**2**	**2**	**4**	**55, 56**
Sept 28	**191**	**Cubs 13 vs. Reds 11**	**3**	**2**	**0**	**2**	**0**

That was certainly the way it looked. In the first game, the Cubs fought back from a 5–0 deficit to tie the game and send it into extra innings. Pitching in relief, Sheriff Blake hurt his back fielding a ground ball, and the Cardinals won the grueling contest in twenty innings, 8–7. The next day, before a Ladies' Day crowd of more than forty thousand, Riggs Stephenson played his first full game since being injured three weeks before and knocked in the winning run as the Cubs won, 9–8. When Chicago won the next day, 16–4, behind Hack Wilson's two home runs, they led by five and a half games with only a month left in the season.

But in winning the battle against the Cardinals, the Cubs had lost the war. The pitching staff was thin. Guy Bush's ERA had soared to more than six runs a game, Root's arm was hanging on by a thread, and Blake's back injury left the Cubs short. All of a sudden, Malone was the only dependable pitcher McCarthy had.

For the rest of the year, the Cubs won only seven games, while the Cardinals surged into first place, winning ten of twelve. By September 14, the first-place Cubs had turned into the third-place Cubs.

A week later, William Wrigley gave a wide-ranging interview. On the one hand, he blamed "ill luck for the Cubs demise." On the other hand, when asked if McCarthy would return, Wrigley gave his manager the kiss of death when he said, "I am a great admirer of McCarthy [but] I will not say McCarthy will be manager next year." Then he backed away, adding that the decision was Veeck's to make.

That sent John Keys of the *Chicago Daily News* scurrying to Veeck, who wisely said, "I'm taking the same position as Mr. Wrigley." In reality, the two men may as well have sat McCarthy with his back to the door at a meeting of Chicago gangsters. They had already made their decision and were simply waiting to carry it out.

Wrigley had always been far more enamored of Rogers Hornsby, a real live major leaguer, than simple Joe McCarthy. After Hornsby was hurt, Wrigley had spent a

The 1929 National League champion Cubs pose for their team picture at the edge of Wrigley Field's famed brick wall. Note the laughter of catcher Gabby Hartnett (front row, left) and first baseman Charlie Grimm (front row, next to Hartnett).

1931

LEADERS OF TEAMS WHICH CLASH IN FIRST GAME OF WORLD SERIES AT CHICAGO TOMORROW

Cub manager Joe McCarthy was matched in his first World Series against Philadelphia Athletics manager Connie Mack, who was making his sixth trip to the Fall Classic. Mack's 1929 Athletics proved themselves to be one of baseball's greatest teams by beating the heavy-hitting Cubs decisively in five games.

great deal of time with his hero, soaking up information from the great man himself. Blunt as usual, Hornsby called McCarthy on every error Hornsby believed the manager had made dating back to the 1929 World Series as he constantly reminded the owner that McCarthy had sent the wrong man to scout the A's and then used the wrong pitching strategy. Wrigley kept nodding his head in agreement, and the *Daily News* later reported that on September 12 Veeck met with Hornsby, not McCarthy, seeking his advice on how the Cubs might halt their slide and how they could be better in 1931.

On September 22, although the Cubs were still mathematically alive in the pennant race, Wrigley pulled the trigger, announcing that Rogers Hornsby would manage the Cubs in 1931.

"I have had my heart set on winning a World Series," said Wrigley. "McCarthy was given free rein in the buying of players, and I believe we have a great team. McCarthy has had five years to prove this, so I don't think there is

anything unusual about not engaging him after a stretch such as that." He then went on to trash McCarthy, again bringing up the use of Joe Tinker as a scout. He blamed McCarthy for the players' popularity and resulting lack of fire, as well as for the lack of discipline that led to the "elaborate scale" at which the players lived while on the road; then he simultaneously blasted McCarthy for his "Czarlike attitude."

McCarthy didn't wait around. With four games left in the season, he "resigned," and Hornsby took over. The Yankees soon hired him, and in New York McCarthy would win eight pennants and six world championships in fourteen seasons.

Although McCarthy may not have been the best strategic manager in Cubs history, he nevertheless deserves credit for taking a last-place team and building a juggernaut, endowing the franchise with a healthy portion of the personality it retains to this day as an offensive force. Under McCarthy, the Cubs nearly became a dynasty, and perhaps should have become one. He was fired for no reason other than the fact that the Cubs fell short in both 1929 and 1930 and Wrigley, after five years and like virtually every baseball owner at one time or another, suddenly decided he knew more about baseball than his manager. If one wishes to chart the eventual demise of the franchise, dumping McCarthy deserves consideration as the starting point.

Although Hornsby made a lot of noise about making big trades to put the Cubs over the top, the club was relatively quiet in the offseason apart from picking up some spare parts for the pitching staff. All things being equal, if the healthy Cubs, particularly Wilson, could even approach their 1930 standard and the unhealthy Cubs, especially Hornsby, bounced back, the 1931 Cubs seemed likely to satisfy Wrigley's desire.

None of those things happened. After the offensive explosion in 1929 and 1930, major league baseball decided to doctor the baseball. With a distinctly softer ball in 1931, it was impossible for Wilson to approach his 1930 performance and impossible for Hornsby to bounce back. And once again, the Cubs were hit by injuries, the worst of which took place in mid-July when Riggs Stephenson broke his ankle.

By then, the season was already over. Hornsby was

1926   [136]

THE CUBS

showing his age. Although he hit .331, he appeared in only one hundred games. And Hack Wilson was showing his decay. A combination of the new baseball and the demon rum caused his average to plummet to .261 with only sixty-one RBIs.

Few players in team history have fallen farther, faster. After his remarkable performance in 1930, Wilson found every barroom door in Chicago open to him. He went through most of them, ordered a round, and was even spotted in the company of gangster Al Capone. He showed up at spring training out of shape, and then deteriorated.

Hornsby was not sympathetic. He treated his own body like a temple, not even attending motion pictures for fear of the effect it might have on his eyes. When Wilson got off to a slow start, Hornsby eventually benched him, which just gave Wilson another excuse to stay out a little bit later.

The Cubs were never in the race, and by late August they had given up. Wilson, who wasn't even trying to disguise his drinking, started taking particular delight in spewing venom Hornsby's way. As one writer delicately put it, Wilson let Hornsby and other Cubs officials know

that they could go "where there are no snowballs." In late August, when he showed up at the ballpark drunk for what was later reported as the fifth or sixth time that season, Hornsby wanted to suspend him, but Wilson turned maudlin and found the one soft spot in Hornsby's heart, and the manager backed off.

But another incident during a train trip in early September sealed his fate. This time Wilson made the mistake of taking pitcher Pat Malone along for the ride. While a sotted Wilson threw more snowballs, this time making the press his target, Malone took his side and punched out two writers.

That was it. On September 6, Wilson, who one *Tribune* reporter described as the "Principal in the act entitled 'From Home Run King to Exile in One Season,'" was sus-

(left to right) William Wrigley Jr., Joe McCarthy, and Bill Veeck Sr. shake hands in the Cubs dugout prior to the start of the 1929 World Series. Each had a reason to smile as the team won its eleventh National League championship and established a home attendance record of 1,485,166, a figure that stood until 1969.

LIGHTS OUT

The longer P.K. Wrigley owned the Cubs, the more the press liked to tell a story about his father, one they told so often that no one ever bothered to check its veracity. After William Wrigley was felled by the heart attack and stroke, he knew his time was running out. Depending upon who was doing the retelling, from his deathbed Wrigley told his son either, "Whatever you do, don't sell the Cubs," or, "Take care of the Cubs"—or words to that effect.

No matter what happened and no matter how much criticism he encountered, P.K. would explain, that was the reason why he would grimly hold on to his father's team. "The club and the park stand as memorials to my father. I will never dispose of my holdings in the club as long as the chewing gum business remains profitable enough to retain it." For better or worse—mostly worse—he fulfilled the promise, holding on to the Cubs until he too passed from this world.

"Smilin' Stan" Hack was both one of the most beloved players of his era and one of the most consistent offensive performers in Cub history. Of the sixteen career offensive categories listed in the Cubs' media guide, Hack ranks in the top ten in nine categories, including leading the pack with 1,092 walks. Upon his retirement in 1947, he ranked second only to Cap Anson with 7,278 at-bats for the Cubs.

Yet, in all likelihood, William Wrigley never passed on such deathbed instructions. The story didn't appear in print until years after William Wrigley's death, when the press and Cubs fans began to express their dissatisfaction with the reign of his son. Besides, when William Wrigley died, his physician, Dr. George Goodrich, said that from the time of Wrigley's initial attack, "until his death, he had medical attention twenty-four hours a day." The club owner "was in a semiconscious condition most of the time since then. . . . rational at times, but for brief intervals. He could be roused for a minute or so, say a word or two, and then would sink back into unconsciousness." Even if William Wrigley did tell his son to take care of the Cubs and never sell them, he unfortunately forgot to add the admonition to win a World Series while doing so. William Wrigley wanted to win, but apparently never passed that desire along to his son. To P.K. Wrigley, a winning team wasn't part of the memorial.

For the time being, however, P.K. Wrigley was just a name on the books. Veeck remained club president, Hornsby was the manager, and after a period of mourning it was business as usual. It took some time before P.K.'s smothering influence would take hold. In the meantime, not much was expected from the Cubs. Only three of sixty-seven baseball writers who participated in a preseason poll picked the Cubs to win the flag, but in reality they were still one of the better teams in the National League.

Then a few things happened that made the Cubs even better. Foremost among them was the emergence of pitcher Lon Warneke.

He came from absolutely nowhere. In 1929 the Cubs purchased the nineteen-year-old pitcher from Alexandria of the Cotton States League for $100. They may have overpaid for him, for over two seasons the Arkansas native had gone only 22–24 in the low minors. In 1930 the Cubs sent him to Reading in the International League, and Warneke was terrible, winning only nine games with an ERA of 6.93.

A true backwoodsman who liked to hunt, fish, and play the ukulele, Warneke was a self-described hillbilly whom sportswriters dubbed "the Arkansas Hummingbird," both for his musical talent and for what one writer called "his sizzling fast and darting form of delivery." But for much of his baseball career he'd been sickly and had fought to stay healthy as much as he did to throw strikes. In the offsea-

son before the 1932 season, however, the mysterious maladies that had afflicted him finally faded. Warneke was suddenly healthy and strong. He already had a good curveball and fine control, and now his fastball had new life. He added at least five miles per hour to the pitch, which now sailed at the top of the zone and sank when Warneke threw the ball low. It was just that simple. All of a sudden he had some weapons. He got Grimm's attention during spring training, made the starting rotation, and was, without question, the best pitcher in the National League in 1932.

The Cubs jumped off to a quick start, winning seventeen of their first twenty-three, then stumbled after Kiki Cuyler broke his foot, an injury that was becoming something of a Cub tradition. But it didn't matter much. The Cardinals, after winning the world championship, slumped across the board. Although Burleigh Grimes didn't pitch that well for the Cubs, the Cardinals missed having him on the mound every fourth day.

No other team in the NL stood out. Cincinnati was awful, but there was little difference between the other seven clubs in the league. In a race marked by mediocrity, Warneke made the Cubs shine.

These were the Cubs, however, and something always seemed to go wrong. Shortstop Billy Jurges, like several other Cub players, kept an apartment at the Hotel Carlos near Wrigley Field. So did a young chorus girl name Violet Valli, who had taken a shine to Jurges during his rookie year in 1931 and had more or less been keeping company with the young shortstop ever since, often with a bottle of gin to complete the threesome. Kiki Cuyler apparently got wind of what was going on. A teetotaler, Cuyler reamed Jurges out and told him to get rid of Valli, who he feared was ruining the young shortstop's career and would railroad him into a marriage he'd later regret.

When Jurges broke things off, Valli was distraught. On July 6, she got drunk and wrote a suicide note addressed to her brother that read, "Life without Billy isn't worth living, but why should I leave this world alone? I'm going to take Billy with me."

That's exactly what she tried to do, confronting Jurges in his room. They argued, and she shot him twice with a small .25 caliber pistol, one bullet striking him in the side and the other in his rear end. Jurges then wrestled her for the gun and in the process was shot again, suffering a superficial wound in the hand, while Valli was struck in the wrist. Fortunately, neither was seriously hurt.

The story was big news in Chicago for a few days, but Jurges refused to press charges. Valli, thrilled with the attention, escaped scot-free and cashed in on her notoriety, taking her act to vaudeville. Jurges spent a few weeks healing and then returned to active duty.

The incident inadvertently sparked a series of events that helped the Cubs reach the World Series. In early July, the Cubs, Braves, and Pirates began to break away from the pack, but after Jurges's injury, the Cubs stalled. The Braves fell back as the Pirates forged ahead and appeared to take command of the race. Woody English filled in for Jurges at shortstop, and rookie Stan Hack manned third, but Hack wasn't hitting, and when Jurges returned he wasn't quite the same player as before.

On July 23, the Pirates beat the Cubs for the seventh consecutive time and opened up a four-and-a-half-game lead. Hornsby, ever blunt, told Veeck the Cubs didn't have it. Had Wrigley been alive, Veeck would have agreed, but he no longer had the owner looking over his shoulder and was becoming his own man. He looked around at the

National League and then decided the Cubs had as good a chance as anyone. If anybody didn't have it, thought Veeck, it was Hornsby and his destructive attitude. By giving up on the season, he was setting a bad example for the younger players, while veterans like Cuyler, who weren't intimidated, tuned him out. Furthermore, Hornsby had compromised his own authority. For all his superior airs, Hornsby had one vice, gambling, and although hitting .400 was a good average at the plate, a similar average at the racetrack or the card table was disastrous. To cover his losses, Hornsby had borrowed money from members of his own team. It was awkward to manage someone he owed thousands of dollars.

At the same time, Hornsby was just about through as a player. He'd had only one great year in a Cub uniform, in 1929, and had never really recovered from his broken foot;

At 5:37 P.M. on September 28, 1938, the sun had already set in Chicago and the Cubs were tied with the Pirates 5–5 in the bottom of the ninth inning when Gabby Hartnett hit the most famous home run in franchise history in a game that virtually assured the Cubs of the National League title. Flash bulbs and flash powder were necessary for photographers to capture the conclusion of Hartnett's home run trot.

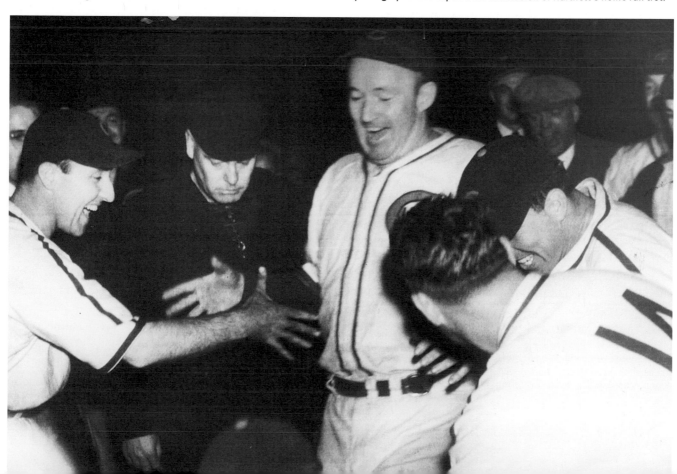

now he was out of shape, old before his time at age thirty-six. He refused to admit it and stubbornly insisted on putting himself in the lineup every once in a while, demonstrating that he could neither hit nor field nor act in the best interests of the ball club.

Veeck spent most of July traveling with the team and assessing the situation. Finally, on August 2, as the Cubs, with a record of 53–46, trailed Pittsburgh by five games, Veeck asked Wrigley if he could get rid of Hornsby. P.K. didn't care—he hardly knew who Hornsby was and admitted at the time, "I don't know much about baseball." Veeck then fired Hornsby as manager and released him as a player. At the press conference announcing the move, Veeck was asked if the two men had quarreled, and he indicated that they had not. He turned to Hornsby for approval and asked, "Right, Rog?"

Blunt as always, Hornsby chimed in and said, "Only big differences of opinion about the ball club and the way it should be handled." Hornsby went home to St. Louis, and Veeck named first baseman Charlie Grimm the Cubs new player-manager.

The man they called "Jolly Cholly" was the perfect antidote to Hornsby, and his opposite in almost every way. Grimm was as easygoing and tactful as Hornsby was driven and curt. The players approved of the move and immediately relaxed. Since first serving as Rabbit Maranville's running partner, Grimm had settled into his role on the club as a slick-fielding first baseman with little power who nonetheless was considered a valuable offensive performer, not unlike the Cub first baseman of the 1990s, Mark Grace. As a manager, Grimm wasn't a dictator and didn't pretend to have all the answers. In a popular move, Grimm named Woody English team captain, then rolled the ball out on the field and let the boys play.

The Cubs made one more move that had its roots in the bad aim and broken heart of Violet Valli. Since being shot, Billy Jurges simply wasn't getting it done at shortstop, and the Cubs needed some help at the position. On August 5, they picked up former Yankee shortstop Mark

The 1932 Cubs celebrate clinching the pennant after beating the Pirates 5–2 at Wrigley Field on September 20. President Bill Veeck Sr. stands in street clothes to the right of winning pitcher Guy Bush, who shakes the hand of player-manager Charlie Grimm.

Koenig, who after four years as a regular in New York had been traded to Detroit and then sent to the Pacific Coast League.

Koenig gave the Cubs way more than they had any right to expect. Not only was his defense superb, but for the next two months Koenig, who had never been known for his hitting, played the best baseball of his career, batting a robust .353 and leading the Cubs in slugging percentage.

The moves coincided with a slide by Pittsburgh, and the Cubs quickly caught up. By August 11, when the Cubs went into Pittsburgh, they trailed the Pirates by only half a game. The Cubs were winning, but that didn't mean they were without worry. In recent days, reports had surfaced that Guy Bush was $38,000 in arrears to a Chicago bookmaker and had openly consorted with what one Chicago newspaper referred to as "two ladies known as blondes" at a racetrack, a report that got the attention of not only baseball commissioner Kenesaw Mountain Landis but Mrs. Guy Bush. Neither was very happy.

While Mrs. Bush dealt with Mr. Bush privately, Landis met the team in Pittsburgh. Since the Black Sox scandal, problems with gamblers were no longer acceptable in major league baseball. Landis started calling players in on the carpet and wanted some answers. For a brief period of time, it appeared as if the scandal would blow the Cubs apart.

Instead, if anything, the threat of a scandal pulled the team even closer together. They ran past the Pirates and right into first place.

But Landis wasn't done with them. He followed the Cubs to St. Louis and kept up the pressure, also talking with Rogers Hornsby. In the end, although Landis didn't exactly exonerate any of the Cubs players, neither did he find any evidence to support the allegations that Bush or any other Cub was in debt to gamblers. He did learn, however, that Rogers Hornsby had been in debt to Bush, Pat Malone, Woody English, coach Charlie O'Leary, and pitcher Bob Smith.

Meanwhile, keyed by Koenig and a series of late-inning rallies, the relieved Cubs embarked on a long winning streak. Chicago got pennant fever. Everyone was playing well as even Burleigh Grimes, winless since June, picked up a victory. The Cubs won fourteen straight before pitcher Dizzy Dean of St. Louis snapped the skein with a 3–0 shutout on September 3.

But there was no stopping Chicago. The Cubs clinched the pennant on September 21, then cruised to the finish as Grimm allowed the Cubs to fool around the last week and play out of position. In the American League, Joe McCarthy led the Yankees on an unimpeded drive to the pennant: New York, behind Ruth and Lou Gehrig, won 107 games to win the pennant by 13 games. To no one's surprise, the Yankees were installed as big favorites in the World Series, and McCarthy looked forward to gaining some retribution against his old club.

Of course, no one remembers much of that today. Just as the performance of Howard Ehmke in game one and the Cubs' collapse in game four overshadowed the rest of the 1929 World Series, one event in game three would similarly overshadow the 1932 Fall Classic.

By then, for all intents and purposes, the World Series was already over. The first game was played in New York, and for three and a half innings Cubs fans had cause to dream.

Cubs rookie second baseman Billy Herman started the Series with a leadoff single, and then English followed with another hit to right. Babe Ruth came in on the ball, but the Bambino was getting old and more and more often played that way, if not at the plate, then certainly in the field.

The ball got past him and rolled to the bleachers. Herman scored, English went to third, and then scored himself when Stephenson singled. The Yankees hadn't come to bat, and the Cubs led 2–0.

But that was the problem. Sooner or later, the Yankees had to come to bat. Guy Bush got through the order unscathed once, but the Yankees had seen enough, and when they faced Bush a second time the result was not quite so clean for Chicago. "I just went wild and got beat," Bush would say later. "There ain't no reasons for it."

Actually there were, because after the game Bush stated the obvious. "All we've got to do," he said, "is stop two men—Ruth and Gehrig."

Truer words were never spoken. Of course, Yankee opponents had been trying to do that for years with little success, and Bush would prove no more successful than anyone else.

Unfortunately, Bush's control deserted him. Combs led off the fourth by working a walk, then Ruth singled, and *boom*, Gehrig homered—the Yankees went from being down 2–0 to up 3–2 in about five minutes. In the sixth, Bush started the inning by walking Joe Sewell, Ruth, and Gehrig, and the Yankees went on to score five times to put the game away. The two sluggers had gone a combined 3-for-7 with three walks, six runs scored, and three RBIs. The Cubs lost, 12–6.

In game two, Cubs fans were happy for a half-inning. Herman again led off the game with a hit—this time a double—and he later scored on a fly ball to put the Cubs ahead. Now all Lon Warneke had to do was stop Ruth and Gehrig.

He couldn't. Warneke started off the first inning by walking the first two hitters he faced before striking out Ruth, only to have Gehrig single home New York's first run; soon Warneke had given up two and the Cubs had fallen behind. New York never trailed again as this time Ruth and Gehrig went 4-for-7 with three runs scored and one RBI in the tidy 5–2 win. There was, noted the *Daily News*, "little hilarity" among the Cubs on the train ride back to Chicago, while the Yankees, in contrast, "were a happy, hilarious gang of marauding baseball spirits. Everyone got on the train for Chicago knowing the Series was all but over."

Still, Cubs fans were optimistic. Some had been camping outside the bleachers for more than a week waiting to purchase tickets, and fans were beginning to notice that it had been an awful long time—twenty-four years—since the Cubs had been world champions. Perhaps they were overdue.

What followed was one of the most memorable games in Series history. Even though the Cubs lost, those who had waited a week for tickets did not do so in vain. They would see history that day.

Batting first in Wrigley Field, the Yankees didn't dispense with any pleasantries. They immediately introduced Charlie Root to the wisdom earlier expressed by Guy Bush. Earle Combs led off with a ground ball, and Billy Jurges threw the ball over Grimm's head, putting him on first. Then Joe Sewell walked, bringing up Ruth.

He liked Wrigley Field. He particularly liked the temporary bleachers in right-center set up on Sheffield Avenue.

In six seasons with the Cubs, right-handed pitcher Lon Warneke won twenty or more games three times and starred in a losing cause in the 1935 World Series, winning two games against the Detroit Tigers and their ace, Schoolboy Rowe.

Ruth hit the first pitch he saw into them for a home run. The Yankees led 3–0, and Cubs fans who had been waiting outside the bleachers for a week began to wonder why they had gone to the trouble.

This time, however, the Cubs fought back. Herman led off the bottom of the inning with a walk, and Cuyler doubled him home. Gehrig got the run back with a home run of his own in the third, but the Cubs came back again. Cuyler homered, and the Cubs scored a second run in the inning on Grimm's double. When Jurges doubled to lead off the fourth and later scored on Woody English's infield hit, the score was tied.

The Cubs, for once, were showing some fire, and when Ruth stepped up to the plate in what Ed Burns of the *Tribune* called "the sad fifth," he noted that "the Cubs were feeling pretty pert." They let Ruth have it.

CUBS ENSHRINED IN
THE NATIONAL BASEBALL HALL OF FAME

PLAYER	CUBS CAREER	PLAYER	CUBS CAREER
Pete Alexander	1918–26	Rogers Hornsby	1929–32
Cap Anson	1876–97	Monte Irvin	1956
Richie Ashburn	1960–61	Ferguson Jenkins	1966–73, 1982–83
Ernie Banks	1953–71	George Kelly	1930
Roger Bresnahan	1900, 1913–15	King Kelly	1880–86
Lou Brock	1961–64	Ralph Kiner	1953–54
Mordecai Brown	1904–12, 1916	Chuck Klein	1934–36
Frank Chance	1898–1912	Tony Lazzeri	1938
John Clarkson	1884–87	Fred Lindstrom	1935
Kiki Cuyler	1928–35	Rabbit Maranville	1925
Dizzy Dean	1938–41	Robin Roberts	1966
Hugh Duffy	1888–89	Ryne Sandberg	1982–94, 1996–97
Dennis Eckersley	1984–86	Al Spalding	1876–78
Johnny Evers	1902–13	Joe Tinker	1902–12, 1916
Jimmie Foxx	1942, 1944	Rube Waddell	1901
Clark Griffith	1893–1900	Hoyt Wilhelm	1970
Burleigh Grimes	1932–33	Billy Williams	1959–74
Gabby Hartnett	1922–40	Hack Wilson	1926–31
Billy Herman	1931–41		

All Series long, the two clubs had been sniping back and forth at each other. The Yankees, led by Ruth, were using profane language to accuse Chicago of being cheapskates, for the Cubs had voted Mark Koenig only a partial share of World Series money. After all, despite his performance, he had played just over thirty games. The Cubs weren't feeling particularly generous. They had also voted not to give Rogers Hornsby, who had managed the Cubs for two-thirds of the season, a single penny.

In response, the Cubs went after Ruth. The Babe was known to have rabbit ears, particularly when harassed with catcalls that questioned his racial history or compared him to an ape, which was precisely what the Cubs did. In game three, Ruth and the Cubs had kept it up all game long.

When Ruth stepped in to lead off the fifth, he was again greeted with racially charged epithets. Grimm and pitcher Bob Smith stood on the dugout steps and waved their fingers at Ruth, putting the "whammy" on him. Ruth laughed it off and dismissively waved his hand back at the Cubs.

He then watched Root's pitch fly by for strike one, which Ruth acknowledged by waving one finger at the Cub bench. When another strike passed, Ruth again kept his bat on his shoulder, and then waved two fingers in the air.

On this much everyone agrees. What happened on the next pitch became the stuff of legend. Root threw again, and as Edward Burns wrote:

> Mr. Ruth smacked the ball right on the nose and it traveled ever so fast. You know that big flagpole just the right of the scoreboard beyond center field? Well that's 436 feet from home plate. Ruth's drive went past that flag pole and hit the box office at Sheffield and Waveland Avenue.
>
> Ruth resumed his oratory the minute he threw down the bat. He bellowed every foot of the way around the bases, accompanying derisive roarings with wild and eloquent gesticulations. George Herman Ruth always enjoys a home run under any circumstances but it is doubtful if he ever cooked one that gave him more satisfaction . . .

The blast gave New York a 5–4 lead. Then, on the next pitch, Gehrig blasted a home run and that was it. The Cubs were finished, and they knew it, even dropping two rou-

tine pop-ups in the ninth inning as the Yanks went on to win, 7–5.

Burns's report, like virtually every other written account of the game, is notable for what it does not include. There was no mention of any "called shot." In fact, no one on either the Cubs or the Yankees, including Ruth and Root, made any mention at the time of such an occurrence.

Only one person did, baseball writer Joe Williams of the *New York Telegram*, sort of. In his game story, he wrote, "Ruth pointed to center and punched a screaming liner to the spot where no ball had been hit before." Some anonymous headline writer, however, deserves credit for the phrase we remember today. The story was headlined: "Ruth Calls Shot as He Puts Homer No. 2 in Side Pocket." The *Telegram* was part of the Scripps Howard Syndicate, and Williams's story got play nationwide. The "called shot" soon became a cherished part of baseball lore—and an ever more controversial tale over the years as baseball

Lon Warneke not only pitched for the Cubs and Cardinals but more than lived up to his nickname of "the Arkansas Hummingbird" while performing country music in the offseason.

writers and historians debated the story's authenticity, bending over backwards to find proof of its existence.

Neither Gabby Hartnett nor Charlie Root, the two players closest to Ruth at the time and the most likely to notice his gesture, ever gave credence to the story, and both got sick of talking about it. Ruth didn't even say he called his shot until later in his life, when he realized that the story was good for his growing legend and that it was futile to deny it anyway. After all, George Washington probably hadn't chopped down a cherry tree or thrown a silver dollar across the Delaware River either, and nobody cared.

In 1999, however, the question, finally, was answered forever. A fan named Harold Warp had attended the game—the only major league game he ever saw—and brought along his new 16 mm movie camera. He happened to film Ruth's at-bat, and when the footage came to light the evidence was irrefutable: Ruth clearly didn't point to center field, he merely gestured toward the Cub bench. The "called shot" never happened.

The next day Root was unapologetic. "If I had to do it again," he said, "I'd pitch the same way." He claimed the pitch to Ruth was a changeup, low and away, but admitted

he was completely at a loss as to how to pitch to both Ruth and Gehrig, who had actually out-hit Ruth thus far during the Series. "You can't guess 'em. You fool them on one, and the next thing you know they'll hit the same ball over the fence." Five times already in the Series, they had done exactly that.

The Yankees didn't play the Cubs in game four so much as they played with the Cubs. Chicago jumped out to an early 4–1 lead, only to watch helplessly as the Yankees inexorably drew them close, then blew them away with a four-run seventh. According to the *Tribune*, this spectacle inspired Cubs fans to "engage in a raspberry serenade the like of which had not been accorded the home team in Wrigley Field in these many seasons." The Cubs deserved it. New York romped to a 13–6 win and swept the Series.

Afterwards, the Cubs had the alibis all ready. Bush claimed that two weeks before the Series he had torn the

---

Elwood "Woody" English was a superb defensive shortstop on three Cub pennant winners. Despite his lack of power, English batted a solid .291 in ten seasons in Chicago. His best year was 1930, when he combined 214 hits with 100 walks.

nail off the index finger of his pitching hand and hadn't been able to grip the ball properly. Warneke, the Cubs claimed, hurt his arm during his first appearance in the Series. Woody English, in a ghostwritten column in the *Daily News*, put it more bluntly. "The entire series had one feature," he wrote, "and that was the lack of strategy to win the games."

No kidding. By any estimation, the Cubs were fortunate to reach the World Series at all, having taken advantage of a year in which no National League team stood out and no National League team could have matched up against the Yankees. One thing was clear. While the Cubs perhaps should have become a dynasty under McCarthy, the fact was that the Yankees had.

Veeck made an enormous mistake after the Series. Despite all evidence to the contrary, he somehow thought the Cubs were, in fact, nearly the equal of the Yankees, and just a player or two away from finishing the season in celebration rather than dismay. In reality, the Cubs were in transition: the guts of the club—Cuyler, Stephenson, Grimm, and Hartnett—were all past thirty.

On November 30, Veeck cut a deal. Outfielder Babe Herman, who had hit .381 and .393 for Brooklyn in Ebbets Field during the overtly offensive seasons of 1929 and 1930, had since moved on to Cincinnati. His production dropped, and despite Herman's presence, the Reds had finished last in 1932. When Veeck came calling, they were more than willing to make a deal.

Herman, who was considered something of an eccentric, was a poor fielder and an erratic base runner. In one overstated example, while with Brooklyn he was once credited with "tripling into a double play." In fact, with the bases loaded, Herman had hit a line drive to right field that appeared as if it might be caught, causing the base runners to hesitate. When it fell untouched and Herman kept running, confusion reigned. Herman, who had safely slid into second, went on to third after the throw went home, only to find it already occupied by not one but two other runners. It wasn't entirely his fault, but Herman's reputation was secure.

Veeck sent the Reds four players—pitcher Bob Smith, outfielders Johnny Moore and Lance Richbourg, and catcher Rollie Helmsley—plus a sizable amount of cash for Herman. They expected a savior; as one anonymous

"Jolly Cholly" Grimm led the Cubs to four pennants as manager, two of those times (1932, 1935) while also serving as a slick-fielding starting first baseman. His 1,739 wins as manager are second only to the 2,274 won by Cap Anson.

Chicago columnist opined, with Herman, if the World Series was played again, "I'd like to see this bunch against the American League champions." Unfortunately, Herman was the wrong Babe.

Spring training was notable only for the earthquake that rattled southern California on March 10, shaking up both the Cubs on Catalina and the White Sox, who trained in Pasadena. For a while, Chicagoans wondered if they'd lost the Cubs as rumors spread that Catalina had been engulfed by an enormous tidal wave, sweeping the team out to sea.

There had been no such wave, but nevertheless the Cubs soon discovered they were in over their heads. In late March, the club suffered its annual injury to a key lower

NEVERLAND

BY RICHARD A. JOHNSON

We are all failures—at least all the best of us are.

—J. M. BARRIE

I'd play for half my salary if I could hit in this dump [Wrigley Field] all the time.

—GEORGE HERMAN "BABE" RUTH

God gave us memory so that we might have roses in December.

—J. M. BARRIE

Have you heard mention of 1908 on the North Side lately? Or possibly the umpteenth recitation of the alleged billy goat curse or the fate of poor old Steve Bartman?

For those of us who have delighted in the Cubs' rich history and relished visits to the friendly confines, isn't Wrigley Field enough? The cover of the Cubs' 1946 scorecard says it all in three words printed in bold type just below a stylized pennant proclaiming their 1945 National League title: "Courtesy, Comfort, Beauty." Such is the credo of a ballyard that is nothing less than baseball's secret garden: same as it ever was and pretty near damn perfect.

Much has and will be made of the century that has passed since the Cubs' last world championship. Nobody is left who remembers the Peerless Leader and his 1908 team of Tinker, Evers, Chance, Steinfeldt, Reulbach, and Mordecai Peter Centennial Brown. They live in sepia-tinted pho-

Workers erect the steel structure for the Wrigley Field scoreboard on August 18, 1937.

Workers build the new bleachers at Wrigley Field, September 1, 1937.

tographs, brittle scrapbooks, and the second- and third-hand memories of fans who barely remember Andy Pafko and the '45 pennant winners, much less a dynasty that captured four championships and two World Series in five seasons from 1906 to 1910.

What fans do remember and hold dear about this team is a park that is 50 percent museum, 25 percent neighborhood tavern, and 25 percent the backyard where you once played Wiffle ball and hit the bat. The only difference being the many backyards that have longer foul lines.

I'd pitched several hundred games at Wrigley Field before I'd actually set foot on the North Side, much less in "the Land of Lincoln."

You see, after having seen Wrigley Field on several memorable broadcasts on the NBC *Game of the Week* in the late sixties, I instantly fell in love with the ivy-covered bricks and the Durocher-led team that spawned the Bleacher Bums and a thousand stories of 1969's Wudda, Cudda, Shudda Cubs.

The back stoop of our house in Worcester, Massachusetts, formed the perfect backstop for a virtual Wrigley Field. Behind me was a chain-link fence covered with an ivy- and bramble-covered lattice. At a distance of twenty-five feet, I'd pretend to face the likes of Mays, McCovey, Kranepool, Agee, Clendenon, and the rest of the National

Cub mascot Paul Dominick strikes a pose at Wrigley Field during the Cubs' pennant-winning season of 1935.

Workers plant the ivy at Wrigley Field in 1937.

Cubs outfielder Augie Galan poses by his car in the players' lot outside Wrigley Field in the late 1930s.

League while pitching tennis balls to a tape-covered target. Called strikes landed between the wooden steps, and gopher balls invariably came as the result of nailing the narrow lip of the soon-to-be-splintered middle step. I especially relished the chance to launch myself against the fence while attempting a game-saving catch and considered the torn T-shirts and pant legs that resulted from these efforts a badge of honor.

The only missing elements were an elevated track, organ music, fellow pitcher Dick Selma leading the cheers from the bullpen, and a prevailing thirty-five-mile-per-hour wind. On more than one occasion, I exclaimed a hearty "Hey-hey" while displaying a full glove to a nonexistent umpire.

In 1978 I finally had my chance to visit the park with which I felt so familiar. While driving back east from graduate studies in Denver, I stopped at a friend's house in Peo-

ria after a nonstop all-night drive. While glancing at the sports page, I saw that the Cubs had a game the next afternoon. Not really knowing how far I'd have to drive, I arose early the next morning and sped north, took a left when I spotted the lake, and arrived at the park about a half-hour before game time.

The details of the game are hazy save for the fact that Bruce Sutter had Willie Stargell flailing at several split-finger fastballs while saving the game for Donnie Moore with a strikeout against the mighty Pittsburgh Pirates' "Lumber Company."

For my part, I spent the better part of three hours utterly enchanted by the whole experience. All too often such a pilgrimage is a total letdown—the circus with scary clowns, sad animals, and stale popcorn. Not only was Wrigley Field much bigger than I'd imagined, but it seemed to exist in a time warp, like the set of a benign episode of *The*

"Good afternoon, thank you for calling the Chicago Cubs. How may I help you?" The Cub ticket office on March 9, 1937.

Opening day at Wrigley, 1937 (opposite). Note the old scoreboard with the two Wrigley chewing gum figures (Double-Mint) on the top as well as the Baby Ruth billboard perched atop a neighboring rooftop. Before the end of the season the Cubs had constructed the bleachers and scoreboard that are now the architectural signature of the park.

CHICAGO CUBS

ADIES DAY TICKET

e are happy to welcome you to Wrigley Field as our
est, subject to the conditions on the back of this ticket.

t A Reminder—You can buy a comfortable, reserved box
t for only $1.25 at the exchange booth inside the park.

CHICAGO NATIONAL LEAGUE BALL CLUB

Ladies' Day was a staple of the Wrigley Field experience for decades.

A view from the grandstand on opening day 1937.

[155]   1938

Untouchables or *The Twilight Zone* where that signpost up ahead said 368 feet to the power alley. Even the Andy Frain ushers seemed like characters from the ballroom scene in *The Shining*.

As I left the park that afternoon, I'd remembered being told that the eccentric team owner, the late Philip K. Wrigley, allegedly kept a small apartment tucked away inside Wrigley Field where he reportedly displayed masterpieces by artists such as Picasso and Miro. As I brushed a hot dog wrapper off my heel and headed toward the exit, I looked for a door in the wall and realized that Wrigley bunked in nothing less than Chicago's biggest and best museum.

The evolution of Wrigley Field was masterfully captured by the photography of Francis Burke and George Brace, and their images accompany this essay. And while there have been a few changes made to the park, over nearly a century the essence of the Wrigley experience remains virtually unchanged since the days when it was known as Weeghman Park and featured the Chicago Whales of the Federal League.

Wrigley Field is best observed from the perspective of a sun-baked bleacher seat, especially after tipping a few cold Old Styles, when it isn't hard to imagine Hack Wilson corralling a liner, Ron Santo clicking his heels, or Pat Pieper shouting today's lineup through a megaphone on an afternoon that lasts as long as our memories.

Photographer George Brace listed this photo from the 1930s as simply "Ciggy Girl/Wrigley Field" in his files. Much of the charm of the park lay in the attention paid to concessions and creature comforts.

RICHARD A. JOHNSON is curator of the Sports Museum in Boston and the author or coauthor of seventeen books, including *Red Sox Century*, *Yankees Century*, and *The Dodgers: 125 Years of Dodger Baseball* (all with Glenn Stout).

The neighborhood of baseball, sans lights, c. 1938. The elevated tracks behind the center-field bleachers still bring riders to Wrigley Field.

extremity, as Cuyler was afflicted again, this time breaking his ankle. And despite the fact that Warneke pitched the Cubs to a 3–0 victory on opening day over Dizzy Dean and the Cardinals, the Cubs never got untracked in 1933. Babe Herman wasn't a total bust, but neither did he bust down the fences: he would hit only .289 with sixteen home runs for the season. The Cubs simply plodded along, never losing too many in a row, but not winning very often either, finishing third behind pennant-winning New York. Chicago was also in the midst of the Depression, and attendance at Wrigley Field dropped dramatically. After six straight seasons in which the Cubs averaged more than one million fans a year, in 1933 fewer than 600,000 fans turned out.

Shortly after the end of the regular season, the club received more bad news. In mid-September, Bill Veeck contracted the flu, but when he failed to get better, doctors discovered that he had an advanced case of leukemia. He died on October 5.

Like William Wrigley, Veeck was a man whose tenure as club president appears better in retrospect than it did at the time, owing in no small part both to what followed and to his son, William Veeck Jr., who went on to serve as an owner and executive for several clubs, including the Cubs, the Indians, and the White Sox, and who earned a reputation as one of the game's good guys. He liked to tell stories about his father, nearly all of them colorful. Veeck's legacy was perhaps put best in one Chicago obituary that stated simply, "He made friends."

Through no fault of his own, Veeck had been forced to learn while on the job, and he was, at first, ill prepared for the general manager–like duties the job of club president then entailed; not surprisingly, his performance during his first few years with the club revealed his inexperience. Just as Veeck was getting comfortable, Wrigley died, and then Veeck himself died before it was really possible to assess him on his own merits. To be sure, he deserves some credit for serving as president during one of the team's most successful eras, but Veeck, like Wrigley, squandered as many opportunities as he optimized. The Cubs probably should have been better during his tenure than they were.

His greatest impact came not in the construction of the team but in the area of promotions. Veeck took Ladies' Days to new heights, regularly holding such events and dramatically increasing the team's appeal to female fans. He kept Wrigley Field comfortable and clean and in some ways was ahead of his time, for he was among the first to suggest interleague play.

Veeck's death left it up to P.K. Wrigley to decide who would run the Cubs. He didn't want any part of it himself. William Walker, the club's second-largest stockholder, succeeded Veeck, first on an interim basis before he was elected to the position by the other stockholders.

That was the only qualification that mattered. Walker had been an investor in Chicago baseball since the Federal League. He had made his money in fish and had no baseball experience, something he would soon demonstrate.

His first act was to pursue a deal that Veeck had been working on for months. Babe Herman clearly hadn't provided the offensive punch the Cubs needed, so as early as May 1933 Veeck had set his sights on Philadelphia Phillies slugger Chuck Klein. In six years as a Phillie, Klein sported a batting average of .359, usually with thirty-five to forty home runs, more than one hundred runs scored, and more than one hundred RBIs. The Phillies needed cash, but the two clubs failed to get a deal done before the May 15 trade deadline. As soon as the season ended, they started talking again, and in exchange for Klein the Cubs gave the Phillies Mark Koenig and two other backup players, plus $65,000.

What the Cubs failed to account for, however, was the effect that Philadelphia's ballpark, the Baker Bowl, had had on Klein's statistics. The right-field fence was only 280 feet from home plate. Although it was topped by a 40-foot screen, Klein had become adept at dropping the ball over the screen. In Wrigley Field, although the fence was only 8 feet high, it was 40 feet farther away.

In essence, the Cubs reenacted the 1933 season in 1934: again they failed to mount a serious challenge and played bland baseball. Klein hit only .301 and managed career lows in everything. Walker made one trade. Grimm was slowing down, so he dumped young first baseman Dolph Camilli and $30,000 on Philadelphia in exchange for Phillies first baseman Don Hurst. Hurst had hit .339 in 1932, but didn't even hit .200 in 1934. Camilli, on the other hand, went on to thrive in Philadelphia and then Brooklyn, leading some baseball historians to consider the deal one of the ten or fifteen worst in Cub history, although in fact it had little impact on the Cubs. Chicago finished third again, a showing as gray and dreary as the Great Depression.

Hurst's failure led the press to unload on Walker, an attack that had less to do with the trade and more to do with the fact that Walker wasn't William Wrigley or Bill Veeck. Walker didn't have the social skills of his predecessors, and he had recently let it be known that he wasn't happy, saying, "The more I see of baseball the more I think of the fish business." Philip Wrigley, who thus far hadn't seemed to be paying much attention to the Cubs, suddenly got a case of rabbit ears. Distressed by the criticism leveled at Walker, Wrigley abruptly decided to buy him out. On October 23, Walker resigned. Although Wrigley said, "There has been no friction between Mr. Walker and myself," in fact it had grated on Wrigley that almost every time Walker was criticized there was open speculation over his own role.

Ever so slowly, P.K. Wrigley was falling into the self-delusional traps that afflict so many men of inherited wealth. Over time he came to believe that somehow his wealth was not the sole product of genealogy, but instead tangible evidence that he himself possessed special gifts and could achieve success in fields for which he had no experience whatsoever. P.K. knew chewing gum; of that there was no doubt, and over time he would prove to be an effective and even innovative steward of the Wrigley Company. But the more he thought about it, the more P.K. was convinced that his success in the manufacture of chewing gum had a parallel in the business of baseball.

That would not be the case, and the failure of his logic would be borne out during his reign over the Cubs. "I have some ideas that may be termed crazy in baseball circles," he said after taking over for Walker, "but I want to prove to my own satisfaction they are good or bad."

Oh boy. A forty-year experiment to test that theory was now officially under way.

P.K. became club president but turned over most personnel duties to Charlie Grimm and club treasurer Boots Weber. They got busy right away.

For all their troubles, in some ways the Cubs were in an enviable position. Second baseman Billy Herman, shortstop Billy Jurges, and third baseman Stan Hack were the best young infield in baseball. Rookie first baseman Phil Cavarretta, only a few months removed from a Chicago

high school, came up late in the year and seemed to fill the hole at first base, hitting .381. More young talent, best represented by outfielder Augie Galan, was on the way, giving the Cubs some flexibility.

Over a three-week period, they remade the pitching staff, first sending Pat Malone, who'd worn out his welcome, to the Cardinals for rookie catcher Ken O'Dea. The deal was lopsided, but it was straightened out a few weeks later. Veteran pitcher Tex Carleton came over from St. Louis for two more nominally youthful arms, Bud Tinning and Dick Ward, and, more importantly, a bagful of money. Thus far, P.K. Wrigley still seemed to be his father's son,

Shortstop Billy Jurges made headlines both on and off the field. In 1932, while playing his first full major league season for the pennant-bound Cubs, he was shot in his hotel room by Violet Valli, a former girlfriend. In 1935, with the Cubs once more headed for a pennant, the native New Yorker needled North Carolina–born teammate Walter Stephenson about the Confederacy in a pregame dustup that started an on-field brawl at Forbes Field.

willing to spend the Wrigley millions on the Cubs, if for no other reason than that he didn't yet know of any other way of doing business. That evolution was still a few years off.

A few days later, the Cubs made another deal, this time landing Pittsburgh pitcher Larry French and outfielder Freddy Lindstrom, a native of Chicago, for Guy Bush, Jim Weaver, and Babe Herman. Grimm thought Galan was ready to take over, and French, a good pitcher with a bad record in 1934, was only twenty-six. No one knew it yet, but the deals had just nudged the Cubs toward another pennant.

It took the new Cubs a while to get untracked in 1935. For the first half of the year, they were barely a .500 club. After losing to Pittsburgh 4–0 on July 5, their fourth straight defeat, Chicago's record was 38–32, and the club was solidly in fourth place, ten and a half games behind the high-flying New York Giants.

Then, suddenly and without warning, it all came together. Bill Lee, in his second year in the starting rotation, emerged as a big winner, teaming with Warneke to give the Cubs the best one-two punch in baseball. French, Carleton, and Charlie Root weren't much worse, and everyone started hitting. The Cubs won twenty-four of their next twenty-seven games to draw within a hair of the Giants.

Then came the annual curse of a lower extremity. In the first game of a double-header split with Pittsburgh in which the Cubs came within one out of catching the Giants, Gabby Hartnett, hitting .347, rolled over his ankle while sliding into home. He stayed in the game, but afterwards the *Tribune* reported that X-rays revealed "the ankle bone sheared off and the ligaments separated."

The injury thwarted Chicago's surge, but in 1935 a broken ankle was not a season-ending injury. For the next month, the Cubs, Cardinals, and Giants all stayed together near the top.

Hartnett returned, and on September 4 the now third-place Cubs, trailing the Giants by three and the Cardinals by two and a half, were ready to begin an eighteen-game home stand. Grimm gathered his charges together and said, "We either do or we don't. But we are going to be loose." That afternoon Augie Galan slammed an eighth-inning grand slam, and the Cubs beat Philadelphia, 8–2.

Such play would soon be expected. The Cubs didn't lose again for more than three weeks, and in twenty of the next twenty-one games Cub pitchers held the opposition to three runs or less. The only time they did not, giving up fourteen runs to Brooklyn on September 14, the Cubs scored eighteen runs and moved into first place. By the time the Cubs lost again, on September 28, they had won twenty-one consecutive games, they had clinched the pennant, and they were preparing to play the Detroit Tigers in the World Series. Like the Cubs, the Tigers had gotten off to a slow start before coming on in a rush behind the pitching of Tommy Bridges and Schoolboy Rowe. On offense, they were led by second baseman Charlie Gehringer, catcher Mickey Cochrane, and first baseman Hank Greenberg. They were hoping to avenge their loss to the Cardinals in the 1934 World Series.

Although the Cubs lacked Detroit's star power, they were nominal favorites, owing to greater depth and the fact that they'd lost only once in the last month. A local astrologer confidently told the *Daily News* that "astrological science" indicated a Cub victory in five games, and Grimm was just as confident, telling the *Chicago Daily Times*, "We'll take 'em in five or six." He also announced that he would go with a three-man rotation, starting Warneke in game one, followed by Root and Lee. Larry French, his only southpaw starter, would pitch in relief, even though the Tigers' usual starting lineup featured no less than four lefties.

The Series opened in Detroit's Navin Field, which was made smaller by the addition of temporary bleachers in left to accommodate extra fans, cutting the distance to the wall by twenty-nine feet. The Cubs took a look around, and Gabby Hartnett sniffed, "It's a soft ballpark." Billy Herman added, "Yeah, *girl's* softball." But when the Cubs took batting practice, only Jurges, Herman, and outfielder Frank Demaree managed to put a ball into those same stands.

In the 1934 World Series, the Cardinals had reportedly rattled the Tigers with their rough play and relentless and often profane chatter. The Cubs decided to incorporate the same strategy. It worked in game one. In fact, everything worked for the Cubs in game one. But it extracted a terrible price. The 1935 World Series was simultaneously unforgettable and infamous.

Augie Galan led off against Schoolboy Rowe, and after smashing Rowe's third pitch past shortstop Billy Rogell's glove into no-man's land, he legged the hit out for a double. Billy Herman then tapped a pitch back to Rowe. The

The 1935 National League champion Cubs whoop it up after clinching the pennant. Starting on September 4, the third-place Cubs nearly ran the table for the rest of the season, winning twenty-one consecutive games on the way to the franchise's fourteenth National League crown.

pitcher threw to first base, but as Herman neared first, instead of cutting across the bag, he leveled Hank Greenberg. Lindstrom bunted him to third, and both runners scored when Hartnett followed with a single to right.

The Cubs led 2–0, and that was all pitcher Lon Warneke needed as he scattered four hits and kept the Tigers off balance all game long, with eight Detroit hitters tapping ground balls his direction. The Cubs won, 3–0, taking the first game of the Series.

The victory, however, cast a vile shadow over the entire World Series. Chicago's bench jockeys went way over the line. They centered their attack on Hank Greenberg, making him the target of not only verbal assaults but, as demonstrated by Billy Herman's play in the first inning, physical assaults as well when the opportunity arose. It worked, because after the collision Greenberg played a skittish game and didn't get the ball out of the infield.

Chicago's assault on Greenberg had less to do with his 36 home runs and 170 RBIs than it did with his Jewish heritage. Billy Herman led the charge and wasn't shy about it. When a reporter later asked him exactly what word he had used to taunt Greenberg, Herman responded by saying, "All of them." The Cubs didn't confine their anti-Semitic remarks to the players either. Jewish umpire Dolly Stark was repeatedly taunted with jeers of "Christ-killer" and similar epithets.

It probably cost the Cubs the World Series. And it should have. While ethnic-based bench jockeying was commonplace at the time, the Cubs went so far over the line that chief umpire George Moriarty felt that he had to step in: over the course of the Series, he repeatedly cautioned the Cubs to knock it off. As the Series stretched on, many Cubs thought the umpire's calls started to favor the Tigers. They may well have been right. The Cubs simply didn't know well enough to stop.

Greenberg got revenge in game two, blasting a three-run home run to deep left off Charlie Root in the first inning, driving him from the game, and putting the Tigers ahead, 4–1. Unfortunately, the Cubs weren't through with Greenberg. After he grounded out in the third, umpire Moriarty stopped the game, went over to the Cubs dugout,

(left to right) Gabby Hartnett, Augie Galan, Walter Stephenson, Billy Herman, Bill Lee, and Tex Carlton celebrate the Cubs' 1935 pennant clincher.

and reamed everyone out. Columnist Westbrook Pegler surmised in the *Chicago Daily News* that it was "safe to assume" the reason was "that the Cubs were firing some dirty talk at Greenberg." Then Pegler added, matter-of-factly, "This sometimes happens to Greenberg." True enough. Greenberg was even harassed in Detroit, the home base of the popular Catholic priest and anti-Semitic ideologue Father Coughlin, whose diatribes were broadcast on the radio.

The Cubs may have been silenced, but they didn't stop their harassment of Greenberg. After Cochrane walked in the seventh inning, Gehringer grounded to second. Cochrane went into second hard, and Billy Jurges didn't even try to turn the double play. Instead, he braced for a collision, and Cochrane gave him one. For a moment, it looked as if the two might fight before Cochrane stalked off.

Greenberg came up to bat next, and relief pitcher Fabian Kowalik, who despite his name was a native of Texas, appeared to retaliate, throwing a pitch up and in. Greenberg turned and ducked behind his hands to protect himself, and the pitch struck him squarely on the wrist. He stayed in the game and later that inning tried to score on a hit to right but was called out in a violent collision

with Gabby Hartnett at the plate. He left the field holding the injured wrist. As X-rays later revealed, it was broken. Not only would Greenberg not play again in the Series, but the injury effectively cost him the following season as well when he reinjured his wrist in the spring of 1936, and the loss of Greenberg cost the Tigers any chance they had to repeat as AL champions. Still, the Tigers won the game, 8–3, to tie the Series.

Commissioner Landis had been in attendance, and he had seen enough. Things were getting out of hand. The two teams adjourned to Chicago for game three, but Landis called a meeting before the contest and read the riot act to representatives of both clubs over the "uncivil and unprintable language" he had heard thus far. For the rest of the Series, the epithets that had been screamed across the diamond now took place in sotto voce.

Nevertheless, the tide had turned. Greenberg's injury did nothing but inspire the Tigers. If anything, it had taken the Cubs outside of their game, and whatever chance they had to win rapidly slipped away. Cub fans seemed to sense the coming demise. Wrigley Field wasn't even full for game three as fully one-third of the bleacher seats remained empty. They'd been sold, but no one wanted to pay the price that scalpers demanded.

Bill Lee started game three and carried a 3–1 lead into the eighth before the Tigers exploded for four runs to go ahead. During the outburst, Grimm, Woody English, and Tuck Stainback were all thrown out of the game by umpire Moriarty. The Cubs came back to tie the score in the ninth, but French coughed up the game in the eleventh, and the Cubs lost, 6–5. The next day, the Tigers put the Series out of reach with a 2–1 win, scoring the winning run on back-to-back errors by Galan and Jurges. The Cubs came back to win game five, 3–1, behind Warneke, but the ace hurt his shoulder. Although he would remain an effective pitcher, from that time onward he would periodically be troubled by arm ailments and would never again be the dominant pitcher he had been from 1932 through 1935.

Game six went down to the wire. The score was 3–3 entering the ninth as Tommy Bridges and Larry French matched each other. Hack opened the ninth for the Cubs with a triple, bringing up French. The situation begged for a pinch hitter, but Grimm let French hit for himself, and Hack failed to score. In the Tiger half, Mickey Cochrane started things off with a hard ground ball to second, but Billy Herman only managed to knock it down. Gehringer followed with another hard grounder to first. Cavarretta took it off his bare hand and, instead of throwing to second, stepped on first for the out, putting Cochrane in scoring position. Goose Goslin followed with a hit to right, scoring Cochrane and making the Tigers world champions.

It was just as well, for if the Cubs had won the 1935 World Series, history might well have ruled against them for their abominable behavior toward Greenberg. At the very least, it was distasteful, and at worst it may have caused him to miss the Series, for it seems unlikely that the pitch that struck his wrist was an accident, and the two collisions, with Herman and Hartnett, may have been more violent than the situation called for. Although Greenberg was much admired for his stoicism, when later asked whether or not such taunts bothered him, he was blunt, saying, "How the hell could you get up to home plate every day and have some son-of-a-bitch call you a Jew bastard and a kike and a sheenie and get on your ass without feel-ing the pressure? If the ballplayers weren't doing it, the fans were. I used to get frustrated as hell. Sometimes I wanted to go into the stands and beat the shit out of them."

Incredibly, as Westbrook Pegler's comments indicated, such anti-Semitism was so widely accepted at the time that

"Big Bill" Lee anchored the Cub pitching staff for a decade, during which time he won twenty or more games for the Cub pennant winners of 1935 (twenty wins) and 1938 (twenty-two wins).

Long before the Sianis family laid claim to the myth of the "billy goat curse," goats were a part of Cub culture. Here Cub owner Philip K. Wrigley (left) and player-manager Charlie Grimm lasso a goat allegedly captured in the wilds near the Cubs' spring training headquarters at the Wrigley-owned Catalina Island in California.

if pretending that the incident never took place helps to preserve the image of the Cubs as benign "lovable losers." Warren Brown's 1946 book, *The Chicago Cubs*, the first narrative history of the club, brushes off the entire incident, even referring to Landis's admonitions to the Cubs over their bad language as "private chuckling." In short, the press gave the Cubs a complete pass. But there was nothing benign about the 1935 Cubs.

In other seasons, the Cubs might well have been snakebitten and may have deserved to win a World Series when they did not, but in this case the loss to the Tigers was well deserved. Not only were the Tigers a better team on the field, but the Cubs' behavior indicates that the Tigers were superior under any yardstick one could choose. Nothing about the Cubs in the 1935 World Series was lovable at all.

If there is anything akin to baseball karma, it was evident over the next two seasons. The Cubs played their way into contention for much of each season, then fell excruciatingly short of the pennant. In 1936 a slow start led to a minor shakeup as a rapidly fading Chuck Klein, Kowalik, and $50,000 were sent to Philadelphia on May 21 for outfielder Ethan Allen and pitcher Curt Davis. The Cubs soon went on a fifteen-game winning streak that put them squarely in the middle of the pennant race, but the New York Giants had Carl Hubbell in 1937, the best pitcher of the year, and the Cubs did not. They faded in the stretch, finishing five games behind the Giants.

Shortly after the end of the season, the Cubs dropped a bomb when they traded Lon Warneke. Although he'd pitched well in 1936, the arm injury he suffered during the World Series had taken just enough away to make him expendable. Phil Cavarretta had slipped in 1936, and Grimm thought the Cubs needed a first baseman. He admired St. Louis veteran Ripper Collins so much that even though Collins had lost his starting spot to rookie Johnny Mize, Grimm had named him to the All-Star team. The Cardinals gladly traded Collins and veteran pitcher Roy Parmalee for Warneke. The local press howled, for Warneke was a favorite. Edward Burns wrote: "As one of the most ardent members of the Warneke Pitching, Squirrel Shooting, Hound Dog Fancying and Arkansas Wisecracking Guild, I am joining in the mourning at Lon's departure."

the incident virtually passed without notice, not only in Chicago newspapers but in those elsewhere. Pegler, in fact, seemed more upset with Moriarty, taking the arbiter to task for having hurled "vile epithets" back at the Cubs and calling him a "Mussolini bully." Even more incredibly, since that time the incident has all but been ignored in most books that purport to tell the history of the Cubs, as

There were other changes afoot as well. P.K. Wrigley continued to open up the family fortune and began a two-year renovation of Wrigley Field, including the installation of the outfield bleachers and the center-field scoreboard, continuing the transformation of Wrigley Field into the now-classic park that is still recognizable today.

The feature that got the most attention was the bittersweet and Boston ivy that Bill Veeck, inspired by a similar feature in an Indianapolis ballpark, had planted in front of the outfield wall. While the ivy is a wonderful aesthetic addition, it has probably been less important for the long-term health of the ballpark than the change that followed at the end of the season and another change that never took place at all. At the end of the 1937 season, more renovations took place, most notably a slight reconfiguration of the grandstand and a reduction in capacity due to an increase in the size of the seats. As a result, unlike other older parks, such as Boston's Fenway Park, the seats have never felt undersized. They are as spacious as seats in any new ballpark, and they keep Wrigley from feeling claustrophobic. The ivy is certainly nice to look at, but the size of the seat is the feature that makes the experience so pleasant and has given the ballpark its longevity.

Wrigley also did not add lights. The Cincinnati Reds added lights at Crosley Field in 1935, and with each passing season night baseball was becoming more and more commonplace. Veeck had tried to convince Wrigley to add lights as early as 1934, and he kept pestering the owner to add the feature, but Wrigley resisted, partly for aesthetic reasons, but also because in the field of baseball Philip K. Wrigley didn't have the same foresight he had in the chewing gum trade. For the remainder of his tenure, Wrigley would keep Wrigley Field in the dark.

The decision revealed an enormous blind spot in Wrigley's character. When night baseball became widespread, major league baseball, for the first time, became readily accessible to the workingman. Since the early days of the game, professional baseball had been played in the midafternoon—a convenient time for businessmen and bankers, but not for factory workers or others who worked a standard daytime shift.

This did not trouble P.K. Wrigley. He never considered the impact that his decision had on the workingman. For him, baseball remained, at best, a pleasant pastime, a leisure-class activity that, like croquet, didn't really matter. He never realized that by preserving Wrigley Field's "aesthetics," he was keeping the vast majority of the team's fan base away, for to most fans the park—and the Cubs—were accessible only during vacations or on weekends. Over time Wrigley's decision would have a dramatic impact on the expectations of the fans, for the fans who could come regularly to Wrigley Field were often far less passionate and intense than those who followed the team from afar in the newspapers, on the radio and on television, and in the local tavern. The passion of the fans who lived and died with the team wasn't always on display at Wrigley Field.

In the end, however, nothing the Cubs did in the offseason made any difference in 1937 because the Giants had Carl Hubbell, the Cubs did not, and Hubbell again proved to be the difference. For the second season in a row, the Cubs entered August in first place, then more or less played .500 baseball the rest of the way as Hubbell led the Giants to the pennant; the process was simply a bit more excruciating in 1937 as the Cubs hung on until the final week and finished only three games back. The late-season swoon was making a comeback.

The Cubs turned the page on the season rather quickly, acquiring Yankees second baseman Tony Lazzeri, who, like Hornsby, Klein, and Collins, was a once-great player well on the way from "great" to "retired." Lazzeri was expected to back up the infield, provide leadership, and, some surmised, perhaps form a line behind Grimm to angle for his job, or at least put pressure on the manager. Since retiring as an active player midway through the 1936 season, "Jolly Cholly" hadn't been very jolly, and his attention had begun to wane. Players began to look to others, such as catcher Gabby Hartnett, for instruction.

By and large, the press blamed the collapse on a lack of pitching, for the Cubs clearly did not have a pitcher who could do for them what Hubbell did for the Giants. And when they complained about lack of pitching, the object of their complaint was P.K. Wrigley. In reaction, he set out to get one.

Brooklyn's Van Lingle Mungo was his first target. Mungo had led the league in strikeouts in 1936, but because he had battled arm trouble ever since, Wrigley believed he might be available. Unfortunately for Brooklyn

THE CHICAGO CUB

1938

LOGAN, HACK, BRYANT, EPPERLY, GALAN, MARTY, C
RUSSELL, JURGES, REYNOLDS, GARBARK, KIMBALL, LOTSHAW, DEAN,
DEMAREE, LEE, FRENCH, LAZZERI, CORRIDEN, GRIMM, JOHNSON, HARTNET
LAPORTA

LETON, MATTICK.
LINS, TRIPLETT, O'DEA, ASBELL.
AVARRETTA, HERMAN, ROOT.

fans, the Dodgers stubbornly held on to the pitcher, and he never resumed full form.

Thus thwarted, in late March Wrigley asked Grimm who the best pitchers in the league were. One of the names Grimm brought up was Cardinal ace Dizzy Dean.

Dean's was probably the only name Wrigley recognized, for the flamboyant flame-thrower may have been the best-known player in America. A bona-fide hillbilly with a natural sense of the showman, Dizzy Dean was a colorful character whose good-natured self-confidence and homespun, fractured use of the English language would one day propel him into a successful career as a broadcaster. He was also, since the retirement of Babe Ruth, the biggest draw in baseball. Wrigley could not have failed to notice that every time Dean pitched in Wrigley Field attendance figures jumped.

He could also pitch. Since 1932, Dean, who, like Warneke, was a native of Arkansas, had won 134 games, including more than 20 games in four seasons, and he had also led the league in strikeouts five times.

He shouldn't have been available, and the fact that he was should have given the Cubs pause, because in 1937 Dean neither won twenty games nor led the league in strikeouts. During the 1937 All-Star Game, Dean's toe had been broken by a line drive. When he tried to pitch again, the sore toe caused him to change his motion slightly, but it was enough to ruin his arm. He probably tore his rotator cuff, an injury that was impossible to treat at the time.

The Cubs should have known this, for in the few appearances Dean made in the second half of the season he was clearly diminished, and he finished the year 13–10. But as Irving Vaughn wrote in the *Tribune*, although Dean had pitched in an "indifferent fashion," after the All-Star break "Dizzy, a foxy lad, probably figured that so long as his team was out of the flag race he would save up for better days." Moreover, in spring training he was reportedly "painfully quiet" and pitched without distinction.

The Cardinals, under general manager Branch Rickey, rapidly concluded that he was done and that they better get what they could. But the Cubs, training out in Catalina, didn't have a clue that Dean was struggling in the spring.

The 1938 pennant-winning Cubs barely edged out the Pirates to win the franchise's fifteenth National League championship.

When Wrigley, through Boots Weber, came calling, the Cardinals could hardly believe their good fortune. Not only did the Cubs want Dean, but they wanted him badly enough to offer three players—pitcher Curt Davis, outfielder Tuck Stainback, and pitcher Clyde Shoun—plus something even better: $185,000 worth of chewing gum profits.

The deal was announced on April 16, and although Grimm cautioned that "it doesn't mean a pennant is a certainty," he added, "I'm tabbing him for twenty victories." Most of Chicago echoed Irving Vaughn, who wrote, "The only risk assumed by the Cubs in making the trade was financial," for Dean earned nearly $20,000.

He earned most of it in his first month with the Cubs. Dean won his first start against Cincinnati, 10–4, and then, on April 24, faced his old Cardinal club. In front of a crowd of nearly thirty-five thousand in Wrigley Field, Dean was magnificent, scattering four hits and winning 5–0.

Close observers, however, noted that this was not the Dean of old. One reporter noted that Dean "put his faith in dipsy-do stuff," mesmerizing the Cards with slow curves and changeups instead of his signature fastball. He was also throwing the ball sidearm instead of using his normal overhand motion. He made his next two starts and won each time; when he ran his record to 4–0 with a 5–2 win on May 3, it gave the Cubs a 10–5 mark for the season.

The next day he was done. His sore shoulder was even more sore than before. Initial reports indicated that he'd torn a deltoid muscle and would be out a month, and it was finally admitted publicly that ever since joining the club Dean had complained about a lame arm. As spring turned to summer, Dean and his shoulder became the daily soap opera. Fortunately, with Larry French, Bill Lee, and Tex Carleton, the Cubs had enough pitching depth until they found a fourth starter. Eventually they would settle on Clay Bryant, who would go on to win nineteen games and soften the loss of Dean.

But it would not be enough to save Charlie Grimm's job. Wrigley had spent money, made an investment, and expected a return. Yet by mid-July, when Dean finally made his return, the Cubs were in fourth place and barely

Player-manager Gabby Hartnett (left) shares a laugh with pitcher and fellow Hall of Famer Jerome "Dizzy" Dean in September 1938. In his first season with the Cubs, Dean won seven games against one loss and helped the Cubs win the pennant.

a .500 baseball team with a record of 45–36. Grimm had been looking over his shoulder all year, and Wrigley finally decided to relieve him of the anxiety, naming Gabby Hartnett as new manager. At the press conference announcing the move, Grimm put on a good act, posing with Hartnett. When the new manager said, "I'm glad you're taking this well, Charlie," Grimm snapped, "What the hell. There's no other way to take it. That's baseball."

For six weeks, Hartnett made no difference. If anything, he threw in the towel, calling his club "highly overrated." Meanwhile, Pittsburgh opened up a big lead by winning forty of their next fifty-four games. The Cubs plugged along, battling Cincinnati and New York for second, third, and fourth place. Hartnett fractured his thumb on August 15, and five days later the Cubs trailed the Pirates by nine games.

The Cubs were still firmly in fourth place on the morning of September 4. After dropping a double-header to Cincinnati, it seemed as if it would take an act of God himself to bring a pennant to Chicago.

Actually, that would be *two* acts of God. And the Cubs, most improbably, got both.

Over the next two weeks, Hartnett returned to the lineup, and the Cubs got hot and, ever so slowly, began to chip away at Pittsburgh's lead. Still, on September 18, with less than two weeks left in the season, the Pirates, who defeated last-place Philadelphia 1–0 and then had a second game end in a tie, led Chicago by three and a half games. Even with a favorable schedule—including two more games against the Phillies followed by a series against seventh-place Brooklyn—it still seemed unlikely that the Cubs would catch the Pirates.

That's when God got busy. A streak of bad weather, culminating in the Great Hurricane of 1938, which battered the East Coast, killing more than six hundred people, left the Pirates idle for the next three days. At the time, there was no mechanism to make up the contests; therefore, all the games were canceled forever. Although the Cubs still trailed by three and a half, the Pirates had lost the chance to win three games and put the Cubs away.

Three days later, the lead was down to a game and a half when the Pirates came to Chicago for a three-game series. Pittsburgh manager Pie Traynor told his club that they needed to win only one game to lock up the pennant. Hartnett knew his club needed a sweep, but also that his pitching staff needed a breather.

It wasn't quite the equivalent of Connie Mack picking Howard Ehmke off the scrap heap to start the World Series, but Hartnett tabbed Dizzy Dean, who hadn't started a game in more than a month, to pitch the first game.

It was a risk, but not a gamble. Although Dean had pitched in only twelve games all year, when he was able to pitch he had been magnificent, and he sported the lowest ERA on the team. Every time he took an extended rest, he came back and pitched well, slathering his arm with a pungent, heat-producing liniment that masked dull pain with pure agony. And he was smart enough to know that fastballs—at least fastballs of the speed to which he was accustomed—were not a part of his arsenal anymore. Slow, slower, and slowest, from every possible angle, was his strategy now.

At first, that didn't appear to be enough. In the first inning, the Pirates sat on Dean. Lloyd Waner ripped his

SO WHAT'S A "GLOAMING"?

"Gloaming" was an archaic word rarely used at the time, and had it not been for some anonymous newspaperman enamored with the alliterative lilt of "homer" paired with "gloaming," it is likely that the phrase would be little known to most speakers of American English. In fact, before Hartnett's blast, the word had appeared in the *Chicago Tribune* only forty times in nearly seven decades, many of those in 1892 when a racehorse named Gloaming enjoyed some moderate success.

What's a "gloaming" then? The word refers to the dusk, or twilight, and is rooted in the Old English word *glom*, which referred to dusk. "Gloaming" has often been used more specifically, however, to denote not just twilight but a time with a certain mystical and even magical character—a time when day is being overtaken by darkness.

In 1938 that was certainly the case for the Pittsburgh Pirates—and, soon enough, for the Cubs as well.

hero. The Cubs scored another run in the sixth, and Dean cruised into the ninth before stumbling, putting runners on second and third with two out.

Dean was through; Hartnett came out and waved for Bill Lee. Although he allowed one run on a wild pitch, he struck out Al Todd to end the game. The Cubs won, 2–1, and now first place was within reach.

The second game against the Pirates is as famous as any regular-season game in franchise history. Both managers emptied their pockets trying to win, the Cubs knowing that a loss would probably knock them out of the race, the Pirates just as certain that a defeat would put the Cubs on top. It was, wrote Edward Burns, "as thrilling an afternoon as any sports carnival could produce. Mob ecstasy choked by bitter disappointment, only to be supplanted by more ecstasy with more disappointment. Heroics nipped in the bud, opportunity hammering and not being heard."

The score was tied at three apiece through the seventh: the Pirates had routed the Cubs' Clay Bryant for three runs in the sixth, only to see the Cubs claw back to tie the score in the bottom of the inning. In the eighth, as darkness began to fall on Wrigley Field, the Pirates went ahead, 5–3, off of Vince Page and Larry French. The Cubs tied it up in the bottom of the inning again before the Pirates' ace reliever, Mace Brown, set them down.

Now Hartnett turned to Root, the old veteran, to keep the game close in the ninth. He did, and the Cubs went to bat in the bottom of the inning with the entire season on the line.

Had this been another game, at another time, the ninth wouldn't even have been played, for the twilight was rapidly wrapping Wrigley Field in shadow and shade. Players on both teams knew that unless the Cubs scored, the game was over. It was too dark to play another inning, and the result would be a tie, making the previous nine innings meaningless.

Mace Brown didn't waste time. He knew the Cubs couldn't see the ball, and he poured fastballs over the plate, easily retiring Phil Cavarretta and Carl Reynolds.

Then Hartnett stepped in. He watched—or heard—two fastballs slip over the plate knee high. Then Brown threw another, this time a little higher.

Hartnett turned on the ball, met it square, and saw it rise into the gloom, a small dark spot rapidly disappearing.

On October 3, 1938, two days before the start of the World Series at Wrigley Field, the City of Chicago feted its pennant winners with a parade down Michigan Avenue. Gabby Hartnett waves from the open car.

second pitch for a hit, and then brother Paul hit a sizzling line drive for an out. After Johnny Rizzo popped up, Arky Vaughn singled to center before Gus Suhr ripped a ground ball straight at Rip Collins. The Pirates were out, but of the eleven pitches Dean had thrown, he had given up two hits and two others that were hit right at someone. The Pirates were salivating at their future prospects.

That was their problem. They became too anxious. In the second inning, catcher Al Todd foolishly tried to stretch a single into a double but was tagged out, thwarting a potential rally. After Rip Collins tripled and scored in the Cub third, Chicago led and put the pressure on the Pirates.

Now Dean could deal, as every Pirate tried to be the

The Cubs surged to the top of the dugout steps, squinting, and thirty-five thousand Cub fans stood, as much in reaction to the sound as to the flight of the ball, for it was hard to see, appearing and disappearing and then appearing again, dropping fast.

The Pirate outfielders gave it away, first running and then slowing and turning, and then the fans in the first few rows of the bleachers in left-center, scrambling and cheering, and then the Cubs who raced after Hartnett and the fans who caught him on his way to second and then third and home, paving the way for him around the bases, now and then frozen in a flash as photographers ran alongside, grappling with their boxy cameras and trying to capture the scene. And when he touched home plate, it was suddenly nearly dark and the Cubs were in first place and hardly anyone believed it. John Carmichael of the *Chicago Daily News* wrote: "We have surrendered to inadequacy. . . . It was almost too much for human flesh and blood to watch. And the hat we do not own is off once more to HIM and THEM." A headline writer summed it up and gave the moment a name: "the Homer in the Gloamin'."

The Cubs were ecstatic in the clubhouse, and the mailman who caught the ball in the bleachers brought it to Hartnett, who gave him a signed ball in exchange.

The Cubs led by only half a game with three remaining, but the race was over. The next day, despite pitching for the fourth day in a row, Bill Lee cut down the Pirates 10–1,

and when the Cubs beat St. Louis in the second game of a double-header on October 1 and the Pirates lost, the pennant was theirs.

But the Cubs' season had ended with Hartnett's home run in the twilight, the curtain coming down and the show over, with the audience standing and cheering for an encore that never came. In the World Series that followed, the Cubs were thoroughly humiliated by the Yankees—out-hit, outpitched, outplayed, and out-thought. New York won in four straight games as the exhausted Cubs lost first behind Lee, 3–1, and then 6–3 after Dean courageously held the Yankees at bay until the eighth. Joe McCarthy's charges then rolled in the next two contests, winning going away by the scores of 5–2 and 8–3. On the train ride back to Chicago, Hartnett bitterly attacked his own club.

In a sense, the night that followed the famous "Homer in the Gloamin'" has never lifted, for ever since the Cubs, with only a few brief exceptions, have dwelled in the darkness. The previous era, in which the Cubs had appeared in the World Series in four of ten seasons and finished either first or second in six seasons out of ten, while never playing below .500 baseball, was over. As Ed Burns accurately noted in a story whose headline read, in part, "Jinx of Post-Season Games Still Pursues Cubs," "The experience of losing in a world series is not a new one for the Cubs."

They were almost a dynasty. Then darkness fell, and dawn has yet to arrive.

WAR STORIES

Although few people knew it at the time, by 1938 Philip K. Wrigley had begun to make good on his promise to test "some ideas that may be termed crazy in baseball circles." In the off-season after the World Series, the Cubs owner was determined to put his ideas into practice. An inveterate tinkerer, Wrigley often told people he was never happier than when he was alone in his garage, working on one of his many cars. For the next three decades, he would tinker periodically with the Cubs. Sometimes he would simply change the oil and kick the tires, but other times he would tear the engine apart and after trying to put it back together again, walk away and leave the parts scattered all over the floor.

Now Wrigley wanted to rebuild the engine. One year before, he had contacted University of Illinois psychologist Coleman R. Griffith. Griffith, who had played baseball while attending Greenville College, gained some notoriety in the 1920s by teaching a course entitled "Psychology and Athletics" and then writing a series of articles on the topic. Impressed, university officials created the Laboratory for Research in Athletics in 1925 and put Griffith in charge,

Chicago native Phil Cavarretta accepts his 1945 National League MVP Award in a ceremony at Wrigley Field. The first baseman–outfielder helped lead the Cubs to their sixteenth National League by leading the league in batting with a .355 average. Cavarretta also led all regular players in batting in the 1945 World Series with a .423 average.

hoping his research could help UI athletic teams. Although Griffith's findings had little impact on the university's teams and budgetary restraints led to the closing of the lab in 1932, Griffith remained a well-respected academic.

Precisely how P.K. Wrigley became aware of Griffith and his work is uncertain, but Wrigley's tenure as president of the Wrigley Company was marked by continuing attempts to apply principles of science and technology to the chewing gum business. Those generally successful efforts led Wrigley to embark on an automation program in company factories that saved Wrigley millions in salaries and benefits.

Increasingly, Wrigley looked at the Cubs and thought that whatever worked in the manufacture and marketing of chewing gum should also work in the business of baseball. He hired Griffith to help, in a sense, automate the "production" of baseball players. Griffith was charged with identifying those traits that differentiated major league—quality prospects from others and highlighting areas that needed improvement for players already on the Cubs staff. Griffith dubbed his project the "Experimental Laboratories of the Chicago National League Ball Club," hired an assistant, purchased $1,000 worth of equipment, including a slow-motion movie camera, and joined the Cubs during spring training.

For much of the season, Griffith and his assistant examined the Cubs as if they were so many microbes in a petri dish. He then prepared a series of reports summarizing his observations and making his recommendations. Everywhere Griffith looked he found something lacking, whether it was in the way practices were structured (he found them "aimless, disorganized, and unproductive"), in the spacing of players while playing "pepper" (they stood too far away from each other), or in manager Charlie Grimm's approach (he yelled too much). Needless to say, Griffith and his reports were roundly ignored by the Cubs players and coaching staff.

Wrigley, however, found them fascinating, and the reports may well have played a part in Grimm's dismissal. When the Cubs went on to win the pennant under Hartnett, Griffith's notions were given further credence.

Wrigley's use of Griffith was, in a sense, an absolutely revolutionary attempt to break the bonds of tradition that were—and still are—endemic in the game and to look at it with an entirely new set of eyes. In the 1970s, the Kansas City Royals opened a baseball academy and tested prospects in all manner of ways, including psychological, and today many teams use sports psychologists. To embark on that approach in 1938 was extraordinary.

At the same time, the entire operation was premature—it was an interesting idea, but one that was not yet wholly practical. Griffith is considered a pioneer in sports psychology because he was the first to recognize that psychology is a factor in athletic performance, but he didn't know exactly why or how. He didn't even really know what to study or look for, and his early work produced only generalities and dead ends. Sports psychology didn't become a valid field of study until the late 1960s, and then on a basis that owed nothing to Griffith.

In short, hiring Griffith to study the Cubs was like hiring the man who first conceived of the atom to create an atomic bomb. Although well intentioned, Griffith was essentially making things up as he went along. He foundered, and the longer he worked for the Cubs the less he confined himself to psychology, his only area of expertise. Griffith studied player performance statistically and studied slow-motion films of Cub players. Although both approaches are now commonplace in professional baseball, and Griffith can be credited with being one of the first people to envision the value of each approach, he was in way over his head, with no real idea of what to do with his information. Only a handful of players, most notably Bill Lee, found the films useful, and then only for what the players saw in the films, not for what Griffith did.

Furthermore, Griffith alienated the Cubs' baseball staff from the outset. An academic to the core, Griffith, despite his collegiate baseball background, didn't understand or value baseball's culture and traditions. The Cubs' baseball staff blanched at the notion of a complete outsider reporting on their activities directly to Wrigley, so even if Griffith had known what he was doing, he had little chance of succeeding.

Wrigley too failed to envision the impact of a person like Griffith on the Cubs. Had Wrigley truly looked at what he was trying to accomplish, he probably should have let Griffith test his ideas with Cubs prospects first. Over time the Cubs could have developed a more comprehensive program, based on Griffith's reports. Then perhaps those findings could have been tested in the Cubs minor league system first before being put into practice on the major league level.

In the early 1920s, Branch Rickey of the St. Louis Cardinals had pioneered the development of the "farm system"—a series of minor league clubs at various levels, stocked with players signed and controlled by the major league franchise, designed to provide a never-ending stream of talent. Before Rickey's innovations, most players were first signed by minor league teams and then sold to the highest bidder or drafted by big league clubs at a set price. Major league teams controlled very few minor league players themselves. The farm system was a much more efficient, cost-effective, and predictable way of ensuring a supply of talent. Rickey himself was particularly adept at using his extra players as fodder for trades. By 1939 there were 292 minor league teams, of which 149 were part of a farm system for one of the sixteen major league teams. The Cardinals had twenty-eight farm teams, while the Indians and Yankees had sixteen and fifteen, respectively.

The Cubs, on the other hand, had *two* minor league teams, the fewest in the major leagues. Even if they had wanted to use their farm system, it would have had little impact. In fact, Wrigley hoped that the insights provided by Griffith would enable the Cubs to avoid the farm system altogether. He simply didn't understand its value. For example, Wrigley owned the Los Angeles Angels of the Pacific Coast League, yet he did not treat the team like a Cub farm team, instead allowing club officials complete latitude to sell players to other clubs whenever they wished.

Wrigley only wanted major leaguers. From his viewpoint, a farm system was just a collection of minor leaguers, and as he once noted, "It's surprising how many ballplayers can play Triple A ball but still not make it to the majors." So instead of building a minor league system and using Griffith and some of his ideas to help develop younger players, Wrigley tried to start at the top. As a result, the Cubs fell far behind every other team in baseball in the development of young talent, something that would turn into a chronic problem under P.K. Wrigley.

At the end of the 1938 season, Griffith produced a final "General Report" that assessed the entire season, evalu-

The Cubs' most consistent pitcher in the 1940s was right-hander Claude Passeau. In 1940 he enjoyed a solid 20–13 record, and he would compile a 124–94 record for nine Cub teams that, save for the 1945 pennant winners, finished an average of twenty-eight games back in the standings. He is shown here with his son, Claude Jr., at Wrigley Field.

ated each player, and made recommendations on whether to trade or retain each player's services. Incredibly, only a few weeks after reaching the World Series, these reports were used by the Cubs as a guidepost for the future.

In December, the Cubs dealt Frank Demaree, Billy Jurges, and catcher Ken O'Dea to the New York Giants for shortstop Dick Bartell, outfielder Hank Lieber, and catcher Gus Mancuso. In terms of talent, the deal was a total wash, an exchange of shades of gray. Apparently, however, it was done in part at the suggestion of Griffith. Later that spring, he produced a detailed report on the batting tendencies of

Hall of Fame slugger Jimmie Foxx hit only three of his career total of 534 home runs, while batting only .191, in limited duty with the Cubs spread over two seasons in 1942 and 1944.

the three new players, something he could not have done in 1938 unless he had known the players would be acquired.

This wasn't Wrigley's only idea that might have been "termed crazy in baseball circles." He had another one, and it was a doozy—crazy not only in baseball circles but in just about any circle one can imagine. According to Bill Veeck, who had remained employed by the Cubs until 1941, at about this time Wrigley hired someone Veeck described as "a little bum" and paid him $5,000 a year, with a promised bonus of $25,000 if the Cubs won the pennant.

It seems that Wrigley had either seen a professional wrestling match or read about one in which a wrestler used an assistant to cast spells and hexes or otherwise put a "whammy" on his opponent. In the arranged world of pro wrestling, the record of the "whammy man" was spot-

less. A very dim lightbulb went off in P.K. Wrigley's head. He decided that the Cubs needed just such a person.

Wrigley apparently had no idea that pro wrestling was fixed, and none of the sycophants he surrounded himself with felt they could tell the boss the truth. Veeck's "little bum" was Wrigley's "whammy man." Although his name is lost to history, the whammy man accompanied the Cubs both at home and on the road, sitting in the stands, staring at opposing players, and giving them the "evil eye" while ominously wiggling his fingers. If it hadn't been so pathetic, it would have been funny. Soon, however, the Cubs and everyone else in baseball would have more important things to worry about.

The Cubs weren't awful in 1939, but they weren't very good either as the whammy man found nine innings quite a bit tougher to influence than a round of wrestling. Ripper Collins was released in the spring, replaced by Rip Russell. The new acquisitions were all right, but the remaining Cubs all fell off just a little, and the result was a very average ball club. In the middle of the year, they acquired veteran pitcher Claude Passeau in trade from Philadelphia in exchange for three players, including pitcher Kirby Higbe. Passeau would go on to have a fine career with the Cubs, but Higbe would later become a big winner with the Dodgers. The Cubs also purchased minor league slugger Bill Nicholson from Chattanooga for $35,000, a move that demonstrated just how vapid their own minor league system was. He more or less replaced rookie Jim Gleeson in the outfield, a perennial prospect the Cubs had acquired in the offseason from the Yankees for $25,000, overpaying wildly for a prospect who was already almost thirty. For the $60,000 they spent on the two players, the Cubs could have bankrolled several minor league clubs. Sadly, several years before, they had passed on a player who could have not only manned the outfield but served as the centerpiece of a championship club. The Cubs once had the inside track on San Francisco Seals outfielder Joe DiMaggio, but they backed off after he hurt his knee. DiMaggio eventually went to the Yankees for $25,000 and five nondescript players.

All year long Griffith kept feeding Wrigley his "reports," most of which focused on Hartnett's failures as a manager. "The center of the whole problem," he wrote "is Hartnett . . . a man who must satisfy his own ego at all costs." Of course, Hartnett had seen what happened to Grimm once Griffith showed up, and he had absolutely no use for the psychologist. Hartnett let Griffith know it too. But Wrigley appeared to give the reports credence, for at a certain point the front office seemed to give up on the season, satisfied to make do with what it had. Fourth place, which was where the Cubs finished, seemed good enough.

Despite Griffith's reports, Hartnett stayed on. He was, after all, a Chicago legend and much beloved, and although he had slowed as a player, he still caught more than half of the Cub contests in 1939.

But the slow erosion continued in 1940. Hartnett hardly played at all. Passeau won twenty games, but everyone else struggled to win, and Dizzy Dean, after struggling through several seasons pitching every month or so, appeared finished as well.

In August, a frustrated Griffith submitted one final report before leaving the Cubs to return to the university. It contained a hodgepodge of advice, very little of it psychological in nature, although he again blasted Hartnett for his "grandstanding, his super-egoism, and his stupidity." One suggestion in particular apparently stuck in Wrigley's brain.

Thus far in his tenure as club owner, Wrigley had been something of a spendthrift, following his father's example and spending whatever it took to acquire players. Chicago was known as a comfortable place for players to play, and the Cubs, in comparison to other players in the league, were considered relatively well paid.

Griffith, who by this time had been completely closed off by the players, thought this was part of the problem. He had come to the conclusion that major league ballplayers were pampered and soft. He advocated a more Darwinian approach, suggesting that Wrigley cut salaries and make them more performance-oriented. Over time Wrigley took Griffith's advice. The Cubs would soon add the adjective "cheap" to their vocabulary.

They also added the phrases "second division" and "sub-.500," for the 1940 Cubs were both, ending the season in fifth place with a 75–79 record, their worst finish since 1925. After a protracted period of speculation, in November the Cubs released an announcement from P.K. Wrigley that "Gabby Hartnett's contract as manager of the Cubs will not be renewed when it expires on December 31." Fur-thermore, the Cubs put Hartnett the player on waivers. If unclaimed, he would be released.

Hartnett, who knew his playing career was just about over, was glad to go and even appeared at the news conference announcing the change with a smile on his face. He knew as well as anyone that the Cubs were in trouble. The few decent players they had were getting old, and the young ones weren't very good.

Even Wrigley seemed to realize that. His written release added, "The success or failure of the club does not depend on any one person, but rather on getting the right combination. We are not blaming Hartnett—he had done everything he could, but we feel it is up to us to try and keep on trying and get the best possible combination of personnel to produce the best possible results. We may be wrong but we are trying."

In fact, the Cubs were cleaning house. After drawing almost a million fans in 1938, by 1940 attendance had dropped to just over 500,000. Boots Weber wanted to resign, so Wrigley, like his father, turned to the world of journalism for a man to run a ball club. He selected former sportswriter James Gallagher to serve as general manager. Like William Veeck a generation before, Gallagher had no experience apart from serving as a backseat driver as he covered the Cubs over the years. Veeck's son Bill, who had worked his way through the ranks of the Cubs and was probably qualified for the spot, became club treasurer. Wrigley himself no longer wanted to serve as club president, but for the time being his plan to step down was, as he termed it, "temporarily clogged" because no one else wanted the job. No one was exactly clamoring to become the Cubs' next manager either. Among the names mentioned in the press were Kiki Cuyler, Braves manager Casey Stengel, or, speculated the press, perhaps some sort of player-manager to be acquired through trade.

The Cincinnati Reds had won the National League pennant in 1940 under manager Bill McKechnie. He wasn't available, so the Cubs went after what they thought was the next best thing. Reds coach Jimmie Wilson was baseball's hero of the moment, for after Reds catcher Ernie Lombardi was injured late in the 1940 season, Wilson, who'd retired as a player, filled in. All he did was hit .353 in the Series and lead the Reds to the title. That was a lot more impressive than his record as a manager. He'd led the

Lennie Merullo was the Cubs shortstop during the war years from 1941 through 1945, during which time he batted .240. He later served the Cubs and major league baseball as a scout.

a result, otherwise average players on each of those two teams suddenly became stars, and stars became superstars.

Foremost among these players was Phil Cavarretta. Since joining the team in 1934 shortly after high school, Cavarretta, a valuable, hustling, and popular player who was perhaps a bit too versatile for his own good, had shuttled back and forth between first base and the outfield. Before the war, Cavarretta never really settled into one spot.

But he was the perfect wartime ballplayer—talented, but with just enough physical maladies to be rejected by the military. Cavarretta had a bad ankle and was plagued by chronic ear trouble. Finally installed at first base full-time in 1943, Cavarretta thrived against wartime pitching, hitting .291 in 1943, .321 in 1944, and a league-best .355 in 1945 with occasional power.

Cavarretta should have been the perfect partner in the Cubs' batting order for Bill Nicholson, whose 33 home runs, 116 runs scored, and 122 RBIs led the National League in 1944 and who should have thrived on league pitching in 1945. But Nicholson, inexplicably at the time, slumped terribly in 1945 and never came close to approaching his previous standard. He didn't know it but he was developing diabetes, which affected his eyesight and eventually cut his career short.

The Cubs started off slow in 1945 while the Giants sprinted to the front. Still, without warning, and buoyed by Cavarretta, the Cubs suddenly got untracked. The war ended in Europe on May 7—VE Day—and as spring turned into summer, news of American success in the Pacific made it clear that the war was winding down there as well. As summer took hold, everyone on the club got hot at once. For the first time since before the war, Wrigley Field was suddenly full of life again, bursting with optimism as more and more fans turned out each day.

It helped that Chicago had a secret weapon in 1945—several actually—double-headers and opposing teams in the second division, particularly the Cincinnati Reds. The Cubs played twenty-nine double-headers in 1945 and swept twenty. Of their sixty-six games against the sixth-place Braves, seventh-place Reds, and tail-end Phillies, the Cubs won fifty-three, including twenty-one of twenty-two against Cincinnati. The two clubs had trained together in French Lick earlier that spring, and the Reds were no mystery to Chicago. For the season, fully fifty-three of Chicago's ninety-six wins came either in double-header sweeps or against the Reds. The Cardinals, in contrast, were barely over .500 against those same three teams.

From early June through early August, the Cubs had the best of both worlds, playing fourteen double-headers and facing the Reds eighteen times. They swept into first place on July 8 and held on.

On July 27, they received some surprising help. In the American League, the New York Yankees, despite the war, were still a powerhouse under manager Joe McCarthy and fighting for the pennant with several other clubs. But the Yankees had a new general manager, the volatile Larry MacPhail. He disliked McCarthy and was looking for a way to get rid of him. He couldn't fire the popular manager, so he decided to drive him away.

Right-handed pitcher Hank Borowy was the ace of the Yankee staff, already the winner of ten games, and 46–25 over the past three seasons. Without consulting McCarthy or anyone else, MacPhail snuck Borowy onto waivers, meaning that any other club in the American League could claim him. If they didn't, Borowy could be offered to teams in the National League.

A few weeks earlier, while shopping for some additional pitching, Jim Gallagher had called MacPhail, hoping to cut a deal for veteran Ernie Bonham. MacPhail steered Gallagher toward Borowy, but the Cub GM didn't believe Borowy would ever clear waivers.

MacPhail may have used some sleight-of-hand tactics to make that happen, because after Borowy passed through the American League, several clubs howled in protest, but when the Cubs saw he was available, they jumped. As expected, the Yankees pulled Borowy back after Chicago claimed him—they weren't going to give him away—but now they were free to make a deal with Chicago. To manager Charlie Grimm, the pitcher was the answer to a prayer he hadn't dared utter—a bona-fide ace delivered in the midst of a pennant race. As Grimm later put it, "We just got him out of the sky."

All MacPhail wanted was money, and Wrigley still had plenty of that. When Gallagher told the owner that Borowy could deliver the pennant, Wrigley—for the last time in a long time—simply wrote a check, this time for $97,000. Borowy was now a member of the Cubs.

There were rumors immediately after the deal that MacPhail had pulled a fast one on Chicago, for Borowy was draft-eligible, but the pitcher had wisely taken an offseason job in an essential industry, a tool and die shop, and was designated 2-B. He was also supposedly bothered by a blister problem and, as MacPhail told the New York press, "appears to have outlived his usefulness with us. Since April he has only pitched four complete games for us, and hasn't been able to go the distance at all since June 24." He forgot to tell Borowy, for the new pitcher won his first two starts with the Cubs and finished eleven of the fourteen games he would start over the balance of the season. Paired with Hank Wyse, Passeau, Derringer, and veteran Ray Prim, Borowy gave the Cubs the best and deepest pitching staff in the league.

Yet despite the presence of Borowy, the Cubs couldn't quite shake the Cardinals, who played the Cubs quite a bit tougher than Cincinnati. Chicago had a chance to put the Cardinals away in series in late August and both early and

mid-September, but the Cardinals won eight out of ten to keep the Cubs close, upping their record against Chicago to 14–6.

When the two clubs met for their final series, a two-game set in Chicago on September 25 and 26, the Cubs led by only a game and a half, with six games remaining in the season. With a sweep, the Cardinals could move into first place.

Borowy got the start, and the Cubs were confident. Since joining the team, he had gone 11–2 and had not pitched a bad game even when he lost.

The game was played in a drizzle, and the Cubs seemed to have the upper hand when in the seventh inning, with the bases loaded, Andy Pafko cracked a two-run double

Center fielder Andy Pafko was the best player developed by the Cubs during the war years. In his nine years in Chicago, Pafko proved to be a superb fielder, batted .294, and socked a career season high thirty-six home runs in 1950. His trade to the Dodgers in 1951, along with pitcher Johnny Schmitz, catcher Rube Walker, and second baseman Wayne Terwilliger, for outfielder Gene Hermanski, pitcher Joe Hatten, catcher Bruce Edwards, and infielder Eddie Miksis, was one of the worst in Cub history.

down the left-field line, clearing the bases and putting the Cubs ahead, 6–3. Pafko cracked his bat on the hit and later said, "It might have curved foul if the bat hadn't busted."

In the eighth, however, the Cards got to Borowy. Marty Marion started the rally with a line drive back at the pitcher. He got his glove up, but the wet ball slipped loose and Marion was on. St. Louis went on to score twice before Ray Prim came on in relief and shut the Cardinals down. The Cubs won, 6–5.

Most of the players thought the pennant race was over. A tub filled with beer and ice greeted them in the clubhouse, and Lon Warneke and Roy Johnson broke out in song, singing "John the Baptist," just as they had after every Cub victory over the past few months.

But St. Louis wasn't dead, for as Ed Burns wrote, the game the next day "was one of the most zany ever perpetrated on Mr. Wrigley's beautiful premises." Forty-two thousand fans got their money's worth.

The Cubs lost, 11–6, but after the game was finished the outcome remained in doubt, for the Cubs filed a protest over a play that took place in the seventh inning. Ray Sanders of the Cardinals lofted a fly ball to right field. Bill Nicholson drifted back and appeared to catch the ball up against the wall.

Or did he? One umpire ruled that he had made the catch, while the other ruled that he had caught a carom off the wall. The base runners didn't know who to believe or what to do. Sanders kept running, but base runner Whitey Kurowski, confused, stayed somewhere between first and second, starting and stopping and starting again as Sanders passed him and then backtracked. After a lengthy argument, the umpires ruled that Nicholson hadn't made a legal catch. Grimm wanted Sanders called out for passing the runner, but the umpires refused to penalize him over the confusion the call had caused. With the pennant in the balance, the decision on the protest filed by Grimm could have determined the NL champion.

Fortunately, it did not. After the game, the Cubs traveled to Cincinnati for a double-header. That made it automatic. The Cubs swept both games to clinch a tie for the pennant and two days later swept a double-header in Pittsburgh to clinch it. The league eventually ruled against Chicago, but by then the question was moot.

The Cubs were National League champions, the last

time that phrase has been uttered in Chicago without irony or as the product of a hallucination. For the ninth time in thirty-six seasons, the Cubs, although they had only one world title to their credit, would play in the World Series. Only the New York Giants and New York Yankees, with ten and fourteen pennants, respectively, had made more appearances in the World Series. The Chicago Cubs, without question, were one of the most successful franchises in the game.

Imagine that.

The Detroit Tigers captured the American League title behind pitcher Hal Newhouser, who won twenty-five games and his second consecutive MVP Award. Like Cavarretta, who won the NL MVP Award in 1945, Newhouser was the perfect wartime player, a skilled pitcher whose "leaky heart" made him unfit for military service. He had to be cautious, for doctors warned him that pitching was life-threatening, but Newhouser thrived against wartime competition and was one of the few wartime stars who continued to produce after the war. Hank Greenberg returned in June after four years in the Army and put the Tigers over the top.

There was intense interest in the Series, for with the victory over Japan on August 14, the Series would be the first played in peacetime since 1940. Still, the war affected the 1945 World Series more than any other. So many soldiers were in transit on the nation's railways that baseball commissioner Happy Chandler, who had taken over from Landis in March, kept travel to a minimum, scheduling the first three games for Detroit and the remainder for Chicago. The rosters of each club were still so depleted— only 9 percent of the players called into service had been discharged by the end of the 1945 season—that prognosticators had a hard time envisioning either team as a world champion. The Cubs were installed as narrow favorites owing to their superior hitting attack, but Chicago reporter Warren Brown probably put it best. When asked by another reporter which team he favored, Brown responded, "I don't think either one of them can win it."

Unfortunately, Brown's estimation was astute, for the World Series that followed was anything but a "Fall Classic." In his history of the team published a year later, he titled his chapter on the Series, which was marred by errors and other poor play, "World's Worst Series." In many ways it was, and that may be one reason it is best remembered by Cub fans today not for anything that took place on the field but for an incident in the stands. Not even Phil Wrigley's "whammy man" could top this one.

The Series opened in Detroit, and at first everything went perfectly for the Cubs. Facing Hal Newhouser, the Cubs jumped all over him, scoring four first-inning runs and then driving him from the game with three more runs in the third. Borowy struggled early, giving up two hits and two walks in the first inning, but Doc Cramer grounded into a double play with two on and no out, and then Rudy York popped up with the bases loaded. Borowy escaped the jam, but struggled through the first six innings, giving up a total of six hits, five walks, and a hit batsman, a performance that led Irving Vaughn of the *Tribune* to describe the performance using one of his favorite words—"wabbly."

In the sixth inning, with two on and no outs, Grimm came charging out to the mound, and for a moment it appeared as if Borowy was finished. But the manager left him in. Borowy retired the last twelve men he faced, Andy Pafko cracked a two-run home run in the seventh, and the Cubs won, 9–0.

But Grimm's decision to leave Borowy in the game may well have cost the Cubs the Series. When he went out to talk to the pitcher, Chicago already led, 7–0. His ace was clearly struggling and, in fact, had shown some signs of fatigue late in the season, not completing his last few starts. The wise move might have been to pull Borowy and allow him to get some rest, preserving him for later in the Series. Borowy needlessly went the distance. The decision to leave him in has haunted the Cubs ever since.

Hank Wyse, who won twenty-two games for Chicago in 1945, started game two opposite Virgil Trucks. Trucks, who spent most of the war pitching for the Great Lakes team and then for something of an "All-Star" Navy club in Hawaii, had been discharged less than two weeks earlier and had pitched only five innings during the regular season. In any other season, he wouldn't have been eligible for the Series, but Chandler allowed each team to expand its roster to accommodate returning servicemen.

The decision was a huge help to the Tigers. Dizzy Trout, who'd led the league in wins in 1944 and served as the Tigers' number-two starter behind Newhouser, ran out of steam late in the season. He hadn't pitched since Septem-

Cub captain and Chicago native Phil Cavarretta was a graduate of Lane Technical High School and spent his entire twenty-year major league career in the Windy City. In eighteen years with the Cubs he was a member of three National League champions and enjoyed his greatest season in 1945 when he won MVP honors while helping lead the Cubs to their last World Series appearance of the century.

ber 23, and at the start of the Series he was fighting a bad cold. The sudden availability of Trucks allowed the Tigers to give Trout some much-needed rest. Trucks came up big in game two, scattering seven hits and giving up only a single run in the fourth when Cavarretta doubled and came home on Nicholson's single. The run put the Cubs up, 1–0, but that lead didn't hold.

Hank Greenberg, the Tigers' other war refugee, saw to that. Unlike Trucks, Greenberg had spent most of the war overseas, serving in the Chinese and Indian theaters as a captain in the Army Air Corps. Although his duties were primarily administrative, he had one close call when he responded to a B-29 that had crashed on takeoff. As Greenberg and others raced to the plane, its load of bombs exploded, sending Greenberg flying through the air and damaging his hearing.

Fortunately, in the 1945 Series he didn't hear the same jeers from the Chicago bench that had marred his 1938 experience. By 1945, Nazi atrocities against the Jewish people were well known. That didn't mean that there were no more anti-Semites in the United States—or in the major leagues—but it did mean that it was no longer acceptable to advertise such leanings loudly and in public. Greenberg extracted a measure of revenge in the fifth inning with a three-run home run off Wyse, driving him from the game and giving the Tigers all the runs they would need in their 4–1 victory.

Game three should be etched in granite, the touchstone of a Cub world championship, for Chicago starting pitcher Claude Passeau hurled one of the greatest games in Series history. He gave up only one hit, a second-inning single to Rudy York, who was erased on a double play, and one walk, to Ed Swift in the sixth. That was it.

Meanwhile, Stubby Overmire was almost as good for the Tigers. The Cubs scratched across two runs in the fourth and another in the seventh to win 3–0, their second shutout of the Series.

Immediately following the game, both clubs boarded a train for Chicago, where the Series would continue the next day. With a 2–1 advantage in the Series and the remainder of the games scheduled for Wrigley Field, the Cubs, on paper, enjoyed a huge advantage.

Instead, although few recognized it, the advantage had actually shifted to the Tigers. Trout was now healthy, rested, and available for game four. Like Newhouser, Trout was not a wartime fill-in. Ineligible for military service owing only to his poor eyesight, he was a bona-fide ace.

In contrast, Chicago starter Ray Prim was the epitome of a wartime player. The thirty-nine-year-old pitcher, nicknamed "Pop" because of his age, had pitched without distinction for the Washington Senators from 1933 through 1935 before returning to the minor leagues, presumably for good. But the war had given Prim a reprieve. He won twenty-two games for the Los Angeles Angels in 1944 and made the Cubs in 1945 during spring training. A natural right-hander, he had learned to pitch with his left arm after hurting his right arm in a childhood accident, an injury that left him ineligible for military service. After starting the season in the bullpen, Prim joined the starting rotation in June and won thirteen games against only eight defeats, his 2.40 ERA second only to Borowy's league-best 2.14. During one stretch in July, he had won five games in two weeks, throwing twenty-seven consecutive scoreless innings. He was a soft-tosser and curveball artist

Pitcher Hank Borowy (left), shown in this 1948 photo with catcher Bob Scheffing, was the key player for the 1945 National League champions. He arrived in Chicago from the Yankees on July 27 in a controversial waiver deal for $97,000. His 11–2 record for Chicago gave the Cubs the necessary boost to capture the pennant by three games over the Cardinals.

whose success depended on a combination of guile and control.

But Prim's eight losses were telling. Like the Cubs, he had fattened up on the bottom feeders of the National League. The Cardinals, on the other hand, had handed him five of his eight defeats.

Wrigley Field was decked out in all its glory for game four, packed to the gills with more than forty thousand people ready to celebrate the end of the war, the return to normalcy, and a world championship for the Cubs. They had yet to realize those last two desires were mutually exclusive.

Prim made it through the Tigers' batting order precisely once, pitching perfect baseball through three innings. It was not an omen of success but rather a sign that the Tigers were simply taking measure of the ancient pitcher Edward Burns delicately referred to as "ripe."

They exploded in the fourth. With one out, Prim walked Eddie Mayo. In a heartbeat, Detroit's third, fourth, and fifth batters—Doc Cramer, Greenberg, and Roy Cullenbine—all teed off, driving Prim from the mound. Then, as the *Tribune* noted, "39-year-old Paul Derringer replaced 39-year-old Ray Prim." Derringer was not much more successful: by the time he got the third out, the Tigers led, 4–0. Meanwhile, Trout put his rest to good use, displaying what the Cubs called the "best fastball" they'd seen all season, striking out six and scattering five hits as the Tigers knotted the Series with a 4–1 victory.

All of a sudden, it was a best-of-three series. In many ways, game five would prove to be the difference.

The pitching matchup was a repeat of game one as the Tigers brought back Newhouser, who had not appeared since getting knocked out, and the Cubs countered with Borowy.

For the second straight time, Borowy staggered at the start. He worked his way out of trouble in the first, but in the third inning the Tigers hit him hard, scoring a run on a walk, a hit, and a sacrifice fly off the bat of Doc Cramer that pushed Andy Pafko to the limit in left-center. Greenberg ended the inning with another screaming drive to Pafko. The Tigers led 1–0, and Borowy wasn't fooling anyone.

He did, however, help the Cubs tie the score with a third-inning double. Stan Hack followed with a hit to cen-

Bill "Swish" Nicholson was the greatest slugger of the war years, averaging 28 homers per season from 1940 to 1944. In 1943 he led the National League in home runs (29) and RBIs (128) and finished second in the MVP vote to Cardinal first baseman Stan Musial.

ter. Irving Vaughn noted that "almost any kind of throw . . . would have cut down Borowy," but defense was a recurring problem in the Series as aging 4-Fers made miscue after miscue. This time Doc Cramer bobbled the ball, and Borowy scored easily. The game was tied.

As Vaughn noted, "A double play between two singles kept Borowy in an upright position in the fifth," but there was no such lifesaver in the decisive sixth. Greenberg was in the middle of another rally, ripping a double in the Tigers' four-run sixth that helped chase Borowy and hitting a flare to the outfield for a second double in the seventh that led to another Detroit run. The Cubs rallied late, but still lost, 8–4.

In the minds of most Cub fans today, what took place on the field during the game doesn't matter nearly as much

THE REAL DOPE
ON THE REAL GOAT

In the 1940s, a Greek immigrant named Bill Sianis operated the Lincoln Tavern at 1855 West Madison Street, a modest establishment opposite Chicago Stadium not much different from any other in the neighborhood, which also featured a number of "girly" bars and illegal but still tolerated casinos.

Sianis was something of a character. Since immigrating to America in 1906 at age fourteen and hopping a freight train to Chicago, he had worked as a newsboy and then sold hot dogs before opening his tavern. Owing to that establishment's proximity to Chicago Stadium, Sianis became acquainted with a number of Chicago sportswriters.

In recent years, Sianis's pet goat, named Sonovia, had gained a small measure of notoriety for his restaurant. Sianis, who told reporters he had once been a goat herder in his native Greece, claimed that in 1933 he'd found the goat with a broken leg on a Chicago street after it fell off a truck. After nursing the animal back to health, Sianis usually kept it in a pen behind the restaurant, but sometimes he also allowed Sonovia to enter the bar, where patrons bought the goat drinks, helping Sianis's bottom line—at the time he claimed to be grossing only $7 a day.

But a goat in a restaurant was a violation of city health regulations. Someone complained, and Sianis was hauled into court.

An attorney for the *Tribune* took notice and told Sianis, "This will be worth a million dollars' worth of publicity for you." He represented Sianis in court, got the charges dismissed, and cajoled the judge into "paroling" the goat into Sianis's custody for life. As Sianis later told a reporter, after all the publicity over the goat, "receipts began to go up $100 a day and more. People came from the Stadium after all the sports events. They stood four deep at the bar and some nights we never closed."

Sianis was smart enough to know that the goat was good business and began to milk the connection for all it was worth. He grew a goatlike goatee himself and soon found himself being called "Billy Goat." His tavern became a popular stopover, and Sianis soon made the acquaintance of just about anybody who was anybody, particularly in the press, as time and time again he and his goat found their way into the newspapers.

In 1938, for example, Sianis, a citizen since 1916, lost his citizenship papers and filed for a replacement copy, submitting a photograph of himself sporting his new whiskers. The federal government didn't recognize the photo, which didn't match the clean-shaven picture he had originally submitted. They rejected his claim, but Sianis took advantage of the situation and got the story into the newspapers. Not only did he receive a new copy of his papers, but the tavern received another shot in the arm from new patrons curious about the two old goats. A few years later, Sianis outfitted his goat with a sign that read BUY DEFENSE BONDS and marched him into the *Tribune*'s public service office. Sianis purchased a $1,000 war bond, and an intrepid photographer snapped his picture for a small story in the paper. Clearly, the goat was good business.

The World Series of 1945 offered Sianis another prime opportunity for some free advertising. Sianis bought two box seats for game five, one for himself and one for his goat, and showed up for the game early, goat in tow. The animal wore a blanket with a sign pinned to it that read WE GOT DETROIT'S GOAT. The game was briefly delayed by rain, and Sianis and his goat were allowed inside and even got to parade around the field for a while before they were ushered into the stands.

The goat, however, wouldn't cooperate and ran back on the diamond, which probably alerted team officials to the fact that having a goat in the stands was not the best idea. There were, after all, more than forty-three thousand fans in Wrigley Park that day, some of whom had paid scalpers as much as $200 for a box seat. Nevertheless, for a time, Sianis and his goat were allowed to watch the game.

Other fans, however, weren't enthralled with sitting next to a goat, particularly one that smelled, sported a pair of sharp horns, and was prone to chewing on anything it could reach. Ushers asked Sianis to leave. He did, but not until he and an usher staged a faux photo op for the press, Sianis waving his ticket, the goat resting its forelegs on the turnstiles, and a smiling usher blocking Sianis's path into the park.

That evening the *Chicago Times* published the picture of Sianis and his goat, and the next day Arch Ward mentioned the incident in his "In the Wake of the News" column in the *Tribune*. Business at the tavern boomed.

All this coverage, of course, made no mention of a curse. Despite the legend and lore that has since grown to surround the incident, at the time there was no suggestion that Sianis placed any hex on the Cubs, what has since come to be known as the "billy goat curse" that would forevermore keep the Cubs from the World Series. The closest Sianis came to that was sending a telegram to Phil Wrigley after the Series that read, "Who smells now?" a ploy that got Sianis yet *another* mention in the papers.

Sianis's curse is as spurious as Boston's "Curse of the Bambino," the utterly fictional claim that Babe Ruth cursed the Red Sox after being sold to the Yankees. The notion of a "billy goat"–inspired hex or curse was a

later product of the press, and Sianis was savvy enough to play along with it. In fact, before the 1990s, when Boston's curse was invented from whole cloth and gave the whole hoary notion a platform, the billy goat curse barely existed apart from a few brief newspaper stories that began appearing in the late 1960s—more than twenty years after the 1945 World Series.

Until December 26, 1967, there was nary a mention of such a thing in the *Chicago Tribune*. Then the *Tribune*'s William Granger, quoting Sianis, mentioned the hex in passing in a story about Sianis and his tavern, but Sianis claimed he had removed the curse at the request of Philip Wrigley, a request Wrigley apparently communicated only to Sianis. Then, as the Cubs challenged for the pennant in 1969, columnist David Condon wrote several columns around Sianis. In the first, which appeared in April, Sianis again "lifted" the curse that hardly

anyone had ever heard of. In the second column, which appeared in September after the Cubs collapsed, the tavern owner had to explain the whole notion to Condon once more. Then he claimed that he had removed the curse and that the Cubs had really lost the pennant because "the New York Mets just played like hell!" Over the next few years, Condon made regular use of the idea in subsequent columns, and other journalists ran with the idea.

The attorney who once said that the goat was worth "millions" was correct. Sianis would eventually rename his establishment the Billy Goat Tavern and move it to Michigan Avenue. Later he opened a second bar near Wrigley Field. For the Sianis family, the curse has been nothing but a blessing and a windfall, absolutely the best thing that ever could have happened.

So too for a generation of Chicago journalists. Like their brethren in Boston, the

Wrigley Field as it appeared for the 1945 World Series. It marked the fifth World Series held at the North Side park. In all, the Cubs have captured only one postseason series of any kind since 1908—the 2003 National League Division Series in which they defeated the Atlanta Braves three games to two. The Cubs' overall postseason record at Wrigley Field is 7–17, with but two victories coming in World Series play.

notion of a curse has made easy copy over the years and been used as an excuse to ignore the real reasons the Cubs have not returned to the World Series since 1945. The true story, like Boston's, isn't quite as cute and cuddly as that of Bill Sianis and his pet goat. Besides, if Sianis had really hexed the Cubs after game five of the 1945 World Series, how in hell did the Cubs ever win game six?

as what took place in the Wrigley Field stands. On that day a local restaurateur named Billy Sianis brought his pet goat to the game. He was asked to leave, and the so-called billy goat curse was born, something that has allegedly kept the Cubs from winning a World Series title ever since.

Still, after game five the Cubs needed to win only one game. Trucks drew the start for Detroit for game six, and Charlie Grimm passed over game two loser Hank Wyse for Passeau, pitching on two days' rest. The veteran pitcher made him look like a genius. The Cubs exploded for four runs in the fifth, and Passeau entered the sixth inning with a comfortable 5–1 lead.

With one out and a man on second, Detroit outfielder Jimmy Outlaw hit a line drive back to the box, Passeau threw up his pitching hand, knocked the ball down, and threw Outlaw out, and then Passeau bent over and started shaking his hand. The ball had struck the nail of his middle finger, tearing it partially off.

The team trainer cut the nail loose, and Passeau continued. He gave up another smash through the middle—this time he knocked the ball down with his glove hand—before collecting the third out on a strikeout.

In the seventh inning, however, the finger began to swell. Still, Passeau should have made it through the inning. Unfortunately, Stan Hack booted Chuck Hostetler's ground ball for an error. Mayo grounded out, and then Cramer singled. Hostetler should have scored easily, but he tripped between third and home and was thrown out. Passeau was now one out away from escaping the inning.

He never got it. Greenberg walked, and then Cullenbine singled to center, scoring Cramer. Hank Wyse came on for Passeau and gave up another hit, making the score 5–3.

The Cubs appeared to put the game away in the bottom of the inning, however, scoring twice on two infield hits sandwiched around three errors. They might have scored more, but with two out, Grimm let Wyse hit, and he struck out to end the rally. Leading 7–3, the Cubs needed only six more outs to tie the Series.

The 1945 National League champions led the league in batting average (.277), ERA (2.98), and fewest errors (121). Their quest to win their first World Series since 1908 was undone in the seventh game when ace pitcher Hank Borowy pitched on only a single day's rest and lost the second of his four decisions in the Series.

CHICAGO CUBS—1945

FRONT ROW—left to right: Paul Derringer, Mickey Livingston, Stanley Hack, Roy Johnson, Milt Stock, Charlie Grimm, Jimmie Chalikis, Bat Boy—seated on ground, Len Rice, Lennie Merullo, Phil Cavarretta, Claude Passeau.

SECOND ROW—left to right: Loyd Christopher, Paul Gillespie, Don Johnson, Andy Pafko, Harry "P-Nuts" Lowrey, Bill Schuster, Eddie Sauer, Dewey Williams, Ray Prim, Harold H. Vandenberg.

BACK ROW—left to right: Paul Erickson, Frank Secory, Eddie Hanyzewski, Bill Nicholson, Hank Wyse, Andy Lotshaw, Heinz Becker, George Hennessey, Red Smith, Bob Chipman, Mack Stewart.

Once again, Cub pitching faltered. Wyse sinned by walking Tiger catcher Bob Swift to start the inning, and then Hub Walker doubled. Mayo singled him home, driving Wyse from the game.

Now Grimm turned to Prim. He got one out, and then Hank Greenberg obtained another measure of revenge, driving the ball over the wall to tie the score.

That was, in effect, the Series, for the tie game, 7–7, forced Grimm's hand. In the ninth, he turned once more to Hank Borowy.

The former Yankee made up for his performance the previous day by shutting out the Tigers over the next four innings. Unfortunately for the Cubs, Virgil Trucks was just as effective for the Tigers.

Finally, with one out in the twelfth, Cub pinch hitter Frank Secory singled to center field. Bill Schuster came in to pinch-run, but Grimm let Borowy hit for himself. He struck out, bringing up Stan Hack, whose two errors had probably cost his team a chance to win in regulation.

Hack rapped a line drive through the hole into left field, a routine play. Greenberg, forced into the outfield upon his return to the Tigers by the emergence of slugging first baseman Rudy York, charged the grounder, then pulled up and started to drop to one knee to make the safe play.

As he did, the ball hit a sprinkler head buried deep in the left-field grass. It hopped up and over Greenberg's left shoulder. Schuster kept running, and the Cubs won, 8–7, to set up game seven.

As the jubilant Cubs poured off the field and into the clubhouse, Grimm reportedly told Hy Vandenberg that he would start game seven. After all, Borowy, Wyse, and Passeau had all pitched in game six, and Borowy had pitched in game five as well. Derringer was rested but had not given the Tigers much trouble. A quirk in the schedule gave both teams a day off before the finale, but Grimm apparently concluded that it was better to go with a well-rested pitcher than one who was already tired.

Hank Wyse thought that he was going to start the game, but moments after Grimm spoke to Vandenberg, Borowy bounced up to Grimm and told him that he would rest up and "I'll be ready for game seven." Just like that, Grimm had changed his mind.

Two days later, hundreds of Cub fans camped out for bleacher seats, and thousands more spent the morning adjusting their antennas to pick up the broadcast on radio. Steve O'Neill of the Tigers had followed Grimm's lead and also gone with his game one starter and ace, Hal Newhouser. The difference, however, was that after starting game five, Newhouser had two days' rest. Borowy, after pitching four innings of relief, had only one.

Most of the Cubs knew what was going to happen before it did. Backup catcher Dewey Williams warmed up Borowy and knew that he had nothing.

The Tiger hitters also knew. Skeeter Webb led off with a single. Then Eddie Mayo singled, as did Doc Cramer, scoring Webb.

Grimm called for Paul Derringer, but the veteran was wild. By the time the inning was over, the Cubs trailed 5–0 and Wrigley Field was silent.

Newhouser didn't have much, but he had enough. He scattered ten hits and beat the Cubs, 9–3, in the last World Series game the Cubs have ever played.

Cub fans can blame a goat if they want to, but if there was any goat that made a difference in the 1945 World Series, it was Charlie Grimm for overusing Hank Borowy. Since then, any number of men connected with the Cubs, from P.K. Wrigley all the way to Sammy Sosa, Dusty Baker, and Alex Gonzalez, can share that same designation.

But Sonovia the goat didn't have anything to do with it.

DOORMATS

They all came pouring back—the players, the fans, everyone.

Now that the war was over, the American military rapidly downsized. By February 1946, hundreds of players were preparing to descend on big league training camps—veterans and minor league prospects returning from the war, wartime suspects and assorted 4-Fs trying to extend their careers, and a larger-than-average crop of youngsters eager to prove themselves and ecstatic to be carrying bats and balls instead of bayonets and grenades. Minor league baseball expanded from eighty-six teams in 1945 to more than three hundred teams in 1946, and the number of Negro League teams doubled. Americans everywhere eagerly looked forward to a return to normalcy—a way of life without war. For many of them, "normalcy" meant professional baseball.

So too in Chicago. In economic terms, the war had been good to Chicago, relegating the Depression to the past. More than fourteen hundred companies had worked

Slugging left fielder Hank Sauer was known as the "Mayor of Wrigley Field" during his memorable seven-year stint with the Cubs from 1947 to 1955. He captured National League MVP honors in 1952 while leading the league in home runs (37) and RBIs (121) for the fifth-place team. His loyal fans in the left-field bleachers often celebrated his home runs by tossing him packets of his favorite pipe tobacco.

directly on the war effort, employing more than one hundred thousand people in addition to those already employed in facilities such as the Great Lakes Naval Training Station. During the war, anybody could get a job—old or young, male or female, and, perhaps most significantly, white *or* black. The war had modernized industrial Chicago and expanded its industrial base beyond the stockyards. As soon as the war ended, Chicago rapidly adapted, becoming a much more varied and textured city than ever before.

Vast numbers of soldiers and sailors had passed through the city during the war or been stationed at the Great Lakes Naval Training Station. Chicago, which had previously been a faceless big city, daunting and intimidating, was now a real place to them, and they had liked what they saw. They'd ridden the El, gotten drunk in city taverns, and taken in a ball game at Wrigley Field or Comiskey Park. Everywhere they looked they'd seen people working.

Chicago had always been a destination for immigrants, but now average Americans looked at the city and said "I want to live there." Soldiers turned citizens streamed into the city. Carl Sandburg's "City of Big Shoulders" was open for business and ready to embrace all those who entered the city limits. The population quickly swelled to more than three million residents.

What was normal before the war, however, was not necessarily normal afterwards. The world had changed. The city of Chicago, the game of baseball, and the Cubs would all have to adapt. It was a different world, and over the next few seasons the Cubs would fully develop the character that still dogs them today—that of a franchise that is not only a failure but inept. For in the years after the war, the Cubs were ill equipped to change. The National League walked all over them.

Drawn by the promise of jobs, thousands of African Americans had streamed into Chicago over the last three decades, leaving the rural South for jobs in Chicago's many industries in what sociologists referred to as "the Great Migration." Many settled in the so-called Black Belt on Chicago's South Side, creating a community that came to be known as "the capital of Black America." The black middle class boomed in Chicago, and a vibrant African American culture came of age as Chicago jazz, blues, and

African American literature all developed their own distinct identity. The black newspaper, *The Chicago Defender*, developed a national readership. The black Chicago American Giants, led by players such as Willie Wells, Cool Papa Bell, and Ted "Double Duty" Radcliffe, dominated play in the Negro Leagues. Beginning in 1933, the annual "East-West" Negro League All-Star Game took place in Chicago at Comiskey Park, and Negro League teams made regular appearances both there and at Wrigley Field. Although the Depression had slowed the migration and hit the black community hard, sending 40 percent of black Chicago onto relief roles, during World War II the pace of migration increased again, and after the war it exploded.

Although Chicago lacked the obvious segregation of the South, it was still very much a divided city; a civil rights leader later referred to it as the most racially segregated city in the United States, a place where "a negro dare not step outside the environs of his race." Redlining and restrictive real estate covenants kept black Chicago relegated to only a few areas of the city. But in the years after the war, black Chicago became impossible to ignore—or confine. The sheer size of the community gave it political clout.

Before the war, in the 1930s, various political groups had begun to pressure major league baseball to break the color line that had been in existence since the era of Cap Anson, but during the buildup to the war those efforts had taken a backseat to the battle against fascism. Once the war was under way, those efforts began anew, and supporters were armed with additional ammunition. Thousands of African Americans were serving their country in World War II, living and dying like everyone else. How then could these men be denied access to major league baseball?

Major league baseball in Chicago was not immune to the pressure. In March 1942, the Chicago White Sox, still training in Pasadena, California, were coerced by the African American press and the Communist newspaper *The Daily Worker* to give Jackie Robinson and another player a tryout. Although the Sox didn't sign either man, manager Jimmie Dykes told the *Worker*, "I would welcome Negro players on the Sox," and stated his belief that if he had been white, Robinson would have been worth $50,000 on the open market.

In Chicago itself, the push to integrate baseball was led by the Citizens Committee for Negroes in the Big Leagues, a group that included Communist and civil rights activist William L. Patterson, Catholic Bishop Bernard Sheil, *Chicago Defender* sports columnist Fay Young, and other community leaders. In December 1942, the groups forced a meeting with Philip Wrigley.

If any baseball club owner was going to break the color line at the time, Wrigley seemed to be the most likely candidate. Nearly 30 percent of his Wrigley employees in Chicago were black, and the Wrigley Company was among the more progressive companies in the country in terms of worker rights and benefits—Wrigley himself was an honorary member of the CIO (Congress of Industrial Organizations) labor union, and the CIO endorsed the efforts of the committee. Moreover, Wrigley had demonstrated his willingness to go against the status quo and take risks in both the creation of the All-American Girls Professional Baseball League and in the hiring of psychologist Coleman R. Griffith. He also seemed sympathetic to the plight of African Americans. According to one report, he had supported the right of an African American who wanted to move to Catalina Island.

Patterson, who had served as the executive secretary of the international defense group that helped represent the Scottsboro Boys, represented the group at the meeting with Wrigley, and he'd done his homework. He told Wrigley that the issue was not simply one of moral obligation but, as reported in the *Defender*, one of necessity: the need to "[buoy] up the morale of the Negro people during wartime" was an argument similar to the one Wrigley had made to advocate the use of chewing gum by war workers. Wrigley reportedly told Patterson that he agreed with him but worried that the country wasn't ready for black major leaguers, saying, "If Negroes are taken into the big leagues without proper public support, I'm afraid some fights will take place if a Negro player rides high into a white. What I'm afraid of is a riot." Patterson responded by pointing out that integrated basketball and football games, which inspired much more physical contact than baseball, had taken place without such incidents, but Wrigley was adamant, saying, "The temper of people in baseball is very high."

At every step, Wrigley deftly parried Patterson. While he admitted that "Negroes will be in the big leagues—and soon," he added, "I don't think the time is now." Wrigley

Cubs owner Philip K. Wrigley once said, "Baseball is too much of a sport to be called a business and too much of a business to be called a sport." Under his stewardship, the Cubs won four pennants before entering a period when they became the perennial doormat of the National League.

claimed that if there was sufficient public demand, "I would put a Negro on my team now," but there wasn't, at least in his mind. He tried to show his empathy for the cause by pointing out that he allowed Satchel Paige's all-star team to play at Wrigley Field and that Cub prospects on the West Coast played regularly with Negroes in "mixed games." He then pointed out that "I have taken a thousand Negro workers into my plant," as if that proved that he, Philip Wrigley, was without prejudice. With that, he dismissed Patterson, saying, "My door is always open," before closing it.

That was no great surprise. Activists like Patterson were accustomed to meeting men who said the right things and then did nothing. Underneath Wrigley's progressive veneer was a deep stripe of paternalism, one that was nowhere more evident than in the way he viewed

The versatile Jack Brickhouse practically lived at the Wrigley Field broadcasting booth while calling Cubs games for forty years (starting in 1948) and Bears games for twenty-four. His distinctive home run call of "Hey Hey" is an essential part of Cubs lore.

African Americans. His concern over "riots" revealed his fear of blacks, while his treatment of Patterson, who was patronized and sent away with a virtual pat on the head, showed he didn't take such concerns seriously. In racial matters, Wrigley's apparent open-mindedness rarely extended beyond his words.

Yet the Citizens Committee for Negroes in the Big Leagues did not give up. A year later, Patterson and another committee member met again with Wrigley, Cubs general manager Jim Gallagher, and Clarence "Pants" Rowland, the president of Wrigley's Los Angeles Angels. Wrigley again said many of the right things, announcing that "I don't see how you can keep them [African Americans] out," before lecturing the men like they were schoolboys, warning them that "the middle of a war isn't the spot to make such a departure from custom." That viewpoint conveniently ignored the fact that war was precisely the time when departures from custom took place, as demonstrated by the millions of American women who entered the workforce during the war.

Wrigley tried to show that, despite all evidence to the contrary, he was not a bigot, telling the men that the Angels were, somehow, pressing for the admission of black players to the Pacific Coast League. Wrigley even promised to scout Negro players, although he admitted that he had no plans to employ any as ballplayers. When the committee members gave Wrigley a list of players who were ready for the big leagues immediately, including Buck Leonard and Josh Gibson—both of whom were eventually honored by the Hall of Fame—Wrigley dismissed the suggestion, saying, "You don't start at the top in any business," although that is precisely what P.K. himself had done. He then added that he thought blacks could be hired around the ballpark in other capacities, such as "trainers."

Those were just words. Over the next two years, Wrigley made no substantive moves toward integration. In fact, after allowing Negro League teams to rent Wrigley Field over the past few seasons, in July 1945 Wrigley abruptly raised the daily rental fee to $5,000 plus 15 percent of the gross above that amount, a move that the *Defender* claimed "practically shuts the door to Negro baseball." The newspaper speculated that Wrigley made the decision because of a fight at Wrigley Field between the Chicago Americans and Memphis Red Sox. The Cubs were close-mouthed. A team spokesman said only that the decision "was not a question of color . . . the park is available for rent if you want to pay the right price." Baseball seemed no closer to integration than before the war.

But in fact it was. Over the past year, Branch Rickey of the Brooklyn Dodgers had been slowly moving in that direction. Finally, on August 28, 1945, he secretly signed Jackie Robinson, the first African American player to be employed by organized baseball since Cap Anson's infamous declaration in the previous century. On October 23, 1945, Robinson's contract became public. Nothing in baseball—and nothing in America—would ever be the same.

It would have been the perfect time for Wrigley to follow up on his words with action, to reiterate his earlier statements over the inevitability of integration in baseball, and, now that the war was over, to announce that the time was right. Instead, he remained silent, making no public statement in regard to integration. In private, however, he worked against Rickey and supported the color line.

The Cubs, like every other team apart from the Dodgers, essentially ignored the news at first and proceeded with business as usual. Neither Wrigley nor the Cubs organization made any public statements concerning Robinson's signing, and Chicago's white press virtually ignored it. Robinson was scheduled to play the 1946 season for Montreal in the International League. For the time being, baseball collectively chose to let him play—and hoped he did not make it in the major leagues.

In 1946 the Cubs paid a price for their success in 1945. When teams that had lost more players to the war than Chicago now got them back, the Cubs were suddenly the oldest club in the league. Shortstop Billy Jurges was thirty-eight. Stan Hack turned thirty-six. Meanwhile, St. Louis and Brooklyn were flush with talent and the class of the league. The only Cub player who was young enough to seem likely to improve was first baseman Eddie Waitkus, a twenty-six-year-old rookie. He hit .304 for the third-place club, the only Cub to break the .300 mark.

Franchises with extensive farm systems rapidly restocked. The Cubs finally, at long last, set out to develop a farm system. In 1942 and 1943 they had operated nine and eleven farm clubs, respectively. After dropping to only seven clubs in 1945, by 1946 the Cubs had reached working agreements with eighteen minor league clubs—the second-highest total in all baseball. But the difference between the Cubs and teams like the Cardinals and the Dodgers was that the Cubs were starting almost from scratch—other organizations were simply resuming normal operations. As a result, at the beginning of peacetime the Cubs were average, at best, and already beginning to lag behind the competition.

Season highlights in 1946 were few and far between. On April 19, fledgling Chicago television station WBKB planned to televise the first Cub baseball game from Wrigley Field, but electrical interference from elevators in the State-Lake Building, where the transmitter was located, blocked the broadcast. They tried again two months later, on July 13, and a handful of Chicago viewers

---

Following the Cub loss in the 1945 World Series, manager Charlie "Jolly Cholly" Grimm (right) remained enthusiastic despite his team's slide from first to last in three and a half seasons. Owner P.K. Wrigley (left) replaced him with Hall of Famer Frankie Frisch after just fifty games of the 1949 season.

watched the Cubs fall to Brooklyn 4–3 as Jack Gibney served as the Cubs' first television broadcaster.

Press reports at the time were less than effusive over the results. The *Tribune* reported that "the baseball figures always appeared in miniature form, perhaps three inches high at best. Only rarely could the ball be seen." Moreover, the umpires "looked like black bears." Nevertheless, the era of televised baseball in Chicago was under way. In 1947 the broadcasts were expanded to include all Cub home games, and broadcasting legend Jack Brickhouse made his debut behind the microphone.

The only other notable event took place on the final day of the season when the Cubs ended the disappointing season on a high note. They dumped St. Louis, 8–3, forcing the Cardinals into a playoff with Brooklyn for the National League pennant. St. Louis won and then rolled over the Boston Red Sox to win the World Series.

But the real baseball news in 1946 was taking place in Montreal, where Jackie Robinson was tearing up the International League and making it obvious to everyone that baseball was on the precipice of a momentous decision. In the offseason, Branch Rickey, the Dodgers' president and general manager, was certain to push for integration.

Major league baseball was already anticipating the move—and preparing to thwart it at every turn. In the middle of the 1946 season, baseball established a joint steering committee to consider "all matters of Major League interest." The committee, chaired by Yankee general manager Lee MacPhail, included both league presidents and three club owners—Sam Breadon of the Cardinals, Tom Yawkey of the Boston Red Sox, and Phil Wrigley. What the committee called "the Race Question" was their main focus of interest.

After seven meetings, MacPhail drafted a report of the committee's conclusions, perhaps the single most damning document in the annals of major league baseball. While the report echoed Wrigley by admitting that "every American boy, without regard to his race color or creed, should have a fair chance at baseball," that didn't necessarily mean major league baseball. The bulk of the document went on to provide a variety of roadblocks and leaps of logic to argue that integration was not such a good idea after all. The committee concluded that there were not enough qualified black players and therefore promoting a

handful to the majors would be simply a meaningless "gesture." Integration would also harm the Negro Leagues and hurt major league club owners who rented their parks to Negro League baseball, etc., etc., etc. While the report was never formally adopted, its conclusions nevertheless represented how baseball felt about the entire issue. On its own, major league baseball, collectively, would never integrate.

Although the steering committee never approved the entire document, significant portions were submitted to the other owners, and both Branch Rickey and Happy Chandler later indicated that the document accurately reflected the wishes of the committee. In regard to Philip Wrigley, his membership on the committee was particularly damaging, for it reinforced the degree to which his previous statements on race were just double-talk—meaningless public pronouncements that sounded progressive, backed up by private actions that only served to block the way. In this, he was like every other man who owned a team in the major leagues not based in Brooklyn—a moral coward embarrassed to reveal his true nature to the public.

Robinson's MVP performance for the Montreal Royals made it clear to everyone that he was on the verge of becoming a major leaguer. The men who owned baseball made one last play to prevent that from happening.

In January 1947, the owners, including Wrigley, met secretly in New York to address "the Race Question" head on. Branch Rickey addressed the group and told them he planned to promote Robinson to the major leagues.

The other owners presented a united front. As the issue was discussed, each of them, including Philip Wrigley, reportedly stood and announced his opposition to Rickey's plan. Rickey then pled his case again, this time asking for a secret ballot, hoping that some other owner, maybe several, hidden behind the veil of secrecy, would support integration.

None did. The vote was fifteen to one. Rickey stormed out of the meeting. The remaining fifteen owners thought the issue was settled and broke out the cigars. Major league baseball would remain as white as it was in the days of Cap Anson. The "gentleman's agreement" still held firm.

But they were mistaken. The agreement had never been codified or put into writing. For all their prejudicial bluster, the men who owned baseball were the ultimate cowards. None of them were willing to put their stated beliefs on paper. As such, there was no written prohibition barring blacks from the major leagues.

Rickey exploited that failure. A few days later, he met with Commissioner Chandler and pled his case again.

Happy Chandler was a pragmatist. The former senator, who still had political aspirations, found the perfect middle ground on the issue, one that allowed Rickey to integrate baseball without forcing Chandler to rule on the matter specifically.

He had no choice, really, or even the authority to do otherwise. Since baseball had never codified its opposition to black players, as long as Robinson's contract was legal, Chandler concluded that he had no authority to disapprove it. Chandler told Rickey that if he submitted Robinson's contract, Chandler would approve it like any other, and if Robinson made the Dodgers, Chandler personally would not stand in the way. As he later claimed, he told Rickey, "I'm going to have to meet my Maker someday, and if he asks me why I didn't let this boy play and I say it's because he's black, that might not be a satisfactory answer." To block Robinson, either the other owners or the players themselves would have to take a public stand against him.

The Cubs spent an uneventful spring in Catalina, making few substantive changes for 1947. The organization had not yet realized that the rest of the league was leapfrogging past them. And nowhere was that more obvious than in Brooklyn.

Robinson made the Dodgers in the spring of 1947, earning the starting job at first base. Opposition to him in the major leagues took place mostly in silence, behind closed doors, as neither the players nor management of other major league teams were eager to go on public record against him.

Behind closed doors it was different. On the precipice of the season, plans for a player strike were secretly being made.

Most Brooklyn Dodgers, while not overtly welcoming to Robinson, realized that their jobs might well depend on their acceptance of him. But a few were adamantly opposed to his presence, among them outfielder Dixie Walker. During spring training, Walker circulated a petition among the Dodger players protesting Robinson's presence.

Fortunately, Rickey got wind of the move and had manager Leo Durocher intervene. Rickey then met with the players and told them that if any individual did not want to play with Robinson, he would accommodate that person with a trade. Still, that offer did not completely halt opposition to Robinson among the players.

The full story remained untold for forty years until it was uncovered by ESPN in 1997 in a report on the fortieth anniversary of Robinson making the major leagues. Immediately before the season opened, players from at least four clubs—the Dodgers, the Pirates, the Cardinals, and the Cubs—were in contact with one another. If Robinson stepped onto the field on opening day in a Brooklyn uniform, the players planned to strike.

The Cubs opened the season at Wrigley Field on April 15 against the Pittsburgh Pirates. According to pitcher Hank Wyse, who was one of only a handful of Cubs players willing to go on the record about the incident, some time before taking the field Cub captain Phil Cavarretta held a team meeting. Wyse told ESPN: "He had a telegram saying all the other clubs would go on strike if Jackie Robinson played." Cavarretta asked the Cubs how they felt about the issue, and according to Wyse, all but one Cub player, whom he did not identify, voted to strike. Other reports suggest that both the Pirates and Cardinals held similar votes. Wyse said that Dixie Walker of the Dodgers was supposed to call the clubhouse to let the Cubs know that Robinson had taken the field in the Dodgers' opener versus Boston, a signal to start the strike.

Robinson took the field, but the call never came. The Cubs fell before the Pirates, 1–0. There was no turning back, and because there was not, the Cubs would soon start to fall even further behind.

Robinson was the story everywhere he went in the 1947 season, including his first trip to Chicago on May 18. While the mainstream press was rather blasé about Robinson's appearance, assigning it no special significance, it was different in the black community, which bent over backwards to make sure Robinson would succeed.

Earlier that spring, Branch Rickey had lectured the black community on their behavior in major league ballparks, warning them that "the biggest threat to his [Robinson's] success and the one enemy most likely to ruin his success . . . is the Negro people themselves. . . . We don't

CUBS
AT WRIGLEY

BY WILLIAM NACK

At the beginning of the Great Depression, back when he was a teenage boy growing up on Cleveland Avenue on Chicago's North Side, Phil Cavarretta used to do what many young Cub fans invariably did just after schools closed their gates for that long summer recess.

Phil would head for his favorite haunt, the old ball yard at Clark and Addison Streets. "We didn't have a dime in those days, not during the Depression, so to get to Cubs Park I'd *sneak* onto the elevated trains that ran through my neighborhood," Cavarretta, who turned ninety in 2006, told me. "Then I'd get off that train and head for the gate by the bleachers around back. There was a policeman there who was so nice to the kids. He'd say, 'Now wait here. I'll give you a boost after the game starts, around the second inning.' We'd be there, and he'd boost us over the fence and into the ballpark."

Once inside the yard, Cavarretta would often walk right past the bleachers and head for the upper deck, to the loftiest seats in the house. "I'd sit by myself and watch the game and dream about playing there someday," Cavarretta says. In fact, the man insists today that he can still remember, as an even younger lad, his first visit to Cubs Park in 1920, the day the dreaming began. He was watch-

ing a game there between Chicago's Lane Tech High School, the Windy City's public school champs, and New York City's High School of Commerce, which had just won the public school baseball title in Gotham.

"Guess who was playing first base for the New York team," Cavarretta says. "Lou Gehrig. I was just a kid, but I remember watching him play. I remember he hit a big home run that day." In fact, with the bases loaded and two outs in the ninth inning, Larrupin' Lou hit a 3–2 pitch over the right-field wall in Wrigley Field to win the game. "When he hit that home run, I said to myself, 'This is my favorite player.'" And eighteen years later, as the fates would so kindly arrange it, there was Gehrig back in Wrigley Field again, this time in the 1938 World Series— by then the aging, ailing first baseman for the New York Yankees—and there was the young Cub outfielder and sometime first baseman, Phillip Joseph Cavarretta.

"It was a big thrill to play against Gehrig at Cubs Park," Cavarretta said. "I'll never forget that. I happened to get on base one day, and I was standing on first and I looked at him and he didn't look too good. His skin was starting to get a little yellowish. I was having a good Series, and he looked at me, he was very very quiet, and he said to me, 'You know, Phil, I've been watching you. You play hard.

You hustle all the time. That's the way to play this game. Whatever you do, don't change.' I'll never forget that. But it was kind of sad too. The next year Lou was gone."

Cavarretta ended up as a baseball institution in Chicago, a native son who played twenty straight years for the Cubs, from 1934 to 1953, competed in three All-Star Games, and played for the last three Cubs teams that won National League pennants but never a World Series—against Detroit (1935), against those damn Yankees (1938), and against Detroit again (1945). Near the end of his playing days, Cavarretta even worked as the Cubs' player-manager for three years, from 1951 to 1953.

"I loved playing for the Cubs," Cavarretta says. "We had good ball clubs back in the old days. And Wrigley Field was great. Not just the park, but the fans. Win or lose, they always came out, even when we had lousy teams. They'd have a few beers and say, 'Well, we lost another one.' And the next day they'd be back. A great place to play. And a great place to watch a baseball game."

Wrigley Field has a place in our cultural history unmatched by any other sporting edifice west of Yankee Stadium. In Chicago it is viewed as a midwestern shrine, especially since they tore down old Comiskey Park after the 1990 season and replaced it with that soulless monstrosity known as whatever. Not even Soldier Field, the site of the famous Dempsey-Tunney heavyweight championship fight of 1927—the combat known in boxing lore as "the infamous Long Count"—can match Wrigley in its long, often bittersweet drumroll of timeless moments. Indeed, Wrigley Field has been the spiritual center of Chicago sports for most of the last one hundred years, a status it inherited immediately after the Black Sox scandal broke on the South Side, and today it stands as a kind of municipal reliquary for that city's sporting life, an aging chamber of memories.

This was where Babe Ruth called his home run shot to center field in the 1932 World Series, then corkscrewed around Charlie Root's next pitch and sailed it into those very seats. This was where, on September 28, 1938, Cub catcher Gabby Hartnett, his team a half-game behind league-leading Pittsburgh—with the score knotted at 5–5 in the ninth inning, two out, the count 0–2, and a hazy darkness falling on Wrigley—hit a game-winning shot forever known as "the Homer in the Gloamin'," ultimately launching Chicago toward that World Series where Cavarretta finally met Gehrig. This was where Pete Rose had them standing in cheery unison when he hit safely for the 4,191st time, equaling Ty Cobb's all-time record for base hits. This was the four-acre field that the Chicago Bears called home until 1970, the field where they won the NFL Championship on a sunny, frigid day in 1963 by beating the New York Giants, 14–10, and where Bear running back Gayle Sayers once turned in one of the greatest performances in pro football history, dashing for a record six touchdowns in a game against San Francisco. Wrigley is where Kerry Wood struck out twenty Houston Astros on the afternoon of May 6, 1998, setting a National League record, and where Ernie Banks hit his five-hundredth career home run, a shot off Pat Jarvis of the Braves that had the old girders vibrating to the roars of the crowd.

Finally, this was where former baseball impresario Bill Veeck was sitting in the right-center-field bleachers on that hazy Friday afternoon of September 14, 1984—a day the Cubs were beating the dreaded New York Mets and were well on their way to winning their division. I was doing a story for *Sports Illustrated* on the resurgent Cubs, and I just happened to find Veeck as I walked among the Bleacher Bums that day. He invited me to join him, so I slipped in beside him and sort of inhaled the passing scene. High hopes were fluttering in the air as visibly as the league's team flags were snapping atop the center-field scoreboard, and that big sheet was rippling in the wind from the upper deck, waving its message to all: HAIL MARY, FULL OF GRACE, KEEP THE METS IN SECOND PLACE. GO CUBS.

Veeck had owned or been involved with assorted teams over the years—at various intervals, he owned the White Sox, the Cleveland Indians, and the old St. Louis Browns—but he had been born in Chicago two months before Wrigley's doors first opened in 1914, and he literally grew up at Clark and Addison. His sportswriter father was named president of the Cubs in 1918, and by the time young Veeck was ten, in 1924, he was at the ballpark every day, vending hot dogs and peanuts to the crowds. He was also a junior groundskeeper. After his father died in 1933, Veeck became the team treasurer; in 1937 he supervised the construction of the manually run scoreboard in center and also decided to decorate the outfield walls by planting about two hundred Boston ivy cuttings along their base.

"I came out here with a crew of groundskeepers and helped set the plants," Veeck said.

Those ivied walls soon became Wrigley's signature flourish, and Veeck had lately become Wrigley's signature Bleacher Bum, a daily visitor to the center-field seats. In fact, I came to view him that day as the very embodiment of what was best and good about the game, and a testimony to the joys of watching daytime baseball at Wrigley, the most ideal and idyllic baseball setting in this whole vast land. Veeck's wife, Mary Frances, had made a large container of spiced lamb chops, and Bill was handing them out to any hungry-looking fans who happened to be sitting nearby or just drifting past to say hello.

Now he was cradling a beer in one hand and helping to pass a tub of popcorn down his aisle. "Why are you here instead of in the grandstand?" a fan called to him from a few rows below.

Bill cupped his hands around his mouth. "Here the beer is colder, the fans much smarter, and you can see better," Veeck hollered back to much laughter. "This is for people who come to enjoy, to relax!"

He turned to me again. "Would you like a lamb chop?" he asked.

They were perfectly done, just like this sun-dappled scene. "Why do you come here every day?" I asked him.

That one hung like a curve at his letters. "To me, a ballpark filled with people is a beautiful thing," he said, spreading his arms as if to embrace the multitudes around him. "It's an epitome, a work of art. This is the prettiest ballpark in either league. Look at it! It's open. You're close to the players. You're a participant rather than a spectator. If you look out from the bleachers or the grandstands, you

see the vines, you see grass. Ballparks should smell like freshly cut grass. That's why artificial turf is such a disaster. People come to the ballpark to escape the asphalt and the city streets. This park is light and airy, and it means outdoors."

Veeck turned and pointed up. His hand traced a circle. "You see the old bleachers and the old scoreboard," he said. "*There is not a discordant note in the appearance of this park.*"

Nor was there an off-key moment the entire day. In the sixth inning, with the bases loaded with Cubs and the home team winning 3–0, catcher Jody Davis came to the plate to chants that rolled in waves around the park: "Jo-DEE! Jo-DEE!" A guy sitting not far from us turned to Veeck and yelled, "A grand slam. Watch this!"

You could hear the crack of that bat from home plate to Highland Park. The ball bucked the headwinds coming in from the lake, looking like it might not have the steam to make it out, before dropping suddenly and settling in the left-center-field seats. And so it was that I turned to Veeck and told him of my finest hour as a denizen of Wrigley Field back in the early 1950s. This was the day that I hopped on the Oakton Street bus in my hometown of Skokie, Illinois, a suburb on the northern border of the city, got off at Howard Street in Evanston, clambered aboard that hot, creaking elevated train going south, and

zigzagged to a noisy stop at Addison Street, the same station where young Cavarretta once disembarked years before.

It was June 11, 1952, a bright and sunny afternoon. For a young lad of eleven, there was truly no journey more exhilarating, no sense of high adventure more keenly to be felt or relished, than the trip by train to that perfectly trimmed patch of lawn in the middle of the great metropolis on Lake Michigan. My parents had grown up on the North Side of Chicago too, and I grew up devouring tales of baseball derring-do that starred the likes of Hall of Famers Three-Finger Mordecai Brown, who once joined my ten-year-old father and his boyhood mates for a game of baseball in Lincoln Park, circa 1912; pitcher Grover Cleveland Alexander and second baseman Rogers Hornsby, who invariably used to tip his hat and wink at my mother as they passed in the mornings at the Addison Street elevated stop, he on his way to the ballpark, she on her way to Edith McCrae's ballet and dance school; and Hartnett and Hack Wilson and friends from the late 1920s, the years when city dwellers went to ball games and then to speakeasies, where my good father played piano for drinks-on-the-house.

What made the June 11 journey so special, of course, had not so much to do with chasing old ghosts long departed as it had to do with following the real-time exploits of the one genuine hero, very much alive, who was playing for the Cubs that year. At six-foot-four, and wielding an enormous forty-ounce bat, Hank Sauer was the newly emerging home run king of the National League. By June 11, the big outfielder already had fifteen homers and fifty-five RBIs, and he was well on his way to winning the league's MVP Award and hitting a league-leading thirty-seven home runs. Arriving at the park before games, with his face tanned and lined by all those days baking under Wrigley suns, Hammerin' Hank looked to us Lilliputians like some kind of gentle warrior-king. He had a one-hundred-watt smile and the patience of Job as he waded through us signing autographs on his way into the yard. What made the prospect of the day especially delicious was the fact that the Cubs were facing Curt Simmons, a hard-throwing lefty on whom Sauer had regularly feasted. In 1950, we all knew, Sauer had smacked three homers off Simmons in one game.

"Hank wore Curt out," recalls Cavarretta.

So I handed my sixty cents for a bleacher seat to the teller at the window and rose up that winding ramp past the mustard stand to the left-field side—the right-handed-hitting Sauer was a dead pull hitter—and waited as Sauer lumbered to the plate. Was there a better place on earth

for an eleven-year-old kid, for a Chicago kid raised on the lore of the once-mighty Cubs, than in the left-field bleachers on a June day in 1952, with Sauer facing Simmons?

Thwack! I can still see that first home run, a towering shot on a 3–2 count in the second inning, as it whistled by over my head and onto Waveland Avenue, where it bounced once very high and caromed off the front of a house across the street.

Pow! The second homer, off a 3–1 count in the sixth, came off another Simmons fastball and smashed hard into the fence above the catwalk. I recall it dropping to our feet, where a half-dozen small legs scrambled for it, only to be swept aside by a three-hundred-pound bearded giant with the hands and reach of an orangutan, who snatched it up and wobbled off with the prize.

Crunch! The third Sauer blast came in the eighth, on an 0–1 count, when he came around just a tad late and drove the pitch into the seats far to my left. I went home that night with mustard on my T-shirt and my head dizzy from all the spinning.

The banner headline, the big one that led the next day's *Chicago Tribune* sports section, told the tale: "Sauer Beats Phils, 3–2, with 3 Homers."

I've been to many games inside that magic egg on Chicago's North Side and can remember many players and many scenes and things—from shoes and ships and sealing wax to cabbages and kings—but when I think of that old place now, I tip my hat to that friendly cop who pushed Cavarretta over the bleacher fence, and I think of Veeck passing out lamb chops in center and planting the ivy one night in '37. But first, and always, there was that joyful day in June when I was on the catwalk in left, Simmons on the mound, and Henry John Sauer knocked out three.

WILLIAM NACK is widely acknowledged as one of the finest sportswriters of his generation. He is the author of *Secretariat: The Making of a Champion* and the collection *My Turf: Horses, Boxers, Blood Money, and the Sporting Life*.

want Negroes in the stands gambling, drunk, fighting, being arrested." Before Robinson and the Dodgers arrived in Chicago, Fay Young of the *Chicago Defender* carried that message to black Chicago, writing, "There shouldn't be the necessity of devoting this column to the unwarranted actions of Negro baseball fans as a whole, yet we cannot avoid warning our fans they are MORE on trial than is Robinson." He then went on to caution fans that "sun and liquor" don't mix and that "telephone booths are not men's wash rooms."

He needn't have worried. Black fans were interested in seeing Robinson succeed. Worries over their behavior turned out to be groundless.

When the Dodgers came to Chicago on Sunday, May 18, black Chicago turned out in force. Just one day earlier, on a Saturday, only ten thousand spectators had turned out to see the Cubs play the Giants. Now a crowd of 46,572 squeezed into Wrigley Field while more than 20,000 additional fans milled around outside, the largest attendance in the history of Wrigley Field since 1930, when the Cubs ended the practice of allowing overflow crowds to stand on the field. Wrigley and the Cubs might not have been happy about Robinson's presence in the Brooklyn lineup, but they had no trouble accepting the money he put in their pockets, despite the clientele.

As Ed Burns wrote in the *Tribune*: "There was no doubt the new paid record was set because Robinson . . . was making his first baseball appearance in Chicago as a big leaguer." Entering the contest, Robinson had answered the critics who thought he might struggle in the major leagues by knocking a hit in fourteen consecutive games. The crowd cheered Robinson at every opportunity as black and white Chicago appeared to embrace the newest Dodger. On the other hand, Brooklyn outfielder Dixie Walker, whose racial feelings were well known, was booed at every opportunity.

Cub pitching held Robinson in check as he went hitless in four at-bats with two strikeouts, but the Dodgers beat the Cubs, 4–2, sending the club to its fifth consecutive defeat. More importantly, however, baseball in Chicago had been integrated without incident. Within a short time, it would be impossible to provide any logical argument why the Cubs should not follow Brooklyn's example.

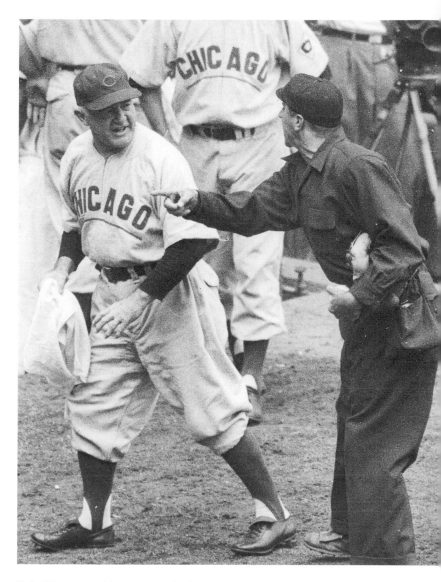

Hall of Fame second baseman Frank Frisch was named to succeed Charlie Grimm as Cubs manager in June 1949. The "Fordham Flash" suffered through nearly two seasons of losing before being replaced by player-manager Phil Cavarretta on June 21, 1951.

Although the Cubs snuck into first place with a record of 29–21 on June 14, they immediately lost ten of their next twelve games and over the balance of the season accumulated the worst record in the National League, finishing in sixth place, near the bottom in virtually every statistical category. Meanwhile, Robinson led the Dodgers to the World Series. The contrast between the two clubs could not have been more striking.

Slugger Ralph Kiner leaving a party with Elizabeth Taylor. By the time he arrived in Chicago via a blockbuster ten-player trade on June 4, 1953, he'd already dated Taylor and led the National League in home runs for seven consecutive seasons.

On July 8, Wrigley Field played host to the annual All-Star Game, an event more notable than the final score, which ended 2–1 in favor of the American League. No one realized it at the time, but the contest would be the last all-white All-Star Game in big league history.

Three days earlier, in fact, on July 5, former Cub employee Bill Veeck, now the owner of the Cleveland Indians, stole some thunder from the midsummer classic. While the Indians were in Chicago to play the White Sox,

Veeck held a press conference to announce that the Indians had signed Larry Doby, breaking the color line in the American League. Although Veeck later said that he made the announcement on the road "to make it as easy as possible for Doby," Veeck was a man who rarely acted without forethought. Making the announcement in Chicago not only ensured a great deal of publicity before Doby's appearance in Cleveland but, with national media already descending on the city for the All-Star Game, made certain that his move would not go unnoticed and would steal some of the limelight.

The St. Louis Browns soon followed suit, signing two black players, and by the end of the season every team in every big league city was under increasing pressure to integrate. That policy had long been advocated in the black press, but in a few places, such as Boston and New York, the white mainstream press led the charge, often behind a crusading columnist, such as the *Boston Record*'s Dave Egan.

In Chicago, however, that was not the case. The white press, particularly the influential *Tribune*, the dominant newspaper of the period, ignored the issue almost entirely. Only Lloyd Lewis, while sports editor and managing editor of the *Chicago Daily News*, had made race much of an issue, but he left the newspaper in 1945 to write historical biographies, and no one else took up the cause. When other writers did address race, they generally did so dispassionately. In practice, if not in reality, the Chicago press was, at best, neutral, as if motivated by the belief that writing anything about the subject, beyond the pure reporting of facts, would offend their readership, either at home or in the Cubs' front office.

Only Fay Young, the black sports columnist for the *Chicago Defender*, pressed the issue. By the end of the season, the Cubs began to feel some heat.

They were already sending the occasional scout to Negro League games, but theirs was a halfhearted effort. Young reported that they first set their sights on George Crowe, the first baseman for the New York Black Yankees, but the Cubs lost interest when Crowe "didn't feel like hustling the days he was being watched." Crowe would later make his major league debut with the Boston Braves in 1952.

In September the Cubs again moved to deflect criticism over their racial policy. Two Negro League veterans were invited to a tryout at Wrigley Field—catcher John Ritchey of the Chicago Americans and another player who was never publicly identified, presumably one of Ritchey's teammates. While the Cubs played out the string in St. Louis, the two men and at least fifty white prospects were invited to Wrigley Field for a workout before three Cub scouts.

Fay Young probably played a role in the selection of the black players. Not only was he present at the tryout—the only reporter known to attend—but he reportedly had to convince Ritchey to attend the tryout. Ritchey already had plans to return home to his native San Diego before being persuaded to remain in Chicago another week.

Ritchey's upbringing was similar to that of Jackie Robinson, whose collegiate background and military experience had helped convince Branch Rickey that he had the proper temperament to make it in the big leagues. As a teenager, the Californian had played for a mostly white American Legion team, where he earned the nickname "Johnny Baseball," a partial homage to San Diego native Ted Williams, who was just a few years older and had been nicknamed "Teddy Ballgame." Ritchey's Legion team reached the national semifinals in 1938 and played in South Carolina, but Ritchey was not allowed to participate. In 1940 the club reached the finals, this time played in North Carolina. Once again, Ritchey was not allowed to play.

After high school, Ritchey attended San Diego State College before joining the military, where he served with the Army Corps of Engineers in both France and the Pacific, earning five battle stars in the process. After being discharged in 1947, he joined the Chicago American Giants of the Negro American League and hit a league-best .381. Only five-foot-nine, Ritchey ran well, hit for average, and was a fine defender. All he lacked was power—and white skin.

After the tryout, Cub official Harold George was guarded. The scouts were unimpressed by the other Negro Leaguer, but they liked Ritchey. "All I can say," said George, "is that we're interested."

Within a week, however, interest in Ritchey had cooled. The *Defender* reported that if the club signed him, he would probably be sent to one of their Single A farm clubs in either Davenport or Des Moines. Ritchey, apparently, was not impressed by the Cubs and had no interest

in a demotion. In the spring of 1948, the Cubs expressed surprise when they learned that instead of waiting for the Cubs to offer him a contract, Ritchey signed with the San Diego Padres of the PCL, becoming the first black player in that league. Over the next decade, Ritchey went on to a productive career, primarily in the PCL, but he was never called up to the major leagues. During that same time period, the catcher's box at Wrigley Field would be manned by a revolving door of mediocre talent, none of whom displayed much more power than Ritchey.

In 1948 it became clear just how badly off the Cubs were. Awful from the start, they spent much of the season in a pitched battle with the Phillies and the Reds for last place. The club had no direction and no future.

The Cubs were in desperate need of players. Had they acted boldly, they could have had the pick of the Negro Leagues. Then again, so could have almost every other club in baseball, for despite the breaking of the color barrier in 1947, integration in the major leagues was painfully slow. Only the Dodgers and Indians continued to act boldly, signing more African Americans in 1948. It would be several more years before a black face on a major league roster was the norm and not the anomaly.

The *Defender* tried to mount a boycott of both the White Sox and the Cubs in 1948. The White Sox, apart from the 1942 tryout of Robinson, were no better than the Cubs in racial matters—since that time they had not even bothered to give a tryout to a black player. But in reality, neither team felt much pressure, either to integrate or to win. The Cubs were not troubled when black fans at Wrigley Field booed the Cubs and gave their support to Brooklyn. The way the Cubs were playing, the fact that anyone showed up at the ballpark was a miracle.

While the Cubs benefited from the fact that the crosstown White Sox were even worse than they were, in the wake of the war attendance was good no matter how bad the baseball was. The Cubs were drawing more than one million fans a year despite their decision, beginning in 1948, to make baseball even more available on television. The *Tribune*-owned WGN (the acronym stood for "World's Greatest Newspaper") began broadcasting on April 5. WBKB also broadcast Cub games, and in 1949 a third station added the Cubs to their lineup, saturating the market. Wrigley wasn't worried about that, saying, "We are confident that television, handled with imagination and understanding, will bring baseball closer to vast numbers of Americans. It will result eventually in bringing many more persons to the ballpark." Somewhat improbably, he was right, at least in the short term, for just as radio broadcasts had made the Cubs a regional favorite and expanded their base, so did television. Over time a Cubs game on TV became the backdrop in many Chicago homes. By the end of the season, WGN, with Jack Brickhouse at the microphone, was by far the favorite station of most fans. As Larry Wolter wrote in the *Tribune*, "Brickhouse is like a friend sitting beside you in a box seat, a friend who understands everything." For a generation of fans, Brickhouse provided the soundtrack to summer. He is one of the reasons why many longtime Cubs fan still look back at the Cubs of the late 1940s and 1950s with such nostalgia. When television was new and televised baseball exotic, Jack Brickhouse was a favorite uncle who showed up every afternoon and took you to the ball game.

At the end of the 1948 season, Jim Gallagher and Wrigley decided that something had to be done. Unfortunately, they had no clue as to what. As a last-place ball club, no one would have blamed the Cubs if they had chosen to rebuild, trading away their few valuable veterans for prospects. Instead, apparently random trades were made, just for the sake of making trades and not according to any long-term strategy.

At the end of the season, Bill Nicholson, after ten years with the Cubs, was sent to the Philadelphia Phillies. In return, the Cubs received, not a prospect, but Dixie Walker's brother Harry, a thirty-one-year-old outfielder. In 1947 he had won an unlikely batting title, batting .363 with the Phillies and Cardinals before returning to earth in 1948, when he hit a soft .292 in part-time duty. Walker was not a bad player, and to be fair, Nicholson's career was on the decline, but he had cracked sixteen home runs in 1948. The Cubs probably could have parlayed that into some kind of prospect. Instead, they seemed ever determined to acquire another veteran a year or two too late.

A few days later, Gallagher sold Philadelphia the Cubs' best young pitcher, Russ Meyer, a ten-game winner in 1948 and precisely the kind of player he should have been trying to acquire. Before the year was up, he made yet another stupid trade with the Phillies, sending away a fading Hank

Borowy and Eddie Waitkus for two pitchers, Monk Dubiel and thirty-nine-year-old knuckleballer Dutch Leonard. The end result was that the Cubs were even older and less talented in 1949 than they had been in 1948, and every time they faced Borowy, he beat them.

The Cubs started slow and then slumped. Even in the moribund Cub front office, it was clear that things were falling apart.

Wrigley wanted to pull down the shades and disappear from view. He did not want to sell the Cubs, but he had tired of his role as club president, a position he clearly did not enjoy. Wrigley tried to find someone to take over, but with few contacts in the game apart from those he already employed, he soon abandoned the idea. Instead, he merely shuffled the deck.

He asked Grimm to move from the bench to the front office and become director of player personnel, taking charge of the minor leagues and taking over most of the general manager duties from Gallagher. Gallagher was not fired but kicked upstairs, becoming vice president and business manager. Then Wrigley told Grimm to hire his own replacement.

The ex-manager picked New York Giant coach Frankie Frisch, a more talented and far more fiery version of himself. The hard-nosed former second baseman had learned baseball under John McGraw and led the Cardinals' raucous Gashouse Gang while forging a Hall of Fame career, but in fourteen seasons as a big league manager with St. Louis and the Pirates, Frisch's clubs had won exactly one pennant despite finishing below .500 only three times. Wrigley announced the changes on June 10, and Frisch took over two days later.

The announcement buried the other Cubs news of the day. As an organization, they were no longer lily-white.

On June 11, Wrigley's Los Angeles Angels signed veteran Negro League pitcher Booker McDaniels. McDaniels, thirty-six years old, was near the end of a fine career. As a pitcher for the Kansas City Monarchs, the hard thrower was nicknamed "Cannonball" and had occasionally impersonated the great Satchel Paige when the Monarchs played before crowds that did not know better.

The Cubs, however, had no intention of bringing him to Chicago, not even after he won his first three starts, including a shutout in his PCL debut. The signing was symbolic—now no one could say the Cub organization had not signed an African American player. But it was also cynical, for by signing a player already past his prime, the organization had a ready-made excuse if it was ever pressured to promote him to the Cubs. They never were, and they never did.

The Cubs were not the only club to use such a strategy. The Red Sox, for example, signed veteran infielder Piper Davis for the same reason. Signings like these bought major league teams time and kept political groups at bay.

The Chicago press was almost complicit in the ploy. Incredibly, even though McDaniels was the first African American signed by the Cub organization, the event was virtually ignored.

Granted, there was a lot going on. Three days after the McDaniels signing, just before the June 15 trading deadline, the Cubs made a deal. Neither the Cubs nor the Cincinnati Reds were going anywhere, so each sent the other a thirty-year-old outfielder and a thirty-two-year-old outfielder: the Cubs' Peanuts Lowrey and Harry Walker went to the Reds for former pro basketball star Frankie Baumholtz and Hank Sauer, an occasional slugger whose brother Ed had played for the Cubs during the war.

It turned out to be one of the best deals the team had made in decades. Sauer had hit fifty home runs for minor league Syracuse in 1947, and he followed up with thirty-five more for the Reds in 1947. But he was streaky and did most of his damage early in the season. When he started slow in 1949, the Reds thought he was a flash in the pan and sent him off.

Sauer fit Chicago like the wind blowing out, his powerful right-handed stroke perfect for dropping the ball just over Wrigley Field's ivy-covered brick wall in left field. As soon as he got to Chicago, Sauer, who had hit only four home runs for the Reds in 1949, got hot, knocking twenty-seven more and driving in eighty-three runs in only ninety-six games. The Pittsburgh native was not blessed with speed, but he always appeared to be giving his best effort. That, coupled with his power, quickly made him a crowd favorite, and Sauer soon earned the sobriquet "the Mayor of Wrigley Field." The Cubs weren't winning, but Sauer made going to Wrigley Field bearable, and the kids who huddled around the TV or listened on the radio every afternoon had a hero.

For a time, however, even this was relegated to the back pages. Hours after the Sauer trade, former Cub Eddie Waitkus, in town with the Phillies, was shot by a young woman, Ruth Ann Steinhagen, in Chicago's Edgewater Hotel.

Steinhagen, only nineteen years old, didn't even know Waitkus, but ever since getting her first glimpse of him on April 27, 1947, while attending a Cubs game with friends, she had harbored an unhealthy obsession. Infatuated, she collected photos and news clippings about Waitkus, celebrated April 27 as their "anniversary," and even took Lithuanian lessons (Waitkus was of Lithuanian extraction). When Waitkus was traded to the Phillies, she was crushed.

Her family knew she was not well and tried to intervene, but Steinhagen moved out, and the mentally ill young lady decided to kill Waitkus. When the Phillies came to Chicago, she bought a .22 rifle, checked into the Edgewater Hotel, and sent Waitkus a note that read, "I have something of importance to speak with you about."

When the ballplayer came to her room, she told him, "I've got a surprise for you," pulled out the rifle, and said, "For two years you've been bothering me and now you're going to die." With that, she aimed the gun at Waitkus's chest and pulled the trigger.

The player collapsed, asking, "Baby, what did you do that for?" Steinhagen then called the front desk and reported the shooting.

The bullet went under Waitkus's heart and lodged near his spine. He missed being killed or paralyzed by inches. Although Waitkus eventually recovered from his wounds and returned to the major leagues in 1950, the leading vote-getter at first base in All-Star balloting at the time of the shooting was never quite the same. Steinhagen spent three years in a mental institution, receiving shock treatment, before being released, and she has since lived in seclusion.

By the time the press turned its attention back to the Cubs, the season, thankfully, was half over. After Grimm, manager Frisch's in-your-face approach was jarring. Like Rogers Hornsby a generation before, Frisch had little patience for players without his talent, and no one on the Cubs, not even Sauer, had Frisch's talent. The manager made no difference, and the Cubs finished in last place, thirty-six games behind the pennant-winning Dodgers. In his third year in the major leagues, Jackie Robinson underscored the idiocy of Jim Crow baseball by leading the league with a .342 batting average and earning the Most Valuable Player Award. The contrast between the two clubs could not have been more pronounced.

The Dodgers were just better—and blacker—as Robinson was joined by two more African American teammates, Roy Campanella and Don Newcombe. The Dodgers were also smarter, something the Cubs would give Brooklyn many opportunities to prove over the next few seasons. With their own farm system barren, the Cubs looked longingly at the pile of prospects accumulated by the Dodgers. Branch Rickey was flattered each time the Cubs came calling. After all, that was part of the reason to have a farm system in the first place.

Rickey was adept at keeping the cream for his own team while selling sour milk for top dollar. He steered the Cubs toward left-handed pitcher Paul Minner, whom the Dodgers could spare, and first baseman Preston Ward. Ward had been a sensation when he first came up to the Dodgers in 1948, but pitchers soon discovered he couldn't hit the curveball, and the Dodgers soon discovered that Gil Hodges could. Ward was sent back to the minors, presumably never to return, until the Cubs again rang up Branch Rickey.

Grimm, Gallagher, and Wrigley fell under Rickey's spell, and by the time he was through he had them convinced that Minner and Ward were the key to the pennant. On October 14, the Cubs gladly turned over $100,000 for two players who had yet to prove themselves.

Charlie Grimm didn't wait around to see them try. The relationship with Gallagher was awkward. On January 6, Grimm quit to take a job in the Texas League, leaving Gallagher in charge again. The longtime GM made one more move, buying pitcher Johnny Vander Meer from the Reds on February 18. In 1938 Vander Meer had set a record by throwing two consecutive no-hitters, but that had been a lifetime ago. Now he was thirty-five years old and coming off a season in which his record was only 5–10. But Vander Meer had thrown a shutout against the Cubs, which was enough to fool them into thinking he had something left. He did not.

A week later, Wrigley made a shocking move, one that seemed, at first, to represent a sea change in his thinking. For once he actually hired a baseball man to run the franchise. At an annual salary of $20,000, Dodger scout Wid Matthews was signed up to serve as the club's new director of player personnel. "In general," announced Wrigley, "Wid will be responsible for keeping Frank's [manager Frank Frisch] needs satisfied and also seeing to it that adequate replacements are ready." Wrigley, it was reported, planned to give Matthews carte blanche and an empty checkbook to acquire talent as quickly as possible. The press reacted as if Wrigley had hired Branch Rickey himself. Indeed, Matthews seemed the next best thing.

Matthews had played outfield for the A's and Senators in the 1920s before first going to work as a scout, under Branch Rickey, for the Cardinals, where he was credited with signing Cardinal star Stan Musial. Matthews then followed Rickey to the Dodgers. Along with Clyde Sukeforth and George Sisler, he had been one of three scouts Rickey sent to evaluate talent in the Negro Leagues before signing Jackie Robinson.

Frisch had known Matthews since his days with the Cardinals and probably recommended him for the position. The hire was seen as a real coup for the Cubs. Matthews was considered the "top talent man" and player evaluator in the Dodger system, the practical genius behind Rickey's more forward-leaning intelligence. Furthermore, as the *Tribune* crowed, "Adding to the jubilance of the Cubs executives was the fact they finally got something from Branch Rickey for nothing."

Those words would prove to be premature. In fact, Matthews would quickly sour under the Cubs' employ. While he had worked for Rickey for fifteen years, that didn't necessarily mean the Mahatma considered him irreplaceable. In fact, Rickey was probably glad to see Matthews go. As historian Jules Tygiel wrote in his book *Baseball's Great Experiment*, when Matthews scouted Jackie Robinson, he was less than enthusiastic, terming Robinson "strictly the showboat type." Tygiel also believed that had the southern-born Matthews known at the time that he was being sent out to scout black players for the Dodgers, he would have accepted integration with reluctance.

Matthews was also no scientist. He was an old-time baseball man with old attitudes, a person who considered a player's handshake an integral part of his evaluation. Despite first impressions, he was hardly the type to lead the Cubs in a new era.

Matthews did very little in 1950, presumably focusing his activities on the minor leagues. But he did sign one player of lasting impact. On April 1, 1950, the Cubs signed their second African American, shortstop Gene Baker of the Kansas City Monarchs.

Baker was no Booker McDaniels, an aging star past his prime. He was young and talented, a player whose best years were ahead of him, and at first blush it seemed as if the Cubs were ready to plunge into the black market. Sadly, that would not be the case. As with the signing of McDaniel, Baker was acquired primarily in order to keep him in the minor leagues.

Baker, a native of Davenport, Iowa, who had starred in basketball and track in high school, played semipro baseball after leaving the Navy and began his professional career with the Kansas City Monarchs in 1948. He quickly developed a reputation as the best-fielding shortstop in the Negro Leagues.

The Cubs assigned him to Springfield in the International League, but after only a few games he was reassigned to Des Moines, where he hit .321 and earned a promotion to the Los Angeles Angels in midseason. Baker was quickly recognized as the best-fielding shortstop in that league too.

But in terms of race, the Cubs were moving with all the haste of a glacier. Although Frisch cleaned house in 1950, the end result was that the Cubs replaced about a dozen untalented veterans with an equal number of untalented youngsters. For the past three seasons, Roy Smalley had manned shortstop, struggling at both the plate and in the field, yet even though Baker impressed everyone from the start, the Cubs seemed unwilling to make a change. For Baker, the phrase "languishing in the minor leagues" would quickly become familiar.

Even worse, with the acquisition of Baker, the Cubs' interest in African American players stopped. Now that they had one black player, the organization did not seem interested in any more. It would be three years before the Cubs signed another African American, outfielder Solly Drake.

It rapidly became apparent that once he was out from under Rickey's direction, Matthews was clueless. At the end of the season, Matthews announced a policy change in regard to the Los Angeles Angels, one of the club's two

ERA CHAMPIONS

1902	Jack Taylor	1.33
1906	Mordecai Brown	1.04
1907	Jack Pfiester	1.15
1918	Hippo Vaughn	1.74
1919	Pete Alexander	1.72
1920	Pete Alexander	1.91
1932	Lon Warneke	2.37
1938	Bill Lee	2.66
1945	Hank Borowy	2.13

Triple A teams, a policy that *Los Angeles Times* writer Frank Finch called "revolutionary." That was the understatement of the year.

"For the past several seasons," Matthews told Finch, "[the Cubs] have refrained from picking off Angel stars," preferring to place those players most likely to be recalled to Chicago with the Cubs' other Triple A team in Springfield, Massachusetts. Now Matthews was making the policy not only official but public. "We will not take any player from the Angels during the season without the express approval of President Don Stewart of the Angels and the Los Angeles baseball writers," said Matthews. In fact, he added, the Cubs were already following that policy. "Frank Baumholtz could have helped the Cubs this year," he said, "but we laid off him." After all, Baumholtz *only* hit .379 in 1950 for the Angels. "Henceforth," he added, "[if a] recall would hurt the Angels more than it would help the Cubs . . . he'll stick with L.A."

What? Matthews was admitting that winning major league games in Chicago was far less important than win-

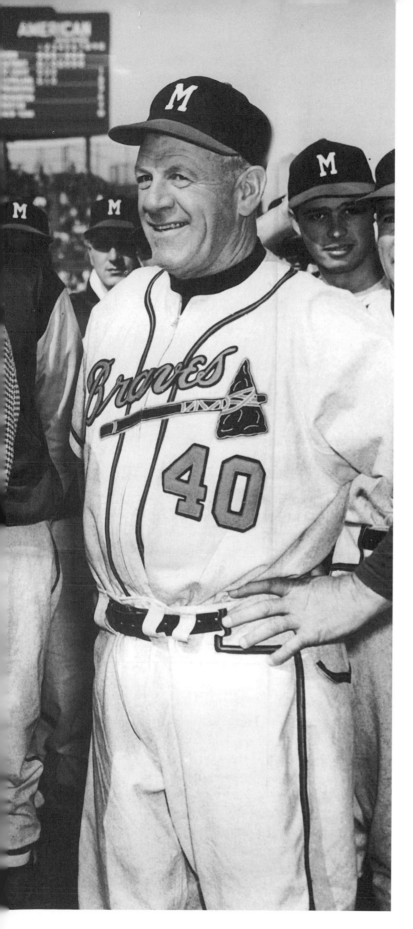

ning minor league games in Los Angeles and that *sportswriters* halfway across the country would have a larger say in who played for the Cubs than he would. The Angels, one of the top two teams in the Cub farm system, and stocked with some of the best talent in the organization, was off limits unless the team president and baseball writers covering the team gave their okay.

Of all the nutty things P.K. Wrigley allowed to take place during his reign or put in place himself, that policy may have been the wackiest. It made no sense whatsoever . . . until one realizes that it conveniently left Gene Baker in Los Angeles for the foreseeable future and took the decision out of the hands of both Wrigley and Matthews. Baker had been an all-star in the PCL in 1950. Why would the Angels ever willingly choose to part with him? Expecting the Angels to act against their own interests was nearly as insane as the Cubs actually acting *in* their own interests.

It would have been akin to the Dodgers leaving Jackie Robinson in Montreal after 1946 or the Giants leaving Mays in Minneapolis in 1951, but the Chicago press did not even ask why. Expectations for the Cubs were so low that no one really seemed to care. It was easier for most of the writers just to show up in the press box for a few hours, eat a sandwich, and then go home rather than try to figure out what the Cubs were doing and why.

Two days later, on October 10, Matthews locked horns with the Dodgers and got taken once again. One year after acquiring Preston Ward to play first base, Matthews dealt backup outfielder Hank Edwards and cash to Brooklyn for two older first base prospects, Dee Fondy and Chuck Connors. Both players had some talent, but more first basemen was hardly what the Cubs needed. At the same time, the Cub farm system was beginning to shrink under Matthews: it was down from twenty-three teams in 1947 to only fifteen in 1950. Television was part of the reason—families all over America were deciding to sit at home rather than go to the ball game—but at the same time the

No single player symbolized the postwar Cubs better than left fielder Hank Sauer. He is shown receiving his 1952 National League MVP Award from *Chicago Sun-Times* sportswriter John C. Hoffman (center), along with manager Phil Cavarretta (left) and Braves manager Charlie Grimm (right). Sauer was a crowd-pleaser for a team that finished as high as .500 only once (77–77 in 1952) during his seven years at Wrigley Field.

Ernie Banks posed for photographer George Brace on his first day at Wrigley Field on September 14, 1953. Early arrivals at the ballpark saw the twenty-two-year-old shortstop hit his first batting practice pitch out of the park. He played his first major league game three days later in Chicago before a crowd of 2,703 batting seventh, going hitless, and making an error. By season's end, however, he finished with a .314 batting average and had won the starting shortstop job.

Cubs acted as if an extensive system was a waste of resources. Wrigley never saw the value in accumulating prospects, always preferring a player with major league experience over one with none, no matter how promising he looked. In only a few years, the already struggling franchise would have one of the smallest farm systems in the major leagues.

The 1951 and 1952 seasons brought little change. In 1951 the Cubs finished last, and Matthews got fleeced by the Dodgers again, trading outfielder Andy Pafko and several others to Brooklyn for a bunch of spare parts the Dodgers didn't want—Gene Hermanski, Eddie Miksis, Joe Hatten, and Bruce Edwards, players who were little better than anyone the Cubs already had on hand. Pafko, who had ably manned center field since 1943, was a four-time All-Star coming off his best season in 1950, when he cracked thirty-six home runs and knocked in ninety-two. At age thirty, he was showing no signs of slowing down and was precisely the kind of player the Cubs had trouble finding: a multi-skilled player who was as valuable on the road as he was at Wrigley Field, a park where small dimensions sometimes masked a player's lack of speed and range and could increase power. Paired with Hank Sauer, he was even more valuable, and Pafko's lunch bucket appeal was undeniable.

This meant nothing to Matthews, who seemed determined to show his baseball acumen by "getting" something from the Dodgers. Instead, Brooklyn did all the getting.

Frankie Frisch did not survive the season. On July 25, the Cubs turned to a tried-and-true strategy—hiring an ex-player to take the job. Even if it did not work, it was guaranteed to keep the press at bay for a while.

Phil Cavarretta drew the short straw, and under his command the Cubs were even worse than they had been under Frisch. They had nothing. Cavarretta, at age thirty-four, was little more than a part-time player, yet he was the only Cub to bat above .300, and Dutch Leonard, at forty-two, was arguably the team's best pitcher. That didn't bode well for the future, and by the end of the season everyone noticed. The *Tribune* pled for the restoration of "major league representation" at Wrigley Field.

Even Phil Wrigley finally seemed out of patience. Having just announced that they were raising ticket prices 25 percent, on January 9, 1952, the Cubs held their annual winter luncheon, a generally dull affair punctuated by optimistic prattle designed to sell tickets.

After the luncheon, Wid Matthews entertained questions and opened the session by saying, "Mr. Wrigley's patience is at an end." Then Matthews launched into a long discussion of catcher Bruce Edwards's sore arm. In Matthews's world, the loss of Edwards—he hit .234 in 1951 after being acquired by the Cubs—was all that kept the Cubs from being a winner.

"Let me interrupt," said Wrigley. He called any hope for

Edwards's return "dreaming," and any thoughts about winning in 1952 "wishful thinking." Matthews then tempered his remarks and took the heat, saying, "If there is anything wrong now, you may lay it at my feet." He then admitted that, indeed, the Cubs had little to look forward to in 1952. "With our young players," he said, "our future is in the laps of the gods." Well, in 1952 God left the young players to fend for themselves. Before the start of the season, *New York Herald Tribune* columnist Red Smith asked Ed Burns of the *Tribune*, "What's your ball club like this year?" Burns responded by extolling their human virtues, calling them "the nicest bunch of kids you ever saw," before pausing dramatically and adding dryly, "They faint at the sight of blood."

About the only player who didn't was Hank Sauer. God apparently sat Sauer down on his knee, pointed to the bleachers, and directed him to hit the ball out there as often as he could.

Sauer might have been helped by the fact that the Cubs abandoned Catalina in favor of holding spring training in Mesa, Arizona. Now the Cubs actually got to face real major league competition in the spring, something that had always been hard to come by in Catalina. Whatever the reason, Sauer got off to a quick start. For the first two months of the 1952 season, Hank Sauer was as good a hitter as the Chicago Cubs had ever had, and as long as he was hitting the Cubs were respectable.

Opening day proved to be typical of the 1952 Cubs. Ransom Jackson hit a home run, and Sauer followed with a grand slam to put the Cubs ahead 5–0 over the Reds. Then it all nearly unraveled. First, second baseman Eddie Miksis pulled a muscle. When his replacement, Bob Ramazzotti, got hit in the head on a pickoff attempt and left the game with dizziness, Cavarretta was forced to insert rookie Bud Hardin into the lineup. A few botched double plays later, and the Reds tied the score before the Cubs finally won in the tenth.

On June 11, Sauer hit three home runs, all solo shots, to account for all of Chicago's scoring in a 3–2 win versus the Phillies at Wrigley Field. The Cubs were in third place with a record of 31–19 and closing fast on both the league-leading Dodgers and second-place Giants. Sauer was leading the known world in almost everything, batting .359, with eighteen home runs and fifty-eight RBIs. If he kept it up,

he'd not only break Babe Ruth's home run record but Hack Wilson's RBI mark. Even a triple crown seemed to be within his grasp.

Of course, it didn't last, and neither did the Cubs' grip on the first division. A five-game winning streak that gave the club a record of 34–19 was followed by a nine-game losing streak. Unfortunately, Hank Sauer had crammed half a season's work into the first fifty games. For the rest of the season, he was barely average, hitting well under .250 and taking another hundred games to match the power he showed in the first fifty. He finished with a batting average of .270 with 37 home runs and 121 RBIs. That was enough to earn him the NL MVP Award, since no one else really stood out. The Cubs slipped back to .500 and finished 77–77, in fifth place behind the Dodgers.

All the 1952 season did for the Cubs was buy Matthews another year and give him a false sense of accomplishment. The Cubs' record of 42–58 after June 15 was more indicative of their true standing than their 34–19 mark before it. Chicago failed to make a substantive move in the offseason, opening 1953 with a roster virtually identical to that of 1952. Of course, apart from Gene Baker, the Cubs did not have much in the minor leagues in either L.A. or Springfield. Despite the fact that L.A. manager Stan Hack recommended that Baker be promoted, in the spring of 1953 Cavarretta sent him down for more "seasoning." After all, with their .500 finish, the Cubs were moving in the right direction. What did they need Baker for?

On March 17, they began to find out. The Boston Braves became the first franchise to move in fifty years, transferring to Milwaukee. Although Wrigley could have fought the move, he chose not to, retreating from his northern border. From Chicago's northernmost suburbs, the Braves were less than an hour away, and hordes of fans in Wisconsin, Minnesota, and Iowa soon changed their allegiance.

The Braves were also a better and far more interesting team, as were the White Sox. Both the Braves and the White Sox had integrated, the Braves making the move with Sam Jethroe in 1950 and the White Sox with Sam Hairston in 1951. Although neither of these players remained with their ball club, both teams put black players on the field every day in 1953. Bill Bruton played outfield for Milwaukee and Minnie Minoso for the White Sox. Each club got out of the gate fast in 1953, both in terms of wins and losses and at the gate—particularly Milwaukee, which played to a packed house almost every day.

The contrast could not have been more dramatic. All of a sudden, the Cubs could not depend on an automatic million-plus fans streaming into Wrigley Field anymore. According to an interview Phil Wrigley gave the *Chicago Daily News* later in the season, since World War I the Cubs had generally turned an annual profit of 4 to 5 percent. They had lost money only twice: in 1942, when they finished $7,000 in the red, and an undisclosed amount in 1950. This was not a bad financial performance given that they had spent over $4 million on the minor leagues and player development since the end of World War II. But those days were gone. Wrigley claimed that the Cubs would lose nearly half a million dollars in 1953.

They were terrible from the start, a situation not helped by the fact that Sauer broke a finger in spring training and started the season on the bench. On June 4, the Cubs were in last place with a pathetic record of 12–27. Attendance was off by more than eighty thousand. Something had to be done.

This time Matthews turned, not to the Dodgers, but to the Pirates. It was a distinction without a difference, for by 1953 Branch Rickey had moved on from the Dodgers to take control of the Pittsburgh franchise. Rickey licked his chops at the opportunity to take some more of Phil Wrigley's money.

Outfielder Ralph Kiner, who had led the league in home runs for the past seven seasons, was too expensive for Rickey's taste. In 1953 Rickey cut his salary from $90,000 to $75,000, but still looked to deal him. The Cubs had expressed some interest in the offseason but balked at the price—Rickey wanted $200,000, or perhaps a bit less if he could get some players.

Now Rickey had the Cubs over a barrel. In the *Tribune*, Ed Burns reported that the Cubs were "the only bidder for Kiner at Rickey prices" and that Matthews "has been spurred to complete the deal . . . to divert fan attention from the failure of the Cubs."

Chicago paid a dear price for their diversion. They sent Rickey "only" $150,000, but also *five* players—Preston Ward, Hermanski, pitcher Bob Shultz, catcher Toby Atwell, and minor league infielder George Freese. In return, the Cubs got not only Kiner but another $50,000 of

salary Rickey didn't want in pitcher Howie Pollet, catcher Joe Garagiola, and outfielder Catfish Metkovich. All told, the deal cost Wrigley almost $200,000 in cash and salary.

Cub fans were not fooled for long. Pittsburgh beat the Cubs 6–1 in Kiner's first game, leading one longtime fan, a salesman named Harry Cox from the North Side, to complain bitterly about the deal in the *Tribune*, saying, "It stinks. You remember when they got Chuck Klein from Philadelphia? It's the same damn deal. Kiner is over the hill." Sadly, Cox would be proved correct. After averaging 37 home runs a year and 102 RBIs for Pittsburgh, in two seasons with the Cubs Kiner would hit only 50 home runs and knock in only 160 base runners.

Wrigley had been more than patient with Matthews, once saying that building a ball club "was like planting an asparagus bed." Well, by midseason it began to become clear that Matthews's bed wasn't going to bear. It was time to look elsewhere.

The Cubs had never given much credence to the logic of the idea that since African Americans had been willing to die for their country they should be allowed to play baseball. But once the Cubs' racial policy started to have an impact on their ability to make money, they paid attention. The presence of black players on successful clubs both in Comiskey Park and in Milwaukee, drawing big crowds and winning games, suddenly made the Cubs' longtime position untenable. Economic self-interest led to instant enlightenment. Kicking and screaming and bleeding red ink, the Cubs were finally ready to break their own color line.

Down in L.A., they suddenly remembered Gene Baker and finally abandoned the bizarre and cowardly policy that had kept him there, taking over his contract on August 31 and announcing that he would join the Cubs after the Angels' season ended on September 13. When Matthews made the announcement, he made no mention of Baker's race.

The Cubs, however, were acutely aware of it. Since midseason, they'd fretted over Baker's impending promotion, which they knew could cause an immediate problem. Most major league clubs brought up African Americans in pairs so that the players could room together. Otherwise, it was just too awkward when the clubs encountered segregated conditions in restaurants and hotels, and baseball was not yet enlightened enough to ask black and white players to room together. The Cubs could not bring up one African American player—they needed two, and the only other African American in the organization, Solly Drake, wasn't ready.

In midseason they had begun scouting the Negro Leagues in earnest, an act that exposed as a lie Wrigley's earlier statements that the Cubs were already scouting the Negro Leagues. They were just in time, because the Negro Leagues were already beginning to falter as more and more African American fans turned their attention to major league baseball and the major leagues stripped the Negro Leagues of talent. Increasingly, rosters were made up of players who were either too old for the majors or, in the minds of the major league scouts, not talented enough. Fortunately for Chicago, one final wave of youthful talent still remained.

The Cubs found Ernie Banks. A native of Texas, Banks initially starred as a semipro softball player before joining the Kansas City Monarchs in 1950. There he first attracted the attention of major league scouts. Following a two-year stint in the service, Banks returned in 1953 to K.C., where a number of observers considered him the best prospect in the league.

Precisely how Banks came to the Cubs' attention—and precisely who was responsible for signing him to a contract—is a bit of a mystery, as several different men, including Monarch manager Buck O'Neill, have claimed responsibility. At any rate, Banks was a standout in 1953, and anyone with half a baseball brain could see that. At some point in midseason, Cubs scout Ray Hayworth spent a week following the Monarchs and came away most impressed by Banks. Matthews then sent three other scouts to check on Banks—Vernie Helms, Jim Payton, and Ray Blades—all of whom gave their approval. Matthews approached Monarch owner Tom Baird and said he wanted Banks, but Baird responded that he had already promised the White Sox and the Yankees first dibs on the young

shortstop. Matthews, however, started talking money, and when he got to $22,000, Baird accepted, also giving the Cubs rights to nineteen-year-old pitcher Bill Dickey.

The deal was made official on September 8. Unlike Baker, Banks would report directly to the Cubs. The team gave him several days to prepare, leaving it unclear whether Banks or Baker would be the first African American to appear in a Cub uniform.

Both arrived in Chicago on September 14, Banks flying in from Pittsburgh and Baker from San Francisco. Unfortunately, Baker had pulled a muscle in his side for L.A. and was immediately sidelined.

Later that day, Banks made his first appearance at Wrigley Field, where early arrivals saw him hit the first pitch he saw during batting practice out of the park. Three days later, when the Phillies came into town, Banks made his debut as part of a lineup that included three rookies—Banks, outfielder Bob Talbot, and pitcher Don Elston.

The trio got a quick taste of what it was like to play for the Cubs in Chicago. Before only 2,703 fans, the Phillies blasted the Cubs, 16–4. Banks batted seventh, went hitless, and made one error in seven chances, a performance that the *Sun-Times* termed, indelicately, "a bad case of buck fever." Banks had an excuse, however. He had forgotten his glove and had to borrow one from Eddie Miksis.

Three days later, Banks gave Cub fans a glimpse of the future, albeit in St. Louis against the Cardinals. He tripled, singled, and homered off Cardinal starter Gerry Staley, who weathered fifteen hits while winning 11–6. Two days later, on September 22, Baker was well enough to play. By then, however, Banks had all but won the shortstop job. Baker played second base for the first time in his career, and for the rest of the season the Cubs lineup included both men, Banks hitting .314 with two home runs and Baker hitting .227 as the Cubs finished in seventh place, 65–89, and forty long games behind the Dodgers.

It would take more than Ernie Banks and Gene Baker, however, to turn the Cubs around.

notoriety and celebrity status opened doors for him in the business world that previously had been closed to blacks. For example, when Banks expressed interest in opening a car dealership, Philip Wrigley personally called Ford and helped Banks become the first African American Ford dealer in the nation, even buying the first car Banks sold.

Still, at times Banks seemed so submissive and compliant that he appeared weak and easily manipulated, which

Center fielder Richie Ashburn was traded to Chicago from Philadelphia in January 1960. His first season as a Cub was a success: he led the league in walks while scoring ninety-nine runs and batting .291 for a team that finished just one game out of last place.

to a degree he was. In 1962 he was drawn into politics by local Republicans, who convinced Banks to run for alderman representing the Eighth Ward; when, in a surprise, he lost the primary, the party unceremoniously dumped him and made Banks appear unnecessarily foolish. And compared to his peers, Banks was underpaid. He allowed Wrigley to keep and invest half his salary on his behalf, essentially agreeing to defer payment. Banks valued loyalty, once telling a reporter that he believed that "loyalty and friendship are the same," and he remained loyal to P.K. Wrigley. At a certain point, Banks could have wielded real influence on the franchise, but he deferred to Wrigley and stayed in his place. Banks never publicly pressed the club to win, called for a trade, or expressed any frustration with losing year in and year out.

His silence spoke volumes, for it gave Wrigley a pass, both with the public and in the Cubs clubhouse. Perhaps that was all for the best. As long as Wrigley owned the team, no amount of complaining would have changed the Cubs, and they were so bad that any other attitude would have inevitably led to frustration.

In the offseason, the press focused on who Wrigley would name as the next Cubs manager, but Wrigley did not appear to be in any rush. In fact, he began to intimate that perhaps there would not be a new manager at all. Once again, he was planning on giving another crazy idea a big league trial.

Instead of hiring a manager who would then hire his coaching staff, Wrigley wanted to turn the usual arrangement on its head. He announced that he planned to hire eight different coaches and employ them throughout the organization, rotating from team to team, with each man taking a turn as one of four or five who would be on the staff of the major league team at any one time. "Our main objective," he announced, "is to standardize our system." He wanted organization men who all believed in the same principles and methods. Perhaps, said Wrigley, those eight men would then choose the club managers, just as a board of directors selects a chairman. "You should put the army together before you choose the general," Wrigley explained. "The dictionary tells you a manager is the one who bosses and a coach is the one who works. We want workers."

Thinking out loud, Wrigley then let slip a notion that even he found revolutionary. Perhaps, he indicated, the coaches would run the team without a manager at all. They would all get a chance, rotating throughout the organization, periodically serving as "head coach."

Uh-oh. Just as Wrigley had once hired Coleman R. Griffith to serve as the team's sports psychologist before he figured out exactly what he wanted Griffith to do, another Wrigley idea was running ahead of practicality. And now that the idea was out, there was no turning back.

On January 12, Wrigley made the full announcement. The Cubs would not have a manager. Instead, a rotating system of head coaches would be put in place. "I don't like the term 'manager'," said Wrigley, "because it says he's a dictator. And I don't want a dictator." When pressed to provide specific details of his plan, such as how he would decide who would serve as head coach, when, and how, Wrigley was secretive. "There's an old expression, 'He who explains is lost.' Therefore we will not try to explain except to say we are not departing from tradition rashly or in haste, but rather only after long and thorough analysis." Then, in a rare moment of candor, he added, "We certainly cannot do much worse trying a new system than we have done for many years under the old."

Oh boy. Just as the hiring of Griffith had had potential as a worthy innovation, so too was Wrigley's new proposal not without its merits. He wanted the game of baseball taught throughout the Cub organization in exactly the same way, so that as a player moved up in the system and then to the major leagues, he would receive consistent instruction and, hoped Wrigley, produce standardized results. There was nothing wrong with that. Under Branch Rickey, the Cardinals and Dodgers had both been run in very much the same fashion, and a number of other teams had, to various degrees, adopted a similar approach.

What was revolutionary was the manner in which Wrigley wanted to codify the system. Not only did the organization reportedly produce a booklet called "The Cub Way," which attempted to put that approach on paper, but Wrigley wanted to take the concept so far that individual coaches, and eventually players, would be completely interchangeable: each player would be taught the same skills and approach by every coach in the organization, with no deviation.

That was where the plan broke down. The concept was sound in theory, but its application was problematic

Philip K. Wrigley's "College of Coaches" managerial scheme met with nearly universal derision.

because Wrigley failed to think his plan through to its logical conclusions. He did not understand people and naively believed that if the coaches were simply told to coach in the same manner, the result would be eight identical coaches, all getting similar results. As long as they were teaching the same principles, Wrigley did not think it made any difference whether they were coaching raw rookies in their first year of pro ball or a team of veterans. And if all the coaches were indeed the same, then why change "head coaches" at all? If the head coaches were not the same, the strategy was doomed to failure, for the very consistency Wrigley valued would not be reinforced but subverted. Wrigley failed to account for the fact that each coach came to the job with his own philosophy, personality, and style, and Wrigley made no attempt to hire coaches who shared similar traits. Most baseball men recognized the flaws in the plan and turned him down. Those who did agree to serve as one of his coaches were already in the organization or desperate for work. Moreover, the plan failed to recognize that basic competitiveness would cause the coaches to work against one another. The result would not be consistency but utter confusion.

People all around baseball raised their eyebrows, scratched their heads, and reacted with other expressions of incredulity. Commissioner Ford Frick said Wrigley was certainly within his rights to put the scheme into place, saying, "The rules only require that nine men be on the field." American League president Joe Cronin found the idea laughable, and NL president Warren Giles said simply, "I've never heard of a team without a manager before," and refused further comment.

The press dubbed the arrangement the "College of Coaches," but from the start few observers thought it represented the result of higher learning. Once again, Wrigley demonstrated that despite the fact that he owned the Cubs, he did not really understand the game. Manufacturing a winning baseball team was not like manufacturing chewing gum. The practical impact of the "College of

Coaches" on the Cubs was so bad, on so many levels, that decades later it still stands as probably the most impractical and bizarre management decision any baseball owner has ever made—which in a world that has included George Steinbrenner, Charlie Finley, and Ted Turner among its membership is saying something. In short, the Cubs were now officially a joke.

No one apparently realized it, but the notion wasn't even original. Wrigley cribbed the idea from the newspaper. Over the past twenty years, *Chicago Tribune* columnist Arch Ward had periodically trumpeted the idea of rotating coaches between different collegiate football programs, believing that such a strategy would decrease the emphasis on winning and build sportsmanship and character. The notion must have intrigued Wrigley, for now his proposal took the same rough concept and applied it to baseball.

The sad part was that Wrigley's experiment was unveiled at the precise time when the Cubs, for the first

---

Vedie Himsl was the first of the Cub coaches to serve as manager-elect during the first two weeks of the 1961 season. He is shown here with Reds manager Fred Hutchinson going over the ground rules at Crosley Field on opening day.

time in years, were actually beginning to develop some talent. In Wid Matthews's final few seasons, the quality of talent in the Cubs' minor league system had begun to improve. In 1955 the Cubs had hired Buck O'Neill, former manager of the Kansas City Monarchs, as a scout, and O'Neill gave the Cubs a real advantage in the black community. When Holland was hired, Wrigley had relaxed his hold on the purse strings, so that by the spring of 1961 a host of young talent was under contract to the Cubs. Ron Santo and Danny Murphy were already in the big leagues, but they would soon be joined by outfielder Billy Williams, infielder Ken Hubbs, outfielder Lou Brock, and others. Although the system wasn't deep, it was producing a few real players.

They all came too late to help Ernie Banks. From 1955 to 1960, Banks averaged forty-one home runs a year while hitting almost .300 and knocking in more than one hundred runs all but once.

Those years were gone. After 1960, Banks was an entirely different player—still very good, but no longer great, and not quite the centerpiece of the organization. He had hurt his knee while playing softball years before, and in 1960 it began to give him real trouble. While the injury was most noticeable when Banks was in the field, where it adversely affected his range, it also cost him some power.

In the offseason, Wrigley and Holland busied themselves interviewing coaches to serve in Wrigley's grand experiment. Candidates were not exactly lining up for the jobs. Most viewed the scheme with skepticism and, like former Cub Billy Jurges, turned Wrigley down cold. Virtually anyone already coaching in the major leagues or serving as a minor league manager was hoping to get a job as a big league manager one day, not serve as some part of an experiment. Those who were willing to give the scheme a try probably were not the best candidates.

At length, Wrigley hired ten coaches in 1961—Vedie Himsl, Harry Craft, Goldie Holt, Lou Klein, Bobby Adams, Elvin Tappe, Dick Cole, Charlie Grimm, Rube Walker, and Fred Martin. By opening day, a play on the phrase "You can't tell the players without a scorecard" had become a cliché.

Wrigley's plan had also evolved and become a little more complicated. He had his minions at Wrigley Company headquarters do a statistical analysis of the Cubs with the help of an IBM computer. The results of that analysis were then delivered to the Cubs manager du jour. It was another good idea, in theory, but premature, for the stats by themselves were meaningless. When one coach made the mistake of telling a sportswriter that he didn't plan to use the cards, Wrigley snapped back, saying, "Anybody who doesn't keep the cards in the dugout won't work for me." So the cards were kept in the dugout . . . somewhere.

Predictably, the 1961 season was a disaster from the start. At the beginning of the season, pitching coach Vedie Himsl was named the first head coach. John Holland told reporters, "Mr. Wrigley felt that Himsl, because he is the oldest in point of consecutive service with the Cubs, had earned the honor by his diligence and contribution to the program." What was so innovative about that? Although it was originally announced that Himsl would serve only two weeks at the helm, he stayed on a month as the new system began to break down almost from the start. Wrigley kept changing his mind—and his reasons—for making the change. The Cubs went 10–21 under Himsl, and then he was sent down to begin his minor league tour of duty, serving as pitching coach in San Antonio. Harry Craft took over and lasted sixteen games, going 7–9, then was replaced by Elvin Tappe, who had served as a backup catcher for the Cubs from 1954 to 1958 before becoming a coach. Tappe remained in place for more than ninety games, but before the year was out he was replaced by Lou Klein. The other six coaches never got a turn.

There were some impressive individual performances among the Cubs, as both Ron Santo and rookie Billy Williams hit more than twenty home runs and more than eighty RBIs, but the lineup was always changing. In late May, Banks, troubled by his bad knee, was exiled to left field. A few weeks later, Banks tried first base, but after playing 717 consecutive games, he had to sit out on June 23. Later in the season, he was bothered by eye trouble and missed more time. Only a few weeks after the start of the season, the Cubs fell to seventh place and hung on for dear life.

Nevertheless, the 1962 season gave Cubs fans some reason for optimism. The National League expanded to ten teams, adding the Houston Colt 45s and the New York

Despite joining the Cubs coaching staff in 1962 John "Buck" O'Neill was denied the opportunity to join fellow coaches El Tappe, Charlie Metro, and Lou Klein as one of the coaches who managed the Cubs on a rotating basis. Thus did Philip K. Wrigley miss a historic opportunity by preventing the former Negro League star from enjoying the privilege shared by five fellow Cub coaches in 1961 and 1962.

were already among the most highly touted prospects in recent Cub history.

Incredibly, and improbably, the Cubs got it right. Injuries and overuse had just about ruined pitcher Dick Drott. The Cubs left him exposed, and Houston gambled on him in the fourth round. One round later, they nabbed journeyman outfielder Al Heist.

Now it was the Mets' turn. They helped out too, plucking infielder Sammy Drake and first baseman Ed Bouchee before dropping $75,000 on Don Zimmer. All were expendable. Drake had failed in several trials with the Cubs. Ken Hubbs was scheduled to take over at second base, and the Cubs planned on moving Banks permanently to first base. The draft hadn't hurt the Cubs.

But it also did not help them. Incredibly, at a time when expansion meant there was even *more* competition for prospects, the Cubs chose to cut back. In the spring of 1962, player personnel director Gene Lawing cleaned out the farm system and released more than forty players, simultaneously cutting the farm system from six to five teams. Except for the expansion clubs, which were still building farm systems, the Cubs now had the smallest minor league system in baseball. Then, in a bizarre move, Wrigley banned his scouts from signing *any* ballplayers in 1962. Once again, it seemed as if Wrigley did not want the Cubs to succeed.

Chicago opened the 1962 season in Houston, and baseball's oldest franchise was swept by the youngest in three games. It was embarrassing. By the middle of May, the Cubs not only trailed Houston's Colt 45s but the lowly New York Mets as well. Although the Mets soon faltered and fell back, Chicago chased Houston for much of the year, catching up to them in late July and doing battle for a month before again falling behind. The Cubs finished ninth, forty-two and a half games behind the San Francisco Giants and six games behind Houston. Only the Mets, who finished sixty and a half games out of first, were worse.

Elvin Tappe, Lou Klein, and Charlie Metro served as head coaches during the season, and if consistency was the goal, they succeeded, for each man was indeed interchangeable as they led the Cubs to a disastrous record. But Wrigley had not so subtly changed the plan. Midway through the 1962 season, the Cubs named Buck O'Neill as the first African American to serve as a coach in the major

Mets. The two clubs seemed likely to fight it out over last place. The Cubs, by default, would probably finish ahead of both clubs.

Each new club was stocked with players through the expansion draft. According to the draft rules, each club was allowed to draft two players from each existing NL club roster at $75,000 each and one more for $50,000. The existing clubs then had to make two more players available at $125,000 apiece.

For an already weak team like Chicago, which at every opportunity seemed ready to expose its incompetence, the expansion draft was fraught with peril. The Cubs could not afford to lose any frontline players, but it was just as dangerous leaving a young prospect exposed. In the final days of the 1961 season, they had brought up outfielder Lou Brock and second baseman Ken Hubbs, both of whom

leagues. Under the Cubs' coaching scheme, that should have put him in line to become the first African American to serve as a manager in the major leagues, even if his title would have been "head coach."

But the Cubs did not want that. As Holland explained, even though O'Neill would be in uniform on the Cubs bench, he was not really a coach, at least not in the way the others were coaches. "Buck will serve as an *instructor*," said Holland, giving evidence that Jim Crow lived on in words. In fact, O'Neill was not even allowed to leave the bench. During his time with the Cubs, he never appeared as a base coach, and the other Cub coaches were told that in the event that one or more of them was thrown out of the game, they were not to give O'Neill the reins. In that regard, the Cubs got precisely the kind of standardization they wanted.

After the season, Wrigley began to intimate that the era of the "College of Coaches" was coming to an end. He invited Chicago native Bob Kennedy, a veteran of the White Sox, to join the coaching staff. In 1961 Kennedy had been the Cubs' farm director, and in 1962 he managed their farm club in Salt Lake City. He was widely considered

an up-and-comer, and there was immediate speculation that Kennedy would serve as head coach.

Wrigley, however, was not quite finished testing out new ideas. Now he decided that what the Cubs really needed was an athletic director, someone to be the boss of the coaches, just as an athletic director was the boss of all the coaches in a collegiate athletic program. In fact, he had recently met the perfect candidate through his cousin, Wrigley Offield, who served as advertising manager for the Wrigley Company. Offield's wife had met the wife of Col. Robert Whitlow, who was serving as the first athletic director of the Air Force Academy. She introduced Whitlow to her husband, who in turn introduced him to Wrigley. According to Whitlow, "Mr. Wrigley told me the Cubs needed a centralized director." Whitlow explained his qualifications, and lo and behold, the Cubs had an athletic director. Could pep rallies be far behind?

Left-hander Dick Ellsworth rebounded from losing twenty games in 1962 to win twenty-two in 1963. Included in the win total was the one-hit shutout over the Phillies being celebrated here with first baseman Ernie Banks (left) and shortstop Andre Rogers (right).

Center fielder Lou Brock spent the first two seasons of his nineteen-year Hall of Fame career with the Cubs before being dealt to St. Louis for pitcher Ernie Broglio in a trade many have judged as the worst in franchise history. Brock is shown here making a leaping catch of a drive by Ron Hunt of the Mets at the Polo Grounds in a Memorial Day double-header in 1963.

Whitlow was obviously pleased, for Wrigley entrusted him with the authority to select the next head coach, who Wrigley then indicated would serve indefinitely. Whitlow said, "I will be responsible for the playing end of the game . . . to make sure our basic plan of play is followed. . . . I may sit on the bench, and in uniform."

That was just what the Cubs needed: someone with no experience in the game picking the manager and sitting on the bench. Had it not been so sad it would have been funny.

Five weeks later, as spring training was about to begin, Whitlow, in his first official act, was allowed to make the official announcement of Kennedy's appointment. As Ed Prell noted in the *Tribune*, "The bare fact was not there but the implication was. . . . Wrigley's Utopian plan of revolving coaches was as dead as the spit ball."

"I have no secret plans," declared Kennedy later that day. "I have no mystery deals. . . . Of course I don't know where we'll finish." That was anyone's guess.

That was also why it came as such a shock that in 1963, for the first time in a long time, the Cubs were not bad. In fact, for much of the first half of the season they were pretty good. Left-handed pitcher Dick Ellsworth, already a veteran at age twenty-three, blossomed into an ace and one year after losing twenty games won twenty-two. Santo and Billy Williams continued their steady improvement, while both Ken Hubbs, who in 1962 had been named NL Rookie of the Year, and outfielder Lou Brock continued to give fans reasons to be optimistic. Hubbs, in fact, had even set a record in 1962 by playing in seventy-eight consecutive games without committing an error.

On June 6, the Cubs were tied for first place with a record of 31–23, and as late as mid-July they were ten games over .500 and still within striking distance of the top. But apart from Ellsworth, starting pitching was inconsistent, and Ernie Banks seemed to be fading fast. At age thirty-two, he hit only .227 with eighteen home runs, most of which came in the first half. In September, the Cubs finally discovered that Banks had been sick for most of the year, suffering from a case of the mumps. Had the Cubs had one more pitcher, and if Banks had been healthy, they might have stolen a pennant. As it was, they finished with the best record in history for a seventh-place team: above .500 with an 82–80 mark, only seventeen games behind Los Angeles.

At last it seemed reasonable to be optimistic. Despite the failure of the "College of Coaches," in Santo, Williams, Hubbs, Brock, and Ellsworth, none of whom were over twenty-five, the Cubs appeared to have a solid core of players to build around in the future.

Hubbs in particular was a fan favorite. The Utah native, a devout Mormon, almost seemed too good to be true, the epitome of an all-American kid. Growing up, he led his Little League team to the national finals. Long, lean, handsome, and single, he left Brigham Young University to sign with the Cubs and help care for his father, a paraplegic. Hubbs reached the major leagues at age nineteen and became a particular favorite of young female fans. Although he had yet to hit for average or power, at age twenty-two he was more than holding his own and seemed destined to improve. After striking out 129 times in his rookie season, he had cut that number by nearly one-third in 1963, a feat that was usually an indication of a bright future.

During his rookie year, he had become interested in flying, often sitting in the cockpit during the Cubs' charter flights and peppering the pilot with questions, in part to overcome his initial fear of air travel. He began taking flying lessons and earned his pilot's license just after the New Year. On February 12, 1964, Hubbs and a friend, Dennis Doyle, flew from Hubbs's home in Colton, California, just east of Los Angeles, to Provo, Utah, to visit Doyle's father-in-law. There was no room in the plane for Doyle's wife, so she took a train.

The next morning, on February 13, Hubbs and Doyle took off in Hubbs's single-engine Cessna and headed toward Colton. It was snowing, and airport officials later described the weather as "very unfavorable for flying," particularly for a pilot as inexperienced as Hubbs.

He flew for less than an hour before realizing that the weather was more than he could handle. He turned the plane around and tried to make it back to Provo.

He never did. Hubbs apparently set his radio to the wrong frequency, and if he made any calls for help, no one heard them. Investigators later speculated that Hubbs became disoriented in the weather and lost the horizon. He crashed the plane into the frozen surface of Utah Lake.

He and Doyle were killed instantly, but no one knew they were missing until Hubbs's father called looking for his son after they failed to arrive in Colton. Two days later,

searchers found the wreckage of the plane. The funeral in Hubbs's home of Colton was so large that it had to be held at the local high school, and Hubbs's teammates attended en masse. In the *Tribune*, Robert Markus wrote: "He used his fielder's glove the way a violinist uses a bow—there was magic in it—and at twenty-two his brilliant future stretched before him."

Understandably, the tragedy knocked the Cubs off course in 1964. Five different players played second base, and none of them made anyone forget Ken Hubbs. The club was out of sync all year. Billy Williams got off to a terrific start that marked him as a star of the first magnitude, hitting over .400 for the first two months of the season before fading, and Ron Santo had another fine year, but the Cubs just did not have enough pitching. Dick Ellsworth and veterans Larry Jackson and Bob Buhl matched up well with the top three starters for any team in the league, but the Cubs could not seem to find a dependable fourth starter.

In late May, the Cubs were in ninth place, but closer to first place than last, in a tangle of teams knotted around .500. Wrigley, Holland, and Kennedy all sensed that the season was slipping away and that unless they did something soon their stopover in ninth place might become permanent. Besides, attendance, which had jumped to almost one million fans in 1963, was slipping again.

Only the Cardinals and the Reds had pitching to spare. The Reds needed a third baseman, but Santo was off limits, and the Cubs had no one else of interest to Cincinnati. St. Louis, on the other hand, was willing to talk.

In 1963 the Cardinals had picked up veteran Lou Burdette from the Braves as pitching insurance, but he was costly and had not pitched very well. The two clubs started talking, and the Cardinals dumped Burdette on the Cubs for former prospect Glen Hobbie. Although this deal has since been overlooked, had it not been made, the next trade between the two clubs, perhaps the most notorious in Cub history, would never have taken place.

Burdette was not the answer for the Cubs, but in his first few starts for St. Louis Hobbie pitched so well that the Cardinals penciled him into their rotation. The Cardinals still had too much pitching, and the two clubs kept talking. Chicago still wanted a starting pitcher, and the Cardinals wanted an outfielder.

1954

For the next two weeks, the Cubs kept pace as the two teams dickered back and forth. On June 15, after winning thirteen of nineteen, the Cubs were .500, with a record of 27–27. Chicago's first three starters, Larry Jackson, Ellsworth, and Bob Buhl, were a cumulative 23–12. The Cubs' other starters, which included guys like Hobbie, Paul Toth, and Sterling Slaughter, were a combined 4–15.

For two seasons, Cub outfielder Lou Brock had seemed on the brink of greatness. Blessed with extraordinary speed and surprising power, Brock was only twenty-five years old. In two seasons as a starter, Brock had made slow improvement, hitting .263 in 1962 and .258 in 1963 while increasing his production in every other category.

However, that was not enough for the Cubs. Because of his speed, the Cubs played Brock in center field. He was out of position there, lacking a strong arm, and he had trouble tracking the ball in the swirling winds in center field, where he often looked awkward. He lacked confidence and had found it hard to relax under the "College of Coaches," for each man had given him different advice, one telling him to hit the ball on the ground and use his speed to hit for average, the next expecting him to hit home runs. Compared to Banks, Billy Williams, and Ron Santo, all of whom had become established stars by age twenty-four, Brock was beginning to look like a failure. New manager Bob Kennedy was not impressed by Brock either. He thought Brock struck out too much and took too many chances on the bases.

That made Brock expendable. The Cardinals, by contrast, did not see Brock for his failures but for what he could do. Their home field, Sportsman's Park, was a big ballpark that favored speed more than power, and the Cardinals already had a spectacular center fielder in Curt Flood. They wanted Brock to play left field, where his speed would be an asset and his weak throwing arm would not be an issue.

Meanwhile, the Cubs lusted after twenty-seven-year-old St. Louis pitcher Ernie Broglio. He had won twenty games

For fourteen seasons Ron Santo was one of Wrigley Field's popular players. The slugging third baseman made his Cub debut as a twenty-year-old in 1960 and soon outslugged Cub icon Ernie Banks in a Chicago lineup that also included future Hall of Fame left fielder Billy Williams. Since 1990 Santo has served as the Cubs' radio analyst, and in 2003 the Cubs retired his number 10 before a packed house.

Ken Hubbs was part of the Cubs' incredible crop of young talent that arrived at Wrigley Field in the early 1960s. Hubbs came to Chicago from Brigham Young University in 1962 and enjoyed an outstanding season in which he played a record-setting seventy-eight consecutive games at second, a feat that helped him earn National League Rookie of the Year honors. Following the 1963 season, Hubbs died on February 13, 1964, when his single-engine Cessna crashed into Utah Lake.

in 1960 and eighteen games in 1963, but had gotten off to a slow start in 1964, going 3–5. Since Hobbie's arrival, Broglio had lost his spot in the Cards' rotation.

That should have given the Cubs pause. Teams do not dump eighteen-game winners for no reason, but the Cardinals floated a story that Broglio was unhappy in St. Louis, and the Cubs bought it.

Broglio was unhappy, but not because he played for St. Louis. His arm was shot, and he knew it. For several seasons, he had been receiving cortisone shots in his shoulder, but now they weren't working very well anymore and his elbow was also acting up. The Cubs did not know that,

and they did not seem to wonder why the Cardinals were suddenly so eager to deal a pitcher with Broglio's pedigree for an unproven outfielder. All the Cubs saw was Broglio's career record.

On June 15, the two clubs agreed to the trade. Broglio, veteran Bobby Shantz, and outfielder Doug Clemens went to the Cubs for Brock and pitchers Jack Spring and Paul Toth. Said Wrigley, "If you want to hit the bull's eye you have to take a shot at it." Added John Holland, "We're taking more than a shot at the flag. We're cutting loose with both barrels."

In fact, the Cubs had just shot themselves in the foot. They had made an enormous mistake, and they had also been snookered, for apart from Broglio's injury, they had strengthened a competitor. On the Cardinals, Broglio had been a spare part, and an injured one at that. Anything Brock gave the Cardinals would be a plus.

St. Louis manager Johnny Keane explained the way the Cardinals viewed the transaction. "The way for the deal was opened for us," he said, "when we landed Glen Hobbie and he looked good in a couple of starts. Hobbie gave us a six-man starting staff and we could afford to part with Broglio for outfield help."

The Chicago press corps was ebullient after the trade; one paper termed the deal "the greatest steal since the Brinks Robbery." It was—for the Cardinals.

As soon as Brock got to St. Louis, he flourished, hitting .348 for the rest of the season with twelve home runs and thirty-three stolen bases, instantaneously becoming the player who would eventually be enshrined in the Hall of Fame. Broglio, on the other hand, immediately broke down, winning only one of his first nine starts and struggling to a total of only four wins for the Cubs in 1964.

The deal seemed to take the air out of the Cubs. Brock sent the Cardinals to the World Series, while Broglio went to the hospital in the offseason for arm surgery, his career essentially over. The Cubs slumped to seventh place as Len Gabrielson, who took over for Brock in the outfield, hit .246.

Over time, the trade of Brock has been viewed as perhaps the worst trade in Cubs history. Cubs fans have assumed that Brock eventually would have thrived as a Cub, and they have wondered how well the Cubs would have done had Brock played during his prime with Banks,

Santo, Williams, and others. For Cub fans, the Brock-Broglio trade is almost the equivalent of the Red Sox sale of Babe Ruth to the Yankees.

They shouldn't wonder about such things, because in the long run the trade of Brock may have been the best thing that ever happened to the team.

The deal exposed all that was wrong with the Cubs—well, almost all that was wrong. Starting with Wrigley himself, virtually everyone connected with the team was either incompetent, inconsequential, or, in the rare case of individuals who were actually proficient, hamstrung by those around them. To this point, it was possible to divide Wrigley's stewardship into two eras, before 1945 and after, and since 1945 the Cubs had been terrible. The problem had not been either the plan or the players—it was, pure and simple, the people in charge. Had Brock remained a Cub, that might not have ever changed, and until it did the Cubs were destined to fail. For the past twenty years, the club had slowly decayed, and what had once been one of baseball's best franchises was now one of its worst.

They proved that in 1965. With Broglio and without Brock, the Cubs went backwards again, finishing eighth, ahead of only Houston and the Mets, in the second division for the nineteenth straight season, a level of failure few other clubs have ever approached. Banks, Santo, and Williams were all fine—each had more than one hundred RBIs and hit more than twenty-eight home runs—but no one else on the team knocked in more than thirty-four, and the pitching staff was near the bottom of the league. As usual, there was the occasional standout individual performance—on September 2, for instance, Ernie Banks cracked his four-hundredth career home run, and both Dick Ellsworth and Bob Hendley twirled one-hitters against the Dodgers. Of course, both men lost—Ellsworth on a home run to Al Ferrara, and Hendley when Sandy Koufax hurled a perfect game for L.A.

Kennedy was fired in midseason and replaced on an interim basis by Lou Klein. Attendance dropped to almost nothing as only 641,000 fans came out to Wrigley Field. They didn't care about the "friendly confines" of Wrigley Field, about how clean and comfortable it was or how brightly the sun shined in the bleachers, about how much ivy grew on the outfield walls, how easy it was to get a seat, or how cold the beer was. In fact, they didn't care about the Cubs at all. Even worse, it seemed as if no one connected to the Cubs did either.

On October 26, 1965, that all changed. Leo Durocher was named manager of the Chicago Cubs.

HERE COMES THE SUN

Had Philip Wrigley appeared at a press conference dressed in a tutu and announced that the Wrigley Company was halting the production of chewing gum to manufacture dental floss, it could not have been more shocking than the decision to hire Leo Durocher. For thirty years, Wrigley usually moved so guardedly and so patiently that at times one wondered if he had a pulse, or recognized that anyone did. Almost every general manager, manager, and coach he had hired was cut, more or less, from the same cloth. They were solid, conservative, compliant company men whom Wrigley hired more for their loyalty than for their baseball acumen. In short, Wrigley hadn't ever really hired a bona-fide manager. He had hired *middle* managers—yes men and milquetoasts often more concerned with keeping their jobs and not making mistakes than winning ball games. Most had played the part so well that they might as well have worn clip-on ties and joined the Jaycees.

When major league baseball teams change managers, they often replace easygoing, player-friendly leaders with someone like Durocher, a tougher, more demanding,

Canadian Ferguson Jenkins was the greatest pitcher in Cub history. Arriving in Chicago with outfielder Adolfo Phillips on April 21, 1966, via a trade with the Phillies for pitchers Larry Jackson and Bob Buhl, Jenkins soon made his mark. Starting in 1967, Jenkins won twenty or more games for six consecutive seasons while setting Cub all-time records for games started (347), strikeouts (2,038), and home runs allowed (271).

hands-on taskmaster who can crack the whip. But when the Cubs hired Durocher, the players weren't the only ones intimidated. Durocher scared everyone.

Leo Durocher was an emperor. As soon as he was hired to lead the Cubs, he took command as thoroughly as if he had seized the club militarily. Wrigley and Holland, overthrown before they realized it, offered little resistance. Wrigley retained the crown, but only as a figurehead, while Holland simply followed orders. Durocher was in charge, and as long as he was, the Cubs were a different team. He towered over the franchise like no man before or since, and almost, *almost*, led them to victory. His rise was breathtaking.

Most baseball fans today remember Durocher as the author of the oft-repeated slogan "Nice guys finish last." Although he never said those precise words, the adage nevertheless fit, for Durocher was often not very nice, at least on the baseball field, and he rarely finished last.

He was a hustler. A native of Springfield, Massachusetts, Durocher grew up poor, spending more time in pool rooms than classrooms. In all likelihood, baseball was all that saved him from a life of petty crime. Signed by the New York Yankees as a shortstop, Durocher played two seasons in New York in 1928 and 1929, palling around with Babe Ruth and studying baseball at the side of Yankee manager Miller Huggins before moving on to Cincinnati and the St. Louis Cardinals. In St. Louis he was a key member of the Gashouse Gang and developed a lasting reputation as a combative competitor who didn't like to lose, wasn't afraid to mix it up, and was more than willing to tell you so. Durocher's loud mouth and argumentative personality earned him the nickname "the Lip."

After the 1937 season, he was traded to the Brooklyn Dodgers. One year later, Lee MacPhail made him manager of the team, and for nine of the next ten years the flamboyant, ultra-confident Durocher led the Dodgers, winning one pennant, in 1941, and earning one season-long suspension, in 1947, for "actions detrimental to baseball," primarily for consorting with gangsters and gamblers. Like John McGraw a generation before, Durocher ruled by the force of his personality, intimidating everyone, arguing with umpires, and fighting with friend and foe alike. His teams often adopted his approach, fighting and scratching for every run.

His players loved him and hated him, often at the same time, for the mercurial Durocher blew hot and cold, fawning over a player one day and then either ignoring him completely or tearing him apart the next. He challenged everybody and everything, played by his own set of rules, cursed like a sailor, and tried to sleep with everything that wore a skirt. He also found trouble where none had existed before, often caused it himself, and left others to clean up the mess. As Branch Rickey once said of him, Durocher "had the ability of taking a bad situation and making it immediately worse."

But he knew baseball—of that there was little doubt. Over time he had earned a reputation as a manager who got his team to perform better than they had any right to expect.

After he was fired by the Dodgers in the middle of the 1948 season, Durocher simply moved uptown and took over as manager of the New York Giants, mentoring Willie Mays and winning two pennants and a world championship in seven and a half seasons before being let go at the end of the 1955 season. He moved with his wife, actress Larraine Day, to Beverly Hills, worked in radio and TV, hung out with celebrities, and got divorced. By the late 1950s, he was sending out signals that he wanted to return to baseball, but apart from a coaching stint with the Dodgers—where he hung on to the false hope that he would one day replace Walter Alston—no offers were forthcoming. Durocher kept getting into off-field scrapes and was hit with two "alienation of affection" lawsuits. By 1965 Durocher was approaching sixty years old, and his many enemies whispered that baseball had passed him by, a perception undercut by the fact that more than half the managers in the major leagues at the time were in some sense protégés of Durocher's, having either played with him or for him. Still, for most owners Durocher carried too much baggage, and no one cared to put up with the headaches they feared he would inevitably cause.

Phil Wrigley was just such an owner, which made it even more shocking when he hired Durocher. In 1956, after Durocher left the Giants, he was rumored to be on Phil Wrigley's short list. Wrigley found that mortifying—Durocher simply wasn't his type of human being. He dismissed the notion as "ridiculous," and when Durocher visited Chicago in September 1956, presumably to meet with

GOLD GLOVE AWARD
WINNERS

Year	Player	Position	Year	Player	Position
			1983–91	Ryne Sandberg	2B
			1988	Andre Dawson	RF
			1987	Andre Dawson	RF
			1986	Jody Davis	C
2005	Derrek Lee	1B	1984	Bob Dernier	CF
2005	Greg Maddux	P	1970	Don Kessinger	SS
2004	Greg Maddux	P	1969	Don Kessinger	SS
1996	Mark Grace	1B	1964–68	Ron Santo	3B
1995	Mark Grace	1B	1968	Glenn Beckert	2B
1993	Mark Grace	1B	1967	Randy Hundley	C
1990–92	Greg Maddux	P	1962	Ken Hubbs	2B
1992	Mark Grace	1B	1960	Ernie Banks	SS

Wrigley, Wrigley left town so that no one would get the wrong idea.

By 1966, however, circumstance had left Wrigley, the Cubs, and Durocher in a similar situation. None of them had anything left to lose. As a human being, Durocher was no more agreeable to Wrigley than before, but in recent seasons Wrigley had found himself in the cross hairs, the target of a crescendo of criticism. A new generation of sportswriters had taken over, and the nature of the local press was changing. They were far less deferential toward Wrigley than their predecessors. The *Sun-Times* in particular was much feistier and more critical of the Cubs than the *Tribune* had ever been, and it forced the more established paper to spice up its coverage, including its criticism of Wrigley. By the end of the 1966 season, P.K. felt like a piñata.

Holland's situation mirrored Wrigley's. He too had been the focus of intense criticism, and he was no more comfortable with that than Wrigley was. When Wrigley asked Holland and his son to find a new "head coach," Holland thought of Durocher.

Durocher was not only the best manager currently not employed but also the best known. Durocher loved the spotlight, which allowed everyone around him to stay in the shadows. That was fine with Holland. Like Wrigley, he was beginning to crave anonymity.

Holland first sold the idea of Durocher to P.K.'s son, William, who was taking on a larger role in the management of the club. The two of them then approached Wrigley, who gave Holland the go-ahead to contact Durocher at the World Series. Even though Durocher was the opposite of everyone Wrigley had ever hired, that wasn't necessarily a bad thing anymore. Besides, wherever he went, Durocher had been the face of his ball club, allowing stars like Robinson, Campanella, and Mays to thrive. With Leo around, no one would be pointing fingers at Phil Wrigley anymore.

As anxious as Durocher was to be in the dugout again, he knew the Cubs needed him more than he needed them. He asked for a three-year deal and he got it, reportedly earning $40,000 a year. As soon as he signed the contract, he took over and changed everything. Wrigley and Holland didn't know what hit them.

Durocher's hiring was announced at a press conference on October 25 at the Pink Poodle, a function room at Wrigley Field. Wrigley didn't make an appearance. In fact, Wrigley hadn't even met Durocher during the entire process, finding the whole notion so distasteful that he had left all the details to John Holland. Wrigley stayed at his Lake Geneva home and released a statement that read: "This is Leo's day. . . . There is no immediate announcement as to Durocher's title. We have found from long experience that it doesn't make any difference what title a team leader has as long as he has the ability to take charge. We have a man whose record shows he knows how to take charge."

He got that right. When John Holland introduced Durocher to the press, the new hire sucked up all the oxygen and everyone else faded away. It wasn't so much a press conference as a coup d'état. Durocher installed himself as the only man who mattered in the Cub organization.

When a reporter asked him what his title was, Durocher barked, "I just gave myself a title—manager—not head coach," putting Wrigley and his policies firmly in the rearview mirror. John Holland looked meekly on, nodding his head in agreement, growing smaller by the second. Then, when a reporter asked whether Durocher or Holland would be making trades, Durocher answered the question, first saying, "It'll be a fifty-fifty thing," taking half of Holland's authority, then making it clear that his

Leo Durocher brought passion, controversy, and winning baseball to Wrigley Field during his six-and-a-half-season tenure as Cubs manager. Not only was he the first Cubs skipper since Charlie Grimm to lead the team to as many as five consecutive winning seasons, but in 1969 his team captured the hearts of millions.

1968

On October 25, 1965, Cub general manager John Holland (left) shakes hands with newly hired Cub manager Leo Durocher. Durocher not only received a three-year contract but also was granted complete authority on the field—a dramatic shift by a team that had just experimented unsuccessfully with a system of rotating managers.

own 50 percent was all that really mattered, adding, "If I don't like a deal John suggests, it won't be made. . . . I'm gonna get the best of any trade. In fact, they'll be one-sided."

The press hung on every word, and Durocher gave them plenty more. "I know the Cubs have been in the second division," he said. "That's why I'm here. . . . I'm gonna change things around here. . . . I like to play a wide open game. The first time I see a safety first player, he won't be around long. . . . If my own brother is on this club, and I've got somebody better, then I'd tell my own brother, 'Go home! We can't use you!' I won't be running any popularity contests."

He also showed that he already knew a lot about the Cubs, saying that young second baseman Glenn Beckert was "my kind of player," that he "liked Santo's spirit," and that Billy Williams "is as good a left-handed hitter as you'll want to see." Santo, Williams, and Banks were untouch-

able, but, added Durocher, "we need a catcher, a center fielder, and a left fielder. . . . This club has a good nucleus. We're not starting with a pad and pencil."

Finally, there was a real live human being in charge of the Cubs, a baseball guy, a man's man. The press swooned over Durocher, as smitten as schoolgirls. In the *Sun-Times*, Jerome Holtzman wrote: "It was an impressive performance . . . totally out of character with the Cubs who for years have had a passive and virtually non-profit approach to professional baseball . . . an attitude generally attributed to Wrigley's limp ownership." In the *Tribune*, Ed Prell was nearly as effusive, writing that Durocher "made a spectacular entrance . . . speaking with the authority of a drill sergeant." That was an understatement.

When the players learned about the move, they were almost as enthusiastic. Santo called it "a great move. He's not used to handling a loser. He must think we're a first division club or he wouldn't have taken the job." Billy Williams added that he hoped Durocher could "put some fire in us," and outfielder George Altman was "elated." Even Mayor Richard Daley weighed in. "Everybody likes a scrapper," he said.

Durocher didn't fool around. In early December, he began remaking the team. The Cubs needed a catcher, and Holland and Durocher traded valuable reliever Lindy McDaniels and outfielder Don Landrum to the Giants for two rookies, catcher Randy Hundley and pitcher Bill Hands. It was a steal. Hundley, a former bonus baby, was considered a prospect, but the Giants had plenty of catching, while Hands had led the PCL in both wins and ERA.

But one trade wasn't going to make a difference, particularly in 1966, and Durocher knew that. He spent much of the season just observing, beginning in spring training. In fact, during the first intrasquad game, Durocher turned the split squads over to Ron Santo and Ernie Banks and let them manage while he sat back and watched.

He didn't like much of what he saw beyond the players he already approved of. Although Durocher had offered that "we're not an eighth-place club, I'll tell you that," he soon realized that the team was a long way away from contending. He took a long view, which made his veteran pitchers expendable. The Cubs had some talented pitchers in the minor leagues. When major league baseball adopted the free agent draft for high school and college players in

1965, the playing field was suddenly leveled and every team had more or less the same opportunity to acquire talent; this change allowed the Cub farm system to catch up quickly. The club concluded that by the time the team was ready to compete, the veterans would probably be finished anyway. If they were traded now, they'd deliver some more much-needed pieces.

Larry Jackson and Bob Buhl in particular had some value. Between them, the two pitchers had won more than three hundred games. Jackson was only one season removed from winning twenty-four games, and Buhl was Mr. Consistent.

Durocher wanted the Phillies' young power hitter, Richie Allen. Although Allen was a third baseman, he had the skills and speed to play the outfield. The two clubs started talking.

The Phillies were still smarting from blowing the pennant in the final days of the 1964 season and believed that another frontline starter or two to back up Jim Bunning and Chris Short could put them over the top. Richie Allen, however, was arguably the best young hitter in the game. He was off limits.

But there were other players in the Phillies organization who intrigued the Cubs. Young center fielder Adolfo Phillips was a five-tool player, young, fast, and powerful, and Canadian pitcher Ferguson Jenkins had been impressive in a late-season call-up. The Phillies made the same mistake as the Giants, trading youth for experience. Durocher was particularly intrigued with Phillips. "Only Willie Mays and Curt Flood are better than he is in center," claimed Durocher.

In 1966, however, the results were hard to watch. Twenty-year-old Ken Holtzman, only one year removed from the University of Illinois, was thrown in the rotation, joining Hands, Ellsworth, and whoever else Durocher could think of. Not surprisingly, they all struggled. Jenkins was the best pitcher on the team, but for most of the year he stayed in a relief role.

The results weren't pretty. The Cubs had the worst pitching in the league. They didn't finish eighth, they finished *tenth*, in last place, with only fifty-nine wins, seven and a half games behind the lowly Mets. Still, obscured by their record, the team made real progress. The Cubs could already score runs with anyone, and with the exception of

Not only was Fergie Jenkins an outstanding pitcher, but he was also a highly recruited track and basketball star. In the offseason of 1966–67, he tried his hand playing a few games with the world-renowned Harlem Globetrotters.

Banks, the entire starting lineup was well under the age of thirty. The tandem of young Don Kessinger at shortstop and Glenn Beckert at second base was one of the best-fielding middle infields in the game. Phillips, although he struggled a bit at the plate, caught everything hit in his direction, while Banks, Williams, and Santo all performed as expected.

Durocher spent most of the season little concerned with wins and losses. A stickler for fundamentals, Durocher also liked to play small ball, playing for the single run. Every player in the lineup was expected to know how to sacrifice-bunt and hit behind the runner. As he tried to get the Cubs to play baseball his way, Durocher also felt confident enough to experiment.

Ernie Banks was not a Durocher favorite. Not only was the longtime Cub star past his prime, but he was far too laid-back and politic for Durocher's taste. He liked players with fire, like Santo, whom he immediately named team captain. Besides, Durocher was the star.

Durocher knew that Banks was untouchable and was smart enough to avoid a direct confrontation, but he wasn't afraid to undermine Banks by chipping away at his playing reputation, in the hope that Banks would play his way out of the lineup—every spring Durocher tried to give his job away. Now in midseason he moved Banks to third base and shifted Ron Santo to shortstop. Durocher didn't expect the move to become permanent, but he hoped that John Boccabella would do well enough at first base to show Wrigley and Holland that the Cubs could survive without Banks, who could bring some value in trade. Boccabella failed to hit, however, and when both Santo and Banks struggled defensively, Durocher abandoned the trial after a week.

For the time being, the press gave the Cubs a pass, although after one particularly poor performance Richard Dozer in the *Tribune* referred to it as a "tragic portrayal of major league baseball." The fans gave the Cubs a pass as well. Despite the presence of Durocher, they kept passing Wrigley Field by. Chicagoans had fallen out of the habit of going to Wrigley Field, and attendance actually slipped in 1966, down another few thousand fans. For all intents and purposes, the White Sox owned Chicago. Some Cub games drew fewer than one thousand spectators.

In 1967, however, the Cubs began to turn the corner. In the offseason, Dick Ellsworth, who had lost twenty-two games despite pitching well at times, was traded for pitcher Ray Culp, who was both younger and a proven winner, and in spring training nearly a dozen young pitchers scuffled for a place in the rotation. Ferguson Jenkins not only made the rotation but was tabbed as opening day starter, and three rookies—Joe Niekro, John Upham, and Rick Nye—also made the staff, joined by Holtzman, Culp, Hands, and Chuck Hartenstein. All were under the age of twenty-seven.

Jenkins beat the Phillies, 4–2, on opening day, and the Cubs slowly gained confidence. In late June, they surged into the pennant race on the heels of a seven-game winning streak, their longest since 1954, and with thousands of kids just released from school for the summer, attendance started to soar. The White Sox were in the middle of the American League pennant race, and Chicago was baseball-crazy. On July 2, more than forty thousand delirious fans turned out and saw Jenkins pitch the Cubs into first place, beating the Reds, 4–1, while smacking a triple and a double. After the game, all forty thousand remained at the

University of Illinois alumnus Ken Holtzman proved to be one of the Cubs' most consistent left-handed pitchers in many seasons. In ten seasons at Wrigley Field, he won eighty games, including successive seventeen-win seasons in 1969 and 1970.

park. Atop the grandstand were flags representing each NL club in order of the league standings. The crowd stayed until the Cubs pennant was moved into first place. Wrigley Field had pennant fever.

The Cubs were close, but they were not quite ready. They were hurt when Ken Holtzman, who started the season 5–0, left to fulfill his military obligations and thereafter was only able to pitch while on leave, and the rest of the young staff suffered growing pains. The Cubs spent a month yo-yoing up and down, following their surge by losing seven in a row and nine of ten, then winning five straight before going into another slide that ended any dream of a pennant as the St. Louis Cardinals pulled away.

By then, Durocher had given up on 1967 and, unfortunately, on several players. The Cubs made several deals for cash, sending the signal that they were already thinking about 1968. The Cubs finished the season with a record of 87–74, good enough for third place, fourteen games behind the Cards, earning Durocher manager-of-the-year accolades. After the season ended, they made two significant trades. The first, for outfielder Lou Johnson, was designed to plug a hole in right field. The second, which they'd later regret, was almost capricious. Durocher had lost faith in Ray Culp, and the pitcher was unceremoniously dumped on the Boston Red Sox for minor league outfielder Bill Schlesinger. He never played an inning for the Cubs. Meanwhile, Culp went right into Boston's rotation and became a mainstay, winning sixty-four games over the next four seasons.

The deal was telling, for it revealed Durocher's Achilles' heel. As the Cubs became more competitive, Durocher became less patient and took fewer chances, particularly with pitchers. As Culp had discovered, the worst thing a young Cub pitcher could do was experience some early success and then falter. Durocher almost immediately lost faith and too often buried the young player. In times of stress, Durocher leaned heavily on veterans and nearly forgot everyone else.

At least now the Cubs had everyone's attention. Attendance was up more than 50 percent as nearly one million fans came to Wrigley Field. A better team helped, but the Cubs benefited from a renaissance of sorts. All those kids born after World War II were starting to reach adulthood. Suddenly, teenagers were everywhere, and in college

Adolfo Phillips could never seem to escape manager Leo Durocher's doghouse, despite the fact that Durocher once said of him, "Only Willie Mays and Curt Flood are better than he is in center." His star-crossed Cub career lasted only for two full seasons and portions of two others. Following his trade to Montreal midway through the 1969 season, the Cubs were never the same without the services of the personable and versatile center fielder.

towns like Boston and Chicago young people began to flock to the ballpark as baseball tapped a chord in the countercultural consciousness as an alternative to the military metaphors of football. From 1965 to 1970, major league attendance rose by nearly 25 percent. In between antiwar protests during the 1967 "Summer of Love," young Chicagoans were beginning to discover the Cubs. For the past twenty years, Wrigley had sat nearly empty, unappreciated by fans, an out-of-place anachronism that inspired little poetry and even less affection. Now a new generation began to discover both the joys of the game and the

Shortly after the arrival of Leo Durocher, the Cubs traded for catcher Randy Hundley, a player the new manager would soon declare was "his field general, the guy who runs things for me." A superb defensive catcher and handler of pitchers, Hundley also slugged nineteen home runs in his first season with the Cubs in 1966.

friendly confines of Wrigley Field. The Cubs were on the crest of a wave.

In a society that was beginning to question institutions, the iconoclastic Durocher became something of an anti-hero to young Chicagoans: the manager said what he meant and meant what he said—or at least gave that impression—and he was the absolute opposite of the Cubs' corporate father figure, Phil Wrigley. Durocher made the Cubs cool, and new fans found many of the younger Cubs easy to identify with. All of a sudden, the Cubs began to matter in a way they hadn't for decades. By the start of the 1968 season, for the first time in more than two decades, there were actually expectations that the club might win the pennant.

One big reason was Ferguson Jenkins. In 1967 Jenkins had won twenty games for the first time, outperforming such luminaries as Bob Gibson and Juan Marichal. Jenkins, who stood a lanky six-foot-five and had such big hands that the ball nearly disappeared in his fingers, was a bona-fide number-one starting pitcher. Although neither as fast as Gibson nor as flashy as Marichal, he was every bit their equal, using impeccable control, a hard curve, and a sinking fastball to dominate hitters. Billy Williams once said of him that "Jenks made it easy for us outfielders. When he pitched I could move to get a jump on the ball. When [Cubs catcher] Hundley gave him a target inside I could move to anticipate the hitter, since I knew Fergie was always on target."

When he was on the mound, the Cubs were competitive against anyone. Durocher built his rotation around Jenkins. Other pitchers were occasionally skipped over or jerked back and forth, but Durocher didn't mess with Jenkins, who was probably the one player on the team Durocher couldn't intimidate. Every fourth day the ultra-confident Jenkins towered over the mound as if he were Durocher's field commander. "I didn't consider pitching to be work," Jenkins once said. "I was having fun getting most hitters out." Had San Francisco Giants pitcher Mike McCormick not won twenty-two games in a career-best performance, Jenkins would have won the Cy Young Award in 1967. Over the course of his Cubs career, he'd win the award only once, but he would finish in the top three on three other occasions.

The whole team seemed on the verge of greatness. Adolfo Phillips, whom Durocher initially found inscrutable owing to a language barrier and cultural differences, finally appeared to be ready to push aside Mays and Flood to become the best center fielder in baseball. He hit seventeen home runs in 1967 and led the team with twenty-four stolen bases. Durocher felt as if he were finally getting through to Phillips, pushing him to play with fire and daring.

But the real key to the Cubs' success was the continuing improvement of Bill Williams and Ron Santo. Both were extraordinary hitters and in their prime. Cubs pitcher Jack Lamabe, who faced both men when he pitched for the Cardinals in 1967, remembers that it was Santo and Williams—particularly Williams—whom pitchers feared, not Ernie Banks. Although they lacked the overwhelming power of hitting duos like Aaron and Mathews or Mantle and Maris, to the Cubs Santo and Williams were just as valuable. Williams's smooth left-handed stroke made baseball scouts swoon and produced line drives like Wrigley's assembly line produced sticks of gum. Although he lacked a strong throwing arm and played left field, Williams did everything else well. Santo played fire to Williams's ice by playing spectacular defense at third and hitting for power while displaying patience at the plate, a rare combination that was little appreciated at the time.

Santo had grown up in baseball, in the shadows of Seattle's minor league Sick Stadium, where as a boy he served as a batboy, hot dog vendor, and clubhouse attendant. As he once told reporter Michael Glab, "I used to shine Vada Pinson's shoes, and three years later I'm playing against him in the major leagues."

He could have gotten more money from another team but signed with Chicago for $20,000 because he thought he could make it to the big leagues faster. He was right. He also found out that he had diabetes; no one else in major league baseball, he would learn, had ever played with the disease. Santo did, and although a few teammates would learn about the disorder, particularly after he started taking insulin, at first he kept his condition a secret.

Although Santo and Durocher eventually had a falling-out—both were intense, quick to anger, and slow to forget—Santo initially thrived under Durocher, once calling the manager "the greatest thing that ever happened to me," and Durocher considered Santo "one of my great assets . . . he gave you everything he had." In a lineup that included two Hall of Famers in Williams and Banks, Santo was often the most dangerous hitter, regularly hitting close to .300 with twenty-five or thirty home runs and one hundred RBIs while playing the best third base in the league. All the while, diabetes hung over him, occasionally sapping his strength. Although one can't help but wonder how much better Santo might have been had he not had the disease, his lifetime performance was nevertheless impressive enough that his failure to gain admittance to the Hall of Fame remains an enduring mystery.

Williams wasn't identified by the Cubs as the instant star that Santo was; he told people later that he signed for a "cigar and a bus ticket." Although Williams, who grew up in rural Alabama, was homesick at first and nearly quit during his first professional season—only to be talked out of it by Buck O'Neill—he hit no matter how he felt, and it didn't take long for the Cub organization to realize what they had. In one famous incident in 1960, the great hitter Rogers Hornsby served as an instructor. He sat down a couple of dozen Cub players and went right down the line bluntly telling all but two that they had no chance of making major league baseball. But he told Santo and Williams, "You can play in the major leagues right now."

The 1961 NL Rookie of the Year, Williams was one of the most consistent hitters in major league history—so consistent, in fact, that it was often easy to overlook him. That, however, was just the way he liked it—staying in the background, doing his job, and leading by example. Recent Hall of Famers Kirby Puckett and Ryne Sandberg both found it necessary to give Williams credit for their own careers in their induction speeches—credit Williams himself never would have claimed.

Santo and Williams, in combination, were of immeasurable help to Ernie Banks. They hit in front of Banks in the Cubs lineup, giving him an opportunity to continue to knock runs in even as his skills eroded over time. Together they extended Banks's effective career by several seasons. Had he been exposed in the Cubs lineup, he would not have remained a run producer. Although he was no longer the superstar he had been in the 1950s, Banks remained a

1966

dangerous hitter; also, his availability to the press took the heat off the other Cubs, while his even temper and quiet encouragement provided a contrast to Durocher's acid tongue. Furthermore, in a period of increasing racial unrest, Banks made white Chicago comfortable.

By the start of the 1968 season, although the Cubs were not favored to win the pennant, they were expected to provide the St. Louis Cardinals with a strong challenge. Ron Santo later said that the 1968 season was the first in which he "expected" to win every game instead of just hoping to. Ernie Banks, who had started coming up with a couplet to summarize the Cubs' chances each year, said, "Don't fear—this is the year." Just before the start of the season, however, on April 4, civil rights leader Martin Luther King Jr. was assassinated in Memphis, Tennessee.

King's death knocked baseball to the back page and spawned riots in African American communities all across the country as simmering racial tensions were suddenly released. Chicago, where African Americans now accounted for fully 30 percent of the population, had been spared when riots hit Newark and Detroit in 1967, but it was not so fortunate this time. The West Side, which had evolved into a nearly all-black neighborhood since World War II, exploded in violence. Although rioting was confined to the neighborhood and manifested itself primarily in the burning of stores and other commercial establishments along Madison Avenue, the resulting destruction of twenty city blocks left nine people dead. Moreover, white Americans, in Chicago and elsewhere, found the images frightening. Inadvertently, the Cubs would soon benefit from the tragedy of these events.

For much of the previous two decades, the White Sox had been Chicago's dominant baseball team, and they had nearly won the pennant in 1967. But images of the riots in the wake of King's death gave many white fans in and around Chicago second thoughts about traveling to Comiskey Park on the South Side, a distinctly African American community, even though it had been untouched

---

By the end of the 1968 season, third baseman Ron Santo had captured five consecutive Gold Glove Awards and was considered, along with Brooks Robinson, one of the finest third basemen of his generation. During the same five-year period, he averaged thirty home runs per season and led the National League in RBIs for four of the five seasons.

1968

by the riots. Most longtime White Sox fans did not transfer their allegiance to the Cubs, but at a time when baseball was otherwise experiencing a boom, the White Sox drew few new fans. By 1970 attendance at Comiskey Park was less than 500,000, barely half of what it had been in 1967. During that same period, attendance at Wrigley Field almost doubled, to 1.7 million.

This is not to suggest that the Cubs benefited because of any enlightened attitude toward African Americans; in that respect, the Cubs were squarely in the mainstream, which is to say that age-old prejudices were still in evidence. They liked their African American players to remain quiet, like Banks and Williams, and minority players who did not had a difficult time remaining on the roster unless they were stars—the Cubs' roster contained far fewer blacks than that of the White Sox, and the Cubs didn't openly court African American fans. The Cubs were the beneficiaries of simple geography, nothing more.

King's death caused the preseason series between the Cubs and White Sox to be cut short, and every team in baseball canceled opening day out of a combination of respect and fear. The Cubs opened the season in Cincinnati on April 10, losing 9–4. The White Sox had the honor of opening the season in Chicago, and their opening day crowd was cause for concern: fewer than eight thousand fans turned out. The team would collapse in 1968, falling well below .500. The Cubs, on the other hand, drew over thirty thousand fans to Wrigley Field for their home opener.

Unfortunately, over the balance of the season, those thirty thousand Cub fans and many thousands more would be disappointed. The Cubs weren't ready. The St. Louis Cardinals jumped to the front, and except for a few days in late May, the Cubs never mounted a serious challenge. For a time, in fact, they seemed headed to the bottom, tumbling all the way down to ninth place in late June after being shut out in five of six games.

It was the "year of the pitcher" in the major leagues. Hitting was down everywhere in 1968—Adolfo Phillips went backwards, knocking in only thirty-three runs for the entire season—and the Cubs scored nearly one hundred fewer runs than in 1967. Pitching, which had appeared to be a Cub strength in 1967, was, in comparison to the rest of the league, only barely adequate. Jenkins won

twenty games again, despite losing 1–0 a record five times, but Ken Holtzman, touted by the Cubs as the "next Sandy Koufax" owing to the fact that he was left-handed and Jewish, struggled to win, and Joe Niekro, who earned the opening day start after a strong spring, finished the season with an ERA of 4.32. While today that figure would earn a pitcher a multi-year, multimillion-dollar contract, in 1968 it was the third-worst mark in the major leagues for pitchers with more than twenty starts. Only reliever Phil Regan, acquired in a trade with the Dodgers, performed better than expected, leading the league with twenty-five saves.

Still, even though the Cubs finished third again, at 84–78, when one looked closely at the 1968 season there were reasons for optimism. After dropping to ninth place, the Cubs didn't quit. They turned their season around, compiling the best record in the league in the second half. By August, after the team had won twenty-two of twenty-nine, the Cubs felt as if they were on their way. Santo said, "I think we're the strongest team in the league." Nonetheless, the Cubs needed a late-season surge and a tongue lashing from Durocher in the final week to finish above .500 at 84–78, good enough for third place. For the first time since 1945–46, the Cubs had finished above .500 in back-to-back seasons.

Cubs fans can be excused if they failed to notice the surge, for by August 1968 the city of Chicago was in turmoil. Ever since the riots after the death of Martin Luther King, Chicago had been a city on edge, as authorities reacted to dissent and civil disobedience over racial issues and the war with intimidation and violence. The SDS (Students for a Democratic Society), the Yippies, and the Black Panthers were all active in Chicago, and the city was a hotbed of the growing antiwar movement. When Robert Kennedy was assassinated on June 5, Chicagoans began to look ahead to the Democratic National Convention, scheduled to be held in Chicago during the last week of August, with real fear.

As the convention approached, dissent increased exponentially and the city became a lightning rod for protests. By the time the convention was under way, thousands of protesters had filled Chicago streets. The City of Chicago and the State of Illinois reacted with force, mobilizing thousands of police officers and National Guardsmen. Over the course of a week, nearly 700 people were arrested, more than 150 were hospitalized, more than 1,000 were treated for injuries, and the reputation of the city was seriously damaged as the police and guards beat protesters and reporters with equal dispatch, and on camera. Mayor Richard Daley's infamous slip of the tongue, "The policeman isn't there to create disorder, the policeman is there to preserve disorder," was weirdly accurate. Although the Cubs were out of town during the convention, it was hard to focus on baseball.

Still, when the season ended, the Cubs and Cub fans were already looking forward to 1969, not so they could put 1968 in the rearview mirror, but because 1968 had been something for the Cubs to build on. Change was coming to baseball, and that gave Cub fans even more reason for optimism.

The lack of offense in 1968 had scared baseball. Only five players hit over .300, and in a few cities attendance had slipped badly. In the offseason, baseball took action, lowering the pitching mound and shrinking the strike zone, both measures designed to help hitters. Every pitcher in the league would have to adjust, but that wasn't the biggest change.

Baseball chose to celebrate its one-hundredth anniversary by expanding for the second time in less than a decade. Each league added two new teams, the American League moving into Seattle and Kansas City while the NL added franchises in Montreal and San Diego. Each league also split into two divisions and instituted a postseason playoff.

For the pennant-starved Cubs, the change was a godsend. After decades of needing to beat out another seven clubs for the pennant—or, after 1961, an even more imposing nine teams—in 1969 the Cubs only had to beat out five ball clubs to make the postseason. Even better, they were placed in the National League's East Division with the Phillies, the Pirates, the New York Mets, the expansion Montreal Expos, and the St. Louis Cardinals. Only the Cardinals had finished ahead of the Cubs in 1968—no other team in the division had finished above .500. The Mets, after six seasons, had yet to win more than seventy-three games or finish higher than ninth, and history suggested that the Expos would struggle to win fifty games. The new schedule was intentionally "unbalanced" so that teams played more games in the division than out of it; thus, the Cubs would face each team in the Eastern Division eighteen times and those in the West only twelve. Over the course of the 162-game schedule, the Cubs would play only forty-two games versus the Cardinals, Giants, and Reds, the only three teams other than the Cubs that had finished above .500 in 1968. The Cubs would play the remaining 120 games against teams that finished .500 or less, including thirty games against expansion teams. All these factors would play an enormous role in the way the 1969 season played out, and by the end of the season nothing would ever be the same again.

The world may have been going to hell, and Chicago may have been in flames, but at Wrigley Field the sun was coming out.

A SERIES OF SWOONS

Nineteen sixty-nine created the Cubs. For most of the past three decades, they had been just another team, almost nameless and faceless, second to the White Sox in the Second City, as bland and gray as day-old chewing gum, a collection of mostly lackluster ballplayers playing in a pleasant but unspectacular ballpark before small knots of fans looking to while away an afternoon.

Not anymore. In 1969 the Cubs came out of hibernation, shook off the accumulated dust, stood in the sun, and preened. All that had come before fell away. Almost overnight, the Cubs were with it. And almost just as quickly, they were not—at least not in the same way. No one who saw it happen will ever forget it.

Just as the 1967 "Impossible Dream" season, despite ending in loss, redefined the Boston Red Sox, and the 1969 "Amazing Mets" came to redefine that club, the 1969 season redefined the Cubs. But it was different in Chicago. Although the 1969 season marked a new chapter in Cubs history, it did not end happily, and

In one of the most haunting photographs in Cub history, third baseman Ron Santo watches a black cat lope behind him as he stands in the on-deck circle at Shea Stadium in the second game of a crucial three-game series that all but decided the fate of the 1969 Eastern Division race.

no one ever wanted to experience it again. It was simultaneously the best and worst season in club history: on the one hand, it created their contemporary identity as the lovable "Cubbies," but it also endowed them with the lasting reputation of not just losing, which had long been the case, but of being *losers*, something infinitely worse. In the end, it inspired a fatalistic sense of disillusionment so intense and so thorough that many fans would never again allow themselves to measure their affection for the team in wins and losses. If the Cubs could not win in 1969, when they should have, there must be no way in the world the Cubs could ever win at all. That was it. Better to sit in the sun, sip an Old Style, and put any notions of a world championship right out of your head.

But this outlook, however genuine and heartfelt, is in some ways flawed. Cub fans couldn't help themselves in 1969. They fell in love, and time has since inflated both the significance of that team and its talent. Like a first love viewed at a distance and stripped of the exuberance of youth, the 1969 Cubs were a fine little romance that in reality had little chance of lasting. A good team but not a great one, the 1969 Cubs nearly parlayed a wealth of personality, a sense of drama, and a few great weeks of baseball into a division title.

In reality, a division title, at best, was never more than a fifty-fifty proposition for the Cubs in 1969. The popular contention that the '69 Cubs were the best team that never won is without much foundation. The Cubs were a contender in 1969 not so much because of what *they* were, but primarily because of what other teams *were not* after the addition of two expansion clubs and the splitting of the league into two divisions. From 1968 to 1969, the Cubs themselves had not dramatically improved. They simply took advantage of a unique situation better than any other team in the league—except the Mets. And that was the reason it hurt so badly in the end. The Mets, who before 1969 hadn't even had a *date*, lived out a fairy tale, sweeping the girl off her feet and living happily ever after while America swooned.

To the Cubs organization, actually losing in 1969 was not nearly as damaging as how that loss was perceived afterwards. The Mets victory was such a shock and ran so counter to common perception that, collectively, the Cubs and their fans believed that they were somehow denied

something they had already gained. To this day, the franchise and many fans haven't gotten over it. Never before in baseball history has so much been made of a second-place team that played .500 baseball for three and a half months and finished eight games back in a divisional title race.

The 1969 season began in earnest just a few days after the end of the 1968 World Series, won by the Cardinals. As in 1962, when baseball stocked the expansion clubs with players from an expansion draft, in 1969 the Expos and Padres would have the same opportunity. The seeds of the Cubs' success in 1969—and their demise—were contained in the draft.

The Cubs escaped the draft relatively unscathed as the Expos focused on veterans, such as veteran Pittsburgh first baseman Donn Clendenon, who knocked in eighty-seven runs in 1968 and had been a valuable player for the Pirates since 1962. The Padres went for youth, selecting players like twenty-four-year-old New York Mets pitcher Dick Selma, who had won nine games in 1968, including three by shutout, with an ERA of 2.76. His availability in the draft was reflective of the vast reservoir of young pitching in the Met organization. Both players would end up having a huge impact on the Cubs' fortunes in 1969.

Each club was allowed to protect fifteen players in the draft's first two rounds, and the Cubs weren't terribly disappointed when the Expos picked young pitcher Bill Stoneman and the Padres tabbed backup infielder Jose Arcia. Stoneman was a prospect, but he had angered Durocher during a brief stint with the Cubs in 1968 by throwing too many curveballs, and Arcia, although a fine fielder, couldn't hit. In later rounds, the Cubs lost no players of consequence. Only Stoneman went on to a significant career, throwing a no-hitter and having several fine seasons with Montreal before arm injuries cut his career short.

In the spring of 1969, everything went according to plan. The only hole in the Cubs' lineup was right field, and Durocher seemed to have settled on a platoon of Jim Hickman and Al Spangler. The Cubs had shown plenty of offense in spring training in Arizona, hitting .285 as a team, and although Adolfo Phillips had broken a bone in his hand, Don Young had filled in. Amid the usual prediction of a pennant from the players, only Leo Durocher, oddly enough, was cautious. Although he wrote a letter to the *Chicago American* that stated, "The Cubs are now ready to go for all the marbles," he later added, "I only wonder about our depth." He was right. The addition of the four expansion clubs left most clubs feeling a little short, but for the Cubs the shortage was critical: they opened the season with neither a bona-fide backup catcher nor a backup infielder. On paper, the Cubs' starting lineup could match up with anyone, but their bench was virtually nonexistent. Durocher also wasn't happy with his fourth starter, Joe Niekro, a fastball-slider pitcher at the time who had ticked Durocher off by fooling around with a knuckleball, the pitch that put his brother, Phil Niekro, into the Hall of Fame and later nearly did the same for Joe.

That didn't matter in April 1969. On opening day, a crowd of nearly forty-one thousand fans, the largest since 1929, turned out at Wrigley Field on a surprisingly warm day to watch the Cubs beat the Phillies. They were not disappointed as the Cubs lit a spark that soon burst into flame and spread as quickly and completely as the Chicago fire, sweeping through the city and sucking in all the oxygen. "It was," wrote George Langford in the *Tribune*, "simply sweet. Exhausting, heart-flipping, but sweet." As it turned out, the opening day contest was a microcosm of the regular season until the very end—as the Cubs surged ahead, were caught, and then struggled to hold on. This time, however, the Cubs won in the end.

Ernie Banks homered his first two times up to put the Cubs ahead 5–1, but the Phillies slowly chipped away at the lead. In the ninth inning, Jenkins gave up two singles he called "flukes," and then rookie Don Money homered to tie the game. Philadelphia went ahead in the eleventh before the Cubs won it on a pinch-hit home run by Willie Smith, sending all the Cubs out to home plate to greet him and a couple of dozen fans onto the field to show him the way around the bases. Cubs fans, wrote Langford, went through "an emotional and physical wringer designed to test even the strongest constitutions." They hadn't seen anything yet.

The Cubs were on their way. For the first few weeks of the season, something remarkable happened almost every day. In game number two, Billy Williams set an NL record with four doubles. In the fourth game, Joe Niekro and Ted Abernathy combined to throw a twelve-inning, 1–0 shutout. Following a loss to Montreal in the fifth game

Bill Hands followed up his breakthrough season of 1968, in which he compiled a 16–10 won-lost record, with a superb season in 1969. He not only won 20 games but also led the staff with a 2.49 ERA while pitching 300 innings in 41 starts.

of the season, the Cubs got revenge by scoring three ninth-inning runs to beat the Expos 7–6, the final run scoring on an Ernie Banks single. On the following day, April 14, Ken Holtzman outdueled Pittsburgh's Bob Veale to win 4–0, putting the Cubs in first place with a record of 6–1, the first of 149 consecutive days the Cubs would spend looking down at the rest of the division. They followed with another five consecutive wins, including shutouts of St. Louis by Jenkins and Hands, to run their record to 11–1.

Everything seemed perfect, but for Durocher it was not perfect enough. After Joe Niekro ended the Cub winning streak with a loss to Montreal in the second game of a double-header on April 20, the Cubs lost their next three contests, and Cubs fans entertained the thought of tempering their exuberance. Ever since the start of spring training,

Durocher had been hassling John Holland to include Niekro in a deal for another starting pitcher. Meanwhile, Dick Selma, the former Mets pitcher picked by the San Diego Padres in the expansion draft, opened the season by striking out thirteen. San Diego knew they weren't going anywhere, and Selma's performance suddenly increased his value.

On April 24, the Cubs fell to the Cardinals, 3–2, leading Cardinal manager Red Schoendienst to announce, "The next time we leave Chicago we'll be in first place." Minutes later the Cubs threw down the gauntlet: Holland announced that San Diego had agreed to trade Selma to the Cubs for Niekro and two minor league prospects. "Selma is the fourth starter we've been looking for," said Holland.

Energized, the Cubs went to New York and immediately resumed their winning ways—taking three of four from the lowly Mets and running their record to 14–6—while the Mets, listed in Las Vegas at 100–1, were a not very lucky 7-11 and showed few signs of increasing their chances for a pennant any time soon.

From New York the Cubs went on to Philadelphia, where they took two of three from the Phillies. The defend-ing champion Detroit Tigers followed the Cubs into Philadelphia for an exhibition game, and on his way out of the clubhouse an anonymous Cub player scrawled a message for the Tigers on a chalkboard. "See you in the World Series," it read. "If you can make it."

The Cubs returned to Chicago the next day and were greeted like conquering heroes. Thousands of fans turned out at the airport to welcome them back, singing the Cubs' unofficial theme song, "Hey, hey, holy mackerel, no doubt about it, the Cubs are on their way," over and over again. Already the Cubs ticket office was being deluged with requests for World Series tickets, and the youthful Cubs suddenly discovered that they were the most popular young men in town. WGN even hired Ernie Banks as an occasional sports reporter. No one noticed that after their 11–1 start, the Cubs, now 16–7, had only played .500 base-ball over the past ten days.

Slick-fielding shortstop Don Kessinger anchored the Cub infield during the team's rebirth in the late 1960s and early 1970s. He and second baseman Glenn Beckert formed the best Cub double-play combo since Billy Herman and Billy Jurges in the 1930s.

1969

In Chicago the New York Mets were waiting, and the Cubs took the first two games of the four-game series. For the finale, a Sunday double-header on May 4, Wrigley Field had been sold out for a week: more than forty thousand fans crowded into the park, leaving another twenty thousand milling around outside. A sweep would give the Cubs a gaudy 20–7 record.

For the young Mets, the season hung in the balance. They were only 9–14, and two more losses would bury them.

Bill Hands, a pitcher the Mets had not beaten for more than a year, started the first game for the Cubs. Opposite him was Tom Seaver, a young pitcher on the precipice of stardom who had yet to take that final step, going 16–13 and 16–12 in his first two seasons with New York.

Seaver was one of a new breed of Mets, a player who did not buy into their legacy of loss. After being a winner at the University of Southern California, he had reached the major leagues after only one year in the minors, and he expected to be great.

At the start of the game, Wrigley was rocking. Over the past few seasons, a group of self-described "Bleacher Bums," whom *Tribune* reporter Skip Myslenski aptly described as a "marauding, raucous troop," had taken over Wrigley Field, figuratively if not literally, wearing yellow hardhats, singing, cheering, and making all sorts of mostly well-intentioned mayhem. After he joined the club, pitcher Dick Selma started whipping them into a frenzy waving a handkerchief, and now handkerchiefs were on full display at Wrigley Field. The Bums were drooling at the prospect of sweeping the pathetic Mets.

In the second inning, however, when Ron Santo stepped to the plate, Seaver, whom the Cubs had already beaten once earlier in the year, announced that he had had enough with the whole business of losing and losing and losing. In the six games against the Mets thus far in 1969, Santo had knocked in ten runs. Seaver was determined to stop him.

When Ron Santo stepped in, Seaver's first pitch knocked him on his ass. Seaver admitted later, "I brushed him back on purpose . . . the man hits me hard. I wanted him to know I was protecting myself." Santo wasn't hit, but the message was delivered—Seaver and the Mets weren't going to roll over.

Bill Hands responded in kind. When Seaver came to bat in the third, Hands hit him in between the shoulder blades, tit for tat. According to baseball's unwritten rules of engagement, it was over. The Cubs and Mets were even.

Not so fast. For the Mets, it wasn't over. "The whole dugout suddenly came alive" after he was hit, said Seaver later. In the third inning, Hands came up to bat, and Seaver drilled him, sending a fastball hard into his left side, doubling Hands over.

Mets manager Gil Hodges and Leo Durocher both rushed from the dugouts. Durocher wanted Seaver thrown from the game, or at least warned, while Hodges argued against it. Hodges won, and as George Langford wrote in the *Tribune*, "The proverbial sleeping dog received a kick in the backside . . . which roused it with a vengeance and the proud Cubs were bitten. . . . The psychological damage had already been done." The Cubs were suddenly compliant. Santo went hitless in both contests as Seaver went the route in the first game of the double-header, winning 3–2, and Tug McGraw did the same in the second, winning by the same score when Ron Swoboda scored from second on Dick Selma's wild pitch.

Despite a banner headline in the *Tribune* that read "Cubs Swoon Before Big Crowd," the Cubs hardly noticed—these were *the Mets* after all—but the sweep was huge for New York, giving the club confidence and probably saving them from a season-ending tailspin. "We put a notch in our belts that day," Seaver said later. "That little bit of throwing, it wasn't too nice, but it proved another issue: that they weren't playing with boys anymore." No one could see it, but the first small crack in the Cubs' facade had been exposed.

It was all forgotten over the next week as the Cubs beat up on the NL West, splitting with the Dodgers and Giants, then taking three in a row from the Padres, the first two by shutout, 2–0 and 19–0, their third shutout in a row. Then the Cubs went to Houston and beat the Astros 11–0, their fifth straight win, by a combined score of 43–2.

They lost Glenn Beckert to a broken thumb in the contest, but it hardly slowed them down. For the next month, the Cubs won two of every three games they played.

Everything was almost perfect. Barely fifty games into the season Ernie Banks had already knocked in fifty runs. Ron Santo had forty RBIs, and Billy Williams was hitting over .320. Ken Holtzman was 9–1, Jenkins had eight wins, and even light-hitting shortstop Don Kessinger was batting almost .300. When the Cubs lost to the Reds on June 9, the loss snapped a seven-game winning streak. They were 36–17, seven games in front, one of only two teams in the division above .500. The other team was the Mets, who were 28–23, but no one was taking them seriously. At the end of the month, the Cardinals were coming to Wrigley. They already trailed by eleven and a half and were not about to fulfill Schoendienst's prediction.

Then the Cubs stumbled. After breaking a bone in his right hand on March 11, Adolfo Phillips returned to the starting lineup on April 27. That was too long for Durocher, who steamed, "He doesn't want to play." Although Durocher had once been Phillips's biggest booster, the manager was now out of patience and had started trying to demean Phillips into fulfilling his potential. In spring training, Durocher had even threatened to give the center-field job to nineteen-year-old Oscar Gamble, who had played all of thirty-four games in Single A. Nothing Phillips had ever done satisfied Durocher, who expected him to be Willie Mays. Phillips was sensitive to Durocher's barbs, which were increasingly personal; also, according to Ferguson Jenkins, Phillips was bothered by a kidney ailment and was rarely healthy enough to play to his potential.

When Phillips returned, Durocher jerked him in and out of the lineup for the next three weeks, then in late May buried him. Don Young, a rookie, became the regular center fielder by default. Young was thoroughly overmatched. In 1968 he had hit only .242 for Single A Lodi, his first season since 1965 in which he had hit above .200. Yet Durocher handed him a job in the starting lineup.

Durocher had made a critical mistake, seeing Phillips for what he was not doing rather than for what he was. What he was not doing was hitting, either very often or very hard. Ever since Phillips had hit seventeen home runs in 1967, including three in one game, Durocher and the Cubs had expected him to blossom into a slugger. He hadn't, and when he returned to the lineup after the broken hand, he hit with even less power than before. By June 11, he had only four extra-base hits and no home runs. In fact, Phillips was hitting only .224, with only eleven hits for

the season. Every time Durocher saw those numbers, he fumed.

What Durocher did not see, however, was just as important, perhaps more so. Phillips might not have been hitting, but he was still playing fine defense, and he was getting on base. In fact, he was walking more often than at any time during his career. His batting average was only .224, but his on-base percentage was a stellar .424. At least fifty points higher than any other Cub's—and more than one hundred points higher than Don Young's—Phillips's OBP was made even more impressive by the fact that, hitting in front of the pitcher, Phillips had been intentionally walked only three times. No matter how frustrated Phillips made Durocher feel, he was not hurting the Cubs.

Durocher didn't see it. No one did. On June 11, Phillips was sent off, traded with reliever Jack Lamabe to the Expos for backup infielder Paul Popovich, a former Cub. While Popovich gave the club some much-needed infield depth, the Cubs should never have made the deal unless they had an adequate replacement on hand, and in an expansion year such players were at a premium. Neither Young nor anyone else the Cubs would later try in center field would be an improvement. Up until that point in the season, the Cubs were twenty games over .500, 38–18. After the Phillips trade, they were barely a .500 team, 54–52, a record that was not entirely coincidental.

Three days later, another critical trade took place, this time between the Mets and Montreal. In combination with the Phillips deal, the balance of power in the NL East was beginning to shift.

Earlier in the spring, baseball had experienced the first rumblings of labor unrest that would, in less than a decade, usher in an era of free agency and change the face of the game forever. For the first time, the Players' Association was flexing its muscles as the players, increasingly politicized, began to question the status quo that made them virtual slaves. In February, they threatened to boycott spring training over pension issues, demonstrating amazing unity—only ten players out of more than five hundred voted against the job action. Ron Santo was the biggest name who disagreed. He broke ranks, saying, "Mr. Wrigley's been good to me, and I'm going to be good to him," a move that did not endear him to his peers. The two sides eventually settled during the last week of February, and a strike was averted.

A month earlier the Expos had traded expansion draftee Donn Clendenon and Jesus Alou to the Astros for Rusty Staub. Clendenon seemed to accept the trade and even negotiated a new contract with Houston for $36,000. But on February 28, just a few days after the labor settlement, Clendenon suddenly retired.

The Astros expected new baseball commissioner Bowie Kuhn to void the trade, returning Staub and Alou to the Astros, but Kuhn inexplicably refused, ordering the two clubs to work out compensation. And so they did: the Expos eventually sent $100,000 and several prospects to Houston in lieu of Clendenon. Then Clendenon, after a protracted period of public hand-wringing, suddenly unretired and signed a two-year, $100,000 contract with the Expos—$14,000 more annually than what he had negotiated with Houston.

Other players immediately noticed that Clendenon's ploy had not only resulted in a significant raise but rescinded a trade he apparently hadn't liked. Met first baseman Ed Kranepool quipped, "Great! If the Mets trade me, I'll retire before I report," presumably to "unretire" with a raise. In early April, Ken Harrelson was traded by Boston to Cleveland and used the exact same strategy.

At any rate, Clendenon did not become an Astro but remained a member of the Expos. Then, in mid-June, the Expos made Clendenon available again. The Mets, with a record of 30–25 on June 14, were still hanging around in second place in the NL East, but they were winning with pitching. Over the past three weeks, they had not scored more than five runs in any one game. Clendenon was a proven run producer, a player who had hit more than one hundred career home runs for Pittsburgh despite playing in cavernous Forbes Field. Desperate for offense, on June 14 the Mets sent several prospects to the Expos for Clendenon.

He would have an enormous impact on the remainder of the season. Having Clendenon allowed Met manager Gil Hodges to install a platoon at first base, where he paired Clendenon with Ed Kranepool, and over the balance of the season Clendenon led the offensively challenged Mets in home runs and RBIs. New York's lineup still didn't scare anyone, but Clendenon gave the Mets just enough punch

NO-HITTERS

August 19, 1880 September 20, 1882 June 27, 1884	Larry Corcoran
July 27, 1885	John Clarkson
August 21, 1898	Walter Thornton
August 31, 1915	Jimmy Lavender
May 12, 1955	Sam Jones
May 15, 1960	Don Cardwell
August 19, 1969 June 3, 1971	Ken Holtzman
April 16, 1972	Burt Hooton
September 2, 1972	Milt Pappas

to make a difference. For the rest of the season, the Mets would go 70–36. In combination, the Phillips and Clendenon deals had made the Cubs worse and the Mets better. It was that simple. The Cubs and their fans didn't know it yet, but the season was effectively over. The torture would soon begin.

For the next month, the Cubs remained oblivious, basking in the attention of the masses and cashing in on their popularity to such an extent that a number of players had to employ an agent to sort through the various endorsement and public appearance offers being thrown their way. It was Cubs, Cubs, and more Cubs wherever one went in Chicago. Ernie Banks took "Mr. Cub" to the extreme as his

Ernie Banks celebrates his five-hundredth home run by tossing the ball for photographers on the day after his feat in May 1970. On May 4, the day of his historic homer, only 5,264 fans trekked to Wrigley Field to see "Mr. Cub" take Braves pitcher Pat Jarvis deep in the second inning of a 4–3 Cub victory.

Gamble—their best prospect—to the Philadelphia Phillies for outfielder John Callison. Durocher immediately named Callison the Cubs' starting right fielder, adding, "Callison not only adds to a solid defense, but he adds another big bat in our lineup. . . . [He] has the best arm in the league outside of Roberto Clemente." John Holland chimed in, saying, "We felt we owed it to Williams, Santo, Banks, and some of the others to give the Cubs a player in his prime when we go for the pennant again next year."

That was fine and well, but Callison wasn't in his prime. While he had once been one of the NL's premier power hitters, cracking more than thirty home runs and one hun-

dred RBIs in back-to-back seasons in 1964 and 1965, since then he had fallen off badly. He seemed to be aging quickly, with diminishing power. It was shades of Chuck Klein—for the umpteenth time in their history, the Cubs traded for a player on the downside, giving away the future in exchange.

But that wasn't the half of it. Selma, like Joe Niekro and Ray Culp before him, hadn't fulfilled Durocher's expectations, so was simply cast away. Now, in addition to a center fielder and their other needs, the Cubs also needed a fourth starter.

They fulfilled none of their needs, and by the time they did, it was too late. Chicago got off to a quick start in 1970, moving into first place on April 22 in the midst of an eleven-game winning streak and then holding on for two months despite the fact that Banks looked finished and Randy Hundley was out of the lineup with a thumb injury.

In a sense, the winning streak came at the worst possible time, for it gave the organization false hope. Instead of trying to plug the obvious holes, the organization acted as if they didn't exist.

Cub fans sensed the truth, tempering their excitement with the knowledge that the Cubs were never very far ahead and were never really playing very well. At the end of June, the Cubs fell out of first place during a twelve-game losing streak. After struggling all season with no center fielder and no fourth starter, the Cubs belatedly made a move to fill both holes, buying pitcher Milt Pappas from the Braves in late June and adding problematic and flamboyant outfielder–first baseman Joe Pepitone in a waiver deal in July.

These might have been the right deals had they taken place in March, but by midsummer, despite forty-four RBIs from Pepitone in fifty-six games and a team-best 2.67 ERA from Pappas in twenty starts, it was just a little too late. All Pepitone and Pappas did was allow the Cubs to stay close. Had they been in place earlier, the Cubs might have been able to sneak in front.

The Cubs gave their fans a final tease, drawing to within a half-game of the first-place Mets and Pirates on September 3 and then acting as if they still might steal a division title. The bullpen, which had been problematic all year, finally came around, and the Cubs responded with a couple of dramatic wins that gave Wrigley Field some late life. Holland and Durocher thought the Cubs had a chance and, almost in a panic, started adding players for depth, picking up outfielder Tommy Davis and reliever Hoyt Wilhelm.

Then came the collapse. Just as it looked as if the Cubs would sweep past Pittsburgh, beginning on September 20 they went into a now-familiar swoon, losing five of six as the Pirates clinched the title. On September 25, following a 7–1 loss to the Phillies, George Langford summed it up bleakly in the *Tribune*. "The Cubs," he wrote, "went about their work today as if they were condemned men without a hacksaw, a listless, punchless group apparently resigned to a fate which is now evident." That could serve as the epitaph for the entire franchise.

It got worse from there. The Cubs ended the season in New York, and Ron Santo sat out. While the Cubs' official line was that Santo was "ill," in reality he had been the subject of death threats.

By 1971 it should have been clear that this generation of Cubs, born in the early 1960s with the emergence of Santo, Williams, and Jenkins, was starting to get a little old and slow. Banks was virtually finished, barely able to run on his arthritic knees, and he played only thirty-nine games. Glenn Beckert dislocated a thumb, Jim Hickman was ill with ulcers, Joe Pepitone had a bone chip in his elbow, and Randy Hundley tore up his knee. Even worse, the increasingly distracted, tired, and sour Leo Durocher was sixty-six years old and acting every second of it. As Edgar Munzel later wrote in *The Sporting News Baseball Guide*: "In 1969 the Cubs led all the way until September 10 . . . they jumped out again in 1970, leading the East division for 64 games. . . . Last season [1971] the Cubs were never in the lead after their first win."

As the season dragged on, the mood turned sour. In late August, Santo and Durocher had it out.

Once upon a time, the two men had been fingers on the same hand, as each recognized in the other a burning desire to win. But as the Cubs had tried and failed, then tried and failed, the once-warm relationship cooled. Durocher now found Santo lacking, later saying of him, "Five runs ahead and he'd knock in all the runs I could ask for. One run behind and he was going to kill me."

Santo made his diabetes public in midsummer, but he got little sympathy from Durocher. Then, after a 4–3 loss to

the Astros on August 22, Durocher called a team meeting and reamed out Milt Pappas for giving up a hit on an 0–2 pitch. Joe Pepitone jumped to his defense, and a complete blowout followed as the players screamed at Durocher and Durocher screamed back and several years of frustration came to a head and boiled over. After Durocher made a backhanded comment about Santo missing batting prac-

Former Phillie standout John Callison was one of a group of veterans acquired by John Holland in an effort to keep the Cubs competitive after their collapse in 1969. In two seasons in Chicago, Callison batted .244 with 27 home runs in 250 games spread over two seasons in 1970 and 1971.

In nineteen seasons with the Cubs, Ernie Banks was recognized both as the first slugging shortstop in modern baseball history and as the heart and soul of the Cubs.

tice, the two men had it out. The Cubs were giving Santo a "day" at Wrigley Field, and Durocher snidely remarked that the only reason Santo was getting a day was because he had "asked John Holland for one." Santo went nuts. By the time everyone calmed down, although no punches had been thrown, Santo was in tears, Durocher had quit, and nobody wanted to be a Cub anymore.

Durocher quickly rescinded his resignation, but the story made the papers, and it was clear to everyone in Chicago that the Cubs and Durocher were done, that this group and this manager would never win a championship. Then, just as the volume started to go down, Phil Wrigley made a bad situation worse.

On September 3, he took out an ad in the *Chicago Tribune*, presumably with the intent of diffusing the situation. But to Wrigley, intent and effect were rarely one and the same. The ad read:

It is no secret that in the closing days of a season that held great possibilities the Cub organization is at sixes and sevens and somebody has to do something. So, as the head of the corporation, the responsibility falls on me.

By tradition, this would call for a press conference following which there would be as many versions of what I had to say as there were reporters present, and as I have always believed in tackling anything as directly as possible, I am using this paid newspaper space to give you what I have to say direct, and you can do your own analyzing.

I have been in professional baseball a long time. I have served under the only five commissioners we have had to date and four league presidents, and I must have learned something about professional baseball.

Many people seem to have forgotten, but I have not, that after many years of successful seasons with contesting clubs and five league pennants, the Cubs went into the doldrums and for a quarter of a century were perennial dwellers of the second division in spite of everything we could think of to try and to do—experienced managers, inexperienced managers, rotating managers, no managers but revolving coaches—we were still there in the also rans.

We figured out what we thought was needed to make a lot of potential talent into a contending team, and we settled on Leo Durocher who had the baseball knowledge to build a contender and win pennants, and also knowing he had always been a controversial figure wherever he went, particularly with the press because he just never was cut out to be a diplomat. He accepted the job at less than what he was making because he considered it a challenge and Leo thrives on challenges.

In his first year we ended up in the cellar, but from then on came steadily up, knocking on the door for the top.

Each near miss has caused more and more criticism, and this year there has been a constant campaign to dump Durocher that has even affected the players, but just as there has to be someone in charge for the corporation, there has to be someone in charge on the field to make the final decision on the spur of the moment, and right or wrong, that's it.

All this preamble is to say that after careful consideration with my baseball people, Leo is the team manager and the "Dump Durocher Clique" might as well give up. He is running the team and if some of the players do not like it and lie down on the job, during the offseason we will see what we can do to find them happier homes.

Phil Wrigley, President
Chicago National League Baseball Club Inc.

P.S. If we could only find more team players like Ernie Banks.

The statement was stunning in a variety of ways, from its syntax to its stubbornness and its simplistic, twisted view of Cubs history, but for the players, the support of Durocher and the backhanded slap against everyone not named Ernie Banks was also a slap in the face. They were not even in Chicago when the ad appeared: playing in St. Louis, the Cubs would hear about the statement secondhand.

Behind a veil of anonymity, they let Wrigley know how they felt. One player the *Tribune* described as "prominent" spoke out, saying that "several of us have come to realize in recent weeks that the whole trouble is not just Leo Durocher. The other guy [Wrigley] has done some things that are hard to believe. The whole situation is sick, sick, sick. He sits at home watching television and decides we're not hustling . . . the last people to know anything in this organization are the players. All we know [is] what we read in the papers and then the owner, instead of talking to us, takes an ad out in the paper."

The season could not end soon enough. The Cubs ended any speculation over where they would finish by losing eight of their next nine games; Wrigley had deflated any slim chance the Cubs had to catch the Pirates.

On September 26, they played their final home game, falling to the Phillies 5–1 before a surprisingly big crowd of 18,505. Most were on hand to see Ernie Banks one last time. When he stepped to the plate in the first inning, he received a standing ovation.

It had been a long, tough year for Banks as age and arthritis kept him out of the lineup. He may well have wanted to "play two," but was usually unable to play at all. He was making only his twentieth start of the year, and in fewer than 100 at-bats he had hit less than .200 with only three home runs, giving him a career total of 512.

Nevertheless, Banks had one more hit left in his bat: he drove a ground ball that Phillies third baseman Deron Johnson fielded behind third base, but Johnson had no play as Banks, improbably, legged out an infield single for his last hit in the major leagues. In three other appearances, he walked, grounded out to short, and, in his last at-bat, popped out to third. Although the Cubs had three games remaining in Montreal, Banks was allowed to stay behind. His wife was undergoing minor surgery the next day.

After the game, the headline for the game story in the *Tribune* made no note of any of this. Banks left the game the way he came in, playing for a team playing out the string.

The headline read: "Cubs Leave Home Losers."

TRIALS AND **TRIBUNE**-LATIONS

Philip Wrigley was as clear and direct as possible. Amid increasing calls for the club owner to fire manager Leo Durocher and speculation that he'd name player personnel director Whitey Lockman as the new manager, on November 18, 1971, Wrigley squashed all those rumors by releasing a statement that read, "With the exception of the rebuilding year of 1966 the Cubs have compiled a record of 430–379, 51 games over .500, under Leo's direction." That was the bottom line, and with that statement Wrigley made it clear that, despite growing evidence that change was in order, Leo Durocher was still his man and that he, Phil Wrigley, after ceding control for several years, was back in charge. The Cubs hadn't won a championship, and they hadn't finished in first place since 1945, but, hey, they *were* over .500.

And night fell on Wrigley Field.

Ever since Wrigley first hired Durocher, a world championship, a pennant—hell, at least a division title—had seemed almost inevitable, hanging tantalizingly close

Bruce Sutter was the "accidental Hall of Famer." Drafted by the Washington Senators in 1970, he went unsigned until Cub scout Ralph DiLullo signed him as a free agent for $500 in 1971. The right-hander would master the split-finger pitch and revolutionize the craft of pitching while saving 133 games for the Cubs between 1976 and 1980.

just over the horizon. After the 1971 season, however, that vision quickly receded. Over the next decade, the Cubs, despite ample resources and opportunities, allowed that goal to slip ever further out of reach. It was almost as if Philip Wrigley, having tried competence, tired of it and decided to go back to the old way of doing business, hiring the unqualified to lead the inept and inert. He went from using his way to using Durocher's way, and then, eventually, to using no way at all. Despite the sunshine that filled Wrigley Field, the Cub organization would spend the next decade wandering around in the dark.

Retaining Durocher, oddly enough, was the first sign that the Cubs were about to reenter the dark ages, for by 1972 Leo Durocher reminded no one of the brash taskmaster who had been hired in 1966, a man who had brought a well-deserved reputation as a master motivator and in-game strategist who could get the most out of a ball club. He had done that in Chicago—at least for a while—and it hadn't been enough. Now his act had grown old, and so had Leo. The veterans had tired of him, while the newer Cubs didn't respect him. To them, Durocher wasn't the genius who had led the Dodgers and Giants to the World Series, but a crotchety has-been and failure whom his own players didn't respect and tried to ignore.

Taking their cues from disgruntled veterans like Ron Santo and Ken Holtzman, both of whom made no secret of how they felt about Durocher, at the end of the 1971 season the press kept up a steady drumbeat calling for Durocher's removal. Wrigley himself then inadvertently added to the noise by waiting almost six weeks after the end of the season to meet with general manager John Holland and make plans for 1972 while every other team in baseball was already moving ahead.

The louder the din, however, the less Philip Wrigley seemed to hear it. Left on his own, he might well have finally come to the conclusion that Durocher needed to be replaced, but instead, every time another Chicago columnist or radio host called for Durocher's ouster, Wrigley took it as another reason to keep him. He had given Durocher a vote of confidence in August, and he was determined to stand by it, telling some reporters in mid-November that if they didn't get off his back, "I'll keep Leo Durocher as manager no matter what."

Besides, under Durocher the Cubs had been more suc-

cessful and, even more significantly, more *profitable* than at any time in their history. From a corporate standpoint, Wrigley saw no reason to replace the manager. After all, the Wrigley Company didn't stop making Juicy Fruit gum just because sales leveled off. Profit was profit, and even better, Durocher was cheap. At age sixty-four, he had started to collect his baseball pension of $24,000 a year, the highest in the game, which allowed the Cubs to pay Durocher less than they would have otherwise.

On November 18, Wrigley not only gave Durocher a vote of confidence and a new contract but also agreed to rehire Durocher crony Pete Reiser as a coach. At the same time, every other coach was let go, and John Holland, not Durocher, hired the replacements—foremost among them first base coach Ernie Banks, who the Cubs announced would be activated as a pinch hitter and given the opportunity to play in the event that the Cubs made the postseason. The team also hired former pitcher Hank Aguirre in a new position as coach of "information and services." What was that? Well, the relationship between Durocher, the players, and the press had deteriorated so badly that Aguirre's main role was to give the other two parties the

logic behind Durocher's decisions, because Durocher himself didn't plan on doing so. It was a sure sign that the lights were starting to dim and the Cubs' brief era of enlightenment was over.

One day later, on November 19, Durocher made his first appearance at Wrigley Field since the end of the season. The manager tried to sound upbeat, dismissing talk of trouble in the clubhouse. Looking forward, he said, "We start at zero." He was unintentionally accurate.

Ten days later, presumably at Durocher's urging, the Cubs traded Ken Holtzman to the A's for outfielder Rick Monday. Holtzman was glad to be going and quipped, "I wouldn't have cared if the Cubs had traded me for two dozen eggs." Since being the number-one draft pick in 1965 out of Arizona State University, Monday hadn't quite fulfilled predictions of superstardom, but he did finally give the Cubs a real center fielder, while rookie Burt

---

In his first full season as a Cub starter in 1972, Burt Hooten delighted fans in his fourth major league start by tossing a no-hitter against the Phillies. On that cold April afternoon, Hooten warmed up by throwing 128 pitches—more than the 118 pitches he threw in the game.

A SUMMER AT WRIGLEY FIELD

BY RICK TELANDER

I n the mid-1970s, when I was in my midtwenties, I lived on Dakin Street, three blocks north of Wrigley Field. That would likely be enough to make a person a Cubs fan, but I already was one.

Growing up in Peoria, not making the Cardinal turn, going to Northwestern University in Evanston (just a handful of El stops north of the Friendly Confines), feeling a childhood reverence for my Ernie Banks card but not much of anything for my Minnie Minoso one—it all conspired to make me a lover of the "lovable losers."

Of course, they weren't known as such back then. The Cubs were just a baseball team that hadn't won in a while. Okay, a long time. But if you went to a game in the early 1970s, there still seemed to be a reasonable connection to the winning past. There were always people in the stands, for instance, who had been to the World Series in 1945, when the Cubs last made it to the peak event. Of course, the Cubs didn't win that one, losing to the Detroit Tigers, four games to three. And yes, the horrifying collapse of 1969 lingered in the air like the waning vapor from a tear-gassing. But 1969 was incomprehensible. So you didn't speak of it.

The beacon was 1908. All my life I have tried to find somebody who attended a World Series game in 1908, the last time the Cubs actually won it all. But I haven't found anybody. I didn't then. I can't now. Once, a few years ago, I put out a plea on a television show. Nothing. Ninety-eight years have gone by since that last crown. I have to figure that anybody who even peeked through a knothole at the Cubs during the Series of '08 is dead.

Regardless, I'm a Cubs fan, living near the park, and I'm pretty much of a party animal. The Cubs played only daytime games at home back then, so if you went to a weekday game, it already meant you were a loser of some form; at the very least you were playing hooky from a job, or else you were unemployed or were a student on summer break without responsibilities. Of course, it could also mean you were a hopeless drunk or a retired senior citizen or low-rent gambler or maybe a professional sunbather. There were all those at Wrigley. But I was a fun-loving partyer with my buddies, and I had the perfect cover to do what I did: I was a freelance sportswriter.

What that title really meant was: no job. I had written a deeply passionate book called *Heaven Is a Playground* in 1974, but it had sold about three copies. I wrote occasionally for different publications—as diverse as *American*

Libraries, *National Wildlife*, *PTA* magazine, the *Peoria Journal-Star*, and the plum, *Sports Illustrated*—and I believed wholeheartedly in the printed word, but I didn't have anything that resembled a full-time job. Maybe playing in my band, the Del-Crustaceans, could go on the résumé as such. But the sporadic Dels gigs often led to even worse problems, such as monumental hangovers. And those were the kind of things that could best be sweated off in the little funhouse down the street.

I got a press pass from the Cubs PR folks, an amateurish piece of white, rectangular, wallet-sized paper with black print that let me into Wrigley for a specified amount of time, the amount of which was typed on the front by a staff member who had used a typewriter. That time varied, depending on how long it would take, theoretically, for me to collect the information I needed for the story I had been assigned. I wrote articles of varying length on Jose Cardenal, Dave Kingman, Andre Thornton, and others. Once I went with the effusive, quirky, mushroom-haired Cardenal, who had told me about missing a game because a cricket kept him awake all night, to a Cuban restaurant where his previous season's glove hung from the ceiling. The Cubs' skinny little slugger looked at the leather orb dangling above him as he waited for his *ropa Viejo*, and I thought he might cry.

"I love my glove," he said, knowing that this one could not be taken back without breaking his countryman–restaurant owner's heart. "I love it more than . . . my teeth."

But most of my "research" time was spent simply wallowing in the quiet, unadorned splendor of summer afternoons at lazy, vine-laden Wrigley. The Cubs were going nowhere, and their record through the years of my writing youth—1973 to 1978—reflected this. They were never above .500, and in fact, if you look at the midseventies on a larger scale, you can see that this subdued half-decade—in which the Cubs finished fifth, sixth, tied for fifth, fourth, and fourth—was actually a fair snapshot of a six-decade malaise during which the Cubs climbed sporadic peaks but mostly lurched along like a burrowing pack of moles.

Indeed, from 1940 to 2000—sixty-one seasons—the cheerful little fellows rang up only thirteen winning seasons. From 1973, when I started to hang out professionally at the park, until 2005—thirty-three seasons—the Cubs finished over .500 only seven times. But why dwell on this?

As I said, here I am, a young man in full bloom in the flowering arena of life, and the arena is good.

Attendance was skimpy. Which was wonderful. I could go anywhere in Wrigley, find a seat, adjust for the sun, peer down on the bullpens, order an Old Style, crack a peanut, jot on a notepad, work at my craft. And because this was so delightful, I began to think of others, of my friends. I'm a friendly guy. Why shouldn't they have some of this heaven?

There were numerous times, I swear, when I would be sitting in my work room in the apartment I shared with three other people (one being my girlfriend, who would become my wife several years later), and I would have the window open, and the sound of the Wrigley Field organ would waft through the pores of the screen, and I would

CHICAGO CUBS
CHICAGO NATIONAL LEAGUE BALL CLUB · WRIGLEY FIELD
NEWS MEDIA WORKING PASS

Admit _____ Rick Telander _____

Sports Illustrated

From _____

FOR NECESSARY DUTIES AT WRIGLEY FIELD
April 26, 1977

Date _____

Good only for areas indicated below:

~~Field~~ ~~Roving~~ Press Box ~~Clubhouse~~ ~~Pink Poodle~~

SUBJECT TO THE CONDITIONS SET FORTH ON THE BACK HEREOF

This pass is issued subject to the condition, and by use of this pass each person admitted hereunder agrees that he will not transmit or aid in transmitting any report, description, account or reproduction of the baseball game or exhibition to which he is so admitted, except that he may transmit news reports of said baseball game or exhibition to the newspaper, press association, television station, or radio station represented by him for the sole purpose of publication or broadcasting of such news reports in the newspaper, or on the television or radio station represented by him or publication in newspapers subscribing for the service of the press association represented by him and for no other purpose.

drift out of the place, down the street, and into the emerald park much as the fairy-tale children followed the Pied Piper into the crack in the mountain. Except I was entering a crack in the world. I may not have been advancing my income or opportunities or reputation, but I was mainlining bliss. I needed company.

I looked at my press pass. Hmm. A light bulb clicked. *This can be duplicated.*

No, there weren't super-high-tech copying machines back then. But there were functional ones at printing stores, those pre-Kinko's places known to all students. Nor was this like copying a Pollock miniature. It was a piece of white paper, for God's sake, with some black words on it. I owned several passes by this time, with expired dates. But what I needed to do was make a master copy, one that

would be the template for my counterfeiting process. Easy enough.

At the top the cards said, "CHICAGO CUBS—Chicago National League Ball Club—Wrigley Field." Just beneath were the block letters: "NEWS MEDIA WORKING PASS." And below that: "Admit _____." And below that: "From _____," and below that: "For Necessary Duties at Wrigley Field," and below that: "Date _____." And at the bottom the card said, "Good only for areas indicated below: Field—Roving—Press Box—Clubhouse—Pink Poodle."

The Pink Poodle, I kid you not. Sounded like a transvestite bar. But it was the cramped little press box feeding area where you could snag a free pregame meal and mingle with announcers like Jack Brickhouse and Vince Lloyd and Lou Boudreau and crusty old baseball writers with half-smoked cigars in their pockets. In other words, it was the cherry on the sundae.

"Pink Poodle" was crossed out on two of my cards. Another card had only "Press Box" valid. But one card had everything wide open. It was a good card. My name was misspelled "Tellander," which reminded me nobody at the park really knew, or cared, who I was.

I bought some Wite-Out. In short order, I had a card that was blank after "Admit," "From," and "Date." I Xeroxed this card, front and back, then did it again, and again, and again. Lots of times. I only copied the original, so the phony cards weren't degraded by the printing process. Still, a number of copies looked a little dubious from the Wite-Out contrast, so I threw those away.

I took the best sheets home and carefully cut the copies from the whole. Following the edge sometimes was difficult, but I had been good with scissors as far back as first grade. I glued fronts to backs, pressed them under a stack of books, and let them dry. When they were crisp and unified, I surgically trimmed the edges to perfection. I then took one card at a time and ever so carefully lined it up on the printing cylinder of the massive electric typewriter we had in the apartment.

Now the business part. I typed in a friend's name after

"Admit," and then put in a time period after "Date" that wasn't too limited but also not overly presumptuous. Something like, "June 17–July 21." Not the whole season. That might raise a flag. I could always make a new card, anyway. Then I had to come up with something to put after "From," which more accurately meant "Representing." This was trickier.

I thought of "Baseball Insider." No, there might be a real one. "The Big Scoop." No, vague with overtones of smart-ass. "Suburban Times"? Better. I needed media titles that were reasonable but mundane, that would not alert the blue-coated, half-witted, nasty Andy Frain ushers who patrolled the park like aging hit men.

I came up with "Sports Journal" and "Midwestern Baseball Monthly," and for the gals in my life, "Women and Athletics" and things of that ilk. The cards looked darned good to me, with their only flaw being that they were double-thick and, of course, fraudulent. To detract from the thickness issue or snooping Frain-ites, who might try to peel the layers apart, I laminated the cards with clear plastic purchased from the drugstore. As far as the fraudulence went, well, what is life without risk?

I gave the cards out to various buddies—not bundles of them, mind you—and advised everyone of the importance of maintaining decorum and keeping a low profile at the park. Do not, for instance, go up to Bill Madlock in the batting cage and start asking about softball swings. Avoid suits. Remember, somebody could call you out and say, who the hell are you and where the hell did you get this? But enjoy yourselves. As I was doing. Revel in the fact that players like Steve Swisher and Ivan DeJesus and Pete LaCock were going to be out there working for you. Get your fill of outclassed managers like Whitey Lockman and Herman Franks. Check out the bricks. The plants.

Embrace the fact that the Cubs were inept and harmless and innocent enough to have a system of entry to Wrigley Field that I had easily and pleasantly breeched, perhaps—at least in my opinion—to the benefit of all. For there were empty seats abounding, and we had no money,

and by God, the Cubs of the seventies needed every supporter they could get.

I don't need to tell you that times have changed or that I have aged. Just as I don't have to tell you that the Cubs still haven't won anything. Or that they now have a gazillion fans around the globe.

But I'd like you to know that I and my friends had a good time back in the day, and the lovable Cubs were serving.

RICK TELANDER is a columnist for the *Chicago Sun-Times*.

Hooten, who'd been signed out of the University of Texas the previous June, took Holtzman's place in the rotation. A late-season call-up, Hooten had been nothing short of spectacular, striking out fifteen in one start against the Mets. In fact, Hooten had been spectacular from the moment he was signed, and had he been brought up earlier he might have made the difference in the season.

Opening day was delayed as the players' union continued to grow in strength and this time walked out over pension issues. After a few days, ownership capitulated and the season resumed, but not until every team in baseball lost a handful of games. The Cubs' season was cut from 162 to 155 games. Rain in Chicago pushed the opener back yet another day, but Hooten's pitching performance in the second game was the story of the early season. On a bitterly cold day, in front of only a few thousand fans, many of whom left early, Hooten, making only his fourth major league start, threw a no-hitter. He struck out seven, and despite giving up seven walks, he shut out the Phillies. The performance was made even more remarkable by the fact that it reportedly took Hooten fully 128 pitches to warm up before the game, in which he threw another 118, many of them his signature knuckle-curve, which drew favorable comparisons to Sandy Koufax's curveball. After the game, Wrigley gave Hooten a new contract with a $2,500 raise.

Leo Durocher, however, missed the performance. He was in the hospital with what his doctor called "persistent fatigue" stemming from a throat infection and complications from an abscessed tooth, and he would miss most of April. He didn't miss much, because the Cubs started slow, opening up 2–9. On May 2, Joe Pepitone, who'd become a crowd favorite with his "mod" haircut and flamboyant clothes, suddenly retired to spend more time tending to his tavern, called Joe Pepitone's Thing. The Cubs briefly got hot, and then on July 1 Pepitone thought better of his career change and rejoined the Cubs, his return coinciding with a teamwide slump.

Once again, there were calls for Durocher to be fired, many from inside the clubhouse. This time he would not survive.

On July 24, Wrigley fired Durocher, although the Cubs officially announced that the manager had "stepped aside." Wrigley still didn't like it. He felt forced into the move and said bitterly that it would "allow the players to find out themselves if they are pennant contenders" without having the excuse of blaming Durocher for their failures. A few weeks later, Durocher was hired to manage the Houston Astros.

Increasingly, Wrigley was finding modern ballplayers lacking. Guys like Ernie Banks and Santo had returned his loyalty with respect and deference, just the way he liked it. But in recent years, that attitude had disappeared. The recent player strike offended Wrigley's paternalistic sensibility, and he had been hurt by statements from players intimating that he was out of touch, more part of the problem the Cubs didn't win rather than part of the solution. Instead of gratitude, which Wrigley expected, he was suddenly on the receiving end of insolence. In a sense, when Wrigley fired Durocher he was cutting the players loose, telling them, "Fine. If you think you're so smart, go ahead and try to win on your own." For the rest of his life he would feel increasingly remote from the Cub players. He didn't quit caring, but he certainly quit caring as much, and the slow decay that soon followed can in many ways be traced to his growing indifference.

Wrigley selected player personnel director Whitey Lockman, who had played for Durocher and was considered his protégé, to be the new Cub manager, and for the rest of the year the Cubs played as if they'd been let out of school early. While it was too late for them to reach the postseason, under Lockman the Cubs played .600 baseball. They finished in second place behind Pittsburgh, but still eleven long games out of first.

Apart from the firing of Durocher, the big reason for the surge was Billy Williams. Since first joining the Cubs for good in 1961, Williams had always been something of an afterthought to many Cubs fans—everybody's second-favorite player after Ernie Banks and, in the minds of many, the Cubs' second-best player as well, first behind Banks and later behind Santo. Year after year, day in and day out, Williams just played and produced. In 1969 he broke Stan Musial's NL record for consecutive games, running the mark to 1,117 games—second only to Lou Gehrig at the time—before finally sitting out a game in 1970.

But Williams was anything but an afterthought to major league pitchers. Former Cub Jack Lamabe, who faced the team in 1967 while pitching for both the Mets and the Cardinals, considered Williams far more dangerous than either Banks or Santo. When asked which hitter he least liked to face among Banks, Santo, and Williams, Lamabe said, without hesitation, "Billy Williams."

As first Banks and then Santo began to fade, Williams, improbably, kept getting better. In 1970 he found his home run stroke, cracking a career-high 42 home runs. But he saved his best for 1972 when, at age thirty-four, he put together one of the best years in Cubs history, hitting .333, with 37 home runs and 122 RBIs, and edging out the Braves' Ralph Garr for the batting title by going 3-for-3 on the final day of the season. He also led the league in slugging percentage, beating out players like Willie Stargell and Johnny Bench. Don Kessinger once said of Williams that he "didn't hit for just one or two days, or one or two weeks. He hit all the time." This observation was deadly accurate, for rarely has a player been more consistent over the course of his career. Although Bench edged out Williams to earn MVP honors in 1972, *The Sporting News* named him Player of the Year, belatedly bringing some attention to a player whose career surpassed that of any other modern-day Chicago Cub. Both supremely modest and supremely confident, Williams didn't talk about himself, believing that his talent did that well enough on its own. Over time, he was proven correct.

In the first half of the 1973 season, the honeymoon that Whitey Lockman had enjoyed in 1972 continued. "Morale is a helluva lot better under Whitey," said Fergie Jenkins on opening day, a 3–2 win over the Expos. In fact, for the first few months everything was a helluva lot better. Rick Monday exploded out of the box with twenty home runs in the first half of the season, Glenn Beckert notched a twenty-six-game hitting streak, and Ron Santo was the best hitter in the league in April. The bullpen, the Cubs' one big area of concern entering the season, was terrific as Cubs relievers went nineteen innings at the start before allowing a run. The ball club even made some his-

---

The Cubs' new manager, Whitey Lockman, is all smiles as he takes the field at Philadelphia's Veterans Stadium on July 28, 1972, after being hired to succeed Leo Durocher.

MONEY IN THE BANKS

He was Mr. Cub, the face of the Chicago Cub franchise, the ball club's biggest star for more than a decade. What Willie Mays was to the Giants, Hank Aaron to the Braves, or Mickey Mantle to the Yankees, Ernie Banks was all that and even more to the Cubs.

But in the "bang for the buck" department, Ernie Banks was second to no one. He was easily the lowest-paid superstar of his generation.

No wonder Banks was Philip Wrigley's favorite player. The Cubs paid Mr. Cub like a pauper.

In 1947 Hank Greenberg reportedly became baseball's first $100,000 player, earning that salary with the Pittsburgh Pirates. By the late 1950s, however, only a few veteran stars, like Ted Williams, were earning a six-figure salary. By the early and mid-1960s, Willie Mays, Mickey Mantle, and Hank Aaron were all approaching the $100,000 mark, and each of these players eventually reached or eclipsed the $100,000 barrier. Mantle and Mays each reached the $100,000 mark in 1963, even as each player had reached his peak and begun a slow decline; Aaron first earned $100,000 in 1970 at age thirty-six. In 1972, when Hank Aaron's production began to slide, he still earned $200,000, the highest salary in baseball, and Willie Mays's salary peaked in 1971 at $160,000.

Then there was Ernie Banks. According to data accumulated by the National League and placed on deposit at the National Baseball Hall of Fame when the two leagues merged in 2002, in 1954, Banks's first full season with the Cubs, he earned $6,000. In 1955 he signed a contract for $10,000 and responded with 44 home runs and 117 RBIs while hitting .295; that earned him a raise to $17,500 for the 1956 season. Baseball business analyst Doug Pappas, using documents he found at the Hall of Fame, calculated that the average NL salary in 1956 was $14,778, making Banks's 1956 salary the first time he earned in excess of the league average. But after hitting 28 home runs in 1956 and 43 in 1957, by 1958 Banks's salary was barely keeping up with inflation: that year he earned $20,000, only $4,000 more than the league average.

He responded with an MVP season: 47 home runs and 129 RBIs earned him a $7,500 raise. A second MVP Award in 1959 brought Banks's salary to $45,000 in 1960. At this point, Banks was everything to the Cubs, and one would expect that over the final decade of his career the club would have recognized that fact and rewarded Banks accordingly, for even as his on-field production peaked and began a slow decline, his importance to the organization grew.

That never happened. After Banks hit 41 home runs in 1960, his salary reached $57,500. For the remainder of the decade, it fluctuated back and forth between this figure and $50,000. In real dollars, accounting for inflation, Banks actually earned less virtually every season for a decade. Then in 1969 Banks signed a two-year deal worth $60,000 annually, before being cut in 1972 to $45,000 for his final season, when he also received another $10,000 for "coaching and promotional duties." In 1973 Banks served as a coach, earning $35,000, plus an additional $10,000 for "public relations services" from 1974 through 1976, before his annual salary was raised to $45,000 in his final season as a coach in 1977.

While Banks's compensation as a coach was generous, it hardly made up for his below-market salary during his playing career, which paled in comparison to what baseball's other stars were paid.

Furthermore, Banks has said that during his career he allowed Philip Wrigley to withhold fully one-half of his salary—cumulatively, more than $450,000—and invest it in a trust on his behalf. In 2001 Banks told Salon.com that when he received the proceeds at age fifty-five in 1986, the trust was worth more than $4 million, an outcome he indicated was more than satisfactory. However, when one considers the annual inflation rate and cost-of-living increases from the beginning of Banks's career through 1986, his return is much less impressive.

What is more significant is not that Banks was underpaid by the Cubs, but the fact that every NL club had access to this information and was thus able to keep salary levels artificially low. Every penny the Cubs didn't pay Ernie Banks allowed other teams to argue that their players' salary demands were comparatively out of line, and thus salaries were depressed across the board.

Over the course of his career, Banks was money in the bank for the Cubs—and for every other team in the league.

tory on May 8 when Whitey Lockman was ejected from the game. That wasn't noteworthy in and of itself, but coach Pete Reiser was out with an injury, and pitching coach Larry Jansen was also absent, caring for his wife after surgery. That left only Ernie Banks available to manage the club. He led them to a 3–2 win over San Diego, becoming the first African American to act as a manager in the major leagues.

By June, Cubs fans were starting to drink the Cub Kool-Aid again, dreaming of red-white-and-blue bunting hanging over the green and golden ivy of October. They were the only team in the division over .500, in perfect position to stretch out their lead and put the division title away early. Yet just as everyone seemed to agree that "this was the year," it most assuredly became the exact opposite. Inexplicably, every single Cub hitter stopped hitting, and a team that was 46–31 on June 29, and in first place by eight full games, fell out of first place less than a month later. On Whitey Lockman's one-year anniversary at the helm, the Cubs' record over that time period was a not too shabby 90–71, but Lockman offered that the anniversary "really wasn't that big." The Cubs proved him correct, losing to the Giants in thirteen innings for their fifteenth loss in their last twenty contests.

It was panic time everywhere but in the Cub front office. Although each loss screamed at the Cubs to make a deal and do something to halt the slide, they didn't. In contrast, the Cardinals, for example, who started the season 5–20, made six deals in June and July to get back into the race. But instead of making some deals and trying to salvage a fine first half, Wrigley and Holland did nothing, as if still determined to punish the players for forcing them to let go of Durocher. It was almost criminal.

And the team hadn't even hit bottom yet. That came in August with an eleven-game losing streak that inspired one local newspaper headline writer to find his metaphor in Southeast Asia, referring to the slide as the "fall" of "Cubodia." Too late, the Cubs finally made a deal, adding creaky Texas outfielder Rico Carty. He couldn't hit anymore and fit right in with his slumping teammates.

In a season that saw the Mets steal the division title with an 82–79 record, the Cubs finished fifth, at 77–84, as Santo ended the season hitting .267, a far cry from his April performance, and Rick Monday returned to form in the second half, going seven weeks without hitting a home run to finish with only twenty-six for the season. Meanwhile, Ken Holtzman won twenty-one games for the Oakland Athletics, who would go on to capture their second consecutive world title.

Someone had to take the fall after the disastrous season, but the front office barely had a pulse. Manager Whitey Lockman stepped into the void and tried to pull a Durocher, taking command by force. But where Durocher did so by the power of his personality and transformed the Cubs he had into the team he wanted, Lockman took an entirely different approach. As the 1973 season was frittered away, he came to the conclusion that just about any player who preceded his tenure was a cancer that needed to be cut out and forcibly removed. After making virtually no deals during the season, as soon as it ended the Cubs traded almost every player who could draw a breath.

Fergie Jenkins was the first to go. In 1973 he had slumped to only fourteen wins, but more significantly, he had also showed an increasing tendency to question authority. At age twenty-nine, he was still a valuable commodity. On October 25, he was sent to the Texas Rangers for third base phenom Bill Madlock, who had hit .351 in September. In rapid succession, the Cubs then dealt Glenn Beckert, Randy Hundley, Ron Santo, Ken Rudolph, Jim Hickman, and Paul Popovich. None delivered as much as Jenkins, for Beckert, Hundley, and Santo were all past their prime. At the same time, Lockman cut loose nearly his entire coaching staff, even exiling Ernie Banks from his social secretary job as first base coach and to the minor leagues as a roving instructor.

It was no accident that the two veterans the Cubs retained, Don Kessinger and Billy Williams, were, as Richard Dozer described them in the *Tribune*, "neither capable of—nor inclined to—'rock the boat.' They are 'house men' of the purest order," and were thus allowed to stay on.

Lockman explained it all by saying, "We're going for speed," but the only velocity that had seemed to matter in the trades was how fast a player was traded after he spoke up. By opening day, one really did need a scorecard to tell the players: eleven new faces had found their way onto the roster, including nine rookies. In theory, there was nothing wrong with that, but in reality the Cubs were two ball clubs: remaining veterans like Williams and Kessinger were going one way, while rookies like Bill Madlock were headed the other. The vets couldn't perform anymore, and the rookies, with the exception of Madlock, who seemed born to hit, weren't ready.

On July 24, as the Cubs puttered about ten games below .500, Lockman decided to declare victory. He resigned, took back his old job as director of player personnel, and named third base coach Jim Marshall manager. Despite all evidence to the contrary, Lockman announced that he was leaving Marshall a team "still in contention" for the pennant. When asked if he had accomplished his goal as the Cubs' pilot, he announced, "Basically, yes."

In a way he had, for the Cub organization had begun to learn something very valuable during Lockman's tenure. As Richard Dozer put it succinctly, "You expect less, and you get it."

During the Durocher years, a new generation of fans had bonded with the team, embracing not only the Cubs but Wrigley Field, which, in contrast to the modern "cookie-cutter" stadiums recently built in Cincinnati, Pittsburgh, and Philadelphia, was a draw in and of itself as it began to be appreciated for what it was—one of the few remaining "classic" ballparks. Wrigley Field and the entire Wrigley Field "experience"—the enjoyment of which didn't entirely depend on whether the Cubs won or lost—was proving to be as much an attraction as the team itself. While attendance still fluctuated somewhat according to how well the Cubs did on the field, there was a growing base of about one million fans who showed up win or lose and no matter what price the Cubs charged for tickets. Their faithfulness more or less guaranteed that the Cubs remained profitable—or nearly so—and allayed any fear that attendance would ever again take a disastrous tumble.

Over the past few seasons, Cub fans had been abused in almost every way possible—their pennant hopes dashed, their favorite players dealt away, and their allegiance taken for granted by the front office—and they'd hardly noticed. After Lockman resigned, the *Tribune* polled a number of fans about the switch and marveled to discover that fully 60 percent "had no opinion one way or the other." In fact, wrote columnist John Husar, "a lot of people didn't even know Marshall was the third base coach. And a lot of them didn't care." One fan summed it up saying, "Leo Durocher came in and I thought things could change a little then. There's something wrong here—and I think it's higher than the field manager." But instead of following that statement by blasting management, the fan added wistfully, "This is the most beautiful ballpark in the world, they should fill it up."

For the rest of the 1974 season nothing much happened, except that Marshall fully abandoned the failed experiment of trying to turn Billy Williams into a first baseman, and Wrigley found himself on the defensive once again over racial issues when Jesse Jackson blasted him for being racist by not making Ernie Banks the manager. Wrigley countered by saying that Banks was "too nice" for the job, and to be fair, there was no indication that Banks wanted the position anyway. Not that the Cubs were immune to bigotry; indeed, in recent years a disturbing pattern had begun to emerge. The Cubs still preferred their ballplayers, particularly their African American players, quiet and compliant, like Williams and Banks. Those who weren't didn't last long unless they had overwhelming talent, like Jenkins, and even he had become expendable as soon as his performance dropped off. This attitude had cost the Cubs, as talented young African American players who didn't fit the mold, like Oscar Gamble and Billy North, were traded away only to thrive elsewhere and marginal African American players in the farm system were cut loose before their white peers. The problem wasn't unique to the Cubs, but the Cubs certainly weren't the most progressive organization either.

In 1975 the Cubs slid to sixth place under Marshall, winning only seventy-five games. In the offseason, the purge that Lockman had started continued. Billy Williams had earned $150,000 in 1974 but hit only .280 with sixteen home runs. Under a new provision negotiated by the players' union, Williams, with more than ten years of major league experience and five years with one club, had the right to block any trade, but when Oakland owner Charlie Finley offered Williams a two-year deal, Williams agreed, and on October 24 he was traded to the Athletics for infielder Manny Trillo and two relief pitchers, Darold Knowles and Bob Locker.

The 1975 season was almost comical as the Cubs

repeated the by now familiar pattern. They got off to a good start, opening the season 12–5, which left them feeling so flush that on May 2 they dealt Burt Hooten to the Dodgers for Geoff Zahn and a minor league pitcher. After his spectacular start in 1971 and his 1972 no-hitter, Hooten had been a disappointment, and after playing winter ball for Tommy Lasorda in Venezuela, he expressed interest in being traded to the Dodgers. The Cubs finally acceded to his wish. "I could say some things about the Cub organization," he said on his way out the door, "but what's the sense? The Cubs organization is the Cubs organization." That it was.

The Cubs held on to first place as late as June 3, when they had a 27–20 record, before folding. Two weeks later, they had slumped to fourth place at 30–29 despite the fact that third baseman Bill Madlock was in the midst of an incredible hot streak, going fourteen for eighteen from June 13 through June 16. With his average a gaudy .360, Madlock pronounced, "I haven't been in a streak like this since Little League." He wasn't the only Cub enjoying a good season, as Jose Cardenal, Jerry Morales, Manny Trillo, and Andre Thornton all exceeded expectations, but the pitching collapsed—the team ERA of 4.49 was the worst in all of baseball. Zahn went 2–7 before hurting his shoulder, while Hooten, freed from Chicago, won eighteen games for L.A. The Cubs finished last again, tied with the Expos.

On the final day of September, Phil Wrigley drove the last nail home that relegated the Durocher-era Cubs to the distant past, making them about as relevant as Cap Anson. John Holland still held the title of executive vice president and, officially, carried out the duties of a general manager (though Wrigley continued to eschew that formal title), but Whitey Lockman had taken over many of Holland's duties. On September 30, Wrigley officially relieved Holland, but instead of putting Lockman in the position or giving the job to Holland's assistant, Blake Cullen, who many thought was Holland's heir apparent, Wrigley pulled a surprise. He reinstituted the position of general manager and gave the job to longtime employee E. J. "Salty" Saltwell.

Some veteran Cub observers didn't even know who Saltwell was, and with good reason, for he had no background in player development and was almost invisible at the ballpark. As the "vice president in charge of park operations," Saltwell primarily oversaw concessions.

Third baseman Bill Madlock came to Chicago along with utility man Vic Harris in the 1974 trade that sent superstar Ferguson Jenkins to the Texas Rangers. In three seasons with Chicago, Madlock became the only Cub to ever win back-to-back batting titles (1975 and 1976) and also was the first Cub named an All-Star Game MVP when he shared MVP honors in the 1975 game.

It was a classic Cub move. After all, this was a team that in the past had hired sportswriters William Veeck and John Gallagher to serve as GM before finally hiring individuals at least partially qualified in Wid Matthews and John Holland. But qualified hadn't worked, so now it was back to "square none"—time to hire someone with absolutely no experience in the job. If that wasn't bad enough, the

Besides playing a solid center field for the Cubs from 1972 to 1976, Rick Monday garnered a share of baseball immortality at Dodger Stadium in April 1976 when he raced from his position to snatch an American flag that was about to be set ablaze by two fans who had run on the field. Monday is shown posing with the flag, which hangs in his living room to this day.

move came just as baseball was entering the free agent era, a time when the general manager's duties would become exponentially more complicated and the financial stakes infinitely higher.

Like Holland before him, Saltwell had served as a minor league GM, following Holland into the position in Des Moines and Los Angeles, but at the minor league level the job was primarily administrative and had precious little to do anymore with signing and acquiring players. Saltwell had joined the big league club as assistant business manager in 1958, proved loyal to Wrigley, and was rewarded with a vice presidency in 1972.

The move was openly mocked. The *Tribune* asked, "What is Phil Wrigley trying to tell us by naming a hot dog vendor as GM?" Columnist Robert Markus offered that, "I don't know what Phil Wrigley is likely to do in a given situation. Except that whatever it is is probably wrong." Wrigley tried to defend the move by claiming that Saltwell had the capacity to "get rough," presumably in contract negotiations, but even Saltwell seemed a bit mystified by his selection, admitting that he had hardly ever watched a game from start to finish because his duties kept him in the office during game time. He did, however, claim that "I see quite a bit of them on TV." Well, if that was all the job required, anybody with a set of rabbit ears that pulled in television station WGN was qualified to run the club. Of course, that was precisely how Wrigley monitored his team.

A month later, Saltwell traded Don Kessinger to the Cardinals for pitcher Mike Garman and a minor league infielder. Not a single player remained who had played for the Cubs in 1969.

That didn't last for long, as Randy Hundley was brought back at the end of spring training for a brief return engagement, but over the next two years injuries held him to a total of only twenty-two at-bats. At any rate, the Cubs of 1976 reminded no one of 1969. This time they didn't mess around: the team swooned at the start and stayed in a swoon all season long.

Although the Cubs could hit a little, the pitching staff was aptly described by one sportswriter as one that "only a foe can love." Both traits were on display on April 17 at Wrigley Field. Over the first four innings, the Cubs took advantage of a twenty-mile-per-hour tail wind to jump out to a 13–2 lead against the Phillies. Then Phillies slugger Mike Schmidt got going. After hitting a single in the fourth, the next four times he stepped to the plate Schmidt drove the ball over the wall. The Cubs lost, 18–16, in ten innings. It was no anomaly. On two other occasions that week Cub pitchers gave up fourteen runs.

Cub outfielder Rick Monday provided the highlight of the season, if not the decade, for the Cubs on April 25 during a game in Los Angeles. In the fourth inning of—what else—a 5–4 loss, a man and his adolescent son ran onto the field, spread an American flag on the ground, and started dousing it with fluid. Like some kind of superhero, Monday ran over and grabbed the flag before the man could light it on fire, and he carried it to safety in the bullpen as security personnel arrested the man and his son. Dodger fans spontaneously started singing "God Bless America," and Monday was lauded for his quick thinking. The Dodgers eventually presented him with the flag, which Monday has displayed in his home ever since.

Unfortunately, the Cubs needed more than a super-hero. All they had was GM Salty Saltwell. In mid-May, with the pitching staff in tatters, he panicked. Despite breaking his wrist, first baseman Andre Thornton had led the Cubs with eighteen home runs in 1975 and showed signs that he was about to become an All-Star. In the spring of 1976, however, he had complained about the Cubs' training facilities and briefly feuded with Jose Cardenal. Those two incidents were enough for the Cubs to label the African American player a troublemaker.

On May 17, Saltwell traded him to the Expos for a .500 pitcher, Steve Renko, and outfielder Larry Biittner, whom the Cubs didn't need. The deal was widely criticized, and it should have been. Thornton later became a star with Cleveland, while Renko and Biittner helped the Cubs finish fourth, twenty-six games behind the champion Phillies.

The offseason ushered in an entirely new era in baseball, one that would soon have an enormous impact on the Cubs: free agency. In 1975 pitchers Andy Messersmith and Dave McNally successfully challenged a portion of the MLB reserve clause, which bound a player to a team for life. Before the 1976 season, both had been declared "free agents," available to the highest bidder. When the players' union and major league baseball signed a new basic agree-ment in July 1976, that right was extended to dozens of other players. After six years of major league experience, players were freed from the reserve clause and made available to other clubs in a "reentry draft" that limited the number of teams that could pursue an individual player. In spite of that restriction, the era of free agency had begun. Two dozen players eventually qualified for this initial draft, including stars like slugger Reggie Jackson and relief ace Rollie Fingers.

Not since the color line was broken in 1947 had so many players suddenly become available. It was a time of tremendous opportunity. In this new age, the richest baseball teams in the largest markets presumably enjoyed an advantage, for they could simply outspend the competition. Rebuilding no longer would take years—in theory, by acquiring the right free agents, a team could rebuild overnight. Similarly, already good teams could become even better.

On September 29, 1975, longtime Cub executive E. J. "Salty" Saltwell was inexplicably promoted from the position of vice president of ball-park operations to general manager. He lasted only one year in the position before returning to his old job.

A few teams, most notably the New York Yankees, realized this immediately. Most, including the Cubs, did not. Wrigley was a wealthy man, and the Cubs were financially healthy. At the time, they could have spent as much money as any other club. They chose not to, and with this decision, they chose mediocrity. Just as they missed out on the first generation of black stars after Jackie Robinson broke the color line, so too would the Cubs miss out on the first few generations of free agents. Over most of the next three decades, few other teams—and none that possessed their financial resources—would be as inactive and cautious as the Cubs. Free agency could have been the Cubs' salvation. Instead, and in the meantime, it became an unnecessary impediment to their success.

While teams like the crosstown White Sox kept their options open in the initial reentry draft, asserting their right to negotiate with eighteen of the twenty-four available players, the Cubs had a much more tepid response, drafting only four players: outfielder Don Baylor, pitchers Bill Campbell and Wayne Garland, and catcher–first baseman Gene Tenace. Saltwell claimed he'd have drafted more, but some players' agents indicated that their clients had no interest in the Cubs. Word was getting around that the Cubs were a mess, and when given the option, few players wanted to go there. To the Cubs the draft was meaningless. They had no genuine interest in paying any of the free agents and made no real effort to sign anyone. They were in transition anyway.

In what was becoming a nearly annual occurrence, Wrigley shook things up. Saltwell returned to ordering hot dogs, and manager Jim Marshall was fired. Wrigley looked to the past again, tapping Bob Kennedy, who had once served as a member of the failed "College of Coaches," to assume GM duties under the title of "director of baseball operations," and Kennedy then hired veteran manager Herman Franks, who hadn't worn a uniform since 1970 or managed a team since 1968. The two men fit the Cubs perfectly—shades of gray on shades of gray. Kennedy promised to shake things up and build from within, admitting that a team like the Dodgers had "about a 10 to 1 ratio of scouts over the Cubs," but he defended the Cub approach, saying that he didn't see the point of just hiring scouts for the sake of numbers. He also didn't think much of base-

ball's new era, saying, "I don't believe in spending millions on free agents."

He should have put a period at the end of the word *spending*, because the Cubs didn't want to spend, period. At the end of the 1977 season, two Cubs, Rick Monday and Bill Madlock, who won the batting title on the final day of the season by going 4-for-4 to edge out Ken Griffey, would soon be eligible for free agency.

Both men approached the Cubs from a position of strength. Monday was coming off his finest season, and Madlock had just won his second consecutive batting title. Each player wanted a multi-year contract at something that would approach what they could get on the open market.

Monday wanted around $200,000 a year, double what he earned in 1976 and roughly in line with the rapid escalation of contracts taking place throughout baseball. The Cubs said no, and on January 12, 1977, they traded Monday to the Dodgers for Bill Buckner and shortstop Ivan DeJesus. "Rick was simply asking for more money than we were willing to pay," said Kennedy. "It was simply a matter of dollars and cents."

Bill Madlock wanted even more, asking for a five-year deal worth $1.5 million. The Cubs said no to him as well. "We can't stay in business paying that kind of money," said Kennedy. Wrigley, who earlier had said that "no ballplayer is worth one million dollars," reportedly gave the order to get rid of Madlock. On February 11, 1977, Kennedy traded him to the Giants for three players, most notably outfielder Bobby Murcer. Murcer was still a good player, but five years older than Madlock.

Madlock ripped the Cubs afterwards for not even trying to negotiate. "They're just trying to make me the scapegoat," he said, disputing the $1.5 million figure. "If they had negotiated, the Cubs could have had me for less." Then Madlock noted that reports from San Francisco indicated that Murcer wanted a similar contract. "They must want to pay Murcer, and not me," he added.

Madlock was probably right—Murcer eventually signed for $320,000 a year, more than what Madlock had wanted. Like Jenkins, Thornton, North, and Gamble, Madlock wasn't Billy Williams or Ernie Banks. A player from another generation, he was unafraid to speak his mind or to go out to the mound after a pitcher. That didn't jibe with the way the Cubs wanted black players to act. White players were held to a different standard. Bill Buckner, for example, was allowed to moan constantly, and the Cubs later overlooked pitcher Dickie Noles's alcoholism past the point where it affected his performance. Black players weren't given the same slack. Batting title or not, Madlock just didn't fit.

On opening day, the Cubs showed little sign of improvement, losing to the Mets and Tom Seaver, 5–3. They were sitting at .500 with a record of 2–2 when one era of Cub history ended and another began. On April 12, 1977, Phil Wrigley died.

His health had been deteriorating for years, and in the last decade he had rarely made an appearance at Wrigley Field or even in Chicago, preferring to remain in family homes in Arizona or Lake Geneva, Wisconsin, as his son William Jr. ran the gum company. In fact, Wrigley hadn't even been seen in the Wrigley offices for more than six months. He was in Lake Geneva, reportedly watching the Cubs on television, when he became ill. He was rushed to a hospital, where he died of a gastrointestinal hemorrhage.

Had it not been for the Cubs, Philip Wrigley would have been just another Chicago-based business tycoon, a mostly anonymous man little remembered outside of the city, memorable mostly because of the brand name he bore, like Philip Danforth Armour III, scion of the meatpacking firm. The Wrigley Company was well known but, in Chicago terms, not particularly significant, worthy of only a small entry in the massive *Encyclopedia of Chicago*. As a businessman, Wrigley had been a reasonably capable steward of the company his father started, and a progressive, caring, and occasionally innovative employer. The Wrigley Company had been profitable, and P.K. Wrigley had expanded into the international markets, but at the same time the company had been oddly static and perhaps had not grown as much as it should have; Wrigley had seemed content with the status quo and a healthy but steady market share.

He had operated the Cubs in much the same fashion: after inheriting a relatively successful team in one of baseball's largest markets, with a pleasant and attractive ballpark, he had held on to that position. For vast portions of his reign, Wrigley seemed content with fulfilling his long-term goal of preserving the Cubs as a memorial to his

Andre Thornton led the Cubs in home runs in 1975 with eighteen, despite breaking his wrist. In May 1976 the budding star was traded by Cub general manager Salty Saltwell to the Expos for .500 pitcher Steve Renko and reserve outfielder Larry Biittner.

father. Everything else was secondary to simple preservation. Attempts to change or improve, while well intentioned, were poorly thought out and executed. As a result, to their fans the Cubs were not unlike a piece of chewing gum that had lost its flavor but, through habit, remained a fixture in the mouth—a simple way to pass the time.

On the plus side, Wrigley had maintained Wrigley Field, a not insignificant accomplishment, for by the 1960s

estate. Although many had speculated over the years that Wrigley was worth hundreds of millions of dollars, after his death the figure turned out to be much smaller. His estate was eventually valued at only $81 million, which included the Cubs, Wrigley Field, and 19 percent of all stock in the Wrigley Company.

Since his father's death in 1932, P.K. Wrigley, who had eventually received 60 percent of his father's $40 million estate, or $24 million, had barely managed to triple the size of his personal fortune over a forty-five-year time period during which the U.S. and world economies expanded exponentially. In fact, he had barely kept pace with inflation. While Philip Wrigley almost certainly had distributed portions of his estate to his family and charities before 1977, it would soon become clear that he was no financial genius. For the moment, nothing changed at Wrigley Field. Well, almost nothing. As if freed, the Cubs started winning.

The reasons were obvious. Husky starting pitcher Rick Reuschel, who looked more like a truck driver on a coffee break than a major league pitcher, parlayed his mastery of the sinkerball into a 15–3 start. And when that wasn't enough, relief pitcher Bruce Sutter was virtually unhittable. He threw a new pitch, a "split-finger" fastball that looked for all the world like a fastball until just before it reached home plate, at which point the ball dropped to the ground and left the hitter swinging at air.

Sutter was, in a sense, an accidental Hall of Famer. Drafted by the Washington Senators in 1970 out of high school in Lancaster County, Pennsylvania, Sutter never signed. He tried getting into college but lacked both the temperament and the grades. He started pitching for a local team known as "Hippies Raiders," and a year later Cub scout Ralph DiLullo signed him as a free agent for only $500.

Rarely did the Cubs ever spend their money better. Sutter injured his arm before the 1973 season, damaging a nerve while trying to learn to throw the slider. Afraid he'd be released if the club found out he had a bad arm, Sutter paid for his own surgery. A year later, Fred Martin, who served as pitching coach for the entire Cub farm system, noticed the scar on Sutter's elbow and his lack of a major league–quality pitch. In a few brief moments, he taught Sutter, who had enormously long fingers, to grip the ball like a forkball but throw it like a fastball—the split-finger fastball, a pitch Martin himself had developed while pitching for the minor league Houston Buffalos in 1941.

"The pitch just came to me," Sutter said later, admitting that he picked it up easily and immediately. From the very start he was able to make the pitch break. It took the better part of one season to learn to control the pitch, but after that he rose rapidly through the Cubs system; when he reached the major leagues in 1976, he was throwing the pitch almost exclusively.

In 1977 Herman Franks used him early and often as, apart from Reuschel, Cubs starting pitching struggled. Franks often went to the bullpen early, first to young left-hander Willie Hernandez, and then to Sutter, often for two or three innings, using him as a true "fireman" to squelch rallies.

Keyed by Reuschel and Sutter, the Cubs surged into first place in May and held on for more than two months. Appreciative Cub fans, as if aware that they had to celebrate whenever they could, began giving the Cubs a standing ovation before the games even started. From May 1 through June 28, the Cubs were a stellar 40–13, good enough for an eight-and-a-half-game lead in the NL East.

Then they all sat back down rather quickly. The Cubs were struggling to score runs and desperately needed a hitter to help take the pressure off the pitching staff. The time was ripe for the Cubs to make a deal or two and secure their lead, but that wasn't the way the front office worked. The only bat they added was that of outfielder Bobby Darwin. After lasting all of twelve at-bats, he would never appear in the major leagues again.

Wrigley's death was partly to blame, for it blurred the chain of command. Wrigley had left the bulk of his assets split between his wife, Helen, and son, William Jr., with smaller portions designated for fifteen other beneficiaries. But Helen suffered a heart attack shortly after her husband died and passed away on June 27. Because her portion of the estate now had to go through probate, an already complicated estate became even more problematic. In the meantime, it was business as usual—which all but ensured failure.

Sutter kept the Cubs afloat for a while, but in mid-July overuse resulted in a sore shoulder. It failed to respond to rest, and on August 3 Sutter finally went on the disabled list. At the same time, Rick Reuschel hurt his back. Once again, the situation screamed out for a trade. Reds manager Sparky Anderson called the Cubs "the most fundamentally sound team in the league," but added, "There's no way the Cubs can win it unless they get Reuschel and Sutter back."

He was right. Two days after Sutter went on the DL, the Cubs fell out of first place. The farm system was barren and couldn't deliver what the Cubs needed; they added only pitcher Dave Giusti, who, like Darwin, was a player in the final days of his major league career. In September, Sutter came back and was magnificent—striking out the Expos' Ellis Valentine, Gary Carter, and Larry Parrish on nine pitches in one appearance—but by then it was too late. The Cubs were a horrific 16–35 over the final six weeks and played out the season in a nosedive, losing eight of nine to finish at .500. The annual Cub swoon was becoming more than a cliché. It was as predictable as a summer thunderstorm.

It was a bad time for a baseball team to be in transition, for free agency was affecting everything, and the Cubs struggled to come up with a coherent response. Starting pitcher Bill Bonham was scheduled to become a free agent in the offseason. Although Bonham had never been a big winner, he was only twenty-eight years old and could be counted on to eat up more than two hundred innings a year. The Cubs needed every pitcher they could get, but balked at giving Bonham a multi-year deal. The pitcher indicated that he planned to test free agency, so the Cubs decided to trade him. Just two days before he became a free agent, the Cubs worked out a deal with Cincinnati. Bonham signed a long-term deal, and in exchange the Cubs received veteran journeyman Woodie Fryman, who had walked out on the Reds in midseason after being removed from the rotation, and minor league pitcher Bill Caudill. Caudill was a real prospect, but he wasn't ready yet. Meanwhile, the deal left a hole in the rotation.

At the same time, a month after they dumped Bonham, the Cubs suddenly shifted gears and took their first tentative steps in the free agent market, making a play for slugger Dave Kingman. Although they'd earlier indicated that they wanted nothing to do with free agency, that was clearly an impossible position. Besides, the Cubs considered Kingman a special case.

Bobby Murcer hit twenty-seven home runs for the Cubs in 1977, but no one else had knocked more than twelve, a pathetic performance in one of the most hitter-friendly parks in all baseball. Meanwhile, in seven big league seasons, slugger Dave Kingman had crushed 176 home runs, twenty of them in Wrigley Field, including ten over the past two seasons. Weak Cub pitching was part of the reason for that, but the Chicago front office salivated at the thought of having Kingman in the lineup at Wrigley Field for eighty-one games. Everybody could do the math and figured that Kingman was good for at least forty home runs, if not fifty or more.

Of course, Kingman also carried a lot of baggage. He was, at best, an indifferent fielder, and each time he came to bat it was all or nothing as he swung for the fences. He averaged a strikeout a game, didn't walk much, didn't run well, and didn't hit for a high average. Teams liked Kingman from afar, dazzled by his power, but once they had him they tended to see what he couldn't do, while his surly demeanor was sometimes a problem in the clubhouse. In 1977 he had played for four different teams—the Mets, Padres, Angels, and Yankees—and twice was dumped on waivers. Now he wanted some stability.

He wanted to play for the Cubs, which the organization found intriguing. Although Kingman had been born in Oregon, he had grown up in Mt. Prospect, a town just northwest of Chicago whose motto was, "Where friendliness is a way of life." The Cubs hoped not only that Kingman would be comfortable in the "friendly confines" of Wrigley Field, but that once he was back home he himself would prove to be friendly as well. A hometown star could have a big impact at the box office, and in September 1977 the Cubs had played before several home crowds of fewer than five thousand fans.

Kingman wanted a five-year deal, and the Yankees had made him an acceptable offer worth $1.25 million. The Cubs could match that, but they balked at guaranteeing all five years of the contract—they still weren't at all sure about this whole business of free agency. Fortunately for the Cubs—at least at the time—Kingman was so eager to come to Chicago that he agreed to accept a deal with only a two-year guarantee, saying, "I can't put into words the feeling I get when hitting at Wrigley Field. Psychologically, I get all charged up."

IT WAS WRIGLEY, NOT SOME GOAT, WHO CURSED CUBS

BY MIKE ROYKO

It's about time that we stopped blaming the failings of the Cubs on a poor, dumb creature that is a billy goat.

This has been going on for years, and it has reached the point where some people actually believe it.

Now a beer company, the Cubs, and Sam Sianis, who owns Billy Goat's Tavern and the accused goat, have banded together to lift the alleged curse that was supposedly placed on the Cubs in 1945—the last time they were in the World Series.

As the story goes, the late Bill Sianis, founder of the old tavern, tried to bring his pet goat into Wrigley Field and was turned away because the goat smelled.

That's when the curse was placed on the Cubs, and they haven't been in a World Series since.

It's an entertaining story, but is only partly true.

Yes, blame for many of the Cubs' failings since 1945 can be placed on a dumb creature. Not a poor, dumb creature but a rich one.

I'm talking about P.K. Wrigley, head of the chewing gum company and the owner of the Cubs until he died in 1977.

In many ways, Wrigley was a nice man—shy, modest, and very good at selling chewing gum. He was a lucky man, inheriting the thriving gum company and a fine baseball team from his more aggressive father.

In baseball, what P.K. Wrigley was best known for was preserving day baseball long after all other franchises were playing most of their games at night.

A myth grew that Wrigley believed baseball was meant to be played in sunshine and, as a matter of principle, kept lights out of his park.

The truth was that he planned on lights very early. But when World War II began, materials needed for lights were needed in the war effort. So he shelved plans for the lights, and when the war ended, he didn't bother.

The only other baseball feat he was known for was running the worst franchise in baseball.

And a big part of that can be blamed on racism. If not Wrigley's, then that of the stiffs he hired to run his baseball operation.

After World War II ended, the best players available were being discharged from the military and returning to the teams they had starred for a few years earlier.

But Wrigley had a unique manpower problem. His best players had remained home during the war because they were 4-F for one physical defect or another or too old to have served.

So as other teams quickly got better, all the Cubs' 4-F team did was get older and more enfeebled.

Because he had a second-rate minor league system, there were few good young prospects moving up.

1972

[310]

But all of that could have been overcome in 1947—two years after the Cubs' last World Series and the end of the war.

That was when Branch Rickey of the Brooklyn Dodgers knocked down the racial wall in baseball by signing ex-Army officer Jackie Robinson.

Although he went on to a fabulous career, Robinson was not nearly the best available black ballplayer at the time. Rickey chose him because Robinson had the education and character to endure the racial abuse heaped on him by fans, press, some of his own teammates, and opposing players.

The old Negro League was loaded with outstanding players. When they played offseason exhibition games against white all-star teams, the blacks won as often as they lost.

By 1947, the year Robinson broke in, the Cubs were already pathetic doormats.

Had Wrigley followed Rickey's lead, he could instantly have had a competitive team. And depending on how many black players he could have tolerated, maybe a great team.

He didn't. His players had made their feelings clear, voting not to play if the other teams boycotted Robinson. And his team's front office wouldn't listen to those who urged them to sign black players.

It wasn't a momentary hesitation. It was not until September 1953—nearly seven full seasons after Robinson arrived—that Wrigley signed two black players.

By then, the Dodgers, with Robinson, Roy Campanella, Junior Gilliam, Don Newcombe, and Joe Black, and the New York Giants, with the amazing Willie Mays and clutch-hitting Monte Irvin, had become dominant teams.

Who did Wrigley ignore? Besides some of the names above, there was Larry Doby, who became an American League home run leader; slugger Luke Easter; Minnie Minoso; the great Satchel Paige; and Hank Aaron, who broke Babe Ruth's lifetime home run record. During the years Wrigley snubbed black players, the black players who were in their late twenties or early thirties when Robinson broke in had aged past their primes.

By the time Cubs management got over their racial fears, the black league was getting ready to fold. Fewer players were available, and better teams competed for them. Other sports, college and pro, began going after black athletes.

So what might have been wasn't. It had nothing to do with a goat's curse. Not unless the goat wore a gabardine suit and sat behind a desk in an executive suite.

Yes, I know, so don't grab your phone: the corporation that owns this paper has owned the Cubs since 1981. So why, you ask, haven't they made it to the World Series?

Because they haven't been good enough. But I do know that if they thought a three-legged green creature from another planet could hit home runs or throw a ninety-five-mile-per-hour fastball, they'd sign it. And we'd cheer.

MIKE ROYKO was a Pulitzer Prize–winning columnist for *Chicago's Daily News*, the *Chicago Sun-Times*, and the *Chicago Tribune*. The author of many books, he died in 1997.

Expectations for the six-foot-six slugger were enormous. The *Tribune*'s Rick Talley speculated that "by Aug. 1 (or thereabouts) Chicago newspapers will be publishing large block numbers showing how many home runs Dave Kingman needs to break the records of Babe Ruth and Roger Maris." But the Cubs needed more than home runs.

They failed to replace pitcher Bonham and entered the 1978 season with question marks almost everywhere. Then Kingman got off to a slow start, and by May 1 the 1978 season was looking like a disaster. Bob Kennedy had become so frustrated with Kingman, who had only three home runs by mid-May, that he traveled to California and supervised a session in the batting cage, trying to get Kingman to relax and stop trying to swing so hard.

Then, as if a switch had been flicked, Kingman gave them everything they expected, at least for a while. In his next game, Kingman singled and hit a home run off Dodger pitcher Tommy John.

For the next few days, the player they called "Kong" (after King Kong) acted as if he'd escaped from the theater. He was so good it was scary. On May 14, Kingman was a one-man wrecking crew, celebrating Mother's Day by breaking up a shutout in the sixth inning with a home run; avoiding a double play in the seventh by beating out a ground ball and keeping a rally going; cracking a game-tying home run in the top of the ninth; then making a game-saving catch in the bottom of the inning before ending things with a towering three-run home run in the fifteenth inning to lead the Cubs to a 10–7 win.

Kingman was ebullient after the game, even asking beat writer Richard Dozer to include a greeting to Kingman's mother in his game story. In only two days, Kingman had cracked four home runs in eight at-bats with ten RBIs.

The outburst keyed a Cub surge, and on May 24 they took over first place with their eighth victory in a row. They entered June still in first place, marking the seventh time in the past eleven seasons that they had held the top spot at the start of summer—all without winning anything yet.

This time the front office took notice. The Cubs made five deals in June, adding outfielders Jerry White and Mike Vail, along with pitcher Lynn McGlothlen and former Cub Ken Holtzman. For once, it appeared as if the Cubs would be proactive and make a move *before* they collapsed instead of afterwards.

Holtzman seemed to be the key. Since leaving Chicago, he had blossomed with the Oakland A's, winning four games in the World Series before being traded, first to Baltimore and then to the Yankees. But Holtzman had foundered in New York, feuding with manager Billy Martin. The Cubs announced that he would start out in the bullpen to build arm strength before joining the rotation.

By then, however, the season was over. Kingman's two-day outburst in May would prove temporary, accounting for nearly 15 percent of his offensive output for the season. By mid-June, Franks was platooning him in the outfield, and Kingman was back to swinging for the fences and usually missing. At the end of June, the Cubs came into Philadelphia leading the division by two games, only to lose four in a row and drop out of first place. Kingman finished with only twenty-eight home runs and seventy-nine RBIs, which was still plenty to lead the Cubs in both categories, but Holtzman was awful and didn't win a game. The Cubs finished third, 79–83, eleven games behind the first-place Phillies.

For Cubs fans, it was becoming difficult to tell one season from the next, and it would be no different in 1979. The club spent most of the offseason trying to work a trade with the Phillies, but when the deal was finally made, it was difficult to tell exactly why. Cub second baseman Manny Trillo had blossomed into one of the better middle infielders in baseball, and he and Ivan DeJesus gave the Cubs a better-than-average double-play combination, which was critically important on a staff anchored by Reuschel and manned by several other ground-ball pitchers.

But for some reason, Cub GM Bob Kennedy thought Trillo was expendable, and for some reason he was also focused on making a trade exclusively with the first-place Phillies. Initially, the Phillies were interested in Bobby Murcer, but their interest cooled after they acquired Pete Rose as a free agent. Kennedy wanted a catcher and had his eye on the Phillies' third-string catcher, Barry Foote. Foote was better than that, but not much. After more than three months of negotiations, the two clubs finally made the trade on February 23, the Cubs sending Trillo, catcher Doug Rader, and outfielder Greg Gross to Philadelphia for Foote, outfielder Jerry Martin, Ted Sizemore, and two minor league pitchers.

At best, the deal was a wash, but Kennedy, reacting as

if he'd won the pennant, claimed that the Cubs had received three regulars in exchange for one. "It was a deal we had to make," he said, adding, "If it blows up in our faces, then I'm dumb." In fact, what went unsaid was the fact that the deal saved the Cubs some money: Trillo was approaching free agency, and when the Phillies had signaled their willingness to part with fleet outfielder Bake McBride as part of the deal, the Cubs balked at his salary.

The result was the same old Cubs. One memorable game in May against the Phillies epitomized the season. As Philadelphia shortstop Larry Bowa said later, "We all knew it was going to be one of those days . . . the Cubs had a field goal kicker warming up on the sidelines for three innings." All the Cubs did was mount the greatest comeback in baseball history and still lose the game.

The wind was blowing out at Wrigley Field that day, and both clubs took advantage. As David Israel wrote in the *Tribune*, "The Phillies had seven runs after the first inning and knew it was not enough. They had 15 runs after three innings and they knew it was not enough. They had 21 runs after five innings, and they knew it was not enough." That was because the two clubs combined for eleven home runs, including three by Dave Kingman. At various times during the game, the Phillies led 16–6 and 21–9, but the Cubs scored seven times in the fifth inning, three more in the sixth, and with three more in the eighth inning they tied the game at 22. Unfortunately, they chose that precise time to stop scoring, and the Phillies won in the tenth inning, after Mike Schmidt homered off Bruce Sutter, by the final score of 23–22.

The Cubs simply didn't have enough. For the first two months of the season, Kingman appeared to have Roger Maris's number, hitting twenty-five home runs in only sixty-four games, but he eventually cooled. This time the Cubs never bothered with actually reaching first place before falling back, but they did hang with the division-leading Expos into September before losing twenty-three of their last thirty-two games to tumble all the way to fifth place. Kingman finished with forty-eight home runs, and Barry Foote and Jerry Martin partially vindicated Kennedy by cracking sixteen and nineteen home runs, but the clubhouse was a mess. As the Cubs fell apart in September, Herman Franks completely lost control.

The Cubs were in open insurrection. In midseason Ted

Slugger Dave Kingman played only three seasons for the Cubs but evoked memories of Hank Sauer when he socked a league-leading total of forty-eight home runs in 1979.

Sizemore had blasted the manager for limiting the Cubs to two bottles of wine per table at a team dinner in Montreal. A few days later, he was traded away and the team came apart at the seams.

On fan appreciation day, AP reporter Joe Mooshil broke the story that Herman Franks had told him that he planned to quit and that "some of these players are crazy,"

The colorful Herman Franks had already made a fortune in business before being hired as Cubs manager prior to the 1977 season. In three years as skipper, he finished just barely below .500, with a won-lost record of 238–241.

calling Bill Buckner, Ted Sizemore, Barry Foote, and Mike Vail "whiners." Franks then showed the reporter a $24,000 check he had written to join a Salt Lake City country club, saying, "Next year, I'll be at the country club every day." Franks could afford it. He had made a fortune in construction in California and in 1965 had nearly purchased the New York Yankees.

When the story broke, the floodgates opened as the players let Franks know they didn't think much of him either. One player said anonymously, "If we're crazy, what does that make him? He's sixty-five, worth millions of bucks, but he wants to waste the last three years being a lousy manager of a lousy baseball team?" Later that day the Cubs fell to the Pirates, 6–0, and former Cub Bill Madlock, now with Pittsburgh, chimed in: "The Cubs have the best team they've had here in years and they're still sixteen games out and in sixth place? What does that tell you?"

It told Bob Kennedy it was time to make a change. Although Franks denied saying everything Mooshil claimed he had said, the damage was done. Franks was let go, and Cubs coach Joe Amalfitano finished out the season, although the Cubs actually finished fifth, not sixth. A few days later, Kennedy, on Franks's recommendation, hired Preston Gomez as the Cubs' new manager, passing over Whitey Herzog, who had just been let go by Kansas City. Gomez almost immediately lost credibility when he exhibited no knowledge of the club. He said that he intended to build the bullpen, because "in the last few years the Cubs have lacked a middle relief man." Not true: Dick Tidrow had been superb in the role in 1979, and in 1978 Donnie Moore and Willie Hernandez had split the role. In fact, over the course of about five or six seasons some of the best relief pitchers of the era played for the Cubs. Unfortunately, few of them stayed for very long.

Bruce Sutter, who won the Cy Young Award on the strength of his thirty-seven saves, said after the season, "The toughest job now rests on Bob Kennedy. He's got to get us some more players. If you don't have the players, you can't win." Once again, the Cubs would not get the players.

But they did have Bruce Sutter. He wanted to stay with the Cubs, and the Cubs wanted to keep him, by locking him up to a long-term deal before he reached free agency.

Sutter was open to the idea and tentatively agreed to a four-year deal worth $400,000 a year, more than four times his current salary.

But when Sutter and his attorneys met with Kennedy and William Wrigley, the deal was off the table. Sutter wanted some of the money deferred, but Wrigley balked, telling Sutter he didn't want to be paying him if he wasn't playing.

What Sutter didn't realize was that Wrigley was beginning to put the Cubs in position to be sold. The death of both parents only a few months apart had hit him with a double inheritance tax, and the team was perhaps the easiest asset to get rid of. He was far more focused on the Wrigley Company, which was rolling out a wide variety of new product lines, and the Cubs were nothing but a distraction. He didn't want any long-term debt or contracts to inhibit a sale of the club.

Instead of signing with the Cubs long-term, Sutter went to binding arbitration, a process in which both the player and the club selected a salary and pled their case before a neutral arbitrator, who would choose one figure or the other. The Cubs offered Sutter $350,000 for the 1980 season, while Sutter and his attorneys, knowing they were already guaranteed to earn at least $350,000, shot for the moon and asked for $700,000.

Sutter won, shocking the Cubs and all of baseball, as he instantly became one of the highest-paid players in the game. Not only that, but the decision led the Cubs to put Sutter on the trade market soon thereafter, and it eventually played a part in William Wrigley's decision to sell the team. He saw the writing on the wall—baseball was becoming too expensive. Although it would be more than a year before he began to shop the Cubs, the seed was planted. In the interim, the Cubs would be like the Yankees of the early 1960s before they were sold to CBS—an organization making itself lean to make the bottom line more attractive to a potential suitor.

The Cubs tried to rebuild in 1980—not with young players, whom they didn't have, but with a series of rejects and retreads, players who had flamed out elsewhere, like second baseman Mike Tyson, formerly of the Cardinals, and ex–Texas Ranger Lenny Randle. Neither player was without talent, but both were role players who were better

suited to a team that was already good, not centerpiece players to build a team around.

Gomez didn't last the season as manager, and Amalfitano took over again in late July, to no effect. The Cubs won only sixty-four games, finishing last despite Bill Buckner's batting title and Bruce Sutter's twenty-eight saves. In July a radio station tried to organize a "Snub the Cubs" boycott to protest "thirty-five years of bad baseball," but backed off when the Cubs threatened legal action. But the Cubs couldn't even get their own players to show up. On August 7 Dave Kingman, out with a shoulder injury, captured the mood at Wrigley Field and he didn't show up either. On a day when the Cubs were giving away 15,000 Dave Kingman T-shirts, Kingman, instead of going to the game, chose to make an appearance for a vendor at a boat show.

The worst-kept secret in Chicago during the offseason was that Bruce Sutter would be traded before becoming a free agent. But unlike, say, Manny Trillo, Sutter was one of the premier players in all baseball; he was widely seen as a player who could make a good team great and a great team fantastic. There was no shortage of suitors for his skills.

The Cubs needed everything and could afford to be choosy. But they also didn't want to take on too much salary. In an ideal world, they were looking for a young superstar or can't-miss prospect who would remain affordable for the foreseeable future, plus a starter or two.

Kennedy knew whom he wanted. Baseball's most highly touted hitting prospect at the time was Leon "Bull" Durham of the Cardinals. After being named the MVP of the American Association in 1979, the powerful Durham came up to the Cardinals in 1980. A natural first baseman, he could hit for average, hit for power, and run well enough to play right field or left, but he didn't have a strong arm or the instincts to play center field. For the Cardinals, that meant he couldn't crack the starting lineup— he was stuck behind Keith Hernandez at first base and Bobby Bonds and George Hendrick in the outfield. In part-time duty, he had hit .271 with eight home runs. The Cubs expected more from him at Wrigley Field—a lot more. They hoped he'd provide the power of Banks combined with the all-around hitting skills of Billy Williams.

The Cardinals wanted Sutter, but it took a few days to work out the details, since the Cardinals also wanted the

Cubs to take third baseman Ken Reitz, who was a fine player but an expensive one: he earned $1 million a year and had a no-trade clause to boot. After several days, Reitz waived his no-trade clause in exchange for another $150,000, and Sutter swapped addresses with Durham and Reitz. "Durham was the key player," admitted Kennedy.

With that bit of business taken care of, the Cubs moved on to other matters. Kingman wasn't happy, and neither were the Cubs anymore. Like every other team he'd played for, the Cubs now found him lacking in almost every regard. The Mets needed a draw, and right before spring training began they took Kingman in a trade, giving up outfielder Steve Henderson.

It made no difference. The Cubs were terrible from the outset, with the worst pitching in the league and, even with Durham, nearly the worst offense. In a television interview, Bob Kennedy admitted as much, saying, "What difference does it make if I finish fourth, fifth, or sixth? I can't put a winner in here this year, or next year either." The truth hurt, but even though Cub fans knew he spoke the truth, Kennedy became a lightning rod for criticism. On May 22, he was fired. Herman Franks left the country club in Salt Lake City and came back to Chicago to serve as interim GM.

He need not have canceled his tee time, because on May 29 the players' union authorized a strike. The players wanted unrestricted free agency, while ownership was determined to place even more restrictions on the movement of players. Over the next few weeks, the two sides tried to negotiate a settlement.

It was too late for the Cubs, who would have been better off if the season hadn't even started. Nothing was working out. On June 4, they had purchased Bobby Bonds, and in his first inning in a Cubs uniform he fell in the outfield and broke his finger.

On June 12, the players went on strike. The Cubs, who had won four of five, were still firmly in last place, with a record of 15–37, and looked for all the world as if they were even worse than that, for at eight o'clock in the morning Herman Franks cut a deal with the Yankees, sending Rick Reuschel and reliever Jay Howell to New York for Doug Bird, Mike Griffin, minor leaguer Pat Tabler, and, most importantly, $400,000.

He'd done his job, dumping Reuschel and his $280,000 annual salary while taking on only about $150,000, making the deal a net gain of more than half a million dollars for the Cubs. Franks admitted that "I know a couple people can't wait to fry my posterior for this trade, but I don't care," adding, "We'll take that [$400,000] and sign up those thirty-three amateur free agents we drafted this week."

True enough, but adding half a million dollars to the team bank account also made the Cubs look a bit more profitable at a time when William Wrigley was in deep negotiations to sell the Cubs. Cub fans didn't know it yet, but after what seemed like forever, the Wrigley era was about to come to an end.

Ever since he had inherited the team, the Cubs had been nothing but a problem to William Wrigley, both on the field and, more importantly, to his bank account. Incredibly, Philip Wrigley had failed to do proper estate tax planning. He did not anticipate the tax burden that his estate would cause for his son, particularly if Helen died soon afterward. This was a critical error and not the kind of mistake a man with P.K. Wrigley's alleged business acumen was supposed to make. As a result, the two estates were taxed as a "package," leaving William Wrigley liable for a $40 million tax bill, which represented almost the entire amount the estate had grown since 1932. According to a story in the *Tribune*, the estate "lacked enough cash or liquid assets to pay taxes," as P.K. Wrigley had only $4 million in cash at the time of his death. William Wrigley wanted to retain full control of the Wrigley Company and had to sell almost everything else in order to do that. The Cubs were eminently expendable.

There was no shortage of potential buyers—people had been approaching the family for years with offers to buy the team, but the Wrigleys had never seriously entertained an offer. A half-dozen well-heeled Chicagoans wanted to put together syndicates to buy the team, as did former A's owner Charlie Finley. Had Wrigley been patient and put the club up for bid, he might have been able to get nearly $30 million for the team.

But like his father, Wrigley didn't plan ahead. While the tax issues were being worked out, he could have shopped the team around. Instead, he waited until the tax bill was due. The timing was all wrong. Selling the team in the midst of a labor stoppage during a nationwide recession wasn't exactly the way they taught you how to do it in business school. Now he needed to sell, and sell fast. He couldn't afford a protracted sale process, financially or emotionally, for in recent years not only had both Philip and Helen Wrigley died, but a Wrigley niece had stabbed herself to death, and Helen Wrigley's sister-in-law had been murdered.

In the spring of 1981, William Wrigley received his tax bill and approached the most obvious suitor around, the Tribune Company. In addition to the newspaper, the company also owned WGN, which still broadcast Cub games and was just beginning to be picked up nationwide on hundreds of cable television systems. The company wanted to protect its asset and was able to move fast and—just as important to Wrigley—pay cash. On June 16, Wrigley and the Tribune Company announced that they had a deal. For $20.5 million, the Tribune Company purchased the assets and liabilities of the Cubs, including Wrigley Field and an option for the property on which it sat, as well as, for tax reasons, an option to purchase Wrigley's team stock. While the deal was subject to the approval of the other National League club owners, there was no question that the deal would be approved.

After more than sixty years, the lights were about to come on at Wrigley Field.

BIG SHOULDERS

Lovable losers.

Once upon a time that phrase was used to describe Brooklyn's beloved Dodgers, the "Bums," a team that, for a time, meant everything to their city but just could not manage to win. That changed in 1955, when the Dodgers won their first world championship. A few years later, the phrase was adopted by New York Mets fans to describe their affection for that hapless club, but as Cub fans well remember, the Mets shed that appellation by winning the 1969 World Series. Then, for a time, some tried to attach the phrase to the Philadelphia Phillies, the only remaining team in existence when the World Series was first played in 1903 that had not won the championship.

When the Phillies won the World Series in 1980, however, "lovable losers" was once again up for grabs. The phrase soon found a home at Wrigley Field.

After the Phillies' victory, the Cubs had the dubious honor of being the National League franchise that had

During the 1980s Chicago sports fans celebrated the achievements of a trio of superstars who symbolized the resurgence of their respective teams: Walter Payton of the Bears, Michael Jordan of the Bulls, and Cub second baseman Ryne Sandberg. Sandberg won the 1984 National League MVP Award while leading the Cubs to their first postseason appearance since World War II.

gone the longest without winning the World Series, a drought that stretched back to 1908. They now became the logical candidate to adopt that infamous expression. It was no accident that the phrase soon began making regular appearances in Chicago newspapers soon after the Tribune Company purchased the team.

The Cubs had completely deteriorated since 1969, a process that only sped up after the death of Philip Wrigley in 1977. Son William may well have wished to do things differently, but he had neither the will nor the means. By the time the Tribune Company purchased the team in 1981, the Cubs were in ruins. They were certainly losers, and perhaps still lovable, but not in a very endearing way, or, like the early Mets, in a way that drew people to the ballpark out of proportion to the team's record.

The *Tribune* newspaper was the first media outlet to make widespread use of the phrase in Chicago, repeatedly referring to the Cubs as "lovable losers" in prepublication promotions for a magazine story by Skip Myslenski entitled "Can the Cubs Be Saved?" that appeared in the offseason after the club was purchased by the Tribune Company. The use of the phrase was telling, for it revealed precisely how the Tribune Company viewed the ball club. The Tribune recognized that the Cubs were awful—in fact, "losers." Yet the company also recognized that the Cubs—make that "Cubbies"—could still be made to be *lovable*: cute and cuddly and worthy of affection, even in defeat.

The team acquired by the Tribune Company was in need of a complete renovation. Since 1976, the club had failed to break even in four of the last five seasons—William Wrigley hadn't even maintained what he had been left, refusing to hold the franchise together with chewing gum and checks.

In recent years, only the ultra-cheap Oakland Athletics, who once listed teenager Stanley Burrell—who later became famous as rapper MC Hammer—as "Executive Vice-President," had a smaller front office than the Cubs. At Wrigley Field, old warhorses like former manager Charlie Grimm, Salty Saltwell, and "College of Coaches" alumnus Vedie Himsl were all still on the Cub payroll. In 1980 in the third-largest market in all of American sports—a city that was the home of hundreds of major corporations—the Cubs had sold a grand total of 954 season tickets.

For the Tribune Company, this would not do. Today the company is a self-described "media industry leader," primarily consisting of newspapers and television and radio stations concentrated in New York, Los Angeles, and Chicago, the nation's top three markets, with annual revenues that exceed $6 billion. In that portfolio, the Chicago Cubs are nothing more than another line in a very big and very fat budget.

It was not always that way, and in that difference lies the logic that led the Tribune Company to acquire the Cubs in the first place.

After the Tribune Company purchased the Cubs, the ball club remained under a corporate umbrella, just as it had been under the ownership of the Wrigley family. The club was neither the focal point of that corporation nor its reason for existence, but rather an outrigger—a piece of a larger whole and thereby subject to both corporate whims and windfalls.

There was, however, one enormous difference between the way the Wrigley Company looked at the team and the way the Tribune Company looked at it. Under the Wrigleys, the Cubs had become an unwelcome anachronism and a source of embarrassment, but the family made no real effort to change the status quo. To the Tribune Company, on the other hand, the Cubs' status quo was unacceptable. While the corporate bottom line had been no less important under the Wrigleys than it was at the Tribune Company, the Tribune motto was essentially: grow or die. Unlike the Wrigleys, the Tribune Company did not buy the Cubs in order to sit idly by and watch the shadows move across Wrigley Field like a sundial as the players dashed back and forth, oblivious to their position in the standings and the number of people in the stands. Neither was the corporation married to the club for sentimental reasons. The Tribune Company didn't just hope to break even— it expected a *growing* financial return, and from day one that marked the difference between it and the Wrigley Company. In virtually every way possible, in less than a decade the Cubs, under the Tribune Company, would achieve a level of success that had been impossible under the Wrigleys and would have remained impossible if the Wrigleys had retained control.

The Tribune Company was both extremely lucky and extremely prescient—it acquired the Cubs at a rock-bottom price and at the perfect time—a few years before the economy began a slow turnaround, just as cable television spread across the landscape, delivering WGN to a nation-wide audience, and a moment before baseball began to experience a boom that in many ways still echoes some twenty-five years later. In the recent history of the game, perhaps only the Yankees, which George Steinbrenner bought for $11 million in 1974 (hardly any of that money his), have turned out to be a better bargain.

The Tribune Company was also looking to the Cubs to give it a presence, an identity, for just as no one had known who William Wrigley was before he purchased the Cubs, outside Chicago, *Tribune* was just a name for a news-paper. Awareness of the parent company was almost non-existent. Tribune officials hoped to take the company public at some point, and the "lovable losers" marketed through WGN could make it stand out.

Over the next several decades, the Tribune would simultaneously try to cater to two distinct constituencies and serve two distinct goals—to satisfy their hard-core fans the company attempted to make the losing Cubs a champion, while enhancing and marketing the "lovable" Cubbies to casual fans less concerned with wins and losses. In a sense, it was selling time shares to a ski resort and try-ing to make sure that even if there was no snow, the party at the lodge would be so good that hardly anyone would notice. Well, when the Tribune bought the club, the slopes were bare and the bar was empty, but in short order the company hired two men they hoped could solve both problems. Dallas Green was brought in to make the snow and groom the slopes for the hard-core, while Harry Caray was hired to lead the party at the bar.

Over time the Cubs would be everything and do every-thing under the Tribune Company but one: win. But they would come close.

To the Tribune Company, the 1981 strike was a bless-ing, for the shutdown gave it some time to figure out exactly what it wanted to do with the Cubs without doing anything very quickly. When—or if—the strike ended, there was no expectation that the Cubs would do anything more than play out the string in 1981.

Management of the Cubs under the Tribune Company landed on the shoulders of Andrew McKenna, president of a local paper company, friend of Bill Veeck, former opera-tor of the Michigan City, Indiana, minor league team, and

On June 11, 1981, William Wrigley III (center) ended sixty-five years of his family's stewardship of the Cubs when he sold the team to the Tri-bune Company for a little over $20 million. The six National League championships that the Wrigley family brought to Chicago were more than matched by a slew of mediocre clubs.

onetime investor in the White Sox. A Chicagoan through and through, McKenna graduated from Leo High School and had once served as the school's sports correspondent for the *Sun-Times* before he went on to earn a fortune in business and serve on the board of directors of no fewer than eleven businesses and as a trustee for two universi-ties. Named chairman of the board of the Cubs by the Tri-bune, McKenna was given free rein to hire whomever he wanted to run the franchise.

McKenna didn't want to be in the spotlight, and he also knew baseball well enough to realize that he didn't have the skills to rebuild the organization himself. He also knew there was no one in the current Cub organization remotely qualified to do so. He started the job search in the most basic way possible: by flipping through baseball's official "Blue Book," a guide to every franchise in baseball.

The first general manager hired by the Tribune Company was former Phillies manager Dallas Green. Not only did Green lead the club to the 1984 Eastern Division crown, but he also traded for 1984 National League MVP Ryne Sandberg and Cy Young Award winner Rick Sutcliffe (at left), and later signed Andre Dawson as a free agent.

One name stood out. Baseball's genius of the moment was Phillies manager Dallas Green. In the early 1970s, he had taken over the Philadelphia Phillies farm system, and during his tenure the Phillies produced one quality player after another, including stars like Mike Schmidt, Garry Maddox, and Lonnie Smith, and captured division titles in 1976, 1977, and 1978. When the Phillies slumped in 1979, Green took over as manager, led them on a late-season surge that carried them past the Cubs and into fourth place, then led those "lovable losers" to their first-ever world championship in 1980. Along the way, he earned a reputation as a tough and feisty hard-ass who drove his team to victory by force of his own personality. Although Green was born in Delaware and his first name was George, his middle name "Dallas" both fit the era and fit Green. At six-foot-five, the swaggering, blunt-spoken, square-shouldered Green seemed to have stepped from central casting. At the time the Dallas Cowboys were in their glory, posters of the Cowboy cheerleaders adorned the walls of adolescent boys everywhere, and the night-

time soap opera *Dallas* was one of the most popular programs on television. Dallas Green was the right guy at the right time.

McKenna approached him before the end of the season and sounded him out about coming to work for the Cubs, not as manager but as GM and vice president. Not only was Green qualified for those jobs, but his appointment would make a splash and send a clear message that the Cubs were under construction. Green, whose Phillies were trying to repeat, initially turned McKenna down, but once the Phillies were bounced from the playoffs, McKenna made Green a solid offer. He would be given a free hand to remake the organization from top to bottom; to hire whomever he wanted, to do whatever he wanted them to do; to make trades; and, flush with Tribune cash, to sign some free agents. While reality never quite matched the promise and Green would eventually chafe under interference from above, he couldn't turn the offer down. It was a challenge, and his ego craved the attention that bringing a world championship to Chicago would bring.

Green was introduced to the Chicago media on October 16 and made an immediate impression. McKenna announced that "my only role is to help Dallas . . . the decisions are up to him." And Green concurred, saying, "It's totally up to me," before launching into a cogent and insightful assessment of his team. "I'm going to look everyone in the eye and tell them if they don't want to work as hard as I do they might as well go home right now." Afterwards, the *Tribune*'s David Condon wrote that "I left with the feeling that sometime, somewhere, I had gone through this scene before. . . . Then it dawned. I long ago had been on a similar scene—when a determined aggressive battler named Vince Lombardi took over Green Bay's hapless Packers. Dallas Green will be the Cubs' Vince Lombardi."

Green got to work immediately. In his first move, he hired former major league shortstop Lee Elia as manager. Just a few years before, Elia had been out of baseball entirely, selling insurance, before he bumped into Green and renewed an old friendship. Green soon gave Elia a reprieve from his desk job and offered him a manager's job in the Phillies farm system. Elia then worked his way back up to the major leagues, serving as Green's third-base coach in Philadelphia.

Elia would not be the last former Phillies employee to join the Cubs: over the next year Green hired a number of trusted allies from the Phillies organization to take over key roles in player development, scouting, marketing, and other areas. Some of it was pure politics, but the Phillies organization was deep not only in player talent but also in the front office. Many old-time Wrigley employees were initially retained for their institutional knowledge, but there was little question that the new guard was taking over.

While Green got familiar with the big chair, the Tribune Company made another big move. Earlier that season, legendary broadcaster Jack Brickhouse had announced his retirement. Cub fans had grown accustomed to Brickhouse's restrained approach, and most expected sidekick Milo Hamilton to take over.

The Tribune, however, had other ideas. The company had to sell the "lovable" aspect of the Cubs for a few years, and to do that it needed the broadcast equivalent of a carnival barker, a man who could get the crowd into the tent and leave them happy no matter what they saw inside.

Harry Caray, whom a local television critic accurately described as "outrageously colorful, a raspy-voiced beer drinker . . . [and a] high-living high-salaried friend to countless bartenders," was all that and more. He was also everything Brickhouse was not. For a voice, he was flamboyant, drawing attention to himself at the ballpark by grabbing foul balls with a fishing net, leading fans in the singing of "Take Me Out to the Ball Game" during the seventh-inning stretch, and earning the well-deserved nickname of the "Mayor of Rush Street" for his late-night conviviality. Broadcaster Jack Drees once noted that Caray and Howard Cosell were the only two sports broadcasters who were able to "overshadow the event."

Caray's big league broadcasting career had started in St. Louis, where he was the voice of the Cardinals from 1947 to 1969. There he was considered "a god," the voice of the

Broadcaster Harry Caray was a legend before arriving at Wrigley Field in 1982. Not only was he the longtime voice of both the Cardinals and White Sox, but he also was a staple of countless World Series and All-Star Game broadcasts. His shift from the White Sox to the Cubs in 1982 was soon embraced by Cub fans, who loved his corny antics and "Take Me Out to the Ball Game" seventh-inning sing-alongs.

fan, a guy who called them like he saw them through his Coke bottle–thick glasses. But in 1969 the Cardinals fired Caray, allegedly for having an affair with the wife of St. Louis owner Gussie Busch's son. In 1971 he landed with the White Sox and received credit for inspiring renewed interest in the club: attendance nearly tripled from pre-Caray levels in his first two seasons. In less than a decade, he was bigger in Chicago than he had ever been in St. Louis.

The White Sox were about to put their television broadcasts on cable, and they expected Caray, whose contract expired at the end of the 1981 season, to lead the transition. But Caray balked. The White Sox cable channel was just getting off the ground, and although he'd undoubtedly be given a raise, fewer than fifty thousand homes would

receive the broadcast and, as much as anything else, Caray craved attention. He asked for an outrageous contract, and when the White Sox hesitated, Caray let the Cubs and the Tribune Company know that he was interested in moving across town.

He was the perfect man for the job. WGN was one of the first cable "super stations": it brought the Cubs to a potential audience of almost thirty million. The Tribune Company knew that the team couldn't hold that audience, at least not yet, but Caray, with his ability to "overshadow the event," could. When fans skipping from channel to channel landed on WGN, they heard Caray and stopped changing the channel. It was just that simple.

He was hired on November 17. Local media critic Ron Aldridge wrote that the hire "shows how radically the Cubs are changing under their new ownership, how determined they are to shake off the dullness of the past."

Many old-time Cubs fans, however, were put off. They still identified Caray with the enemy, the Cardinals and White Sox, and they hated Caray and hated his style. The Tribune Company ignored their complaints, which was a measure of just how eager the company was to change. It did not care if it alienated old fans. Change was in the air, and first with Green, and now with Caray, the public face and voice of the franchise were in place. Now all it needed were a few players.

Green got off to a slow start as he learned his way around Wrigley Field. He knew as well as anybody that the Cubs weren't going anywhere in 1982. Rather than make a big splash and spend big for free agents who weren't going to make much of a difference, Green used some restraint. On December 8, he brought back Ferguson Jenkins and signed free agent reliever Bill Campbell. Jenkins was thirty-eight, and Campbell was no longer the dominant reliever he'd been a few years before, but both gave the club a veteran presence. On that same day, Green made his first deal and just as many other front-office hires do, he looked to the organization he knew best, his last one. He traded pitcher Mike Krukow and cash to the Phillies for two Phillies pitchers, Dickie Noles and Dan Larsen, and catcher-outfielder Keith Moreland.

His big move, however, came in January. Once more it involved Philadelphia.

Philadelphia thought shortstop Larry Bowa was both

Leon Durham came to the Cubs as part of one of the more unfortunate trades in team history. On December 9, 1980, Chicago dealt future Hall of Famer Bruce Sutter to the Cardinals for Ken Reitz, Tye Waller, and Durham. Despite this stigma, Durham enjoyed a solid career as a first baseman–outfielder from 1981 to 1989.

past his prime and too expensive, making him and his out-spoken personality expendable. He had recently popped off over some front-office moves he disagreed with, and the Phillies were eager to get rid of him. Cubs shortstop Ivan DeJesus, despite coming off a bad year, was several years younger, a better fielder, and, most importantly, far quieter.

Green knew the Phillies were looking to move Bowa when he proposed the trade, but he didn't want to make a one-for-one swap. The Cubs needed more.

In November 1981, Cub infielder Steve Macko died of cancer. A fourth-round pick in 1977, Macko, who could play third, short, or second, appeared to be on the fast track to the major leagues after earning a call-up at the end of the 1979 season. In 1980 he returned to Triple A Wichita, but made his way back to the majors in midseason.

In one of his first appearances, former Cub Bill Mad-lock steamrolled him while Macko tried to turn a double play, injuring his thigh. While treating his leg, doctors dis-covered that Macko had cancer. He remained on the ros-ter—and often in uniform in 1981, in one of the Wrigleys' more compassionate moves—but would die sixteen months later.

His death left the Cubs short of infielders, for neither Pat Tabler nor young Scott Fletcher was showing any abil-ity to hit major league pitching. Meanwhile, Green knew there was a player in the Phillies' farm system who could plug that hole.

Ryne Sandberg had been drafted by Green in the twenty-first round out of high school in Washington State. Almost immediately, it became clear to some in the organ-ization that Sandberg was a real find, a low-round draftee who was better than expected. He ran well, fielded well, threw well, hit well, worked hard, and kept quiet. The only thing he couldn't do was hit for power.

Fortunately for the Cubs, in the Phillies organization Sandberg had almost been overlooked. The Phillies were flush with young infielders and had already identified nineteen-year-old Julio Franco as a future star. In the mean-time, Manny Trillo, Mike Schmidt, and—if they could acquire him—Ivan DeJesus would give the Phillies a solid infield for at least another three or four years. Despite his obvious talent, Sandberg was far down on the Phillies' depth chart.

Green knew this and knew Sandberg would be avail-able. Although some have later described Sandberg as a "throw-in," Green made it clear at the time that unless the Cubs received Sandberg, they had no interest in Bowa and DeJesus would remain a Cub.

Philadelphia agreed to the deal on January 27. In retro-spect, it almost seemed predestined that Sandberg, who shared the same phonetic last name with the poet Carl Sandburg, who had termed Chicago the "City of the Big Shoulders," would play for the Cubs. During his career in Chicago, Ryne Sandberg would supply the big shoulders and carry the Cubs. "I look at it this way," said Lee Elia of the acquisition. "Sandberg can play any one of three posi-tions for us: second base, third base, or center field."

Unfortunately, he couldn't play all three. After a terri-ble start that saw him go hitless over his first twenty at-bats and only 1-for-32, he settled in for most of the season at third base, where he was a pleasant surprise to everyone but Green, scoring 103 runs and hitting .271. The Cubs, however, were not much better than they had been in 1981, even with a top-notch bullpen anchored by Camp-bell and young Lee Smith. But they were more exciting. Green and Elia had the team running—Durham, second baseman Bump Wills, and Sandberg stole more than twenty-eight bases each—and Harry Caray worked his magic on the airwaves, selling Wrigley Field as much as the action on the field. Attendance bounced back to pre-strike levels, but the resurgent White Sox, who battled for the division title before finishing third, still ruled Chicago.

The Cubs, despite their slow improvement, still didn't have the players. "There are," said Lee Elia just before the end of the season, "a lot of guys I hope aren't here next year. You get tired of looking at garbage in your own back-yard."

In the offseason, the garbage truck backed up at Wrigley Field, not so much to remove players, although Green did make several small deals in December, but to remove the last vestiges of the Wrigley administration from the front office; many of them were replaced with people known to Green from his time with the Phillies. Longtime fans and some remaining Wrigley partisans blanched at the way the Tribune Company seemed oblivi-ous to tradition, but in reality much of that tradition had been nothing more than mold. The company embarked on an ambitious renovation program at Wrigley Field, replacing the scoreboard and, over the next few seasons, enlarging player facilities. It also continued to suggest that "day only" baseball at Wrigley Field would soon come to an end. Simple baseball economics demanded that teams do everything possible to get fans into the ballpark, and daytime baseball was too inconvenient to most fans.

Green tried to make a splash in the free agent market by making a run at Dodger first baseman Steve Garvey. Garvey turned the Cubs down and signed with San Diego, a decision that would resonate throughout both organizations a few years later, but the mere fact that Green entertained signing Garvey sent a not too subtle message to the Cubs, particularly first baseman Bill Buckner, that no one was safe.

Since joining the Cubs in 1977, Buckner had become one of the club's most popular figures, the kind of player who somehow got his uniform dirty every day and looked as if he was playing hard even while making routine plays. In Buckner's case, however, injuries to his feet and ankles had caused the once-fleet outfielder to move to first base, and he ran as if both shoes were coated with layers of heavy clay.

Buckner often clashed with Cub management. He had once called former manager Herman Franks "a clown," and Franks considered Buckner selfish and self-centered, saying, "I thought he was the all-American boy . . . [but] he's nuts. He doesn't care about anything but getting a hit." Buckner was born to hit in Wrigley Field, however, lining line drive after line drive into the gaps. By 1982 Buckner was the highest-paid Cub.

After Garvey turned him down, Green moved to plan B. Dodger third baseman Ron Cey was not a free agent, but he was expensive, and after Cey hit only .254 in 1982, the Dodgers were eager to deal him. Green, thinking Cey would hit well in Wrigley Field, traded two minor league pitchers in exchange for the third baseman. Although the local press criticized the deal at the time, in reality Cey was a much better hitter than Garvey, and his acquisition

From 1977 to 1983, first baseman Bill Buckner was the Cubs' most consistent player. In 1980 he captured the National League batting title with a .324 average and batted an even .300 in his eight seasons at Wrigley Field.

1984

On April 29, 1983, Cubs manager Lee Elia unleashed a tirade in the Wrigley Field clubhouse that has since become an essential part of Cub lore. Among other things, Elia bellowed, "Eighty-five percent of the world is working. The other fifteen percent come out here."

They didn't really want him, but they knew that the Cubs wouldn't let him go and that by announcing their intention to draft him, they would force the Cubs into making a trade to reacquire Jenkins's rights. On January 26, in exchange for not drafting Jenkins, the White Sox dumped two pitchers they didn't want on the Cubs, Steve Trout and Warren Brusstar, for four players they did want, reliever Dick Tidrow, young starter Randy Martz, and infielders Scott Fletcher and Pat Tabler. Jenkins's agent summed up the general feeling over the deal when he said, "The Sox held the Cubs hostage."

It was hard to see, but the deal actually ended up helping the Cubs. The pieces were nearly there—although some were not yet in the right place—as the Cubs' lineup began to feature a mixture of savvy veterans and young players on the rise. Sandberg settled in at second base, surrounded by veterans in Bowa, Buckner, and Cey. Catcher Jody Davis took over behind the plate. In a push, Leon Durham played in center field—though he was a natural first baseman—flanked by rookie Mel Hall and Keith Moreland, giving the Cubs one of the most potent hitting attacks in the National League. But the pitching staff, apart from closer Lee Smith, was a disaster. Jenkins was nearly finished, and the remaining starters—Chuck Rainey, Steve Trout, and Dickie Noles—were either in over their heads or hurt. Scoring runs wasn't a problem for the Cubs in 1983—nor, unfortunately, was it a problem for their opponents.

They opened the season with six straight losses and then struggled, falling out of the race early. Cubs fans had been patient in 1982, but they expected some improvement in 1983. When they didn't get it, even though it was only April, things turned ugly.

Following a 4–3 loss to the Dodgers on April 29 in which Lee Smith wild-pitched home the winning run in the eighth inning, Keith Moreland and Larry Bowa were both doused with beer by fans from atop the dugout. Moreland had to be restrained from going into the stands.

It was no more welcoming in the clubhouse. Elia, livid after the loss, closed the door and reamed his team out for a full fifteen minutes before opening the clubhouse to reporters. He calmly answered a few innocuous questions before suddenly going off, complaining that he was sick of hearing about "Phillieitis," one local newspaper's term for the Philadelphian orientation of the Cubs. Elia then lost it

allowed the Cubs to move Sandberg to second base, where Sandberg could make better use of his speed and quickness.

One last deal sent the local press into hysterics. The Cubs exposed Fergie Jenkins in the short-lived free agent compensation draft, which allowed teams who had lost free agents to select replacements from other clubs, much in the same way an expansion draft worked. The Cubs didn't protect Jenkins, who had bounced back to win fourteen games in 1982, figuring that no one would want to take on the $500,000 salary of the thirty-nine-year-old pitcher, who was only twenty-two games away from three hundred career victories, a pursuit whose impact on the box office the club was looking forward to. But the White Sox pulled a surprise and announced that they intended to select Jenkins.

in a legendary, profanity-laced tirade, insulting Cub fans and unintentionally revealing the organization's attitude toward beloved Wrigley Field by saying, among other things, "Eighty-five percent of the world is working. The other fifteen percent come out here."

Elia's explosion was caught on tape by radio reporter Les Grobstein and caused an immediate media firestorm. In the *Tribune*, Robert Markus called it "the most sizzling footage recorded since the Nixon tapes," while John Schulian, in the *Sun-Times*, wondered why Elia went after Cub fans, whom he spoofed as "gentle souls . . . pensioners, Little Leaguers and account executives playing hooky."

Green played a copy of the tape for Elia a few hours later, and the manager apologized, admitting that he had "lost it" and blaming the outburst on "frustrations." Cub fans were not amused. A liquor salesman interviewed at the Cubby Bear, a watering hole just outside Wrigley Field, asked one reporter to "bring me the head of Lee Elia. I've got a real job and I'm unhappy about this. Get rid of him." Elia hung on to his job—barely—as both McKenna and

THE TIRADE

Manager Lee Elia's tirade following a 4–3 loss to the Dodgers at Wrigley Field on April 29 was captured by several reporters on tape. Challenged by his admonition to "*Print it!*" they took him at this word. The tape was replayed countless times on Chicago radio stations with the profanities bleeped out. Since then, however, the tirade has taken on a life of its own. More than twenty years afterwards, it remains a popular shared audio file on the Internet.

Owing to its profanity, however, it has rarely appeared in print. With some creative word substitution from the vegetable kingdom and the world of insects, here is a sanitized version of Elia's tirade:

Potato those potatoin' fans who come out here and say they're Cub fans that are supposed to be behind you, rippin' every potatoin' thing you do. I'll tell you one potatoin' thing, I hope we get potatoin' hotter than coconuts, just to stuff it up them 3,000 potatoin' people that show up every potatoin' day, because if they're the real Chicago potatoin' fans, they can kiss my potatoin' ass right downtown and *print it*.

They're really, really behind you around here . . . my potatoin' ass. What the potato am I supposed to do, go out there and let my potatoin' players get destroyed every day and be quiet about it? For the potatoin' nickel-dime people who turn up? The mother-potatoers don't even work.

That's why they're out at the potatoin' game. They oughta go out and get a potatoin' job and find out what it's like to go out and earn a potatoin' living. Eighty-five percent of the potatoin' world is working. The other fifteen percent come out here. A potatoin' playground for the bumblebees. Rip them mother-potatoers. Rip them potatoin' bumblebees like the potatoin' players. We got guys bustin' their potatoin' ass, and them potatoin' people boo. And that's the Cubs? My potatoin' ass. They talk about the great potatoin' support the players get around here. I haven't seen it this potatoin' year. Everybody associated with this organization have been winners their whole potatoin' life. Everybody. And the credit is not given in that respect.

All right, they don't show because we're five-and-fourteen . . . and unfortunately, that's the criteria of them dumb fifteen mother-potatoin' percent that come out to day baseball. The other eighty-five percent are earning a living. I tell you, it'll take more than a five-and-twelve or five-and-fourteen to destroy the makeup of this club. I guarantee you that. There's some potatoin' pros out there that wanna win. But you're stuck in a potatoin' stigma of the potatoin' Dodgers and the Phillies and the Cardinals and all that cheap bugaboo. It's unbelievable. It really is. It's a disheartening potatoin' situation that we're in right now. Anybody who was associated with the Cub organization four or five years ago that came back and sees the multitude of progress that's been made will understand that if they're baseball people, that five-and-fourteen doesn't negate all that work. We got 143 potatoin' games left.

What I'm tryin' to say is, don't rip them potatoin' guys out there. Rip me. If you wanna rip somebody, rip my potatoin' ass. But don't rip them potatoin' guys 'cause they're givin' everything they can give. And right now they're tryin' to do more than God gave 'em, and that's why we make the simple mistakes. That's exactly why.

Green, while defending their manager to a point, called the speech "a fireable offense."

The players had a different reaction. They appreciated the fact that the manager had gone out on a limb to defend them, and for a time the Cubs played somewhat better, almost reaching .500 and drawing to within only a few games of first-place Montreal.

But in the long run, nothing could mask the Cubs' lack of pitching, and in the second half they tumbled. In a little over a year, Green had made more than a dozen deals and doubled the payroll, but the Cubs appeared no better off than before. On August 22, under pressure from McKenna and Tribune executives, Green fired Elia, throwing him under the bus by saying, "I told Lee he didn't manage up to his capabilities." Although the local press didn't shed any tears when Elia left, they also were not fooled. Most agreed with Jerome Holtzman, who blamed Green, writing that he had "oversold his team to the public" and that Elia was simply taking the fall for Green's failures.

Veteran manager Charlie Fox was hired to replace Elia, but it soon became clear that he was simply an interim appointment. The Cubs limped to the finish, finishing nineteen games out of first and twenty games below .500.

As the season neared its end, it became clear that Green would not escape some blame for the club's performance—the Cubs were still losing, and thus far, despite Harry Caray's best efforts, the Cubs hadn't enjoyed a surge in attendance, although television ratings were up. McKenna was spending far more time on the Cubs than he had expected, and the Cubs' performance over the last eighteen months had caused some at the Tribune to begin to doubt the wisdom of giving Green so much power and authority. Although Green's job was safe, Jim Finks, who was better known as a former pro quarterback and GM of the Vikings and Bears in the NFL, was hired as club president. The former minor leaguer took over some of the duties of both McKenna and Green. Green wasn't entirely enamored of the arrangement, as he had been promised the presidency when he was first hired, but it did free him

---

Pete Rose nicknamed his Phillie teammate Gary Matthews "Sarge" for his take-charge attitude. Matthews's arrival in Chicago in March 1984 with fellow outfielder Bob Dernier signaled a new day for the once list-less Cubs: both would play dynamic roles in the team's resurgence.

from numbing administrative duties to focus on his strength, player development.

At the end of the season, interim manager Fox resigned to take a job in the front office, and Green soon hired former Kansas City Royal manager Jim Frey to replace him. Green knew Frey—his Phillies had beaten Frey's Royals in the 1980 World Series. The appointment seemed to be just another shuffling of the deck of the old boys' network, but it would soon become clear that there was some substance to Frey's appointment. Frey had served as Earl Weaver's caddy in Baltimore for ten years, and in a short time the Cubs would become a lot like the Baltimore clubs of the 1970s, the 1980 Kansas City Royals, and, for that matter, the 1980 Phillies: all were flexible, well-balanced teams that could win with speed, power, pitching, or defense, and though rarely overwhelming in any single area, all were solid from top to bottom. Green, who was starting to run out of time, was determined to put just such a team on the field. Besides, unlike Elia, Frey was also low-key, a not insignificant factor in the organization, for Green still sucked up most of the oxygen and a new Cub manager had to realize ahead of time that Green would take credit for any success.

Going into the offseason, the Cubs clearly needed more pitching, as they had ranked twelfth in the NL in that department in 1983. Jenkins, after winning only six games and racking up fifteen no-decisions, was on the trading block and didn't expect to return, and the other starters—Dick Ruthven, Dickie Noles, Chuck Rainey, and Steve Trout—hardly inspired confidence. Lee Smith anchored the bullpen, but the problem was getting to him.

Fortunately, the Cubs were not without resources. They had plenty of offense and were flush with young hitters, ranging from Durham, Sandberg, and Mel Hall in the majors to minor league first baseman Carmelo Martinez and outfielders Harry Cotto and Joe Carter, both top-notch prospects. On December 7, Green dealt from a position of strength, working a three-way deal with San Diego and Montreal that landed starting pitcher Scott Sanderson, a sixteen-game winner in 1980, while giving up reliever Craig Lefferts and Martinez. Sanderson immediately became the de-facto ace of the staff. Unfortunately, by the start of spring training Green was unable to add another starting pitcher.

The Cubs were awful in the spring, losing badly and acting worse as the phrase "laughable losers" came into vogue. Training camp was marred by two fights, one between minor leaguers Reggie Patterson and Bill Johnson, and the other between Dick Ruthven and outfielder Mel Hall, who described himself as "unable to keep my mouth in my pocket." His pockets were reserved for his batting gloves, so that they waved "good-bye" when Hall toured the bases after a home run, a move that impressed no one but himself. Ferguson Jenkins was late reporting to camp, and on March 17, after failing to make a deal, the Cubs released him. "It was inevitable," said Jenkins. He wanted to keep playing, but it soon became clear that no one was interested in a forty-year-old pitcher with 284 wins. "There's a time and a place to say, 'Hey, it's all done.'" Still, the release wasn't popular in Chicago, and Green's reputation took another hit.

Bill Buckner was the next source of trouble. He had been ticked off when he was moved to the outfield in the 1983 season while Martinez and Durham played first, and at spring training Buckner hit the ground moaning. He had nearly been traded to San Francisco as part of a package for Chili Davis, and he blamed Charlie Fox, now working as a special assistant to Green. His days as a Cub were numbered.

On March 25, the Cubs' spring record was a pathetic 3–16. To a point, that was both meaningless and understandable, since Frey was getting to know his team and testing both Mel Hall and Joe Carter in the outfield, pairing them with Moreland and Durham. But when only ten players showed up at a voluntary dinner courting radio and TV advertisers, Green, not manager Jim Frey, unloaded on his team. Two days later, he started cleaning house.

He once more turned to Philadelphia. The Phillies wanted to get younger and cheaper and decided to move outfielder Gary Matthews, a sometime All-Star coming off an MVP performance in the 1983 NLCS. The aggressive, outspoken Matthews was precisely the kind of player the old Cubs never used to acquire, or soon got rid of if he came from their own minor league system, but he was the kind of player this team urgently needed—an attitude enforcer. Pete Rose once said of Matthews, "His statistics don't really reflect the contributions he's made. . . . He's a very take-charge guy. That's why I named him 'Sarge.'" He went to the Cubs along with speedy backup outfielder Bob Dernier, whom the Phillies were preparing to send to the minors, for reliever Bill Campbell and two others. The trade gave the Cubs a glut of outfielders that pushed Leon Durham back to first base and sent Mel Hall, Joe Carter, and Bill Buckner to the bench. "I can't see Bobby Dernier coming in here and taking my job," said Hall. "I don't think he qualifies." Carter and Bill Buckner were similarly miffed. Green indicated that more trades were on the horizon, but he wasn't able to pull any off by opening day. A disappointed Joe Carter was soon sent back to the minors, Hall and Dernier shared center field, and Bill Buckner was relegated to the bench, a sour situation that everyone knew would not last for long.

At the start of the season, the *Tribune* offered that the Cubs began the year with "a sense of urgency for immediate improvement," but answered the question of what else the Cubs could hope for with pessimism, responding with: "certainly not a pennant." They were not alone. In the off-season, the Cubs had been installed as 100–1 underdogs to win the pennant.

There were, however, two dissenting views. Before the start of the season, a San Francisco astrologer named Bob Marks predicted that "the Cubs will start slowly. They will fight among themselves but make their move August 18 and be totally awesome." Another prediction, a more "scientific" excerpt from a book, appeared in the *Tribune* on April Fools' Day.

In an excerpt entitled "Cubs Appear Ripe for Miracle Season," the author suggested that the Cubs were uniquely qualified to pull a surprise in 1984, noting that there had been only a twenty-two-game difference between the first- and last-place team in the NL East in 1983 and that the difference between the number of runs the Cubs scored in 1983 and the number they gave up indicated that they should have had a record near .500. The author also made note of several other subtleties not usually noticed at the time, such as the discrepancy between their performance on grass and artificial turf. He advised readers to "take it" if anyone offered 100-plus odds against the Cubs, although he also cautioned that, despite the headline, "I am certainly not saying that the Cubs will be a miracle team and win the division. . . . I expect the Cubs to play about .500. In this division, that puts them in the race."

CY YOUNG AWARD WINNERS

1992	**Greg Maddux**
1984	**Rick Sutcliffe**
1979	**Bruce Sutter**
1971	**Ferguson Jenkins**

The author was Bill James, and the excerpt came from the 1984 edition of his *Baseball Abstract*. A heretofore obscure author whose self-published volume had achieved cult status among members of the Society for American Baseball Research, James was just entering the mainstream with his studious, statistically inspired analysis. His estimation of the 1984 Cubs would soon prove accurate, although not entirely for the reasons he cited. Miracles needed pitching, and lots of it.

Nevertheless, on opening day in San Francisco, the Cubs, behind Dick Ruthven, dumped the Giants 5–3, only their third opening day victory in the past eleven seasons. Their sharp play continued for the rest of the month, and in a "shades of 1969" moment, they entered May tied with the Mets for first place with a 12–8 record—already nearly three weeks ahead of their 1983 victory pace. Catcher Jody Davis had hit safely in fifteen of eighteen games, Gary Matthews led the club in almost every offensive category, Leon Durham was playing well back at first base, and the Cubs were chugging along nicely as Sandberg and Bob Dernier, whose speed was a revelation in center field, were given the green light to run whenever they wished. Dernier led off in front of Sandberg, and the press soon dubbed the combo the "daily double" for their propensity to get on base back to back.

Still, by the end of May few people were penciling the Cubs into the playoffs, particularly after a spate of injuries temporarily sidelined Scott Sanderson, Ruthven, and Lee Smith. On May 25, in an exchange of the disgruntled, Bill Buckner, who wasn't playing, was shipped to the Boston Red Sox for pitcher Dennis Eckersley. Although Eckersley, a former twenty-game winner who was in the process of partying his way toward baseball purgatory, got off to a slow start, he provided some stability at a critical time. The sportswriters liked the ever-quotable pitcher too. After taking his first look at Wrigley, he quipped, "Fenway is bad enough. But this place is worse. . . . I can give up home runs anywhere." Although the Cubs didn't exactly burn up the league after his arrival, they didn't fall off the table either.

The real key to the season was delivered on June 13. Manager Jim Frey was in his office as the Cubs waited out a rain delay in an eventual 7–4 victory over Montreal. The Cubs' record at the time was a respectable 33–25, which put them in first place by a game and a half, but they were just one bad week away from fifth place, since only five games separated the top five teams in the division. The pitching staff was still thin, and just a few days before the Cubs had learned that backup catcher Steve Lake would miss the remainder of the season with hepatitis.

Dallas Green burst into Frey's office and asked, "You little son of a bitch, do you think we've got enough talent to win it now?" Frey gave him a look and said, "Give me another starting pitcher. I've got to have another starter." All season long he'd been pressing for more.

"You've got him," Green shot back. He had just completed a trade that sent Mel Hall and Joe Carter to Cleveland and delivered starting pitcher Rick Sutcliffe, reliever George Frazier, and catcher Ron Hassey.

Green had been after Sutcliffe for weeks. A member of the All-Star team in 1983 after winning seventeen games, Sutcliffe threw hard, carried a big salary, and had gotten off to a slow start in 1984 because of complications from a root canal. Meanwhile, Hall and Carter were potential stars. Hall, despite his cockiness and tendency to talk before thinking, had finished third in Rookie of the Year balloting in 1983, and Joe Carter was a genuine five-tool player whom everyone expected to succeed. For weeks Green had refused to include both outfielders in the deal, but after Lake became ill and the Indians offered to include Hassey, Green felt that he had no choice but to make the deal. At the end of the day, the Cub payroll went up by nearly \$2 million. When a sportswriter asked Frey if he was worried that all the trades would adversely affect team chemistry, Frey quipped, "Chemistry to me is a pinch-hit double with the bases loaded."

Sutcliffe won his first start on June 19, but by then the Cubs had fallen to third place behind the Mets and Cardinals. Another swoon seemed imminent.

The season turned on June 23 in a nationally televised game against the St. Louis Cardinals. One day before, the Cubs had stopped a slide in which they had lost six of seven with a 9–3 win, but they were still hanging on by the slimmest of margins. Behind rookie pitcher Ralph Citarella, the Cardinals jumped out to early leads of 7–1 and 9–3, and Wrigley Field, which was half full of Cardinal fans, sounded like Busch Stadium, while the NBC broadcasters trotted out the same old tired jokes about the same old tired Cubs. Joe Garagiola had once described them, painfully, as "like Rush Street—a lot of singles, but no action." No one would be thinking anything like that by the end of this day.

The Cubs started their comeback in the sixth by loading the bases on two walks and a hit batsman. Richie Hebner then singled, Bob Dernier doubled, and Sandberg singled to knock in two and draw the Cubs to within one run of the Cardinals.

Still, when the Cubs came to bat in the ninth inning trailing 9–8, their chances of victory seemed infinitesimal, for Bruce Sutter was on the mound for the Cardinals. Since leaving the Cubs, he had only gotten better, and in 1984 he was in the midst of his greatest season, on his way to forty-five saves and an ERA of 1.54.

But Sutter wasn't the only player having his greatest season. Ryne Sandberg was just beginning to emerge. In his first two major league seasons, he had been more than adequate, a slick-fielding, speedy infielder, but hardly a star. In spring training, Jim Frey challenged him to drive the ball. It was difficult at first, but over the previous ten days, although no one had noticed as the Cubs slumped, he had turned a corner, hitting almost .500 and, more importantly, hitting with surprising power. To this point in his career, even Cubs fans didn't know how good he was.

Sandberg stepped to the plate to lead off the ninth looking for—what else?—a split-finger fastball. That did

him little good because batters had been stepping in against Sutter for years looking for the pitch and had been unable to hit it. This time was different, however, because Sandberg was different. He drove the ball into the bleachers, stunning Cardinal fans into silence and sending Cubs fans into hysterics.

The celebration seemed short-lived, because in the tenth the Cardinals scored twice off Lee Smith to take an 11–9 lead. Then, with two outs in the bottom of the inning, Dernier walked, bringing Sandberg up again. As he said later, "To go up there and think I'm going to hit a home run again is unbelievable." But that's just what he did, tying the score with his fifth hit, second run, and sixth and seventh RBIs of the game. An inning later, the Cubs won when pinch hitter Dave Owen singled home Leon Durham. On WGN, Harry Caray went overboard with his signature "Cubs win" call as the Cubs poured from the dugout and the crowd at Wrigley Field stood and screamed and cheered, and all of a sudden everyone, from the players on the field to the fans in the stands to the rest of the league and everyone watching at home, had the same thought— the Cubs were for real, and Ryne Sandberg was a star.

Dallas Green tossed the proverbial dice on June 13, 1984, when he struck a mega-deal that sent promising young outfielders Mel Hall (above) and Joe Carter to the Indians in exchange for starter Rick Sutcliffe and reliever George Frazier. Sutcliffe did nothing less than help deliver the first Cubs title in a generation, and both Carter and Hall enjoyed outstanding major league careers.

Cardinal manager Whitey Herzog thought that too, referring to Sandberg after the game as "Baby Ruth" and "the best player I've ever seen." The Cubs were off and running, and the next day they added an exclamation point as Sutcliffe hurled a shutout, striking out fourteen, and Sandberg smacked a triple, his tenth of the season, and the Cubs won again, 5–0, despite the fact that both Durham and Cey were out with injuries.

"Cubs Fever" was sweeping the country, and fans everywhere began tuning in to WGN to check out this Sandberg kid and then got hooked on Harry and the rest of the Cubs. Owning the Cubs finally began to fulfill the hopes of the Tribune Company. It helped that the season seemed to be playing out like 1969 in reverse as over the next month the Cubs stalked the first-place Mets. This time, however, the

The legend of Ryne Sandberg was forged on a blistering afternoon in June 1984 as he went five-for-six in a nationally televised game against the Cardinals at Wrigley Field. In helping the Cubs surmount a 7–0 deficit and beat their rivals in twelve innings, Sandberg socked two game-tying home runs off former Cub and future Hall of Famer Bruce Sutter.

Cubs were the lovable losers, the underdogs everyone was falling in love with.

In 1969 the Mets had had their "nine crucial days" in which they buried the Cubs; in 1984 the Cubs would have two crucial weeks in which they played the Mets eight times. Nineteen-year-old phenom Dwight Gooden beat the Cubs 2–1 in the first crucial game on July 27 to drop the Cubs four and a half games back, but the Cubs came back to take the final three games of the series, surging into first place on August 1 and then burying the Mets by sweeping a four-game series in New York a week later. Now the Cubs led by four and a half games, a nine-game swing in two weeks.

Almost everyone was playing well as the Cubs had a new hero every day, but Rick Sutcliffe in particular was magnificent. After coming over from the Indians, he lost only once as he gave the Cubs a bona-fide ace for the first time since Fergie Jenkins dominated the league in the late 1960s. No less important was Gary Matthews. He set the example and laid down the law in the clubhouse, barring his young teammates from delivering high-fives before the seventh inning.

Still, Cubs fans tried to keep their enthusiasm in check into September, although most found it impossible. Others expected the fall to come, but day after day it did not. No big losing streak marred the final month, no devastating injury sapped the team's momentum, and no tragedy thwarted the Cubs' march to the postseason.

They clinched the division title on September 24 in Pittsburgh, with Sutcliffe on the mound and Cub fans parading around Three Rivers Stadium behind a banner that read 39 YEARS OF SUFFERING IS ENOUGH, a reference to the Cubs' last appearance in the postseason, the 1945 World Series. Leading 4–1 with two outs in the ninth, Jody Davis barked at Sutcliffe, "I want the ball," and Sutcliffe provided it, striking out Joe Orsulak to spark the celebration.

In Chicago, crowds poured out onto Rush Street, and at Wrigley Field a crowd of 1,500 or more stumbled from the bars and started singing, dancing, and climbing on the ticket booths. One writer noted that 60 million Americans had been born since the last time the Cubs played a meaningful game in October.

Now it seemed as if all 60 million were Cub fans, at least for the time being. Most were smacking their lips and already looking forward to the World Series. The Detroit Tigers, who started the season 35–5, seemed a lock to beat the barely .500 Kansas City Royals in the playoffs. Of course, to get there the Cubs would first have to beat the NL West champion, the San Diego Padres. To most Cubs fans, that didn't seem much of a challenge. Compared to the fuzzy Cubs, who had captured the imagination of the nation, the Padres, despite the presence of stars like Steve Garvey, Graig Nettles, young batting champion Tony Gwynn, and reliever Goose Gossage, were boring. They didn't even have an ace like Sutcliffe, who was 16–1 since joining the Cubs, but only six almost interchangeable starters who didn't scare anyone.

From a Chicago perspective, the Padres lacked history, color, and almost everything else. Many Cub partisans agreed with Mike Royko, who wrote, "Because we have fairness, equity, truth and justice and the American way on our side, we're going to slaughter those wimps." Not only that, but the Padres appeared to have peaked early. Over the last two months of the season, they were only one game over .500, while the Cubs were on a roll.

Yet when one took off the Cubbie bear sunglasses, it was possible to see that the Padres, underneath their garish brown uniforms, were a very good team. They'd split with the Cubs during the regular season, outscoring Chicago in the process. With veterans like Garvey, Nettles, and Gossage, all of whom already had a World Series ring, they weren't easily intimidated or rattled.

The five-game series opened in Chicago on October 2. If Cubs fans were concerned at all, it was over the umpires. The regulars were on strike, and the game was manned by arbiters more accustomed to college baseball. The fatalists expected a bad call by a replacement ump to cost the Cubs the pennant.

At dawn, Wrigley Field was unveiled, wrapped in bunting, and from first light fans began arriving, first in a trickle and then in a deluge, anxious for the game to begin. One fan was overheard asking, "Are we dead and this is heaven?" As game time approached, the answer was a resounding "Yes!" as all Chicago appeared to slow and then stop, eyes and ears tuned to Wrigley Field. They had all waited a long time for this, and even those who hadn't, the nouveau fans who had jumped on the WGN bandwagon, pretended like they had and tried to fit in with the Bleacher Bums. Ernie Banks threw out the first pitch and then took a place in the Cub dugout, in the postseason at last.

Rick Sutcliffe, pitching on seven days' rest after a regular season in which he had thrown a career-high 244 innings, took the mound for the Cubs. He started strong, setting down the side in order before Bobby Dernier stepped in to lead off the bottom of the inning against the Padres' Eric Show. Unlike Sutcliffe, who was a power pitcher, Show depended on finesse and control. Normally, Dernier, who hit three regular-season home runs, wasn't much of a power threat, but as he commented later, "This was a June 1 day instead of an October day." It was sunny and warm and a twenty-mile-per-hour breeze was blowing out to center field.

Show's first pitch was a slider, a ball that Dernier let

pass, but his second pitch was a fastball up. Dernier got it up into the wind and the ball took off, landing on Waveland Avenue for a home run. Gary Matthews, in the hole, threw his bat in the air in celebration and almost hit Ryne Sandberg. That would be the only miss the Cubs would have all day. Sandberg struck out, and Matthews followed with a home run of his own.

Like Hank Borowy in 1945, Rick Sutcliffe helped lead the Cubs to the postseason while winning twenty games and pitching in the service of teams in both the American and National Leagues. Sutcliffe went an amazing 16–1 for the Cubs and also won the opening game of the National League Championship Series at Wrigley Field.

Sutcliffe homered in the third, and by the end of the inning the Cubs led 5–0. The Padres made exactly one run at the Cubs, loading the bases in the fourth, but then ex-Cub Carmelo Martinez lofted a short fly to right. Normally, the soft fly would have dropped in for a hit, but on this day the wind pushed it out, and Keith Moreland, running like a truck that had lost its brakes, charged in, dove, and caught the ball.

That was it. The rout was on. After six innings, it was 13–0, and the party that started at dawn was getting a second wind. Frey, thinking ahead, pulled Sutcliffe after seven shutout innings. He had given up only two hits but had thrown a lot of pitches as he struck out eight and walked five.

Cubs fans saw the score and thought destiny, if not dynasty. By the end of game two, they were thinking Detroit.

On another perfect day, although without the wind, Dernier got things started for the second game in a row, this time with a single. Sandberg followed with a routine grounder to third base. Dernier made it to second easily and then, mindful that Steve Garvey, the Padres' first baseman, couldn't throw, just kept going, sliding into third base well ahead of the ball and sending the message that the Cubs did not need home runs to score, a point he underscored a moment later when he crossed the plate on Gary Matthews's groundout.

On the mound for Chicago, Steve Trout was nearly as dominant as Sutcliffe. The sinkerball pitcher gave up only a single run in the fourth and carried a 4–1 lead into the sixth. Once again, the Padres received one chance to take the Cubs down.

With one out, Alan Wiggins walked, bringing up Tony Gwynn. He pulled a chopper down the first-base line. Two innings before, Leon Durham had drawn the applause of the crowd when he stopped Garvey's hot smash, then beat him to the bag. The reception represented quite a turnaround for the slugger. On opening day, Durham had been booed as Cubs fans expressed their displeasure over the benching of Bill Buckner. Since then, however, Durham had won them over, knocking twenty-six home

Cubs fans celebrate their first postseason appearance since the Truman administration.

runs and ninety-six RBIs and playing surprisingly good defense.

Now he got Cub fans cheering once again. Gwynn's ball took a huge bounce and seemed about to go over Durham's head and into right field for at least a double, probably scoring Wiggins, when Durham suddenly went up and up and came down with the ball, then beat Gwynn to the bag. Padres manager Dick Williams later called the play "a big one. . . . We thought the ball was going through." Trout took advantage and escaped the inning. He pitched into the ninth, and Lee Smith slammed the door as the Cubs won, 4–2. One more victory would put them in the World Series.

The Padres seemed done, outscored 17–2 in two games. "If the wind had been blowing out," moaned Eric Show after the game, "we probably would have lost 10–4." After the game, thousands of Cub fans refused to leave Wrigley Field, as if they were already staking out their places for the World Series. Nearly an hour after the game, ushers finally had to herd them out of the park.

As both clubs boarded planes for San Diego for game three the next day, Cub fans knew it was over. As Fred Mitchell wrote in the *Tribune*, "Barring a minor miracle and pending notification of next of kin, the San Diego Padres can be pronounced dead." The national media had the same idea, leading the Padres' Tony Gwynn to note, "It's like we're in the 'National League playoffs, starring the Chicago Cubs, also with the San Diego Padres.'"

On the flight to San Diego, some Cubs felt that way too. Veterans like Bowa and Matthews tried to warn their younger teammates about getting too cocky, but it was hard not to. Even the front office had gotten into the act and was already squabbling with MLB over the starting time for game five of the World Series against Detroit. The Cubs' lack of lights was beginning to stick in the craw of the TV networks that ruled the postseason, and to ensure that the game would not be called because of darkness, the scheduled start had to be pushed to 1:15 P.M. EST, earlier than the network wanted.

So far the Cubs had taken advantage of every break. In game three, they seemed poised to do so again. In the second inning, Moreland led off with a double, and Ron Cey singled him home to put Chicago ahead, 1–0. San Diego starter Ed Whitson was in obvious trouble.

But Frey let him off the hook. He gave Bowa the bunt sign, but the shortstop popped the ball up to shortstop. Then Eckersley tried to bunt, and he too popped up. When Dernier lined out, Whitson had wiggled free.

Eckersley wasn't so lucky. After scuffling through the first few innings, in the fifth the Padres broke through for three runs and had another rally going in the sixth before Frey, too late, took Eckersley from the game and the Padres rolled to a 7–1 win. Cubs fans were disappointed, but most saw the loss as just a brief delay in the trip to the Series. After all, the Cubs needed to win only one more game, and Sutcliffe would pitch one of those. He was a lock.

That's what Jim Frey thought too. He toyed with the idea of bringing Sutcliffe back on three days' rest in game four, but he wanted the pitcher rested, both in case there was a game five and, if the Cubs won game four, for game one of the World Series. It made sense to hold him back, but by the start of game four, Sutcliffe had had three and a half days' rest, and since game four was a night game and game five was scheduled to be played in the afternoon, there really wasn't that much difference between the two. Saving Sutcliffe forced Frey to turn to Scott Sanderson in game four. Sanderson had been bothered by back trouble for much of the year and had won only two of his last ten starts. The move also pushed game two winner Steve Trout out of the rotation and into the bullpen.

So far the Cubs had kept their own history at bay. Hardly anyone had brought up their legacy of failure since 1908, and even now, those who did so only pointed out the contrast between then and now. As Bernie Lincicome wrote, "The Cubs' perpetual failure has always been an important certainty . . . but now look at what they're threatening to do."

The Padres were pleased to learn that Sutcliffe wouldn't be pitching in game four. He was on a roll and had already beaten the Padres three times in the 1984 season, including game one. Although Sanderson was talented, the Padres knew their ex-teammate and knew that after fighting back trouble for much of the season, he was subpar.

Neither Sanderson nor San Diego starter Tim Lollar was sharp, and neither survived the fifth inning. The Cubs scored three in the fourth on home runs by Davis and Durham, but neither Sanderson nor any other Cub pitcher could stop Steve Garvey.

Reliever Lee Smith enjoyed a banner season in 1984, winning a career season high nine games to go with his thirty-three saves.

Garvey won the game almost single-handedly, collecting hits in his last four at-bats, answering the Cubs at every turn, smacking an RBI double in the third, knocking in a run with a single in the fifth and in the seventh, and then, in the ninth with the score tied, cracking a home run off Lee Smith. San Diego won, 7–5, to tie the series.

Now the burden of history draped itself around Chicago's neck and started the slow squeeze. Anyone who thought the Tribune Company was immune to the Cub experience began to think better of it. Fans who had been ebullient two days before bit their lips and slept fitfully. The only good part was that the Cubs still had Sutcliffe, but many fans were already looking ahead and realizing that even if the Cubs managed to beat the Padres, without Sutcliffe available for three starts, beating the Tigers, who had dumped the Royals in four games, was a dream.

Under a bright sun, and with temperatures that pushed ninety degrees, the Cubs got off to a quick start in game five. With two outs, Matthews walked, and then Durham followed with a home run to put the Cubs ahead, 2–0.

After the Padres went down in the bottom of the inning, Jody Davis homered, and when Sutcliffe singled, San Diego manager Dick Williams didn't hesitate. He pulled Show and put the game in the hands of his bullpen.

They shut down the Cubs, but it didn't seem to matter. After all, Sutcliffe was pitching, and thus far he had been perhaps the greatest midseason pickup in the history of the game, better than Hank Borowy in 1945. He cruised through five innings, giving up only two hits. Out in the bullpen, Steve Trout started asking his teammates if they had extra Series tickets. Trout was a Detroit native. His father, Dizzy, had starred for the Tigers a generation before. In fact, he had pitched in the 1945 World Series, winning game four and losing game six in relief. If the Cubs won, Steve Trout, who had been born in Detroit, was scheduled to pitch, and he'd need every ticket he could get.

Then suddenly, as Mike Royko wrote later, "it was as if some malevolent spirit breathed on us. Sutcliffe sagged before our eyes." Alan Wiggins opened the sixth inning by pushing a bunt down the first-base line to Durham, who played the ball stiffly, allowing Wiggins to beat it out for a bunt single. For the first time in the game, the Padres had the lead runner on, and now Sutcliffe would have to get three outs pitching from the stretch. The heat was also starting to take a toll on him—Chicago hadn't played in really warm weather for over a month. Tony Gwynn, who later said, "It looked like he was starting to get tired," singled to left. With Garvey up, Sutcliffe pitched around him, walking him to load the bases. Sutcliffe then managed to retire Nettles and Terry Kennedy on fly balls, but Wiggins and Gwynn were able to tag up and score. The Padres were within one run of tying the game.

Everybody in the Cub bullpen was available, plus Steve Trout, but Frey stuck with what had gotten him there, hoping Sutcliffe would get a second wind. After all, his right shoulder had carried the club since the middle of June. But in the seventh inning, Sutcliffe clearly wasn't the same pitcher who had won seventeen of eighteen decisions in a Cub uniform. All of a sudden, he couldn't find the plate, walking Carmelo Martinez on four pitches to lead off the inning, but with the eight and nine hitters due up, Frey left Sutcliffe in.

Garry Templeton sacrificed Martinez to third, and then Padres manager Dick Williams pinch-hit Tim Flannery for the pitcher. He rolled a soft ground ball to first base.

Two years before, Dallas Green had tried, and failed, to sign first baseman Steve Garvey. Eventually, that led the Cubs to move Leon Durham to first base and trade Bill Buckner to the Boston Red Sox. Chicago fans cannot help but wonder how the history of all three clubs might have been different had Garvey signed with the Cubs.

Durham, whose glove had saved the Cubs in game one and who, with his first-inning home run, had looked as if he'd be the hero of game five, bent at the waist and dropped his hands to field the ball, just as he had done more than one hundred times during the regular season, making only seven errors on more than one thousand total chances, and just as he had done tens of thousands of times as a young player while learning the game. He had never felt comfortable in the outfield and had been delighted when the Cubs returned him to first base, what he considered his "natural" position.

In baseball, repetition breeds success, and after fielding thousands and thousands of ground balls, a player develops a sixth sense, anticipating the hop, the bounce to the glove that makes the routine ground ball routine. This time, however, the routine ground ball that always took the charity hop into his glove stayed down, hugging the ground. It scooted under Durham's glove and rolled into right field.

All over the country, Cub fans sagged. Durham looked to his glove and then to the ball. Martinez, running to third, kept going. The game was tied.

But that was all—the game was tied. The Padres had a chance, but the game was only tied. Even if Durham had made the catch, Martinez would have been on third, and in position to score on a hit. As it was, the game was tied, Flannery was on first, and Sutcliffe was still one hard ground ball away from a double play and a tie game.

But Sutcliffe couldn't get it. Alan Wiggins hit a soft single to left, and Flannery stopped at second. Sutcliffe was still one pitch away from preserving a tie, and in a perfect world Cub fans prayed that Tony Gwynn would hit a ground ball to Sandberg, Mr. Automatic, and he would turn the double play and the game would stay tied.

They got half their wish. Gwynn hit the ball to Sandberg, but it was a rocket, a hard one-hopper. Sandberg, knowing the Cubs needed a double play and perhaps recalling how Durham had stayed up, expecting the hop, only to have the ball stay down, stayed down, poised for the sharp hop and then the double play. Only this time the ball, instead of staying down and scooting, took a bigger than expected hop, a big bounce over his glove, and then, on the hard pan of Jack Murphy Stadium, shot into the gap, a potential double play turned into a double. Flannery scored and Wiggins scored and Gwynn went to third on the throw home, and the deluge of memories began . . . Don Young dropped the ball in center field and Durocher went to summer camp . . . the billy goat got the boot and Hank Borowy got the ball. Then Garvey—who else?—singled, and it was 6–3, and the Cubs were losing.

That was it. Trout came in, too late, and slammed the door, but the Padres turned to Goose Gossage, who had been there before. He set the Cubs down in the eighth and the ninth. The Padres won, and the Cubs remained the Cubs, more so than ever before.

For an entire season, Cubs fans and the Chicago press

had enjoyed the ride, but after the Cubs went up two games to none, they finally, for the first time, expected more. Now that it was gone, they turned on the team. Bernie Lincicome began his column: "Today's word, boys and girls, is choke. Can you spell it? Will you ever forget it?" It was a cheap shot, but after the Cubs had lost three in a row, an understandable emotion.

Durham got the blame, although Jerome Holtzman noted, "To say he prevented the Cubs from winning the pennant . . . would be neither accurate nor fair." Sutcliffe tried to take the heat, saying, "The key was those four pitches to Martinez," but it didn't stick. It stuck to Durham—not Sutcliffe, not Sandberg, not Frey, and not the Cub hitters, who collected all of two hits over the final seven innings. "We had them by the throat," said Dallas Green, "but we just didn't go for the jugular."

"I've got to let it go," said Durham. "I make that play two hundred times in a row."

Even the Padres, in the midst of celebrating, stopped to mourn the Cubs. "What's it like in Chicago?" asked Goose Gossage rhetorically, then answered by saying, "It's got to be awful depressing. They got to be dying in Chicago today, like finding out the day before Christmas there's no presents."

Actually, it was worse than that. A lot worse. As soon as the last out was made, the bars in Wrigleyville and on Rush Street emptied quickly as fans who had come expecting a celebration found they were in no mood to attend a wake. When the Cubs flew back to Chicago, barely one hundred fans greeted the plane, and the players, as if embarrassed, were allowed to circumvent the terminal. The *Tribune* tried to smooth things over in an editorial that claimed, "They exorcised the ghosts of the past with their excellence. That means next year is all theirs."

It would not be that simple. Winning would prove to be a harsh mistress, and beginning in 1984, each loss would only make the Cubs a little bit harder to love, and the phrase "loser" a little harder to swallow.

DAYS OF GRACE AND DISGRACE

"The Cubs," wrote Chicago sports columnist Bob Verdi before the start of the 1985 season, "simply, yet unbelievably, appear too good to lose."

That was the consensus in Chicago, for even after losing to the Padres the previous year, the Cubs still looked like a contender for the foreseeable future. Jim Frey was named the NL Manager of the Year. Dallas Green won the *Sporting News* Executive of the Year Award. Ryne Sandberg was a near-unanimous selection as National League MVP, and Rick Sutcliffe was the unanimous choice for the NL Cy Young Award. Lee Smith was one of the game's premier relief pitchers. In the second half of the 1984 season, the Cubs' pitching staff had been the best in baseball. With the exception of the shortstop and third base positions, where veterans Larry Bowa and Ron Cey were both nearing retirement age, every starter was either in his prime or, like Sandberg and Durham, a star presumed to be on his way to superstardom. And waiting in the wings was the 1982 number-one draft pick, shortstop Shawon Dunston, a player many considered a lock for Cooperstown.

First baseman Mark Grace won the *Sporting News* Rookie of the Year Award in 1988 while batting .296. In 1989 he boosted his average to .314 and led the team with seventy-nine RBIs.

Then there was general manager Dallas Green. By taking the Cubs to the brink of the World Series, he seemed to answer any lingering questions about his approach. No one complained about "Phillieitis" anymore. Just a few weeks after the World Series, he solved the biggest challenge of the offseason. Rick Sutcliffe was eligible for free agency, but he spurned an $8 million offer from San Diego to re-sign with the Cubs in a five-year deal worth $9 million. Green also consolidated his power. He'd been miffed when Jim Finks was named club president, but as the Cubs surged in 1984 Finks's power had diminished, and he resigned at the end of the season to return to football. Green took over. Now Dallas Green and the Chicago Cubs were as synonymous as the Cubs and Leo Durocher had once been.

Everything appeared to be in place. The Cubs had the players, and after drawing more than two million fans in 1984, Green also had the confidence of the Tribune Company and, even more importantly, a blank check. If the Cubs were not quite a dynasty, they appeared on their way to becoming one. What else could the Cubs possibly need?

But underneath all the optimism, the loss to San Diego had inspired a deep sense of fatalism, and a certain portion of Cubs fans began truly to believe that, no matter what, the Cubs would never, ever, *ever* quite go over the top. Verdi seemed to recognize that too, for in the same column in which he espoused his belief in the Cubs, he also predicted that even though the Cubs would make it to the World Series, in the end Leon Durham would spill Gatorade on Ryne Sandberg's glove, causing the team to lose to the Blue Jays.

Of course, in reality, they weren't close at all. Apart from their tragic history of loss, if there is one characteristic that defines the Chicago Cubs over the past three or four decades, it is the fact that virtually every time they have challenged for a championship, they have lost and in the wake of defeat the Cubs and their fans have overestimated the strength and potential of the club, often disastrously. Not once have they been inspired by defeat to seek improvement. Instead, they have treated each loss as an anomaly. Instead of resolve, such abject disappointment has bred only failure.

It would be no different after 1984. Far from making that year the beginning of a new era, in ten of the next thirteen seasons the Cubs, despite the presence of Hall of Famer Ryne Sandberg on their roster, would finish below .500. They would make a lot of money and garner a lot of attention, but they would not, unfortunately, win a lot of games.

On opening day of 1985, however, the Cubs were still bristling with confidence. "I feel a personal responsibility to finish up the job we started," said Sutcliffe. Many Cubs had shown up for spring training up to three weeks early, and the only problems they encountered were those born of competition. Larry Bowa bristled and then moped when Shawon Dunston was given the starting shortstop job, leading Don Zimmer to call him "the most selfish player I've ever seen." Apart from signing Sutcliffe, the Cubs had been quiet in the offseason, adding only relief pitcher Ray Fontenot and outfielder Brian Dayett from the Yankees. "I think it will be more a matter of execution than anything else," said Green. "Sometimes you just have to hold tight and look at what you've got in your hand." The problem in 1985 would not be with what the Cubs had in hand. It would be that they didn't have enough hands.

Sutcliffe beat Pittsburgh 2–1 on opening day, and the Cubs were off, winning seven of their first eight to surge into first place. The ivy was green and the stands were full in mid-May when the Cubs got their first dose of bad news. Dunston wasn't ready and was sent back to the minor leagues, making Bowa the starting shortstop again. Then Sutcliffe pulled a hamstring. He missed almost three weeks, but the Cubs kept winning, and when Sutcliffe threw a 1–0 shutout against Pittsburgh in his return, all seemed right with the world again.

After beating the Expos for their sixth straight win on June 11, the Cubs, with a record of 35–19, led the second-place Mets by four games and were already four games ahead of their division-winning pace in 1984. With a scoring differential of nearly fifty runs, they were making Bill James proud. On pace to win more than one hundred games, the Cubs seemed immune to a long losing streak. Since Sutcliffe had pitched his first game in a Cub uniform, they were a stellar 95–55.

Then, all of a sudden, it was over. Injuries to Dernier, Matthews, and Davis took effect all at once and suddenly left the Cubs scrambling for runs. Over the next thirteen games, the Cubs were shut out four times, and they would score more than two runs on only four occasions. They lost all thirteen times.

In only two weeks, the combined genius of Jim Frey and Dallas Green evaporated. Green started sniping at Frey for playing for the three-run homer, saying, "That's fine when it works, [but] we have to play situation baseball." For his part, Frey wanted some offense, but Green suddenly discovered that no one was very eager to deal with the Cubs. "They've got us down and they're kicking the hell out of us," he said of other clubs. "They've got the leverage now."

At the same time, the Tribune Company was hoping to use the Cubs' success as a hammer to wield over Wrigleyville and finally convince neighborhood residents to allow the Cubs to install lights. Had they reached the World Series in 1984, MLB had already decided that the Cubs wouldn't have had home-field advantage, solely because of the lighting issue, and in the offseason baseball commissioner Pete Ueberroth had warned the club to resolve the light question, or "baseball would have no alternative but to resolve the situation on its own." The Cubs had filed suit to get permission to put in lights, but in the meantime, as the process dragged through the courts, they tried to convince local officials to give in. That responsibility had been Jim Finks's when he was club president, but now, in the midst of the losing streak, Green had to get involved and try to assuage the concerns of local community groups that opposed lights at Wrigley because of concerns over traffic and noise.

Green wasn't adept at playing politics. The local community, with backing from both the state legislature and city hall, was pushing for temporary lighting to be used only if the Cubs made the postseason, but the Cubs wanted permanent light and a limited schedule of night games. "They want it their way," Green said about the community. "I'm not even sure they even care about winning anymore." As far as Green could tell, the local attitude in regard to the Cubs was: "Don't change anything, don't trade anybody, don't do anything, but stay in Wrigley Field and keep feeding the animals." It was all unraveling way too fast. "The lawyer's got us, the legislature's got us, the neighborhood's got us," bitched Green. "It's a lousy year." It was bad enough that the Cubs were losing, but by insulting their fans, Green revealed that he was also losing control.

Following his selection as *Sporting News* Executive of the Year in 1984, Cubs general manager Dallas Green stopped all the complaints of "Phillicitis" as he appeared poised to lead his team to the promised land of a National League and world championship.

Even after the Cubs ended the losing streak by beating the Mets on June 26, things rapidly went from bad to worse. As soon as the offense got going, the pitching started to falter. Rick Sutcliffe developed a sore shoulder, sat out a few weeks, returned, and eventually went on the disabled list. Doctors traced the trouble to a subtle change in his delivery after he returned to action following the hamstring injury.

On the morning of July 19, the Cubs were 45–42, barely above the water line, six and a half games behind the Cardinals, when, in a letter from Green to season ticket holders, the team announced that if the Cubs made it to the World Series, they wouldn't play *any* games at Wrigley Field "because of the light situation." The club had already

Shawon Dunston was not only the best Cub shortstop since Don Kessinger but also the first everyday player developed by the Cub farm system since Kessinger arrived nearly a generation before. Dunston was at his best in 1989, when he sparked the Cubs' September drive to their second division title.

turned down an offer by the White Sox to use Comiskey Park and instead were said to be considering such far-off sites as St. Louis and Pittsburgh. Green termed the situation "embarrassing."

Huh? Had the Cubs been in first place, that threat would have been taken a bit more seriously. As it was, with the Cubs in fourth place and still falling, Green's threat was met with skepticism, particularly when he started intimating that the Cubs should build a new ballpark with lights somewhere in the suburbs. Combined with the Cubs' performance in the standings, Green's standing was shot. He'd gone from genius to disingenuous in less than a month.

The rest of the season was a disaster as every other member of the starting rotation ended up injured. Steve Trout took the door prize for the best story when he got hurt falling off a bicycle. When he first came to Chicago, Green had made a lot of noise about rebuilding the farm system and appointed another crony from Philadelphia, Gordon Goldsberry, to run the operation. Goldsberry had succeeded, but unfortunately the best prospects were still a few years away and there were no pitchers ready to start in the major leagues. Guys like Steve Engle and Johnny Abrego were rushed to the majors and got hammered. Despite another MVP-quality season from Sandberg, who seemed oblivious to all the turmoil surrounding him and pounded the ball, hitting .305 with twenty-six home runs, the Cubs barely edged out the Phillies for fourth place, finishing 77–84, twenty-three and a half games back.

In the offseason, the Cubs did nothing. Green expected all the injured starting pitchers to bounce back, and at the start of the season, at least in Chicago, the Cubs were expected to fight for the division title with the defending champion Cardinals and the New York Mets. Paced by young fireballer Dwight "Doc" Gooden and slugger Darryl Strawberry, the Mets were on the verge of becoming the deepest and most talented team in baseball. After finishing second to the Cardinals in 1985, in 1986 the Mets were unstoppable.

The Cubs, on the other hand, were eminently stompable. The offense was all right—although Durham seemed to be stagnating as merely a good, but not very good and certainly not great, player—but the pitching was horrible. Sutcliffe, Trout, Eckersley, and Sanderson all threw like

Pitcher Steve "Rainbow" Trout enjoyed his best seasons as a Cub starter in 1984 and 1985, when he went 13–7 and 9–7, respectively. He hurled a gem in the second game of the 1984 playoffs, beating the Padres 4–2 at Wrigley Field.

pitchers coming off arm injuries, giving the Cubs the worst pitching in the league. Closer Lee Smith led the team in victories with nine.

Jim Frey didn't survive the season. On June 12, Green fired both Frey and third base coach Don Zimmer, who'd gone to high school with Frey. Coach John Vukovich filled in for a few days, and Green then hired former Yankee manager Gene Michael to replace Frey. Michael was thrown out of his first game as Cubs manager and made no difference. Without pitching, the Cubs were exposed, and it didn't matter who managed the team.

The most entertaining event that happened in 1986 was that fresh-faced ball girl Marla Collins, who'd become something of a local celebrity, took off her clothes for *Playboy* magazine. When the Cubs found out, she was fired too.

The Cubs were lucky to finish fifth in 1986, thirty-seven games behind the Mets. Even if by some miracle they had won the division in 1986, Chicago wouldn't have seen a playoff game. MLB continued to play hardball with the Cubs over the lighting issue and insisted that if the Cubs made the playoffs, they would have to play in St. Louis.

Chicago clearly needed something in 1987, namely pitching, but in the offseason the Cubs and every other team in baseball secretly and illegally colluded with one another to keep salaries down, agreeing not to pursue free

agents from other teams. That secret strategy made it impossible for the Cubs to go after pitchers, or anyone else, in the free agent market.

Instead, in a bizarre move, a free agent sought out the Cubs. Montreal Expo outfielder Andre Dawson was a free agent. After playing his entire major league career in Montreal, he was desperate to leave. His knees simply couldn't take the constant abuse caused by playing on Montreal's artificial turf, one of the least-forgiving surfaces in baseball. Dawson had once been blessed with a sprinter's speed, but in recent years running had become less and less a part of his game as the once-genuine five-tool player saw one of those precious gifts slip away. It would not be overstating the case to say that the damage to Dawson's knees caused by the turf cost him a chance at the Hall of Fame.

He was still one of the best players in baseball, yet because of the collusion between the owners, no team made a significant bid for any free agent of real ability. The Expos made the only offer for Dawson, $2 million over two

One of the Cubs' best free agent signings came in the wake of the owners' collusion on March 6, 1987, when outfielder Andre Dawson signed a two-year, $2 million contract. He more than earned his paycheck by capturing the 1987 National League MVP Award.

son went to the Cub camp, and while peering at the Cubs through a chain-link fence, held court among sportswriters, telling them how badly he wanted to play for Chicago.

Green was livid—he was simply following orders and didn't like being boxed in. He couldn't reveal why he wasn't interested in Dawson and told the press that the outfielder could "take his dog-and-pony show elsewhere," but he soon realized that he had to make some kind of offer—if he didn't, it would appear even more suspicious than it already was. He did. Dawson accepted, signing a contract for only $500,000 for the 1987 season. Rick Sutcliffe said it "feels like Christmas Eve."

Dawson was a nice prize, but the Cubs still had mostly coal in their stocking. Keith Moreland moved from right field to third base to make room for Dawson, and during spring training the Cubs decided to retool their starting pitching staff. Sutcliffe, healthy again, anchored the staff, but every other spot in the rotation was up for grabs. Steve Trout pitched his way back into the rotation, as did veteran Ed Lynch, who had been acquired by trade in 1986, but the remainder of the staff consisted of two youngsters, second-year man Jamie Moyer and twenty-one-year-old Greg Maddux.

Moyer and Maddux were two of three pitching prospects drafted in 1984 whom the Cubs believed were on the cusp of stardom. Number-one pick Drew Hall was supposed to be the real prize, but he had been slow to develop. Left-handed Jamie Moyer, whom the Cubs had acquired with their sixth pick, was the first to reach the major leagues, winning seven games in the second half of the 1986 season. At the time, Moyer threw hard, and the Cubs expected him to be a big winner.

Hall and Moyer were drafted out of college, whereas Greg Maddux was drafted out of high school in Las Vegas with the Cubs second-round pick in 1984. Standing just five-foot-eleven and weighing only 150 pounds or so, Maddux, unlike Hall, hardly fit the profile of a major league prospect. His fastball didn't touch ninety miles an hour, and given his build, Maddux didn't project well. He wasn't likely ever to become a hard thrower.

What set Maddux apart, however, was his control, pitching acumen, and mechanics. Maddux looked like a pitcher and was able to spot the ball like a much more

seasons. The players sensed what was going on but could do nothing about it at the time.

Dawson, however, decided he wasn't returning to Montreal under any circumstances. He and his agent decided that Chicago would be the perfect place for him. If he was a Cub, he'd get to play on grass, and Wrigley Field would enhance his power. And to be honest, the Cubs needed all the help they could get. Dawson and his agent, Dick Moss, made it clear that they wanted Dawson to come to Chicago, but Green wouldn't bite—his hands were tied by the secret agreement.

In a stroke of brilliance, Moss sent Dawson to Arizona and, in essence, had him stalk Green and the Cubs. Daw-

experienced pitcher. His older brother, Mike, was already pitching professionally, and scouts were intrigued by his bloodline.

He flew through the farm system, not because of his stuff, but because he out-thought hitters at every level. His fastball developed a little life, occasionally reaching ninety miles per hour, and the pitch moved as Maddux learned to cut it and make it sink; he also threw a breaking ball and a changeup. Both he and Hall had been brought up the previous September, and although Maddux had been knocked around a bit, he hadn't been severely overmatched. In the spring of 1987, at age twenty-one, he outpitched Hall to earn a spot on the staff as the fifth starter.

For the first half of the 1987 season, the Cubs were competitive. Dawson thrived in Wrigley Field, Sutcliffe was again one of the best pitchers in the league, Moyer and Maddux were hanging in, and the Cubs featured one of the most potent offenses in baseball, on their way to leading the majors in home runs. But in the second half, the Cubs' young pitchers ran out of steam. Both Moyer and Maddux began to struggle, and each responded by trying to throw harder, which only led to less control and more hits. Unless Sutcliffe or Smith was on the mound, it was a merry-go-round on the bases. Over the course of the season, Green was ordered by Tribune executives to start shedding salaries, and he dealt away players like Gary Matthews. Gene Michael came to the rapid realization that general manager Green, not manager Michael, really ran the club, and the two clashed frequently. Michael resigned on September 8, saying, "I have no respect for Dallas Green."

Increasingly, neither did anyone else. At the end of the season, in which the Cubs finished last in the division, Green charged that the players "quit, with a capital T," but it had been the organization that chose not to pursue free agents, and the organization that chose not to spend money and take on salary in trades. Few were fooled. Andre Dawson had earned every penny of his salary by hitting forty-nine home runs and winning the NL MVP Award, but apart from him, nearly everyone else drawing a salary from the Tribune Company had been disappointing, and that included those in the front office.

When Michael quit, Green had toyed with the idea of taking over as field manager himself, which would have

In the second round of the 1984 amateur draft, the Cubs surprised observers when they selected a boyish 150-pound pitcher who stood a shade under six feet tall. Within two years Greg Maddux was pitching at Wrigley Field, where his combination of control, poise, intelligence, and toughness led him to ninety-five wins in his first six full seasons as a Cub.

Following the 1987 season, third base coach Don Zimmer was promoted to manager and in 1989 led the Cubs to a 93–69 record and their second-ever Eastern Division title. In a little over three seasons as manager, Zimmer led Chicago to a 265–258 record.

29, after meeting with Tribune officials, Green abruptly "resigned," citing "philosophical differences with management," the major difference being that Green himself would no longer be the only voice in management that mattered.

Like Leo Durocher, he had given the organization a much needed jolt when he first arrived, and he nearly took the Cubs to a pennant; in those terms, Green was a success. During his watch, the Cubs made money and, for a time, won games. His mistake had been to believe that he was almost solely responsible for both of those accomplishments, and then, once the Cubs stumbled, not to accept responsibility for their failure. Had Green not taken on so much, or not made himself such a central figure, he might have stayed on, and he might have built a successful organization. But he did not, and one can almost trace the club's demise back to the point at which Green began to increase his power.

Baseball was changing, and by the late 1980s it was impossible for one man to be responsible for a franchise both on and off the field. In a sense, Green was a victim of the changing game. Furthermore, in the end he seemed to forget that the Tribune owned the team and he was just a cog in a much larger corporation. He didn't act like a corporate man, and in the end the corporation simply had no room for someone like him.

Under the direction of Cub chairman John Madigan, the Cubs turned back the clock, in their minds trying to recapture the spirit that had infused the club only a few seasons before. Former manager Jim Frey, who'd been in the broadcast booth since being fired as manager, was brought back, this time as general manager. In turn, he hired Don Zimmer as manager, essentially undoing the changes Green had made less than a year and a half before. It was a funny way to do things, but then again, without Green around, the Cubs were essentially being run by committee, and the suits at the Tribune had been listening to Frey snipe at the Cubs for the last year and a half.

Frey's first move as GM was his worst. On December 8, he traded Lee Smith to the Boston Red Sox for two pitchers, Al Nipper and reliever Calvin Schiraldi, who had been shell-shocked ever since the 1986 World Series.

The deal made no sense at all, except to Frey. Very quietly, for Lee Smith saw little reason to talk to the press,

given him every important position in the organization except owner, but when Green's overseers with the Tribune balked at the move, he hired Frank Luchessi, a former manager with the Phillies, to finish the season. As soon as it was over, Green began a protracted process of interviewing candidates to take over the team in 1988, making runs at Bobby Cox, Joe Torre, and the Twins' Tom Kelly. While Green was busy doing that, Tribune executives had time to ponder what they thought the problem was; increasingly, they decided it was Green. On October

Smith had become one of the best and perhaps the most consistent relief pitcher in baseball, setting a league record in 1987 with his fourth consecutive season with thirty or more saves. Smith threw hard and was durable, a rare combination. Pitchers with those skills were at a premium, and although Smith was well paid, his salary wasn't out of line; in addition, the Cubs' payroll, after shedding a host of high salaries over the past year or so, didn't need significant paring.

Frey's problem with Smith was one of style. He simply didn't like Smith's demeanor, whether on the mound or in the clubhouse. When he wasn't pitching, Smith acted as if he didn't care, which was probably part of the reason he was able to succeed at a job that was all highs and lows. Frey preferred take-charge holler guys, and that wasn't Lee Smith. He simply got the job done, but that wasn't enough for Frey. Fans took their cue from management, and the reliever, like almost every Cub not named Ryne Sandberg, received more than his share of boos. Smith asked to be traded.

The Cubs had initially asked Boston for starting pitcher Bruce Hurst, a proven winner, but the Red Sox countered by offering Nipper and Schiraldi, both of whom were coming off terrible seasons. Schiraldi, in particular, had become persona non grata in Boston ever since he helped blow the sixth game of the 1986 World Series. The Red Sox were desperate to move him. The offer was meant to be a starting point for negotiations, and when the Cubs agreed, the Red Sox couldn't believe their good fortune. They'd acquired one of the game's great closers for almost nothing.

The move caused a ripple effect on the Cubs roster. Zimmer planned on trying Schiraldi in the starting rotation, so now the Cubs needed a closer.

To get one, Frey signed Vance Law to play third base, which turned Keith Moreland, who hit twenty-seven home runs in 1987, into trade bait. He was sent to the Padres for Goose Gossage, who'd lost a few miles on his fastball and, as a result, his job in San Diego. On paper, the Cubs had just become worse at two positions, giving up a closer and a home run–hitting third baseman for a third baseman with no power and two pitchers who showed no recent signs of turning their careers around.

The big news in the offseason, however, was a resolution of the lighting question. Back in 1983, the Chicago city council, under pressure from neighborhood groups, had passed an ordinance that effectively prevented the Cubs from playing at night. But in February 1988, under intense pressure from MLB and the Tribune Company and after a survey indicated that a majority of Chicagoans were in favor of lights, the council rescinded the resolution, freeing the Cubs to put in lights and allowing them to play postseason games at night, eight regular-season night games in 1988, and eighteen annually from 1989 to 2002.

Although the purists still howled, it was a reasonable compromise to a situation that had become anachronistic. No matter how aesthetically pleasing fans found day baseball, in the free agent era teams were forced to do everything possible to maximize revenue. To do anything else was corporate suicide, and exclusively day baseball was costing the Cubs thousands of fans each year—not to mention ratings points on WGN. The compromise allowed the Cubs to compete while retaining the most distinctive feature of the franchise, and the protracted battle over the issue, in the end, worked to the Cubs' advantage. Through WGN and the publicity over the issue, fans all over the country became intrigued by the notion of day baseball, which was becoming rare elsewhere. Moving eighteen games to the evening made the remaining day games even more distinctive, and after lights were installed, day baseball became an even bigger draw as tourists began to consider a day at Wrigley a standard part of the Chicago experience. It was the best of both worlds.

Still, entering the 1988 season, the Cubs weren't fooling anyone, and no one seriously believed they were a contender. With attendance holding steady at around two million fans regardless of their record, the Cubs were not under any great pressure to win and could embark on a modest youth movement.

Maddux, Moyer, and Hall weren't the only young talent in the Cubs system. Outfielder Rafael Palmeiro and catcher Damon Berryhill were ready for the major leagues, and first baseman Mark Grace and pitchers Jeff Pico and Mike Harkey were not far behind.

Although the Cubs won their first three games of the 1988 season, by the end of April they were hovering around .500 and clearly not in the same class as the New York Mets, which made more changes possible. Over the past few seasons, Leon Durham's career had stalled. As he

aged, he lost many of the skills that had once led the Cubs to view him as a potential superstar. He no longer ran well, his fielding at first base was barely adequate, and his power numbers had slipped. In 1987 he knocked in only sixty-three runs.

The Cubs had tried to trade him in the offseason but found no takers, or at least no one willing to give up anything of value. When Durham got off to a slow start in 1988, the Cubs didn't wait around. On May 1, they brought up Triple A first baseman Mark Grace and handed him the job, announcing that Durham would only play against the occasional left-hander.

Grace was an unlikely candidate to replace one of the most ballyhooed prospects. A fine college player, Grace wasn't drafted until the twenty-fourth round in 1986. Scouts knew he could hit, but Grace didn't overwhelm them with his other skills. He played a solid first base but couldn't run or throw, and he lacked the power that most clubs wanted from the position.

But once Grace reached professional baseball, his hitting ability stood out, and he demonstrated just enough power to make him valuable. A line drive hitter, he reminded some of the Yankees' Don Mattingly, another low-round pick who simply hit his way to the major leagues.

Grace, who'd been disappointing in spring training, got off to a slow start in Triple A Iowa. He later admitted that he was trying to pull everything and to hit home runs to get the Cubs' attention. Frey went down to take a look, met with Grace, and told him that the Cubs were thinking about bringing him up and that he better start hitting. Grace immediately went on a tear, making the decision easy. He made his debut on May 2.

Two weeks later, the Cubs sent Durham to the Cincinnati Reds for a journeyman pitcher, Pat Perry. Sadly, the Reds soon discovered that at least part of the reason for Durham's slide was drug use. He entered rehab shortly after the trade and missed most of the season before suffering a relapse and leaving the major leagues for good in

After decades of debate and months of neighborhood meetings and protests, the Cubs installed lights at Wrigley Field during the 1988 season.

1989. To his credit, Durham has since recovered and remains in the game as a hitting coach.

Unfortunately, there was no rehabbing the Cubs. Although many of the kids began to fulfill their promise, the Cubs were still barely a .500 ball club, and the only reason they were even that good was Greg Maddux. After going 6–14 in 1987, in the first half of 1988 he was almost unbeatable. It wasn't an accident.

In the offseason, the Cubs sent Maddux to winter ball in Venezuela. While there, coach Dick Pole remade Maddux by insisting that he throw thirty changeups in every game he pitched, regardless of the score or situation. This forced Maddux both to develop a feel for the pitch and to realize the importance of changing speeds. To this point, his control and the movement on his fastball had allowed him to succeed in the minors, but major league hitters found the pitch hittable, particularly the second or third time they faced him. But once Maddux had the faith in his changeup to throw it in any count, hitters couldn't sit on the fastball, and Maddux began changing speed on that as well. He shut out the Braves in his first start of the season, and through June he was almost perfect, going a stellar 14–3.

He was also exhausted. Zimmer leaned on Maddux hard, using him to give the bullpen a breather. In one game, he threw more than 160 pitches, and by midseason he was on pace to pitch nearly three hundred innings, milestones that most teams were beginning to realize were damaging to young pitchers. Maddux faded in the second half, winning only three games but, perhaps more significantly in the long run, forcing Zimmer to cut back on his workload, a move that may have saved his career. The Cubs, who at one point hauled themselves to seven games over .500, also faded.

As they did, the media turned its attention to the impending end of day-only baseball at Wrigley Field. The Cubs began installing lights in April, and by midseason they were ready. On July 25, they celebrated the lights installation with a $100-a-head charity affair featuring Ernie Banks and Billy Williams that also gave the team a chance to test the lights and make any needed adjustments.

The first night contest was scheduled for August 8 against Philadelphia, and the meaningless game between two clubs going nowhere was hyped out of all proportion. Nearly six hundred media credentials were issued, the

THE LIGHTS
THEY FINALLY LET BE

Although Phil Wrigley once had light stanchions stored under the grandstand, ready to be installed, by 1988 they were long gone, donated to the military during World War II. When the Cubs received permission to light Wrigley Field in 1988, they started from scratch.

The Osborn Engineering Company of Cleveland, Ohio, a firm that had built or renovated a number of ballparks, was hired to design the lighting plan. It posed a significant challenge, not only because the Cubs needed to remain sensitive to neighborhood concerns as well as ballpark aesthetics, but also because the location of the park in an urban environment made it impossible to install light towers outside the park. After considering at least two dozen different schemes, and at a cost of more than $5 million, the club agreed to a plan that called for three banks of lights installed atop the grandstand on each side of the field, with auxiliary lighting used elsewhere for concessions and the grandstand, allowing the field lighting to focus almost entirely on the field of play.

The lighting banks, while sufficient to light the field, do not overwhelm the ballpark—the towers themselves are only thirty-three feet high, in scale with both the neighborhood and the existing grandstand. Furthermore, apart from the auxiliary lights used to illuminate the scoreboard and other public spaces, no lights were installed in the outfield, so that fans in the grandstand can look toward the outfield without looking directly into lights. Thus, what is essentially the same view that has greeted fans for generations was preserved.

The towers were preassembled and lifted into place by helicopter in April and June 1988. Osborn used a computer program to pre-aim the floodlights to ensure that the field was lit evenly, and each of the 540 1,500-watt floodlights, which measure 23 inches across, can be aimed individually. Each spot on the field is lit by at least two sides. More than 33 miles of cable and conduit were used in the installation, and at the time of installation the electrical costs for each game were approximately $1,000. Each lamp has a life of 3,000 hours and is expected to last nearly 30 years. During which time, those same lights might possibly illuminate a championship.

At 6:09 P.M. on August 8, 1988, ninety-one-year-old Harry Grossman, who attended his first Cubs game in 1906, proclaimed, "One-two-three, let there be light," and thus ended the Cubs' string of 6,852 consecutive home day games.

most in baseball history at the time. A crowd of more than forty thousand—what one newspaper called "essentially a celebrity audience" made up of those more concerned with being seen than seeing baseball—turned out to witness ersatz history, and thousands more roamed the streets outside figuring they could see the lights come on just as well from there. As Mike Royko later wrote, "It was a historic evening I won't soon forget. Although I'll do my damnedest to try."

The honor of turning on the lights went to ninety-one-year-old Cub fan Harry Grossman. He called out, "Let there be light," and then, with the assistance of Jack Brickhouse, led a three-count before flipping the switch.

The crowd roared and oohed and aahed, although in reality it was still light outside, and Wrigley Field with lights looked like . . . Wrigley Field with lights. No matter. Then the Chicago Symphony Orchestra broke into song— "Also sprach Zarathustra"—before both Billy Williams and Ernie Banks threw out the "first pitch," and the ceremonies concluded with the national anthem, sung by PA announcer Wayne Messmer. Rick Sutcliffe took the mound for the Cubs, and with the crowd cheering as if it were the World Series, he fired the first pitch at 7:01 P.M. Wrigley Field was never brighter, for as Sutcliffe let go of the ball,

thousands snapped photographs and light bulbs flashed from every corner. After 6,852 home day games, the Cubs were now able to play after dark.

The spell was broken on pitch number four, which Philadelphia outfielder Phil Bradley slammed out of the park to left field. The blast hushed the crowd, and from that moment on, apart from a brief appearance by Morganna—the "Kissing Bandit," who was thwarted in her attempt to embrace Ryne Sandberg—it was just another baseball game.

Except that, officially, it never happened. In the third inning, lightning was seen and thunder was heard, then rain began spitting down, sending many of the forty thousand fans either home or to huddle beneath the stands as the game continued. In the fourth inning, the heavens opened up, and after a delay of more than two hours, the game was canceled. None of it counted, giving those who opposed the lights one last day to preen. Comedian Bill Murray had the line of the day when he quipped that he thought it was "a wrath of God type of thing. I thought we were all going to be electrocuted for coming to a night game at Wrigley Field."

One day later, they tried again, this time versus the New York Mets. Mike Bielicki threw out the first pitch to the Mets' Lenny Dykstra, who made the first out on a fly ball. It was just another game, somewhat more festive than normal, but apart from the nighthawks fluttering around the lights, not very different from the nearly seven thousand games that had come before. The Cubs beat the Mets, 6–4, then over the next six weeks finished out the season, ending in fourth place, 77–85. Maddux finished with only eighteen wins but with his right arm intact, and Mark Grace hit .296 in his rookie season. Jamie Moyer suffered a severe sophomore slump, neither Calvin Schiraldi nor Al Nipper helped out much, and Rich Gossage was a bust in the bullpen. Former Cub Lee Smith, on the other hand, saved twenty-nine games and helped the Red Sox win a division title.

The Cubs' bullpen—or lack thereof—was the talk of the offseason. The Cubs needed help—badly—and most teams they talked trade with realized that and held out for a dear price.

The Cubs knew what they wanted—a guy like Lee Smith, who threw hard. To get him, they were willing to give up Shawon Dunston. Although Dunston was only twenty-five, it seemed clear that he was never quite going to be the superstar the Cubs had hoped. He was erratic in the field, and although he hit with some power, he struck out too much, never walked, and didn't hit for a high average. There were a lot of players like that in the major leagues, and the Cubs hoped to find a team that still believed in Dunston's potential.

They didn't, so they had to pare back their search for a premier closer to guys who found their existing closer lacking and thereby expendable. Texas Ranger pitcher Mitch Williams was just such a player.

The left-handed Williams threw hard, of that there was no doubt, slinging the ball violently toward home, then almost falling over from the effort, before regaining his balance by turning around almost a full 180 degrees. Left-handers found him nearly impossible to hit, but then again, batters didn't always need to hit Williams to get to him, for the young pitcher had a hard time finding the plate. In sixty-eight innings in 1988, Williams had struck out sixty-one, but he also walked forty-seven—the kind of performance that had threatened to give youthful Texas manager Bobby Valentine prematurely gray hair. Williams seemed to live on the line between success and utter disaster, with one foot in the Hall of Fame and the other in agate type: he was as likely to walk the bases loaded as he was to strike out the side, something he occasionally did in the same inning. When Williams notched a save, he *earned* it, for he usually put the game on the line before wiggling free.

The Cubs, blinded by Williams's ninety-five-mile-per-hour fastball, fell in love with his potential. They thought they could do what the Rangers couldn't—teach Williams to throw strikes.

The Rangers were willing to deal, but they wanted something in return. The two clubs spent several days dickering, adding more players into the mix, until finally they agreed to a nine-player swap: the Cubs received Williams, pitcher Paul Kilgus, infielder Curt Wilkerson, and three minor leaguers while giving up—and giving up on—Drew Hill, Jamie Moyer, and Rafael Palmeiro. Zimmer admitted that, in Williams, the Cubs were receiving a player with "just possibilities." The trade was an enormous gamble, but Zimmer had run out of patience with Moyer, who couldn't win in Wrigley; with Hall, who couldn't get anyone out in the majors; and with Palmeiro, who hit .307 in 1988 and had the sweetest swing seen in Wrigley Field since Billy Williams, but who was, in Zimmer's view, a singles hitter. Zimmer ignored the fact that Palmeiro had cracked forty-one doubles in 1988.

In the long run, it was an awful deal, the kind that often gets cited in lists of worst trades. Eventually, both Moyer and Palmeiro would prove to be star-caliber players, while no one the Cubs received, including Williams, would even be in the major leagues seven years later. But in the short term, for one single season, the trade provided the Cubs with everything they expected, and even more. For in the history of the Cubs, few players have had as dramatic—or as entertaining—an impact as Mitch Williams.

Despite the acquisition of Williams, by spring training the Cubs faced few expectations. Even for the most optimistic fans, modest improvement to a .500 season seemed a stretch.

Nothing took place during the spring to indicate otherwise. The Cubs were a pathetic 9–23 during spring training. Rich Gossage was released, and uber pitching prospect Mike Harkey did not make the team, but Double A center fielder Jerome Walton did, along with a handful of other youngsters such as catchers Rick Wrona and Joe Girardi and outfielder Doug Dascenzo. The Cubs appeared at least a year away from respectability and more than a few years away from first place. With a payroll of only $11 million—a full million dollars less than in 1988 and half of what some clubs were spending—the Cubs seemed committed to rebuilding and to raking in a profit.

On opening day against the Phillies, the Cubs provided a glimpse of how things would be in 1989. Sutcliffe started the game, and in the second inning both Joe Girardi and Jerome Walton showed what could happen when a club depended on rookies, as both made errors. Sutcliffe escaped the jam without giving up any runs, and in the third inning Girardi and Walton both singled to help the Cubs score their first run. Chicago went on to take a 5–3

lead into the eighth inning before Mike Schmidt made it a one-run game with a leadoff home run off Calvin Schiraldi. Zimmer had Mitch Williams start throwing, and one batter later he entered the game with the bases empty and one out.

For Williams, few situations were more dangerous than having the bases empty. After a fly-out, he proceeded to walk Dickie Thon, balk him to second base, and then walk Rickey Jordan. As forty thousand Cubs fans sat on the edge of their seats, Williams, surrounded by Phillies, could finally relax and he retired Steve Lake on a fly ball.

One inning later, he walked to the mound to start the ninth inning, needing only three outs to secure a Cubs win, and again, of course, the bases were empty. Three singles later, Cubs fans were screaming themselves hoarse as

---

In December 1988 the Cubs acquired hard-throwing reliever Mitch "Wild Thing" Williams in a nine-player deal that sent soon-to-be slugger Rafael Palmeiro to the Texas Rangers. Williams was a major contributor to the Cubs' 1989 division title, saving thirty-six games.

First baseman Mark Grace tips his hat to the crowd.

Mike Schmidt, in his final season but still dangerous, stepped to the plate. Williams, who, Mark Grace once said, "pitches like his hair's on fire," was his frenetic best and struck out Schmidt, fooling the slugger by throwing the final pitch straight down the middle.

Sufficiently relaxed, Williams then proceeded to do the same to Chris James and Mark Ryal, somehow saving the game and not giving up a run despite allowing three hits, two walks, and a balk in only one and two-thirds innings.

Afterwards, Williams was the talk of the game. "If I've seen it once I've seen it thirty times," pitcher Paul Kilgus, Williams's teammate in Texas, told reporters. "I'm telling you, it's amazing. If you just put three guys out there [on the bases] where there's no place to put 'em, he'll get the guys out."

Over the next few weeks, Williams and the Cubs proceeded to do just that as they opened the season 8–2. Those first games weren't always works of art, but they were victories.

At the time a movie entitled *Major League* was in theaters. The character of Rick Vaughn, played by actor Charlie Sheen, was a wild-looking, Mohawk-wearing, wild-throwing pitcher who entered every game accompanied by the Troggs' old hit "Wild Thing" and who earned the same nickname. A reporter asked Williams, who had just seen the movie, whether he'd like to hear the song when he took the mound, and Williams was smart enough to say, "That would be great!" The Cubs' organist took note, and Williams soon had not only a theme song but, in the life-imitating-art department, a new nickname. "Wild Thing" he was.

Williams set the tone, and the Cubs' season played out like an extended version of one of Williams's relief appearances as the club surged and slumped and teetered but refused to fall, with every winning streak followed by a losing streak, inexplicably followed by a winning streak. Fans were simultaneously afraid to watch and even more afraid not to as the Cubs lost games they should have won and won games they should have lost. Every player Zimmer put into the lineup seemed to surprise: Girardi hit over .300, while Damon Berryhill was hurt. Jerome Walton hit far better than expected, and after being recalled in April, rookie outfielder Dwight Smith started playing almost as well as Walton, who would later be named Rookie of the Year. Williams continued his successful stroll upon the tightrope, and with Maddux, Sutcliffe, and Mike Bielicki anchoring the rotation, Cubs starting pitching was far better than anyone had hoped, while Sandberg and Grace keyed an energetic, opportunistic offense built around speed. The Cubs were young, perhaps too dumb to know they were playing as well as they were, and obviously having fun. So were Cub fans. Wrigley Field hadn't been so exciting since 1969.

On July 4, their record was 42–38. After losing eight of the next ten, the Cubs seemed poised for the obligatory swoon, yet they surprised everyone by hanging in. They ended July by winning six of seven to pull to within two games of the first-place Expos, pulled into a tie for first on August 5, then, oblivious to pressure, dumped the Expos in three straight games a few days later to take over first place, one of the most unlikely first-place teams since the 1969 New York Mets. One day later, however, they showed their schizophrenic nature by blowing a seven-run lead before losing to the Phillies, 16–13. Meanwhile, Jerome Walton was in the midst of a thirty-game hitting streak, and Damon Berryhill was lost for the season with a rotator cuff injury. Every day, it seemed, the Cubs faced another crisis, and every day they somehow pulled through, coming up with one late-inning rally after another.

As September approached, the situation screamed for a trade. Eons-old baseball logic said that the Cubs needed a veteran presence down the stretch, particularly another starting pitcher, or perhaps a third baseman or veteran catcher. Frey, unsure how the Cubs were winning and afraid to mess it up, did virtually nothing. Watching the Cubs play down the stretch was like watching a baby crawl out on a ledge.

On August 29, the Cubs played the game of the year. After falling behind to the Houston Astros 9–0, Zimmer began to empty his bench, taking Andre Dawson from the game and, as he later admitted, almost removing Sandberg; he left Sandberg in only because he was afraid "that will look like quitting." In the sixth inning, with two outs and Mark Grace on base thinking about where he would go after the game, the Cubs were ready to step off the ledge.

Shawon Dunston then hit a chopper to Houston pitcher Mark Portugal for what should have been the final out, but Portugal threw the ball away and Mark Grace scored, ruining Portugal's shutout and changing everything as the baby started doing back flips. Of the next twenty-eight men the Cubs sent to the plate, nineteen reached base on thirteen hits, four walks, and a hit batsman, the last being Dwight Smith, whose tenth-inning single ended the game and gave the Cubs a most improbable 10–9 win.

That sealed it. Now not only did the Cubs believe, but so did their fans and, more importantly, the rest of the NL East. The next day Frey finally made a deal, sending Schiraldi to the Padres for outfielder Marvell Wynne and infielder Luis Salazar. Salazar immediately took over at third base and for the next month played the best baseball of his career, hitting .325.

The division title was theirs. In September, despite a few stumbles, neither the Mets nor the Cardinals were able to mount a serious charge, and the Cubs won the division with ninety-three wins, six games better than the Mets. The press took note of the Cubs' small payroll, and Chicago entered the postseason as the sentimental favorite.

The World Series, however, was still in the distance. In the playoffs, they faced the San Francisco Giants, whom the Cubs seemed to match up well with. The Giants lacked a bona-fide ace—their number-one starter was former Cub Rick Reuschel, who was enjoying a renaissance at age forty. On offense they were top-heavy, led by first baseman Will Clark, who hit .333 with 111 RBIs, and outfielder Kevin Mitchell, who knocked 47 home runs. No other Giant had more than 50 RBIs.

Greg Maddux had a chance to win his twentieth game on the final day of the season, but he told Zimmer to hold him back for the series opener. The Giants, meanwhile, had been pressed to the end and picked Scott Garrelts, a native of Buckley, Illinois, and admitted Cub fan, to start the first game in Chicago.

Maddux took the mound on a cold and blustery night. Giants center fielder Brett Butler led off with an opposite-field single, was sacrificed to second, and then went to third when a pitch got past catcher Rick Wrona. Will Clark stepped up and, true to form, spanked a double to put the Giants ahead. Mitchell followed with a single, and then rookie Matt Williams drove in both sluggers with another hit. The Cubs trailed 3–0, and late arrivals hadn't even found their seats.

The Cubs bounced back with two runs of their own in the bottom of the inning as Sandberg singled and Grace got one into the wind for a home run, but Maddux didn't have it. The Cubs trailed 4–3 in the fourth when the Giants put the game away on Clark's grand slam. San Francisco rolled to an 11–3 win behind Clark's six RBIs. When a reporter asked Zimmer about Clark's big night, the manager responded, "I'd say he had a hell of a week." Now the Cubs needed a hell of a week if they were to survive the Giants.

All year long the Cubs' great strength had been their youth and inexperience, which had allowed them to bounce back after losses that a more experienced team

THE JOKE GOES ON
FOREVER

BY JOHN SCHULIAN

If you subscribe to the theory that comedy is born of pain, it's no wonder you've embraced the Cubs as you might the Three Stooges. Year in, year out, the feckless wonders of Wrigley Field break your heart by hitting you in the face with baseball's equivalent of a cream pie, and still you come back for more. I can only assume it's because you find rampant hilarity in the life lessons the Cubs teach every time they obliterate their chances for glory with a pratfall. And don't even think about shifting the blame for their enduring status as a punch line onto a bar owner's goat or the unfortunate Steve Bartman. The Cubs are a joke of their own making.

Even Sammy Sosa became a source of as much amusement as adulation when Wrigley's bleacher dwellers had to remind him how many outs there were; Sammy, it seems, was preoccupied thanking God and his pharmacist for the muscles he needed to hit all those home runs. Though he ultimately departed in scorn, Sosa may have been the perfect hero for a franchise that once had a hot dog salesman for a general manager and employed one outfielder who lost a ground ball in his cap and another who missed a game because his eyelid was stuck. It is not, after all, excellence that is the Cubs' hallmark. Excellence calls to mind Ernie Banks and Ryne Sandberg, and what were they but aberrations in a history as warped as a reflection in a funhouse mirror?

The true measure of the Cubs was Roy Smalley Sr. heaving the ball from shortstop and splintering the box seats behind first base. The aptly named Boots Merullo did no better when he was out there. They are members of a most peculiar society, Smalley and Boots, one filled with names the mere mention of which conjures up decades of Cub ineptitude: Bob Ramazzotti, Bill Serena, Doyle Lade, Toby Atwell, Eddie Miksis (as in "Fix Us," which he didn't). I think of them now, and of how many others have been part of the joke, and I pat myself on the back for not mentioning Brock for Broglio—but there, I've done it. And I have no regrets. I feel the way those tragic urchins outside Wrigley must have years ago when they made more than a fashion statement by wearing T-shirts that said, CUB FEVER—CATCH IT . . . AND DIE!

None but a blockhead would argue that the Cubs are more an improv troupe than a baseball team, and yet it can take a while to wrap your head around the truth. In my case, the truth really didn't hit me until the day a best-forgotten Cubs manager named Herman Franks wanted to hit me.

This was in 1978, the second of my seven years as a newspaper sports columnist in Chicago, and the flashpoint for the contretemps was Jose Cardenal, he of the stuck eyelid. My lasting image of Jose involves a cap sitting atop his billowing hairdo like a VW Bug on the deck of an

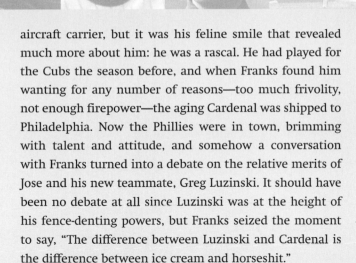

aircraft carrier, but it was his feline smile that revealed much more about him: he was a rascal. He had played for the Cubs the season before, and when Franks found him wanting for any number of reasons—too much frivolity, not enough firepower—the aging Cardenal was shipped to Philadelphia. Now the Phillies were in town, brimming with talent and attitude, and somehow a conversation with Franks turned into a debate on the relative merits of Jose and his new teammate, Greg Luzinski. It should have been no debate at all since Luzinski was at the height of his fence-denting powers, but Franks seized the moment to say, "The difference between Luzinski and Cardenal is the difference between ice cream and horseshit."

I knew a good quote when I heard one, even if I had to sanitize it for the children and the easily offended in my readership. And then, imagining myself to be devilishly clever, I harked back to the quote at the end of my column, paraphrasing it to say that the same difference separated Cardenal and Franks.

The next time I visited Wrigley, as I stood beside the batting cage watching the Cubs hit, Franks waddled up, a scowl darkening his doughy countenance. "So," he said, "you think I'm horseshit."

"You must have read the paper," I told him.

"Smart son of a bitch," he said. "Let's go under the grandstand."

That was when I started laughing. What Franks had done, in the vernacular of his generation of baseball red-asses, was challenge me to a fight. I pointed out that not only was he thirty years older than I was, but that we had both graduated from the same high school in Salt Lake City, and that we had both been catchers, and that neither of us had really been much of a hitter. All of which meant I wasn't going to fight him.

My refusal only made him angrier. Or maybe it was my laughter. Whatever, he finally stomped away, bleating profanely. And he never confronted me again, unlike, say, Billy Martin, who would have waited for a chance to sucker-punch me, or Frank Robinson, who was legitimately scary and would have sent me running if indeed I had summoned the courage to get wise with him in print. Franks and I didn't resume speaking until a few years later,

when he was hired for a second try at managing the Cubs. I was as mystified by his return as he appeared to be, and when I prodded him for an explanation, he said, "Hey, why the hell you asking me?" What a funny guy.

And the Cubs are a funny team, the keepers of a joke that has lasted since their last World Series championship, in 1908. But when I first started hearing about them, they seemed possessed of mystery and even, dare I say it, gravitas. My father was working in a Chicago hotel when Gabby Hartnett hit his "Homer in the Gloamin'," and once I was old enough to appreciate such heroics, he passed the story along to me, seasoning it with his memories of ballplayers who removed their tobacco chaws only when they ate, just parked those sodden brown lumps by their plates and popped them right back in as soon as they were finished. That was vivid fare for a kid in Los Angeles, then still years from the Dodgers' arrival and largely dependent on Mutual Radio's *Game of the Day* for its connection to the big leagues. If the Cubs appeared on TV, I don't remember it. Most likely they didn't—so it goes for losers. Their day games at Wrigley made them a radio staple, though, and when I heard about the ivy on the walls, they seemed more magical than ever.

Radio was also how I heard about Hank Sauer, who didn't let the Cubs' last-place finish in 1952 prevent him from becoming the National League's most valuable player. Thirty-seven homers, adoring bleacherites showering him with packages of Beechnut tobacco—no wonder I decided to read his biography. Of course, by the time I discovered there was such a book in the Inglewood, California, library, Sauer wasn't a Cub anymore. But the librarian told me something that rendered his trade inconsequential: he lived just down the street from her. Suddenly I cared more about having a big leaguer in my neighborhood than whether or not that big leaguer was a Cub. Call it my first lesson in perspective.

It was soon forgotten, however, as the Cubs kept luring me back, first with Ernie Banks, a far more compelling star than Sauer, and then with a 1958 team that featured six players with twenty or more homers. Box scores sustained my fascination as I lurched into adolescence, moving from L.A. to Salt Lake and going to six different schools in six

years. Come 1968, however, when I was a grad student at Northwestern, the Cubs were transformed into something vastly more important to me: a refuge. Weary of academe and prime fodder for the military draft, I fled to Wrigley Field and lost myself in the spectacle I found there. Bleacher seats cost a dollar, gamblers bet openly beneath the manually operated scoreboard in center field, drunks tiptoed from left field to right atop the ivy-covered wall, and the public address announcer was a relic from the megaphone era. In a word: nirvana.

It should have been good-bye to all that when the Army caught up with me, but the Army is full of surprises. After a detour to basic training in California, I was shipped to Fort Sheridan, Illinois, which was farther north than Northwestern but still well within range of Wrigley. Getting there was simply a matter of timing. I worked on the weekly post newspaper, and if we put it to bed by 11:00 A.M. on Thursday, I could hustle back to the barracks, change into civilian clothes (nothing, alas, could disguise my military haircut), take a commuter train to Evanston, switch to an El train that stopped at Addison Street, and be in the bleachers before the top of the first was over. That was how I won the war.

Foolish me, I thought the Cubs were going to win something too. It was 1969, and I was there on opening day when Banks hit two home runs and Willie Smith, with a name straight out of witness protection, won the game with a pinch-homer in the eleventh. It happened like that over and over all summer, and I was just as swept away as everybody else who cared about the Cubs and didn't realize that the victory cigars everybody planned on smoking were tricked up to explode.

No need to go into the gory details. I'll just tell you that the next year everybody was back at Wrigley, not as though the Mets hadn't happened—that would have been like saying the Great Chicago Fire hadn't happened—but with the fervent belief that nothing so terrible could befall the Cubs again. And in a way, it didn't. They were such bland also-rans that the only lasting memory I have of that season concerns the last game I went to before the Army discharged me. The crowd was singing "Take Me Out to the Ball Game"—no celebrity warblers back then—and Pat

Pieper, the ancient PA man, accidentally turned on his microphone. Out in the bleachers, I could hear his beautifully tinny voice above everybody else's, a voice that had called out the names of Hack Wilson and Phil Cavarretta and all the other Cubs who had entered into legend without benefit of victory. The old man sounded like Cubs history itself.

Saying so makes me realize that once upon a time I could be as softheaded as anyone about the Cubs. My only consolation is in knowing that Mike Royko, the crustiest newspaper columnist Chicago ever saw, and the best one who ever worked anywhere, could be even worse. You might find that hard to believe if you remember the laughs he got with his annual Cubs quiz, which always asked for the identities of "the Quicksand Kids." (Answer: That was the outfield that featured the fleet but unfortunate Frankie Baumholtz in center between Hank Sauer and Ralph Kiner, both of whom moved as if up to their chins in quicksand.) It was Royko who also believed that the best time to visit Wrigley, at least in the days before wire-to-wire sellouts, was during September, when the Cubs were long out of the pennant race and you could lie down in the bleachers and take a nap.

But one steamy August night in 1984, as he watched a game on the TV in Billy Goat's Tavern, I saw him turn to the woman who would become his second wife and say, "If the Cubs win, we'll dance in the street." There was cause for that kind of behavior then—Ryne Sandberg emerging as a thoroughbred, Rick Sutcliffe looking as though he'd never lose another game—but this was Mike Royko, nobody's fool. He never cared that the owner of the bar put a curse on the Cubs when they refused to let his pet goat attend the 1945 World Series. Nor did Royko appear to pay any attention to the lifting of the curse the very same year the Cubs were making him forget his skepticism. He just did what he felt like doing. So a couple of hours later, on the corner in front of the bar, with newspaper delivery trucks rumbling past and the fire hydrant leaking, he took his future bride by the hand and they whirled and dipped to music only they could hear.

You know what happened not long afterward, of course. That fateful ground ball went through Leon

Durham's legs, and the music stopped. Chicago was in my rearview mirror by then, but I still thought I could hear Royko laughing about how the Cubs had duped him and the entire city. He had a connoisseur's appreciation of a good scam, be it in politics or baseball, and he knew that a wise victim always laughs as hard as whoever snookered him.

The joke with the Cubs is that the story always ends the same way. In the years I was paid to watch this annual lesson in inevitability, it was easy to be enthralled by Bill Buckner's courage as he won a batting title on one leg, and Bruce Sutter's unhittable split-finger fastball, and even weird Dave Kingman's forty-eight-homer dalliance with what he might have been. But I always knew that sooner or later the trap door beneath them was going to open, and they would be gone, gone, gone.

Nothing changed when Chicago's Tribune Company bought the team in 1981, or when the lights finally went on in Wrigley Field seven years later—and nothing will change as long as the Cubs pack the joint, sustain a cable TV network, and sell all manner of trinkets and gimcracks without ever winning a game that means anything. Critics may still complain that a media conglomerate shouldn't own something it's supposed to cover with a wary eye, but nobody seems to pay attention anymore. It's apparently easier to be comfortably numb, to buy into the idea that the Cubs need be nothing more than cute or quaint or droll. Sure, the first general manager hired by the Tribune Company severed the team's ties with Ernie Banks, who was merely the walking personification of the Cubs. But Banks was eventually restored to the payroll, and besides, that was a long time ago. What you should realize, however, is that if the Cubs' owners think that little of the team's greatest hero, they think even less of the paying customers. So it is that when the ticket windows at Wrigley are sold out, there's a legalized, Tribune-owned scalping operation up the street that is still wheeling and dealing.

This may strike you as harsh, but some Cubs fans deserve to be fleeced, absolutely beg for it in fact. And there are some, of course, who don't. In the latter category are the old-timers who wish better things for Derrek Lee and Mark Prior than Mark Grace and Andre Dawson ever

got, and the savvy youngsters who have taken it upon themselves to understand that it isn't the Lou Brock trade that epitomizes the Cubs' status as a laughingstock, it's the Andy Pafko trade.

And then there are the dummies who don't have a clue who Andy Pafko was, or any apparent interest in finding out. (He was, for the record, perhaps the nicest guy who ever wore a Cubs uniform, he played a sweet center field, and he knocked the ball lopsided until he got swapped to the Dodgers in '51 for mystery meat.) The faux fans who clutter Wrigley these days treat the park as if it were no different than their favorite Starbucks or J. Crew, just one more place to make the scene. They put on their Cubs gear, and they cheer for their Cubbies, a diminutive that always makes me want to fwow up, and they tried to run Steve Bartman out of town too. Bartman was the souvenir-seeker who snatched a foul fly ball away from Moises Alou in the 2003 playoffs and got himself blamed for the Cubs' collapse against the Florida Marlins. Of course, everybody else in Wrigley would have done the same thing Bartman did if they'd had the chance. But the phonies pilloried the poor guy while those fans with a sense of perspective shrugged off his gaffe as the latest variation on the joke that is the Cubs.

There's no winning with them, there's just learning to laugh. With that in mind, I offer you a story that could happen today though it comes from 1948, just three years after the Cubs' last World Series appearance. They were having trouble scoring runs, so their manager, Jolly Cholly Grimm, dispatched the team's talent hunters to the hinterlands to find a heavy hitter. His plea produced the following message from a scout: "Spotted a pitcher who stopped a good team cold for nine innings. Only one ball hit out of the infield and that was a foul fly."

"Forget the pitcher," Grimm wired back. "Send the guy who hit the foul."

JOHN SCHULIAN was a sports columnist for two Chicago newspapers, the *Sun-Times* and the *Daily News*. He went on to a career in Hollywood that, among other things, saw him co-create TV's *Xena: Warrior Princess*. He remains a special contributor to *Sports Illustrated*.

might have found devastating. They did so again in game two. It took them all of four pitches to prove it.

After Mike Bielicki retired the Giants in the first inning, Jerome Walton hit Reuschel's first pitch for a single. Zimmer put on the hit-and-run play on the next pitch, and Sandberg tripled to the right-field corner. On Reuschel's third pitch, Dwight Smith lined out, but Mark Grace sent Reuschel's next offering off the wall. Four pitches into the game the Cubs led 2–0.

The rout was on, and Chicago went on to win easily, 9–5, as Mark Grace collected three hits for the second game in a row. Rick Sutcliffe, scheduled to start game three in San Francisco, was ebullient afterwards and reminded writers that the Cubs had survived losing streaks of five, six, and seven games during the regular season, only to find their footing. "This team has been knocked down so many times before," he said. "I've seen the headlines 'Cubs Collapse' or 'Wait Till Next Year.' This was just another situation where we had to bounce back."

They went to San Francisco on a high and started game three by scoring two first-inning runs on four consecutive hits. But the Giants batted around on Sutcliffe in the bottom of the inning to take the lead, 3–2. The game stayed close, and the Cubs led 4–3 leading into the seventh inning. With one out, Brett Butler singled off reliever Paul Assenmacher, and then Assenmacher threw a ball to Robby Thompson before Zimmer decided to make a change. He came out to the mound and waved for reliever Les Lancaster. As Zimmer said later, "I usually remind a pitcher of the count in a situation like that, but I honestly don't remember if I did last night."

He didn't, and neither did catcher Joe Girardi. Lancaster thought the count was 2–0. He threw a ball, and then, with what he thought was a 3–0 count on Thompson, threw the obligatory get-it-over batting practice fastball right down the middle.

Thompson knew the proper count and jumped out of his shoes at the 2–0 fastball, smacking it over the fence for a home run. The Giants now led 5–4.

The Cubs had one more chance. In the top of the eighth, Grace opened the inning with a single, putting the tying run on base. Andre Dawson then followed with a high fly ball to deep left-center. Grace took measure of the ball, retreated to first base, and then took off for second as soon as Mitchell caught it.

The outfielder appeared startled to see Grace tag up, but he recovered and threw a strike to second. Bang. Grace was out, and one inning later so were the Cubs. They may have been able to survive one critical mistake, but two such errors in back-to-back innings was too much even for them.

Lancaster tried to take the blame, saying, "I screwed up, and I won't forget it for a long time." Taking Zimmer off the hook, he added that it was his responsibility to know the count ahead of time. Grace did the same, admitting that he was running on his own.

Down two games to one, you could see it coming. The Cubs were running out of games to bounce back in. In game four, Garrelts outpitched Maddux again, putting the Cubs on the brink, and the Giants pushed them over in game five. The game was tied 1–1 in the eighth when Mike Bielicki, with two outs, walked Candy Maldonado and then Brett Butler. Zimmer came out to the mound and, incredibly, left without taking his pitcher with him. Bielicki then walked Robby Thompson on his 127th pitch of the game.

Now Zimmer called on Williams, who was pretty good when he loaded the bases himself but less so when they were already full when he arrived on the mound. Will Clark, who hit .650 for the series, singled, and the Giants led 3–1.

The Cubs didn't give up, bunching three singles in the ninth to score a run and bringing Ryne Sandberg to the plate with the tying and go-ahead runs on base. But he grounded out to second, and the game, the series, and the season were over. The Cubs had come close again, but still went home while others were left playing. "Today," said Sutcliffe after the game, "[there] are twenty-four to thirty guys in this clubhouse who feel like they're going to throw up."

Just as some had blamed Zimmer after his Red Sox lost the 1978 playoff game to the Yankees, Zimmer had provided plenty of fuel to second-guess his decisions in this playoff series, but the Cubs were such a surprise that few members of the press had the heart to press him afterwards. At the postgame press conference, Zimmer thanked them for their kindness, and they even gave him an ovation as he walked away. That would be the last time the press was that kind to a Cub manager, but then again, in the next few seasons there would be no reason to be kind. Just as the Cubs had faltered after reaching the playoffs in 1984, after the 1989 playoffs the Cubs seemed to exhaust the available supply of good luck, good fortune, and good decisions. They rapidly fell flat.

Just as the organization had stood pat after the 1984 season, they made the same mistake in 1990. Instead of building on success, they sat on it. The whole season was out of focus as the Cubs got off to a slow start and then injuries hit both the outfield and the pitching staff. Jerome Walton and Dwight Smith struggled in their sophomore seasons, Sutcliffe was hurt and missed most of the year, while Mitch Williams battled a bad knee. Mike Harkey showed some promise, winning ten games, but Greg Maddux went 15–15, at one point going thirteen straight starts without a victory. Only Sandberg, Grace, and Dawson performed close to their accustomed standard, and the Cubs were never in the race, finishing a desultory 77–85, tied with the Phillies for fourth place.

To the Tribune Company, that was far less important than another number. The Cubs had drawn almost 2.5 million fans in 1989 and nearly as many in 1990. With the team payroll still only about $14 million, the Tribune had been printing money in Wrigley Field. In 1991 they gave Jim Frey permission to almost double the payroll.

That represented a real change. Ever since free agency had been in effect, the Cubs had played it conservatively, signing hardly anyone of consequence apart from Dawson, who had fallen into their lap. Like the Yankees and the Dodgers, the Cubs, in a top-three market and with the backing of the Tribune, certainly were one of the few teams that had the resources to be a player in the free agent market, but up to this point they never had done so. Now they seemed willing to spend to win.

In the widest sense, Frey had the right idea. The Cubs needed an outfielder—preferably with some power—a starting pitcher, and a reliever. There was some talent available both on the free agent market and in trade: outfielders like Darryl Strawberry and Dwight Evans, for example, were free agents, and Joe Carter was known to be available. It was a buyer's market for pitchers: Zane Smith,

MOST VALUABLE PLAYERS

1935	Gabby Hartnett	C
1945	Phil Cavarretta	1B
1952	Hank Sauer	OF
1958 1959	Ernie Banks	SS
1984	Ryne Sandberg	2B
1987	Andre Dawson	OF
1998	Sammy Sosa	OF

Dave Righetti, Teddy Higuera, Mike Boddiker, Bob Welch, and Tom Browning were all on the market.

Unfortunately, although Frey acquired an outfielder and two pitchers, they fulfilled the Cubs' needs by the dictionary definition only. The best free agents generally prefer to go to a team they feel can win, and the Cubs were not yet one of those teams. Failing to attract the players they really wanted, the Cubs were left to overpay and choose primarily from among the dregs. Toronto outfielder George Bell won the AL MVP Award in 1987 but hadn't approached that standard since, first losing his power and then his batting average, and Cincinnati pitcher Danny Jackson won twenty-three games in 1988 but had suffered from a sore arm ever since. The Cubs were Bell's only suitor, but they gave him a three-year deal worth almost $10 million anyway. They also handed Jackson $10.5 million over four years, and Houston reliever Dave Smith, who was coming off a good year but was

General manager Larry Himes came to the Cubs from the White Sox in 1992 and scored a major coup in trading a slumping George Bell for a budding superstar named Sammy Sosa. Himes also presided over the regrettable departure of free agent Greg Maddux to Atlanta and the sudden retirement of Ryne Sandberg in June 1994.

thirty-six years old, received a two-year deal worth nearly $5 million. The Cubs would have looked great after the signings—if it had been 1987.

For 1991, the outlook wasn't quite so bright unless you were either Jim Frey or a writer for the *Tribune*, which praised the deals out of all proportion. Frey said, "We put ourselves in position to win. This is the strongest team we've had since I've been here"—which after the 1984 and 1989 seasons was the equivalent of saying that he thought the Cubs would make it to the World Series. Going into spring training, most Cubs fans thought the same way. Expectations were huge.

It did not take long for them to be disabused of that notion. Zimmer handed the closer's job to Dave Smith, and on April 7 the Cubs sent Mitch Williams, who'd fallen out of favor, to the Phillies. Every player the Cubs had acquired

for Palmeiro and Moyer was gone, as was any resemblance the 1991 Cubs had to the division-winning 1989 club. Bell and his bloated contract pushed Dwight Smith to the bench, and the Cubs' image went from a bunch of snotty-nosed kids to a bunch of snobby free agents. When the Cubs got off to a sputtering start, the Tribune Company demonstrated that with an increase in budget came increased scrutiny. Shortly after the start of the season, Cub president Don Grenesko, a Tribune executive, told a reporter that according to standard corporate policy, Zimmer would be evaluated at the end of the year. To Zimmer, who'd never worked a day in his life outside of baseball, it sounded like he was being set up to take the fall in the event that the Cubs missed the postseason. He tried to call the Cubs' bluff, asking the team to make a decision by July 1.

They weren't bluffing, and they didn't wait that long. On May 20, with the Cubs' record at 18–19, Grenesko fired Zimmer, saying, "There's too much talent on this team to be a game under .500." Abandoned, Zimmer said he felt like "a piece of garbage in Lake Michigan."

The company was already starting to sweat the big contracts to Bell, Jackson, and Smith. Jackson promptly landed on the disabled list, as did Mike Harkey, and Smith would soon follow. In the meantime, Bell, while hitting the occasional home run, played left field with all the range of the Boston ivy attached to the wall and reminded no one of the player who had once won the MVP Award. Rather than pay big for a name manager, the Cubs promoted Jim Essian from Triple A Iowa to manage the team.

He tried, but it didn't matter: the Cubs finished fourth again, and at the end of the season the Tribune Company, which had promoted Grenesko, decided to start all over one more time. Stanton Cook, retired Tribune Company CEO, was named Cubs chairman, and he began to call the shots. In November, Essian and Frey were fired. Former Dodger Jim Lefebvre became the new manager, and ex-White Sox general manager Larry Himes became GM.

Through it all, Grace, Sandberg, Maddux, and Dawson somehow continued to shine. For a while, those four players were enough to get Cub fans to continue to come to Wrigley Field, no matter what.

Dawson, the senior statesman, was, like Billy Williams, quietly appreciated for his professionalism and grit. Everyone knew his knees were shot, yet Dawson played and played hard regardless of how he felt or where the Cubs sat in the standings, and he maintained order in what otherwise might have been a tumultuous clubhouse. Grace fell comfortably into the role of the workingman's hero, in the tradition of guys like Hank Sauer and Bill Buckner— good but not great players who carried lunch-bucket appeal. He was the Cubs' everyman, the guy who got dirty, the player everybody wanted to have a beer with and, if they picked the right place, often could.

Sandberg, on the other hand, was the poster boy, the pinup, the classic all-American superstar who made girls swoon and made little boys want to be just like him. At the time, he was performing at a level rarely seen in a middle infielder. Although today a middle infielder with power is the norm, Sandberg, one of the first middle infielders to combine fielding prowess, speed, and the ability to hit for a high average with power, was an anomaly at the time.

Then there was Greg Maddux. He was almost easy to overlook because he didn't strike out an enormous number of batters and, on the Cubs, his won-lost record wasn't gaudy, but Maddux's sixty-seven wins over the past four seasons was still the best in the National League. He was a true ace, the kind of pitcher who held a staff together, ate up innings, saved the bullpen, tutored the young, and, in the case of the Cubs, prevented a complete and total free fall. His nickname, "Bulldog," appeared to belie his style, but National League hitters knew the name fit. Maddux simply didn't give in, and when a Cub batter was hit by a pitch, Maddux was always quick to retaliate.

Since 1989, the presence and day-to-day excellence of these four popular players had made it easy for Cub fans to compartmentalize their affection. They fell for Ryno, and Gracie, Bulldog, and the Hawk (Dawson), Wrigley Field and Harry Caray, and ignored the rest of it. No matter what mistakes the Tribune Company and the front office made, it was still possible to cheer their heroes and enjoy the game. Over the next few seasons, however, their patience would be tried.

After spending nearly $25 million and seeing very little return, the Tribune tightened up the purse strings, a corporate decision made without regard to the current situation. Rick Sutcliffe, who had spent too much time on the disabled list over the past two seasons, was allowed to leave as a free agent. Greg Maddux was only a year away from his

first year of free agency. He wanted to remain a Cub, and in the offseason his agent, Scott Boras, began negotiating with the Cubs. They quickly came to a tacit agreement on a five-year deal worth nearly $5 million a season.

As Boras and the Cubs negotiated the finer points of the deal and Maddux and his wife went house-hunting, the Tribune Company grew impatient and suddenly pulled the deal off the table. The company then turned around and signed Maddux to a one-year deal at $4.2 million, leaving the star scratching his head.

Ryne Sandberg was in a similar position. He too was due to become a free agent at the end of the 1992 season and wanted a long-term deal. Like Maddux, he was willing to take a little less to stay in Chicago, and he set a March 1, 1992, deadline to get a deal done. Otherwise, Sandberg was prepared to walk, which to most Cub fans would have been like seeing Wrigley Field sacked and burned.

At the same time, Himes was prepared to start over. He wanted to gut the club and build from within. An early advocate of statistical analysis, Himes was, in a sense, ahead of his time, but he also lacked the personal skills to convince the Tribune Company to allow him control. When he proposed trading Sandberg for prospects, Stanton Cook vetoed the scheme. Instead, Cook began looking to sign up Sandberg long-term.

Himes's plan to trade Sandberg was heresy, but not entirely without merit. Sandberg was thirty-two years old, and ever so slowly his skills were beginning to erode. At the same time, the Cubs farm system was barren; the gains achieved under Dallas Green were gone, and recent drafts had been poor. Trading Sandberg would have helped replenish the system, and to be frank, over the next few seasons not even Ryne Sandberg could have turned the Cubs into a first-place team.

The March 1 deadline passed, but the Cubs and Sandberg remained in deep negotiations. One day later, Sandberg signed the most lucrative contract in the history of baseball, a four-year deal worth nearly $30 million. When the Cubs made Sandberg baseball's first $7 million man, other owners were angered; they thought Cook had needlessly overpaid Sandberg and had helped to escalate salaries everywhere.

Signing Sandberg to such an enormous contract only made sense if Sandberg was to be the centerpiece for a

1985

team that was prepared to surround him with talent. But the Cubs were not that organization. The team was pulling against itself, with Himes headed one way, Cook another, and the players confused in the middle. It was both disgraceful and wasteful as the Cubs cynically took advantage of the fact that Cubs fans, like victims of chronic violence, would put up with just about anything. Over the next few seasons, the Tribune Company would treat Sandberg and, to a lesser extent, Grace as the 1990s equivalent of Banks and Williams—great players kept on board to keep the turnstiles spinning while the organization spun its wheels.

A month later, Himes was able to make a trade for a prospect and acquire a player who would one day, for better and worse, change the direction of the franchise. Like Dallas Green, Himes looked toward his former organization, in this case the White Sox, for help.

Several years before, Himes had traded the White Sox hitting star Harold Baines to the Texas Rangers. One of the players he asked for and received in turn was a young Dominican outfielder named Sammy Sosa. Sosa was incredibly raw but blessed with a set of skills rarely seen. He was fast, had a strong arm, and, if he could ever learn to make consistent contact, showed remarkable power. Himes thought he would be a star.

But in two years with the White Sox, Sosa had been little more than a tease. In 1990 he seemed on the precipice of greatness, for despite hitting only .233, he knocked fifteen home runs with seventy RBIs while stealing thirty-two bases—pretty good production for a twenty-two-year-old. Himes had been booted by the White Sox in 1990, and in 1991 Sosa went backwards. The White Sox returned him to the minor leagues, and in spring training in 1992 Sosa rarely played, platooning in the outfield with former Yankee phenom Dan Pasqua.

The White Sox wanted a veteran hitter, and Himes wanted to dump George Bell and his $3 million salary. When Himes asked for Sosa, the White Sox readily agreed, and they also included pitcher Ken Patterson in the trade.

By the early 1990s the Cubs had returned to their stock role as National League doormats. However, their loyal fan base kept Wrigley Field filled on a regular basis. In the summer of 1993 the fourth-place club failed to attract thirty thousand or more fans to Wrigley Field only three times.

1994

Sosa was still a few years away from contributing, but not even Babe Ruth would have made much of a difference to the Cubs in 1992.

The Cubs buried themselves early, going 7–13 in April to end the season before the leaves came out on the ivy. Greg Maddux, pitching for a contract, epitomized the Cubs' woes. At midseason his ERA hovered just over 2.00 and opponents were hitting barely .200 against him. Nevertheless, his record was only 10–8. Maddux and Boras tried negotiating with the Cubs and, given the way Maddux was pitching, upped their demands. As a negotiating ploy, they were now asking for a five-year deal worth close to $40 million, which would have been the biggest contract in baseball at the time; even Boras, notorious among agents for asking for the moon and then getting it, did not think the figure was realistic. Stanton Cook and the Cubs took offense and balked at the figure, virtually cutting off negotiations. During the All-Star break, Maddux made it clear that time had run out, saying, "I'm going to go ahead and become a free agent at the end of the year. I wouldn't say I'm bitter. I am disappointed."

He wasn't the only one. The Cubs seemed to have adopted fourth place as a permanent address and finished there again, six games under .500. Maddux won twenty games for the first time, with a career-best ERA of 2.18, which was made even more impressive by the fact that he pitched half the time in Wrigley Field. In the offseason, the Yankees and Braves made bids for the pitcher, who tried one last time to approach the Cubs, but they were not interested. He signed with the Braves for $28 million, a devastating loss for the Cubs, for as Maddux would soon demonstrate, he was entering his prime and over the next six seasons would be perhaps the greatest pitcher of his era.

Andre Dawson left as a free agent, and in the offseason all the Cubs did was throw players together and stir the pot. Grace and Sandberg remained, since the presence of both players on the field ensured that the Cubs would make a profit regardless of whatever else happened. The Cubs simply made sure they had seven other players on the field each day. A few were surprising—catcher Rick Wilkins, for example, inexplicably hit thirty home runs—but the Cubs were solidly .500 all year long before a brief late-season surge pulled them a few games above the mark

of mediocrity. Incredibly, however, attendance went up to nearly 2.7 million fans, the highest figure in club history.

There were several reasons for that, including a change in accounting that allowed the Cubs to base attendance figures on tickets sold rather than a turnstile count, but at the same time the club's performance on the field was becoming ever more insignificant to the bottom line. Beginning with the construction of Baltimore's Camden Yards ballpark in 1992, baseball was experiencing a surge of nostalgia. Camden Yards aped the few "classic" ballparks that still remained in use, such as Wrigley Field and Fenway Park. Increasingly, fans from all around the country were making Wrigley Field a destination. The fact that the Cubs were playing there hardly mattered: even meaningless contests were near sellouts. In the summer of 1993, for instance, the Cubs failed to draw more than thirty thousand fans only twice.

At the end of the season, Jim Lefebvre was fired and replaced by Tom Trebelhorn, but few people noticed. The Cubs shed salary in the offseason, and amid some optimism that under baseball's new divisional system—which placed the Cubs in the Central Division and added two teams to the league playoffs—they had a better chance of reaching the postseason, they started the 1994 season by losing their first twelve games at Wrigley Field. In fact, they went nearly eight months between home victories before finally winning on May 4, when they lifted their record to a pathetic 7–18. In the *Sun-Times*, Dave Van Dyck captured the mood perfectly by taking Cubs fans to task and chiding them for their passive acceptance of the status quo: "Lighten up. Lay off this team. You should be proud, not embarrassed of what your loving little Cubbies have done this year. . . . Without your Cubs being the 'worst' something, what would you have to talk about?" He was right. Expectations were lower every year. Many fans had simply given up on winning and were content to sit in a classic park, cheering Ryno and Gracie and drinking Old Style, regardless of the score. It was both comfortable and comforting, for diminished expectations also meant there was virtually no chance of disappointment. For Cub fans, the choice was not between love and loss. They embraced both.

Yet on June 13, 1994, even the most hard-core Cub fan was shaken. Ryne Sandberg, explaining that "I don't feel I am currently performing with the focus or the standards I expect from myself," announced his retirement, saying that he planned to return to his family and their home in Arizona.

For nearly a year, there had been inklings that something was wrong. Sandberg, bothered by injuries, had an off year in 1993, hitting only nine home runs, and in spring training he'd appeared frustrated and even blasted management for failing to get some pitching, a rare expression of emotion from the quiet star. He'd gotten off to a decent start in 1994 but had recently slumped: with only one hit in his last twenty-eight at-bats, his batting average had dropped to .238.

The local press lauded his decision, which appeared selfless. With a labor dispute on the horizon, he appeared not to be driven by money. By retiring, he was walking away from nearly $16 million in guaranteed salary.

Sun-Times columnist Jay Mariotti wrote, "The man is too noble to say it, too quiet, too classy. So let me say it for him: Ryne Sandberg told the troubled game of baseball, the cold business of sports in the '90s, to shove it Monday. He told a bumbling bottom-line conglomerate called Tribune Co. He told a new age of selfish, money-grubbing players. He said goodbye to all the greed and b.s. . . . This is how bad he wanted out of Cubbie Hell." That was the consensus opinion. Former teammate Larry Bowa said that Sandberg was "disgusted with the managers and general managers going through here," and Don Zimmer added that he had to be frustrated when "every six months [he was] playing for a new manager."

The Cubs were completely taken aback. They'd had no inkling of his plans and were thoroughly unprepared.

But as it turned out, there was more to the decision than Sandberg revealed. A short time after he announced his retirement, his wife Cindy filed for divorce. At the time, Sandberg said the divorce had nothing to do with his decision, but several years later *Sports Illustrated*, after reviewing court documents, revealed that the divorce and Sandberg's fears over a custody battle for his two children played a huge role in his decision to retire. For now, however, Sandberg assumed the status of a saint in Chicago, where he was touted as the only living ballplayer not driven by the dollar bill.

An already bad season rapidly got worse. Harry Caray hadn't been well, and ten days after Sandberg's retirement he blacked out and collapsed owing to an irregular heartbeat, the third such episode of the season. This time he was off the air for a month before returning.

He didn't have much to say when he returned to work, because on August 12 baseball went on strike. The players and owners had failed to come to an agreement over a new contract and were choosing to wait each other out.

In what turned out to be their last game of the season, the Cubs' 5–2 loss to the Giants broke their stranglehold on fourth place. They finished last in the five-team Central Division, at 49–64. "Those Cubs," wrote Dave Van Dyck, "they sure know how to pack." As in, pack it in.

Just a few days before, when it became obvious that the strike was inevitable, Larry Himes had lashed out at the ball club he'd help create. He called the Cubs' performance "sick" and "pitiful," particularly at home, where they were only 20–39 for the season. "This sucks for me," he added.

At the time, he could have been speaking for just about everyone who cared about the Cubs.

1995–1998

SAY IT AIN'T SO, SAMMY...

Thirteen years.

That's how long it had been since baseball had experienced a major strike, and that's how many unlucky years the Tribune Company had owned the Cubs. Over those thirteen seasons, the Cubs had undergone a number of changes, but in the end not a great deal had changed on the field.

Cubs fans, however, had changed, or at least enough new members had climbed on the couch that the crowd looked different. Since 1981, over the course of those thirteen seasons—particularly after the playoff losses in both 1984 and 1989—many fans had cut a kind of Faustian bargain with the club. They hadn't sold their souls to win, but they had traded hope of victory for something less. Rooting for the Cubs was like staying married to avoid eating takeout every night. The Cubs were the ultimate comfort food.

When the strike began in 1994, the Cubs were so awful that they were almost *guaranteed* to be better when they

In the four seasons following the strike of 1994, Sammy Sosa helped rekindle Cubs and baseball fans' passion with consecutive seasons of one hundred or more RBIs and a steady increase in home run totals. In 1998 his battle with Mark McGwire for both the National League home run title and the all-time single-season home run record received enormous media play.

returned to action. Of all the teams in major league baseball, none was better inoculated against the effects of the strike than the Cubs. The ball club would suffer financially during the work stoppage, but the Tribune Company could easily absorb the economic loss. While other teams worried that fans might not return when the strike ended—and in Montreal, for example, they did not—in Chicago those fears were groundless. Cub fans willingly accepted ever-increasing doses of pain and agony and hardly blinked.

The Tribune Company clearly realized this. Just as it had used the 1981 strike to retool, it took the same approach in 1994, for even the Tribune Company had come to realize that the Cubs were, to use a term just coming into vogue at the time, "dysfunctional." Stanton Cook was eased to the side, and another Tribune executive, number-two man Jim Dowdle, became the Cubs' caretaker. His first order of business was to find somebody who knew baseball to run the show, and in early September he settled on Andy MacPhail, the executive vice president and general manager of the Twins.

MacPhail was baseball royalty. Grandfather Larry Mac-Phail once owned pieces of both the Dodgers and the Yankees and served as an executive with each, while his father Lee served as GM of the Orioles and the Yankees and as American League president. Both men were in the Hall of Fame, and as soon as he graduated from college, Andy MacPhail used those connections to get a job in baseball and had never done anything else. His first job was with the Cubs. He served initially as business manager for their rookie league team in Bradenton, Florida, then worked in player development before leaving to join the Astros in 1981. In 1985 he had moved on to the Minnesota Twins. In Minnesota, he earned a reputation for being an effective and efficient executive, and the Twins won the World Series in both 1987 and 1991. Now, as Joseph Reeves of the *Tribune* noted, "the Tribune Company was willing to go outside to hire MacPhail because the Cubs have become an embarrassment."

Dowdle named MacPhail president, handed him the office keys, and promised to leave him alone—at least as long as the Cubs continued to serve their corporate purpose. While others would later come to praise Dowdle for his foresight in allowing MacPhail to "cut the cord"

between the Cubs and the Tribune Company, in reality Dowdle was treating the Cubs precisely as what they were in the larger corporation—a nearly trivial, albeit high-profile, component of the rapidly growing company. The Tribune still didn't need the Cubs to win—company stock took a brief 9 percent dip in the weeks leading up to the strike but rapidly recovered. One financial analyst remarked at the time that "the company's fundamentals have rarely been better." One could not say the same about the Cubs.

MacPhail was no revolutionary. He moved conservatively, bringing in his own people. In October, he fired Himes and hired former Cub pitcher Ed Lynch, who had spent several years working in the Padres' front office, as general manager; then Lynch and MacPhail fired Trebelhorn and hired someone Lynch felt as close to as a "brother," Padres manager Jim Riggleman. Riggleman had the distinction of having the worst managerial record in baseball over the past two seasons, making him uniquely qualified to lead the Cubs.

While the local press was happy to see some change taking place, they quickly realized that this was not quite as dramatic a change as when Durocher or Dallas Green came on board. In fact, even the *Tribune* reacted critically. Columnist Bernie Lincicome wrote, "There is sense, there is nonsense, and there is Cubs sense. This is Cubs sense." He criticized the team for hiring a president who'd never been president of anything, a general manager "who never has managed, generally, or specifically, anywhere before," and a "lifetime minor leaguer" who was "the losingest manager in baseball." With the World Series canceled and the strike still in place, apart from the charade of recruiting replacement players to attend spring training, no one in the new regime had a great deal to do in the offseason.

At long last, on April 2, 1995, the strike ended. Over the next few days, as the real players made their way to spring training and the replacements were quickly forgotten, Lynch and MacPhail did what they could to put together a team. As their first order of business, they re-signed Mark Grace, who was making noise about entering the free agent market and who, after Sandberg's retirement, was a player they couldn't afford to lose. They were nominally successful, adding some talent to the club in center fielder Brian McRae, pitcher Jaime Navarro, and infielder Howard Johnson. None were stars, at least not anymore, but McRae and Navarro in particular were far better than most of the other Cubs players.

One player they already had who was beginning to attract attention was Sammy Sosa. He'd become a solid player for the Cubs in 1993, hitting thirty-three home runs to go with thirty-six stolen bases, only the fifth player in baseball history to go "thirty-thirty," and in 1994 he'd emerged as one of the better hitters in the league, batting .300 with twenty-five home runs. He was no longer a skinny kid from the Dominican who had gone to work at age seven shining shoes, but an emerging star who at age twenty-six had just signed his first really lucrative contract, earning $4 million in 1995. Increasingly self-aware and comfortable, Sosa had applied for permanent resident status in the United States as an "athlete of extraordinary ability." He would be a free agent at the end of the year and was savvy enough to say all the right things, telling reporters in spring training that "if you don't have a ring on your finger when you retire, it's not the same. I want to see the Chicago Cubs win a world championship."

That wasn't very likely in 1995, and everyone knew it. Although the Cubs appeared somewhat improved, many fans had never seen the Cubs play without Ryne Sandberg. They opened the season with two straight wins in Cincinnati, then won the home opener in Wrigley on April 28, 4–3, as Sosa cracked a long home run over the center-field TV booth, which caused the camera man to yell at his producer, "It's coming right at me!" Actually, it sailed over his head, the first ball to clear the booth in thirty-two years. One veteran sportswriter thought that only Dave Kingman had ever hit a ball farther at Wrigley Field. Over the next few seasons, Sosa would do so more and more often.

The crowd at Wrigley was a bit tepid, some six thousand fans shy of capacity, and the next day they expressed their displeasure at the strike by spontaneously hurling their magnetic calendars out onto the field, causing a five-minute delay, but they left happy as Sosa cracked another home run and the Cubs opened the season 4–0, their first such start since 1969.

They held to that happy thought through May as Sosa got off to a quick start and the Cubs moved into first place and stayed there until early June before falling back. After making a run at making the playoffs as a wild-card team in late August, they fell back again in early September before

On September 9, 1995, the Cubs named Andy MacPhail as their president and chief executive officer. MacPhail, the son of former American League president Lee MacPhail and the grandson of the legendary Dodger and Yankee executive Larry MacPhail, had come to Chicago after winning two World Series as general manager of the Minnesota Twins.

finishing with a rush, winning eight straight games to draw to within two games of a wild-card berth with only two games left. Unfortunately, they also needed the Colorado Rockies to lose two games. Instead, the Cubs lost while the Rockies won. Still, the Cubs finished 73–71, in third place in the Central Division, their highest finish since 1989. Sosa and Grace were a big part of that decent showing. Sosa, hitting cleanup, went 30–30 again with 36 home runs, 34 stolen bases, and 119 RBIs, and Grace benefited from the protection he received in the lineup, hitting .326. The Cubs appeared to have turned the corner.

They took what appeared to be another huge step on October 1. After a year and a half in Arizona, Ryne Sandberg decided to return to active duty. In July, his divorce from his ex-wife Cindy was finalized, and six weeks later Sandberg married his Phoenix neighbor, Margaret Koehnemann. The couple was at Wrigley Field on the final day of the season, and she turned to her husband and said,

"You're going to go back and play." It wasn't the first time marital issues had played a part in the brief retirement of a baseball superstar. At the end of the 1954 season, Ted Williams had "retired" while getting divorced. As soon as it was finalized in 1955, he "unretired," signing a new contract unencumbered by alimony.

The decision pleased the organization, which welcomed Sandberg's return. Attendance had dropped slightly in 1995 following the strike, and Sandberg was certain to help. The decision also pleased most Cub fans, many of whom worshiped all things Ryne. But it may not have been the best thing for the team, which had been rebuilding for a year and a half and now had to shift gears. Shawon Dunston left as a free agent in the offseason, and Rey Sanchez, who had played second in Sandberg's absence, shifted to shortstop.

The Cubs stalled in 1996. Even though Sandberg returned and hit twenty-five home runs, he showed some rust and hit only .244. After a quick start, the Cubs fell back, stayed nominally in contention thanks to a weak division, and then, with a 62–62 record, on August 20 fell apart. Sammy Sosa, who already had forty home runs and one hundred RBIs with nearly one-quarter of the season remaining, broke his hand when he was struck by a pitch thrown by Mark Hutton. Chicago went 14–24 the rest of the season to land in fourth place with a thud, yet still only twelve games behind the first-place Cardinals. Had Sosa stayed healthy, the Cubs might well have snuck into the playoffs.

That thought may have permeated the front office, because in the offseason the Cubs held to the status quo. They seemed to think either that they were better than they were or that the division wouldn't improve. They lost Jaime Navarro as a free agent and replaced him with Kevin Tapani, lost outfielder Luis Gonzalez to free agency, then signed Shawon Dunston, re-signed Sandberg, and signed pitchers Terry Mulholland and Mel Rojas, who was expected to become the closer. The deals weren't necessarily all bad, but they weren't very dynamic. So far, MacPhail, Lynch, and Riggleman didn't seem to have much of a pulse.

They should have checked the schedule before the start of the 1997 season. Had they done so, they might have noticed that the Cubs would open the season with ten games against the Florida Marlins and the Atlanta Braves. They would face starting pitchers Kevin Brown, Al Leiter, Alex Fernandez, Denny Neagle, Greg Maddux, John Smoltz, and Tom Glavine—seven pitchers who, combined, had won 117 games in 1996.

The Cubs made certain that all seven enjoyed similar success at the start of the 1997 season. By the time the ten games were done, the Cubs were 0–10, and then they promptly lost to Colorado, 10–7. After the game, the *Sun-Times* asked of fans, "Why do they come? Do 12,000 people have no lives, nothing better to identify with than a ruptured sewer main of a baseball team? Cubs' fans have been beaten into such a masochistic pulp for so long, they seem to derive warped enjoyment from the futility, a perverted pride from the nationwide attention of what now is a historic losing streak. Throw the home-run ball back? Try getting a damned clue. You do not have a brain in your skull if you don't boycott this team."

The newspaper ran a poll asking if the Cubs would break the Orioles' 1988 record by starting the season with a twenty-one-game losing streak. Cubs fans, by a slim margin, didn't think they could beat the Orioles either, as 51 percent answered no.

Club president Andy MacPhail was the speaker at a luncheon sponsored by the Broadcast Advertising Club and was surprisingly calm, saying of his club, "You have to let them play. . . . The only judgment call becomes 'How much time do you give them?'" He might as well have been talking about himself, Lynch, and Riggleman. He took questions from the crowd, and when someone referred to the "billy goat curse," a notion growing more popular by the day, Harry Caray, sitting nearby, piped up and said, "Shoot the goat."

They didn't shoot the goat, or beat the Orioles' record, but the Cubs did go until April 20, when they were 0–14, before winning their first game. By then, the season was over. All that was left was six months of carping in the press.

There was plenty to complain about. Mel Rojas was awful, as was just about anyone else who tried to throw a ball from the mound in Wrigley Field while wearing a Cub uniform. Cub hitters weren't much better, and most responded with subpar seasons.

With winning out of the question, players played other

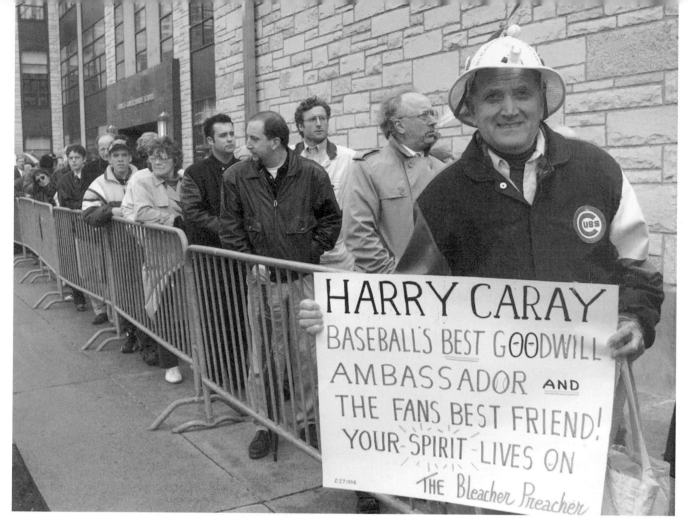

For nearly a generation, broadcaster Harry Caray was the Cubs to millions of fans. His death on February 18, 1998, came just after his retirement and marked the end of an era.

games. Sammy Sosa was about the only Cub doing anything, but even he wasn't performing as expected. He seemed to swing from his heels on every pitch, trying to hit home runs and sometimes succeeding, but as the season progressed Sosa began to resemble Dave Kingman more than Willie Mays. His strikeout rate skyrocketed, his batting average and every other element of his game appeared to plummet, and he sported both a career batting average and on-base percentage well below the league average. Whereas Cub fans cheered every move made by both Sandberg and Grace, Sosa became the target of their boos, the player viewed as emblematic of all that was wrong with the Cubs.

There was intense speculation that the Cubs, going nowhere, would trade Sosa for prospects, since there seemed little sense in trying to forge this team into a contender; Sandberg was likely to retire, and Mark Grace, after hitting .331 in 1996, was entering his midthirties. It was not the three highest-paid players on the team who represented the future of the Cubs, but third baseman Kevin Orie, outfielder Doug Glanville, and nineteen-year-

old minor league pitcher Kerry Wood, who was expected to be the next Roger Clemens.

General manager Ed Lynch, however, thought otherwise. On June 27, just as criticism of Sosa was reaching a crescendo, Lynch stunned everyone by signing Sosa to a four-year contract worth $40 million, making him one of the highest-paid players in the game. Lynch said, "We see a five-tool player who is coming into his prime years who couldn't find the trainer's room." Instead of retooling, he thought the Cubs were just a player or two away from being a contender, something he looked to the free agent market to rectify.

In the long run, the Sosa contract would prove to be a financial bonanza worth every Tribune Company penny, a terrific financial investment. Yet at the same time, given the questions about the use of performance-enhancing drugs that now surround Sosa, Mark McGwire, and other

THE MEANING OF CUBNESS

BY SCOTT TUROW

Several years ago, I was excited to learn that a little organization I belong to in Chicago had snagged Andy MacPhail, the Cubs' president, as a dinner speaker. When I arrived at the event, I was nearly delirious to discover that the luck of the draw had put me next to MacPhail at the table. There had long been something I was burning to ask any Cubs executive I met.

My question concerned my father. He was nearing eighty and in failing health. Since my dad was five or six years old, not a day had passed during a baseball season, save the time he was overseas at war, when he had not made it his business to find out whether the Cubs won or lost. My father was an OB-GYN who routinely worked fourteen hours a day and whose chances of naming any of his children's birth dates was no better than one in three hundred sixty-five. But the Cubs were always on his mind. Just as he had brought me up to be a Cubs fan, so his father had done with him. One of my dad's boyhood friends, Ed Brody, often recounted to me how during the 1930s Ed's dad and my father's father would sit in their respective apartments listening to the Cubs broadcasts on the radios. Between innings, the two immigrants would charge outside and yell at each other over the fence in Yiddish, more often than not lamenting what had just occurred.

So as it is with religion, table manners, and other things imprinted in our early years, my dad just couldn't help himself when it came to the Cubs. He made his daily inquiries about the score even though the years of defeat, especially the smoking rubble of the Ernie Banks era when even a .500 season was a dream, had turned him into a hard-bitten cynic. Now and then during my childhood when I'd ask him to share his information on the Cubs' fortunes that day, he'd respond, "They won. They didn't play." But still he inquired, hope residing side by side with reason.

Which brought me to what I had to ask MacPhail. Given my father's lifelong travail, could it really be that he was destined to pass from the planet without the ultimate reward for which every fan yearns, a World Series victory? Could life, fate, and baseball be so cruel that my dad's loyalty would never be rewarded? Would he actually live and die without the Cubs ever winning it all?

These were the questions with which I was prepared to confront Andy MacPhail. I didn't want to jump on him, of course. I would wait to limn this tale of heartbreak until our acquaintance had been secured with more pleasant conversation. Andy is from a longtime baseball family, and eventually the talk at the table turned to the unique challenges he had experienced when he came to the Cubs.

"I'll tell you what's hard on me," MacPhail said. "It's all these guys calling me up and giving me hell because their parents died without ever seeing the Cubs win the World Series. As if I've been here for the last ninety-five years."

I kept my mouth shut after that. I guess he'd gotten the message.

Not long after, my father sailed into the great beyond and joined that vast parade of Cubs fans who have come and gone without ever seeing a championship, a column headed by Harry Caray. I imagine them all marching through heaven, where they have to be, since they did their time in purgatory here on earth. It occasionally staggers me to consider what's gone on since the last time the Cubs won it all. Haley's comet has passed by twice. Forty Olympics have been held, and sixteen presidents have been elected. The NFL, NBA, and NHL were formed. When the Cubs were last champions of the world, Oklahoma, Arizona, New Mexico, Alaska, and Hawaii weren't even states, and neither radio nor TV had been invented.

Being a Cubs fan is, in my view, a completely different enterprise than rooting for any other team. The role of sports in culture is the subject of complicated anthropological theories. There are Jungian hypotheses that emphasize the totemic names we give our teams—Giants, Bears, Hawks, the same mythic creatures invoked by Native American tribes in legend and personal naming. This view sees sports as an expression of the primordial struggles harbored in the collective unconscious. Other theories hold that sports is a healthier outlet for the same aggressive impulses that lead to war. There's probably something in all of that, but my take is simpler. Generally speaking, sports represents the life that's better than life. Heroes emerge. Victory is complete. It's a version of experience we all yearn to adhere to from time to time, one that allows for total victory or wholesale defeat in a life where, generally speaking, winning and losing is measured on a much grayer scale. Life's other successes can be somewhat ambiguous. You get promoted—over your friend. Your invention's a winner, but now that you have some money, you worry about spoiling your kids. In sports, when your team wins, so do you, and in a way that requires no second thoughts. It's totally elevating—at least until you have to take out the garbage.

Given human nature and the intense identification of fans with their teams, it goes without saying that virtually all supporters go to the stadium to root their team to victory. Yankee fans, for instance, are virtually addicted to the thrill of winning. To me it's like rooting for Microsoft. But the Yanks' supporters never seem to care that it's unfair for one team to win all the time—that it is, in a few words, not really sporting. They want to roll over everybody, and more often than not they do.

Cubs fans, of course, approach baseball from another perspective. For us, sports—at least this sport—is about hope and reason. Reason and experience say that they're going to lose. They have lost, eventually, every year since their "dynasty" period, 1907 and 1908. But still we show up, we watch—and sooner or later we suffer. Being a Cubs fan means growing accustomed to misfortune.

Some Cubs fans claim they are in it for the glories of Wrigley Field, which is not only a spot of antique architectural glory but also these days, for many, the world's largest singles bar. Wrigley's a great place. But it's not the home of winners. While nobody ever wants to mention it, the Chicago Cubs have never, ever won the World Series in Wrigley Field. They moved into the park in April 1914, five seasons already past since their last world title. Wrigley was most aptly characterized by the late folk singer and composer Steve Goodman, another Cubs fan whose life was cut far too short by leukemia. Among the treasures he left behind was "A Dying Cubs Fan's Last Request," including a lyric that goes:

> Do they still play the blues in Chicago
> When baseball season rolls around
> When the snow melts away,
> Do the Cubbies still play
> In their ivy-covered burial ground?

That's Wrigley, a place where hope expires annually, about the same time as the vines on the walls lose their leaves.

There have been so many disappointments, it seems hard to focus on any one of them. Before Boston won the Series in 2004, Red Sox fans used to claim they were worse off than the Cubs followers because their hopes had been raised so often, only to be smashed. I thought this was ridiculous. The Sox fans had seen their team in the Series several times in living memory, even if they'd blown it, most famously when that grounder dribbled through ex-Cub Bill Buckner's legs in 1986. To me, it was like somebody with a nice house in the suburbs complaining because he didn't live in a mansion.

The Cubs, of course, have never gotten even that far during my lifetime, and the bitterness of it all still rots my heart. I think of game five of the 1984 NL Championship Series when the Cubs led 3–2 in the seventh. Their first baseman, Leon Durham, made not one error but two, the second on a grounder that even Bill Buckner would have had. The following winter there was a popular joke in Chicago: "Leon Durham got hit by a bus, but don't worry. It went right through his legs."

Of course, the most recent wound still hurts the worst for me, not simply because of the extraordinary nature of the defeat, but because of the company I was keeping. In October 2003, just as the National League Championship Series started, I was obliged to tour the United States to promote a new book. I was in a New York City hotel room to see the end of game one when Sammy Sosa had probably his greatest moment for the team—as opposed to his many moments of glory for his own sake—when he hit a two-out, two-run homer off the Florida Marlins' Ugueth Urbina in the ninth to send the game into extra innings. The Cubs lost eventually, but that little puff of magic seemed to propel the team to victory in the next three games. Carlos Zambrano did not get the elusive fourth victory that would send the Cubs to their first World Series since 1945, but as a Cubs fan, I was as confident as I have ever been. They were on their way back to Wrigley, where the Marlins would face Mark Prior, then, if necessary, Kerry Wood, the most dynamic duo of arms in baseball that year.

By then, my book tour had taken me to the other side of the country to the Bay Area. I finished my promotional event in time for the first pitch of game six, and it was an extraordinary moment for me, because I was with my son, who was an undergraduate at Stanford. Although Gabe had been the kind of baseball player I had only dreamt of being, he was not a committed fan. But he understood this was important to me, having grown up watching me pass hours in some galaxy far far away as the image of the Cubs on their way to defeat flickered across the TV.

We found a fusty sports bar, ate, drank, and watched the Cubs near the pinnacle they hadn't reached since 1945. My palms and armpits were moist. My heart flew around like a butterfly. Worst of all, the long-dormant six-year-old inside me had awoken from hibernation, the poor child who believed in Santa Claus, Superman, and the Cubs as champs of the world.

Mark Prior, nearly invincible, took the team into the eighth with a 3–1 lead. We all know what happened next. Steve Bartman, with the game blaring in his headphones, reached out anyway for the foul ball that Moises Alou would have caught. Yes, of course, Alex Gonzalez, an acolyte at the altar of Buckner and Durham, muffed a sure double-play ball moments later with the Cubs still leading, an error that in real-world terms was far more costly to the Cubs' hopes for the game and the pennant.

But who could ignore the poetry of Bartman, an ardent member of the Cubs' long-suffering nation, actually opening the door to defeat? Let's face it, the players are rich vagabonds who pitch, catch, and hit for the highest bidder. Ken Reitz, one of the long line of failures who followed Ron Santo to third base for the Cubs, said, "The only bad thing about being released by the Cubs is that they made me keep my season tickets." It's the fans who are eternal. And if even they could not ignore the siren call of perpetual defeat, how could we expect the mere hired guns who embody our hopes on the field to do any better?

In a single, thoughtless gesture, Bartman invited back onto the field the Cubs' century-long history of failure and dim expectations. The Cubs had largely stayed positive all

season, believing they had bettered the goat curse and the dead weight of destiny with the aid of their new manager, Dusty Baker. A proven winner, Dusty seemed to have the juju to overcome whatever it was that ailed the Cubs. And then there was Bartman. Baseball players are intensely superstitious by nature. Players do not step on the baseline when they return to the dugout; no one speaks to a pitcher working on a no-hitter. And at some level it makes sense for them to accept that kind of voodoo. Science has yet to explain the micrometric differences in timing that turn a slump into a hot streak. But that inclination made them uniquely vulnerable to the mess of doom that seemed to tumble from the closet when Bartman stuck out his mitt. Something bad was back in Wrigley. Jim Brosnan, the former Cubs reliever who went on to become a good writer, put it this way about the sad era when he played for the team: "You have to have a dullness of mind and spirit to play here. I went through psychoanalysis and that helped me deal with my Cubness." Bartman brought back Cubness. And that poor six-year-old found the hole in my heart where he'd been hiding and climbed back in.

For my son, I think it was also a seminal moment, the first time the parent-child dynamic had fully revolved and he felt himself in the grip of unbearable sympathy for me. He took me out and bought me a bottle of wine and drank with me while I tried to recover. Looking back, I realize that the worst thing of all had happened. He felt at that moment the same impulse that had led me to want to confront Andy MacPhail. He wanted to protect me. He wanted the boys in blue to win for my sake, just as I wanted them to win for my father. In other words, my son had crossed the Rubicon. He had become a Cubs fan.

After the Cubs were closed out in the seventh game of that series, a close friend called me near tears. "How could I have done this to my children?" he asked about his boys who had been immobilized by devastation. This is a question that has echoed among Cubs fans for generations.

All of this left me pondering the even larger question we all dwell with from time to time. Never mind our children. Why do we do this to ourselves? My wife, a person who is learned and sincere about her faith, thinks I'm engaging in sacrilege when I insist that rooting for the Cubs has the aspect of religious experience. But I still believe it: if rooting for the Cubs isn't an act of belief that casts away doubt in the face of massive countervailing evidence, I don't know what is. One of my friends, who regularly wears a Cubs cap on which the team name is spelled out in Hebrew characters, gives a personal devotion about the Cubs every year at his synagogue during the daylong service on Yom Kippur, the day of atonement. In 2005 his discourse concerned Adam Greenberg, the first Jewish Cub since Jose Bautista, who pitched for them in 1993–94. Greenberg's major league career, at least to date, lasted a single pitch. With his parents in the stands on July 9, 2005, Greenberg was beaned by the first delivery he saw from Valerio de los Santos and spent weeks recovering from the concussion before being returned to the minors. Now there is *glatt* Cubness. This is how God tests our faith. By giving us the Cubs. We atone for our other transgressions on a daily basis from April to October.

Whether religion is a fair comparison or not, there remains a special meaning in being a Cubs fan. It makes sports more profound. It teaches the hardest lesson of all: there is no life that's better than life. Hope dignifies our experience on the planet. But there will be defeat for all of us in the mortuary. With the Cubs, as a writer-friend once said of Hollywood, "You learn to take the bitter with the bad." You accept hope as an essential, irrational part of the human condition that will never be fully borne out.

It's existential.

It's tragic.

It's the Cubs.

SCOTT TUROW is a writer and practicing attorney. He is the author of eight best-selling novels about the law, including *Presumed Innocent* and *Limitations*, and the nonfiction works *One L* and *Ultimate Punishment*.

In 1998 right-hander Kevin Tapani enjoyed a career-best season while helping to lead the Cubs to a playoff berth. Despite a hefty ERA of 4.85, he won nineteen games while losing only nine.

sluggers of the era, it was a terrible mistake, emblematic of nearly everything that was wrong with baseball in the poststrike era, and it casts a shadow over Wrigley Field to this day.

In 1997 the shadow was one created by loss. The Cubs never recovered from their disastrous start. They finished last, with a record of only 68–94, the fourteenth time since 1900 they had finished with a winning percentage of .420 or less. Incredibly, attendance was almost identical to what it had been in 1996. Who needed to win?

Before the season had finished, Lynch was already looking ahead, trading Brian McRae and several others to the Mets for outfielder Lance Johnson and also shedding both Rey Sanchez and Shawon Dunston. As expected, Ryne Sandberg retired at the end of the season, this time for good, leaving another hole in the Chicago lineup.

The Cubs were more active in the offseason than usual, shuffling their way through a half-dozen players, signing free agent shortstop Jeff Blauser, trading for outfielder Henry Rodriguez, swapping Doug Glanville for second baseman Mickey Morandini, and adding reliever Rod Beck.

But much of what the Cubs did in the offseason was overshadowed by the death of Harry Caray at age eighty-three on February 18. Four days earlier, he'd suffered a devastating heart attack while celebrating Valentine's Day with his wife. Over the past few seasons, Caray's health had been precarious, and he no longer went on the road with the team. But even as the quality of his broadcasts deteriorated, most Cubs fans didn't care. Even many of his critics had come to realize that, for better or for worse, listening to Caray made whatever else took place on the field somehow more palatable. There was the real game and there was the game Harry saw, and they weren't always the same anymore, but Harry's version was usually a little easier to take and far more pleasant.

Public reaction to Caray's death demonstrated just how valuable he had been to the Tribune. For many younger fans and for Cubs fans weaned on WGN, Harry Caray was the Cubs. As Dave Van Dyck wrote in the *Tribune*, "Caray lived his life in italic spurts and capitalized exclamations . . . his love of life and his love of the game showed through on his broadcasts: because it was *REAL*." As would soon become clear, not much was anymore.

Nothing happened during the spring to indicate that the 1998 season would be one of the most unforgettable in recent history. The Cubs, despite the presence of new faces like infielder Mickey Morandini and reliever Rod Beck, didn't look all that different from the 1997 team. Particularly short of starting pitching, they had pinned most of their hope on Kevin Tapani and young Steve Trachsel, and most observers thought the Cubs would be lucky to reach .500.

They were tempted to install twenty-year-old Kerry Wood into the rotation. Since being drafted in 1995, he had shown the potential to be a thoroughly dominating pitcher. He had a fastball that pushed one hundred miles per hour and a Star Trek breaking ball that seemed to dematerialize on its way to the plate and then appear about a foot and a half away from its expected path, leaving batters swinging at air. A native of Texas, Wood stood an intimidating six-foot-five and invited natural comparisons to both Roger Clemens and Nolan Ryan.

The only question surrounding Wood was his health. The right-hander threw across his body, putting enormous torque on his arm, and had spent time on the disabled list in 1996. The Cubs were trying to be patient with him, and in a little more than two minor league seasons he had pitched fewer than three hundred innings. Having Wood in the organization and then not using him, however, was like driving a sports car five miles under the speed limit. Sooner or later you had to floor it.

Cub pitchers were among the majors' worst during spring training. Terry Mulholland paced the staff with an 11.35 ERA, as the opposition hit .425 off him, and Tapani, Trachsel, Mark Clark, and Geremi Gonzalez all sported ERAs way over 5.00. Nevertheless, the Cubs sent Wood to Triple A Iowa in late March, Riggleman saying, "He needs some fine-tuning." That seemed fine with Wood. "I'll take a number and wait my turn," he told the press. "If it's not this year, then hopefully it'll be next year. I'm not in any hurry."

The Cubs opened the season in Florida against the defending champion Marlins. They were hardly the same club that won the world championship the year before, as owner Wayne Huizenga had broken the club apart, but nevertheless the Cubs were mildly encouraged when they opened the season winning two of three, then six of seven against the Mets and Expos. Ten games into the season they were 8–2.

Wood made one start for Iowa and pitched like a fifteen-year-old in Little League, giving up one hit and striking out eleven. Terry Mulholland opened the season pitching like he had in spring training, and when reliever Bob Patterson got hurt, the front office decided to take Wood out for his long-awaited joy ride and called him up.

He started his first game on April 12 in Montreal and scuffled, losing 4–1, but he struck out seven in four and a third innings. The Cubs started scuffling too, and by the end of the month they were hanging around .500. So far they were way down on the list of baseball stories in 1998. Cardinal first baseman Mark McGwire, who had hit fifty-eight home runs in 1997, got off to a hot start, hitting eleven home runs in April and renewing talk that he might challenge Roger Maris's home run mark. In the American League, the Yankees got off quick and seemed nearly impossible to beat. The Cubs? Who cared?

That changed on May 6 in the fifth start of Kerry Wood's career, against the Houston Astros. He was domi-

In 1998 the Cubs took a gamble and inserted twenty-year-old Kerry Wood into their pitching rotation. The six-foot-five right-hander brought excellent control and a ninety-nine-mile-per-hour fastball to Wrigley Field.

nant from the start, fanning leadoff hitter Craig Biggio to start the game, then striking out Derek Bell, who was hitting almost .300 at the time. Wood finished the inning by freezing Jeff Bagwell for another strikeout.

The Astros didn't have a chance. They couldn't catch up to his fastball, adjust to his curve, or even believe his slider, which seemed to move in a way no other pitch on the planet could duplicate. In the third inning, Houston shortstop Ricky Gutierrez hit a hard ground ball to third that glanced off Kevin Orie's glove and into the outfield for a hit, the kind of play that had it happened in the eighth inning of a no-hitter would probably have been called an error, but in this situation was scored a hit. It would be the closest the Astros came all day to catching up with Wood.

Entering the fifth inning, the Astros seemed to know they were overmatched. They tried waiting Wood out, hoping he'd lose command, but Wood's control was as good as his stuff, and he struck out the side, all on called strikes. After "resting" in the sixth inning, striking out only one, he fanned the side in both the seventh and the eighth. In the ninth, with the crowd on its feet, Wood struck out Bill Spiers, retired Biggio on a ground ball, then struck out Derek Bell for his twentieth strikeout of the game, which

On May 6, 1998, in the fifth start of his Cub career, Kerry Wood tied a major league record by striking out twenty Houston Astros in nine innings at Wrigley Field. He also became the first pitcher since seventeen-year-old Bob Feller to strike out as many batters as his age.

set a National League record, tied Roger Clemens's major league record, and made Wood the first pitcher since seventeen-year-old Bob Feller to strike out as many batters as his age.

There was nothing to say after the game except to note that in the minds of most observers it was the most dominant pitching performance anyone had ever seen, and that it came against a good club. Wood had thrown 84 of 122 pitches for strikes, and only three balls had reached the outfield—Gutierrez's hit and two routine fly balls. Wood hadn't walked a batter and had hardly come close. Twice his fastball was timed at one hundred miles per hour.

It was a legendary performance, remarkable for any pitcher, made even more so by Wood's age. Now the comparisons to Clemens and other youthful phenoms like Feller and Herb Score appeared warranted. Wood was one of them now, and only the possibility of injury stood between him and the Hall of Fame.

And suddenly the Cubs were a contender, or close to one. Wood gave them precisely what they lacked, a dominant starter, and the Cubs won ten of their next thirteen games to challenge Houston for the division lead.

Most of the headlines, however, were still going to Mark McGwire. On June 1, he had twenty-seven home runs, and baseball was already in full "home run record" mode. For much of the year, Sammy Sosa had been an afterthought as he quietly put together a nice season that was beginning to justify the size of his contract, but he wasn't headline material.

In the last week of May, however, that began to change. On May 25, Sosa smacked two home runs, his tenth and eleventh of the season, and over the next two weeks he hit nine more, bringing his season total to twenty, still nine behind McGwire, but enough to inject his name into the conversation when anyone began discussing a new home run record.

Sosa had always been a streaky hitter, but he had never had a streak like this before. Moreover, Sosa's home runs weren't just sneaking over the fence. He was hitting a fair number of soaring moon shots that cleared *everything*. On June 15 against Milwaukee, Sosa cracked three home runs, all of which traveled well over four hundred feet, the last one clearing the left-field bleachers and bouncing off the

roof of a building on Waveland Avenue, leading Mark Grace to say, "I've seen a lot of his home runs. That's the longest I've ever seen."

Sosa explained the turnaround as the combined result of the extra work he put in with Cubs hitting coach Jeff Pentland and patience. "I just have in my mind to go up there, make contact and go to right field," he said. Fans were becoming familiar with the sight of the ball rocketing off Sosa's bat and Sosa taking a sideways skip and hop down the baseline, then running quickly around the bases and, upon his return to the dugout, pounding his chest, kissing two fingers, and pointing to the camera. It looked contrived at first, but soon became so familiar that fans looked forward to it almost as much as the home run itself.

And the home runs just kept happening. In the month of June, Sosa hit twenty home runs, including twelve over his last thirteen games, to set a home run record for a single month, giving him thirty-three for the season, only four behind McGwire. Several other players, such as Ken Griffey Jr., Andres Gallaraga, Greg Vaughn, and ex-Cub Luis

Cub fans came prepared for Kerry Wood's historic twenty-strikeout game. They are shown marking the occasion in the bleachers with large K signs.

Gonzalez, were also hitting home runs at a prodigious pace, and even hitters not known as power hitters were suddenly in double digits with the season not even half over. And, oh yeah, the Cubs had slumped to 44–39; they were second in the division and second in the wild-card race, but hardly anyone noticed. The home run chase, not the pennant race, seemed to be all that mattered.

From today's perspective, it seems incredible that no one stood back, took a breath, and asked, "What the hell is going on?" But it was as if a gigantic mass hallucination had taken over baseball, a mental dance of veils to try to explain how so many players, all of a sudden, without warning, precedent, or explanation, were suddenly hitting so many home runs, so long, and so often, and making it look about as hard as spitting sunflower seeds into a paper cup.

There were, of course, rumors that something wasn't quite right and hadn't been for quite a while. While observers in many other sports had long known about the effects of steroids and other performance-enhancing drugs and those substances had long been banned in Olympic competition, baseball, with a long-seated prejudice against weight training, had ignored the problem. After all, it wasn't until Carl Yastrzemski of the Boston Red Sox credited weightlifting for his triple crown batting performance in 1967 that any high-profile ballplayer publicly admitted to using weights, and as late as the early 1990s those who did were still in a minority. Team weightlifting facilities were usually limited to a handful of free weights and perhaps a small, self-contained weight machine.

But recently something had changed. Howard Bryant, in his groundbreaking book *Juicing the Game*, traces the change back to the 1994 baseball strike. During the strike, players began working out in gyms en masse and interacting with body builders, and for the first time a number of baseball players began experimenting with steroids and other questionable "supplements," a catchall phrase that included anything that could be bought over the counter without a prescription and wasn't illegal—yet. Many play-

First baseman Mark Grace and catcher Sandy Martinez congratulate Kerry Wood on his twenty-strikeout performance.

1995

ers returned from the strike bigger than ever, some saw the effects on the field, and those effects were then enforced by larger contracts.

From there it spiraled. Ever since Babe Ruth stopped pitching and started hitting home runs, home run hitters have reaped the benefits in fame and fortune. For a team, home run power translates into wins. For the game at large, particularly in the wake of the 1994 players' strike, an increase in offense appeared to lead to an increase in attendance, concessions, souvenir sales, and television ratings. Everybody connected to the game in any capacity, from those on the field to those in the front office, in the press box, in the stands, with the union, on the bookshelves, in front of the computer, or on the couch, benefited. In 1998 the home run hit baseball like a shot of crystal methedrine. Addiction was instantaneous. Put it all together and it was as if a dam had broken and lifted everyone up at once.

At some level, however, everyone knew, or suspected, what was going on. In 1991 baseball's executive counsel, of which Bud Selig was a member, discussed steroids' potential impact on baseball, and when Selig took over as acting commissioner in 1994 he met with owners over the issue, but did nothing. Reporter Pete Williams wrote a frightening story about supplement use entitled "Lifting the Games" in *USA Today's Baseball Weekly* on May 7, 1997, that should have given baseball a reason to pause. Although the story was ignored by baseball, at the same time it alerted anyone not yet on the program that not only was the use of such substances commonplace, but failure to use might put one at a disadvantage. Almost overnight, players had gotten huge. Film of baseball players from only eight or ten years before was jarring. Compared to the contemporary player, yesterday's stars looked like kids in junior high school awaiting the onset of puberty. Actually, it was the contemporary player who was malformed, pumped up on testosterone, steroids, and God knows what else, but apart from the occasional wisecrack, no one wanted to break the spell.

When the issue was addressed at all, it was done so only obliquely. Just before the All-Star Game, Phil Rogers of the *Tribune* offered up the standard reasons put forth by observers for the surge in home runs, "a pitching pool diluted by the addition of four teams in six years, muscle-

ROOKIES OF THE YEAR

1998	Kerry Wood
1989	Jerome Walton
1962	Ken Hubbs
1961	Billy Williams

bound hitters strengthened by weight-lifting and nutritional supplements and warm spring weather brought by El Niño. There is probably some truth in all of them. But before suggesting the favorable conditions diminish the hitters' accomplishments, consider this: The fans don't care."

That was it. And because the fans didn't care, neither did anyone else. The frenzy of home runs led to an increase in attendance and ratings and interest, thereby resulting in an orgy of cash for everyone. Beat writers wouldn't look into the problem because if they did they risked losing their access; independent reporters rarely had the connections needed to investigate the story, and besides, every newspaper, network, and other baseball-oriented media group was making money off the situation. It was easier for everyone to turn their heads and cash their checks.

Everyone was complicit, but some more so than others. No media company benefited more from 1998's home run race than the Tribune Company, not even Fox or ESPN, which shared MLB's national broadcast contract. The Tribune owned not only the Cubs but other broadcasting and media outlets and other markets, many of which spent considerable resources either broadcasting baseball locally or otherwise covering baseball. All benefited from the cash generated by the home run race; in fact, as the *Tribune* newspaper reported, the Tribune Company "outpaced the industry in almost every respect." By 1998, the Tribune

In 1998 the rash of tape measure home runs hit baseball like a shot of crystal methedrine as addiction was instantaneous. Sammy Sosa's season-long duel with Mark McGwire for slugging supremacy made front-page news for weeks.

to 673,508. Even better, the home run race attracted younger fans, a much-sought-after demographic, allowing all these outlets to increase advertising rates out of proportion to the already significant raw increases in ratings and circulation. That didn't even include the specific financial benefit that came solely from the Cubs. Attendance soared during the regular season: the Cubs would draw more than 2.6 million fans for the season, up more than 400,000 from 1997. The Cubs helped the company's "entertainment division," of which it was a part, post a 72 percent gain in revenue over the previous year.

Although becoming an affiliate of the Warner Brothers Entertainment Television Network forced WGN to cut the number of Cub games it broadcast from 139 to 92, those other 47 games were all broadcast on WGN's cable-based "sister station," CLTV. Almost entirely because of Sosa and the home run chase, ratings for Cub games on TV were up 38 percent from 1997, and the games also delivered the highest ratings in CLTV history while immeasurably increasing the fledgling channel's profile. For the Tribune Company, Sosa's home run surge was a win-win-win-win-win-win-win-win situation. Any who dared question the veracity of the home run chase was either ignored or drowned out by a combination of applause and the sound of printing money. It was feeding time, and everyone fought for a place at the trough.

To be fair, Sosa and most other sluggers of the era have denied using steroids and other performance-enhancing drugs, and anyone who did use steroids is only slightly more culpable than all those who suspected what was taking place and did nothing, like the press; those who benefited financially and stayed quiet, like management; and those who encouraged the use of "supplements" with their applause and fawning attention, like the fans.

Sosa's denials have followed him into retirement. As late as November 2006, he reiterated his oft-repeated claim that he never used steroids, telling the *Tribune* that "I put up those numbers by going to bed at nine o'clock at night in Chicago because I have to play a day game every day at one o'clock. I prepared myself for that." But as even Sosa appears to recognize, his quick collapse as a player, coupled with his sketchy testimony before the House Governmental Reform Committee on March 17, 2005, has led many observers to question his performance during what

owned television stations in nearly twenty markets, including New York, Los Angeles, Philadelphia, Dallas, and Boston, all of which also benefited from renewed interest in baseball—what baseball commissioner Bud Selig termed a "baseball renaissance," with higher ratings. According to the company's annual report, in the wake of the 1998 season broadcast revenue increased 15 percent, and the publishing division, spearheaded by the *Chicago Tribune*, "turned in a record performance." Circulation of the *Tribune*, after falling slightly from 1996 to 1997, increased dramatically in 1998, from a daily average of 652,199 in 1997

has been called baseball's "tainted era." Sosa, together with Mark McGwire, who was exposed by Jose Canseco in his 2004 book, *Juiced*, and Barry Bonds, whose involvement with BALCO was revealed during a federal investigation, has come to represent the era. At the end, Sosa, a player who at the age of thirty owned Chicago and seemed like a lock for the Hall of Fame, was, at age thirty-eight, without a contract and without a friend in the city where he made his mark.

But as Phil Rogers noted, "The fans don't care," and at the time that was certainly true. They turned out in record numbers at the ballpark and tuned in their TVs in record numbers as well. Without question, the fans were enjoying themselves, but in retrospect the experience was more akin to watching pro wrestling than watching baseball, because what was taking place on the field had little to do with reality.

Excitement built over the month of July as Sosa chased McGwire, and then Steve Wilstein, a reporter for the Associated Press, noticed a supplement called androstenedione on open display in McGwire's locker. Although legal, the supplement was considered performance-enhancing by both the NFL and the International Olympic Committee, both of which banned its use. McGwire, who pled innocent and kept repeating the words "it's legal," like he was trying to chant his way into heaven, downgraded its effect on his performance as if it were a multivitamin, and virtually everyone chose to look the other way. Temporarily distracted, McGwire went into a mild slump. Sosa virtually avoided the controversy entirely, brushing off questions about androstenedione by professing utter ignorance of not only that substance but any other. He was totally unbothered by the revelation, and as McGwire slumped Sosa pulled ever closer in the home run chase. After cracking two home runs on August 5, he trailed McGwire by only two. The Cubs then traveled to St. Louis to play the Cardinals.

The Sosa and McGwire show took center stage, completely overshadowing the rest of the series. The Cubs came into St. Louis with a record of 64–51, four and a half games behind Houston in the Central Division, but one and a half games ahead of the San Francisco Giants in the wild-card race. The Cardinals were well below .500 and out of the race completely.

Neither player stood out during the three-game series; each hit only one home run, and the Cardinals swept the Cubs, winning 16–3, 9–8, and 2–1. When the Cubs left St. Louis, the division title was out of reach. They trailed the Astros by seven and a half and led the Mets by only half a game in the wild-card chase.

A week later, the Cardinals came into Chicago, and it was all Mark and Sammy and sunshine one more time. McGwire, who had appeared nervous and suspicious the last time the Cardinals faced the Cubs, now seemed to realize that every time Sosa hit a home run or opened his mouth, everything was easier on him. McGwire played the straight man to the press and let Sosa get all the attention. To his credit, Sosa seemed nearly oblivious; smiling and happy to be in the spotlight, he said all the right things about how great it was to be Sammy Sosa playing baseball in the major leagues and advised the St. Louis slugger to relax and have fun.

Sammy Sosa and Mark McGwire embrace following McGwire's record-setting sixty-second home run at Busch Stadium on September 8, 1998.

An interesting dynamic was beginning to take place. On the one hand, the Cubs were trying to make the playoffs and in fact had made several deals to help push them over the top, and they would make even more, adding players like third baseman Gary Gaetti for the stretch drive. But with each passing day, the home run chase seemed ever more important.

Both men went hitless in the first game, a 4–1 Cub win, but in the second game a much more relaxed Mark McGwire cracked two home runs, including the game winner in the tenth inning, his forty-eighth and forty-ninth of the season, as Cub pitchers inexplicably chose to pitch to McGwire rather than pitch around him. Sosa hit only one home run, his forty-eighth. Despite chants from the partisan crowd at Wrigley of "MVP, MVP" every time Sosa came to bat, the Cubs lost, 8–6. Now the Cubs trailed Houston by eight and a half and the Mets by one.

The renaissance wasn't quite done with McGwire and Sosa. McGwire was now back on track, and over the next two weeks both men went on a tear and the Cubs pulled back into a lead in the wild-card race. However, Cub playoff fortunes soon suffered a debilitating blow. On August 26, Kerry Wood pitched his second-best game of the year, striking out sixteen while beating the Reds, 9–2. Five days later, he struck out ten in only six innings to beat them again, running his record to 13–6. But he'd thrown a total of 249 pitches in those two starts, and after the second game his elbow started bothering him. Although it wasn't yet clear just how severely he was hurt, Wood had damaged his ulnar collateral ligament. He would miss the rest of the regular season, then all of 1999 as well. In fact, he would never fulfill the promise he had shown earlier in the season. In retrospect, the Cubs had fallen victim to temptation, pitching Wood too hard and too often too early in his career. It cost them a potential Hall of Famer, something they would refuse to admit as they spent the next seven seasons expecting Wood to become the pitcher he had shown he could be back on May 6, 1998. As it was, his loss for the remainder of the season effectively ruined any chance the Cubs had to advance in the postseason—if they made it. Without Wood, they simply didn't have enough pitching.

When the Cubs returned to St. Louis on September 7 for their final two games against the Cardinals, it was as if everyone was acting out a script entitled "Maximum Publicity"—postseason be damned. McGwire, with sixty home runs, was on the precipice of passing Maris, and Sosa was only two behind.

This time Sosa and McGwire were trotted out before the press in tandem, the epitome of Bud Selig's "baseball renaissance" and a marketing dream: white and black, Anglo and Latino, the privileged son of a dentist and the poverty-stricken shoeshine boy, brought together by baseball, hand in hand, massive arm in massive arm, stars of the biggest magnitude.

If anything demonstrated the degree to which the home run chase overshadowed the race for the postseason, it was that joint press conference. The two sluggers mugged for the cameras and traded one-liners as if they were a veteran comedy team, Sosa calling McGwire "the man" and joking that "baseball has been very, very good to me," as McGwire, looking more relaxed than he had been in weeks, chuckled along with everyone else.

The last thing Sosa and the Cubs should have been doing was *anything* that potentially could help Mark McGwire. Chicago was in a pitched battle to make the playoffs and needed every single win. Living under the corporate umbrella of MLB and the Tribune Company, however, did that really matter? The home run chase was not only a bigger story than the Cubs' attempt to earn a postseason berth as a wild-card team but a far, far more lucrative one, with payoffs all around for everyone. The dual press conference provided ample evidence of that.

The players on both teams couldn't help but notice. As the Cubs' Mickey Morandini said at the time, "In some ways, it's not even baseball anymore. It's not who's winning, who's losing, who's good, who's bad. It's just who's going to hit the most home runs." No kidding. Sosa and McGwire were a team unto themselves. Everybody else might as well have been shagging flies.

The answer to the question of who was going to hit the most home runs would be Mark McGwire. Sosa went homerless in the two contests, but McGwire tied Roger Maris by hitting home run number sixty-one in the first inning on September 7 off Mike Morgan and setting the record with number sixty-two in the fourth inning off

Steve Trachsel on September 8. As McGwire shook the ground running the bases, Sammy Sosa clapped and then even raced in from right field to embrace him, trading high-fives and playful stomach punches. The game was stopped for eleven minutes while the celebration continued, and after the game there were even more ceremonies.

And, oh yeah, the Cubs lost both games, 3–2 and 6–3, dropping into a tie with the Mets for the wild-card berth.

Now, at least, they were done with the Cardinals. Sosa continued to chase McGwire but began to press, and the Cubs stumbled. On September 23, he broke the slump and tied McGwire when he hit two home runs against the Brewers, but the Cubs lost in excruciating fashion. Steve Trachsel carried a 7–0 lead into the seventh inning before losing it, giving up four quick runs on four singles and a walk. Still, entering the ninth, the Brewers trailed 7–5 against closer Rod Beck. Although he'd been terrific all season and had become a fan favorite—glowering at batters from beneath his mullet, his right arm swinging back and forth like a metronome—on this day Beck bent, loading the bases. Brewers' outfielder Geoff Jenkins then lofted a fly ball to deep left for what should have been the last out. Cubs' outfielder Brant Brown, inserted into the game for defensive purposes, camped under the ball but dropped it.

For the first time in a long time, Sosa and the home run chase wasn't the story. All three runners scored, the Cubs lost, and a new generation of Cubs fans were introduced to the name Don Young as Brown's gaffe became the second most notable outfield error in Cub history, as local newspapers reminded readers the next day. After nearly a full season of sun and excitement, it was all starting to sour.

Two days later, Sosa briefly passed McGwire when he hit what would be his last home run of the season, number sixty-six, but McGwire tied him forty-five minutes later, on his way to a season-ending seventy home runs. The Cubs lost again, dropping them into a tie with both the Mets and the Giants for the wild-card berth.

For a time it appeared that the Cubs would miss the playoffs altogether. On the last day of the season, they blew a 3–1 lead, then lost to the Astros in Houston, 4–3, in eleven innings in what now appeared to be a classic Cub collapse. The Giants appeared to sew things up, taking a 7–0 lead over Colorado. Fortunately for the Cubs, the game

In 1998 relief pitcher Rod Beck enjoyed his greatest season following his free agent signing with the Cubs. He is shown here celebrating his fifty-first save in the Cubs victory in their one-game wild-card playoff against his former team, the San Francisco Giants, on September 28, 1998.

was played in Colorado's Coors Field, where no lead was safe. The Rockies stormed back to win 9–8, leaving the Cubs tied with the Giants and setting up a one-game playoff to determine which team would earn the wild-card berth. "You have to be a pretty good team," cracked Cub infielder Mickey Morandini after the game, "to play 163 games." The Cubs had backed into the postseason, but then again, so had the Giants.

The two clubs met on September 28 at Wrigley Field, the first one-game playoff in Cubs history. In the long history of the Cubs, it had all come down to the final day of the regular season only once before, in 1908, when the Cubs and the Giants met in the infamous replay of the "Merkle's Boner" contest. All Chicago hoped for a similar result. Steve Trachsel, who until his last start had been horrible since giving up McGwire's sixty-second home run, got the ball for Chicago.

He was at his gutsiest best, taking a no-hitter into the seventh inning despite walking six, hitting a batter, and throwing a ton of pitches. Entering the ninth, the Cubs led, 5–0, as Gaetti cracked a two-run home run and pinch hitter Matt Mieske singled in two more. All the Cubs needed were three more outs.

Normally, Jim Riggleman would have waved for closer Rod Beck, but in recent days Beck had begun a slow metamorphosis into Mitch Williams, at least in terms of results. Riggleman had ridden him hard, and Beck never refused the ball, even as his velocity dropped precipitously and his arm, swinging back and forth before each pitch, looked as if it might just work loose and drop onto the ground. The Giants had used him up at the end of the 1997 season, and when he joined the Cubs in 1998 all he had left was his heart. He was done, cooked, and Riggleman knew it, but for most of the season Beck's heart had been enough, and he was still better than anyone else the Cubs had. Yet in the aftermath of the 1998 season, Beck would never again be the dominant pitcher who had collected 250 saves in nine seasons.

Riggleman hoped to save Beck for the playoffs, so he turned to Kevin Tapani in relief of Trachsel. He gave up two hits to start the inning, and Riggleman replaced him with Terry Mulholland. He immediately gave up a single to Stan Javier, putting the Giants on the board, then walked Ellis Burks before Barry Bonds almost took him deep, lining out hard to score another run on a sacrifice fly.

On September 13, 1998, Sammy Sosa enjoyed the greatest day of his best season as he hit two home runs, numbers sixty-one and sixty-two, in an 11–10 ten-inning victory over the Brewers in Chicago. Following his second blast, Cub fans gave him a six-minute-and-twenty-five-second standing ovation.

1998

Mark Grace watches quietly as the Cubs lose to the Braves in the 1998 division series. Despite enjoying a superb regular season in 1998 in which he batted .309 with thirty-nine doubles, he managed to hit only .083 in his second postseason series.

Beck was up and throwing. For the eighty-first time that year, he strolled to the mound, this time pitching on memory.

He retired Jeff Kent on a ground ball that scored another run to make the score 5–3. Then Joe Carter, whom the Cubs had traded so long ago, stepped to the plate. Everything was in place for a final fall.

But Beck didn't teeter. Carter popped up to Mark Grace, and the Cubs were in the playoffs.

After sixty-six home runs by Sammy Sosa, fifty-one saves from Rod Beck, and assorted other heroics in a season that, once one stripped away the home run chase, saw the Cubs come from behind to win forty-nine times, including twenty-four times in their final at-bat, the Cubs figured that maybe, just maybe, they were due—maybe this was their year. After all, went the logic, if Sosa got hot during the National League Division Series against Atlanta, he could, all by himself, lift the team to victory, for in addition to his sixty-six home runs, he had also hit .308 with 158 RBIs and 134 runs scored, good enough to win the MVP Award over McGwire.

The Atlanta Braves disagreed. Before the start of the NLDS, a headline in the *Atlanta Journal-Constitution* summed up their attitude. It read: "Cubs a Veritable Bye in Opening Round." In other words, the Cubs didn't have a chance. The Braves had won 106 games to only 90 for the Cubs. No Brave had hit sixty-six home runs, but then again, the Braves hadn't needed anyone to. A season defined by the home run had been dominated by two teams, the Braves and the Yankees, who, with 106 and 114 wins, respectively, had played the game the old-fashioned way. Andres Gallaraga had led the Braves in home runs with what now seemed a modest total—forty-four—and no one on the Yankees had hit more than twenty-eight. As opposed to the "all or nothing" approach of the Cubs, the Braves countered with a fair amount of everything.

It was over fast. In game one, Braves pitcher John Smoltz carved the Cubs to pieces, giving up only a solo home run, as Michael Tucker and Ryan Klesko both cracked early home runs to put the game away early. The Braves won, 7–1.

In game two, at least the Cubs had a chance, carrying a 1–0 lead into the ninth. Earlier in the year, Riggleman probably would have turned to Beck to finish the game, but now he left the game in the hands of starting pitcher Kevin Tapani. With one out, Javy Lopez let the air out, tying the score with a home run. Then in the tenth inning, with Terry Mulholland on the mound, the Braves' Walt Weiss walked and Tony Graffanino bunted. Mulholland missed the bag after catching Mark Grace's awkward flip. Then Braves third baseman Chipper Jones knocked in the winning run with a single, and the Cubs were in their most familiar postseason posture, one game away from elimination.

All they had to do to survive was beat Greg Maddux, who since leaving the Cubs had secured his spot as perhaps the most dominant pitcher of his generation, winning 107 games in six seasons. The Cubs decided to counter with Kerry Wood, pitching his first game in a month.

Common sense said that they should have sat him down, particularly since they were already losing the series two games to none, but common sense hadn't had a place at the table in regard to Kerry Wood since he struck out twenty. His elbow didn't implode—yet—and he pitched well enough to win, giving up only three hits in five innings. Unfortunately, Maddux pitched better, and in the seventh inning, after Wood left the game, Mulholland and then Beck both got ripped. The Braves won going away, 6–2, to take the series and pull the curtain on an unforgettable, unbelievable summer. Sammy Sosa ended the season as he had started it, quietly, going only 2-for-11 during the series with no home runs.

Still, the 1998 Cubs had given Chicago hope, and with Sosa and Wood the future looked bright. Perhaps Wood would win twenty games in 1999 and break his own strikeout mark. And Sosa? What couldn't he do? Another sixty home runs seemed automatic, and seventy wasn't as much a barrier as a reasonable goal. This wasn't 1984, or even 1988. These Cubs, everyone agreed, seemed different.

The 1998 season, wrote Dave Van Dyck in the *Tribune* after the final game, "was a natural thing. Something impossible to be manufactured or faked."

Not so. Consider this: at the end of the season, *Time* magazine named Mark McGwire "Hero of the Year." What once appeared to be a season to remember is, in the long run, perhaps better off forgotten.

CUBS WIN!!! . . . DOH!

As soon as the 1998 season ended, anyone schooled in the history of the Cubs should have run screaming down Waveland Avenue as far away from Wrigley Field as possible. For the next few seasons, the "friendly confines" would not be very accommodating. The Cubs would not just be confined by their history, but almost incarcerated by it.

Although the Cubs had reached the postseason in 1998, most observers without an office at Wrigley Field or with the Tribune Company realized that they were a long way from becoming a genuine contender. Despite Sammy Sosa's bloated home run total, the Cubs had scrambled to win ninety games with a pitching staff that, with few exceptions, scared no one. They weren't close to challenging the Houston Astros, who had won 102 games in 1998, for the division title, or the pennant-winning Atlanta Braves—the only pitchers on the Cub staff who conceivably might have made the Braves' pitching staff were Rod

In the sixth game of the 2003 National League Championship Series, the Cubs were just five outs away from their first trip to the World Series since 1945 when disaster struck. With one out in the eighth inning, Cub starter Mark Prior had a three-run lead with no one on base. When Luis Castillo of the Marlins lofted a foul ball toward left, it appeared as though Moises Alou would grab the second out. A small group of fans, including the now-infamous Steve Bartman, jockeyed for the ball, which fell away from Alou. The Cubs lost their composure and lost the game, and Bartman was immediately and unfairly made a scapegoat.

Beck and Kerry Wood, and now both were damaged goods. As the 1999 season approached, the smart money said to remember 1985 and 1990, the last two seasons following a Cub appearance in the postseason. In those two seasons, the Cubs had finished under .500, in fourth place, twenty-three and a half and eighteen games out of first place.

Yet Cub fans hadn't seen anything yet. Over the next few years, the Cubs would give fans of recent vintage a crash course in Cub-ology.

At first, however, the Cubs appeared as if they would be able to avoid the post-champagne hangover. The Tribune Company had more than earned back its investment in the Cubs in 1998, and there seemed to be no reason why the company wouldn't choose to reinvest in the team—through either free agent signings or trades—secure the advances they had made, and ensure a profitable future. After all, Sosa's contract—suddenly cheap in terms of his recent production—had several more years to run. The future was now. The Cubs, despite their position in baseball's third-largest market and the backing of the Tribune Company, only had baseball's tenth-largest payroll. The farm system, apart from Wood, wasn't producing. The choice was to spend or die.

Unfortunately, the Cubs chose to spend the offseason fumbling with their wallet and dropping change on the floor. They couldn't even get on the same page. Manager Jim Riggleman told the press that he thought all the team needed was some "fine-tuning," while GM Ed Lynch said, "We're looking for a number one," as in a number-one starter. There was plenty of talent available through free agency, ranging from Yankee outfielder Bernie Williams to slugger Albert Belle to frontline pitchers Kevin Brown and Randy Johnson, and the Toronto Blue Jays were looking to trade pitcher Roger Clemens. The addition of any one of those players would probably have secured Chicago's place in the standings.

Instead, despite the fact that injuries had both Kerry Wood and Rod Beck entering the offseason with question marks, the team made no real move to replace either player, gambling that not only would each return to form, but that each would be even better than in 1998. In fact, the Cubs didn't make a genuine run at anyone significant. They re-signed pitcher Terry Mulholland, picked up catcher

Benito Santiago, and, after losing pitcher Mark Clark to free agency, traded outfielder Brant Brown and his bad memories to Pittsburgh for pitcher Jon Lieber.

In spring training, Wood was a mess from the beginning, battling the stomach flu and a bad head cold. He didn't even make his first spring appearance until March 13 against Anaheim, and his performance made everyone else ill. He threw his first warm-up pitch ten feet over the catcher's head and didn't get better. Of the twenty-six pitches he threw, only ten were strikes.

There was a good reason why. The ligament he first damaged in his right elbow in 1998 had torn completely loose. Three days later, the Cubs announced that he would undergo "Tommy John" surgery to replace the ligament and would miss the entire season.

In retrospect, Wood was lucky. Because there was very little of the 1999 season not worth missing.

The Cubs actually got off to a decent start in 1999. The pitching was somewhat better than expected, and Sosa picked up where he had left off in 1998. On May 21, the Cubs finally recognized that Beck was done and traded for Twins closer Rick Aguilera. After a brief slump pulled the Cubs down to .500, they went on a bit of a tear against the league's also-rans and on June 8 were 32–23, only one game behind the division-leading Astros.

It was a mirage. Cubs pitchers were giving up home runs at an alarming rate. They were swept by the White Sox in interleague play, and over the next two weeks Cubs pitchers gave up ten runs or more six times. By July, they were in free fall.

Everything fell apart. From July 23 through September 12, the Cubs won only ten games while losing forty. Sosa kept hitting home runs as he and McGwire indulged in another session of home run derby, but it wasn't nearly as exciting the second time around. Sosa finished the year with sixty-three home runs, two fewer than McGwire, but as the Cubs fell back the rest of his play suffered, particularly on defense. The Cubs finished last with a record of 67–95, thirty games back.

On October 4, they fired Jim Riggleman, but he hadn't been the problem, not really. The organization was messed up, and that wasn't going to change very quickly.

Former Colorado manager Don Baylor was hired to

take over. Baylor was old school, a tough, no-nonsense guy and a player who had once won the MVP Award with the Orioles. Like Sosa, Baylor, an African American, was a minority, and the unspoken message was that he had been hired because it was thought that he could both relate to Sosa and get tough with the star—for despite all the home runs, Sosa was playing like he was on cruise control, living large and starting to piss people off. He ruled the clubhouse, playing salsa music at high volume almost incessantly, and he was beginning to rub his teammates the wrong way. The Cubs hoped Baylor, who wasn't intimidated by anything, could reel him in.

Then again, they also hoped that Kerry Wood would come back and win twenty games. As if to underscore that desire, they once again did virtually nothing in the free agent market beyond losing pitcher Steve Trachsel to the Devil Rays.

During the 2000 season, Baylor did light a bit of a fire under Sosa, whose average climbed to .320, but Sosa moped anyway, politicked for a new contract, and tried to get the Cubs to trade him. The Yankees almost bit, but in a rare moment of restraint, backed off. Kerry Wood, back from surgery, won only eight games, and the Cubs finished with the fourteenth-worst ERA in the league. Coupled with the thirteenth-lowest batting average and twelfth-lowest slugging percentage, the Cubs were lucky to win any games

and finished in last place again, 65–97, their worst back-to-back finish in almost forty years.

General manager Ed Lynch was the first casualty. He didn't last the season and was fired on July 19. As Mike Kiley wrote in the *Sun-Times* a few days earlier, "Problem is . . . being decent seemingly has been the Cubs' highest priority for too long. The organization's 'let's get lucky' philosophy for demanding economic times has paled and shriveled after years of rolling the dice and throwing snake eyes." Andy MacPhail took over general manager duties, saying, "Either I'm going to get it right or it's going to kill me," but nothing really changed.

On December 8, an era ended when Mark Grace, after thirteen seasons as a Cub, left as a free agent, signing a two-year deal with a one-year option with the Arizona Diamondbacks for only $3 million a year.

Grace hadn't wanted to leave, and everyone knew it. He loved being a Cub and realized that he was appreciated in Chicago like he would have been in no other place—he even painted the Wrigley Field ivy on his motorcycle to make his feelings clear. He held out hope that, at the

Former American League MVP Don Baylor managed the Cubs from 2000 to midway through the 2002 season. His best season was 2001, when the Cubs finished above .500 for the first time since the 1998 wild-card team.

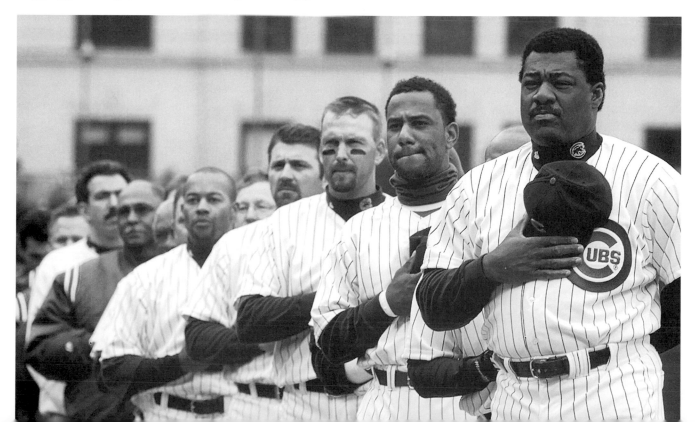

very least, the Cubs would offer him arbitration, but Grace had done some sniping at MacPhail in 2000, and the Cubs never even made him an offer. "When your employer doesn't want you back, you have to find work elsewhere," said a resigned Grace at the time, adding that "I'll miss the city so much. It sounds sappy, but there are people on the first base side I've gotten to know over thirteen years." MacPhail explained that the Cubs were ready to go with youth and believed that both Julio Zuleta and Hee Sop Choi were ready for the major leagues. Besides, Sosa would soon be due for a new contract, and the Tribune was keeping a tight hold on the purse strings.

Chicago did make one big move, signing closer Tom Gordon as a free agent, and a lot of little moves as Matt Stairs eventually replaced Grace at first base, and Gary Matthews Jr. and Rondell White replaced Henry Rodriguez and Damon Buford in the Cubs outfield. After throwing a tantrum for the better part of the year, Sosa was rewarded in March by the Cubs with a four-year contract extension worth $72 million. After finishing in last place two years in a row, they realized they were probably better off, in the long run, trading Sosa, but he'd priced himself out of the market. The few teams that could afford him, like the Yankees, didn't want him, and no one was offering adequate prospects in return. Besides, a certain element of Cubs fans had a huge blind spot in regard to their star, and now that Grace was gone, the club couldn't face another PR hit, for Sosa was still wildly popular. There were enough of these fans who were satisfied watching Sammy regardless of whether or not the Cubs won. Historically, that satisfied the organization by keeping attendance, TV ratings, and corporate profits in the black.

For the first time in a long while, the Cubs got lucky in 2001. Kerry Wood bounced back and for much of the year proved to be surprisingly resilient. At times he pitched as if he still might become that pitcher who had once struck out twenty batters in a game. Jon Lieber, after several season of mediocrity, kept his sinker down all year long, and the bullpen, keyed by Gordon, slammed the door. A happy and wealthy Sammy Sosa bounced back with his best all-around year since 1998, and the Cubs actually led the division by six games on June 7 and stayed in first place into August.

That wasn't indicative of reality. Despite the addition of slugging first baseman Fred McGriff at the end of July for the stretch run, both the Astros and the Cardinals proceeded to lap the Cubs as Wood left the rotation in mid-August with tendonitis. In the end, the Cubs just didn't have quite enough to stay with either team, and they finished second behind Houston and St. Louis, winning eighty-eight games.

For a change, they were active in the offseason, trading for second baseman Mark Bellhorn and shortstop Alex Gonzalez and, in a big splash, signing outfielder Moises Alou as a free agent, a move that not only helped the Cubs but hurt the Astros, for whom Alou had hit ninety-five home runs over the past three seasons. With Sosa hitting behind him, the Cubs expected Alou to thrive in Wrigley Field. They planned to insert a player many expected to become another Lou Brock into center, rookie Corey Patterson. Furthermore, the farm system seemed ready to produce another phenom fully the equal Wood. In 2001, with the second pick of the draft, the Cubs selected pitcher Mark Prior. Most observers expected him to race through the minor leagues and make it to Wrigley in a year or two.

He wouldn't be ready in 2002, however, and in spring training the Cubs felt they were just a pitcher or two away from being a contender. When Tom Gordon went down with an injury, they moved quickly.

The Florida Marlins had decided to build their club around young pitching and wanted to shed some salary. The Cubs wanted closer Antonio Alfonseca, and the two clubs worked out a deal, the Cubs sending fifth starter Julian Tavarez to the Marlins along with the player the Marlins really wanted, minor league pitcher Dontrelle Willis, for Alfonseca and pitcher Matt Clement. At the time, it looked like a steal: the Cubs replaced Tavarez with Clement, who was younger and potentially much better, and received an established closer. The Cubs liked Willis but thought his exaggerated wind-up might cause arm trouble, and with Mark Prior and Carlos Zambrano already in the farm system, they considered him expendable.

Now the Cubs actually looked like a contender entering the 2002 season. That scenario should have caused Cubs fans to shield their eyes from what was about to happen.

By May 1, it was "wait till next year" as the Cubs got off

to an 8–16 start. Injuries were part of the reason, but Cub hitters deserved most of the blame. On May 15, the Cubs had a record of 13–25, and only a handful of Cub players were hitting above .250. Most were well below that mark, including Fred McGriff, who was hitting .213, Moises Alou (.164), and Todd Hundley (.128). There were already calls to fire Don Baylor, but MacPhail, who had put the team together, deserved most of the blame.

On May 18, the Cubs dropped their ninth game in a row to fall to 13–27, already twelve games out of the division lead and even further behind in the wild-card chase. The Cubs had to change the conversation, and fast.

Even though they really needed hitting and they'd already rushed Kerry Wood to the major leagues with disastrous results, the Cubs chose to call up Mark Prior despite the fact that he'd pitched all of nine games and fifty-one innings in the minor leagues. If nothing else, it gave the sportswriters something else to write about. As Greg Couch noted in the *Sun-Times*, "Prior's job is simply to show promise, blaze one fastball; maybe save one game. Also save the manager's job, the general manager's, save a season, win a pennant, make us forget about strike dates and All-Star boycotts, and generally boost morale, not to mention lower our handicap, straighten out our kids and maybe find us a parking spot."

The Cubs pooh-poohed the notion that they were rushing Prior, who they felt was a completely different pitcher than Wood. For one thing, Prior was older, already twenty-two years old. Wood had signed out of high school, but Prior had spent three years in college, first at Vanderbilt and then USC. Moreover, Prior had been preparing to pitch in the big leagues for more than a decade.

While growing up in San Diego, his parents had placed him under the tutelage of former big league pitcher and coach Tom House. For years House had worked with Prior using the latest available methods—medical, technological, nutritional, and psychological. As House told Couch, "He is not going to fail. . . . Mark has been exposed to, and taken advantage of, the best research available." But if that was so, why then had he ever been allowed to sign with the Cubs?

In his first game, on May 22 against Pittsburgh, Prior was everything advertised: he struck out ten in six innings,

Outfielder Moises Alou arrived in Chicago in 2002 as the classic rent-a-star. The former Astro All-Star enjoyed three solid seasons in Chicago, especially during 2004, when he hit 39 home runs and drove in 109. Alou was especially effective in both sets of playoffs in 2003: he batted .500 against Atlanta in the divisional series and .310 in the championship series against Florida.

wowed the crowd with his fastball, and left after 103 pitches with a three-run lead. The Cubs even won, 7–4.

Prior was already good, and potentially great, but he could only pitch every fifth day, and he couldn't really hit at all. In the end, he made no real difference in the Cubs' performance. One day after the Fourth of July, they threw in the towel.

MacPhail cleaned house, firing Baylor and . . . himself. Baylor got the word at the team hotel in Atlanta and left without comment. As the season had spun out of control, he'd been the object of all sorts of anonymous sniping, and as Mike Kiley wrote in the *Sun-Times*, the season had been "rife with stakes to the heart. Baylor was killed off slowly by his own players." Cubs coach Bruce Kimm took over.

At the same time, MacPhail named Jim Hendry general manager, stepping down from the position himself and saying of Hendry, "He will be in charge of all personnel decisions." A former college baseball coach and minor league manager, Hendry had been serving as vice president of player personnel for the Cubs and was credited with reviving the team's farm system. They hoped he could do the same at the big league level. Of his new job, Hendry said, "I consider it one of the greatest jobs in professional sports," at once demonstrating a capacity for self-delusion and an utter ignorance of history. The Cub GM job was many things, but one of the greatest jobs in sports was not one of them.

Former USC star pitcher Mark Prior was selected by the Cubs with the second overall choice in the 2001 draft. He was pitching at Wrigley Field within a year and by 2003 had won eighteen games for the Cubs, including an amazing 12–1 run down the stretch. Arm trouble has hampered his career since that time.

The Cubs played out the string, finishing with fewer than seventy wins for the third time in four seasons, the first time they'd done that since 1957. And they still drew 2.7 million fans.

Hendry fired Bruce Kimm at the end of the season. He wanted his own man. The franchise was at a nadir. As Jay Mariotti noted in the *Sun-Times*, "Nothing remains the same in this world except the Cubbies," and that didn't seem likely to change very fast. He blamed MacPhail, calling him out for his failures and writing that, "from this point on, the Peter Principle is known as the Andy Principle."

This time the Cubs took their time finding a manager. For a time it appeared as if they'd hire Ken Macha, who later became manager of the Oakland A's, but when veteran Dusty Baker became available after the Giants lost in the World Series to the Anaheim Angels, the Cubs turned their attention to him.

He was intriguing for a number of reasons. A native of California, Johnnie B. Baker earned the nickname "Dusty" from his mother for his propensity to get dirty while playing. Drafted by the Braves, Baker signed without his father's permission, and the elder Baker, who had wanted his son to accept a basketball scholarship, took his son and the Braves to court to try to stop him. Baker went on to a nineteen-year career with the Braves—where he was a teammate of Hank Aaron—the Dodgers, the Giants, and the A's. He had most of his success with Los Angeles, where even on a team of media darlings like Steve Garvey and manager Tommy Lasorda he was the acknowledged leader in the clubhouse.

Entertaining and glib, Baker was both bright and street-smart, referring to everyone as "Dude" with his signature toothpick hanging out of the side of his mouth. In 1988 he joined the Giants as a coach, and after becoming manager in 1993, he put together an enviable record, finishing first or second eight times. Known as a player's manager, he had managed successfully to navigate the volatile psyche of Giants slugger Barry Bonds, a not insignificant achievement. Baker loved to talk, was good copy, and was certain to attract good press. The Cubs knew that just by hiring Baker they'd receive a pass for the next year or two.

Those who had watched Dusty manage the Giants, however, warned that his clubhouse prowess was undercut by his relative lack of dugout skills during critical moments. He didn't over manage, just sent his players out to play, a strategy that usually worked but had failed at some critical moments. His critics cited two examples. First, when trailing 2–0 in the fifth inning of the elimination game against the Mets in the 2000 playoffs, he failed to pinch-hit for pitcher Mark Gardner with two out and the bases loaded. Second, in the seventh inning of what could have been the winning game of the 2002 World Series, pitcher Russ Ortiz entered the seventh inning with a two-hitter, leading 5–0. Then, with one out, he gave up two singles. Baker pulled him, but then tempted fate by handing Ortiz the ball as he walked off, presumably to keep for a souvenir as the winning pitcher of the final game of the World Series. However, reliever Felix Rodriguez then gave up a home run, and the Angels stormed back to take the game and the Series.

Nevertheless, the Cubs decided Baker was the man to lead them out of the desert, and the man to get Sosa back on track, for not only was Sosa losing some skills, but he was losing in the clubhouse. As his performance became ever more mortal, his teammates became ever less enamored with the Sammy show. Just as important, Baker wanted the job: he would later tell people that his mother had told him on her deathbed that he would one day end up in Chicago. Baker promised to get "on the same page" with Sosa and predicted that free agents would be more likely to come to Chicago now that he was in place. What

Cub general manager Jim Hendry (left, with Alfonso Soriano) had worked for the organization since 1994 in both scouting and player development before being hired as general manager in 2002. The former Creighton University coach was the architect of the 2003 Central Division champions and made headlines when he signed free agent Alfonso Soriano in 2006 at the same time he underwent emergency angioplasty.

Former Giants manager Dusty Baker (right, with Nomar Garciaparra) signed with the Cubs in the wake of San Francisco's heartbreaking loss in the 2002 World Series. He nearly made it back to the Fall Classic in his first season at Wrigley Field, but his team lost an unforgettable championship series to the Marlins in seven games.

went unsaid was the fact that the Cubs, who agreed to pay Baker nearly $4 million a year, also agreed to spend a bit more on players. Baker was the boldest hire since Leo Durocher, and the first manager hired since Durocher who was expected not just to win, but to win sometime soon.

Soon after Baker signed on, the Cubs made some moves in that direction. They remade the right side of the infield, trading for Eric Karros and Mark Grudzielanek of the Dodgers, and signed three free agents, outfielders Troy O'Leary and Thomas Goodwin and utility man Lenny Harris.

Still, by the time the Cubs opened the 2003 season, it was hard to see how this club would play into October. They started the season with a pitching rotation of Wood, Clement, Prior, Shawn Estes, and Carlos Zambrano, a potentially good staff, but neither Prior nor Zambrano had yet spent a full season in the majors, Wood had a history of

injuries, Clement was inconsistent, and Estes, the veteran, was coming off a terrible season.

Nevertheless, the Cubs burst out of the box quick, beating the Mets 15–2 on opening day behind Wood as center fielder Corey Patterson knocked in seven runs and seemed on the precipice of stardom. A few days later, Sammy Sosa garnered the headlines by cracking his five-hundredth home run in Cincinnati, but the Cubs gave little indication that they were more than a .500 ball club. The starting pitching, apart from Estes, was actually better than expected, as everyone else finally seemed to be reaching their potential, and Wood and Prior both looked like top-of-the-rotation studs. But the Cubs offense was spotty. On April 20, Sosa was hit on the ear by a pitch from Salomon Torres of the Pirates. Although he wasn't seriously hurt, afterward he seemed gun-shy, backing off the plate and bailing out on the ball, and the Cubs offense suffered. Mark Bellhorn, after hitting twenty-seven home runs while playing second base in 2002, moved to third and didn't hit anything. Every week or so the Cubs would score runs in bunches and then would struggle. Fortunately, no other team in the NL Central seemed capable of putting the division away. The Cubs stayed just close enough to keep things interesting.

On June 3, the Cubs led every sports broadcast, but not for any reason they were proud of. As the Cubs faced the Tampa Bay Devil Rays at Wrigley Field in the first game of interleague play, Sammy Sosa came up in the first inning facing Geremi Gonzalez with two men on base. Gonzalez came inside—since Sosa had been hit in the head, *every* pitcher was trying to jam him—and Sosa hit a ground ball to second. His bat exploded as he made contact, breaking in half, leaving Sosa holding the handle as the barrel, split up the side, went wheeling out into the infield.

Sosa ran to first and was thrown out, but by the time he turned around the umpires were already examining his bat, or what was left of it. Clearly, a hole had been drilled in the barrel and filled with cork, an age-old and illegal baseball trick believed to result in increased power.

Home plate umpire Tim McClelland called Dusty Baker onto the field, showed him the bat, and tossed Sosa from the game. Meanwhile, his other bats were confiscated from the clubhouse. The Cubs won, 3–2, in eleven innings, but all anyone wanted to talk about was Sosa.

He apologized immediately and profusely, explaining that he had used the bat by mistake, that it was a batting practice bat, saying, "I apologize to my teammates, the fans, the commissioner, and major league baseball. I take the blame, it's a mistake." He explained that during batting practice the corked bat helped him entertain fans, who expected him to hit home runs.

That may well have been the case—the seventy-six bats in Sosa's locker as well as five in the collection of the Baseball Hall of Fame were all examined and found to be normal—but Sosa's credibility took a hit, and those who already suspected that much of his home run prowess came from performance-enhancing substances looked at Sosa with even more suspicion. He went from being Babe Ruth to Hack Wilson, a Hall of Famer to a has-been, in about half a second. Sosa was eventually suspended for seven games. In the meantime, the New York Yankees visited Wrigley Field for the first time since the 1938 World Series. The Cubs took two of three as Wood and Prior outpitched Roger Clemens and Andy Pettitte, but the comparisons between Sosa and Yankee sluggers like Babe Ruth and Joe DiMaggio didn't do the Dominican star much good.

By midseason, the Cubs were still hanging on, but not by much. As June turned into July, the Cubs slowly slipped toward .500.

In almost any other season, they would have kept slipping. But in 2003 no team in the Central Division seemed able to run away with the title. On June 30, the halfway point of the season, both the Cubs and Astros trailed the Cardinals by only one game.

Cub fans wanted the club to make a deal, but GM Jim Hendry hesitated. Then Corey Patterson hurt his knee and was knocked from the lineup, and the Cubs, already struggling to score, struggled even harder. Now the Cubs needed both a center fielder to replace Patterson and a third baseman to take over for Bellhorn, who was worse than awful. Hendry had his eye on Florida third baseman Mike Lowell, but the Marlins wanted younger pitching, something Hendry was loath to give up. Carlos Zambrano was the player most clubs started asking about, but Hendry knew that if he traded Zambrano, it would leave a huge hole in the starting rotation.

On July 11, that hole opened up anyway. Prior collided with Atlanta second baseman Marcus Giles, and his golden right arm was bent back awkwardly. As he rolled on the ground in pain, any hope for a postseason berth seemed to disappear in the grimace on his face. At first Prior seemed okay, but ten days later he went on the fifteen-day disabled list.

The Cubs seemed likely to throw in the towel, and there were rumors of a rift between Hendry and Baker, with Baker pushing for a deal while Hendry and MacPhail wanted to pack it in. On July 23 came evidence that if there was a rift, Baker had won.

On June 3, 2003, not only did the Cubs play their first-ever regular-season game against the Tampa Bay Devil Rays at Wrigley Field, but Sammy Sosa experienced an unwanted share of the spotlight when he shattered his cork-filled bat while stroking a first-inning grounder to second base. His transgression led the Hall of Fame to X-ray the bats from his record-setting season in 1998 to see if they'd been doctored. Fortunately for Sosa, they were clean even as his reputation began to tarnish.

For the umpteenth time in recent years, the Pittsburgh Pirates, losing money and losing on the field, wanted to get rid of some salaries. Shedding third baseman Aramis Ramirez, scheduled to earn $6 million in 2004, and Kenny Lofton, earning $1 million, could nudge the Pirates toward the black.

They didn't want much in return. Hendry offered minor league pitcher Matt Brubeck, Jose Hernandez, and a player to be named later for both men. The Pirates accepted. It was an out-and-out steal, a deal driven by money and nothing else. Pittsburgh columnist Bob Smizik described it as "a trade that rips out what little heart was left in the Pirates."

Ramirez and Lofton, who had played with Baker in San Francisco, were exactly what the Cubs needed, and together with the return of a healthy Prior in early August, they made the difference in the division race. At the time of the deal, the Cubs were 50–50 and trailing the Astros by five and a half games and the Cardinals by four. For the rest of the season, the Cubs would go 38–24, while both the Cardinals and Astros struggled to play .500 baseball. The Cubs didn't score more runs, but Lofton helped the defense, Ramirez forced the opposition to pitch to Sosa, and the Cubs offense was far more consistent than before the trade. In the meantime, both Wood and Prior seemed to grow up overnight. They were huge down the stretch as each pitcher appeared to come into his own, not just winning but dominating.

The Cubs clinched the division with two days left in the season on September 27, sweeping the Pirates at Wrigley Field and sending Cubs fans into a frenzy. Sammy Sosa ran

Following his trade from the Pirates in 2003, third baseman Aramis Ramirez batted .300 for the Cubs while slugging 120 home runs in three and a half seasons through 2006. He has proven to be the best Cub third baseman since Ron Santo.

around the field in a victory lap, his corked bat and other questions temporarily forgotten, and then he carried a bottle of champagne into right field and sprayed the crowd.

There was plenty to celebrate. Not since 1984 had the Cubs entered the postseason with a legitimate chance of moving forward. The postseason favored teams with strong starting pitching, particularly teams with dominant starting pitching, and in Woods and Prior the Cubs had that. Prior had gone 18–6, Wood was 14–11, and both pitchers struck out more than a batter an inning. Together they had the potential to shut down any team, anytime.

Yet there was also some reason for pause. Prior had never pitched so many innings before, and Wood was at his limit. Both pitchers were entering unknown territory. Since coming back from the disabled list, apart from his first start back, Prior had thrown 100 or more pitches in every start he had made, usually throwing 120 or more, and he topped 130 pitches several times. Wood had been ridden just as hard. Neither had had an opportunity to rest or to skip a start, and both entered the postseason running at full velocity. In fact, for the first time since 1975, four Cub pitchers had thrown more than two hundred innings.

In the first round against the Atlanta Braves, it all went according to plan. For years the Braves had entered the postseason with the best starting staff in baseball, but that wasn't the case anymore. Tom Glavine was gone, Greg Maddux was finally slowing down a bit, and John Smoltz, after elbow trouble, was in the bullpen. The Cubs, with Wood and Prior, had the advantage, and it showed. In the five-game series, the Cubs won the three games started by Wood and Prior—Wood won games one and five, 4–2 and 5–1, and Prior picked up a win in game three, 3–1—and Carlos Zambrano was nearly as impressive and successful in his start. When Chipper Jones of Atlanta broke a 0-for-11 slump with a home run to win game four for Atlanta, 6–4, a reporter asked him what was the difference compared to the first two games. "The difference?" asked Jones incredulously. "I finally saw some pitches that weren't ninety-eight miles an hour and on the black."

While the Cubs were beating the Braves, the Florida Marlins, with their young pitching staff finally maturing, surprised the San Francisco Giants to reach the NLCS. Meanwhile, in the American League, the Yankees and Red Sox were facing off for the pennant, causing media in New

Reliever Joe Borowski was once traded for Pete Rose Jr. and bounced around eleven minor and three major league teams before signing with the Cubs as a free agent in 2001. In 2003 he experienced a breakthrough season, converting thirty-three of thirty-seven save opportunities for the Central Division champs. Borowski is shown here after striking out Andruw Jones to beat the Braves in the deciding game of the 2003 divisional series.

York, Boston, and Chicago to go ga-ga, since a World Series featuring the Cubs and either the Yankees or the Red Sox was a potential marketing and ratings bonanza. If the Yankees played the Cubs, it would be Joe McCarthy and Babe Ruth and his called shot 24/7, with the cuddly Cubs in stark contrast to the mercenary Yankees. If the Red Sox won, it would be dueling curses, the Bambino versus the Billy Goat, ad infinitum and ad nauseam. Every sportswriter in all three cities already had his columns all written. All he needed was to know the opponent and then fill them out like sportswriting "Mad-Libs." Before the start of the series against the Marlins, Jay Mariotti asked in the *Sun-Times*, "Can anyone, even the Yankees, overcome Wood

Right-hander Matt Clement enjoyed a career-best season in 2003 while winning fourteen games. His finest hour was his victory in the fifth game of the 2003 championship series in Miami, where he beat the eventual champions by a score of 8–3.

and Prior in a seven-game series?" Cub fans weren't just saying no—they were screaming it.

The Marlins were the only naysayers around. They had gotten off to a terrible start and in late May were 20–29 before turning their season around and making the play-offs as the wild-card team under ancient manager Jack McKeon. But over the last month of the season, very quietly, they had gone 20–8, the best record in baseball, better than even the Cubs. They could play.

Before the start of the series, all the talk in Chicago was about how different these Cubs were from past contenders, and Baker was given all the credit. He addressed his team almost like a new-age preacher, with metaphor and allegory, getting rid of negative thoughts and replacing them with the positive. He laughed off any talk of the

role that "history" would play in the postseason. Ever since he'd first been hired, whenever anyone started bringing up the Cubs' star-crossed past and all the reasons they'd never been able to win it, Baker had just laughed and asked, "Why not us?" So far the players seemed to be buying it. Most were too young to know the history of their own team anyway. That was for radio talk shows and newspaper columnists.

The degree to which that was so was on display in game one against the Marlins in Chicago. It was a heartbreaker, precisely the kind of game that in the past would not only have crushed the Cubs but exposed them as inadequate and flawed. With Carlos Zambrano starting for Chicago opposite the Marlins phenom Josh Beckett, the Cubs launched into the postseason with four first-inning runs, the key blow a three-run home run by Moises Alou. But the Marlins came storming back against Zambrano, scoring five times on three third-inning home runs.

Yet Zambrano and the Cubs seemed oblivious. They didn't buckle and quit. The young pitcher weathered the onslaught, and when he left the game after six innings, the score was tied 6–6 and the Cubs were fighting history to a standoff.

Entering the ninth, the score was still tied, and the Cubs turned to closer Joe Borowski. Borowski had been knocking at the door of the major leagues since 1995, and before the 2002 season he had always found it locked, once even being released by the Cincinnati Reds. But in 2002 he pitched well, and in 2003 he surprised everyone by taking the closer's job from Alfonseca, saving thirty-three games. He didn't have great stuff, but he was like Rod Beck. He didn't care, so it didn't matter. He threw strikes and dared hitters to beat him.

It usually worked, but not this time. After giving up a leadoff double to Todd Hollandsworth, he walked Juan Pierre. Then Luis Castillo rolled a ball to Grudzielanek at second base. He tried to tag Pierre, who was twisting out of the way, and did, but the ball fell free. Everyone was safe. Ivan Rodriguez singled, and suddenly the Cubs trailed, 8–6. They looked finished, and Joe Borowski looked like the pitcher released by Cincinnati.

The Cubs faced Marlin closer Ugueth Urbina in the bottom of the ninth, and he appeared to do his job, getting two outs around a Kenny Lofton double, bringing up Sammy Sosa, the tying run, with a man on and first base open. Three or four years before, Sosa would have never been allowed to bat in the ninth inning with the game on the line. It was a measure of just how far he had fallen that the Marlins chose to pitch to Sosa rather than Moises Alou. They'd pitched around Barry Bonds in the NLDS, but before facing the Cubs, manager Jack McKeon had announced that the Marlins were going to pitch to Sosa. He wasn't otherworldly anymore.

Sosa, however, still seemed to think he was. Twice during the series against the Braves, Sosa thought he'd hit a home run and followed his swings by giving his signature little hop and skip before starting around the bases, but each time his celebration had been premature, as both fly balls landed short of the seats, something that was happening to him more and more often. He'd taken some heat over that. Ever since the corked bat incident, Sosa had been about as popular as former *Tribune* columnist Bob Greene, the onetime Chicago icon whose squeaky clean image had been exposed as fraudulent ever since it was revealed that he'd had a liaison with a high school student. So too with Sosa. Now when he came to bat, there was an expectation of failure, not success. His batting record in the postseason was pathetic, 5-for-31.

Urbina threw, and Sosa, who later said, "I just tried to stay calm," connected and once again gave a hop and skip. For a brief moment it was 1998 again as the ball rocketed over the fence for a home run, Sosa dashed around the bases, pointing to the sky when he crossed home plate, and a sound never before heard rang out over Wrigleyville, a deep, unrestrained roar that lifted Cub fans halfway out of their shoes and seemed to herald the passing of an era and the beginning of a new one. The Cubs didn't do this in the postseason, but they just had. The score was tied.

Alou made an out, and when Sosa ran out to right field to start the tenth inning, the bleacher crowd gave him a mass group salaam, welcoming him back into the fold. He was in position to be the hero, but in the eleventh inning the Marlins' Mike Lowell, the player Jim Hendry had tried to get earlier in the season, quieted the crowd with a lead-off home run off Mark Guthrie, and a game that had seemed unlikely to end suddenly raced to the finish. The Cubs went down quietly, and the Marlins emerged with the 9–8 win. Maybe it wasn't the start of something new.

After the game, Baker seemed unaffected, even bemused. He stayed calm. This was nothing new to him. Both as a player and a manager, he was accustomed to being in the postseason, and now he said simply, "That's playoff baseball. It was full of emotional twists." But these were also the Chicago Cubs. Even though Mark Prior was scheduled to pitch game two, after a game like this the Cubs were hardly a lock. With their luck, Prior could pitch a no-hitter and Chicago would still lose.

Not this time, however, and perhaps not this year. In game two, the Cubs scored early, often, and off just about everybody the Marlins sent to the mound, scoring two runs in the first, three in the second, and three more in the third, piling up runs in a panic as if they were building a dam to protect against a flash flood. Prior was magnificent—well, not really, but close enough. After five innings, he led 11–0, but Baker left him in and he pitched through the seventh, giving up two runs and throwing 116 pitches. The Cubs won, 12–3. With Wood scheduled to pitch in game three against the Marlins' Mark Redman in Miami, the advantage tilted toward Chicago.

Like Prior, Wood wasn't quite right either, and anyone looking to worry could have started there, for both Cubs aces seemed to have left their best games on the mound against the Braves, and the way they were pitching now didn't make victory quite as automatic as it had been when either pitched in September.

Wood made it into the seventh, but left losing 3–2. Unlike game one, however, Chicago's bullpen held—barely. After the Cubs scored twice in the top of the eighth, Florida tied the game off Kyle Farnsworth. After that the Cubs pen held firm, and this time the Cubs came through in extra innings as two late-season pickups won the game, Doug Glanville slamming a triple and Randall Simon finishing it with a home run. The Cubs won, 5–3, winning both games behind Prior and Wood, and now the Cubs had command of the series.

In game four, Matt Clement pitched the game of his life and ex-farmhand Dontrelle Willis couldn't find the plate for the Marlins, walking the first three hitters before Aramis Ramirez banged a grand slam and the game was over. Cubs fans couldn't believe it. It was actually easy, an important game with absolutely no accompanying anxiety. The Cubs led the series three games to one, and the young Marlins team seemed to be crumbling.

Suddenly, the Cubs were there, right on the edge, needing only one more game to reach the World Series for the first time since 1945. After the game, fans poured out of the bars around Wrigley Field . . . happy. The Cubs had three chances to win one game, and they figured out all the angles. The Cubs hadn't lost three games in a row since mid-August, and in even the worst-case scenario, if Carlos Zambrano lost game five, Prior would pitch game six and Wood would pitch game seven, and the last time the Cubs had lost consecutive games started by Prior and Wood was more than 120 games ago, back in May, when the Pirates beat Wood 5–2 and Prior lost to Houston two days later. Sweet.

Fans a bit older, however, started thinking about 1984. Rick Sutcliffe had been a mortal lock then as well, but he had lost, and so had the Cubs. But they dismissed those thoughts as quickly as they surfaced. Prior and Wood were like having two Sutcliffes. That made losing twice as unlikely, right?

Of course the Cubs did lose game five behind Zambrano, 4–0, as the Marlins' Josh Beckett was almost perfect, facing only three batters over the minimum. The Cubs didn't seem too concerned, and after the game Dusty Baker, knowing that every writer in Chicago was certain to dredge up all the bad moments in Cub history, dismissed it out of hand, telling his players, "Don't watch it, don't read it, and don't believe it." Baker seemed to realize that if there was any curse that hung around his club, it was the curse of negativity that came from the constant drumbeat of doom and gloom. Over the last few years, a new generation of Cubs fans seemed almost to wallow in the *Cliff's Notes* version of their history they picked up from TV and radio that blamed their situation on everything from Mrs. O'Leary's cow to the billy goat. At the same time, as the Red Sox and Yankees fought it out in the American League, the Red Sox and their specious Babe Ruth curse and their history of failure were getting a lot of play. It was almost as if some Cubs fans and some members of the media were weirdly jealous and out to prove that the Cubs, not the Red Sox, were more miserable.

Actually, it was the Marlins who should have been worried. They were facing Prior, and in his last thirteen starts he was 12–1 with a minuscule ERA of 1.55. And although few fans would say it, many were actually happy that the Cubs had lost game five. They were looking forward to celebrating the victory in Wrigley Field. They deserved that.

It was clear and chilly on the evening of October 14— World Series weather. At the end of the night, that's exactly where the Cubs wanted to be, and for two hours that's exactly where the Cubs appeared to be headed for the first time since 1945.

They nicked Marlin starter Carl Pavano for three runs, the first when Sosa doubled home Lofton in the first, and the second in the sixth when Sosa singled, moved to second on Alou's hit, went to third on a double play, and then scored when Dontrelle Willis, in relief, threw a wild pitch. The score was 2–0, and the Marlins were facing winter. Cubs fans started to enjoy themselves.

Mark Prior was the same Mark Prior who had gone 12–1 in his last thirteen starts, or at least close enough. He had struggled a bit early, giving up a hit and a walk in the first, then seemed to get stronger. He started the sixth by striking out the Marlins' two most dangerous hitters, Ivan Rodriguez and Miguel Cabrera, and when he retired the Marlins with a clean inning in the seventh, he still seemed strong, although a close observer would have noticed that the last four batters had hit the ball to the outfield. He wasn't fooling the Marlins anymore.

The Cubs then gave him room to breathe. Catcher Paul Bako singled, and with Prior on deck, Dusty Baker didn't hesitate at all. Prior never looked over his shoulder. He wasn't coming out of this game, and he deftly sacrificed Bako to second.

Lofton struck out, but then Grudzielanek singled, moving Bako to third and bringing up Sosa. It seemed as if the home run in game one had taken all the pressure off him, and all of a sudden he was playing the best baseball he had in years, not swinging for the fences, not sucking up all the air, but letting the game come to him. He followed with a single, Bako scored, and now the Cubs led 3–0. The Cubs weren't just going to win and change their personality forever—they were also going to restore Sosa's reputation. All of a sudden, even former owner P.K. Wrigley didn't seem like such a bad guy.

Cubs fans started calling friends on cell phones, checking their scorecards, counting down the outs, all while looking for signs of impending doom. So far, there were none. Boxes of pennant-winning T-shirts were already being delivered to concession stands, but none of the vendors would sell them yet, even as people begged. Staff members were wrapping the locker room in plastic to protect it from champagne, not being arrogant, just realistic. No one was dancing yet in the dugout, but they were starting to dance in the stands, staying on their feet. Prior seemed strong, determined, confident. The Cubs hadn't squandered any grand opportunity to score a half-dozen runs that would come back to haunt them, and the Marlins weren't showing signs of life. There was no reason to turn to the bullpen, not yet—perhaps in the ninth, but with the ninth hitter due up to start the eighth, then Juan Pierre and Luis Castillo, this was no time to make a change. Prior was throwing strikes.

Shortstop Mike Mordecai led off and with the count 2–1 lofted a soft fly to left field. Moises Alou circled under the ball, and you could see it now. Alou caught it soft, certain, and sure, counting the outs himself. Six to go now turned to five.

Juan Pierre stepped to the plate. He was, in a way, the Marlins' biggest threat, a guy who could turn a ground ball into a base hit, perhaps force a bad throw and make it a double, or hit a ball into the gap, take advantage of a bobble, and turn it into a triple. So far he hadn't really hurt the Cubs, and in the fifth inning, after he singled, Bako had thrown him out stealing.

But Pierre was tough. He battled and worked the count to 2–2, then spanked a pitch to left and took off. Shifting gears faster than any player in the game, he made second base for a double.

The party just getting started slowed a little bit, but did not stop as Cubs fans stayed on their feet and for the most part stayed gleeful. It was okay. The Cubs could afford to give up a run. Just keep the tying run from coming up. Get Castillo out and go from there.

Prior still had good stuff, but now, for the first time since the fifth inning, he was forced to pitch from the stretch, a subtle change, one that might have cost him one, perhaps two miles on his fastball, and maybe a bit of command. He'd been in a groove. Pierre had gone the

RETIRED NUMBERS

10	Ron Santo	3B
14	Ernie Banks	SS
23	Ryne Sandberg	2B
26	Billy Williams	OF
42	Jackie Robinson	

other way, and now so did Castillo, the ball slicing off his bat. He hit a soft pop-up down the left-field line, the kind of pop-up that once it gets in the air starts to slice toward the stands.

Moises Alou was there. He knew Castillo went the other way, and he was playing him shallow and toward the line. The ball went up and Alou started to run. The ball hung in the air, and Alou had time. There was a stiff breeze blowing in from the northwest, over the stands, pushing the ball, just enough to keep it in play, and Alou had room. He ran and he raised his glove, the brick wall along the left-field foul line looming and drawing closer with each step, a mass of Cubs fans in front of him, all of them looking up at the ball, arms in the air. Alou placed one arm out to brace himself and touch the wall, then reached up with his glove hand over the wall as the ball dropped down.

He was not alone. Four, five, six, ten pairs of hands in the stands were all reaching out for the ball, and they all missed, every single hand—except one. And that was the hand of an every fan named Steve Bartman, a twenty-six-year-old guy wearing a Cub hat thrilled to be at the game where the Cubs would finally win, with a good seat, and now here was the ball, and he rose from his seat—aisle 4, row 8, seat 113—rose up like everyone else and reached out and over heads, and only he, Steve Bartman, touched

THERE'S NO CRYING IN BASEBALL

BY PENNY MARSHALL

It was early June in 2003, and the New York Yankees were about to play the Chicago Cubs for the first time since the 1938 World Series.

I was born in the Bronx and grew up a die-hard Yankee fan, so there was no way I was going to miss this historic rematch, especially with Yankee pitcher Roger Clemens going for his three-hundredth career win.

But to me there was something else that would make this trip to Wrigley Field every bit as special, every bit as historic. Wrigley Field was where the tryouts took place for the girls who played in the All-American Girls Professional Baseball League, the inspiration for the movie *A League of Their Own.*

After World War II, the league was but a forgotten moment in time. The girls' contribution to the national pastime went sadly unnoticed. But the movie brought their story out of the shadows. Their feats were recognized. Their place in baseball history was solidified. After nearly half a century, these women finally received the recognition they deserved.

Since the three-game series was going to be played in Chicago, I called Jim Belushi, an old friend and native Chicagoan, and left a message asking him what he could do about getting me tickets. Back in the day, Jim stayed at my house for a few years, so I figured this would be a good way to pay me back.

Jim returned my call while he was having dinner at Chicago's famed steakhouse, Smith and Wollensky. Since it's a favorite restaurant of so many athletes, he put me on the phone with Chef Hans, a local god and the go-to guy when it comes to filling such requests. All Chef Hans needed to know was how many tickets I needed and how I like my steak.

Four and medium rare.

It turned out my niece, Penny Lee Hallin, a Chi-town schoolteacher and Smith and Wollensky regular, had already gotten tickets for Friday's opener, and Cubs manager Dusty Baker had lined up tickets for Sunday. So Chef Hans got us seats for Saturday's game, as well as on-field passes for the entire series.

To put things into historical perspective, the Yankees swept the Cubs in the 1938 World Series and swept them the first time they met in the Fall Classic back in '32. Since those were the only two years the Cubs and Yankees ever faced each other, it meant the Cubs had never beaten the Yankees in the history of baseball. *Ever.* 0-for-ever is a bad streak. And I wanted to be there to see if that streak would continue or end.

FRIDAY, JUNE 6

I love Wrigley Field, an old neighborhood ballpark with ivy on the outfield walls and a guy inside the scoreboard put-

ting up the numbers by hand. Everything about the atmosphere that day was electric. Everything except the scoreboard.

The starting pitcher for the Yankees was my friend David Wells. Boomer was really excited about pitching in Wrigley Field because he's a huge Babe Ruth fan, and Wrigley Field is where Ruth hit the famed "called shot" in the 1932 World Series against Charlie Root.

When we got to the ballpark, the tarp was covering the infield. Rain delay. Not good. I don't want to see history get rained out.

While waiting for the skies to clear, Cubs and Yankees fans drank together at the bars surrounding the ballpark. Then they'd head into the gift shops, where everyone was buying T-shirts, hats, programs, and any other kinds of memorabilia that commemorated the series. At one of the stores, I bought whatever I could find made out of 100 percent cotton, including a button-down Yankees shirt. I love all-cotton. I'm First Team all-cotton.

When the rain let up long enough for the teams to get in some running and batting practice, I went onto the field to say hello to my Yankees.

Got some G-rated love from Derek Jeter, Bernie Williams, Jason Giambi, and manager Joe Torre. The usual hugs and hellos. For many of them, it was their first trip to Wrigley Field. They were amazed at all the people watching from bleachers on the rooftops across the street from the ballpark.

Jeter asked me if I had been to Wrigley Field before.

"Not to see a game. Just to shoot *League*."

I told him my brother Garry, who played league owner Walter Harvey, was modeled after Phil Wrigley. But we couldn't get the rights to the Wrigley name, so we changed it to Harvey, which not so coincidentally happens to be my grandson's last name.

Many of the players were talking about the media circus following Clemens in his bid for his three-hundredth career victory. Roger was scheduled to pitch Saturday's game, and all the players were hoping he'd get the win and have everything return to normal. Okay, "Yankee normal."

Joe Torre walked with me as I headed over to say hello to Dusty Baker, who was standing by the batting cage, watching his hitters take BP. I thanked Dusty for the tickets and congratulated him on the great job he was doing in his first season with the Cubs, who were in first place in their division. The Cubs hadn't been to the World Series since 1945, and this year had all the signs of a possible return to the Fall Classic.

When we got to our seats—first row behind the third-base dugout—a peanut vendor came over to me and said, enthusiastically, "I'm the 'get the clap' kid!"

"Excuse me?"

"I'm the 'get the clap' kid!"

I had no idea what he was talking about. And one doesn't usually associate such enthusiasm with getting the clap.

It turned out, when he was around six years old, he was in *A League of Their Own*. He shows up in front of the girls' boarding house with a baseball in his hand and approaches Jimmy Dugan (based on Jimmie Foxx and played by Tom Hanks) and asks him for his autograph.

Dugan signs the ball: "Don't get the clap. Jimmy Dugan," then tells the kid, "That's good advice."

Just not the kind of advice you often give to a six-year-old.

After I bought a bag of peanuts from the "get the clap" kid, the grounds crew removed the tarp, and after a rain delay of almost an hour and a half it was time to play ball.

In the top of the first, the Yankees jumped out to a 2–0 lead on Jason Giambi's home run into the left-center-field bleachers off Cubs starter Carlos Zambrano.

Even though this was my first game at Wrigley Field, I knew about the long-standing tradition of Cub fans throwing the opposing players' home run balls back. Never mind that this was a historic game. Never mind that this was the Yankees. Never mind that this was the kind of souvenir that would be handed down from generation to generation. Throw it back. My feeling is, if you want to throw something back, go fishing. If you catch a home run in a historic game, keep the ball. The fan threw it back. Bad move. Good arm.

In the fourth inning, with the Yankees leading 5–2, something took place on the field that sent shock waves throughout the entire Western Hemisphere.

"Boomer doubled."

Those words had never been spoken before.

Boomer doubled.

Since the game was played in a National League ballpark, there was no DH, so Boomer had to hit for himself. They might as well have asked him to do a routine on the balance beam. It wasn't going to be pretty. But then I heard a *crack!* Boomer got good wood on the ball, sending it to deep left field, over Moises Alou's head. It was beautiful. There was Boomer, standing on second base. Standing where one swing of the bat had never taken him before. On that day, Boomer was both a dominant pitcher *and* a great hitter. If only for a day, David Wells *was* Babe Ruth.

With one on in the Cubs' sixth, Sammy Sosa came to the plate. Sammy with his three sixty-plus home run seasons. Sammy with his finger-kissing, chest-thumping routine after each dinger. Sammy was in the lineup while appealing an eight-game suspension for getting caught using a corked bat three days earlier against Tampa Bay.

Boomer threw Sosa a breaking ball, and Sammy drove it deep to right field. Sammy did his trademark hop as he left the batter's box. And when he hopped, I rose to my feet, along with all the fans in the ballpark. The fans watching from the rooftop on Sheffield Avenue did the same. Seeing a well-hit ball sailing through the air is like a moment frozen in time. The world stops until the result is known. Fans in the right-field bleachers prepared to attempt a barehanded catch. Kids put on their mitts. Drinks are spilled. Food falls off disappearing laps. Nothing matters but the ball. Nothing matters but catching a Sammy Sosa home run against the Yankees. Raul Mondesi drifted back to the warning track, looked up . . . and made the catch for the out. Cub fans let out a collective sigh—as did I—but mine was one of relief.

Sammy went 1-for-4 and made a spectacular diving catch. Maybe they should've checked his *glove* for cork.

In the bottom of the seventh, the Cubs sent in a pinch hitter for reliever Antonio Alfonseca, a guy who can count to eleven on his fingers without using any finger twice. I imagine there must be some advantage to having six fingers on his pitching hand other than being able to give a "high-six."

Something else about the moment struck me. The player coming in to pinch-hit was Troy O'Leary.

O'Leary.

Wasn't it Mrs. O'Leary's cow that started the Chicago Fire? Is this the name Cub fans want to pin their hopes on in a crucial spot in a historic game? In Chicago, if you want to put a bat in a guy's hands and get results, put in a guy named Capone.

But not O'Leary.

O'Leary did nothing to help Chicago that day either, grounding out in his only at-bat.

Mariano Rivera came in to close things out in the ninth, giving Boomer the win, and the Yankees took the first game of the series, 5–3. The 0-for-ever streak was still alive.

After the game, we went to Smith and Wollensky for dinner, where Chef Hans gave us a tour of the meat locker. Chef Hans is very proud of his slabs of beef. They're like works of art to him, except instead of hanging at the Louvre, they're hanging on meat hooks.

When we got out of the meat locker, we ran into three of the four members of the umpiring crew—Dan Iassogna, Jim Reynolds, and Laz Diaz. All great guys despite the earful they constantly get from managers, players, and fans. So when I suggested they go into the meat locker, I think they took it the wrong way.

SATURDAY, JUNE 7

Sunny, seventy-five degrees, no threat of rain. The kind of day when Ernie Banks would say, "Let's play two!"

I've never seen so many people who weren't part of the teams on a field before. You don't see people hanging around on the field at Yankee Stadium like that. I just never thought of the playing field as a place to be catching up with old friends.

"You're going to the game? Great. Where are you sitting?"

"Don't go to the seats. Just meet me on the field."

"You can do that?"

"Sure, it's the Cubs."

We might as well have had a barbecue.

Saturday's on-field convention included my friends John and Annie Cusack. Annie played Shirley, the girl who couldn't read, in *A League of Their Own*. Saturday she was in the Cubs dugout. Was she gonna play?

Also in the dugout was "Mr. Cub," Ernie Banks, who called out, "Penny, I've got a project for you!" And you know, he was right! Now Ernie and I have a project together.

Tommy Lasorda and Michael Milken, who were in town for a fundraiser, were also leaving their footprints on the soggy Wrigley Field grass.

But I loved it. It only added to the event.

I talked to David Wells and congratulated him on getting the win. I gave him a stack of sports sections from the Chicago and New York newspapers, with articles about the game.

And of course, we also talked about his double.

"Why didn't you ask for the ball? You expecting to hit more doubles?"

"I'll ask for the ball if I hit a triple."

"You'll be asking for oxygen if you hit a triple."

Saturday's game was a classic pitching matchup. Two strapping right-handers from Texas. Roger Clemens was going for his three-hundredth career win against Kerry Wood, who was looking to earn career win number fifty.

During the seventh-inning stretch, with the Yankees leading 1–0, John Cusack sang "Take Me Out to the Ball Game," followed by Harry Caray's signature line, "Let's get some runs!"

With two on and one out in the Cubs' seventh, Yankee manager Joe Torre took the Rocket out and brought in Juan Acevedo. Clemens had thrown only eighty-four pitches, but he was battling a respiratory infection, and Joe felt it was time to make a move. Yankee and Cub fans rose as one, giving Clemens a standing ovation as he headed to the dugout.

Maybe it was Harry Caray watching from above, or maybe it was Johnny Cu's Irish luck working its magic, but on Acevedo's first pitch, Eric Karros took him deep, hitting a three-run homer. Just like that, Clemens's bid for career win number three hundred was over.

Just as a side note, I did get to see Roger Clemens's three-hundredth win the following week at Yankee Stadium against the Cardinals. Tino Martinez, who was on deck when the game ended, handed me a foul ball. So I do have a ball from Clemens's milestone victory.

The only reason Karros was even in the game was because of a very scary moment that happened in the

fourth inning. On an infield pop-up on the third-base side of the mound, Cubs first baseman Hee Sop Choi collided with Kerry Wood, and both players fell to the ground. Wood got up, but Choi remained on the ground, unconscious.

My niece, Penny Lee, said, "They need an ambulance. How are they going to get one on the field?"

Having shot *League* there, I knew how my film equipment trucks got in. I told her, "The right-field gate will open, and it will come through there." I believe it was the first time an ambulance ever appeared on the field.

Choi was taken to the hospital, where he was treated for a concussion. And that's what set the stage for Karros to enter the game and become a hero.

The Cubs won 5–2—their first win ever against the Yankees.

The Cub fans went crazy. Good crazy. They weren't yelling, "Yankees suck!" They didn't get out of control. Maybe they were just being respectful of the history-making event, I don't know. But whatever the reason, the Cub

fans showed a lot of class and sportsmanship in the way they celebrated.

After the game, we went back to Smith and Wollensky. And since some new people had joined our group, that meant another tour of the meat locker. Personally, I like it in there. I'm a big fan of cold rooms.

After dinner, we went to the Vic Theatre to see Dan Aykroyd and Jim Belushi perform as the Blues Brothers, then went to Le Passage, a great Chicago nightspot. It's a bottle service place, so some of the people I was with got very drunk because they didn't want any of the liquor to go to waste.

Everywhere we went, everyone was talking about the Cubs and Yankees. Waiters and waitresses, cab drivers and bell captains, the whole city had a singular focus—adversarial in their allegiances, yet extremely good-natured.

When we left the club, I ran into Alfonso Soriano, who was standing behind the velvet rope, waiting to get in.

"What're you doing out?" I asked. "You've got a game tomorrow."

"I like to dance."

"It's three in the morning!"

But Soriano wanted to dance.

I told the bouncer, "Let him in. He's a Yankee."

They were happy to let him in. They hoped he'd dance all night and would be exhausted for Sunday's game.

SUNDAY, JUNE 8

Yankee southpaw Andy Pettitte was scheduled to go against Mark Prior for the Cubs.

Since game time wasn't until 7:00 P.M., I had time during the day to go say hello to Art Garfunkel. He was performing that night at Ravinia, about thirty miles north of the city. Artie and I used to go out during the same time my friend Carrie Fisher was seeing Paul Simon. So one of the great music duets of a generation had hooked up with Princess Leia and Laverne.

I told Artie that the talk in Chicago was that he and Paul Simon were going to be doing a tour together. He told me the rumors were true and that the tour would begin later in the year. It was nice to hear that, in their sixties, Simon and Garfunkel finally got along.

Leaving Ravinia, we got stuck in traffic, so we got to the ballpark too late to go onto the field, where we would've run into God-only-knows-who. Probably the Pope and Jimmy Buffet. I hear they're big Cub fans.

We settled into our seats, and before I could call out my first "Yo!" to any of the vendors, the Yankees were already down 6–0. Where's the "get the clap" kid? Yo! Peanuts!

During the game, home plate umpire Jim Reynolds came over and handed me a bunch of baseballs. I'm telling you, this Wrigley Field is better than room service. You get stuff without ever making a call.

I gave out the baseballs to all the kids in the nearby seats. Here I am, a Yankee fan in a hostile environment, wearing all my Yankee garb, and not one kid booed me. Maybe it was getting a free ball or maybe Laverne supersedes baseball.

The seventh inning included a Cub milestone when Sammy Sosa got his two-thousandth career hit—an RBI single. The crowd chanted, "Sam-my! Sam-my!" Sosa tipped his corked helmet to the crowd.

Yankee catcher Jorge Posada hit a two-out, two-run single in the ninth, and suddenly it was a one-run game.

Charles Gipson came in to pinch-run for Posada. Good. Speed on the bases. Raul Mondesi, who had homered in his previous at-bat, stepped to the plate.

The stage was set for great drama.

On the hill for the Cubs was their closer Joe Borowski. Two strikes on Mondesi.

Borowski looked in and got the sign from catcher Damian Miller.

From the stretch, Borowski wheeled and threw to first, and picked off Gipson to end the game.

Picked off to end the game???

I never saw a game end that way before. Not in person, not on TV, not in the movies. Redford in *The Natural* didn't get picked off. Neither did Gary Cooper in *Pride of the Yankees*. Kevin Costner's character in *Field of Dreams* didn't search for Moonlight Graham because he got caught leaning. In *A League of Their Own*, it never occurred to us to end the movie that way. Kit Keller steps up to the plate. Her sister, Dottie Hinson, catching for the Peaches, tells the pitcher that Kit can't lay off the high ones. The pitcher gets the sign from Dottie. Working from the stretch, the pitcher wheels and fires to first. Out! Fade to black. Roll credits. Not gonna happen.

But it happened that day at Wrigley Field. And the Cubs won 8–7.

A lot of things happen in life that could never happen in the movies. And until that fateful weekend in June, there was something that could only happen in the movies, never in life. Seeing the Cubs beat the Yankees. Times were changing. History was being written. It was an emotional ending to a great series—the kind of ending that brought tears of sadness or tears of joy.

I guess there *is* crying in baseball.

PENNY MARSHALL is an actress, producer, and director.

the ball. It glanced from his hand and fell into the stands as Alou, instead of catching out number two, caught only air and the fans scrambled to find the ball amid their feet. Alou backed off, looked up, slammed his hands onto his knees, then looked again and started yelling, looked toward the umpires and, angry, threw his glove to the ground.

It was not fan interference. The ball was foul, and no one reached from the stands into the field of play to catch it. Had they done so, the umpires could have called Castillo out, and they did not. It was close, but it was a foul ball. In every ballpark in the world, when a foul ball heads toward the stands, fans reach out and try to catch it. They never sit on their hands and wait, deferring to the fielder, not in spring training and not in the World Series, and no one ever raises their hands and tries to hold the crowd back, even though perhaps they should. Every time the ball goes in the air, the fans raise their heads, their eyes, their arms, and watch the ball and track it and see it grow large in the sky, then come down fast, and they try to catch it, kids again, a dozen times or more each game.

It was a foul ball. A strike. But these were the Cubs, and the fans started to boo because they'd been told this would happen, or something would happen, and ever so slowly they decided this was it. It was a foul ball, but it would soon be more than that.

Still, Castillo was at bat. Nothing had happened really, nothing that hadn't happened probably a hundred times during the regular season: a batter hits a foul ball right at the edge of the stands, it falls in, the fielder glowers, the batter smirks, the pitcher sighs, and everybody forgets all about it. Nothing had really happened except that now when the ball fell, and then when Alou threw a tantrum instead of just shrugging it off, maybe, just maybe, the Cubs, who to that point had listened to Dusty saying, "Why not us?" and had listened to him when he told them, "Don't watch it, don't read it, and don't believe it," maybe when that happened they stopped and started to think and took a quick knowing glance at each other. And just as important, maybe the Marlins—almost without hope—started to believe they could win.

But Mark Prior was still on the mound. There was still one out and one on, and the Cubs still led 3–0. Now he needed something extra, and he tried to reach back and find it, but he was pitching from the stretch, and Castillo,

still alive, kept fouling him off and fouling him off, and then, with the count 3–2, Castillo walked and the pitch went past catcher Paul Bako and Pierre went to third.

The walk was bad, the wild pitch was awful, but both happening on the same pitch was worse. Now Prior, with more than one hundred pitches for the game and more than fifteen just this inning alone, was in trouble, suddenly tired and struggling, and the tying run stepping to the plate.

It was time for Dusty Baker to call time and stroll out to the mound, twisting his toothpick in the side of his mouth, to stand in front of Prior for a moment, to say something, anything, just to slow the game down and let everybody breathe.

Dusty Baker watched. He could have and should have called time, gone to the mound, given Prior a breather, but he didn't. Maybe Dusty started thinking too. He watched as Prior threw one pitch for a strike, then another.

Then, with the count 0–2, Ivan Rodriguez lined a single, and Pierre scored, and Castillo, playing it safe, stopped at second. In five minutes, Wrigley Field had gone from fun to funeral. Except for a growing contingent of fans starting to pelt Steve Bartman with refuse and chanting obscenities, Wrigley Field fell silent.

Miguel Cabrera, a rookie but a good one, stepped to the plate, and Baker stayed in the dugout. There was still time. The score was only 3–1. Prior was still one pitch away from getting out of it, one pitch away from saving Steve Bartman and saving the series and saving the Cubs from themselves.

He threw a near-perfect pitch. Hard. Down. Away. Cabrera was young, wanted to be the hero. He tried to pull the ball.

He hit a ground ball, an almost perfect double-play ball, to the perfect man, shortstop Alex Gonzalez, who had made only ten errors all year long. Gonzalez took a few quick, smooth steps to his right as Grudzielanek floated toward second, and Cabrera ran to first, watching the inning end as the ball hit Gonzalez's glove . . . and then bounced out, spinning on the ground. Gonzalez tried to pick it up and at least get the force at second, but it was too late and now the bases were loaded.

It was over, that was it. Anyone who still believed the Cubs were going to win stopped. Derrek Lee ripped a double, and the game was tied. Now Baker came out and pulled Prior, but Farnsworth came in and walked Lowell on purpose, and then Jeff Conine hit a sacrifice fly, and now the Cubs were behind. Another walk followed, and then a double, and the Marlins were running around the bases and the numbers were changing on the scoreboard like that Bugs Bunny baseball cartoon, and when they finally stopped spinning the Marlins had scored eight runs. Steve Bartman had been escorted from the stands, and the Cubs didn't come back, and fans walked like zombies out of Wrigley Field and into bars and drank hard. The Cubs had lost, 8–3. They had lost a game they should have won, lost a game in which Mark Prior threw about twenty pitches that could have gotten him out of the inning, lost a game in an inning in which the Cubs made an error and threw a wild pitch and Dusty Baker sat on his hands when he could have walked to the mound.

And when it was over they blamed Steve Bartman, and they blamed the billy goat.

After the game, they said it didn't matter, but it did. Prior said, "I gave it everything I possibly had," and he had. "You can't blame the entire game on that play," he said.

"It has nothing to do with the curse," said Dusty Baker. "It has to do with fan interference, the very uncharacteris-tic error by Gonzo. They just started hitting . . . it has to do with their bats."

"History had nothing to do with this game. Nothing."

He was right. When it was happening, history had nothing to do with it. But now that it was over, the game belonged to history, and history would have its way with it.

Everybody piled on in one great big heap, as if they all decided that if they couldn't come together to celebrate, they sure as hell could come together to wallow in it. In the *Sun-Times*, an anonymous paean pleaded, "Won't somebody please find Mrs. O'Leary's cow, lead it to Wrigley Field and convince the heifer to kick over another lantern?" In the *New York Daily News*, Lisa Olson wrote about Steve Bartman, "Don't worry about him. It's not like his life is ruined. He doesn't have a life. He's a Cubs fan." Variations on the theme appeared in every paper in the country.

It was worse, far worse, than game four of the 1929 World Series when the Philadelphia A's scored ten runs to

---

Steve Bartman will forever live with the unfairly directed enmity of some Cub fans who wrongly blame him for the Cubs' loss in the sixth game of the 2003 championship series. What these fans fail to acknowledge is that their team squandered many opportunities to seal the win following the foul ball incident.

beat the Cubs. That Cub team was behind in the Series three games to one. This team was ahead.

And it was worse than 1969. That team hadn't really come close to winning the pennant. They'd lost soft, over a period of weeks. This was a heart attack.

There was still game seven, but the series was over, just as it had been over for the Red Sox in 1986 when the ball rolled between Bill Buckner's legs and the Mets came from behind to win game six. The Red Sox took the lead in game seven but still lost anyway.

That's exactly what happened to the Cubs. Exactly. In game seven, history had its way with the Cubs. The Cubs went ahead 5–3 before faltering. The Marlins took the lead, and then Josh Beckett, who had stopped the Cubs cold in game five, came on in relief and shut the Cubs down. The Marlins won 9–6 and went on to win the Series, and the Cubs, who gave up seventeen runs to the Marlins in the last two games, went back to being the Cubs, perhaps more so than ever before.

It was the worst thing that could have happened, because until game six, the Cubs and their curse had been sort of a cute side story, but nothing anyone except kids

and lazy TV reporters took seriously, and it had never been a real excuse for anything. It had been impossible really to look at the Cubs and, with the possible exception of 1969 and 1984, think that they should have won more than they did, that fate had somehow cheated them out of a world championship. For so much of their history the Cubs simply haven't been very good, and everyone, including hardcore fans, has realized that even the 1969 and 1984 Cubs probably didn't have enough to win the World Series anyway if they had ever made it there. But after this loss to the Marlins, the media and many fans all drank from the same soup. Younger, more casual fans bought the whole thing, and wherever you looked it was suddenly billy goat this and billy goat that, blow up the Bartman ball and all that crap. And one of the reasons they blamed Bartman with such venom and violence was that, deep down, just about every Cub fan in the world knew that, given the chance to catch that ball, he or she would have reached for it too.

The lovable losers were back and for sale on every street corner and on every T-shirt. Almost overnight the Cubs had become the Red Sox, self-flagellating, self-absorbed, and sliding toward self-parody, a silly, stupid cliché. Boston didn't help matters when they blew the ALCS against the Yankees a couple of days later and gave everyone another chance to underscore the relationship.

Everybody blamed Steve Bartman, but they might as well have blamed the wind, because if it hadn't been blowing at fifteen miles per hour from the northwest that night, snapping the flags atop the grandstand out straight, the ball would have landed three, four, five rows deep, and it never would have mattered. That's one reason. And there are dozens more, for when a team loses a game it should have won—particularly late in the game, with a supposedly safe lead—it is never one thing that leads to loss but a dozen, two dozen, a thousand subtle ways the universe combines to spit things out, because in the end, no matter what the stat freaks say, baseball is art, not science, and art is never predictable, not ever, not once.

But if it was the worst thing that ever happened, it was also maybe, just maybe, the best thing that ever happened.

Huh?

Steve Bartman may have helped lose the game, but in doing so he just might have saved something more. A lot has happened since 2003, and much of it has been unsavory. No one thought about it at the time, but if the wind hadn't been blowing, or Bartman hadn't reached for the ball, or if Gonzalez had turned the double play and two innings later 39,574 fans spilled out of Wrigley Field and celebrated long into the night, and then if a week or ten days later the Cubs had beaten the Yankees to become world champions, what would history say about that now?

It might just say that when the Cubs won the World Series, they won it with Sammy Sosa. It might just say that the Cubs won it with the help of steroids. Since steroids entered baseball's consciousness, history hasn't had to say that yet about a World Series, because apart from Jose Canseco's 1989 Oakland A's, those players most under suspicion over the use of steroids and other performance-enhancing drugs haven't won the World Series. The Giants didn't win with Barry Bonds, so they never said it about the Giants. The Cardinals never won it with Mark McGwire, so they never said it about the Cardinals. And the Yankees never won it with Jason Giambi, or the Orioles with Rafael Palmeiro, so they never said it about them, and they didn't say it about the Marlins or the Angels or the Red Sox because none of these players played for those teams.

But they might have said it about the Cubs. Not right away, but in another year or two or three they'd have whispered the word "tainted" when they mentioned the World Series, just as they whisper that same word now when they mention all those home runs.

Blame Bartman? Go ahead, but if not for him and the wind and the universe, the Cubs wouldn't still have a chance to win it and receive credit for winning it clean and without any questions, and now they do. And besides, now that the Red Sox have won and the White Sox have won, it's just the Cubs, and when it happens it will be bigger, way bigger, than it would have ever been before.

Still, the loss to the Marlins was devastating and sent shock waves through the Cub organization, some of which have yet to fully play out. The loss shook the organization to its foundations, but it did not inspire fundamental change. These Cubs were not like the Cubs of 1984, 1989, or 1998. They hadn't been lucky—they were genuinely talented, and with Wood and Prior and Zambrano, the future looked bright. The Cubs kept their promise to Baker and kept spending in the offseason. When the Marlins decided to break their team apart, the Cubs traded Choi for Derrek Lee, then signed both Todd Walker and Greg Maddux as free agents.

Maddux was supposed to be the key. Although he was no longer a twenty-game winner, he could still pitch, and the Cubs hoped he'd rub off on Wood, Prior, and Zambrano. But despite the improvements, the Cubs got off slow in 2004. Prior injured his Achilles tendon in the spring and was sidelined for the first few months of the season, then took time rounding into form. Wood, too, was injured, as his balky elbow started acting up.

The Cubs scuffled all year. They had plenty of offense, even as Sammy Sosa, battling back spasms caused by a sneeze, missed almost a month and started to slide toward mediocrity. Carlos Zambrano emerged as the team ace, the kind of workhorse the Cubs had always hoped Wood and Prior would become, but the Cubs were out of sync and couldn't seem to get anything going. At the trading dead-line, they added Boston shortstop Nomar Garciaparra and hoped for the best.

He helped, but what helped the Cubs the most was the fact that, apart from the St. Louis Cardinals, who were on pace to win more than one hundred games, there wasn't another standout team in the National League. That left the Cubs to battle it out in the wild-card chase with the Giants and Astros. Entering September, each team needed only one hot streak to make the playoffs.

The Cubs, improbably, got it. On September 10, after the Cubs split a double-header with the Marlins, losing behind Wood but winning with Prior, they got hot. For the next two weeks, it all came together. The Cubs won thirteen of sixteen to move a game and a half in the lead for the wild card, and with both Prior and Wood pitching well again, plus Zambrano and Maddux, well . . . Cubs fans started thinking those thoughts again.

Then *it* happened again. On September 25 against the Mets, the Cubs lost a game they should have won, and the flashbacks killed them. Mark Prior was on the mound again, pitching in the eighth inning once again, leading 3–0. Only this time Prior and the Cubs made it through the eighth. It was the ninth inning that flatlined them.

Joe Borowski had been injured and lost his job. LaTroy Hawkins had filled in admirably, but Baker had used him in six out of the last seven days, and with a three-run lead he turned the game over to Ryan Dempster. The game quickly went into the Dumpster. He walked two and with two out gave up a game-tying home run to Victor Diaz. Then in the eleventh the Cubs lost it when Craig Brazell hit a home run. As Mike Kiley wrote in the *Sun-Times*, "All that was missing was Steve Bartman," but he and the billy goat weren't missing at all—they were in every column and story about the game.

The collapse that followed was classic—it was the swoon to end all swoons, made worse by the fact that it came in the last week of September rather than the third week of July or some other time. The Cubs finished the season losing seven of nine, three of them in extra innings, five by one run, most under circumstances too painful to recount. The Astros made the playoffs, and the Cubs went home.

Actually, one of them went home early. On the last day of the season, Sammy Sosa, who knew he wasn't going to

play, didn't even arrive at Wrigley Field until a little more than an hour before the game. He did not bother dressing, and then he left early. Sosa said later that "I was in the clubhouse until the seventh inning, when I left. I was in there with the other guys like I always do when he gives me a day off. I always stay inside."

There was just one problem with that. Well, to be precise, two problems. Sosa hadn't asked Dusty Baker for permission to leave, and he hadn't stayed until the seventh inning. Sosa denied it until Jim Hendry found a videotape that showed Sosa leaving early. He was fined $87,400, and with $17 million remaining on his contract, he had just made his final appearance at Wrigley Field.

It was over. If nothing else, the collapse at the end of the 2004 season gave proof that an era of Cub history was over. Although the 2003 and 2004 seasons were their best back-to-back performances since 1937 and 1938, it was over. The Cubs decided to erase the past.

On February 2, 2005, they traded Sosa to the Orioles, washing their hands of him and the era he represented, but it would take more than that to change the Cubs. For far too long they'd dreamed and depended on the fantasy of Wood and Prior at the top of the rotation. For a few brief months in 2003, it had been everything they expected, but now it was a lodestone around the franchise, weighing it down. Both pitchers were injured again in 2005, Wood with his elbow and Prior with shoulder miseries, and despite a fabulous season by Derrek Lee, the Cubs were back to their accustomed position of mediocrity, 79–83.

This time there would be no quick improvement. Hendry and MacPhail shifted gears in 2006, aiming to rebuild around speed by signing Juan Pierre, but Derrek Lee was hurt early, Wood couldn't pitch at all, and Prior threw less than fifty not very effective innings. The Cubs finished last again—probably the most common sentence in this entire book—with a record of 66–96.

The Cubs hit the bottom so hard that it could even be heard in the air-conditioned offices of the Tribune Company. Things weren't going so great for them either, as the newspaper industry was experiencing a long, slow decline, leading to speculation that the company would sell off some of its print resources and perhaps even the Cubs, for there was some fear that the club would begin to under-perform financially just as it had on the field. At the end of the season, Andy MacPhail was asked to leave, and the Tribune installed John McDonough, the team's senior vice president of marketing and broadcasting, as the new club president and CEO. The move was generally well received, but while some considered McDonough a marketing genius and gave him full credit for pushing attendance above three million a year, some questioned how much that accomplishment could be traced to him and worried that putting a marketer in charge might not be the wisest approach. Marketing the Cubs has never been the problem—everything else has—and it is uncertain precisely how McDonough plans to change that.

He said the right things, however, telling the press, "The immediate goal and the future goal is to win. We have to win as soon as possible. . . . It's a grandiose statement, but I think our fans need to have something to wrap their hands around. You have to give your fandom hopes and dreams." Manager Dusty Baker was also let go, although GM Jim Hendry was retained, and McDonough promised to let him make all the baseball decisions.

The Cubs went looking for a new manager. At first they appeared inclined toward former Cub catcher Joe Girardi, who had been let go by the Marlins after only one season, despite being named NL Manager of the Year, after a personality clash with owner Jeff Loria. After a period of interviews, Hendry and McDonough settled on veteran manager Lou Piniella instead. As Piniella described himself, "I'm basically a blue-collar-type manager." Piniella's passionate attitude promises to sit well in Chicago, at least for a while, and his hard-charging personality will be a departure. Piniella has won elsewhere, but the Cubs should prove to be a challenge nearly equal in scale to that of his last managerial job in Tampa Bay. There he never had the resources to win. He'll have those resources in Chicago, but he will have to run counter to the momentum of history—perhaps a greater task.

If there has been anything positive to come from the past few seasons, from the losses of 2003 and 2004, the victories of the Red Sox and White Sox, and the last-place finish in 2006, it is this: the Cubs have to win now. After decades of polite acquiescence, the patience of Cub fans finally seems to have reached a limit. They cannot take any more. They will not put up with excuses for long, and neither do they have the patience for yet another rebuilding

In 2005 Cub first baseman Derrek Lee not only won his second Gold Glove Award but nearly won baseball's first triple crown in nearly forty years as he batted .335 to lead the league while also belting 46 home runs and knocking in 107 runs.

plan. In the end, that alone may actually have caused the Cubs to act with some urgency, a rarity in their history.

In rapid succession at the end of the 2006 season, as if trying to make up for thirty years of paralysis, the Cubs threw money into the free agent market. They re-signed Aramis Ramirez for five years at $75 million, signed pitcher Ted Lilly for four years at $40 million, re-signed infielder Mark LaRosa, and, most shockingly of all, signed free agent outfielder Alfonso Soriano to an eight-year deal worth $136 million. The contract was notable not only because it was the fifth-largest contract in baseball history, but also because it was backloaded, leading many to view the deal as an indication that the Tribune Company may be looking to sell the team. While these moves and others in the offseason have certainly given Cubs fans a reason for some optimism, they are not likely to be enough, on their own, to make victory certain. The Tribune is still hedging its bets, for just after the Soriano signing a story in the *Tribune*'s business section sought to defend the Tribune Company legacy by arguing that the team's winning percentage of .507 since being purchased by the Tribune was evidence of the success of that relationship.

Millions of Cub fans would disagree. The only success that matters anymore is a world championship, a pile of Cubs in one huge happy scrum on the mound at Wrigley Field, a conga line coming out of the Cubby Bear Lounge, and the biggest parade in the history of Chicago.

What, then, will it take to change the history of the Cubs and make that happen? Why has it been so very, very hard for the Chicago Cubs to win?

Standing at six-foot-five and weighing nearly 260 pounds, pitcher Carlos Zambrano has been an intimidating presence for the Cubs since his first appearance at Wrigley Field as a twenty-year-old in 2001. In his first four full seasons, Zambrano averaged fifteen wins per season and in 2006 was named to the National League Silver Slugger team.

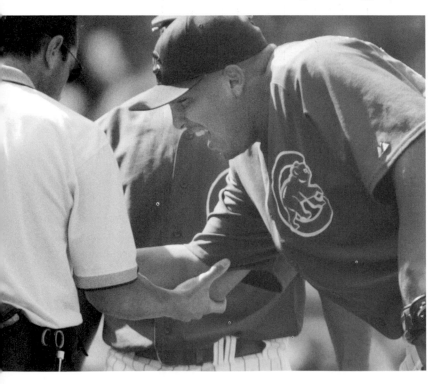

For a long time, it was easy to answer that question by blaming the Cubs' on-field failure on the mixture of sunshine and Wrigley Field ivy, as if in combination they cause every season to sour prematurely. Although some players have blamed the summer heat for causing undue fatigue, studies of the Cubs' home record indicate the opposite. The Cubs are the only team to still play the bulk of their home games in the daylight, but that was not the case until after World War II. From that time until 1988, when Wrigley Field remained naturally lit, the Cubs actually enjoyed a rather dramatic home-field advantage. Cub players have been more comfortable and accustomed to conditions at Wrigley Field than their opponents. If anything, daytime baseball has probably helped the Cubs far more than it has hurt.

Neither does it make much sense anymore to blame their futility on Wrigley Field. For a brief period in their history, in the 1970s and 1980s when the multipurpose stadium was in vogue throughout baseball, Wrigley Field was an anachronistic anomaly, its dimensions smaller and radically different from those of other National League parks. Perhaps during that era playing in Wrigley Field worked against the Cubs by making it difficult for their hitters to adjust to bigger parks elsewhere, while hitters from other teams thrived in Chicago, and pitchers, particularly free agents, may not have wanted to pitch in Wrigley Field. All of this would also have been true in Boston in regard to the Red Sox and Fenway Park. But over the last decade or so, the proliferation of retro "classic" ballparks has rendered these excuses moot: parks in Pittsburgh, St. Louis, Philadelphia, and Milwaukee are now nearly all just as cozy and quirky, if not as genuine and authentic, as Wrigley Field. If the ballpark was ever a detriment to the Cubs on the field, it is not now, and it has never harmed them financially.

Neither can one blame any version of some inane billy goat curse, a premeditated publicity ploy given legs for far, far, far too long by those too lazy to either learn the facts or look at them objectively. As an organization, the Cubs would do well to distance themselves from the idea and abandon what appears to be a tacit attempt to market the notion—please, please spare us the appearance of any more goats at Wrigley Field to lift the curse. It has morphed from an entertaining, colorful sidelight to a semi-serious concept that is now used as a universal excuse, ready for any occasion, deflecting blame from where it truly lies.

It is interesting to note the degree to which the curse is, in reality, a recent phenomenon. As of this writing, the billy goat curse has been mentioned in the *Tribune* and the *Sun-Times* more since 2003 than it was in the previous twenty years. Media outlets love the story because it is quick and easy and allows them to ignore less comfortable aspects of Cubs history almost entirely. The local media, in general, have been incredibly deferential toward both the Wrigleys and the Tribune Company, and every time they write about the curse it allows them not to write about something less comfortable. As an example, the Cubs' racial legacy is nearly as unsavory as that of the Red Sox, yet it has rarely been examined in detail. Mike Royko's famous column on Phil Wrigley, reprinted in this book, was the exception, not the rule.

The national media, and, in particular, the national electronic media, have been even less interested in the truth. A recent HBO documentary on the history of the Cubs, for instance, entirely ignored Gabby Hartnett's "Homer in the Gloamin'," a true highlight in the history of the Cubs, in favor of ad infinitum fawnings over the faux history of the billy goat. Please, let's send this tired cliché to the rendering plant. Most true Cubs fans are already sick to death of it and realize that the longer they allow such hoary notions to be used to hide the truth, the easier it is for the ball club to take their passion for granted and take advantage of their affection toward the team. In short, it's time for reality, not fantasy, to take over at Wrigley Field.

To that end, there is one factor that has been in place around the Cubs more or less from the beginning and that deserves an enormous measure of blame for their performance. Ever since Albert Spalding used the old White Stockings to serve as a foil for his sporting goods business, the Cubs have usually been owned by an individual or a corporation more committed to another business than it has been to the Cubs. For all his many faults, it is interesting to note that Charles Murphy, the Cubs' most successful owner in terms of wins and losses, was also the last owner of the team whose primary business was the Cubs and whose own financial fortune depended on whether the

Cubs won or lost. Since then, the Cubs have never been the main business of their owner. After Murphy, Taft was just a caretaker, and Weeghman used the Cubs to prop up his restaurant chain. Then the Cubs fell under the umbrella of the Wrigleys.

William Wrigley wanted the Cubs to win and made that a priority, but in the end he didn't have the baseball knowledge to make it happen and, rightly, was far more concerned with the Wrigley Company than with what happened in Wrigley Field. The Cubs were a lovely diversion, one he thoroughly enjoyed, but in the end they were nothing more than a very expensive hobby, and one that had the side benefit of making him a very well known man.

Once William Wrigley died and the club and the company passed into the control of his son Philip, the Cubs' subservience to the Wrigley Company ossified. P.K. Wrigley treated the Cubs like a captive insect in a matchbox—taking them out every so often for some experiment, pulling off a leg to see if it would grow back, then, when it did not, hiding them away again. It is no accident that the longer P.K. owned the Cubs, the harder it was for them to win, for under P.K. Wrigley the Cubs were just another one of P.K.'s holdings, always subservient to the Wrigley Company. He measured the Cubs with the same yardstick he used for the gum company, not by winning or losing, but by black and red, profit and loss. Oh, winning would have been nice, but unlike profit, it wasn't necessary, and he certainly wasn't about to go out of his comfort zone and make a bold move to make that happen by embracing either integration or free agency.

When the Cubs were finally sold to the Tribune Company, the fiction of family ownership was finally stripped away and the team's relationship to its corporate parent was made increasingly transparent. The Cubs became a wholly owned subsidiary, a slave to the larger corporation, nothing more than a line item on the budget, a conduit for circulation and ratings, and a cute little perk for stockholders. Under the Tribune Company, winning hasn't been a bad thing, but until very, very recently, since there has been little apparent relationship between winning and profit, it has rarely been considered a necessity. The Cubs have delivered profits regardless.

Both Wrigley and the Tribune Company spread the fiction that the Cubs had to be self-supporting instead of

Following a disastrous season in 2006 in which they lost ninety-six games, the Cubs hired Lou Piniella to lead a crew of seasoned veterans and well-heeled free agents such as Alfonso Soriano. In his first meeting at spring training, the fiery manager told his troops to "relax and have fun."

telling the truth, which is that the Cubs, a team in one of the top three markets in professional sports, helped both corporations make millions of dollars. From the moment the franchise was first conceived, the Cubs have always been one of the wealthiest franchises in the game and, potentially, one of the most powerful. Their peers have never been the *have-nots*, like the old St. Louis Browns or the Brewers and the Pirates, but the *haves*—the Cardinals, the Dodgers, the Yankees, the Red Sox, and, in recent years, the White Sox.

Had either the Wrigleys or the Tribune chosen to invest their resources in the team instead of simply using the Cubs for other purposes, the Cubs would have been successful, for they have always had the resources not just to compete but to *outcompete* almost every other team in baseball. This has been particularly true over the last thirty years, during baseball's free agent era, when financial muscle has meant more in the game than ever before.

Yet with only a few exceptions, the Cubs have rarely chosen to use their advantage and have rarely chosen to compete. P.K. Wrigley sat and watched while other clubs signed African Americans and pursued free agents, and until very recently the Tribune Company has sat and watched while other clubs moved aggressively in the free agent market. The Cubs have spent most of their time waiting, in vain, for the farm system to produce a champion on its own. Their peers have not been so foolish or so patient.

The way out is clear. In a sense, the Cubs have outlived their corporate usefulness. The Tribune Company found itself in the awkward position of being tied to a team that was no longer cute and cuddly but defined by loss and incompetence, hardly a desirable connotation for company stockholders. By the spring of 2007, there was rampant speculation that the Tribune Company, looking to become leaner and more efficient in an era of declining media profits, was looking to sell the Cubs. On April 2—the day after April Fool's Day—the Cubs went on the block, with a sale date targeted for the fall. Suitors began lining up almost immediately.

One can only hope that after decades of corporate servitude the Cubs will be emancipated someday soon, purchased not by a company that hums along with cool efficiency but by a person with a heartbeat and an ego, someone who laughs and cries, someone who will measure both his or her own success and that of the Cubs by the same stick: wins and losses at first, and then by a ring on the finger and nothing else. While there is certainly no guarantee that new ownership will lead the Cubs to victory in late October, after nearly one hundred years of failure there is some reason to hope that it will, and plenty of evidence that the old way doesn't work.

Cubs fans deserve that. They deserve a team owned and operated by one of them, by someone who has sat in bleachers because that's where he or she wanted to be, rather than where they wanted to be seen. By someone who has slammed down the clicker in anger, switched off the TV, and turned it back on twenty minutes later because, well, just because they're the Cubs. By someone who loves the Cubs unconditionally but does not love what *they* have done to this team over the years. By someone who does not love what the Cubs have become at the expense of what the Cubs *could* become.

The Cubs have not won since 1908 because there hasn't been a single season since then in which the Cubs have been the best team in baseball. Not one. That has had nothing to do with curses and goats and everything to do with talent. It is impossible to look at the Cubs' near-misses over recent years—the Cubs of 1969, 1984, 1989, 2003, and 2004—with any objectivity and conclude that they deserved to win it all in any of those seasons. Yes, they did experience some bad luck. Don Young dropped the ball, and no one covered second. Bull Durham missed a grounder. Les Lancaster forgot the count, and Don Zimmer forgot to remind him. Steve Bartman acted like a fan, and Moises Alou acted like it was the end of the world. That is how slim the margin has been for the Cubs. For any of these teams to have won, *absolutely everything* had to go absolutely perfectly, but everything did not. The smallest errors—a hazy sky, a funny bounce, a mental slip, an excitable moment—have been enough to knock the Cubs off track and send everyone home crying in their beer. But if any of these clubs had been better teams, they could have and would have overcome these inconsequential obstacles. That's what championship teams can do.

They haven't won because they haven't been the best team. In fact, in only a handful of seasons have they even belonged in that conversation, and quite frankly, considering how the Cubs have been run over the years, what is even more shocking than the fact that they haven't won is the fact that they've come close as often as they have. Give the players some credit for that. In many of the seasons cited earlier, the Cubs were actually better than they should have been.

Now that the other long-sufferers—the Red Sox and the White Sox—have won their world championship, there is a strong belief that now it is the Cubs' turn. While true in an artistic sense, that will not happen by magic. Someone will have to make it happen, not by ignoring the past, but by looking to the past to see what lessons it might contain. We hope that this book may be of some small help in that regard.

As it stands now, it is difficult to approach the history of the Cubs with unbridled joy. They are baseball's oldest story, but theirs is also a story that is not finished. They desperately need a happy ending, one that has yet to be written. Since the championship days of Cap Anson, Albert Spalding, and Frank Chance, it is as if every man who has subsequently played for the Cubs—from Hippo Vaughn and Gabby Hartnett to Phil Cavarretta and Hank Sauer, from Ernie Banks and Billy Williams and Ron Santo and Fergie Jenkins, to Rick Sutcliffe, Ryne Sandberg, and Mark Grace—is still there somehow, in Wrigley Field, poised at the top of the dugout step or settling underneath a lazy fly ball, standing on the mound or rounding third base, only one out, one run, or one pitch away, waiting, at last, to celebrate.

THE CUBS' ANNUAL RECORD

YEAR	LEAGUE	RECORD	FINISH	MANAGER
2006	NL Central	66–96 (.407)	6	Dusty Baker
2005	NL Central	79–83 (.488)	4	Dusty Baker
2004	NL Central	89–73 (.549)	3	Dusty Baker
2003	**NL Central**	**88–74 (.543)**	**Division Champion**	**Dusty Baker**
2002	NL Central	67–95 (.414)	5	Don Baylor, Rene Lachemann, and Bruce Kimm
2001	NL Central	88–74 (.543)	3	Don Baylor
2000	NL Central	65–97 (.401)	6	Don Baylor
1999	NL Central	67–95 (.414)	6	Jim Riggleman
1998	**NL Central**	**90–73 (.552)**	**Wild Card Champion**	**Jim Riggleman**
1997	NL Central	68–94 (.420)	5	Jim Riggleman
1996	NL Central	76–86 (.469)	4	Jim Riggleman
1995	NL Central	73–71 (.507)	3	Jim Riggleman
1994	NL Central	49–64 (.434)	5	Tom Trebelhorn
1993	NL East	84–78 (.519)	4	Jim Lefebvre
1992	NL East	78–84 (.481)	4	Jim Lefebvre
1991	NL East	77–83 (.481)	4	Don Zimmer, Joe Altobelli, and Jim Essian
1990	NL East	77–85 (.475)	5	Don Zimmer
1989	**NL East**	**93–69 (.574)**	**Division Champion**	**Don Zimmer**
1988	NL East	77–85 (.475)	4	Don Zimmer

YEAR	LEAGUE	RECORD	FINISH	MANAGER
1987	NL East	76–85 (.472)	6	Gene Michael and Frank Luchessi
1986	NL East	70–90 (.438)	5	Jim Frey, John Vukovich, and Gene Michael
1985	NL East	77–84 (.478)	4	Jim Frey
1984	**NL East**	**96–65 (.596)**	**Division Champion**	**Jim Frey**
1983	NL East	71–91 (.438)	5	Lee Elia and Charlie Fox
1982	NL East	73–89 (.451)	5	Lee Elia
1981	NL East	38–65 (.369)	6	Joe Amalfitano
1980	NL East	64–98 (.395)	6	Preston Gomez and Joe Amalfitano
1979	NL East	80–82 (.494)	5	Herman Franks and Joe Amalfitano
1978	NL East	79–83 (.488)	3	Herman Franks
1977	NL East	81–81 (.500)	4	Herman Franks
1976	NL East	75–87 (.463)	4	Jim Marshall
1975	NL East	75–87 (.463)	6	Jim Marshall
1974	NL East	66–96 (.407)	6	Whitey Lockman and Jim Marshall
1973	NL East	77–84 (.478)	5	Whitey Lockman
1972	NL East	85–70 (.548)	2	Leo Durocher and Whitey Lockman
1971	NL East	83–79 (.512)	4	Leo Durocher
1970	NL East	84–78 (.519)	2	Leo Durocher
1969	NL East	92–70 (.568)	2	Leo Durocher
1968	National League	84–78 (.519)	3	Leo Durocher
1967	National League	87–74 (.540)	3	Leo Durocher
1966	National League	59–103 (.364)	10	Leo Durocher
1965	National League	72–90 (.444)	8	Bob Kennedy and Lou Klein

YEAR	LEAGUE	RECORD	FINISH	MANAGER
1964	National League	76–86 (.469)	8	Bob Kennedy
1963	National League	82–80 (.506)	7	Bob Kennedy
1962	National League	59–103 (.364)	9	Elvin Tappe, Lou Klein, and Charlie Metro
1961	National League	64–90 (.416)	7	Vedie Himsl, Harry Craft, Elvin Tappe, and Lou Klein
1960	National League	60–94 (.390)	7	Charlie Grimm and Lou Boudreau
1959	National League	74–80 (.481)	6	Bob Scheffing
1958	National League	72–82 (.468)	6	Bob Scheffing
1957	National League	62–92 (.403)	8	Bob Scheffing
1956	National League	60–94 (.390)	8	Stan Hack
1955	National League	72–81 (.471)	6	Stan Hack
1954	National League	64–90 (.416)	7	Stan Hack
1953	National League	65–89 (.422)	7	Phil Cavarretta
1952	National League	77–77 (.500)	5	Phil Cavarretta
1951	National League	62–92 (.403)	8	Frankie Frisch and Phil Cavarretta
1950	National League	64–89 (.418)	7	Frankie Frisch
1949	National League	61–93 (.396)	8	Charlie Grimm and Frankie Frisch
1948	National League	64–90 (.416)	8	Charlie Grimm
1947	National League	69–85 (.448)	6	Charlie Grimm
1946	National League	82–71 (.536)	3	Charlie Grimm
1945	**National League**	**98–56 (.636)**	**Win NL Pennant**	**Charlie Grimm**
1944	National League	75–79 (.487)	4	Jimmie Wilson, Roy Johnson, and Charlie Grimm
1943	National League	74–79 (.484)	5	Jimmie Wilson

YEAR	LEAGUE	RECORD	FINISH	MANAGER
1942	National League	68–86 (.442)	6	Jimmie Wilson
1941	National League	70–84 (.455)	6	Jimmie Wilson
1940	National League	75–79 (.487)	5	Gabby Hartnett
1939	National League	84–70 (.545)	4	Gabby Hartnett
1938	**National League**	**89–63 (.586)**	**Win NL Pennant**	**Charlie Grimm and Gabby Hartnett**
1937	National League	93–61 (.604)	2	Charlie Grimm
1936	National League	87–67 (.565)	2	Charlie Grimm
1935	**National League**	**100–54 (.649)**	**Win NL Pennant**	**Charlie Grimm**
1934	National League	86–65 (.570)	3	Charlie Grimm
1933	National League	86–68 (.558)	3	Charlie Grimm
1932	**National League**	**90–64 (.584)**	**Win NL Pennant**	**Rogers Hornsby and Charlie Grimm**
1931	National League	84–70 (.545)	3	Rogers Hornsby
1930	National League	90–64 (.584)	2	Joe McCarthy and Rogers Hornsby
1929	**National League**	**98–54 (.645)**	**Win NL Pennant**	**Joe McCarthy**
1928	National League	91–63 (.591)	3	Joe McCarthy
1927	National League	85–68 (.556)	4	Joe McCarthy
1926	National League	82–72 (.532)	4	Joe McCarthy
1925	National League	68–86 (.442)	8	Bill Killefer, Rabbit Maranville, and George Gibson
1924	National League	81–72 (.529)	5	Bill Killefer
1923	National League	83–71 (.539)	4	Bill Killefer
1922	National League	80–74 (.519)	5	Bill Killefer
1921	National League	64–89 (.418)	7	Johnny Evers and Bill Killefer
1920	National League	75–79 (.487)	6	Fred Mitchell

YEAR	LEAGUE	RECORD	FINISH	MANAGER
1919	National League	75–65 (.536)	3	Fred Mitchell
1918	**National League**	**84–45 (.651)**	**Win NL Pennant**	**Fred Mitchell**
1917	National League	74–80 (.481)	5	Fred Mitchell
1916	National League	67–86 (.438)	5	Joe Tinker
1915	National League	73–80 (.477)	4	Roger Bresnahan
1914	National League	78–76 (.506)	4	Hank O'Day
1913	National League	88–65 (.575)	3	Johnny Evers
1912	National League	91–59 (.607)	3	Frank Chance
1911	National League	92–62 (.597)	2	Frank Chance
1910	**National League**	**104–50 (.675)**	**Win NL Pennant**	**Frank Chance**
1909	National League	104–49 (.680)	2	Frank Chance
1908	**National League**	**99–55 (.643)**	**Win World Series**	**Frank Chance**
1907	**National League**	**107–45 (.704)**	**Win World Series**	**Frank Chance**
1906	**National League**	**116–36 (.763)**	**Win NL Pennant**	**Frank Chance**
1905	National League	92–61 (.601)	3	Frank Selee and Frank Chance
1904	National League	93–60 (.608)	2	Frank Selee
1903	National League	82–56 (.594)	3	Frank Selee
1902	National League	68–69 (.496)	5	Frank Selee
1901	National League	53–86 (.381)	6	Tom Loftus
1900	National League	65–75 (.464)	6	Tom Loftus
1899	National League	75–73 (.507)	8	Tom Burns
1898	National League	85–65 (.567)	4	Tom Burns
1897	National League	59–73 (.447)	9	Cap Anson
1896	National League	71–57 (.555)	5	Cap Anson

YEAR	LEAGUE	RECORD	FINISH	MANAGER
1895	National League	72–58 (.554)	4	Cap Anson
1894	National League	57–75 (.432)	8	Cap Anson
1893	National League	56–71 (.441)	9	Cap Anson
1892	National League	70–76 (.479)	7	Cap Anson
1891	National League	82–53 (.607)	2	Cap Anson
1890	National League	83–53 (.610)	2	Cap Anson
1889	National League	67–65 (.508)	3	Cap Anson
1888	National League	77–58 (.570)	2	Cap Anson
1887	National League	71–50 (.587)	3	Cap Anson
1886	**National League**	**90–34 (.726)**	**Win NL Pennant**	**Cap Anson**
1885	**National League**	**87–25 (.777)**	**Win NL Pennant**	**Cap Anson**
1884	National League	62–50 (.554)	5	Cap Anson
1883	National League	59–39 (.602)	2	Cap Anson
1882	**National League**	**55–29 (.655)**	**Win NL Pennant**	**Cap Anson**
1881	**National League**	**56–28 (.667)**	**Win NL Pennant**	**Cap Anson**
1880	**National League**	**67–17 (.798)**	**Win NL Pennant**	**Cap Anson**
1879	National League	46–33 (.582)	4	Cap Anson and Silver Flint
1878	National League	30–30 (.500)	4	Bob Ferguson
1877	National League	26–33 (.441)	5	Al Spalding
1875	National Association	30–37 (.448)	6	James Wood
1874	National Association	28–31 (.475)	5	Fergy Malone and James Wood
1871	National Association	19–9 (.679)	2	James Wood

ALL-TIME CUBS TEAMS

1876–1908

EXECUTIVES

William Hulbert

The Cubs president from 1876 through 1881, Hulbert also played a key role in the creation of the National League.

Albert Spalding

As a player, manager, executive, and equipment manufacturer, Spalding, who served as team president from 1882 to 1891, was a baseball pioneer.

MANAGERS

Frank Selee (1902–1905)

Selee came to the Cubs from Boston, where he had helped turn the Boston Nationals into a dynasty. As manager of the Cubs from 1902 to 1905, he laid the foundation for the Cub teams that captured pennants in 1906, 1907, and 1908.

Frank Chance (1905–1912) 753–379

The "Peerless Leader" led the Cubs to four pennants and two world championships in his eight-year tenure as player-manager.

Cap Anson (1879–1897) 1,282–938

Anson led Chicago to five pennants in the first eight of his eighteen seasons as Cub manager.

FIRST BASE

Frank Chance (1898–1912) .297 BA, 404 stolen bases, 80 triples

Chance was considered one of the great leaders and tough guys in an era when grit more than matched skill as a factor in winning games.

Cap Anson (1876–1897) 2,276 games, 3,041 hits, .334 BA, 1,715 RBI, 1,719 runs

Anson remains the career leader in the following Cub offensive categories: batting average, hits, runs scored, doubles, singles, and RBIs.

SECOND BASE

Johnny Evers (1902–1912, 1916) .270 BA, 291 stolen bases, 1,339 hits

The fiery Evers was the driving wheel of four pennant winners and two world champions.

Fred Pfeffer (1883–1889) .252 BA, 79 HR, 233 stolen bases

The keystone of Chicago's famed "Stonewall" infield, Pfeffer was considered the best-fielding second baseman of his era.

SHORTSTOP

Tommy Burns (1880–1891) .264 BA

The shortstop of the "Stonewall" infield also played third base while helping lead Chicago to five pennants in his twelve seasons in the Windy City.

Joe Tinker (1902–1912, 1916) .260 BA, 93 triples, 304 stolen bases
The shortstop of the famed "Tinker-to-Evers-to-Chance" double-play combination helped lead Chicago to dynastic status with four pennants and two world titles in five seasons from 1906 to 1910.

THIRD BASE

Ned Williamson (1879–1889) .260 BA, 80 triples, 1,050 hits
Cap Anson once called Williamson "the best all-around ballplayer the country ever saw."

Harry Steinfeldt (1906–1912) .268 BA, 696 hits
Steinfeldt was the "silent partner" of the Tinker-to-Evers-to-Chance infield and led all Cub batters in the 1907 World Series sweep of the Tigers with a .471 batting average.

CATCHER

Frank "Silver" Flint (1879–1889) 680 games, .240 BA
Known for his defense, Flint's career began in an era when the pitcher still threw underhanded, and it ended in the modern era.

Johnny Kling (1900–1908, 1910–1911) 1,024 games, 960 hits, .271 BA
A stalwart during the club's glory years, Kling was also a two-time pro billiards champion.

LEFT FIELD

Jimmy Sheckard (1906–1912) .257 BA, 163 stolen bases
Sheckard possessed one of the great throwing arms and also was a master at drawing walks, with 147 in 1911 and another 122 in 1912.

Abner Dalrymple (1879–1886) .295 BA, 933 hits
The former railroad brakeman batted leadoff for five pennant winners in his eight seasons in Chicago.

CENTER FIELD

George Gore (1879–1886) .315 BA, 933 hits
The speedy Gore, nicknamed "Piano Legs," was a player who, according to Cap Anson, was a hard hitter and a fine thrower and fielder, but whose downfall was wine and women.

Bill Lange (1893–1899) .330 BA, 1,055 hits, 399 stolen bases
Nicknamed "Big Bill" and "Little Eva," Lange was a five-tool player who may have been the best all-around outfielder of the 1890s before retiring to marry a woman whose family strongly disapproved of his profession.

RIGHT FIELD

Jimmy Ryan (1885–1889, 1891–1900) .310 BA, 2,102 hits, 1,410 runs, 142 triples
Ryan was second only to Cap Anson as Chicago's most productive player of the nineteenth century.

Mike "King" Kelly (1880–1886) .316 BA, 899 hits, 728 runs
The versatile Kelly (he also pitched and played catcher and infield) twice led the National League in batting average while establishing himself as one of baseball's first media stars.

Frank "Wildfire" Schulte (1904–1915) .272 BA, 1,590 hits, 743 RBI, 117 triples, 214 stolen bases
"Wildfire" Schulte batted .309 in twenty-one World Series games for Chicago and led the National League in both home runs (21) and RBIs (121) in 1911.

RIGHT-HANDED PITCHERS

Mordecai Brown (1904–1912, 1916) 188–85, .689 win %, 50 shutouts, 1.80 ERA
The Cub all-time leader in ERA, Brown won twenty or more games for six consecutive seasons from 1906 to 1911.

Ed Reulbach (1905–1913) 136–64, 31 shutouts
The tall Notre Dame graduate was 2–0 in World Series competition and led the National League in winning percentage for three consecutive seasons from 1906 to 1908.

Larry Corcoran (1880–1885) 175–86, 253 complete games, 1,086 strikeouts, 23 shutouts

Corcoran averaged nearly thirty wins per season during his six years in Chicago.

John Clarkson (1884–1887) 136–57, .705 win %, 2.39 ERA

Clarkson averaged nearly forty wins per season while establishing a franchise-best career winning percentage.

Bill Hutchison (1889–1895) 181–154, 317 complete games

Hutchison had an incredible stretch from 1890 to 1892 in which he led the league in wins, innings pitched, and complete games for consecutive seasons.

LEFT-HANDED PITCHERS

Jack Pfiester (1906–1911) 70–40, .636 win %, 1.86 ERA

Pfiester's side-wheeling delivery baffled many a batter as he pitched his best games against the hated New York Giants, crafting a 15–5 record (including seven shutouts) against his rivals.

1908–1945

EXECUTIVES

Charles Murphy

Although many considered him incompetent, in terms of wins and losses Murphy's seven-year reign as team president from 1906 through 1913 was the most successful in club history.

William Wrigley

The chewing gum magnate renamed Weeghman Park, hired Bill Veeck Sr. and Joe McCarthy, and reestablished the Cubs as a National League power.

MANAGERS

Joe McCarthy (1926–1930) 770–442, .579 win %

McCarthy led the Cubs to the 1929 National League pennant but achieved lasting fame as the skipper of the Yankees dynasty of the 1930s.

Charlie Grimm (1932–1938, 1944–1949, 1960)

The charismatic Grimm led the Cubs to pennants in 1932, 1935, 1938, and 1945.

FIRST BASE

Phil Cavarretta (1934–1953) .292 BA, 1,927 hits, 968 runs

The Chicago native played twenty years for the Cubs and captured MVP honors in 1945 while helping lead the Cubs to their last National League title of the twentieth century.

Charlie Grimm (1925–1936) .296 BA, 1,454 hits, 270 doubles

"Jolly Cholly" was a consistent performer as well as a clubhouse leader. In two World Series (1929, 1932), he batted .364 for the Cubs.

SECOND BASE

Billy Herman (1931–1940) .309 BA, 1,710 hits, 346 doubles, 875 runs

The Hall of Famer enjoyed his best season in 1935, helping to lead the Cubs to a pennant while batting .341 with league-leading totals in hits (227) and doubles (57).

Rogers Hornsby (1929–1932) .350 BA, 392 hits, 91 doubles, 58 HR

In 1929 Hornsby set Cubs single-season records for batting average (.380), runs scored (156), hits (229), and on-base percentage (.459).

SHORTSTOP

Woody English (1927–1936) .291 BA, 1,248 hits, 218 doubles

English was a strong defensive shortstop who also played third. He was an expert at drawing walks and scoring runs and also played in the first All-Star Game in 1933.

Charlie Hollocher (1918–1924) .304 BA, 894 hits, 145 doubles
The diminutive, five-foot-seven Hollocher was a tremendous hitter who led the league in hits (161) as a rookie while contributing to the Cubs' 1918 pennant. Severe stomach trouble led him to retire at age twenty-eight.

Billy Jurges (1931–1938, 1946–1947) .254 BA, 928 hits
Jurges survived a hotel room shooting by a former lover and was a solid performer for three pennant winners in his ten seasons in Chicago.

THIRD BASE

Stan Hack (1932–1947) .301 BA, 2,193 hits, 363 doubles,
 1,239 runs
An exceptional fielder and solid line-drive hitter, Hack was the most popular Cub of the 1930s and '40s and also served as manager from 1954 through 1956.

Heinie Zimmerman (1907–1915) .304 BA, 1,112 hits, 80 triples
Zimmerman was one of only twelve players to ever reach the hitting zenith of a triple crown. In 1912 he batted .372, socked 14 homers, and drove in 103 runs to achieve one of baseball's rarest feats.

CATCHER

Gabby Hartnett (1922–1940) .297 BA, 1,867 hits, 391 doubles, 847
 runs, 1,153 RBI
Hartnett was the first major league catcher to reach the plateau of two hundred home runs, and on September 28, 1938, he clouted the most famous home run in Cub history—the famed "Homer in the Gloamin'"—to beat the Pirates and help lead the Cubs to a World Series date with the Yankees.

Jimmy Archer (1909–1917) .254 BA, 630 hits, 104 doubles
The Irish native succeeded Johnny Kling and was a solid defensive catcher whom sportswriter Ring Lardner rated with Ray Schalk as the best in the game. Archer also was the first big league catcher to throw from the squatting position.

LEFT FIELD

Riggs Stephenson (1926–1934) .336 BA, 1,167 hits, 237 doubles
Not only is Stephenson's lifetime batting average of .336 one of the highest for a non–Hall of Fame player, but he also batted .378 in two World Series for the Cubs.

Augie Galan (1934–1940) .277 BA, 912 hits
The speedy Galan twice led the National League in stolen bases (1935 with 22 and 1937 with 23) and once in runs scored (133 in 1935).

CENTER FIELD

Hack Wilson (1926–1931) .322 BA, 190 HR, 768 RBI
Wilson led the National League in home runs four times and in RBIs twice in his six seasons with the Cubs. His remarkable 1930 season included a major league record 190 RBIs and a home run record of 56 that was only recently surpassed.

Andy Pafko (1945–1950) .294 BA, 1,048 hits, 126 HR
Pafko was a versatile four-tool player who also played third for one season (1948) with the Cubs before being moved back to center, where his graceful fielding and powerful arm helped make him a Wrigley favorite.

RIGHT FIELD

Kiki Cuyler (1928–1935) .325 BA, 1,199 hits, 220 doubles,
 161 stolen bases
Along with Hack Wilson and Riggs Stephenson, Cuyler was part of the greatest outfield in Cub history. He led the National League in stolen bases for three consecutive seasons, from 1928 to 1930, and helped lead the Cubs to three pennants in his eight seasons in Chicago.

Bill Nicholson (1939–1948) .272 BA, 1,323 hits, 205 HR, 833 RBI
Nicholson was the premier National League slugger during the war years, and in 1943 and 1944 he became the first National League hitter to lead the league in homers and RBIs in consecutive seasons.

RIGHT-HANDED PITCHERS

Charlie Root (1926–1941) 201–156, 605 games, 177 complete games, 1,432 strikeouts

No pitcher ever served the Cubs longer or with more versatility. Root served as both a starter and a reliever and is listed in the top ten in most every Cubs lifetime pitching category.

Orval Overall (1906–1913) 86–44, .662 win %, 1.92 ERA, 28 shutouts

Overall helped lead the Cubs to four titles in his six seasons in Chicago and had a superb 3–1 record and 1.58 ERA in four World Series.

Claude Passeau (1939–1947) 124–94, 2.96 ERA, 23 shutouts

Passeau was the ace of the wartime Cubs and for eight consecutive seasons never had a losing record. He started and pitched well in two of the three games Chicago won in the 1945 World Series.

Pat Malone (1928–1934) 115–79, 3.57 ERA, 107 complete games

Malone led the National League with twenty-two wins in the Cubs' pennant-winning season of 1929 and also led the league with twenty victories the following season.

Bill Lee (1934–1943, 1947) 139–123, 3.51 ERA, 364 games, 25 shutouts

"Big Bill" Lee pitched shutouts in his first two major league starts and also won five games during the Cubs' incredible twenty-one-game winning streak down the stretch of the 1935 pennant race.

Lon Warneke (1930–1936) 110–72, 2.84 ERA, 17 shutouts

The "Arkansas Hummingbird" led the league in wins with twenty-two in the pennant-winning season of 1932 and went on to beat Tiger ace "Schoolboy" Rowe twice in the 1935 World Series.

LEFT-HANDED PITCHERS

Hippo Vaughn (1913–1921) 151–104, 2.33 ERA, 177 complete games, 35 shutouts

Not only did Vaughn make history as part of baseball's only double no-hitter in 1917, but he also averaged twenty wins per season for seven of his nine seasons as a Cub.

Larry French (1935–1941) 95–84, 3.54 ERA, 87 complete games, 21 shutouts

French's best season in Chicago was his first, when he won seventeen games for the 1935 National League champions.

1945–2006

EXECUTIVE

Dallas Green (1981–1987)

Under Green's dynamic tenure as manager, general manager, and team president, the Cubs acquired Larry Bowa, Ryne Sandberg, and Rick Sutcliffe for their 1984 division champions and later signed free agent Andre Dawson prior to his career-best MVP season of 1987.

MANAGERS

Jim Frey (1984–1986) 173–149, .537 win %

Frey led the Cubs to their first postseason appearance since the 1945 World Series and later served the Cubs as general manager from 1987 to 1991.

Leo Durocher (1966–1972) 535–526, .502 win %

The Lip brought the Cubs back to respectability after nearly two decades in the baseball wilderness and led baseball's most famous also-rans in 1969.

Dusty Baker (2003–2006) 322–326, .497 win %

Under Baker, the 2003 Cubs nearly made it to the World Series for the first time since 1945 before blowing a three-game lead over the Marlins in the National League Championship Series.

FIRST BASE

Mark Grace (1988–2000) .308 BA, 2,201 hits, 1,057 runs,
456 doubles

The slick-fielding Grace led all major league players in the 1990s with 1,754 hits and 364 doubles. Not only did Grace win four Gold Glove Awards, but he retired as the Cubs' all-time best-fielding first baseman.

Bill Buckner (1977–1984) .300 BA, 1,136 hits, 235 doubles

Buckner was a consistent hitter for the Cubs, capturing the 1980 National League batting title with a .324 average. He was also one of only twelve Cubs to make 200 or more hits in a season, with 201 in 1982.

Derrek Lee (2004–present) 417 hits, 86 HR, 235 RBI, 98 doubles

For much of the 2005 season, Lee threatened to become the first major league triple crown winner since Carl Yastrzemski in 1967, and the first Cub since Heinie Zimmerman in 1912. He finished with a career-best and league-leading .335 batting average, 46 homers, and 107 RBIs.

SECOND BASE

Ryne Sandberg (1982–1994, 1996–1997) .285 BA, 2,385 hits,
282 HR, 1,061 RBI

Not only did Sandberg capture nine consecutive Gold Glove Awards from 1983 to 1991, but in 1984 he became a folk hero to Cub fans while capturing MVP honors and leading the Cubs to their first Eastern Division title.

Glenn Beckert (1965–1973) .283 BA, 1,423 hits, 672 runs

The scrappy Beckert not only was Leo Durocher's favorite Cub but was also the National League's All-Star second baseman from 1968 to 1972. In 1971 he enjoyed a career-best season while batting .342.

SHORTSTOP

Ernie Banks (1953–1971) .274 BA, 512 HR, 2,583 hits, 1,636 RBI,
407 doubles

Banks was the first slugging shortstop, winning back-to-back MVP Awards in 1958 and 1959 while hitting forty-seven and forty-five home runs, respectively. The affable Banks later moved to first base and finished his career as the Cubs leader in many lifetime offensive categories, including games, at-bats, home runs, total bases, and extra-base hits.

Shawon Dunston (1985–1995, 1997) .267 BA, 1,219 hits,
226 doubles

Dunston was a National League All-Star in 1988 and 1990 and in 1989 batted .400 in September while helping lead the Cubs to their second Eastern Division title.

THIRD BASE

Ron Santo (1960–1973) .279 BA, 2,171 hits, 337 HR, 1,109 runs

The combative Santo was a nine-time All-Star and five-time Gold Glove Award winner for the Cubs. His home run total of 339 is fourth-best among third basemen behind Mike Schmidt, Eddie Mathews, and Graig Nettles.

Bill Madlock (1974–1976) .336 BA, 498 hits, 86 doubles

During his three seasons with the Cubs, Madlock became the first Cub to win All-Star Game MVP honors (1975) and also won back-to-back National League batting titles in 1975 (.354) and 1976 (.339).

CATCHER

Randy Hundley (1966–1973, 1976–1977) .240 BA, 758 hits,
111 doubles, 80 HR

Hundley was a superb handler of pitchers, including twenty-game winners Ferguson Jenkins and Bill Hands. He holds the Cub single-season catching records for total chances (1,065), fielding percentage (.996), putouts (978), and games played (160).

Jody Davis (1981–1988) .251 BA, 834 hits, 122 HR

The two-time Cub All-Star enjoyed a banner season in 1984 when he helped lead the Cubs to a division title and batted .359 in the Cubs' crushing five-game defeat in the National League Championship Series against the Padres.

LEFT FIELD

Billy Williams (1959–1974) .296 BA, 2,510 hits, 392 HR, 1,306 runs,
1,353 RBI

Williams emerged from the shadow of Ernie Banks in the early 1970s when he broke Stan Musial's National League consecutive-games-played streak in 1970 and also led the league in hits (205) and runs (137). In 1972 he won the National League batting title with a .333 average.

Hank Sauer (1950–1955) .269 BA, 852 hits, 198 HR

Hank Sauer slugged an average of 28 homers per season for the Cubs and won National League MVP honors in 1952 while leading the league with 37 homers and 121 RBIs.

CENTER FIELD

Adolfo Phillips (1967–1969) .256 BA, 346 hits, 46 HR

The trade of Phillips, a budding five-tool star, to the Expos on June 11, 1969, may have cost the Cubs their shot at a division title.

RIGHT FIELD

Keith Moreland (1982–1987) .281 BA, 100 HR, 491 RBI

The versatile Moreland caught and played third and the outfield for the Cubs while supplying surprising power.

Sammy Sosa (1992–2004) 1,811 games, 545 HR, 1,418 RBI,
1,985 hits

The Cubs' all-time leader in many offensive categories, Sosa's most productive seasons took place in an era now tainted by the specter of widespread abuse of performance-enhancing drugs throughout baseball.

RIGHT-HANDED PITCHERS

Ferguson Jenkins (1967–1973) 167–132, 401 games,
2,038 strikeouts, 29 shutouts

The greatest Canadian major leaguer won twenty or more games in his first six full seasons playing for the Cubs. In 1971 he was awarded the Cy Young Award after leading the league in wins (24), complete games (30), and innings pitched (304).

Greg Maddux (1986–1992, 2004–2006) 130–112, 1,305 strikeouts,
14 shutouts

Greg Maddux departed Chicago and won 194 games for the Braves before returning in 2004 to Chicago, where he won his three-hundredth game and had Cub fans wondering what might have been had Cub management not allowed him to depart after the 1992 season.

Larry Jackson (1963–1966) 52–52, 3.26 ERA, 11 shutouts

In 1964 Jackson enjoyed one of the best seasons for a Cubs pitcher since Charlie Root won twenty-six games in 1927. Jackson went 24–11 in 1964 and was the workhorse of the Cub staff for the three full seasons he spent at Wrigley Field.

Rick Reuschel (1972–1981, 1983–1984) 135–127, 3.50 ERA,
17 shutouts

"Big Daddy" went from being a spot starter and reliever to the Cubs' top starter for eight seasons starting in 1973. His best season was 1977, when he went 20–10 for a fourth-place team.

Bob Rush (1948–1957) 110–140, 3.71 ERA, 1,076 strikeouts,
13 shutouts

Despite losing twenty games for the 1950 Cubs, Bob Rush established himself as one of the best Cub pitchers of the 1950s. His best season was 1952, when he won seventeen games and also secured a win for the National League All-Star team.

Bill Hands (1966–1972) 92–86, 3.18 ERA, 900 strikeouts,
14 shutouts

Bill Hands joined with Ferguson Jenkins and Ken Holtzman to form one of the better pitching staffs for the Cubs during the late 1960s and early '70s. Hands's best season was in 1969, when he went 20–14, had a 2.49 ERA, and pitched eighteen complete games.

LEFT-HANDED PITCHERS

Ken Holtzman (1965–1971, 1978–1979) 80–81, 3.76 ERA,
988 strikeouts, 15 shutouts

Holtzman was regarded as the second-best Jewish pitcher of his era and invited comparisons to Sandy Koufax as he pitched no-hit games for the Cubs in 1969 and 1971.

Dick Ellsworth (1958–1966) 84–110, 3.70 ERA, 905 strikeouts,
   6 shutouts

The epitome of a good pitcher on a bad team, Ellsworth was the Cubs' winningest pitcher of the 1960s. He accounted for 20 of the 1962 Cubs' 103 losses and came back to win 22 games the following season.

RELIEF PITCHERS

Bruce Sutter (1976–1980) 32–30, 494 strikeouts, 133 saves

Bruce Sutter's split-finger fastball proved almost unhittable and started a revolution as a generation of pitchers sought to emulate the bearded right-hander.

Lee Smith (1980–1987) 40–51, 644 strikeouts, 180 saves

The bearlike Smith drilled his fastball past hundreds of batters while establishing himself as one of the great relief pitchers of all time.

Randy Myers (1993–1995) 4–11, 177 strikeouts, 112 saves

Myers set a Cubs single-season record with fifty-three saves in 1993 and averaged thirty-seven saves per season in his three seasons with the Cubs.

Page numbers in italics
refer to illustration captions.

Waller, Ted, *324*
Walls, Lee, 231–32
Walsh, Ed, 53, 54, 56, 66
Walsh, Tom, *50*
Walton, Jerome, 230, 359, 360, 361, 366, 367, 389
Waner, Lloyd, 121, 169–70
Waner, Paul, 121, 170
Ward, Dick, 159
Ward, John Montgomery, 24
Ward, Preston, 214, 220
Warneke, Lon, 142, 147, *147, 149,* 151, 160, 161, 163, 164, 180–81, 188, 215, 441
Warner Brothers Entertainment Television Network, 390
Warp, Harold, 150
Washington Nationals, 3–4
Watson, George, 138
Weaver, Jim, 160
Webb, Earl, 120
Webb, Skeeter, 195
Weber, Boots, 168, 177
Weeghman, Charlie, xvii, *75,* 80, 82, 83, 89, *97,* 98, 106, 427
Weeghman Park, *73,* 80–81, 82, *86,* 89. *See also* Wrigley Field
weightlifting, 388
Weimer, "Tornado Jake," 41, 45
Weis, Al, 277
Weiss, Walt, 397
Welch, Bob, 367
Welch, Curt, 21
Welch, Mickey, 17, 19
Wells, David "Boomer," 415, 416, 417
Wells, Willie, 198
Western League, 32
West Side Grounds, *20,* 26–27, *55,* 81, 82
West Side Park I, 17, 24, *30,* 43, 56, 58–59, 81
West Side Park II, 81
WGN, 227, 234, 268, 317, 321, 324, 390
Whales, 81, 82
"whammy man," 176
Whisenant, Pete, 229
White, Deacon, *3,* 8
White, Doc, 54, 56
White, Jerry, 312
White, Rondell, 401
Whiteman, George, 90, 91, 92, 95
White Sox. *See* Chicago White Sox
White Stockings. *See* Chicago White Stockings
Whitson, Ed, 340
Wicker, Bob, 41, 49
Wiggins, Alan, 338, 342
Wilhelm, Hoyt, 148, 285
Wilkerson, Curt, 358
Wilkins, Rick, 372

Willey, Carl, 235
Williams, Bernie, 400, 415
Williams, Billy
    statistics, 23, 230, *281,* 296, 297, 443
    in Hall of Fame, 148
    acquisition, 239
    1961 season and Rookie of the Year, 239, 259, 389
    1963 season, 242
    1964 season, 243
    and Durocher, 254
    1966 season, 255
    views on Jenkins, 258
    1967 season, 259
    background, 259
    1969 season and NL record, 267, 269–70
    1972 season, consecutive games record, Player of the Year Award, 296
    kept during 1973 purge, 299
    leaving the Cubs, 300
    charity dinner, 356
    first pitch of first night game, 357
    retired number, 410
Williams, C. G., *50,* 70
Williams, Cy, 32, 77, 82, 83, 120
Williams, Dewey, *194,* 195
Williams, Dick, 340, 341, 342
Williams, Lefty, 98
Williams, Matt, 361
Williams, Mitch "Wild Thing," 358, *359,* 359–60, 366, 367, 368
Williams, Ted "Teddy Ballgame," 119, 378
Williamson, Ned, 15, 17, 19–20, 21, 22, 23–24, 32, 438
Willis, Dontrelle, 402, 411, 412
Willis, Vic, 61
Wills, Bump, 325
Wilmot, Walt, 32
Wilson, Artie, 84
Wilson, Jimmie, 177, 179, 181, 433–34
Wilson, Lewis Robert "Hack," xvii
    statistics, 32, *115, 126, 129,* 440
    acquisition, *117,* 118
    alcohol abuse, 118–19
    expertise, 120, 121
    1929 season and World Series, 123, 124, 126, 127
    1930 season, hitting records, and decline, 128, 130–33, 134
    1931 season and decline, 137–38
    leaving the Cubs, 138
    in Hall of Fame, 148
    unpopularity and resignation, 183
    batting record, 230
Wilson, Owen, 61
Wiltse, Hooks, 48

Withlow, Col. Robert, 241–42
women and baseball, 116, 182, 199. *See also* Ladies' Day; *A League of Their Own*
Wood, James, 5, 436
Wood, Kerry, xvii
    statistics, 103, 205, *387, 388*
    1997 season, 379
    1998 season, strikeout record, and injury, 205, 384–87, *385, 387, 388,* 392, 397
    1998 Rookie of the Year, 389
    1999 season, injury, and illnesses, 392, 400
    2000 season, 401
    2001 season and injury, 402
    2002 season and injury, 403
    2003 season, 103, 406, 407, 408, 417, 418
    2003 NL Division Series, 409
    2003 NL Championship Series, 411, 412
    2004 season and injury, 423, 424
    2005 season and injury, 424
    2006 season, 424
"work or fight" order, 86, 88
World Series (unofficial), 14, 19–20
World Series (1903), 41–42, 99
World Series (1906), *47,* 48, 53–57
World Series (1907), *52,* 57–59
World Series (1908), *50, 52,* 70–71, 79
World Series (1910), 76
World Series (1912), 80, 99
World Series (1917), 85
World Series (1918), 89–95
World Series (1919), 98–99, 106
World Series (1927), 121
World Series (1929), 124–27, *136*
World Series (1932), 146–47, 149–50, 414, 415
World Series (1934), 160
World Series (1935), *147,* 160–63
World Series (1938), 171, 414
World Series (1945), 188–91, 194–95, 341
World Series (1946), 202
World Series (1955), 319
World Series (1969), 281, 319
World Series (1980), 319
World Series (1994), cancelled, 376
World Series (2002), 405, *406*
World's Fair of 1893, 26
"World's Worst Series," 188
World War I, *75,* 85–88, *86,* 91, 95, 98, 113
World War II, 179–80, 181, 183, 184, 186, 187, 188, 197, 200
Wortman, Chuck, 93
Wright, George, 4, 5
Wright, Harry, 4, 6
Wrigley, Ada, 138